THE WRESTLING OBSERVER YEARBOOK 1997

Online: F4Wonline.com

Twitter: @davemeltzerWON

Twitter: @WONF4W

Email: dave@wrestlingobserver.com

THE WRESTLING OBSERVER YEARBOOK 1997

THE LAST TIME WWF WAS NUMBER TWO

Dave Meltzer

Published by Titan Insider Press

This book is set in Garamond

10 9 8 7 6 5 4 3 2 1

This book was printed and bound in the United Kingdom

Contents

Chapter One

The Future of No Holds Barred Fighting

JANUARY 27

It was the same old story in a new place on a new day for the Ultimate Fighting Championships this past week. The media controversy that has come and largely gone in recent months, resurfaced in the city of New York stemming from a front page article on 1/15 in the New York Times and subsequent follow-up articles the next two days, and the fact that Extreme Fighting Championship is planning on holding its 3/28 PPV from an undisclosed site in Manhattan.

The controversy began with a front page story entitled "Outcast Gladiators find a home: New York," written by Dan Barry. The story, while having a negative tone toward UFC and EFC as most media stories do, was a fairly written piece on the sport talking about New York becoming the first state to sanction UFC legally (which technically is true but in reality it is fully sanctioned by government agencies—i.e. boxing commissions in Iowa and Oklahoma and has been held in several other states in the South like Georgia, Mississippi and Alabama without any controversy over the past year) and the dichotomy of area politicians getting the first EFC show booted out of Brooklyn, and then state politicians legalizing the sport in a bill that goes into effect in a few weeks, just in time for UFC's 2/7 PPV show from Niagara Falls. This has resulted in both the next UFC and EFC shows in the state.

The irony of the story is that the legalization of UFC and its genre in New York overcame strong opposition of both Governor George Pataki and State Senator Roy Goodman, who wanted it banned. However, it was Goodman who introduced the very bill to legalize it, and in his own press release claimed that the bill imposes rules (which were actually with a few very minor modifications—basically just time limits being held to 20 minutes per match—and most importantly, that the state would be able to collect a tax on the gate for the events to help fund the athletic commission) that would end the so-called human cockfights and turn it into an athletic event. But in newspaper stories this past week Goodman called UFC "animalistic." And it was Pataki who signed the bill.

What happened next was that the Times, while bringing up the strangeness on the surface of the very politicians who were the most publicly and violently opposed to the first EFC event being instrumental in the bill becoming law, didn't even mention the key provision that the bill didn't change any real rules of the event but simply allowed the state to tax the event. And naturally Pataki and Goodman publicly had to change positions once again.

Zenia Mucha, the Governor's communications director, put the blame on the state legislature because they wouldn't adopt a bill banning it and had enough votes to override a Governor's veto of the bill. Mucha said, "The Governor finds this competition revolting and does not consider it a sport. We are going to reintroduce our bill (to ban it in New York), and we are going to keep doing it until we hopefully get it banned."

Goodman introduced the bill to legalize it after being so publicly against it. He was praised in some media circles for his role, along with New York Mayor Rudolph Giuliani and Brooklyn District Attorney Charles Hynes, in getting the first EFC event out of New York state and moved literally one day before the event to North Carolina and perhaps in a sense ruining the show in the process due to all the stress and problems such a move created. "He still wanted to do a ban," said his spokesperson, Kathy Lenhart, "but there's a lot of people who just don't think it's all that bad of a deal—that boys will be boys."

As the Times goes, so goes the New York media, so Thursday was one of those feeding frenzies where many of the local television and radio stations did their own UFC stories, most half-cocked with both group's main promoters, Bob Meyrowitz of UFC and Donald Zuckerman of EFC, getting on several television and radio stations. There were films of boxers being interviewed saying that unlike boxing, UFC is all brutality and has no skill involved. There were the requisite doctors who had never seen a fight talking about the potential damage. Meyrowitz said that in the entire onslaught which saw him interviewed by all four major network affiliates and several the area newspapers and radio stations that there was only one reporter who had talked with him who had actually seen an event.

This led to second day stories in both the Times and New York Daily News, largely based on Giuliani and New York City Council President Peter Vallone saying they were going to work together to get the EFC event on 3/28 banned from the city.

"I think extreme fighting is disgusting, it's horrible," said the Mayor. "I happen to be a boxing fan, have been all my life. And I know there are issues regarding boxing, and they are serious ones. But this is way beyond boxing. This is people brutalizing each other."

However, state athletic commission spokesperson Gwen Lee said that the city can't overrule the state legislature (which has legalized the event).

The original Times story gave the impression that the local politicians were running for cover on the issue, despite the fact that legislation to regulate and thus legalize UFC in New York passed by a landslide in both houses after SEG sent a major lobbyist to try and keep legislation from passing that would ban the events and gave testimony with stats showing a lower injury rate than in boxing or football.

State Republican majority leader Joseph Bruno came forward and said that he had studied statistics on injuries in these events and said that it showed these events were less dangerous than boxing matches. "We ought to regulate it in the same way that we regulate boxing. If someone can prove me wrong, then we will revisit the issue."

It's pretty clear that one serious injury in the next two PPV shows will at least threaten the current status of the sport, unlike boxing, football or auto racing which would be able to survive numerous deaths without any threat.

It may not even take that. Reports we've received is that there is even more heat behind the scenes politically on both EFC and UFC than is apparent even from the media, to the point that Penthouse, which backs EFC, has scheduled a major meeting on 1/24 where the subject of dropping EFC altogether because of the heat will be brought up.

Meanwhile, the story got some press in the Niagara Falls Gazette where Hynes and Meyrowitz traded editorial viewpoints on the subject in the local newspaper. Hynes article showed he was clearly unfamiliar with the event he was trying to ban stating things like there was no opportunity for a doctor or second to examine an injured fighter during a match (because there are no round breaks), which is clearly not the case, and that the event was without mercy, which the tap rule (which Hynes on the Phil Donahue show in arguing this same issue didn't even know existed) is almost a contradiction to as well.

In the midst of all the public media clamor, the subject of pro wrestling, in particular, ECW was brought up by Vallone. On WABC radio on 1/16, Vallone said he saw a tape of ECW wrestling and talked about the blood and the chairs and said if there would ever be a show within his district (Astoria, Queens) he would make sure the police shut the show down. ECW has a date scheduled in Queens on 2/20 and has received word from the athletic commission to tone the show down at least a little in regard to things like fighting over the railing and gotten friendly warnings that this isn't the time to do something that will make the papers.

It culminated on both 1/17 and 1/19 with editorials in the Times and Daily News respectively. The Daily News editorial was short and to the point saying "Extreme Fighting is extremely brutal and stupid and should be banned." The Times editorial, entitled "Ban This Extreme Barbarism" stated:

Merely regulating a barbaric act does not change its nature. Nor does posting doctors at ringside to prevent the combatants from killing each other turn a bloody public spectacle into a legitimate sport.

The commercial sponsors of "extreme" or "ultimate" fighting maintain that such bouts are safe because no contestant has yet to be killed. But that fact is more a testimonial to the novelty of these competitions than to their safety value. Unfortunately, the promoters managed to sell that line to gullible state legislators who passed a law last year making New York the first state to sanction extreme fighting, which Illinois and Missouri have outlawed as dangerous.

Extreme fighting puts two contestants in a ring surrounded by a chain-link fence. They are allowed to pummel each other into pulp until one of them becomes unconscious or surrenders, or until a doctor stops the action because a contestant has sustained serious injury. Head butts, kicks to the groin, punches to the kidneys are all allowed. The rules prohibit only eye-gouging, biting and, in New York State at least, kicks to the throat. No one wins points for style; the promoters hawk violence, blood and pain, not athletic technique. The fact that audiences may relish seeing men bleed, and that some fighters will risk any amount of injury for prize money or glory, does not justify the state's approving these exhibitions of brutality.

State Senator Roy Goodman of Manhattan, Governor George Pataki and New York City's Mayor, Rudolph Giuliani, worked to block an extreme-fighting match at Brooklyn's Park Slope Armory in 1995. But Mr. Pataki eventually signed the new state law because his veto would have been overridden. As a result, the politicians may now be powerless to block a match scheduled by the same sports promoter in Manhattan in March.

Supporters of extreme fighting contend that legalization will allow the State Athletic Commission to regulate the events. But in fact, the commission will not change the nature of the contests, which are distinguished by their lack of rules. The new state law may also make it difficult for communities to ban the repulsive fights by pre-empting local ordinances. Mayor Giuliani will test that issue with his proposed ordinance to ban the fights in New York City.

Governor Pataki has vowed to reintroduce a bill to ban the fights statewide. At the very least, communities ought to have a say in whether they want such events taking place in their midst. Repeal of the new law would give communities that prerogative. It would also nullify the promoters' efforts to enhance their sport's acceptability throughout the country by brandishing the official blessing of New York. In a culture awash in violence, there is no need for another form of savagery as entertainment.

FEBRUARY 3

In a reversal of position largely due to media pressure, in particular the New York Times editorial on 1/17, the future of NHB fighting in New York state is in serious jeopardy.

On 1/27, New York state Senate majority leader Joseph Bruno and state Assembly speaker Sheldon Silver indicated the new law that goes into effect in a matter of days regulating and thus legalizing NHB events under the state athletic commission was under serious reconsideration.

Largely due to pressure from both the media, and then from Governor George Pataki and New York City Mayor Rudolph Giuliani, Bruno brought up a bill which would give local governments the power to ban the events.

According to a New York Times article on 1/28, Bruno said the outrage of New York city leaders (Giuliani, City Council speaker Peter Vallone and State Senator Roy Goodman) persuaded him to restudy the matter. Bruno said he talked with Pataki who said he would sign an ordinance giving local authorities the power to ban the events although the Governor indicated he would rather the legislature sponsor a bill to ban the events entirely in New York.

Pat Lynch, a spokesperson for Silver, said that speaker was looking for nothing less than an outright ban. "He believes that it is a barbaric exercise that can permanently maim individuals who participate and as such, should not be a sporting event in the state."

A bill to give localities the power to ban the event or to simply ban it stateside could come up for a vote as early as 1/29 because the tide in both houses of the legislature, which passed the bill to legalize and regulate NHB by a landslide margin late last year, has totally turned.

"Everybody thinks, it seems, it ought to be banned," Bruno said. Bruno was the lone politician last week who publicly backed the original bill saying that the statistics on injuries simply don't justify banning the event, pointing out boxing has a higher injury rate and there is no call to ban it. The irony is the same politicians who were the most vocal in passing the original bill are the ones publicly making the most of the latest controversy and trying to get a new bill passed for a statewide ban. Bruno said he favors allowing localities to impose their own rules as opposed to the state-wide ban. Both bills were introduced to committee on 1/24.

Goodman, on 10/11, after his bill regulating the sport passed, said, "We heard from public officials and medical professionals, as well as from the fighters themselves, and were able to pinpoint the problems with the sport. My legislation addresses those problems, protecting both the participants and the public.

This legislation will put an end to unbridled human cockfighting which can seriously injure contestants and which sets a terrible example to our youth."

On 1/28, Goodman sent out a press release claiming he is battling lobbying Jiu Jitsu experts to outlaw what he called "human cockfighting."

"These fights are no different from street brawls. Contestants use brutal techniques, including kicking, chopping, head butts and choke holds." Goodman said the recently passed legislation (which, he was the one who authored and got passed) doesn't change its fundamental nature or turn a bloody public spectacle into legitimate sport (basically word-for-word what the Times editorial that changed the sentiment of the state legislature stated)."especially disturbing is the terrible behavioral example which these contests set for our impressionable youth."

No legislation would go into effect in time to threaten the 2/7 UFC PPV show from Niagara Falls, which has sold just under 3,000 tickets.

However, the Extreme Fighting PPV show scheduled for 3/28 in Manhattan will probably be moved to Iowa. "From a practical point of view, it's highly unlikely that the event is going to take place in New York City," said EFC promoter Donald Zuckerman.

The state boxing commission in Iowa has a set of rules for shootfighting, which are far more stringent than the rules previous EFC events have been governed under.

The proposed legislation would also place UFC's tentative date for what it was planning as a major breakthrough show in the Nassau Coliseum on 5/30 in grave jeopardy. The date, which was dependent upon the Islanders being eliminated from the playoffs early enough to begin local advertising, would have been the first UFC event in the New York City market. UFC has lost a great deal of popularity in the Northeast in 1996 due to it not being carried by Cablevision systems, which services much of that portion of the country.

"My reaction is confusion," said SEG President Bob Meyrowitz. "It seemed to me that New York state had taken a very intelligent step. Now, with absolutely no facts, people are pushing the New York state legislature to make a change in what seemed like a good law, an intelligent law."

Jose Torres, a well-known former world light heavyweight champion boxer, noted boxing author, former head of the New York State athletic commission, and current EFC commissioner (which isn't a figurehead position), wrote a letter back to the Times decrying its editorial.

Your call to ban extreme fighting in New York (editorial, Jan. 17) was unfounded. When I was inducted into the Boxing Hall of Fame last week, I had occasion to reflect on the sport that has been a part of my life for over 40 years. I concluded that boxers use every bit of skill, trickery and determination to win. Interestingly, the champions are usually those men with the best character.

This is exactly the case with extreme fighting, the combat sport you inaccurately denounce as one in which fighters "pummel each other into pulp until one of them becomes unconscious or surrenders." Last October, I became commissioner of a group that promotes extreme fighting. I accepted this appointment only after assuring myself that the fighters in no way attempted to maim or kill their opponents. The fighters wear protective gear, and the matches are supervised by a referee and overseen by doctors with full, independent discretion to stop a bout.

While there have been injuries and deaths as a result of boxing matches, auto racing and high school football have claimed even more lives and serious injuries. Yet your newspaper routinely covers these sports. For you to then call for the ban of a sport that has never caused a death or serious injury because it is too brutal seems spurious.

My endorsement of extreme fighting is based on a long history of actual participation in combat sports. Your criticism seems based more on perception than reality. Just because politicians who may never have seen an extreme fighting match want to ban it, that is not a good reason to join the politically popular parade. If censors and politicians succeed in banning these events, their next target may be our religion, our sexual preference or the books we read.

FEBRUARY 10

As is nearly always the case, in the days leading to up the UFC PPV, it is the courts that are providing most of the hype and action.

Semaphore Entertainment Group filed suit on 2/3 against the New York State Athletic Commission and Chairman Floyd Patterson and Commissioner Rose Trentman after the Athletic Commission introduced a series of rules that would totally change the face of UFC and were obviously designed not to make the show safer, but to ruin the show.

The lawsuit, filed in U.S. Federal Court for the Southern District in Manhattan, NY, claims the imposition of the new regulations at the last minute violates Article I of the U.S. Constitution which prohibits states from passing laws that interfere with existing contracts, as well as provision for due process. The suit was filed not only to get a legal order immediately preventing the state athletic commission from implementing new rules for the 2/7 show, but also an attempt to get a federal ruling in their favor stopping the state from being able to squash the proposed 5/30 show at the Nassau Coliseum.

While there is no question that an event under UFC rules will take place on PPV on 2/7, actions of the Athletic commission in New York put into question whether it would emanate from Niagara Falls, NY as is scheduled. At press time on Tuesday, SEG was planning for the event to take place in Niagara Falls and UFC officials believed the chances of a last-minute move to a secondary site somewhere in the South were very slim. Many SEG officials and several of the fighters and other people associated with the event were already in Buffalo and Niagara Falls as of press time.

Due to pressure from numerous politicians in New York, the athletic commission sent both SEG and Battlecade Inc. (which promotes Extreme Fighting Championship which is still publicly scheduled for Manhattan although the odds of it happening within the state of New York on 3/28 are extremely slim) an extensive rule book publicly designed to make the matches safer but realistically designed to force the show on 2/7 to be moved out of New York since, because a law was passed legalizing the event, the politicians won't be able to enact a law that would go into effect rescinding the new law in time to prevent the show.

Among the rules stipulated by the commission were banning chokes, the most prevalent submission move used in UFC matches; kicking above the shoulders or below the knee; head-butting; any strikes to the throat (which had previously already been banned in the existing law); striking an opponent while down; usage of knees and elbows to strike; any strikes to the neck or spine areas; attacking the groin area; mandating combatants wearing eight ounce boxing gloves as opposed to the fingerless grappling gloves; mandating all combatants wear protective headgear ala amateur boxers; implementing five weight classes and banning any matches in which the two combatants aren't in the same weight class (thereby destroying the planned tournament line-up for Friday); having the matches fought in five-minute rounds to be judged by athletic commission boxing judges on the ten point must system; and making it mandatory for an octagon if used, to be at least 40-feet in diameter. The octagon used by UFC is 32-feet in diameter so this rule in essence shows the real intention of the law since it would force UFC to have to build a new octagon which it couldn't do so quickly and thus force them out of the state.

The word we've received is that if forced to use those rules, the event will be moved out of the state. The rules aren't fair to the fighters based on their skills and how they've trained as it basically turns it into a tough man contest with headgear. Ironically, tough man contests, like boxing and other sports including forms of hard hitting and high flying worked pro wrestling have a higher injury rate than UFC but haven't become political hot potatoes. In the UFC controversy, both in the city council in New York and on talk shows and among politicians in Buffalo, EFC and ECW have been confused and interchanged regularly with people talking about banning the events where they use chairs and tables on each other. The mandated gloves and banning of chokes takes away the wrestling and submission skills which actually makes the fights much safer because they consist of something other than banging to the head with gloves to protect the hands in a long fight. In fact, chokes, while misunderstood by people with no experience or understanding of judo, are probably the safest finishing technique in a UFC event. A PPV under those rules would destroy subsequent buy rates for the rest of the year, not to mention several of the fighters would have to seriously consider pulling out.

APRIL 14

The bill to ban NHB, not only from live events but also events to air on PPV, won approval from committee in the Hawaii state senate and was considered likely to gain full senate approval. The Hawaii house of representatives had already passed the proposal. Hawaii has its own regular NHB promotion called UFCF that runs shows every few months at the Blaisdell Center Arena in Honolulu, with the next show planned for 4/16 with Kimo vs. Brian Johnston as the main event, generally drawing about 3,000 to 4,000 per show. The local debate was no different than anywhere else. Senator Rosalyn Baker stated, for example, "There is no level of skill required. It's anything goes. It's the kind of thing that if they were doing this outside the ring, people could end up on aggravated assault charges, attempted murder charges, or even attempted manslaughter charges.

MAY 19

The NHB world suffered its latest in what seem to be weekly political blows with the announcement that Time-Warner Cable systems will drop carrying its PPV shows, believed to take effect after the 5/30 UFC show, a blow so devastating to the genre that it caused the Extreme Fighting Championship to tap out for apparently the final time.

"As of this afternoon, my show's over," said EFC promoter and booker John Perretti to Vale Tudo News on 5/7. "We're finished. The powers that be have beaten us."

EFC, which first went out of business on 4/14, liquidating the company known as Battlecade Inc., got a new investor, believed to be Japanese, and re-opened the company under the name Extreme Fighting and scheduled a PPV show on 8/15 in Davenport, IA. That show was canceled this past week.

Many Time-Warner systems, mainly in the Southeast, pulled the plug literally at the last minute on the most recent EFC show even in systems that were still advertising the show even after the pullout. SEG promoter David Isaacs said he believed Time-Warner systems would carry the 5/30 UFC on a system-by-system decision basis. Other Time-Warner systems decided not to pull the last EFC show because so much advertising had been out and there.

Time Warner is the second largest cable operator in the United States, behind only TCI, which officially pulled out of carrying NHB events after the 3/28 EFC show.

Time Warner's decision came on the heels of National Cable Television Association President Decker Anstrom urging all the cable operators to pull out of carrying NHB shows in the 5/5 Cable World trade journal. Anstrom said he felt it would be the politically correct thing to do because Congress, which is contemplating regulation of the cable industry, is putting pressure on the cable industry to curtail violent programming and banning NHB events would politically look like the cable industry is taking a step in the right direction.

At the same time, Semaphore Entertainment Group officials have been meeting with TCI about reversing its position. It is believed TCI will come to a decision yay or nay sometime this coming week. It is believed that SEG has offered several rule alterations in UFC as a concession to get TCI to agree to carry future shows, perhaps even the next one, including making the wearing of gloves mandatory, a position Isaacs admitted is more designed to make it look like sport to outsiders than one which would actually in reality minimize the brutality and injury risk.

TCI expressed major concern which led to the decision not to carry the events which included Leo Hindery, who has been anti-UFC coming on board as new company President, but also claimed the New York (and perhaps Hawaii law) could be interpreted as banning the events to be able to be aired (in Hawaii, there is no interpretation as a television and PPV ban is specifically spelled out) and they didn't want to be on the wrong side of the law. They wanted SEG to present the event to where it looked more like sport and less like a spectacle, and because Americans think of boxing as sporting, the gloves were a compromise offered in that vain.

The thought process seems to be that if the industry leader, TCI, reverses its position, that Time Warner would likely follow suit, leaving only Cablevision, the seventh largest cable operator, as the lone major not carrying the programming. In addition, a reversal of positions may stop what has basically been a domino effect of systems looking into and officially dropping NHB shows. As of press time, the events are no longer available throughout Canada, which was the strongest market for UFC in its heyday, and in 35 to 40 percent of the American PPV universe.

With EFC officially folding and releasing all its fighters from their contracts, SEG signed EFC heavyweight champion Maurice Smith on 5/13. Smith is expected to be introduced on the 5/30 UFC show, possibly in the role of color commentator, to build up a 7/27 PPV champion vs. champion match against UFC champion Mark Coleman. Exactly how Smith's EFC championship will be addressed on the UFC broadcast is unknown at press time but it is believed his EFC championship and WKA heavyweight kick boxing championship would both be acknowledged on the next broadcast.

Negotiations to hold that show at the Yokohama Arena in Japan, as a co-promotion with the Samurai 24-hour fighting cable channel, appear to have fallen through for many reasons. Among them is that Smith is under contract to RINGS in Japan and thus wouldn't be able to appear on a UFC show taking place in Japan, and the inability to put together a show that would mean something both in Japan and the United States.

The Japanese promoters, H2O promotions out of Nagoya, were wanting a Don Frye vs. Genichiro Tenryu match, and UFC officials didn't like that pairing because of the risk of Tenryu, 47, getting seriously injured in such a match. The Japanese promoters wanted to use pro wrestlers Koji Kitao and Koki Kitahara as well for their name value because they were close to the WAR group, and UFC didn't want that close a connection to pro wrestling and thought such a show would lack interest in the United States which is still where the promotion has to draw from. The Japanese promoters didn't want Yoshiki Takahashi because of his affiliation with Pancrase, even though a Takahashi vs. Jerry Bohlander match seems to be a natural from a booking standpoint stemming from the 2/7 PPV show. There were also numerous technical problems with producing a show in Japan for broadcast in the United States that needed to be worked out but time was running out on getting it done with enough time to properly put together the show. There is still talk of holding a show in Japan later in 1997.

MAY 26

The dominoes kept falling this week, leaving the future of no-holds-barred fighting on PPV in the gravest of situations.

After TCI officially turned down the attempts by both fans of NHB and by Semaphore Entertainment Group to get the company to reconsider its ban on allowing its systems to carry future shows, an even bigger blow followed when Request television informed SEG that after the 5/30 show, it would no longer carry future events due to the fact that so many of the systems it carries programming for (roughly 50% or more of the systems Request serves) wasn't going to be airing the shows. It is believed that Jones Cable, another of the nation's largest conglomerates, had followed in the footsteps of Cablevision, TCI and Time-Warner Cable in deciding not to carry Ultimate Fighting Championship PPV shows after the next program.

For those keeping track with a scorecard, Cablevision, TCI and some Time-Warner systems won't be carrying the 5/30 show. The remainder of the Time-Warner systems, Jones and Request are pulling out after the next show.

Due to the lack of penetration into the PPV universe, it is nearly impossible to see any kind of a bright future for the Ultimate Fighting Championships, coming on the heels of the folding of the Extreme Fighting Championships for exactly the same reason.

Leo Hindery Jr., the President of TCI, wrote a letter on 5/14 to Bob Meyrowitz, the CEO of Semaphore, the parent company of UFC, stating:

Thanks for the constructive effort you and your colleagues have made to meet some of our objections to carriage by TCI of Ultimate Fighting Championship events. However, we have decided to maintain our current position regarding carriage of the telecasts.

A primary reason for our decision is that states in which TCI has millions of customers do not allow the events to be held within their jurisdictions. This is a clear indication that regulatory authorities in these states consider the events inappropriate, given their current format.

The long-term solution obviously is to seek the type of widespread state sanctioning that is common for other athletic events of this type. Please keep us informed if you make progress in this regard.

Meyrowitz and SEG had been in heavy negotiations for weeks with Hindery, to the point that Meyrowitz had been heavily praising one of his long-time critics in the media. SEG had offered numerous rule concessions in an attempt to get TCI to reverse its position and was actually fairly confident of a reversal, which would be a major victory at a time the company needed one, so the news hit like a ton of bricks. While we are not aware of all of them, one of them was to make wearing gloves mandatory in UFC matches and certain types of strikes were going to be banned.

There will be no rule changes for the 5/30 show, but it is expected there will be significant changes in an attempt to get cable companies to reverse their positions and attempt to get boxing commissions in key states to sanction the events which is apparently what the industry leader, TCI, is wanting, before the 7/27 show. That's another political problem because of the heavy boxing influence in most of the key commissions, which simply don't want this around, as the actions of the commission in New York showed by implementing the ridiculous last minute rule book to kill the February event. What the new rules will be haven't been finalized at press time but it is believed they'll include both mandatory gloves and banning attacking the fingers (a tactic which has never been used in a UFC fight up to this point anyway).

SEG is still working on doing a follow-up show on 7/27, rumored to be in Mobile, AL after the attempts to run a show in Japan on that date fell through. After doing the math, SEG feels the show will still be available in 17 million homes because at present, Viewers Choice is the carrier of choice in 61 percent of the PPV universe in the United States. With scaling back costs, it is still enough homes to make the show potentially viable if the buy rate is decent. There is talk of running a show later this year in Russia, and perhaps still going to Japan by the end of the year as well. Running a show from a foreign country is only going to result in an overall more expensive production coming at the same time SEG is said to be re-working the budgets so the next shows should be scaled way back from a production and talent standpoint.

While these dominos have all fallen in recent weeks, the dye had been cast months ago. At a national cable convention, one leading pro wrestling promoter had informed us that the talk of the convention was that UFC and EFC were "done." They saw the pattern with buy rates no longer being what they were, combined with the fate of cable in the hands of a committee empowered by Sen. John McCain of Arizona, that it would be the politically wise move to jump off the NHB bandwagon.

David Isaacs, who heads the UFC division for SEG, said that the letter sent by National Cable Television Association President Decker Anstrom two weeks ago urging all the cable operators to pull out of carrying NHB events was a potent factor in the dominos falling, far more than he realized at the time the letter went out.

"Our buy rates have been good, but not great, but the others (EFC, MARS) have been crappy," Isaacs said. "These changes have made it so the other events aren't going to be able to continue. By getting rid of the other events, the buy rates for the entire genre are going to start looking better."

The fact is, in the court of public, media and private opinion, UFC and its competitors had always fared poorly. While they could continue to point to the lack of serious injuries in the competition as compared to numerous other sports, they were constantly haunted by their own over-the-top promotions before running afoul of political and media problems promising the bloodiest most violent sport around, and their own promotional bragging about it being banned in so many states during the early days of the genre when it actually wasn't banned anywhere. That kind of hype likely led to buy rates rapidly escalating in the sport's early days.

UFC gained popularity initially under the guise that they were pitting champions from various combat sports and putting them in a tournament to see not only who the toughest fighter in the world is, but is the best fighting style. Even from the start, credentials of fighters were exaggerated and even created out of thin air in some cases, and the early successful shows turned into a commercial for the wonders of Brazilian Jiu Jitsu as practiced by unbeaten champion Royce Gracie, who made himself the biggest martial arts star on the planet through winning three of the first four tournaments. But as the years went on, it became apparent that the key issues that drew curiosity in the early shows were no longer there.

Ironically, for the most part, the quality of the fighters has increased greatly from the early shows, but the public generally doesn't recognize that and has still seen star after star from UFC walk away without being clearly beaten and sees the current crop as second rate in comparison to the early stars. Nobody was kidding anyone any longer that the winner of a UFC tournament gave a guy a legitimate claim to being the toughest man alive or proof of a superior fighting style. While most of the shows were well received by people who bought the shows, with no outside hype mechanism and little done to create and make stars, the novelty noticeably began wearing thin in 1996, which some blame on the Dan Severn vs. Ken Shamrock match in May, although that would be far too simplistic an explanation.

The fact is creating a new viable sport is never easy, and even when UFC was drawing the monster buy rates in 1995, the media rated it as a level below tough man contests on their respectability scale. For long-term success as something other than a novelty, it either needed to be able to control its own hype, like pro wrestling, or to be treated in the media as a serious and important sport, thus getting the benefit of that kind of hype.

Their own contradictions on the glove issue, which UFC officials and its spokesperson when in political jams, referee John McCarthy, would point out the lack of gloves inherently make the matches safer, yet the fact was they did allow competitors to wear gloves and it did turn the matches into bloodier and less technical bouts. While UFC talked about having Olympic caliber medal wrestlers and top caliber martial artists on its shows, the competitions were also stacked in many cases with fighters who obviously didn't belong chosen above the numerous world-class wrestlers and judo players that had expressed interest in competing.

At times the company seemed to want to run tournaments and title matches to set up what its fan base wanted, to find out who the toughest man alive was, although none ever worked out exactly as hoped for. At times the company seemed to have an attitude of putting almost anyone in and that the public would pay to see the UFC name with the idea of doing tournaments with a few big names and rounding out the tournament with guys who didn't have a prayer.

Once it became clear that the wrestlers were dominating the field, numerous world class wrestlers, Tom Erikson in particular, were avoided because of the thought, in his case, he didn't look right, was too much like another Dan Severn, and because in reality few thought that there was anyone around who could beat him and they were afraid of him being a dominant force. While publicly trying to portray themselves as a mixed martial arts contest, the company continually attempted to build and push Tank Abbott because of his charisma, but who also was the flesh and blood representative of everything their critics claimed they were. While Abbott came out of UFC's most successful event, a July 1995 show in Casper, WY, as its most talked about fighter, a September 1996 show built around Abbott's return which was geared toward a match between he and Mark Coleman that never happened, drew UFC's weakest buy rate to date.

Isaacs has continually maintained that SEG is in the UFC for the long haul, and that as satellite dishes grow in popularity, there will come a time that they'll be able to be in enough homes without having to worry about cable companies and cable carriers. But those days aren't soon even under the most optimistic of projections, and with lower quality shows due to budgetary cutbacks on the horizon, and less exposure in much of the country, realistically the genre won't be able to maintain even its current level of interest even if that day arrives in a few years. Isaacs is confident, however, that with a lot of outside publicity in recent weeks for UFC, from being featured in two episodes of "Friends" (which finished No. 4 in the ratings in the episode where Abbott has a brief cameo), on MTV, the Learning Channel and expected strong hype over the next few weeks on WWF television, that the 5/30 show will produce a solid number.

JUNE 16

In an effort to save its sport from a political extinction, Semaphore Entertainment Group is expected to formally announce a series of rule changes within the UFC effective on the 7/27 PPV show. The official announcement should come within the next two weeks in an attempt to regain PPV coverage by Request, TCI and Time Warner.

The rule changes are designed to not change the basics of what the sport has grown to be. The rule changes include no attacking the fingers or toes (which nobody has done to date in the history of UFC), mandatory grappling gloves, no throat strikes (another thing that nobody has actually ever been able to do in a UFC match to date), no groin shots (which has been done a few times although not in a notable sense any time recently), no hair pulling (which really only came into effect in the Royce Gracie vs. Kimo match in 1994), no elbows to the back of the head, no stomping and no pressure point striking, whatever that is supposed to mean. Most of these were rules designed to alleviate questions that state athletic commissions have had with UFC, because TCI said that if the states where the commissions won't approve UFC will change their viewpoints, that they would be happy to carry the shows.

The political problem here is that the commissions aren't banning UFC for its potential danger but in most cases making a political statement to protect the powerful boxing interests that control the commissions in key states like New York, California and Nevada. For example, the idea of pressure point striking comes from martial arts mythology of things like paralyzing and death blows that are what's known as voodoo martial arts and not one blow of the type has ever been done in a UFC and they don't occur in sports like karate, boxing or kick boxing. There was pressure additionally to ban knees, elbows and head-butts, but SEG refused to acquiesce to those requests feeling it would change the basic nature of what the sport is.

John Peretti, who was the booker for the defunct Extreme Fighting promotion, has resurfaced once again, this time claiming to be in the process of inventing a new sport without the political headaches. The sport would basically be submission wrestling with no striking at all allowed, fought with three three minute rounds, overtimes, a point system for takedowns and throws, five weight divisions and no draws. He's talking about debuting this sport on PPV in October using players from Judo, Freestyle wrestling, shootfighting and Jiu-Jitsu. Realistically, this has no chance on PPV. Eliminating the striking should logically get rid of all governmental opposition although logic has never played a part in these decisions. However, Americans aren't going to buy in any great numbers a combat sport that doesn't involve striking in some form to the face. Pancrase, which had open hand striking and kicking along with submissions, failed to make a dent.

JULY 14

The problems financially stemming from the bans from various cable companies continues to threaten the future of UFC. As mentioned last week, SEG has pulled Carlos Barretto and Murillo Bustamante off the 7/27 PPV show because of the costs of flying them and their entourages in from Brazil and replacing them with fighters with lesser name value. Apparently SEG has done the budget and figures that this upcoming show is going to lose money no matter what, and they are trying to keep the losses as low as possible.

The current plan is that the heavyweight tournament will have Mark Kerr vs. Daniel Bobish and Brian Johnston vs. Moti Horenstein and the light heavyweight tournament will have Kevin Jackson vs. Youri Valouns and Joe Moreira vs. Todd Butler. SEG will no longer use the term No Holds Barred in advertising its events and the term has been banned for usage on its television shows, instead the events are to be called either reality fighting or mixed martial arts.

In addition, the scheduled 9/26 PPV show from Russia is being moved to 10/17 and the change in date means the show won't be in Russia. They are moving it back three weeks because they are crossing their fingers and hoping that with the new rules that some cable systems will agree to carry the follow-up show, and three weeks gives them more time to attempt to get systems to reverse their position, something at this point there is no groundswell to do.

JULY 21

More bad news as it relates to the future on PPV. Despite the rule changes, there appears to be no movement in regard to cable companies that have pulled UFC changing their minds nor is there any indication any reconsideration will take place. SEG lost a lot of money two shows back because of the last second move, and lost money on the last show because TCI joined the other systems in not carrying the show. The 7/27 show is going to be the third money losing show in a row because there just isn't enough distribution, particularly with Request TV not carrying the show, which makes the future questionable because how long will they continue to produce shows that simply because of outside forces be unable to turn a profit?

Chapter Two

Major Changes to WWF Programming

FEBRUARY 3

Don't be surprised to see either major or minor changes in regard to Monday Night Raw. The rating on 1/20, where WWF came the day after a major PPV show where it changed the world title and had a controversial Rumble finish and opened a hot Raw show with Bret Hart quitting, and Nitro still won the hour handily and scored a tremendous second hour rating were major causes of concern for both WWF and USA Network.

At press time no changes were official, but what has being talked about by both sides didn't include switching Raw to a new date, but was more along the lines of going live as frequently as the schedule permits and increasing the show to two hours so that the first hour of Raw on USA doesn't end up providing the second hour of Nitro on TNT, its rival network, with a tremendous lead-in.

The cost of doing a show of that type would run into six figures weekly, so it's an interesting question how the bill would be split between USA and Titan Sports. When WCW went live weekly with Nitro, both USA and WWF officials publicly talked about how much money Turner was wasting doing that, but it turned out to be the difference in TNT beating out USA last year as the top network in prime time which is big-time bragging rights that USA will do almost anything to reverse.

WWF announced a Raw taping on 2/24 at the Manhattan Center, which would be a live show coming just one week after the live show on 2/17 from Nashville. The WWF word is that the Manhattan Center show was just an experiment at this point.

FEBRUARY 10

As of press time on 2/4, there was still no deal between the WWF and USA Network regarding doing a weekly two-hour generally live Monday Night Raw show head-to-head with Nitro.

There has been much talk between the sides, and Raw was expanded to two hours on 2/3 and it is believed that will continue on 2/17 and 2/24 although even that hasn't been confirmed. It appears the WWF and USA Network both want the two-hour live format, but the hold up appears to be what percentage each side is going to pay of the estimated $100,000 per week plus it would cost to do a weekly live shoot.

The WWF has been working toward the probability of a two-hour live show most weeks, and at one point last week USA Network even told advertisers of the format change as a long-term deal, but has since shied away in being committed past the end of February. The first two-hour show, taped three nights earlier at Sky Dome in Toronto, was basically a last week deal as WWF didn't get the official word from USA as to whether the show would be one hour or two hours until the evening of 1/29, although there had been talks and it was well known by the previous weekend it was a strong possibility.

The impetus for the change is coming more from USA than WWF, because it's highly touted new series "Le Femme Nikita" is struggling in the ratings against TNT's "Robin Hood." The reason the changes are being rushed is because February are sweeps month where the basic advertising rates are determined based on overall prime time ratings so it's more important for all TV stations to hotshot this month, particularly USA and TNT because of their close battle to bragging rights of being the top rated prime time cable network.

The belief at the USA Network is that the one hour Raw is providing TNT was a tremendous lead-in for the second hour of Nitro, which did 4.4 ratings on both 1/20 and 1/27 while the USA 9 p.m. programming has gone down the tubes in competition. While Nitro beats Raw in the head-to-head hour every week, the margin of the victory is much closer than in the second hour with Nitro hour two against whatever USA puts in the 9 p.m. hour.

The original plan, due to February sweeps, is that USA wanted the WWF to air the entire Royal Rumble on the one-hour show on 2/3, which was pushed all week as "Royal Rumble Monday." The reason is that the highest rated pro wrestling show in the history of the USA Network was the 1988 Royal Rumble, which did an 8.2 rating (broadcasted live one year before it became a PPV fixture), and that's the type of thing you copy during sweeps.

However, after agreeing to air the Rumble, Request and Viewers Choice protested and apparently there is some kind of exclusivity protection in their PPV deals so instead what aired of the Rumble on the two-hour show ended up being three different 30 second clips rather than the entire 50 minute match. At the same time, USA now wanted a two-hour show so the decision was made to turn the 1/31 house show in Toronto, which had a huge advance, into a Raw television taping.

However, with all the pressure on both sides for the first two-hour head-to-head confrontation, both shows were major disappointments despite each drawing a large live crowd. From a ratings standpoint, the margin of WCW's victory, as expected, was cut noticeably from previous weeks as Nitro did a 3.04 rating and 4.6 share to Raw's 2.64 rating and 3.9 share which is the first sign of what the effects of a two hour show will be.

The Nitro rating has to be a disappointment since the teased but never outright announced that there would be a Hulk Hogan vs. Roddy Piper title match later in the show. The first hour was very close, with WCW with a 2.76 to 2.64 edge, but WCW was still the show that picked up steam and easily won the second hour 3.31 to 2.63.

WWF opened with a sizable lead with Austin vs. Vader at 2.67 against Dragon vs. Mendoza and Kidman vs. Glacier at 2.34. That was the only point WCW trailed. Ice Train-Parka against Vega-Funk was a 2.55 tie. Steiners-Heat vs. the beginning of the tag title bout saw a huge 3.17 to 2.46 gap and Enos-Malenko vs. tag title finish was 2.99 to 2.87 (although trailing at this point, the tag title match was the WWF show's peak rating). Page-Renegade against Crush-Goldust was 2.99 to 2.74 edge for WCW. Wright-Calo vs. the Michaels-Hart interview segment was 3.24 to 2.74 WCW edge. Konnan-Benoit vs. Mero-Helmsley was 3.37 to 2.43 WCW edge, and the Jarrett deal and mainly Hogan-Piper confrontation against the Undertaker match was 3.64 to 2.61 WCW edge.

WCW drew the first real sellout to pro wrestling at the Mid South Coliseum in Memphis since a March 1986 match with Jerry Lawler & Dutch Mantel vs. Bill Dundee & Buddy Landel (hey, you should have seen the television show building up that match). The actual attendance was nowhere near record breaking since production killed several thousand seats with the total crowd at 8,173 (6,946 paying $77,128) while the aforementioned sellout was closer to 11,000. On television they announced thousands were turned away but it was more like a few hundred. The gate was the fourth largest for pro wrestling ever in Memphis.

The WWF drew 25,628 (an estimated 22,000 paying $324,326) to Sky Dome, which they billed several times as the largest crowd in the history of Monday night television. Vince McMahon called it a capacity crowd even though the place holds more than 65,000. McMahon and Jim Ross threw frequent barbs through the two-hour live voice-over of the taped matches, making numerous references to bait-and-switch tactics, presumably on

Nitro, saying they deliver what they advertise and will deliver the complete matches they say they will and aren't teasing with a match that may or may not take place (in reference to WCW opening the Nitro show teasing that there would be a Hogan-Piper match which ended up simply being a confrontation angle and no match). Of course, with USA plugging airing of the Rumble heavily for one week and it being only 30 second clips, one has to say this wasn't the week for WWF to be name-calling about those tactics.

Both shows were disappointments. The Sky Dome was poorly lit, the crowd wasn't well miced and most of the matches were disappointments. It came off as a dead show, reminiscent of one of those bad WWF house shows that used to be featured on the old "Prime Time Wrestling" two hour show in the 80s, leaving many to question whether the WWF has the talent depth to put on a weekly quality two-hour show. They do on paper, but this show wasn't a good argument supporting that case.

WCW had a hotter crowd on television, but killed the crowd on a show where seven of the nine matches were very bad, and the finishes up and down were even worse, particularly a double-run-in finish during a Steiners vs. Harlem Heat match that killed the crowd dead in its tracks for the next several matches. The only high point of the show was a closing Hulk Hogan-Roddy Piper angle where Piper brought his son out, said he wasn't accepting the match with Hogan, got insulted for a while, and came back brawling and accepting the 2/23 Cow Palace match.

The current working ideas for the WWF, all subject to change, is if the two-hour live format goes into effect on 2/17, the road schedule would change completely. Shows that already have advertising out and international tours will go on as scheduled. They are attempting to book Monday night dates where none exists in buildings near to where the Sunday live event matches are being held, so the idea that most of the tapings will be done at the Manhattan Center isn't the case. The scheduled Tuesday Superstars tapings in cities where advertising is already out, such as 2/18 in Birmingham, AL, should the changes be made, would turn into regular house shows, although eventually the shows where there is no advertising out that have been planned as Superstars tapings would likely end up being canceled.

Over the long run, the plan would be for all house show tours to last from Friday until Monday, with the wrestlers then off until the next Friday, although it will take some time under any circumstances where this will be fully implemented. The Monday show would be a live two-hour Raw taping followed by a one-hour Superstars taping for the show that airs six days later so everything on Superstars would become more current, and a dark main event match or two to keep the crowd from leaving during the Superstars taping. Superstars would contain fewer matches than in the past, maybe around four, and they'd last longer. The two-hour Raw would contain longer matches than Nitro and the attempt would be made because of that to have a better match quality, exemplified by the 2/3 show which had six matches as opposed to WCW which has anywhere from eight to 11 matches. Numbers aside, neither side succeeded that night when it came to match quality.

No final decisions have been made provided the switch to two hours live goes through, but it is believed it would also affect the weekly Shotgun Saturday Night tapings, that are done generally in New York. There has already been a lot of complaints from the wrestlers that work the Shotgun tapings, because the top stars are under downside guarantees that basically mean their price per show averages out to $1,300 to $1,700 per night minimum (even though payoffs in some cities may not reach that level, it averages out to that level if not quite a bit higher).

Between appearing on shows that look shabby and minor league, payoffs of only a few hundred dollars, most of which is eaten up in road expenses of having to say overnight in expensive New York City, poor locker room facilities and having to work past night screwing up the already screwed up sleep patterns, you can see the complaints. The fact the shows have generally been poor doesn't help matters.

Shotgun was done to give WWF a live weekly television show, but if Raw goes like weekly, the idea that the production staff would have to put together a midnight show on Saturday, a live Superstars taping the next Sunday morning and then go on the road for a live shoot every Monday is a killer in many ways and ups to the potential for Monday night live screw-ups caused by fatigue. Because of that, there is talk of taping several Shotgun shows at a time. But none of this is confirmed because the USA deal hasn't been completed.

If the deal is completed, Raw will be taped live on 2/17 in Nashville, 2/24 at the Manhattan Center, the 3/3 show will be taped from Berlin, Germany on 2/26 presumably headlined by the European title tournament championship match, 3/10 will be live from Worcester, MA, 3/17 will be live from Syracuse, NY and 3/24 will be live from Rockford, IL.

FEBRUARY 17

The World Wrestling Federation and USA Network officially confirmed on 2/10 what had been negotiated on and had been largely expected the past few weeks—a two-hour generally live Monday Night Raw would become a fixture.

If there had been any trepidation going in, the rating results on 2/3 would have ended them as the taped two-hour Raw from Toronto's Sky Dome came closer to Nitro's dominant ratings than any week in months, trailing by a 3.04 to 2.64 margin. In addition, for the first time since the two shows debuted, USA Network's prize new show, "La Femme Nikita," paced by the stronger lead-in of the second hour of Raw, beat TNT's prize new show, "Robin Hood" by a 1.5 to 1.3 margin, for the first time. The two sides had been negotiating on what percentage of the added costs, believed to be in the range of $100,000 per week, would be picked up by USA as opposed to WWF.

The first live head-to-head shot will be on 2/17 when Raw emanates from Nashville the day after the Chattanooga In Your House Final Four show, while Nitro takes place as part of the State fair in Tampa. Raw will be live every week through 3/24 with the exception of 3/3, when the show will air on tape coming from Berlin, Germany. As of press time, no final decision has been made regarding the Raw shows on 3/31, 4/7 and 4/14 while the WWF main crew will be out of the country touring South Africa, India and Kuwait. Raw will be done live from 4/21 in either Binghamton and every week thereafter for the foreseeable future.

As reported here last week, and has since been confirmed, both Raw and Superstars will be done together every Monday, with the one-hour Superstars show that airs on Sundays being taped after the completion of the live Raw show. The Tuesday shows that were originally scheduled as Superstars tapings that advertising is already out on will become regular house shows. The WWF is attempting to reschedule its tours so that when the transition period is completed, there would generally be no house shows Tuesday through Thursday every week, so wrestlers would be booked on a weekly Friday through Monday schedule.

Shotgun Saturday Night is being "reinvented," but a final decision as to what that entails hasn't been made. At least one new format idea under discussion would be to air a combination of matches from the previous weeks Raw and intersperse the show with TNT (as in the mid-80s Tuesday Night Titans television show, not the current Turner Network Television) like skits that would be taped earlier in the week at the Titan TV studio. There has also been talk of taping the show less frequently but having first-run matches. At least at present there are no more tapings scheduled which lends credence to the former as opposed to the latter.

The show on 2/8 was basically a complete throwaway featuring some 31:00 of the Godwinns, Crush and Faarooq to where there were large chants of boring the second time the two teams faced each other on the same show (first in a regular tag, second after interference as part of a six-man tag). The "boring" chants from the Penn Station crowd were so loud that Vince McMahon had to acknowledge them on the air and tried to act as if the fans were bored with the NOD. In addition, there was no announcement as to where a 2/15 show would emanate from, which theoretically would have to be in the Chattanooga area since the entire crew by Saturday night would already be in town for the PPV which means this week's show will probably combine taped matches with hype for the next day's show.

I don't know what the end result of the head-to-head two hour Monday night war is going to be as far as an ultimate winner and loser. It should, and probably will be, in the short run, the best thing for wrestling fans because both sides will be forced to put on more competitive shows. But I do believe the costs, more than monetarily, on the personal lives and sanity of those in the thick of the battle will be more than anyone has considered up to this point.

The WCW Nitro on 2/10 showed key people self destructing, either from the pressure or lack of perspective (depending upon whom we are talking about) already. The show was totally devoid of direction and it was obvious by one interview after another going nowhere that nobody has a clue where they are going. Some people have some nasty habits that they better get in check or far bigger problems than losing in the ratings are ahead. And the battle doesn't even start for another week.

MAY 19

The ever-changing Monday night wrestling wars will begin yet another chapter in August with the USA Network moving the time slot of the WWF's Raw in War show.

Due to network programming changes, which are not believed to be primarily due to any situations within pro wrestling, USA Network is moving La Femme Nikita to Sunday nights, and opening up its prime time Monday night schedule with reruns of the Chuck Norris show, "Walker: Texas Ranger." This will result in Raw most likely being moved to a 9 p.m. to 11 p.m. time slot beginning on 8/4. Neither USA network nor WWF would confirm this at press time as being official, although within the industry everyone believes this to be the most probable scenario. In theory it would enable the show to get more risqué with the later time slot. Although nobody has said as much, the belief seems to be that if the WWF was left to make the choice on its own, this wasn't a decision it would have made.

At press time, the story is so fresh that there is no definite response from WCW or feeling one way or another on what will happen. The initial feelings we've heard is that WCW won't follow WWF and move one hour later because the feeling is the earlier time slot is superior because of the ability to draw more of a kids audience both for television and to the live event which would have to end at 11 p.m. (or later for the live crowd if they were to present dark match main events) on a school night.

Eric Bischoff, at a meeting with the wrestlers on 5/12, did hint at the idea of Nitro going three hours although never expressed as they would do so to give WWF competition as much as because TBS wants a prime time wrestling vehicle and due to the work load and costs, at this point the idea of doing a second live show on another weeknight has been on hold. If Nitro expanded to three hours, the possibility would be that the third hour would be on TBS instead of TNT, that way TBS gets its live weekly prime time wrestling show to boost ratings, and the added costs of running another live taping every week would be avoided.

USA Today in its 5/12 edition reported on the time change without even mentioning the Raw show, reporting it as the network struggling with its new shows on Mondays and Saturdays this season and is going to focus its promotion on its Sunday night line-up, which is why La Femme Nikita, one of the first-run shows the network has pushed hard, is moving to Sundays starting on 6/22.

JULY 21

There is expected to be some major changes when it comes to WWF television come the fall season in September. Exactly what this entails hasn't been confirmed, but the belief at press time was that Raw would switch from being a live show weekly to taping two shows every other week since going live weekly has quadrupled expenses of doing the show without any significant movement in ratings. How that would affect the Shotgun show wasn't clear. WCW is also discussing minor changes for Nitro for the fall season to possibly counter the expected unopposed 10-11 p.m. second hour of Raw, particularly after the success WWF had during that hour for the experiment on 7/14.

The biggest news that is confirmed was the shocking 3.75 rating and 6.43 share drawn in the 10-11 p.m. time slot on 7/14 by the WWF's SummerSlam special. The show aired highlights of SummerSlam shows dating back to the first show in 1988 with Hulk Hogan & Randy Savage vs. Ted DiBiase & Andre the Giant in Madison Square Garden.

The show, built in advertising around the biggest names in wrestling of the past decade, most of whom are now in WCW with Hogan's name leading off the advertising, drew a lot of speculation within wrestling. Some felt that WWF would try in updated commentary to bury the former headliners or show them in an unflattering manner, neither of which turned out to be the case.

The show aired interviews and angles along with the original commentary on the finishes of the headline matches at the previous nine SummerSlam PPV shows, along with news clips from the same time period. Besides clips of Hogan, Savage and Elizabeth, Ric Flair, Roddy Piper, Curt Hennig (as Mr. Perfect), Scott Hall, Lex Luger and Kevin Nash (as Razor Ramon and Diesel), all of whom are now in WCW, also prominent on the show either on clips or in commentary were announcers Gene Okerlund, Bobby Heenan and Tony Schiavone and even on the first SummerSlam, in commentary, the voice of Superstar Billy Graham, not to mention a wrestler they are involved in legal action against in Jim "Ultimate Warrior" Hellwig.

It was a strange nostalgic look at WWF wrestling over the past decade, with the main impressions being just how roided up the top guys were up through five years ago, how much worse the main events were in those days, and the fact that overall the crowd heat, as impressive as if often seems today, was generally even more impressive on those clips.

What that number means is the big question. Is it only an affirmation to the masses that all the big names in WWF have gone to WCW, making it the "place to be?" Did it show that WWF can draw a big rating in an unopposed 10-11 p.m. Monday night time slot in the fall? Did it show WCW's headliners to be generally small and much older as compared with in their "WWF" prime? Does it mean in a battle of star power, that WWF will in the future roll out the archives in the ratings war? Was the rating largely drawn (as quarter hour breakdowns indicate) by people who tuned in from TNT after Nitro ended, and then slowly watched the nostalgia and by midway in the show were tuning out? And in the long run, aside from one very impressive rating, does this mean anything in the weekly wrestling war?

JULY 28

The World Wrestling Federation confirmed last week the story mentioned in last week's Observer that starting in September they would no longer be taping Raw live every Monday night.

In addition, the In Your House concept has been dropped effective immediately and the WWF will go to monthly nearly three-hour long shows all with a $29.95 price tag. The change will be effective with the 9/7 PPV from Louisville.

The 7/21 live Raw is War show from Halifax, Nova Scotia, going unopposed since Nitro this week aired on 7/22 due to a TNT mini-series, drew a 4.1 rating and 6.1 share. The rating would be the highest for a Raw show in more than one year and among the company's biggest television audiences for any show in several years. The show drew a 3.8 in the first hour and grew to a 4.3 for the second hour, headlined by a capture the flag on a pole match with The Hart Foundation vs. Steve Austin & Undertaker & Dude Love.

While the rating may have been slightly higher than expected, the WWF was expected to do a monster rating because all of wrestling has been geared this year toward Monday nights and Raw was the only game in town this week. The figure represents 66 to 70 percent of the combined audience the two shows would receive on a typical Monday night.

TNT can't be unhappy about the preemption because the Civil War mini-series drew a 4.1 rating as well, which is well above what Nitro does in that time slot. Nitro ratings weren't available as of deadline but nobody believed, even unopposed, that the number would come close to the Raw rating because Tuesday isn't the night where four plus million homes are patterned to watch wrestling at 8 p.m.

The new television format, effective with 9/8, would consist of television tapings on alternate Mondays and Tuesdays. For example, the 9/8 live Raw from Cincinnati, OH would be done exactly as in previous weeks with a Shotgun taping for 9/13 and a live Raw shoot. However, instead of taping on 9/15, that Raw show and the 9/20 Shotgun show would be taped on 9/9 (site hasn't been finalized for this show at press time) and it would continue that way with tapings on 9/22 and 9/23, no taping on 9/29 and tapings on 10/6 and 10/7. Raw will be continuing in its two-hour format, but moving back one hour from 9 p.m. to 11 p.m. on the USA network starting on 8/4.

That's not the only format change in wrestling as WCW will, to counter in some part the change in the Raw schedule, implement a semi-regular series of three-hour Monday television shows called Nitro-plus, running from 8 p.m. to 11 p.m. Eastern time. The current idea is that Nitro-plus shows would take place about once per month, with little warning in advance as to when they'll take place. The first Nitro-plus will take place on 8/4, which not coincidentally in the least, is the first week WWF's Raw moves back one hour. This plan to do shows like this was discussed before the shocking WWF rating came in for its taped SummerSlam special on 7/14, although no doubt that rating sped the wheels into motion that much faster.

The reason for the change in the WWF live every Monday format was largely budgetary cost cutting. WWF has been trying to cut back on expenses both in running live every week and also in transportation which, depending upon where the taping is held can run from $15,000 to $30,000 per week. Because the Tuesday shows would be booked in arenas within driving distance of the Monday shows, it would cut flight expenses for personnel not already on the tour doing house shows in half with the new format.

There are numerous signs of late that the WWF is taking the financial situation very seriously. For example, for the 7/21 show in Halifax, NS there were many regulars who are always brought to Raw tapings that weren't flown in as a cost-saving measure and lots of regular wrestlers were featured instead in taped segments rather than brought in to do live new material. Those who were flown in (and I believe this includes Vince McMahon himself) were brought in on Saturday as opposed to Sunday to get the benefit of the cost-savings of a Saturday stay over flight.

The Friday-through-Monday road schedule that the WWF has been following the past several months, since the move to live weekly two-hour Raw tapings, has also been overhauled. There is no set guidelines as to how the schedule will be done. The feeling is that because of the time and expense of flying wrestlers to and from their homes, that it doesn't make sense either economically or for the stress level of the wrestlers themselves, to fly wrestlers home-and-back for just a two day break. So for the weeks where tapings will be on Mondays and Tuesdays, either they will add Wednesday and Thursday house shows making it a ten-day run, or they'll cancel Friday house shows and the wrestlers would have Wednesday through Friday off and return on Saturday and continue the tour with Mondays. There will be situations where WWF will be running a live house show on Monday night going head-to-head with its taped Raw show on USA.

A lot of people will talk about these changes as like a throwing in the towel in the highly (and largely over) publicized Monday night ratings war, ironically coming during the same week when the group drew its best rating in more than one year. The change is in a sense an admission that it wasn't the fact that WCW was live every week and WWF wasn't as to why WCW was drawing significantly better ratings each week. WWF up until this past week didn't make a significant difference in the ratings being live every week nor could it cut a significant amount into WCW's weekly margin of victory despite offering a largely better product than it had even a few months back and spending a lot more money to do so.

As mentioned here many times, in the past when Raw was taped three out of every four weeks, there was no significant difference in the ratings of the live show as compared with that of the taped shows. Theoretically, because word travels faster in wrestling now than ever before, there will be more people than ever before aware of much of what will occur on the taped shows before they happen, but there is no evidence that anywhere close to enough people know or if they do it makes enough of a difference to have any kind of a measurable effect on the ratings.

The WWF's decision to drop the two-hour In Your House concept of a reduced price PPV comes on the heels of WCW successfully running monthly nearly three hour long PPV shows this year at $27.95 and not showing any effects of the price tag cutting down on buys. Both groups for average shows seem to hover between a 0.5 and 0.65 buy rate, but WCW this year is substantially ahead in PPV revenue because of charging the higher price on every show. Now it will be back to WWF charging the higher price, as it had been up until the past year.

To keep WrestleMania in its position as a special event, that show will be priced at $34.95. The 1995 WrestleMania, which was something of a major disappointment, was priced at $34.95 and there were many who blamed the price tag as the reason the show didn't come close to early projections. Obviously the WWF believed it as well as it cut the Mania price back to $29.95 the past two years. However, there is every economic indication this year that the wrestling audience is far more willing to spend more money to see what they perceive as a premium event, and all forms of entertainment are charging more for tickets than a few years ago.

In a sense, this would remove the "specialness" of the other four of the formerly big five shows of the year (Rumble, King of the Ring, SummerSlam and Survivors) since all the shows would have to be marketed more as equals to the other monthly events, however WCW has been running this year under similar circumstances while passing WWF as the industry PPV leader. While the future of UFC-type events for 1998 doesn't look positive, one would expect added competition from at least three ECW events on PPV and several WCW-sponsored Lucha Libre events.

In fact, within wrestling there is now the theory that up to a certain point, not only is price inelastic in wrestling but that higher ticket prices may actually encourage buys. Zane Bresloff, who promotes most of the house shows for WCW, which has recently increased its prices across the board to a significant degree and at the same time has shown a significant increase in attendance while doing so (June was the single biggest month for arena attendance in the history of the company) has noted that particularly in the major markets, selling tickets at $35 is easy and they are generally snatched up the first day. But it's very difficult to sell tickets at $10 or $12. He believes there is a psychological deal where people will take dates or go out with buddies for high priced tickets but won't do so when tickets are cheap because somehow they see that as a sign of seeing a minor league level entertainment product or being part of the peanut gallery.

A similar but opposite situation that gives the same message in wrestling took place in 1992 when Kip Frey was in charge of WCW. To make himself fan-friendly, one of his first moves was to decrease prices at the arena shows. The end result of that was an actual decrease in live attendance, not an increase. It must be noted that pro wrestling when it comes to drawing mainstream fans is in competition with other sports and entertainment events, and for all the talk that $35 is too much for a family of four to buy tickets, the fact is the tickets are still far cheaper than events like pro football, the NHL, the NBA and other major league sports events that routinely sellout their shows in most markets.

CHAPTER THREE

THE ORIGINS OF WCW THUNDER

FEBRUARY 24

Just a few days before the World Wrestling Federation began its own generally weekly live prime time wrestling show, World Championship Wrestling has upped the ante again.

TBS, Ted Turner's original cable superstation that basically got off the ground nearly two decades ago through Atlanta Braves baseball and Georgia Championship Wrestling, has decided its future is to go back to its past. TBS will begin its own live two-hour prime time wrestling show at some time in the not too distant future, perhaps as early as the May sweeps. Although it has been heavily rumored within the industry about it being a Thursday night show, and the odds are probably better than it will be on Thursday than any other night, the decisions as to what night and when it will start will probably not be made for another few weeks.

The idea of doing the show had just come up in the past week or two, and was finalized by Eric Bischoff in a meeting with TBS on 2/14. The show would largely be funded by TBS with a weekly financial package that would make it basically impossible for WCW to be a money-losing proposition at any time in the near future. It is expected that WCW will now try to add talent, rather than subtract, in order to fill up four live hours plus five other taped hours between national major cable and syndication every week.

The show will either air on Tuesday, Wednesday, Thursday or Friday on TBS. Obviously Monday is out the window, Sunday would conflict with the PPV shows, and Saturday already has its traditional show. Thursday is the most likely date because the other nights would have too many baseball preemptions during the summer.

Of course this brings up the obvious question of what point does over-saturation hit. It was largely believed in September of 1995 when Bischoff and Turner came up with what became Nitro, a prime time show to go head-to-head with Vince McMahon's successful Monday Night Raw, that the competition would drive down both live attendance and PPV buy rates for both companies, plus divide up a finite group of wrestling fans so both show's ratings would be unimpressive. As history has shown, that turned out not to be the case. If anything, the addition of Nitro revitalized a wrestling industry that had been largely at a lull since a combination of scandals, weak booking and an inability to create new stars had taken it down several levels in 1992.

The competition changed the entire face of pro wrestling booking. Long-term ideas for the most part were dropped based on constant changes made both to fool a public with more access to information and to win on Mondays. By loading up on established names from the past, creating new stars, particularly high fliers who were generally thought to only have a career internationally, and booking PPV quality matches on a weekly basis, Nitro held its own with Raw from the start. The combination of expanding to two hours and the introduction of Kevin Nash and Scott Hall, both of which happened simultaneously in late May, led to WCW dominating the ratings each and every Monday.

If anything, this expansion only picked up live attendance even more. Both companies ran house shows far more successfully and profitably in 1996 than either had in several years—both increasing attendance for the year nearly 60% As mentioned a few weeks back, ironically WWF actually increased on a per show basis at a slightly greater margin than WCW.

On PPV, WWF's buy rates and revenue decreased slightly in 1996 as compared with 1995, even with increasing the In Your House price tag from $14.95 to $19.95 and making the five big PPV events all at $29.95. In 1995, WWF ran ten PPV shows averaging an estimated $1.80 million per event, while in 1996 they ran 12 events averaging an estimated $1.66 million and buy rates did decline an estimated 11% (an estimated 0.75 to 0.67).

WCW slightly increased its buy rates (0.63 to 0.64) while increasing from nine PPV events to ten in 1996 and increasing the per-event revenue from an estimated $1.72 million per event to an estimated $1.80 million.

So, while overall buy rates have declined slightly over the past year and per-event revenue has stayed about the same, the addition of Nitro hasn't had any significant negative effect at least at this point on that end of the business.

So after more than 30 consecutive Monday night defeats, WWF upped the ante starting on 2/17 with its own version of a live weekly show. WCW responded by adding its own prime time show which would go unopposed when it comes to wrestling competition, although if it goes on Thursday nights against the NBC blockbuster line-up, it is hardly without entertainment competition.

However, those same points were brought up when Bischoff started Nitro on Mondays thinking about how the combination of the NFL in the fall and WWF every week would leave that show in ratings dust. And all the points about overexposure were brought up and to this point haven't come to fruition. However, there is a saturation point in every entertainment industry. And we're quickly heading, in this industry, to the real-life night the line was crossed.

APRIL 21

There is absolutely no talk about doing that live Thursday night show on TBS nor are any arenas booked for live Thursday tapings as they'd have to be months in advance for planning a start. TBS offered big money for the show, but apparently common sense may win out after all since it'll destroy the personal lives of most of the office and a lot of the wrestlers, not to mention possibly dilute the winning Monday night formula.

MAY 26

The latest on the Thursday live TBS prime time show are that Bischoff doesn't want to do the show unless TBS can guarantee them a time slot where they won't be preempted by other sports events, and at this point with all the baseball coverage every summer, there was no night TBS could make that guarantee.

AUGUST 25

World Championship Wrestling is expected to officially announce shortly the addition of a second two-hour weekly live television show starting at 8 p.m. on Thursday nights with the kick-off date planned for January on TBS.

The show had been in the talking stages for months. At one point it appeared to have been a definite, as TBS, in its own ratings war with USA, Nickelodeon and sister station TNT for the top spot in cable, wanted the kind of weekly boost TNT has gotten from its wrestling show. With the money figure offered by TBS for the show, believed to be about $12 million for the year, substantial enough to insure the company as being easily and majorly profitable despite its huge talent costs (which likely will be increasing), at first it appeared to be an easy decision.

However, many in WCW feared the new show in a big way, both from a personal standpoint because of the increase in work load, and the fear of television overexposure prematurely ending the current boom period and talent morale problems from adding 52 more dates per year on the road. Nevertheless, when WCW drew a strong 3.8 rating off its traditional Monday night on 7/22, and followed it up with the 4.34 on 8/4, the betting line was that the company would be dragged by the network, kicking and screaming if it had to, into adding the second show.

A memo was sent internally to WCW officials on 8/13 about the second show, although Eric Bischoff was telling people, perhaps in an attempt to come off as the good guy in a situation that wouldn't be taken well, that he was going to resist doing the show unless it was specifically ordered by Ted Turner. However, high-level internal meetings were scheduled in how to put together the new show on 8/19 in Atlanta.

TBS may change its weekend four hours of taped wrestling programming schedule although no change will be made in the Saturday night show. The belief, stemming from statements Bischoff made on Nitro and other bits and pieces we've picked up is that one of the two weekly shows would become more NWO-oriented with Bischoff as the host, and the other more WCW-oriented and that they'd try to portray the two groups even more as two entirely different promotions that are feuding and have the PPV and arena shows become more inter-promotional in focus.

Of course this brings up the obvious overexposure question. Thus far in expansions, from WCW expanding Nitro to two hours, followed by WWF expanding Raw to two hours, it has only resulted in more fans watching wrestling on cable than in many years. There is an over-saturation point as wrestling history has shown, both in the 50s and again in the late 80s and early 90s where television has fueled a boom period and then within a few years gobbled it up and left the scraps struggling for financial survival. Even with all the new programming, there is still far less wrestling available on television in most markets than in the mid-80s when so many regional promotions had syndication before they went under one-by-one. As has been historically the case with wrestling every boom period, more television is added until it chokes itself through decreased ratings.

But at the same time, right now there is no evidence whatsoever based on falling ratings—if anything the opposite looks to be the case—that pro wrestling as it stands right now is overexposed. The ability to add another live show without a creative drain on those writing the shows (not to mention the problems because of the top guys re-writing their own storylines) not to mention the physical drain and increased injury rate from the wrestlers who will have to carry the bulk of the time through their ring work is just another item to consider.

SEPTEMBER 1

Meetings were held this week regarding the new TBS Thursday night live show. If you hear any rumors about what it'll be, they are just rumors because literally nothing has been decided. The only things made clear is that the show has to be as good as Nitro because TBS with all the money they are paying for the show won't settle for a second-rate Nitro.

There were talks about adding stars from the past or about using the Thursday show to focus on the Guerrero, Malenko, Benoit types and give them more time to have better matches, or even using ex-UFC fighters to give it more of a shooting aura. Based on things at the meeting and what Bischoff is saying on television, it seems his idea is to make Nitro a two-hour NWO show and the new unnamed show a WCW show and make it seem more like a promotional war between the two. For reasons alluded to earlier, it's a risky proposition on Mondays.

SEPTEMBER 8

The first episode of the new Thursday show will be on 1/7 from Daytona Beach. While nothing is certain, it appears that one of the two shows, likely Nitro, will be the NWO show. The Thursday show will probably be the WCW show and focus on history and tradition with features showing things through the years like they did with the open of Nitro on Anderson.

NOVEMBER 24

The current plan still seems to be that starting in January, the Monday show will become NWO Nitro, perhaps built around a feud with Hogan's NWO with he and Savage, against the Wolfpack, with the members splitting up and taking sides. Some talk that Bischoff and Rick Rude would do the announcing for this show, which after the job Rude did in ECW, would be good for about one week at the most. Thursday would be WCW Thunder, built around Flair, Sting, Giant, Luger and Bret Hart and they'd feud amongst themselves. What would then make the PPV shows special is that all the big stars would be on the PPV and you'd have theoretical inter-promotional battles there. This could and probably will change 100 times between now and January, which is actually coming up shockingly quickly.

DECEMBER 8

The announcement of the Eric Bischoff vs. Larry Zbyszko match for Starrcade '97 in Washington, DC with Nitro at stake appears to be the beginning of Bischoff's biggest gamble to date—messing with the winning Monday night formula.

As mentioned previously, the working idea for 1998 is to split WCW and NWO into somewhat separate entities, each having their own television show and often running separate house shows. The groups would combine on the major arena house shows and the PPV events, to make those shows have even more of a special aura. This could all change simply by changing the Bischoff-Zbyszko ending as even though things are only a few weeks away, there is shockingly little completed as far as planning for the changes January brings.

The grandiose idea behind all of this would be to make the WWF into the third biggest wrestling company in the United States. The risk involved in this move is tampering with what in 1997 has been overall an incredibly successful formula making WCW incredibly profitable and resulting in its peak of popularity when it comes to Monday ratings (although TBS wrestling ratings have never been lower in the history of wrestling on the station), house show attendance and the recent Havoc show drew more revenue than any WCW PPV in history, a mark that will almost surely to broken again come Starrcade.

Not to mention re-opening the door for the WWF, a company that won't be diluting its own product by splitting up talent and trying to produce two live prime time shows per week, to regain control of the bulk of the Monday night audience, which seems to be the most important item from a psychological standpoint to both companies in the entire business.

Without question, as we've seen everywhere, going too long with a pat hand in pro wrestling tends to create a stale environment, but wrestling fans, particularly from a television ratings standpoint, put up with staleness for years before it starts to show in the numbers. Messing with a winning formula before it has shown economically to have started its decline is rare in any business, particularly this business.

The plan as things stand at press time is for Bischoff to win the match, no doubt with oodles of outside interference from the NWO, and likely Scott Hall in particular because they are obviously building toward a Zbyszko vs. Hall match. This would give the NWO control of Nitro, and move the WCW show to the new Thursday night live 8 p.m. to 10 p.m. slot on TBS. The planned announcing teams are Bischoff, Rick Rude and Mike Tenay on Nitro, and Tony Schiavone, Zbyszko and Bobby Heenan on the Thursday show (which will be moved to Wednesday once baseball season starts in April), which is as of yet unnamed, and for the most part not really very planned out either.

The talent would largely be split between the two shows rather than having the same wrestlers headline both shows. Whether that means Tenay turns heel and is revealed as the WCW turncoat that gave Hogan and Bischoff the info every week as to when Sting wasn't going to be around for all their grandstand challenges (there had been talk internally for months about turning Tenay heel) or he'll be used to counterbalance Bischoff & Rude is unknown, although if it's the latter, he's probably not the right person for the job since his forte is his ability to impart information while remaining non-confrontational at all times.

The original idea of the show being called Thunder appears to have been dropped as on checking the availability of the name, ESPN owned the "Thunder" name for television for a motor sports show. In theory, splitting the talent at the shows should create more of an opportunity for the second-level talent such as the Chris Benoits, Eddie Guerreros, Marcus Bagwells and Rey Misterio Jr.'s and such, many if not most of whom have been largely unhappy with the lack of upward mobility among those without the right friends no matter how much their matches get over.

There are even greater risks involved in this change than the risks Bischoff took when creating the Nitro show in 1995. At that time, WCW literally had nothing to lose when putting on a show opposite the WWF. The WWF was considered the industry leader, and just being a competitive second would have been considered a success. As it was, WCW gained attention early by putting on PPV-marquee level matches every week on television like Hogan vs. Sting, Hogan vs. Luger, Flair vs. Savage, etc. and were dueling evenly for months with the WWF that concentrated on the old formula of a few squashes, a few competitive matches, and saving the marquee matches for where the company would make the most money.

But the tables turned in the summer of 1996, when three things happened—Nitro expanded to two hours going on one hour earlier than Raw and giving them a jump-start, the NWO angle got off the ground with Kevin Nash and Scott Hall jumping and Hulk Hogan going heel, and the company started blowing away its competition inside the ring by signing so many smaller wrestlers who could do things the larger more plodding wrestlers on the other show couldn't do, making WWF, in comparison, look like slow-motion wrestling. Since that time, WCW has dominated every Monday with no end seemingly in sight.

The game changes again in January. Will the WWF be moved a step lower down the totem pole, or will it be the greatest Christmas present Vince McMahon ever received?

The pressure is on Bischoff because if it doesn't work, he's given back the store and screwed up a proven winning formula. Even if it becomes obvious after a few weeks and they make the necessary changes back to the 1997 formula, it would have to be an admission of failure and wrestling promoters are often very slow to make that admission.

It's risky to be sure, since previous attempts to do all-NWO programming have been nothing short of a disaster. The NWO segments in the empty arena on the Saturday night show were funny for a few weeks, but lived out their shelf life in less than one month. Attempts to "take over" Nitro for 30 to 45 minute segments have, without exception, all been disasters. Even the five minute segment on 11/24 where Bischoff and Rude did the commentary during the Hogan-Giant match came off poorly. The NWO PPV show was not only among the worst PPV shows of all-time, but far more importantly—and something that has been forgotten by most—is that it died on the buy rate, and that's with a Hogan vs. Giant main event which on paper should have done nearly twice as many buys as it did if it were advertised as a typical WCW event, and a huge advertising budget.

It is known that behind-the-scenes Kevin Nash was trying to get the NWO show to be the Thursday show. From a risk standpoint, it's better for his and the NWO's position. Even if the new show were to bomb on Thursday, let's say, do about a 2.0 to 2.5 consistent rating, it can always be explained as being a new night for wrestling fans and the competition of going against blockbuster network programming in "Seinfeld" and "Friends." With no wrestling track record to judge it against, anything can be said to be a success.

More importantly, without competing wrestling programming, and also because even though "Seinfeld" and "Friends" are two of the hottest shows on television, when it comes to the demographic that watches WCW wrestling, Monday Night Football is far bigger competition, the actual potential for the ratings in the long run may be greater on Thursday than Monday, although not right away. Because TV viewership is based so much on people being creatures of habit, the Thursday show, like Nitro, is likely to build an audience rather than, like running consistent house shows in a market, do a blockbuster early and then subsequent crowds trickle downward. Of course, come January, the football competition becomes a moot point.

On Monday, there is a track record to live up to. Anything below consistent numbers between 3.8 and 4.0, particularly with no football competition, is a decline, and that's a hell of a standard to have to live up to. By all rights, with no football competition, all things being equal, the ratings should increase from the current level in January by about .3 every week. Anything below what the WWF does, which would mean the show would have to go into an almost immediate free-fall which is an unlikely scenario, will be nothing short of outright disaster.

DECEMBER 22

As best we can tell, the plan is for Nitro to remain as it is on Mondays, as in why mess with a successful formula, and the new formula show will be NWO Thunder on Thursdays. Being that this is 90s wrestling, nothing is for sure until it happens, including Sting winning the title at Starrcade, although Hogan not doing the job on this show, and he has the contractual right not to (which means he's going to hold the company up for whatever he can get), after all this build-up would let a lot of the air out of the Sting balloon.

DECEMBER 29

If there was a chance that the NWO was going to take over Nitro, it almost surely ended on Tuesday afternoon when the ratings came in. And now the prospects for the Thursday NWO show also have to be questioned.

On the 12/22 Nitro from Macon, GA, at the one hour mark of the three-hour show, the NWO, mainly Marcus Bagwell, Konnan and Scott Norton took over the show and they spent about 20 minute tearing down all the WCW equipment and replacing it with new NWO equipment. The rest of the show had a new graphics package saying NWO Nitro, new lighting, new banners and a new insignia for the entrance area. Obviously this is all designed to get people to believe that Eric Bischoff is going to beat Larry Zbyszko and that the NWO is going to take over Nitro starting on 12/29 in Baltimore. It would seem silly to put together all the graphics, logos, banners, etc. saying NWO Monday Nitro just for one television show, although since at the time it was a swerve, it in theory was a brilliant idea. Except it wasn't.

Although Nitro defeated Raw on 12/22, it was the closest margin over the head-to-head period of the entire 1997 calendar year. The approximate head-to-head numbers over the 9 p.m. to 11 p.m. period had Nitro at a 3.3—about .8 lower than its average over the past few months, and Raw at 3.15, about .4 above its average. Overall Nitro did about a 3.5 rating (4.0 first hour; 3.6 second hour; 3.0 third hour) while Raw's 3.15 was a 3.1 first hour and 3.2 second hour, which means that for the first time probably in all of 1997 in a head-to-head full hour, Raw beat Nitro 3.2 to 3.0 which shows just what a disaster the show was for WCW. Quarter hour breakdowns weren't available at press time.

Raw was by no means a blow-away show, in fact it was a bad show, just not bad on the same level as Nitro. Considering just how much of the audience tuned out Nitro when the NWO took over, the message was clear that it was people switching over to WWF because they didn't like WCW and not visa versa.

This was the second crushing business blow for the NWO gimmick, the first being the NWO Souled Out PPV show which did a poor buy rate despite a Hogan vs. Giant main event and tons of advertising going into the show. NWO is cool as an outside force, but despite what the survey says most weeks, it wasn't what people are coming to see all by itself. The quarter hour breakdowns of personnel, where Ric Flair is the top ratings getter and the two biggest ratings losers are Scott Hall and Eric Bischoff should tell the story.

Zbyszko was scheduled to win the match likely not all along, as word we were given is that Bischoff was at first scheduled to win due to interference from Scott Hall, but that about the same time the Observer cover story came out, reality hit and the decision was made to make Bret Hart referee to lead to a Zbyszko win, giving the NWO the Thursday show. Again, this puts less pressure on the NWO show because it has no great ratings track record to blow or have to live up to while trying a new concept, and if the concept doesn't fly, it won't make it appear Vince McMahon is winning once again.

For more on this mystery, in local advertising for the 1/8 Thursday show in Daytona Beach and the 1/15 show in Lakeland, the advertising only lists WCW wrestlers like Luger, Page, Giant, etc. and no NWO wrestlers are listed in the local advertising. So either they are going to great lengths to fool people or they are doing some major league false advertising in those markets. Probably it's the former causing the latter. At the same time, when the show ended, they were strongly teasing that Bret Hart was against the NWO and with Sting, and usually they like to swerve in that direction as well. Having said all that, it was probably the single worst Nitro as if we weren't Bischoff'd to death last week, we were overdosing on it this week between four interview segments, all except the first pre-taped one that had already aired on Saturday night were bad, and some even worse play-by-play announcing.

This hardly bodes well for adding the Thursday show doing two hours live every week with this format. Rick Rude's forte simply isn't announcing. He was bad in ECW, and that's with Paul Heyman feeding him lines in carefully produced segments. Going in live without a net is even worse. Bischoff's new character is such that he's always been a turn-off in lengthy segments. When he went into this heel role, he gave up for a long time, until people have forgotten the role, any chance of being effective as the lead broadcaster. Bobby Heenan has been largely worthless for a long time, it's just that Tony Schiavone and to a lesser extent Mike Tenay have done a great job of carrying him to where some haven't noticed. But in the second hour without Schiavone, it was all too clear.

But this rating may have been a positive in that it was the wake-up call needed before the show goes on live on 1/8, and it's always best to do the format tinkering before the debut show then debut with a bad show. At the same time, WCW needs on 12/29 from Baltimore to get Nitro back on track before the ratings erosion turns into a pattern, and to get some mileage out of Bret Hart who they've invested heavily in and due to having to keep his positioning secret for the PPV show, have been unable to let loose to do an interview or start a wrestling program.

Chapter Four

Shawn Michaels Loses His Smile

FEBRUARY 24

Perhaps the strangest week in World Wrestling Federation history ended up with three WWF title changes, the tease of the end of Shawn Michaels' career, a strange twist in the working relationship with ECW, the beginning of the live Raw, a television special, a PPV event, a surprise IC title switch, numerous long-term plans switched, steroids appeared back to being somewhat in vogue, and perhaps not even limited to the male performers, and the beginning of WrestleMania hype all crammed into five days.

When the dust settled, Sid was back with the WWF title—a belt that Shawn Michaels never lost and that Bret Hart never beat anyone for in becoming a one-day wonder, and probably wondering himself if he made the worst career move of his career, as second guessers and many in the industry were saying by the end of the week. Undertaker vs. Sid will headline WrestleMania on 3/23 in Chicago, at least as of this week.

Michaels' career was teased as being over due to a knee injury portrayed on television Thursday as being so bad even reconstructive surgery may not to able to repair the damage as a teary-eyed Michaels, whose problem was clearly in the interview not a knee injury, said farewell to the WWF in a classic interview repeated to death on television and PPV about 100 times in the ensuing weekend.

It wound up only to have noted orthopedic surgeon Dr. Jim Andrews say Michaels' knee injury wouldn't even require surgery at all, and that after four to six weeks of rehab, he may be able to return. And at press time, it appears the plan is for Michaels to now be put back into the WrestleMania mix, although not as a wrestler, perhaps doing announcing or as a special referee, wrestle a few major shows during the summer and return full-time in the fall.

We're not sure whether plans had been changed at the last minute where Michaels was scheduled to drop the title to Sid on the 2/13 special, but we do know that Michaels' short-term departure threw a total monkey wrench in all the house show and WrestleMania plans. To the WWF's credit, they didn't pressure Michaels into staying at a time when it appeared emotionally he needed the break, but it was surprising they didn't do an angle to build heat on an opponent for his eventual return.

Rocky Maivia, the former Dwayne Johnson, with less than one year in the pros, was surprisingly given the IC title on 2/13 from Hunter Hearst Helmsley. There had been some question that Maivia's push was going to wind up in a Van Hammer/Erik Watts like situation, that fans wouldn't buy a green wrestler being shoved down their throats and push back. If there was any doubt, during the match even before the title had changed there were chants of "Rocky sux."

The before-the-camera working relationship with ECW (which has been going on behind-the-scenes to some extent for months now), which had a test run before planned angles were abruptly dropped a few months back, will pick up with a new twist on 2/24 at the Manhattan Center for the second live two hour Raw show. However, this time it appears ECW won't be the heels or the invaders but that ECW will become, like AAA, a babyface promotion working with the WWF. The exposure in that position pretty well guarantees that whatever chance there was that ECW would totally flop on PPV is now exceedingly slim, because the exposure on a wrestling show with actual large mainstream viewership should at least arouse enough curiosity to do a break-even buy rate.

But the biggest story was not the three WWF title changes, the Michaels vacancy on Thursday, the Hart win under Battle Royal rules on Sunday and the Sid win over Hart due to Steve Austin's outside interference on Monday; but the entire strange circumstances involving Michaels, the wrestler who carried the WWF in the ring throughout 1996, and appeared to be breaking down emotionally from pressure at the same time he was wowing crowds in the ring.

On the Raw special, it was announced at the beginning of the show that Michaels would be vacating his title. In a memorable, but now totally over played and emotional interview, Michaels talked about a knee injury so bad it may be beyond surgical repair, how he wouldn't return to wrestling if he was anything less than 100%, and then broke down talking about this past year as being the top man in the business being the happiest year of his life because he got to do everything he dreamed of, and saying it would be okay if it never happened again because at least he got to do it for one year, thanked Vince McMahon for letting it happen, broke down even worse, said he needed to go home to find his smile because he lost it somewhere, and ended it by saying that he needed to go home now as he hugged McMahon in the ring.

This sent shock waves throughout the industry because it was all totally unexpected—apparently the WWF higher-ups received word at about 6 p.m. the previous night from Michaels that he was taking time off when Michaels informed WWF officials that his doctor in San Antonio had told him his knee injury could be career ending. WWF sources claim that they chose this tact rather than do an angle on Michaels' knee with a wrestler like Sid or Steve Austin to give him a grudge match upon his return, because they were afraid of doing any further damage to the knee.

Perhaps the real-life situation involving Brian Pillman, where both he and the WWF wanted to use him so much when he should have been rehabbing that his ankle healed improperly and he wound up having to have everything redone and start from scratch in an ordeal that will end up keeping him out of the ring for more than one year when all is said and done. Of course, at that same point in time, even with all the damage to Pillman's ankle, they still did the in-ring angle for the storyline explanation and the grudge match built up for the eventual return.

It was announced with the title vacant, that the Final Four match on the Sunday PPV, which was to determine who would get the title shot at WrestleMania, would instead be for the title, and that the original title contender, Sid, would get the winner the next day. One day before the match, the rules of the Final Four were amended to being Battle Royal rules, which meant eliminations would be by throwing someone over the top rope as well as pins or submissions, although as it turned out all eliminations were over the top, which allowed them to placate more delicate egos and saved all three from doing jobs in a match set up originally to where at least three key performers were going to have to do jobs.

Bret Hart captured the title for the fourth time, clotheslining Undertaker over the top when Undertaker was distracted by Austin. The next night it was announced the Hart-Sid winner would face Undertaker at WrestleMania for the title in the main event. After two re-starts due to Austin jumping both men before the match started, in a gimmick designed to get off to a ratings jump on the most important Monday night ratings war to date (well, at least until next Monday), the match, which started at the beginning of the show wound up as the final match on the show with Sid winning when Austin hit Hart over the head with a chair as Hart had the sharpshooter on Sid.

It appears the top matches at WrestleMania will be Sid vs. Undertaker, Bret Hart vs. Austin, Hunter Hearst Helmsley vs. Goldust and a Chicago Street fight with Ahmed Johnson vs. Faarooq. The original plan was for Owen Hart & Davey Boy Smith vs. Doug Furnas & Phil Lafon with the tag team title switch that occurs on nearly every WrestleMania, but that may have already changed. It may be that Hart & Smith, who are more valuable than ever because they need people who can carry time every week with the two-hour live show, will be getting some perks in exchange for dropping the straps.

With Michaels out of commission, house shows over the weekend, originally scheduled as Bret Hart & Sid vs. Austin & Michaels main events, changed first to triangle matches with Michaels removed, and then changed again with an injury to Ahmed Johnson, to double mains with Sid vs. Faarooq and the same Final Four with Bret, Undertaker, Vader and Austin that would be on the PPV show on Sunday, giving the wrestlers two try-out matches to get out the kinks. Major house show main events when the group returns from the European tour which starts this week are going to be triangles with Bret Hart, Sid and Austin. With most of the big names gone to Europe, there will be a skeleton crew for the live show at the Manhattan Center, and they are going all out for shocks and surprises for that show.

Exactly what is the true story involving Michaels is anyone's guess. There is no doubt there was a knee injury. Anyone who does what Michaels does is going to wind up with knee damage. Obviously there are serious problems that were a lot more important to address than any knee problems. Just because someone appears on the surface to outsiders to lead a charmed life, in that they have money, looks, ability and can entertain outsiders and are admired and even worshiped by people who don't know them, doesn't mean that on the inside they are any less immune to the same problems that face each of us. A broken heart and broken dreams don't hurt any less if you have a million dollars in the bank or nothing in the bank, or if you have people clamoring for your autograph or blowing smoke up your ass. In fact, if anything, in Michaels position, he's a lot more susceptible because he was put under a microscope and put in a pressure cooker position.

You have the illogic from a professional standpoint in his mind that he may be unable to come to grips with. He rose to the top in his profession by doing things a certain way. All the people riding the bandwagon with them on the road up there, many suddenly turn against him and point out his flaws for doing exactly the same thing he did to make it to the top, once he's under the microscope.

Despite performing in good matches most nights and great matches on the big shows, and more importantly from the top man position, house show business with him as the key draw and headliner being the best in years—everything he dreamed about being important on paper was going exactly according to plan, suddenly everyone focused on TV ratings and suddenly he was a failure as champion. He was the standard bearer, the quarterback of sorts, on a team that people wrote was on a 33-game losing streak, going downhill fast, despite it really being the most successful it had been in years.

And being a perfectionist to his craft in an imperfect world where others make mistakes often, his immaturity showed, particularly when his big buddies left him. If anything, it made the injuries, and the injuries on the inside that are a lot more painful than back and knee hurts, hurt that much worse. And his starting QB position was going to be being taken away either by the former starter who walked out making it somewhat public he was waiting for his rival to self destruct, and came back in with the biggest money offer in company history looking like the wisest clairvoyant in the 20th century; or by someone who couldn't lace his boots but whom fans chanted for while he did the most important and closest to real interview of his life, a cry for help that some people may have understood, but that the fans for the most part thought and the promotion treated as being just business as usual.

And maybe his problems had little or nothing to do with the profession that he called his entire life. Maybe it was the fact at 31, he stepped back and realized outside the profession he didn't have a life, which is awfully scary. Maybe it was simply he needed time off to get his house in order, and maybe simply because he was setting up a new home in San Antonio and there's stress moving and all this was to get time away from work to move everything in. Or all of the above. Or none of the above. Maybe his best friends know and are disappointed he isn't getting the help they think he needs. Maybe they don't.

The last word appeared to be Michaels returning in a non-wrestling role at Mania, probably to do an angle to lead to his in-ring return, and then he'd work some major shows over the summer before going full-time in the fall, ironically not all that different than the original plans Bret Hart made after he had to drop the title.

Rumors will flourish, most of which won't be true and some of which will. The fact WWF after the fact played it up for all it was worth turned it into just another fake-shoot wrestling angle. Michaels has been in them before. The irony was just last year, the last time they played this game and teased Michaels never wrestling again, set him up for the biggest run of his career. Perhaps he forgot, or hoped people wouldn't remember that when he talked in the interview about a doctor telling him he may not be able to wrestle again for the first time in his life, that it may have been the first time a doctor actually said that to him, but it wasn't the first time that story had been told about him.

It was the third time Michaels hadn't lost a WWF belt in the ring. In September of 1993, he walked out as IC champion, only to return a short time later. In October of 1995, after being mugged, he wasn't able to return in time for a PPV show and gave back the IC title.

MARCH 3

The story on Shawn Michaels at press time appears to be that it is becoming more acknowledged within the WWF that more likely than not his leaving had to do with being burned out from all the travel and pressure and needing a break, combined with the timing of having to put over Sid for the WWF title on the 2/13 special and knowing he was going to follow it up in his next high-profile match having to put Bret Hart over at WrestleMania. Michaels saw how Hart improved his stock by walking out last year and that may have affected the decision, combined with the fact he's good friends with Kevin Nash, Scott Hall and Sean Waltman, all of whom appear to be very smart in handling their personal business and using whatever leverage at the right time to make the right moves.

While there is little doubt there was sincerity in his now-famous interview, it was also a clever business maneuver to build himself into a major sympathetic character to build interest in his eventual return. The WWF continued on that same path with attempts at touching music videos this week regarding Michaels. By leaving before doing the job and giving that interview, Michaels made himself the man of the hour in a positive way, plus both avoided losing the title in the ring and put off the inevitable favor for his legitimate rival.

There is little dispute that he had a knee injury but the belief is that it was something he could have continued to work on had he wanted to, although it was bad enough that any doctor would have recommended taking time off and this was the opportune time.

While it was reported here last week that the expectation is for Michaels to return in a non-wrestling role at WrestleMania, the last word we've received is that at present there are no plans for Michaels to appear on the show, although that could change at any time.

It has been confirmed that Michaels is not in any kind of rehab, other than for his knee, despite rumors within the business to the contrary. Friends of his have also said that in the ten days since walking away and being away from the pressure, he's found that lost smile he talked about.

Michaels has five years left on a lucrative contract with the WWF and the idea of him going to WCW is at best remote because it would require the WWF releasing him from the deal. We've had it confirmed that Michaels did show up at the Continental Arena in East Rutherford, NJ on 2/9—three days before telling the WWF about his knee injury and that he was giving back the title since his doctor said he couldn't work the title change match with Sid or do an angle. However, it is also said that as far as there being any kind of serious heat for doing so has been blown way out of proportion in that he did do it but that nobody considered it as either important or a warning sign of anything.

CHAPTER FIVE

WWF VS. ECW VS. USWA

FEBRUARY 24

Several people were sent to the USWA this week by WWF. Sunny did color commentary on the television to work with Lance Russell and began a feud with King Reginald's Queen Nikki. WWF sent in a team called The Truth Commission who are doing a gimmick that they are from South Africa. They are trying out the gimmick here first. The team consists of Barry Buchanan, formerly The Punisher in SMW and Sunset Sam McGraw in Georgia; and Mike Halac, formerly Mantaur in the WWF and Bruiser Mastino in Europe. They have a manager who is actually from South Africa who is an actor from that country who is friends with Bret Hart that Hart worked with in doing the television series "Sinbad." Brooklyn Brawler was also at television, and Doug Gilbert returned to a big babyface pop saying he's coming in to get rid of the Nation of Domination and team with Brian Christopher. Gilbert had been working opposition shows in Louisville for Ian Rotten. Ken Wayne was also at television looking really heavy.

MARCH 3

In yet another of the weekly versions of the most important Monday night in history, WWF threw shock after shock—the debut of ECW wrestlers, the debut of Ken Shamrock, the return of the Road Warriors and the return to the Manhattan Center in an attempt to reverse its ratings woes. WCW countered by coming one day after a PPV headlined by Hulk Hogan vs. Roddy Piper.

The result on 2/24 was a slight closing of the gap from the previous week but still a victory for WCW Nitro, doing a 2.97 rating and 4.50 share to Monday Night Raw's 2.43 rating and 3.56 share. On 2/17, the first live head-to-head two-hour week, Nitro did a 2.96 rating and 4.40 share to Raw's 2.08 rating and 3.03 share. However, the live two-hour Raw is producing an effect for the later night USA programming, as on 2/24, La Femme Nikita did a 2.4 to Robin Hood's 1.6, and the previous week La Femme won 1.7 to 1.0. Robin Hood had been winning that race handily before Raw went to two hours.

While the consensus was that WWF on 2/17 had one of its best Raws in a long-time, clearly winning the quality battle over a fairly good Nitro, on 2/24 the roles in that regard were definitely in reverse. There is a strong argument that the overall ratings of a show in regard to going up and down from week-to-week are largely determined by the quality of the show the previous week as opposed to the current week. However, the quarter-by-quarter breakdowns show changes that are indicative of viewership patterns and likes and dislikes about the individual show.

That being said, 2/17 was really strange. WCW held a 2.5 to 2.2 lead off the blocks with Rey Misterio Jr. vs. Super Calo opposing the first tease of the Bret Hart vs. Sid title match. WCW maintained the lead throughout. With a weaker show, WCW's numbers steadily increased as the show went on, while WWF's declined most of the way. At the start of the second hour, when WCW had Nick Patrick vs. Randy Anderson and Chris Benoit vs. Roadblock opposing the second tease of Hart vs. Sid, WCW held a shocking 3.2 to 1.9 lead. Clearly the idea of teasing the match throughout the show was a ratings negative once they did it the second time because ratings sputtered for the remainder of the second hour until Hart and Sid finally got into the ring and started their match. The Bret Hart vs. Sid match itself did pick the rating to a 2.4, still trailing WCW's 3.0 for a Giant handicap match and Lex Luger/Eric Bischoff angle.

On 2/24, despite or maybe because of all the surprises on WWF, depending on your point of view, Nitro had the far superior show. The so-called legendary atmosphere of the Manhattan Center turned into a romantic myth that couldn't hold up to its fantasy as WCW had far more enthusiasm in Sacramento, not to mention the smaller Manhattan Center looked bush league from a television standpoint in comparison. The Manhattan Center reacted well to ECW, but died for the WWF matches, making the show almost come off like someone playing a practical joke on the WWF.

McMahon, noticeably exhausted and for good reason, reacted like he recognized things were going badly. Nevertheless, even though WWF lost even with the advantage of coming from New York and the Internet hype on ECW, the scariest thing of all for WWF is that the ratings were slightly stronger during the ECW segments. While the three ECW segments drew a 2.5 average against Nitro's 2.9, the first segment with ECW, with WWF's Raw having the Stevie Richards/BWO show against Nitro's deadly double of Jim Duggan vs. Galaxy and Hugh Morrus vs. Joe Gomez saw Raw ahead 2.7 to 2.6. But at that point, Raw went down slightly and Nitro went up. With Taz vs. Mikey Whipwreck opposing Faces of Fear vs. Eddie Guerrero & Chris Jericho, Nitro led 2.9 to 2.5. With Tommy Dreamer vs. D-Von Dudley opposing Dean Malenko vs. Ultimo Dragon, the gap increased to 3.1 to 2.3. Nitro peaked at a 3.4 for the final segment with the Luger/Bischoff confrontation, while Raw never again reached the 2.7 mark it had when the BWO came out.

Even though the ECW segments didn't play well on WWF television, they blew away what the WWF offered with most of its big names in Germany. WWF had a poorly designed 11:00 long Road Warriors debut that saw them do a double count out with Head Bangers (at the same time WCW presented Rey Misterio Jr. vs. Juventud Guerrera and held a 3.1 to 2.5 lead); a dull Savio Vega vs. Goldust match which debuted Miguel Perez doing a run-in to feud with Vega; and a negative star Undertaker vs. Faarooq match.

But there is no question the appearance, even if it was a letdown in many ways, was a positive for ECW in that more people saw the product than ever before and they were allowed to plug their PPV. It is both amazing and mind-boggling to see a television show four weeks before WrestleMania have more hype for a supposed rival promotion's PPV than for their own biggest show of the year.

Still, ECW came off as a minor league promotion on big-time television since Vince McMahon didn't even know who the wrestlers are and when the fan at home sees that arguably the most powerful man in the industry and the voice they recognize in wrestling doesn't even know or seem to much care about these guys, how important can they be?

The positive of the segment was the work of Jerry Lawler, who as the heel foil to Paul Heyman, was nothing short of phenomenal in his knocks of the product as a heel putting it over. The irony is that Lawler truly does hate Heyman and ECW but as a pro put his job in front of his personal feelings. He also made it if he and Heyman worked it out, if he worked for ECW, he'd go in as the hottest heel the promotion has ever had.

The plan going in was for the ECW wrestlers to return on the 3/10 Raw from Worcester, MA, but after this first appearance, the consensus of Tuesday morning quarterbacks in the industry seems to be WWF would be better off pulling the plug now because it's a bad mix. For ECW, it's pretty much a no lose proposition at this point.

Raw on 2/24 from Manhattan Center drew a sellout 1,000 paying $13,000 as Blackjacks beat Godwinns in 5:50 when Windham pinned Phineas in a DUD match. Phineas had his leg under the ropes and after the match, Henry slopped the ref who took a few pratfalls outside the ring. Eliminators did the total elimination on a non-wrestler to a big pop. Stevie Richards beat Little Guido in 3:39 of a good squash match. Raven showed up. McMahon called him Stevie Ray and Paul Heyman said that McMahon needs to watch the tapes Bruce Prichard puts on his desk every Monday morning. Marlena beat Sunny via DQ in arm wrestling when Sunny threw powder in her eyes. Savio Vega came out to threaten Marlena and Goldust hit the ring and they started their match, which went 11:45 ending in a DQ when Crush interfered. Miguel Perez, who was doing color, made the save. Bad match. Taz beat Mikey Whipwreck in 3:33 with the choke. During the match Sabu dove off the R on Raw onto the members of Team Taz. Taz looked really short in that big ring. Road Warriors double count out Head Bangers in 10:53. Bangers carried it so it wasn't that bad, but it was a terrible debut having Warriors last that long. They did the double impact on Thrasher after the match. Tommy Dreamer pinned D-Von Dudley after a DDT on a chair in 4:25. They used the frying pans and chairs but it was pretty bad. McMahon as an announcer blew off some of their object spots and never acknowledged when Beulah gave D-Von a low blow. After Buh Buh ran in, Sandman made a save with some chair shots and smashed a beer can on his forehead and juiced. Apparently McMahon didn't want the cane being used. They took the camera off the blood almost immediately. Undertaker beat Faarooq via DQ in 14:00 of a -*1/2 match. Just awful. DQ finish when Vega and Crush ran in, and Warriors made the save.

MARCH 3

There was real heat on the 2/17 Raw between Paul Heyman and Jerry Lawler when Heyman brought up the neighborhood watch program, alluding to Lawler's legal problems a few years back and Lawler shot back about cracking his jaw—which he did with a punch in Haiti, MO in 1987 when Heyman was a rookie. Although both sounded like they hated each other on 2/24 and both probably meant the majority of what they said, everything on that show was worked out beforehand as WWF talked with Heyman on 2/20 about what he couldn't say about Lawler on the air and that the two were to act professional with each other.

MARCH 10

The ECW angle was continued with separate phone calls with Jerry Lawler and Paul Heyman and to the surprise of many, including Heyman himself, ECW will be on the live Raw as originally scheduled on 3/10 in Worcester, MA. This will no doubt lead to even more speculation as to why this is happening so close to a WrestleMania that needs all the help it can and that won't at this point have any ECW involvement.

While the ECW segments drew slightly better overall than the WWF segments on the 2/24 Raw when it came to ratings (actually it was only the Stevie Richards BWO segment that did any better), the overall consensus was it was among the worst Raw shows ever from a technical standpoint and something of a disaster from the WWF end. There was a lot of talk after the show that while any exposure was a plus for ECW, the mix was not beneficial to WWF and the plans for 3/10 would be pulled.

Bret Hart, who has long hated ECW, ripped on them in his column in the Calgary Sun and it's no secret that Jerry Lawler's line on Raw about a lot of the WWF wrestlers being mad at the association was a shoot although at the 2/24 Raw there was no sign of problems by anyone and even Jim Cornette and Heyman grudgingly shook hands. Even Heyman himself wasn't sure of whether or not his crew would be invited back until the afternoon of 3/3 when he was asked to phone in on Raw to hype being there for next week. WWF did hype the ECW wrestlers on most of its weekend programming and put together an excellent video package for Raw, completed with digitized footage of the violence, that Heyman himself couldn't have done a better job of to get his company over as something different.

There are total denials from Heyman in regard to WWF having any financial stake in ECW or its upcoming PPV show. There are many within the industry who don't believe that, although nobody who believes it has any tangible evidence of it. The best argument is simply noting the ECW PPV show got more hype and air time to be promoted on WWF programming than the Leonard-Camacho fight did, and the WWF definitely had a financial stake in that show; and that WWF of late has had an iron-clad policy of not letting anyone appear on television that wasn't locked into a contract and yet now all of a sudden there are guys all over its television, any of whom its rival promotion could theoretically take on a moments notice.

It does create curiosity and talk, and WWF does need that, and without question a promotion vs. promotion feud would boost business for both sides in the short-run. But does WWF need it at the expense of its own product rather than adding to its own product, since by all accounts the traditional wrestling approach of a promotion vs. promotion deal isn't part of the plans, particularly with WrestleMania around the corner?

And the other question is, why, if you've got the single greatest angle possible in recent times that always works wonders when done correctly (or even done incorrectly as New Japan vs. UWFI and WCW vs. NWO have been at times), you instead have the outsider group play babyface and feud only with the company heel court jester rather than a serious star, and set up no plans for inter-promotional matches?

There's no doubt an ECW vs. WWF feud would work to the short-term benefit of both groups. But in the long-term, it would be more difficult because Paul Heyman's company doesn't appear to be in the financial straits that other companies who lay down and play dead for New Japan and turn into pro wrestling super novas have been. WWF exposure is good, but they don't need WWF, at least not today, for survival. If they do poorly on PPV, that may change, but as it stands today, ECW is a cult merchandising bonanza and its house show business isn't spectacular, but it fills up small halls most weekends. Ken Shamrock was also announced as appearing on the show although there was no context or explanation as to a storyline reason as to why.

Hart's half-worked column about ECW, saying it was the first time he and Lawler ever agreed on anything, stated, among other things:

> *...to call ECW second rate isn't accurate because to me, it doesn't even rate. It is interesting ECW wants to be on Raw. ECW cult guru, Paul E. Dangerously (Paul Heyman) has brainwashed his followers into believing ECW is a rebel group that won't dilute the extreme nature of its style to conform to TV censors or arena administrators. While this philosophy has cultivated ECW's loyal following in their home area, it has kept them from expanding into other venues and limited them to poor TV time slots in only a few markets. It is not surprising Heyman is now trying to convince the cable companies his product is similar to WWF and WCW. What better way to show them that ECW has the WWF's stamp of approval than to be on Raw. The style of ECW matches on Raw was changed to make them acceptable to censors and fans. You'd think ECW followers would be outraged the ECW matches on Raw weren't hardcore. You'd think they'd turn on Paul E. for selling out everything he has been preaching to them. Instead, they all waved at the cameras.*

APRIL 14

Some notes about the wrestlers in the USWA who are under WWF contract and developing. The Commandant, who is the friend of Bret Hart's from South Africa, appears to be a decent run-of-the-mill heel manager. Of the Truth Commission guys, Tank, who used to be Mantaur in the WWF, is as bad as ever, maybe even slower than before. The one who is Barry Buchanan isn't good, but is easily the best of the three, and the tall Canadian guy is really horrible. Brakkus is surprisingly animated in the ring for a guy who literally had never even seen a wrestling match until a few months ago, but is super green and stiff as a worker. He is a lot better than either Jim Hellwig or Steve Borden were when they came through Memphis in 1985 with a similar level of experience, so who knows.

MAY 26

This week's ECW television is largely focused on making Rob Van Dam into the top heel in the group for appearing on WWF television and being affiliated with Jerry Lawler. Paul Heyman is once again interested in bringing Lawler into the ECW Arena to shoot an angle because Lawler would be the most over heel ever in

ECW. Van Dam was suspended (since he's on the Japan tour) but will return likely on 6/7 at the Arena.

Bruce Prichard apparently has been clamoring for more ECW stuff on the WWF television because it gets Internet reaction. In addition, everyone at WWF was surprised at just how over Van Dam got at the Raw last week. The idea is to build to a Sabu & Van Dam vs. Tommy Dreamer & Sandman feud for the summer. Van Dam did receive an offer from WCW and WCW at one point was confident he'd be going, although it wasn't like they saw him as being another Curt Hennig or anything like that. I'd suspect that up until the PPV show, he probably was going and when the angle of his leaving got him over so strong, from that point on I'd figure his leaving was a work.

JUNE 9

ECW and USWA have agreed at least to a limited inter-promotional angle between the two companies, which would also be pushed on WWF television.

The angle actually started a few weeks back when they hooked up Rob Van Dam with Jerry Lawler on Raw. On Memphis television on 5/31, Lawler issued a challenge to anyone from ECW to come into the USWA and face him, which will probably be announced this coming week to set up USWA's return to Memphis on 6/14 with Lawler vs. Tommy Dreamer. Lawler was scheduled to accompany Van Dam to the ECW Arena in a surprise angle on the 6/7 show, although at press time due to a lot of booking changes being done in ECW due to injuries, that is not a definite, although one would expect Lawler will eventually appear.

There was supposed to be an angle involving ECW, probably Dreamer and Paul Heyman, with Lawler on the 6/2 Raw show, however due to all the booking having to be re-worked in ECW, Heyman and Dreamer had to cancel, but they, along with Van Dam, are scheduled for the 6/9 Raw in Hartford.

JUNE 16

The ECW, WWF and USWA feud geared up this past weekend with incidents in all three promotions.

The biggest angle, perhaps ever, in ECW took place on 6/7 at the ECW Arena where Jerry Lawler debuted to a thunderous heel reaction. Lawler's crowd pop for his monologue and where he, Sabu and Rob Van Dam destroyed several ECW wrestlers with chair shots, was said to be perhaps the loudest in the history of the promotion, and certainly the loudest for any incident in the Arena where a woman wasn't getting piledriven, choke slammed or power bombed by a man.

That morning, on USWA television, they officially announced that Tommy Dreamer had accepted Lawler's challenge and would face him on 6/14 in Memphis. Dreamer did a taped interview where he said how Lawler had sold out the USWA, and said how he was a big fan of Memphis wrestling growing up and blamed Lawler's selling out on the reasons the promotion is in the state it's in, doing what was basically an approved shoot style interview. Dreamer and Paul Heyman taped a second interview to air on the 6/14 Memphis television show.

Lawler, Van Dam, Dreamer and Heyman also appeared both on the live Raw is War show on 6/9 in Hartford, CT, and also did a second angle on the Shotgun Saturday Night show. The current plan is to continue this feud on Raw is War, although complete details haven't been worked out, to culminate in a match most likely at SummerSlam on 8/3 at the Continental Arena in East Rutherford, NJ.

Sources in ECW have said that the match would be at SummerSlam with Van Dam & Sabu vs. Dreamer & Sandman, which is the same main event match Heyman is headlining most of his major shows including the 6/28 ECW Arena show with. Sources in the WWF say that it's better than 50% such a match will take place at SummerSlam and it's tentatively penciled in for the show, but that it'll be Lawler & Van Dam as the tag team against Dreamer & Sandman or whomever Heyman picks to oppose them.

Heyman has in the past expressed concern about using Sandman against Lawler feeling that Sandman's style and Lawler's wouldn't work well together. It is also being considered having the match on the 9/7 In Your House from Louisville, KY rather than the Meadowlands, since Lawler's name would mean so much to be involved in a program for a match in that city.

Both Sabu and The Sheik are claiming to be appearing on the 6/23 Raw is War show which will be from

Sheik's old stomping grounds, Detroit's Cobo Arena, to do an angle that would set up their involvement in SummerSlam. Paul Heyman claimed he knew nothing about that.

The 6/7 ECW Arena angle started after Dreamer finally pinned Raven in Raven's final ECW match, a double-juice brawl that was said to be one of the best matches the two had ever had. The show, before a sellout 1,350 with a few hundred more turned away, was advertised on television as there being a major surprise appearance at the show.

The lights went out and when they came back on, Van Dam and Bill Alfonso were in the ring and destroyed Dreamer with a chair. The lights went out a second time, and when they came on, Sabu was in the ring helping them. The lights went out a third time, and when they came on, Lawler was in the ring. Lawler began talking over the house mic about ECW being Extremely Crappy Wrestling and did some swearing and the like, and joined in destroying Dreamer with a chair.

While this was all going on, Louie Spicolli was holding Beulah and forcing her to watch the carnage. The Gangstas did a run-in, but they were destroyed by Sabu and Van Dam. Ditto Balls Mahoney. At one point Shane Douglas came out and fans expected he'd save the ECW side but he got on the stage and said he had no problem with Sabu, Van Dam and Lawler and just watched it happen. WWF is said to be interesting in using Douglas for his mic work as part of the feud.

Heyman ran in after Lawler said he was the biggest piece of crap of all, and naturally he was destroyed. Sandman ran in and he was destroyed as well. Finally Taz came and everyone left, although Sabu wanted to go after him and he was held back by Van Dam and Lawler. The feeling among many is this may have been the best angle in the history of the promotion. Lawler is scheduled to wrestle Dreamer on the 8/17 PPV show, but Lawler will probably work ECW before that point as well.

In Hartford two nights later on Raw, they showed about a 10 second clip of the angle, and Heyman and Dreamer, with his forearm taped to sell an injury from two days earlier, came down through the crowd to sit in the front row. They got a surprisingly huge reaction with "ECW" and "Paul E" chants, to the point they stole center stage and killed the Doug Furnas & Phil LaFon vs. Head Bangers match that was going on in the ring. A few minutes later in the show, Van Dam beat Flash Funk in a fairly good short match. Heyman and Dreamer than hopped the guard rail and went after Lawler and Van Dam, largely with Lawler pummeling on Heyman and the other two going back-and-forth.

Vince McMahon tried to sell it as if Heyman and Dreamer were in the wrong because they hopped the barricade and were there because they had bought a ticket as wrestling fans, almost as if he was reacting the way Heyman told him to react rather than how he normally would in such a situation. It was a good heated brawl, although that couldn't be said about the second angle.

On the Shotgun show, The Head Bangers were wrestling Lawler & Van Dam, which ended in a DQ when Dreamer attacked Lawler and Van Dam. This brawl lasted way too long and didn't get much heat, much of which will be edited off television and took place after the cameras had turned off. It was largely afterwards considered a mistake by all parties, particularly since they kept brawling for so long it held up the taping of the rest of the show.

JUNE 23

USWA's return to Memphis on 6/14 at the Big One Flea Market drew about 560 fans and $2,800 for the Jerry Lawler vs. Tommy Dreamer match to start the USWA vs. ECW feud here. Dreamer was at the live television show that morning and they had security guards protecting announcers Lance Russell and Michael St. John because they portrayed Dreamer as an out-of-control mad man.

There were several fans wearing ECW t-shirts at the studio and chants of "ECW" throughout television. While on one hand the promotion was happy that people knew about ECW, there were feelings hurt about how popular ECW was and that the crowd didn't take to ECW as a heel promotion as they did during the SMW feud.

Dreamer first showed up trying to attack Lawler as he had a TV match against his cousin, Mr. Wrestling (Carl Fergie), however the security held back Dreamer and threw him out of the building. Finally late in the show,

Dreamer broke through security and beat up USWA commissioner Elliot Pollock and pretty well destroyed the television set, threw bleachers and a garbage can in the ring and while this was going on, the fans were cheering Dreamer like crazy. He also attacked the two security guards who sold the attack poorly.

This led to the house show later that afternoon where Lawler and Dreamer went to a no contest. There were a lot of fans with ECW t-shirts, but in reality the crowd wasn't helped much by Dreamer being there as they had been drawing about 500 fans to recent Saturday afternoon house shows (the weeknight house shows at the big one were drawing closer to 250) and hadn't run in six weeks. There were chants of both "ECW" and "ECW sux."

Dreamer came out shaking fans hands and got a babyface reaction, and didn't play heel at all during the match. Lawler also played face and was cheered more than Dreamer during the match. This feud will be continuing although not sure in what fashion. Paul Heyman was said to be coming in for the next house show, although with it scheduled for 6/28, that won't be the case because it's the same day as the ECW Arena.

JUNE 30

There were some major problems backstage with Sabu and Rob Van Dam. Sabu was complaining about having to do a double count out with Funk. Van Dam was supposed to do a match with Jesse Jammes on Shotgun where Lawler would get involved and Van Dam would end up counted out. Van Dam made the comment that it would be like Bret Hart going to ECW and losing to one of their job guys. Several WWF officials, Gerald Brisco in particular, found it insulting that Van Dam would compare himself to Bret Hart and there were a lot of complaints about Van Dam thinking he was much bigger of a star than he really is.

It nearly killed the ECW/WWF deal completely but Paul Heyman's ability to play both sides looks to have saved it. It may be Heyman's game to if things go bad and his guys are put in a position to put over WWF talent to then pull off WWF TV and claim his group was too extreme for the WWF or that may be the position if things don't work out and he'll make that claim if WWF pulls out of the deal.

There was considerable heat in WWF with Van Dam not doing their planned finish. Of course from an ECW standpoint, it is a WWF prelim wrestler (Jammes) that an ECW main eventer (Van Dam) wasn't able to beat in a television match so you can see their political side of trying to protect themselves from being devoured when working for a major group like the groups who have worked with New Japan have ended up and how SMW ended up when working with WWF.

JULY 7

Jim Cornette debuted with ECW on 6/28 in Philadelphia in an angle very similar to the one a few weeks back with Jerry Lawler.

In this case, during the main event with Sabu & Rob Van Dam vs. Tommy Dreamer & Sandman, the lights went out in the middle of the match and when they came back on, Lawler was in the ring and they worked over Dreamer & Sandman. This time, Dreamer & Sandman made a comeback and the lights went out again, and when they came back on, Cornette was in the ring and laid out both Dreamer and Sandman and about half the dressing room with his tennis racket.

During the finish, there were two referees knocked out, and then Tod Gordon came in to referee and he ended up being hit with a chair by Van Dam and sent through a table by Sabu and the match ended with Sabu pinning Dreamer and Van Dam pinning Sandman simultaneously.

Cornette's appearance was said to have gotten an even bigger response than the debut of Lawler at the previous show and the angle was said to have come across every bit as strong. During the angle, Lawler caned Dreamer low and Dreamer was legitimately injured to the point he couldn't work the next day and wasn't going to be anywhere near 100% for his match in Tokyo for WAR on Sunday. Much of the dressing room emptied and got their clocks cleaned. The angle ended, similar to the first Lawler angle, with Taz' music playing and him walking to the ring and the heels all leaving.

Taz then spotted a fan wearing a WWF "Raw is War" t-shirt and asked for the shirt. The fan wouldn't give it to him which started what could have been a bad scene as the crowd was looking to jump on the guy. Taz said if he didn't give him the shirt that the fans in the building were going to beat him up and get the shirt anyway. The guy still didn't give him the shirt and Taz finally said that he respected the fan for standing up for himself, at which point the fan gave him the shirt and Taz burned the WWF t-shirt in the ring to end the show.

Cornette debuting ended about a week's worth of negotiations, largely with Chris Candido as the middle man between Paul Heyman and Cornette. Heyman wanted to bring Cornette into the Arena feeling he was the last person anyone would expect to do an angle with ECW. Cornette, who has a longstanding hatred of both Heyman and ECW but also hadn't been in a position to do the kind of angles that he loves for a long time, originally laughed off the suggestion but did it since Heyman met a number of his stipulations.

The main stipulation would be that Heyman would apologize to Cornette's friend and long-time rival promoter Dennis Coraluzzo about the incident where Coraluzzo was double-crossed regarding the NWA title tournament a few years back when ECW hosted the tournament in late 1994, then had Shane Douglas throw down the belt and actually used the tournament to create Douglas as the first ECW world champion instead.

Both sides agreed to bury the hatchet in their longstanding war in that Coraluzzo wouldn't try to cost ECW dates, and ECW would allow Coraluzzo to use ECW talent when there isn't a conflicting date without putting heat on the boys for working Coraluzzo's show. Cornette would also be in control of the angle that would be done. Heyman sent a limo to pick up both Coraluzzo and Cornette and bring them to the Arena and apologized to Coraluzzo, and Coraluzzo started to apologize back when Heyman said that both would start with a clean slate.

Exactly where this angle is going is hardly clear, although Cornette is expected to manage Lawler on 7/11 in Asbury Park, NJ and perhaps on the other dates Lawler will work in ECW. Lawler only has a few dates booked with ECW, the Asbury Park show, the 7/19 show at the ECW Arena, and the 8/17 PPV show. Cornette is expected to be cutting at least one interview to build up his future appearances although nothing is 100% Supposedly Cornette also wanted Heyman to apologize to Coraluzzo in front of the boys and let the boys know they could work for Coraluzzo and it was sort of agreed that would take place some time in the future. Cornette was only in the dressing room for a short period of time before doing the angle while Coraluzzo never left the limo.

JULY 7

Paul Heyman was listed on the format sheet as the new co-host of Shotgun Saturday Night which is why they did the angle "firing" Pillman from the show. However, Heyman claimed he didn't even know about it and that WWF had sent him a ticket to Des Moines for a surprise but he has no interest in hosting the show. Don't know who the new co-host will turn out to be.

Heyman and Vince McMahon had a meeting on 6/27. Word has it McMahon was furious at Heyman for bringing up Eric Bischoff's name on Raw and mentioning Nitro, but Heyman said McMahon never brought either subject up at the meeting but said the relationship between the two groups could be hitting the rocks and said there was a lot of heat between McMahon and Van Dam over the finish the previous week.

Some WWF wrestlers are also hot about the double standard on their own show when it comes to ECW. The feeling is that almost anyone if they're allowed to break tables could get over but the WWF guys aren't allowed to do it and Sabu was allowed to brawl and Van Dam allowed to do topes into the guard rail which WWF guys aren't allowed to do and it got both of them over at a time when so many WWF wrestlers are having a hard time getting over.

JULY 7

There is a lot of talk that USWA is going to shortly wind up being a WWF satellite company, particularly since Tom Prichard is moving to Memphis to head the WWF training program which will include working this promotion. Currently the group is being funded by a guy from Cleveland who runs a chain of massage parlors.

JULY 14

The much talked about ECW/WWF relationship appears to be very close to falling apart as the so-called ECW match was pulled from the SummerSlam PPV.

Technically, a match involving Jerry Lawler (or Sabu) & Rob Van Dam vs. Sandman & Tommy Dreamer was at no point ever officially on the card, but there was at least a working understanding that they were building to that match likely for SummerSlam, or if not, for the subsequent PPV show in September in Louisville. Given that USWA is pushing a similar feud currently on its television, it shouldn't be a surprise if a deal is put back together for that match in Louisville.

To say the situation between the two companies over the past week is hard to figure would be an understatement. Paul Heyman claims the WWF had discussed with him doing an ECW match at SummerSlam but the two sides hadn't finalized an agreement, both financially and otherwise, regarding such a match. WWF claims that match wasn't in the plans for SummerSlam of late.

WWF sources said that Heyman agreed to co-host Shotgun Saturday Night beginning with the show taped 6/30 in Des Moines, IA, which is why they shot the angle on 6/23 to eliminate Brian Pillman from the broadcast booth. Heyman claimed he was never asked to do the show, only that they sent him a ticket to Des Moines and indicated they had a surprise for him. Heyman's name was on the format sheet as the co-host with Jim Ross for the Shotgun show in Des Moines, but since he wasn't there, he was replaced by his "good friend" Jim Cornette.

All week long WWF officials attempted to get hold of Heyman from the afternoon when he wasn't in Des Moines, with no success. WWF officials were doubly frustrated claiming that Heyman never called the building in Des Moines to say he wasn't going to be there, but only left a message on Bruce Prichard's answering machine at home, knowing full well Prichard was in Iowa at the time. In addition, Chris Candido was in Des Moines as he is at most Raw tapings to accompany his fiance, and WWF officials claimed Candido also couldn't get a hold of Heyman, although other sources indicated that Candido and Heyman were actually in regular contact that day via the cell phone.

As late as Thursday, when voice-overs were being done for the weekend Shotgun show, WWF officials were still trying to contact Heyman figuring they could chromo key him in the studio since almost all the actual voice-over work for the show is done in studio later in the week and the live show is mainly just for stand-ups and live interviews. As of press time, there has been no contact between Heyman and WWF, although there probably will be before any of you read this and once that happens, the entire situation could change again. Since there has been no contact, the situation seems to be that nobody really knows where this thing is headed.

Heyman's feeling is that while he was intrigued with the idea of doing the Ch. 31 show in New York which WWF is paying $7,000 per week to get weekly broadcast syndication back in the market and doing New York specific commentary, particularly since ECW has a 2 a.m. time slot coming on the same station, that there were too many problems and wasn't as interested in doing commentary on the national version of Shotgun. He felt he couldn't, for example, put over Owen Hart & Davey Boy Smith as a great tag team on WWF without bringing up the Dudleys or Eliminators, that he couldn't talk about Ken Shamrock as a shooter without putting over Taz, put over Sasuke's high risk moves without bringing up Sabu, etc. with the fear he'd turn his territory into what Jerry Lawler turned USWA into where it became obvious to the home folks that they were a minor league group.

All of this came on the heels on the problems on 6/30 in Detroit at the Raw taping where WWF officials were upset with the behavior of Sabu and Rob Van Dam in complaining about or not doing, respectively, the asked for finishes. Talks with WWF and Heyman give a totally different viewpoint on where Heyman stood in that situation. The WWF claimed Heyman was totally apologetic and embarrassed about the behavior of Sabu and Van Dam in Detroit, while Heyman himself says he backed Sabu and Van Dam all the way and it was largely he that was upset about his main eventers not going over on WWF preliminary wrestlers on television.

Heyman and McMahon had a meeting on 6/27 where McMahon complained to Heyman about the behavior of Sabu and Van Dam at the tapings both in not doing the finishes asked and also of Sabu running through the crowd but the meeting didn't end on a note where anyone figured the relationship was over.

As in any situation of this type, both sides become subconscious over who is getting the better of the deal. ECW was getting its company publicity and adding visibility in new markets to its cult following. The appearances of ECW talent haven't appeared to have made any positive difference in the Raw ratings, which was the WWF's hope, but nor have they been a detriment in the ratings, as was many people's fear.

In yet another aspect of this situation, Joey Styles (real name Joe Bonsignore) has been making noises about suing the WWF because he appears in the Steve Austin video and the WWF never asked for his permission. Styles, citing the Jesse Ventura verdicts as a precedent, was in specific referring to the Austin interview while in ECW where he mocks Hulk Hogan and Styles is part of that interview.

The footage to promote the video aired on Raw on 6/30 with the tag line courtesy of ECW. Heyman claims that WWF only asked his permission to use an Austin interview where he calls Nancy Sullivan a $5 piece of ass and says that he can't help it if she married a midget, and Heyman said that he was asked for it to be on broadcast television as opposed to being in a home video, which go under totally different guidelines legally. Yet in this day and age, particularly in the wake of the Ventura verdict, it is hard to believe the WWF would make such an elementary mistake in packaging a video without getting specific written permission in regard to any outside footage.

ECW and USWA are continuing their angle, with the 7/13 show in Memphis including matches with Lawler & Brian Christopher vs. Sandman & Dreamer and Taz & Candido vs. Sabu & Van Dam. Lawler and Jim Cornette are both scheduled to work for ECW on 7/11 in Asbury Park, NJ and Lawler is booked on at least two other ECW dates—the 7/19 ECW Arena show and the 8/17 PPV show. USWA officials are trying to book ECW talent into Louisville, since the first Lawler vs. Dreamer match, which only drew about 560 in Memphis, drew 900 into Louisville a few nights later.

JULY 21

Latest on the Paul Heyman claims and counterclaims. According to sources in the WWF, not only did they have Heyman's permission to put the short Austin ECW clip on the Stone Cold video, but that it was Heyman who brought them the clip personally. They also claim that Heyman and Vince McMahon specifically discussed the Shotgun co-host position and Heyman accepted it, but they held off announcing it because Heyman said he wanted to break it to his wrestlers before it became public knowledge.

This version is somewhat corroborated by the fact it was something of common knowledge within the WWF the week before Des Moines that Heyman was going to replace Pillman as the co-host on Shotgun starting with the 6/30 taping. WWF version is they shot the Pillman angle on 6/23 to get him off the show since Heyman had agreed. They also claim that as it regards the 6/30 flight to Des Moines, that Heyman specifically talked to WWF in regard to getting the ticket as to what time leaving and coming back and what airport to fly out of would be most convenient for his tight schedule, and that they had rearranged the voiceover day from Friday to Thursday for Shotgun because Heyman had told them Thursday would be easier on his personal weekly schedule.

Heyman's version is that the WWF has to lie about everything so they come off publicly looking good since they tried to double cross him on the finishes in Detroit. Dennis Coraluzzo said that both Heyman and Chris Candido had promised that Heyman would apologize to him in front of the boys as a concession to get Jim Cornette to work the last ECW Arena show and that Heyman's version of the story in the Observer last week was a total lie.

He said that Candido told him during the week to come to either Wildwood, NJ or Asbury Park, NJ to the ECW show and Heyman would apologize to him in front of all the wrestlers. Coraluzzo said that he decided even for Heyman that would be too humiliating and only wanted him to tell the wrestlers it was okay to work his shows. Candido told him Heyman told the wrestlers over the weekend that it was okay to work for Coraluzzo, but Coraluzzo claims when he talked to wrestlers he was interested in using, they told him they had never been told it was okay by Heyman and that the only thing said over the weekend in that regard was that Dreamer and Tod Gordon told wrestlers it was okay to work for Robin Hunt.

Supposedly Cornette's take on the entire situation is that he never trusted Heyman but that he got a limo ride, a free meal, a good payoff and some good press for doing the angle so he figures it turned out okay, but that he's not doing the 7/19 show and has no plans of going back.

As far as the WWF/ECW situation goes, neither side would categorize it as dead although with the exception of Heyman being talked with on Candido's cell phone when Candido was in Edmonton for Raw on 7/7, there has been no conversation between Heyman and WWF officials.

Heyman said that he's interested in getting an ECW match on SummerSlam, both because it would expose his main events on a PPV with a solid sized audience, and also politically it would be a smart move because numerous cable systems, most notably on the Viewers Choice side and Time Warner in New York, still aren't carrying the 8/17 show. It would be hard to justify that decision when his main eventers were just on a WWF PPV show two weeks earlier and didn't cause any furor. Obviously at this point there are no plans in the WWF to put an ECW match on SummerSlam and odds against that changing appear to be quite slim. But who knows, tomorrow it could all change.

JULY 28

Paul Heyman said it's absolutely untrue that he gave the WWF the tape of Steve Austin doing Hulk Hogan impression for use on the Stone Cold video that has turned into such a controversial situation. Joey Styles is still said to be planning on suing WWF over the video. Heyman said if you see the tape it's obviously dubbed from VHS because of the quality and not dubbed from 3/4 or Super VHS as a professional dub would be.

AUGUST 11

Heyman had a meeting on 7/31 at Titan Towers with Vince McMahon, Bruce Prichard and Jim Ross basically opening up the closed lines of communication. While nothing definite, as far as a date and an angle was confirmed, McMahon apparently told Heyman that if he had any ideas on angles that would benefit both companies to present them to him, and both sides talked a lot about the 9/22 live Raw show from Madison Square Garden, but saying that ECW will definitely be part of that show appears at this point to be premature, but certainly a possibility. Most likely nothing of that nature would happen before the MSG show, so Heyman won't be able to get last-minute WWF exposure to attempt to bolster the buy rate of his 8/17 PPV show.

The war of words, with each side calling the other liars in regard to every aspect of the break-up, of Heyman's not doing the Shotgun show as WWF said he had agreed to do, and of the Steve Austin video with the brief ECW clip, will apparently slow down for a few weeks as both are allies against the common WCW enemy. Sources in the WWF claim Heyman had been on the WWF payroll for quite a while before the relationship cooling off when, from the WWF side, Heyman no-showed the 6/30 show in Des Moines, IA where he was scheduled to start as the color commentator on Shotgun Saturday Night.

The WWF had claimed Heyman had told them to keep that news quiet because he didn't want his wrestlers finding out before he told them himself. He then never told them and never showed up either in Des Moines or for the voice-overs. Heyman still insists he never agreed to do it and even still claims it was never even brought up to him before hand. According to other WWF sources, while most of the key people in the organization were soured at the conduct of Sabu and Rob Van Dam at the Detroit taping, the door has not been shut to potentially doing business with them again should WWF find it beneficial.

SEPTEMBER 15

There has been a lot of talk of late of WWF taking over the Memphis territory if the current ownership group pulls out. WWF wants to use the territory and control the booking of the territory as a way for its younger wrestlers under contract to gain experience.

The ECW relationship is different. The belief is that ECW fans are both too impatient and unforgiving for inexperienced wrestlers to work there and not be psychologically driven right out of the business, plus the style that they'd learn to get over in ECW wouldn't be applicable to the style they'd have to work in WWF. However, WWF does want to send contracted talent that they haven't used correctly and have talent and experience such as Al Snow and P.J. Walker to ECW to get repackaged. Paul Heyman inquired about using Furnas & LaFon when they're ready under similar circumstances.

DECEMBER 1

There had been some kind of an unofficial agreement between WWF and ECW that WWF would help publicize the PPV show. Originally Paul Heyman was supposed to shoot a taped segment for Raw, but he never sent the tape for either the 11/10 or 11/17 shows because they were going to be so dominated by the Bret Hart situation and he felt anything about his company would be so secondary that from a positioning standpoint it would be buried.

Heyman offered WWF a Sandman & Dreamer vs. Sabu & Van Dam tables and ladders match for the 11/24 Raw in Fayetteville which the WWF turned down. He did send two quick bumpers to the 11/24 show, however they didn't air, and the show was only mentioned once in passing by Jim Ross and then Jim Cornette basically ran it down. They did mention ECW had bought ads which would be seen on the weekend programming.

Chapter Six

WCW Attempts to Purchase NJPW

MARCH 3

Yet another story with some almost mind-boggling political implications involves Eric Bischoff and WCW's attempt to have Turner Broadcasting purchase at least some of New Japan Pro Wrestling.

The story actually started in January when Bischoff, Sonny Onoo and Kevin Sullivan of WCW met with Masa Saito and Nagashima of New Japan Pro Wrestling in Hawaii. During the meeting, there were discussions involving many potential facets involving WCW buying the company, starting a rival company in Japan or other forms of working together.

New Japan over the past few years has not only been the most successful pro wrestling promotion when it comes to house show business during the period, but also most likely in the history of the industry with numerous $5 million plus houses at the Tokyo Dome, figures no other company in history has ever achieved. In 1997, the company at present has five Dome shows scheduled, and if successful in most or all of them, would reach up to yet a new level this year.

However, the future of pro wrestling on a worldwide basis is clearly not house show driven, but driven by not only PPV, but as a provider of cheap television programming that can draw better than competitive ratings on stations that only need fringe ratings to survive.

The Japanese world, as it relates to television, is going to change, much as the American world as it related to television, and then how that related to pro wrestling, changed with the explosion of cable and PPV. It's too soon to know what those changes will be. The belief is that because of zoning laws and the like, that cable television as it exists in the United States will never be that kind of a force in Japan. The belief is that instead it will be things like small dishes, new companies opening in Japan such as DirecTV and PerfecTV, that will open up Japan to more than just the basic VHF television stations the way television existed in the United States into the early 70s.

Japanese wrestling has flourished with cable and the likes in its infancy, generally because of the stronger print media coverage and larger influence of wrestling magazines on driving the industry, plus, even though the shows air in past-midnight time slots, All Japan and New Japan do impressive ratings and are broadcast nationwide on major network stations weekly, and All Japan Women have frequent fringe time slot television specials on a third major network.

Both JWP and RINGS have monthly television shows on the WOWOW channel, which would be equivalent in the U.S. to HBO, broadcasting the major shows without commercial interruption similar to what would be a PPV special tape delayed a few days. Gaora, a smaller cable station runs Pancrase on a few days tape delayed about once per month, along with fairly regular coverage, but not on a weekly basis, of smaller groups like Michinoku Pro, FMW, Gaea and others. The new 24-hour wrestling and martial arts Samurai! channel, along with numerous pro wrestling related features, broadcasts live and taped cards also from the smaller offices, however that station to this point has incredibly limited viewership and thus far cable and dish penetration in Japan is exceedingly minimal.

Ultimately this will all change and when it does, pro wrestling in Japan in some form will change. The only question is what the changes in television will evolve into being, and how wrestling evolves within that picture.

How this relates to Bischoff and New Japan is Bischoff's belief that New Japan, as a house show promotion, isn't ready for whatever changes the future brings and that WCW, with Turner behind them, are major players in that world. Of course, with New Japan being part owned by Rupert Murdoch, one would think whatever advantages Turner has, his rival Murdoch could match.

While a scant few were aware of this for the past two months, Bischoff made it public somewhat in an Internet chat on 2/18 where he vaguely talked about buying New Japan. The question actually related to where WCW would go to get new talent and Bischoff's answer was, "There is a tremendous wealth of talent in Japan and Mexico. Right now we are looking at either buying New Japan Pro Wrestling or creating our own promotion in Japan to attract new talent as well as expanding our efforts in Mexico. I believe a tremendous amount of talent will come from Japan and Mexico in the next few years." Bischoff later elaborated on that point in at least two subsequent occasions over the past week.

The reality is, that buying New Japan outright would be next to impossible. However, Bischoff does have a trip to Japan scheduled around 3/20 to either buy into the company, which wouldn't be all that difficult given the number of different stockholders the company has; perhaps set up WCW running in Japan on its own in a building like the Tokyo, Osaka or Nagoya Dome, a process that would likely be doomed to failure even if WCW was going to break its relationship with New Japan and raid some of its top talent and management.

As in every situation of this type, if Bischoff is given the okay by Turner to spend the money and money is available, there will be more than a few willing people both in management and in the ring that will avail themselves to the money; working with New Japan on major show ventures but increasing WCW's influence and financial stake in those ventures; or some combination of all of this.

The politics of purchasing the company outright would have to be considered nearly impossible in that majority interest in New Japan, Inc. couldn't be sold by any one person or company, and in addition, there is no prevailing interest among the major shareholders to sell the company. New Japan is owned by numerous conglomerates, the largest being TV-Asahi, one of Japan's four major television networks. TV-Asahi is a Rupert Murdoch affiliate and that's where the trickiness politically lies in the idea that Turner and Murdoch, being huge business rivals, could both have ownership in the same corporation.

The other major conglomerate that owns points in New Japan is Sagawa-Express, which would be Japan's equivalent to Federal Express in the United States. In addition, there are numerous individual wealthy businessmen that have points in the company as well as numerous veteran wrestlers and front office employees owning stock like Antonio Inoki, Seiji Sakaguchi, Riki Choshu, Tatsumi Fujinami, Masa Saito, Kengo Kimura and numerous others.

MARCH 10

In a move totally unrelated to pro wrestling, but related to a story in last week's issue, the Rupert Murdoch organization on 3/3 divested itself of all interest in TV-Asahi, which is the major shareholder in New Japan Pro Wrestling. Murdoch sold its financial interests in TV-Asahi, one of the major networks in Japan, to concentrate its Japanese business on what many expect to be the future of Japanese mass communications—satellite television dishes. So whatever political problems it would create for a Turner group trying to buy into a company where Murdoch has key financial interest is no longer the case. Still, from all reports from Japan, there doesn't appear to be any significant interest in Japan from the major stockholders of New Japan to sell to Americans.

Chapter Seven

Ken Shamrock Signs with the WWF

FEBRUARY 24

Serious negotiations have gone on this past week to build for an Antonio Inoki and Satoru Sayama promoted show outside the auspices of New Japan at the Tokyo Dome on 4/12 to be headlined by Shinya Hashimoto vs. Ken Shamrock for the IWGP heavyweight title.

New Japan and Shamrock have been negotiating seriously for the past week. New Japan may have contacted Pancrase, which still has Shamrock under contract for four more matches, to buy out his contract with the group for the proposed Dome show. At present time, no other matches for the proposed Dome show have been announced, nor has Shamrock signed a contract with either Inoki's side company or with New Japan.

Shamrock hasn't wrestled on a Pancrase show since January due to both UFC commitments and injuries, and his contract from a time standpoint with Pancrase has run out, but Pancrase has claimed he's got four matches left on a nine match deal. After a bitter dispute over the contract, his position booking the foreign talent and as manager for the American fighters within Pancrase, the two sides split under less than acrimonious circumstances. The dispute came up when Shamrock agreed to work on a proposed Vale Tudo event at the Fukuoka Dome on 12/15, the same day as a major Pancrase show at Tokyo Budokan Hall. Shamrock eventually had to pull out of the match and the card itself was canceled.

Before gaining fame as a shooter in both Pancrase and UFC, Shamrock worked as a pro wrestler in the Carolinas under the name Vince Torelli and did one tour with All Japan while he was really green and basically didn't have a clue what was going on before gaining pro wrestling fame as one of the top foreign stars with the old UWF and Pro Wrestling Fujiwara Gumi. He became recognized as a top martial arts star after leaving PWFG along with Minoru Suzuki and Masakatsu Funaki in 1993 to form Pancrase, and helped give both himself and that company major credibility that same year when UFC debuted and he quickly became one of that company's top stars as well. It is believed, if the negotiated deal is finalized, that Shamrock will work this show and perhaps others with New Japan along with continuing in UFC.

MARCH 3

While there have been bigger stories over the years in wrestling, there has never been a story with as many implications in so many places as Ken Shamrock's signing with the World Wrestling Federation on 2/24.

Shamrock, 33, signed a three-year guaranteed exclusive contract with the WWF for a low seven figure downside guarantee and signing bonus. In addition, Vince McMahon has the option after three years to continue the contract for an additional three years without Shamrock having the option to test himself at that point on the free agent market. The contract is exclusive, ending Shamrock's participation in the Ultimate Fighting Championship or in any shootfighting events. At least at press time appears to kill what some Japanese insiders were expecting to wind up being the biggest money live match in pro wrestling history—a proposed 4/12 match at the Tokyo Dome against Shinya Hashimoto for the IWGP championship.

Shamrock debuted on Monday Night Raw later that evening at the Manhattan Center, portrayed as a celebrity in the audience attending the matches with his father Bob and wife Tina. They showed him early in the show in the crowd. He was put over as a major star with them talking about him as a superstar from the controversial Ultimate Fighting Championship events and called him a UFC champion and said he was called by ABC-television as "the World's Most Dangerous Human Being".

About 45 minutes into the show, he was interviewed by Jerry Lawler who tried to claim they were best friends and he had taught him all his submission holds with Shamrock acting as if he didn't know who Lawler was. The segment really didn't work. Later in the show he was interviewed again, this time by Todd Pettengill, and asked about the two WrestleMania main event matches. At this point Faarooq came out and got in his face and made a disparaging remark about UFC. Shamrock did a wrestling promo back. For some reason, the camera wasn't on him as he made his comeback and said he'd take him on one-on-one if Vince McMahon would sign the match. This segment didn't come off as either good nor bad.

Shamrock is going to have to get the mega-push from WWF to justify the contract, so it's pretty well acknowledged he's either going to wind up as a major superstar in American wrestling or a flop. There is no in between, and based on his first appearance, there is no hint at all of which it will end up being. It was a positive that the live crowd took to him like a star, popped big for him and the mentions of UFC, and chanted his name during his interview. He does have the look and charisma to be a superstar and has the potential to do great 90s style shoot interviews, particularly since he has credibility coming in as the real deal. But he's never worked American style pro wrestling at this level.

Shamrock was a name pro wrestler in Japan doing shoot style pro wrestling with the old UWF and Pro Wrestling Fujiwara Gumi and made himself a star in Japan doing worked matches before the days of Pancrase and UFC, so he can do believable style worked matches. He has done American style pro wrestling but is limited in his experience at it, and it would be the best thing from a marketing standpoint for him to not wrestle American style because he'd then be just another pro wrestler, and rather work a UWFI style like a more believable and less acrobatic version of Dean Malenko, with the idea that his image will take him to a higher level. McMahon is taking a huge risk, that will either pay off in the end as a great investment and a franchise player, or a better working more charismatic version of Mark Henry.

The signing ends a pressure-cooker of a week for Shamrock, who was torn between offers from UFC, New Japan, WWF and a potential meeting with WCW. It starts another pressure-cooker, going into the world of pro wrestling and on the road with the natural resentment of wrestlers who have paid more dues and because of experience are for the most part at this point better performers that won't be making as much money or getting as much of a push. Nevertheless, these are the risks a promotion has to take from time-to-time or they wind up like All Japan Pro Wrestling—a stagnant company that is a slave to workrate with the inability to fill holes when they open because not many can be super workers.

WCW took it with Hulk Hogan, paying him more than any wrestler in history has ever earned, and gave him the world title despite its most loyal fans resenting it because he was the outsider being put over the home team's superstar and basically telling the most loyal fans the product they love was really not the best. In this case, it'll cause resentment originally by some fans as it portrays a UFC star as being equal to the top WWF wrestlers on their turf. He also gives WWF a chance to give its product a level of credibility and believability it is sorely lacking and is the foundation of those record-breaking houses in Japan.

New Japan Pro Wrestling held a press conference on 2/19 and announced officially what we reported here last week, that they were running a Tokyo Dome show on 4/12 headlined by Hashimoto vs. Shamrock for the IWGP championship. The announcement was made before Shamrock had signed the proposed four-match contract that would include him headlining subsequent events on 5/3 at the first Osaka Dome show ever, 8/10 at the first Nagoya Dome show, and 11/2 at the Fukuoka Dome.

The immediate interest in Japan for this match was such that comparisons were made to the first Keiji Muto vs. Nobuhiko Takada match, the $6.1 million record-setting gate at the Dome on October 9, 1995 which is considered by many as the biggest match in the history of Japanese wrestling. In many ways, this match, pitting New Japan's top star against a superstar from the world of martial arts, combat sports or a rival wrestling promotion's top star, was simply just the latest sequel in the match that New Japan has been the experts in promoting dating back to the legendary Antonio Inoki vs. Shozo Kobayashi match in 1974 and continuing with the likes of Willem Ruska, Muhammad Ali and so many others.

In the case of Shamrock, they had the first New Japan world champion's opponent who fit into all three of the perfect rival categories at the same time. To make things even hotter, it was announced that they were retiring the old IWGP heavyweight title belt and designing a new belt, valued at $90,000—making it the most expensive title belt in pro wrestling history. The strap would first be on public display on 3/27 at New Japan 25th anniversary party at Keio Plaza Hotel, and would be worn to the ring by Hashimoto for the first time in the title match. They also announced Great Muta vs. Masahiro Chono in some sort of a stipulation match, perhaps along the lines of if Chono wins, Muta has to join the NWO, and a J Crown title defense by Jushin Liger against Great Sasuke. In addition, Naoya Ogawa, three-time world judo champion and 1992 Olympic silver medalist in judo, is expected to sign his New Japan contract sometime this week and make his pro debut on the card.

Tickets for the show were announced as going on sale on 3/10 and even though the top and bottom prices, 30,000 ($270) yen and 5,000 ($45) yen, are typical for the Dome, the mid-level prices were increased. The sellout, which was considered more of a question as to how fast as opposed to if it would, would set the all-time record gate.

On Monday night—actually Tuesday afternoon in Japan, the Japanese media and New Japan were stunned to find out the news of Shamrock appearing on the WWF Raw show. Technically it is not 100 percent out of the question that the match won't take place, although realistically there is almost no chance. To book Shamrock, New Japan would have to book him through McMahon. The original price and contract New Japan sent Shamrock, and most believe would probably have included an IWGP title reign (he would join only Hulk Hogan and Big Van Vader as Americans to have held that title), would have to be renegotiated and approved through McMahon. With New Japan being tied to WCW and having no business relationship with WWF, it would make maintaining that main event almost an impossibility.

Forgetting about money and the WCW politics, McMahon would almost surely insist on Shamrock not losing, which means he'd have to win the title or do a screw-job, the latter which would be totally unacceptable in Japan in such a match. The IWGP title reign appeared to have been part of the original plan. However, that would mean a WWF wrestler would be holding the IWGP title, the sister organization of WCW.

For McMahon, who still has designs on promoting in Japan, it would be in his best interest to negotiate to have Shamrock do the New Japan dates. Even losing in this high profile of a situation still makes one a bigger mainstream star in Japan than never having played in the big game. And this is the biggest game of all. Shamrock is already a wrestling superstar in Japan, but if he were to headline four major Dome shows in one year, even if he were to lose once or twice, he would become a far bigger attraction for McMahon in Japan if WWF wanted to promote there, than he would be having never been put in this position.

The word is McMahon indicated to Shamrock he would negotiate with New Japan for him to keep the dates, but preliminary word from New Japan is that they aren't interested in negotiating with McMahon. However, it leaves New Japan with a Dome show, one that wasn't on the books to begin with and was specifically put together in the last two weeks when Shamrock contacted them a few weeks back and expressed interest in working for their promotion, and no main event.

By late Tuesday, the word out of New Japan is that they believed that had been double-crossed by Shamrock and were looking for a new opponent for Hashimoto. Dan Severn's name came obviously to mind, and under other circumstances, a Hashimoto vs. Severn match would be a good draw in Japan. However, Severn would come in under the present circumstances with the feel of being a substitute main eventer and some feel it would be better to go in a different direction, such as using a K-1 champion like Peter Aerts or Andy Hug, but politically with K-1 and New Japan rivals in that they are both promoting several Dome shows this year, that would also seem a political impossibility.

This past October, New Japan had planned a Dome show around Antonio Inoki vs. Royce Gracie, but was unable to get Gracie to do pro wrestling business (ie. the job) and the entire show, which was also almost a guaranteed sellout, was canceled.

The belief is that Shamrock will debut with the WWF in a non-wrestling role at WrestleMania with much of the speculation backstage at the Raw tapings that he would wind up as a guest referee for a submissions only match with Bret Hart vs. Steve Austin, which would lead into some sort of an angle to build to his debut in the ring. The Pettengill interview hinted as such as they asked Shamrock about the match and he refused to pick one or the other as a winner. He'll likely be training with Tom Prichard in Connecticut for whatever style of work it is WWF envisions they want him doing.

From the announcement on Wednesday in Japan of the legendary match that will apparently never happen, things have been in a constant turmoil for both Shamrock and the various promotions with designs on using him. Upon hearing the word, SEG immediately called and offered him a two-match deal for slightly more per event than New Japan was offering but not as much overall, for matches against Tank Abbott and provided he won, a title shot against Mark Coleman or whomever the champion was. However, it was their insistence that he could work New Japan, but that he doesn't lose any matches, or they were pulling the deal off the table.

WWF's deal offered more long-term security than the Japanese deal and far more than the UFC deal, but would require far more work and travel. WWF insisted on exclusivity. The Japanese deal was for a great amount of money, more than any foreign wrestler has ever received on a per show basis in Japan except for Hulk Hogan, for a limited amount of work. But the contract would expire in November.

WWF, which also immediately sped up negotiations on 2/18—the day word broke throughout pro wrestling that the Hashimoto match was being planned and about to be announced—pressured him to make the decision immediately and must have upped the ante since he flew back to Connecticut to sign the deal rather than meet with Eric Bischoff in San Francisco. For his purposes, WWF for many reasons looked like a better fit than WCW because WWF is looking to create new superstars while WCW has the top of its shows locked up and the booking is more controlled by wrestlers looking to maintain position.

WWF wanted him on as a surprise on Raw on 2/24 with so much talent away in Germany and all the key injuries, plus coming off the weak ratings for the first two-hour live show on 2/17 and were looking to pack every shock possible into the show to try and reverse the weekly ratings defeats. Several months back, WWF and Shamrock had a meeting at their offices about a deal, which fell apart when Shamrock's asking price was $500,000 per year. At that time, Shamrock had guaranteed fighting contracts with both UFC and Pancrase, both of which were to expire in the latter stages of 1996.

With WWF looking for the home run that will put them back in the ball game, the two sides ended up back talking. Shamrock was looking toward pro wrestling for career longevity at the age of 33, recognizing his shooting days were near the end, after the reality of the hand injury eliminated him after the first round of the Ultimate Ultimate tournament and a lucrative Japanese booking fell through due to his legal problems with Pancrase.

In addition, Pancrase, which still claims he's under contract with them for four more matches, was making noises once the New Japan match got out. While New Japan did try and negotiate with Pancrase about buying out the remainder of the contract, the two companies at this point are major business rivals. The old school pro wrestling mentality still remains that the shoot style and actual shooting that goes on in Pancrase exposes traditional pro wrestling as being worked and somehow threatens it because of that, despite New Japan doing record breaking business these days, with much of the style popularity coming from incorporating genuine shoot moves into the pro wrestling framework.

At the 2/22 Pancrase card in Tokyo, President Masami Ozaki, whose public statements about Shamrock in Japan after the two sides had the contract problem turned his image in Japan slightly negative publicly, said that the company would take legal action against New Japan if they used Shamrock. However, whatever negativity there was regarding Shamrock disappeared totally when the announcement of the Hashimoto match went public due to the huge buzz on the match.

MARCH 10

Probably the No. 1 topic of conversation this past week, perhaps more within the UFC world than the pro wrestling world, was Ken Shamrock's decision to go to pro wrestling and the WWF in particular. Realistically, the pro wrestling decision was made weeks ago with the Shinya Hashimoto match the first step of a new career and not simply a one-shot deal.

While some may try and portray this as Shamrock being afraid of Mark Coleman, or Shamrock leaving real fighting because he's injury prone—and there may be a measure of truth to the latter—the switch to pro wrestling is more a matter of economic reality. Shamrock went into the Ultimate Ultimate with the idea that he'd likely face Mark Coleman in the finals so the idea he got out because of fear of Coleman is unfounded. By all accounts, Shamrock was very confident in his chances to the point he was willing to risk an already made reputation going into a tough tournament. And remember, in the original Ultimate Ultimate plans, his first round opponent was to be Vitor Belfort. So forget the idea that his leaving was trying to duck Tank Abbott's acceptance of his challenge or anything people wanting to bury him on the way out may come up with.

The future of so-called real fights is now in question, both from the political angle and the economic angle. EFC is hanging by a thread. UFC is licking its wounds and has been stagnant as far as PPV buys since taking the big drop starting in July and is the only real name brand in the game. The other organizations have no concept for economic viability and are going to bail out as quickly as they arrive. And Japan and Brazil are no less uncertain. Even if economic and political conditions were different, Shamrock wasn't getting any younger and his long-term prognosis would still be the world of pro wrestling, if not right now, maybe another year or two down the road.

Shamrock was quoted in the Dayton Daily News as saying, "What closed the door to me with no-holds-barred fighting was that I couldn't make enough money to support my family. If I do something I like and can support my family, I will continue to do it. The minute I can't, I've got to do something else."

Why WWF, where his success is far less certain than New Japan, where it would be almost a given? Simply, the WWF put more money on the table. They made the investment, and after losing out on major talent in the past, it's up to the WWF to make that investment pay off. Whether they have the foresight to pull it off is a question. Whether they have the patience to pull it off is a question. And whether it can be pulled off in the United States is also not totally certain, because it requires educating fans to something new which is never a lock that it'll work although a good promotion with patience more often that not can pull that process off.

The WWF is not expecting to build the company around Shamrock by any means. Despite winning an incredible bidding war for Bret Hart, it's clear the company isn't going to be built around him either. Despite being arguably the best all-around performer in the States and a proven drawing card, the company had decided not to build around Shawn Michaels either. Although WWF is very different from New Japan, they are taking the current New Japan plan where there is a group at the top, that any of the top guys on a given night can beat any of the other top guys.

The top level at this point is Undertaker, Sid, Steve Austin and Bret Hart. Shamrock will no doubt be put in a position to join that quartet, as will probably one or two others like perhaps Davey Boy Smith when he makes his complete turn, and Shawn Michaels will undoubtedly be back at that level if and when he returns.

And everyone recognizes Shamrock can't get there if he's portrayed as just another babyface wrestler. George Scott years ago saw him as the next Ricky Steamboat in the Carolinas, right down to working the same angles to get him over with Paul Jones than he had done with Steamboat an era earlier. But before he came anywhere close to that level, Scott's promotion went under and he became a star in Japan doing worked shootfights, and later doing real shootfights. But for him to fulfill the stardom Scott saw in him, the last thing he needs to be is another Steamboat.

It's no secret what needs to be done, basically educating the audience to submissions with Shamrock portrayed as the master of that game. Will it work? Perhaps not immediately. So the question becomes patience, something pro wrestling promotions have lacked greatly in these days of a new head-to-head ratings battle every Monday night.

For the short run, Shamrock is not going to be a guy who makes a difference in the ratings and a new style isn't going to be understood or over with the new audience for him by next Monday night. I don't know if any one person can be a one-man ratings changer, but certainly if there was, it isn't him. But with the right build-up and booking, and the right opponent, he should be someone who can draw money and interest on PPV for the right match with the right build. If this becomes the beginning of a new road with more emphasis on matwork, realism, and submission finishes, thus enabling wrestlers to get away with less acrobatic and risky high spots and save their bodies in a business where the injury rate and risks seem to get higher by the week, it's better for everyone.

But a change like that can't happen overnight. This happened in Japan, as much by necessity because the top guys were breaking down from the punishment, as by someone with a long-term focus deciding to change it. And pro wrestling is all psychology. All Japan got a simple move like Mitsuharu Misawa's facelock over as a killer finisher a few years back. How? Because Jumbo Tsuruta submitted to the move and presto, that's all it needed. If the WWF has Shamrock make the top stars tap to whatever maneuver or maneuvers he's pushed as having as his finishers, they'll be recognized by people as deadly finishers. If they're treated the way the WCW announcers treat those same submissions when Dean Malenko has them on, as an excuse to babble about Roddy Piper, then the resulting fan reaction to them will be the same as in WCW.

In the U.S., with more bodies to choose from and stars that can get away with coasting on the road, or avoiding the road altogether, it isn't the necessity to get simple maneuvers like facelocks, sleepers, kneebars and armbars over and change what the classic match builds to as it was when similar changes were made in Japan to protect the bodies of the guys on top that need to headline for years to come.

And another point needs to be made in a business so ratings driven. When these changes were made within the Japanese business, while arena business largely stayed strong and in some cases got even stronger as the matches increased their believability factor, the fact was, initially, ratings dropped. They eventually rebounded, but there was a period where they got dangerously low across the board. The casual audience wasn't as entertained at the same time the more serious audience was able to suspend disbelief, take the product more seriously and thus increasing the drama quotient, and the end result was more tickets sold for the major matches. As we've noted many times and as history shows clearly both short-and-long-term, drawing money at the gate and drawing television ratings are two entirely different animals which require two entirely different approaches to the game.

It's also funny the reaction I've received to the Shamrock signing. Several veteran legends of the not too distant past (some of whom are still around today) thought he'd be the perfect person to put the world title on because of his credibility, and put on quickly. A few current wrestlers who follow UFC also believed his potential for stardom was great and that the WWF made a tremendous move for the organization.

But there are dissenting views as well. If the WWF thinks that because Shamrock is on its television or on its PPV shows that UFC fans that saw him as a major superstar will suddenly buy the WWF product, I don't see it happening. And while there is a crossover between the two audiences, it's not significant enough to instantly make someone a superstar anymore than bringing in a pro football star and not doing a good job of hyping him makes him a drawing card.

Kevin Greene and Steve McMichael, and to a greater extent Lawrence Taylor, were all legitimate pro football stars and pro football is one hell of a lot bigger entity than either UFC or pro wrestling. And the initial angle for all these men was given tons of pub and put over as if it was the biggest event of the year within those respective companies. WWF would hit a home run if Shamrock's angle was done anywhere near as well as the angles leading to the debut of Taylor, Greene and McMichael were done. Yet both angles bombed on PPV when it came to buy rate even though the matches in both cases were much better than anyone could have hoped for going in.

Simply put, fans of those athletes from real sports, have no interest in seeing them in something they consider a joke. The Shamrock UFC fans have no interest in seeing Shamrock participate in something they consider a joke. The few super hardcore Shamrock fans who will order pro wrestling if he's on it don't number enough to make any difference in a TV rating or a buy rate just as the name Kevin Greene, coming off a Pro Bowl year and with media publicity, won't make a difference in a national buy rate unless his angle is strong enough on its own to make that difference. However, if any of the above mentioned names made the transition to being wrestling stars, were given the right training and push, they could very quickly become major stars.

McMichael, with very little training and ability in the ring, certainly nowhere close to what Shamrock has, is a legitimate star with less than one year and only a handful of matches largely due to charisma and a lot of help in positioning by being put in a high-ranked group. And at this point while in the ring, his NFL legitimacy was a major help in him getting there. In the case of Shamrock, with the right angle and push, he'll have an easier time getting over because of his legitimacy to the new audience. But nobody from the outside has a strong enough name to get over with the lack of that right angle and push in American wrestling.

New Japan is in a major bind. Everyone knows the story and they made a major mistake. In this day and age, you can't announce a match publicly until the match is signed. By jumping the gun, New Japan left its business even flatter than the WWF's is at this point. The idea of pro wrestling is to tease the audience into wanting to see a specific thing, and then when interest is at a peak, giving it to them. New Japan had a winner of an idea and knew it, and told the public about it before it was etched in stone. Now they have an empty public, all waiting and wanting to see something they can't deliver.

Unless they pull a major rabbit out of their hats, whatever they can deliver is going to look second rate in comparison. Very similar to WWF spending nearly one year building up the idea of Bret Hart getting another crack at Shawn Michaels' title, and then pissing it away by looking for short-term answers, abandoning it as a feature, and then losing out on it completely.

UFC, the company because of its non-worked nature that has far less control over its bookings, allowed Shamrock to do strong hype for a match that may have drawn the most interest of any match it could present as far as to the general public. And now it can't deliver the match either. As worked pro wrestling, both in the U.S. and Japan, look for outsiders to either do the New Japan special angle or pop in as a surprise American mystery partner angle, UFC stars, whether they have pro wrestling experience or not, are going to be looked at.

And don't think nearly every one of them would be interested. Pro wrestling offers more money, more security, more stability and less danger. Martial arts fans may want their sport to be this pure things where people compete for honor and wanting to prove their skills, but that thought process doesn't last long once you're in the world of professional entertainment and you're the economic commodity. And the problem with UFC is, once someone reaches the top level, there are only two places to go. Down—or somewhere else.

Chapter Eight

Naoya Ogawa Signs for NJPW

MARCH 17

New Japan Pro Wrestling officially announced at a press conference on 3/7 that Naoya Ogawa, the 1992 Olympic silver medalist in judo in the 209 pound weight class, would replace Ken Shamrock as Shinya Hashimoto's opponent in the main event on the 4/12 show at the Tokyo Dome. It was announced two days later that the match wouldn't be for Hashimoto's IWGP heavyweight title because it would be under martial arts rules—no time limit and must be a finish by either submission or knockout with pinning not applicable to the match.

Virtually all the sports pages in Japan on 3/8 listed the Ogawa-Hashimoto announcement as that day's lead sports story on the front page, which was a level of publicity that a Hashimoto-Shamrock match wouldn't have been able to achieve. As of press time, only two other matches on that show have been announced, the Great Muta vs. Masahiro Chono and the J Crown title defense of Jushin Liger vs. Great Sasuke.

The feeling in Japan from just about everyone close to the situation is that this main event should draw a sellout, which because of raised mid-level prices, would likely be the largest live gate in the history of Japanese pro wrestling. However, with the yen falling as compared to the dollar of late, the gate wouldn't in U.S. dollars top the all-time record of $6.1 million for the Nobuhiko Takada vs. Keiji Muto first match.

While Ogawa, 28, is not the name Shamrock is to pro wrestling fans in Japan, he is a far more famous name among the general public. In addition, he's a legitimate national sports legend since he won three world championships and seven national championships in a sport invented and popularized in Japan. This will result in far more mainstream media publicity for the match as a lot of media outlets that would shy away from coverage of a match involving a pro wrestler against an Ultimate Fight star, would give coverage to the pro wrestling debut of a national legend in judo in a Tokyo Dome match against the IWGP champion.

While Ogawa at the press conference hinted that he would be receiving 100 million yen (about $825,000) for the match, it's doubtful that figure is anything even close to resembling a legitimate number as the figure Shamrock was offered for the same position on the same card which would have sold out just as easily wasn't anywhere close to that figure.

When Ogawa made the decision to go into pro wrestling, apparently feeling he'd gone as far in judo as he could after finishing fifth in the 1996 Olympics in Atlanta, he at first contacted Giant Baba and All Japan Pro

Wrestling. Baba turned down Ogawa as he didn't want to offer a huge financial guarantee to someone unproven when it came to pro wrestling since his company is essentially a workrate promotion almost devoid of gimmicks.

In addition, a generation ago, Baba did a similar experiment and signed an Olympic gold medalist in judo, Anton Geesink of the Netherlands, to a huge money (at the time) deal and pushed him immediately to the top of the cards as the No. 2 babyface in the company behind Baba himself. While the 6-foot-8 Geesink's presence in pro wrestling drew a lot of publicity in the early 70s, he never got the knack of it, was a poor worker, and his career was over within a few years. But All Japan did get good short-term results at the gate and in casual interest from the two similar experiments in its history in Geesink and a retired sumo grand champion named Hiroshi Wajima in the 80s, who was also a flop in the ring and only lasted a few years but garnered a lot of early interest.

However, New Japan jumped at the chance since some of the biggest matches in the history of the company have involved bringing in outsiders from other sports, including former judo stars like Willem Ruska, Allen Coage (Badnews Allen) and Shota Chochyashivili with ballyhooed mixed matches against Antonio Inoki.

APRIL 21

The pro wrestling debut of Naoya Ogawa, a national sports hero in Japan for being the country's No. 1 heavyweight judo player for much of the past decade, was considered a major success.

The 4/12 Tokyo Dome, the show originally added to the schedule because of the belief it was going to be the largest gate in history almost automatically with a Shinya Hashimoto vs. Ken Shamrock IWGP title main event. Ogawa was to debut on the undercard. The show changed its face with Shamrock signing with WWF and Ogawa moved to the main event. While Ogawa's name wasn't as strong with the ticket buying pro wrestling fans in Japan as Shamrock's, he was far better known to the general public.

New Japan garnered tons of mainstream publicity which led to a crowd announced at 60,500, which everyone was thrilled with since the show's advance wasn't promising at all. This would probably be a gate around $5 million which will make it wind up as almost surely the second biggest money show of 1997 behind only the 1/4 Dome show when it comes to total revenue. The show wasn't sold out but was fairly close to capacity and we're told that announced figure sounded about right.

More than 50 magazines and 250 press photographers covered the main event, and a photo of the finish appeared in color on the front page of a few sports newspapers the next morning. Stories of Ogawa training with Antonio Inoki and Satoru Sayama for his pro wrestling debut ran daily in many newspapers all week leading up to the match, and it spurred enough general public curiosity interest that the television show airing on tape the next afternoon with the main matches from the Dome drew a 13.0 overall rating (Hashimoto vs. Ogawa itself drew a 13.6 rating), making it the highest rated pro wrestling television show in Japan in many years.

Ogawa used the same choke sleeper that was his main finisher in winning seven national titles and three world titles in judo in what was billed as a martial arts match, in 9:25, and referee Masao Hattori stopped the match. This was a disputed finish in that Riki Choshu and Kensuke Sasaki immediately hit the ring screaming that Hashimoto hadn't tapped out. Hashimoto then after the match asked for a rematch, putting up his IWGP title, which will headline the 5/3 Osaka Dome show. Hashimoto also requested to be pulled off the house show schedule for April so he could train uninterrupted for the rematch.

For those interested in "what would have happened" trivia, the plan originally if Shamrock was there was for Hashimoto to pin Shamrock on this card, but for Shamrock to capture the title in the rematch in Osaka. It was pretty well known by insiders that Ogawa was going to win the non-title match to set up the title match, and put him on the map from the start of his career as a big time player in Japanese wrestling.

Ogawa, now 29, was the youngest world champion in the history of judo at the age of 19 in 1987. He followed it up with world title wins in 1989 and 1991. In 1992, he won the silver medal at 209 pounds at the Barcelona Olympics losing to Russian David Khakhalesheivili, who currently works for RINGS and is the current heavyweight world champion in Sambo. He placed fifth in the Atlanta Olympics in 1996, and officially retired from competitive judo last September and began negotiating first with All Japan which didn't come close to meeting his money figures, and later New Japan, which did, to go into pro wrestling.

There was great intensity in the match since New Japan wrestlers Choshu, Sasaki, Satoshi Kojima and Takashi Iizuka were all in Hashimoto's corner doing the gimmick of representing their world champion in the battle against the top judo star in the country, who had Inoki in his corner, which guaranteed heat. It's the gimmick the New Japan promotion has specialized in almost from the inception of the company, and really the direction WWF should have taken Shamrock, as the outsider challenging the champion of the WWF, for maximum initial impact and value.

The wrestlers were screaming at Hashimoto to throw kicks, which he did, but Ogawa snatched him in a cross armlock and Hashimoto made it to the ropes. Hashimoto came back with hard chops and thigh and chest kicks but Ogawa caught a kick and took him down going for an armlock but Hashimoto escaped. Hashimoto, who was a high school champion in judo before getting into pro wrestling, did some judo spots of his own but Ogawa ended up on top in "his" game catching the arm again and Hashimoto again went for the ropes to break it.

Hashimoto unloaded with the hard kicks and finally knocked Ogawa down past the 6:00 mark and did his chops to the shoulder and kicks to the stomach and Ogawa rolled out of the ring. Hashimoto got his trademark bloody nose at this point. Hashimoto unleashed more kicks and knocked Ogawa down for a count of seven. Ogawa made the comeback using a judo throw which will become his trademark pro wrestling winning move called the STO (Special Tornado Ogawa) and clamped on the sleeper with a body scissors on the mat for the finish.

The match was said to have been successful in that it accomplished what it set out to do—appear believable and come off real looking and get Ogawa over to set up his career and the impending rematch. Obviously Ogawa in his first pro match didn't have a classic good match.

MAY 12

The first pro wrestling event at the new Osaka Dome, New Japan's "Strong Style Evolution" headlined by the Shinya Hashimoto vs. Naoya Ogawa rematch for the IWGP heavyweight title broke just about every record for pro wrestling in that city.

The show drew basically a full house of 53,000 fans (a number that was said to look legit as there were scattered empty seats and about 8-9,000 seats on the field in a building that holds 45,000 for baseball), which translated into an approximately $4 million house, another $800,000 in merchandise sales and another $400,000 paid by TV-Asahi for the television rights to the show.

Because the dollar has gotten much stronger against the yen over the past few years, a gate of 500 million yen, as this show drew, would be $4 million today as opposed to a couple of years ago when the same size gate would be a near all-time record $6 million. This is one of the reasons the Muto-Takada 1995 gate record really isn't in any jeopardy until there are global economic changes well out of the realm of the pro wrestling industry.

Besides the Hashimoto-Ogawa rematch pitting New Japan's world heavyweight champion against a multi-time world champion in judo, coming off Ogawa's victory on 4/12 at the Tokyo Dome, the show also featured numerous WCW performers including Senior Vice President Eric Bischoff, Kevin Nash and Scott Hall, with the NWO contingent going 3-0. Hashimoto retained his title in 10:20 of the main event, billed as being under martial arts rules, when he made a comeback on Ogawa and destroyed him with brutal leg kick after brutal kick until Ogawa's second, Tiger King (Satoru Sayama) threw in the towel so they did a martial arts style finish as opposed to a traditional pro wrestling finish.

The finish was set up a few days before the match when they did an angle where Ogawa injured his knee doing mountain climbing with his trainers Sayama and Antonio Inoki and Hashimoto worked on the "injury." To sell the power of the leg kicks, the 1992 Olympic games silver medalist was unable to get back to his feet after the match and did a stretcher job, allowing New Japan Pro Wrestling to once again "prove" their top fighter was superior to a world champion in another combat sport. Ogawa, now having been defeated by the top New Japan wrestler, will join New Japan full-time starting with the next tour in two weeks.

We've had a mixed response from those who attended the show live. The basic feeling is that the regular wrestling fans who attend all the big shows thought it was a so-so event, and in particular didn't get into the American style matches with the NWO wrestlers saying it was like they cut a hole through the middle of the card. However, the NWO merchandise sold like crazy, particularly to kids, who popped big for all of their ring entrances although didn't react much to the matches themselves, and the majority of the fans who attend events like this that draw crowds in those kind of numbers were probably attending their first or second ever live show and those type of fans respond to star power and the spectacle of attending a major event. The matches will air on 5/10, 5/17 and 5/24 on the New Japan television show.

Chapter Nine

Dennis Rodman Signs for WCW

FEBRUARY 10

Dennis Rodman's people told WCW that he had a $500,000 offer to do WrestleMania and be in Goldust's corner, to set up the two as a tag team for SummerSlam. Since he'd previously worked for WCW, they gave them the opportunity to match the offer. The belief is WCW would have but Rodman's NBA probation may not allow him to be part of pro wrestling angles.

MARCH 17

Dennis Rodman became the latest media star of the moment brought into pro wrestling as a publicity stunt in an announcement made by WCW over the weekend.

Rodman, the regularly suspended current leading anti-hero of the NBA's Chicago Bulls, who has a movie coming out this week, will be part of the NWO group and appear on the WCW Uncensored PPV show on 3/16 in Charleston, SC and make what is believed to be two additional appearances with WCW as a participant in matches, the first of which is tentatively planned for the 7/13 Bash at the Beach PPV in Daytona Beach.

WCW was able to outmaneuver the WWF, which was also pursuing Rodman. The WWF had offered Rodman a two-show deal reportedly for a $1 million fee. The first of which would have been WrestleMania, to appear in Goldust's corner to attempt to help the faltering Goldust character get over stronger as both a babyface and as a mainstream bizarre cult figure. The second of which was the SummerSlam PPV in August where he and Goldust would have formed a tag team.

However Rodman's representatives, since Rodman worked a WCW PPV in July of 1995 as Hulk Hogan's corner man for the Bash at the Beach in Huntington Beach, CA, went to WCW to match the offer. WCW pulled the deal off for an undisclosed figure although you'd have to figure they at least matched the WWF's offer if not topped it in some fashion, since there were several incentives for WCW to do so. Besides nixing a WWF publicity ploy with a star that would have gotten them mainstream play, WCW was able to get a front page story in the Chicago Sun-Times just two weeks before WrestleMania with the breaking of the story, although WCW had for the most part completed the deal more than a week earlier.

In the Chicago market, where Rodman has to be one of the two biggest sports celebrities right now behind only Michael Jordan, WCW stole much of WWF's local thunder as they built for WrestleMania, although Mania is going to sellout or come close to it anyway. Rodman, who has been a fan of Hogan's for years, taped a segment with Hogan that promoted both Rodman's movie that comes out this coming weekend and the Uncensored PPV two days later, which aired toward the end of the 3/10 Monday Nitro television show.

Rodman's contract with the Chicago Bulls wouldn't prohibit him from passive participation in something like pro wrestling (ie he could be in the corner, but not get physically involved to any real degree) during the season. When the season ends, Rodman will be an unrestricted free agent, and thus without an NBA contract, would be free to perform in a pro wrestling match.

WCW got some mainstream pub over the next few days, although not nearly as much as they pretended on the Nitro show. Most newspapers didn't carry the story, and aside from the Sun-Times, the few that did just ran a line or two in the AP sports rundown. It did get play, treated as a joke, on both the NBC and ABC radio network top of the hour newscasts on Saturday morning.

Perhaps the most play was Hogan & Rodman appearing on the Howard Stern show on 3/10, with reports from the show saying Stern pretty much blew off Hogan's attempts to plug the WCW PPV to concentrate on talking to Rodman. Apparently something on that show must have been said by Stern about Roddy Piper, since Piper lashed into Stern (among others) that evening on Nitro. It is expected over the next week that some of the entertainment television shows with carry the story.

Actually there was more mainstream press for the story in Japan, where Rodman appears on many television commercials. It was carried in prominent fashion in the sports pages, and on 3/9, New Japan President Seiji Sakaguchi said that he'd like to have Rodman wrestle at one of the Dome shows this year in a tag team match with Scott Hall and/or Kevin Nash but thought that his price would be too high and gave the indication that he didn't believe there was a realistic chance of it happening.

It's doubtful Rodman's appearance in Charleston, SC in the corner will have any effect on the buy rate for the show, since Rodman already did a similar thing in Los Angeles and it had no effect at that time. His match in July will probably garner a lot of mainstream press, and if he appears on Nitros frequently building up the event, he may cause a positive effect on television ratings similar to the Lawrence Taylor deal in the WWF, which spiked the Raw ratings for its duration but resulted in a disappointing buy rate on PPV.

It seems to be at this point that a major celebrity in wrestling causes a lot of talk and mainstream curiosity which is good for ratings, but that those type of people aren't going to spend $27.95 to see someone on television in an activity still largely considered a joke that they are used to seeing regularly on television for free. However, the mainstream pub, whether the buy rate is strong for the July show or not, does get the name brand WCW over and buys the company great publicity. It's certainly a better investment in that regard than buying a bunch of race cars.

Chapter Ten

Dr. Death Arrested

MARCH 24

Steve Williams, the top American star of All Japan Pro Wrestling who also works for ECW and was involved in serious negotiations with the World Wrestling Federation over the past week was arrested on the morning of 3/17 at the Laredo, TX International Airport on drug possession charges.

Williams was caught for at least a third time in his pro wrestling career coming through airports with drugs, in this case inspectors found undeclared pharmaceutical drugs inside luggage belonging to Williams and two traveling companions who are not involved in pro wrestling. The three were charged with a felony possession of a controlled substance and were released from Webb County jail after posting $25,000 bond each.

Drugs seized included 80 boxes of Neo-Percodan, 17 boxes of Valium, 16 boxes of Halcion, 15 boxes of Tamegesic, 26 boxes of Darvon and eight boxes of Ritrovil. The drugs are all pain killer type drugs, most of which are very popular today with more pro wrestlers than you'd think, for obvious and not so obvious reasons. Laredo is a city just across from the Mexican border.

The story ran on the AP wire and was carried in numerous newspapers around the country. While we haven't received any official word of this, one would think it would be very likely that this arrest would at least temporarily kill the WWF's current interest in bringing him in. We say temporarily since WWF brought Crush back more than one year after his arrest on steroid and weapons charges and actually used that arrest as part of his angle. The general belief is that Williams was being brought in as a potential opponent for Ken Shamrock. It is also unclear how this will effect his position with All Japan, but the arrest received significant play in Japan as well, since Williams is the third most popular foreign wrestler in the country.

The WWF already signed Del Wilkes, another of All Japan's top foreign stars, who is better known as The Patriot, to a multi-year contract.

Wilkes, who was last week voted in Weekly Pro Wrestling Magazine as the fifth most popular foreign wrestler in the country, is believed to have signed sometime within the past ten days. He hadn't worked All Japan since the December tag team tournament, where he was the partner of Kenta Kobashi, due to an injury, but apparently during his recuperation had decided to explore the WWF option and the two sides had on-again off-again talks for at least a month or two.

Those close to Williams believed it was most likely that he would be signing with Titan, which has been after him on-and-off for the past two years, but that was all before the arrest and there is no word on how or if the situation in regard to Titan's interest in him will change or how this would affect his status with All Japan, where he was scheduled to return for the Champion Carnival tour, which no doubt he would play a major role in, beginning 3/22.

The news of Williams' arrest will almost surely be carried in a somewhat prominent role in many sports sections in Japan on 3/19, and at press time we do know that All Japan was very concerned with both the story itself and the press reaction to the story in Japan. If he were to not be able to appear on this tour, it would require a major re-doing of all the booking since these tours are very carefully planned.

The situation with Williams, who turns 37 in May, negotiating seriously with Titan points out a major shift and change in the wrestling structure over the past few years. The job Williams and the other American regulars had with All Japan as recently as a few years ago was considered one of the most plum positions in the entire industry. The money was very good, you had basically 24-30 weeks a year off, there was far less political b.s. as in the States. Job security was considered much better than in the U.S. where positions change rapidly every time the wind changes, the situation was favorable since it was an athletic environment with virtually no gimmicks or screwiness involved. The funny thing is that All Japan really hasn't changed all that much, but the industry as a whole has changed greatly.

Both WWF and WCW offer guaranteed contracts which both pay for injuries suffered on the job and wrestlers are paid when injured. The level of pay is equal to or better than All Japan in regard to the talent they are wooing. The travel schedules in each company is not nearly as demanding as had been the case in the past. That, coupled with lesser physical demands in the U.S. and the bonus of not being in Japan for a month at a time which can play serious mental games, you can see why All Japan, which hasn't changed its salary structure or how it treats foreign talent while the market has changed, is rapidly losing much of its talent base.

Wilkes follows in the heels of Phil LaFon (formerly Dan Kroffat) & Doug Furnas as All Japan regulars who have left the promotion in recent years. But it would be the loss of Williams that would be the most damaging.

Williams, has been positioned as All Japan's top foreign star since his return to the company one year ago—and held that position before a year-long suspension as well. While Stan Hansen has more name recognition, it is well established Hansen is long past his prime and exists largely on two decades of name identity and is no longer featured regularly on top as a single.

Williams had a well-known reputation at the University of Oklahoma as a college football and four-time NCAA place-winner heavyweight college wrestling star. He handed Dan Severn his only pinfall defeat in four years of college competition in 1981 and lost a close decision as a senior to Bruce Baumgartner in the NCAA tournament finals in 1982 before going to work for Bill Watts' Mid South Wrestling. He was regarded in many circles as arguably (Meng was generally the other person with that rep) the single toughest person legitimately in the pro wrestling business for many years.

He eventually migrated to New Japan and switched over to All Japan for a famous run as tag team partner of Terry Gordy. He eventually worked his way up the All Japan ladder both from a workrate and position standpoint to where he was considered one of the best performers in the world in 1994, and the premier American wrestler in the All Japan style.

His rise, and for a short while his career, came to a halt after being banned from going to Japan in March of 1995 when he was caught at customs with a small amount of marijuana. He had a previous offense in the United States in 1988 when on a Japanese trip, at the Detroit airport he was caught carrying controlled substances including steroids and cocaine which nearly cost him his job with Jim Crockett Promotions.

Williams showed surprising loyalty to Giant Baba after the 1995 problem, by turning down WWF offers and working very few independent dates over that year, and waiting until he could return to Japan. The feeling is Baba had to pull major strings and it showed just how powerful Baba really was in getting Williams back in one year, since Paul McCartney for a similar offense wasn't allowed back in Japan for more than a decade.

He returned and performed better than just about anyone could have expected going from a one-year layoff right into such high level of competition at last year's Champion Carnival, but as the months in Japan went by, his work wasn't the same. Even so, his June 7, 1996 match at Budokan Hall teaming with Johnny Ace in a loss to

Mitsuharu Misawa & Jun Akiyama was voted the Observer's 1996 match of the year. In addition, his Champion Carnival final match loss to Akira Taue and the later match where he and Ace won the belts from Misawa & Akiyama were close to that level.

However, the first two tours of 1997 appeared to show a noticeable decline in his work and he really didn't get over in ECW where he's made several appearances between Japan tours. Given his age and the physically demanding style of All Japan, it really is the right time for him to make a move if he ever would want to try WWF—although this last minute snafu could throw a red flag on those plans.

The negotiations aspect of the story is actually bigger in regard to All Japan than WWF, although Williams would get at least the chance to reach a level of American stardom that he never quite reached in the past by going to WWF. The jury is out on whether, if he makes the move, that from a WWF standpoint it isn't two years too late. Either way, it is largely expected Williams will work the upcoming Champion Carnival tour for All Japan even if he signs with the WWF, but after that is unknown.

As far as All Japan, by failing to keep pace with what is offered elsewhere, it is in danger of turning into the AWA of the 90s. All Japan was progressive at one point in regard to offering good money and regular positions with its talent. Just a few years ago All Japan was different from just about any company in the world in that the talent did nothing but rave about the company, were thrilled to be there, and praised their boss, with only the minimal grumblings that are inherent in a company of top athletes as part of a business where winners, losers and your position in the promotion are decided by forces often out of the wrestlers' control.

But nothing has changed since that time except everything else in every other major promotion, and All Japan's policy of no insurance coverage, only paying for treatment of injuries if the wrestler gets his treatment in Japan, and not paying wrestlers for time off while recuperating from injuries, which actually was progressive at one point in the business that just ignored injured talent, is today behind the times. By relying so heavily on workrate, it has a harder time filling spots when wrestlers leave when they get better offers, particularly now when the list of available free agents in wrestling who are super workers is decidedly thin or non-existent.

In addition, its core talent base is all, with the exception of Kenta Kobashi and Jun Akiyama, in its mid to late 30s and the physical style has taken its toll on every key member of the company. While the company survived quite well in 1995 without Williams, losing him at this point, even if his work isn't at the same level, would be more damaging because Hansen is two years older and it would leave Gary Albright as the only foreigner who could headline as a single as it's questionable whether Johnny Ace could draw as a single in a top spot.

MARCH 31

The political power of Shohei Baba in Japan was made evident to everyone as he was able to get Steve Williams into Japan for the Champion Carnival tournament that began on 3/22.

Williams, arrested days earlier for possession of a large amount of pain killers at the Laredo, TX airport—his third similar such arrest over the past ten years—was thought to have gone from being a sought after commodity in the WWF to someone whose pro wrestling career was in jeopardy due to the surprising amount of media coverage his arrest received worldwide.

According to those who work in the law in this kind of field, Williams was very lucky on several accounts. The first is that he was allowed to post bond, the second is that with such a large amount of drugs allegedly found on him and the two people he was traveling with that he wasn't charged with intent to distribute and only with illegal possession without a prescription, the third is that the government didn't take his passport away from him and the fourth is the Japan let him back in the country, the latter of which showed Baba's considerable pull.

As mentioned last week, Baba's power in Japan was shown by his ability to get Williams back in the country in one year when the biggest rock promoters in the world weren't able to get Paul McCartney back into Japan for decades for a similar offense.

After learning of the arrest, Baba told reporters on 3/19 that the Carnival tour would go on as planned with Williams' involvement. The explanation was apparently something along the lines that since Williams wasn't caught with marijuana, the drug that led to him being booted out of Japan in 1995, that he would be allowed into Japan. One can only speculate why his U.S. passport wasn't pulled with a felony charge hanging over him, but perhaps since his means of earning a living is his job in Japan, not allowing him out of the country would cost him his job.

Williams worked the ECW show on 3/14 in Downingtown, PA and was scheduled to win a handicap match on the 3/15 ECW Arena show to set up some sort of a confrontation with Taz, but didn't appear at the Arena show and was arrested the morning of 3/17.

Williams arrived in Japan, professing his innocence to the charges, and worked a six-man tag on opening night at Korakuen Hall teaming with Johnny Smith & The Masked Tornado (Richard Slinger) to beat Maunukea Mossman & Stan Hansen & Giant Kimala II. The next night he debuted in the Carnival tournament with a pin on Kimala II.

Chapter Eleven

Pay-Per-View Censorship

MARCH 24

The future of the Ultimate Fighting Championships, Extreme Fighting Championships and the success of the upcoming Extreme Championship Wrestling PPV shows all took turns for the worst over this past week due to what basically amounts to a controversial issue of cable system PPV censorship.

The NHB industry took a major hit this past week with the announcement that Tele-Communications Inc. (TCI Cable), the largest cable chain in the country, will no longer carry the shows. The decision will not effect the upcoming EFC show on 3/28 but either that or the 5/30 UFC show will likely be the last carried by TCI as some reports are saying this decision will go into effect on 6/1. An article in the 3/17 Multichannel News indicated the 3/28 show would be the final one carried. UFC officials stated that it was doubtful the 5/30 show would be carried by TCI but they were still hoping.

TCI systems comprise between four and five million of the remaining 20-21 million addressable homes that were still carrying the shows. Between addressable cable homes and satellite dish owners, there were 26.2 million homes with PPV accessibility in total as of last month (within the industry and media reports will give a higher number but this is the realistic figure), and NHB had lost five to six million of them already when Viewers Choice of Canada, the Cablevision systems in the U.S. and Inter Media Partners systems had decided to no longer carry the programming. But the TCI hit is the biggest one yet because not only is it the largest carrier, but the most influential and there is legitimate fear this will create a domino effect that will reverberate throughout the cable industry and wind up as the fatal blow for NHB on PPV.

With EFC basically hanging by a thread and already being in critical financial condition leading up to the current show, it likely signals the final death knell of the promotion after the 3/28 card. About the only thing that could save the promotion is a huge turnaround in the buy rate coupled with TCI changing its mind. Those close to the situation have indicated that if this decision had come down sooner, the 3/28 show may have been canceled by the promoters even though TCI would still have carried it largely because the idea was that this would be a show to help build an audience for the future, and now there doesn't look to be much of a future. The show is going on in Des Moines, IA since much of the costs of running the show have already been incurred so they might as well go ahead with it.

UFC had taken several recent hits of late, but promoter David Isaacs of parent Semaphore Entertainment Group said that his company was in the business for the long haul. He cited a belief that it is a combination of the fallout from the controversy in New York and the hiring of a new President of TCI from San Francisco—Leo Hindery—to attempt to turn around that company's ailing financial situation, that led to the recent decision.

Hindery, who was named President of TCI last month by CEO John Malone, is an arch-conservative who was CEO of Inter Media Partners, the first system to decide to not carry NHB PPV programming. Although Hindery had been a long-time foe of NHB, including participating in a debate at a cable conference with SEG President Bob Meyrowitz, the decision hit the genre from left field.

The belief of late had been that Hindery had come around to the realization the matches weren't as violent or dangerous as their political foes had made them out to be. In fact, Inter Media had changed its position a few months back regarding NHB and carried the 2/7 UFC show. However, Jedd Palmer, Senior Vice President of programming for TCI said the decision came directly from Hindery. ECW had expressed that its product is theater and not sport to TCI to attempt to differentiate itself from the NHB genre which it is mistakenly lumped into and painted with the same brush.

Isaacs confirmed a loss of TCI systems would mean a significant change in business but said they were in the game for the long haul and that the company's business plan was to hang on and wait until dishes gain more popularity, at which time the company won't be as dependent upon decisions made by cable companies. That could be a long ways in the future. It would be a drop of between 15 and 25 percent in revenue for the shows provided buy rates stayed the same, depending upon whose stats you use—virtually all of which will work against the bottom line. This forces SEG, which is not one of these vanity promotions with no business concept, to cut costs in order to remain financially viable.

This means purses for the fighters, already a controversial issue, would have to be scaled back once again to coincide with the dropping revenue. This would make it more difficult for SEG to bring in the top quality names. Even before the TCI loss, losses from the previous show due to the last minute move had caused purse cutbacks for the upcoming show which will cause the 5/30 show to not feature any kind of a championship match.

The complete 5/30 line-up was finalized this past week with a Vitor Belfort vs. Tank Abbott main event. The site hasn't been revealed, but inside rumors indicate Augusta, GA or a site near Augusta as the prime candidate. There will also be a four-man under-200 and over-200 pound weight division tournaments. The original triple main event single match format with one tournament was dropped due to purses being scaled back, and that was among the reasons that champion Mark Coleman, Don Frye and Marco Ruas, all of whom had been negotiated with and appeared to be on the show at one point, won't be appearing.

For the money offered, none of the potential match-ups involving those three were able to be put together as Frye wanted more than what was offered to face either Coleman or Ruas, and Coleman wanted more to face Ruas. In addition, there were political problems in that Belfort's camp had claimed they weren't going to allow to him to participate in the show if he was lower on the card than Ruas (a secondary plan was to put Belfort and Abbott as the lead attractions in a heavyweight tournament), who he was willing to fight, but SEG sees the 19-year-old Belfort as one of its biggest potential drawing cards and doesn't want to risk him this early against the likes of Ruas or Coleman.

The under-200 division will include Ensen Inoue of Satoru Sayama's shooting promotion in Japan (who lost in 47 seconds last year to Igor Zinoviev in Japan but has extensive experience in both Vale Tudo and Brazilian Jiu-Jitsu tournaments and a strong shooting background), Guy Mezger of Pancrase (2-0 UFC record), Christophe Leninger (0-1 UFC record with a loss to Ken Shamrock in UFC III, but a U.S. nationally ranked 189 pounder in judo) and Royce Alger (A highly-regarded amateur wrestler who is Dan Gable's assistant coach at Iowa). The tournament winner theoretically will face Jerry Bohlander to determine the first under-200 UFC champion in July. Although it is against the rules of Lions Den to allow Lions Den fighters to fight each other, both Ken and Bob Shamrock waived the rule at the request of Mezger as SEG wasn't going to allow him in the tournament if he wouldn't agree to fight Bohlander should he win.

The heavyweight tournament line-up includes NHB veteran David Beneteau (2-3 UFC record, 4-4 overall) and 300-pound pro wrestler Tony Halme (Ludvig Borga in WWF), who was a boxer in Finland many years ago and is currently training under Gene LeBelle for NHB competition. Halme is best known as a fighter in wrestling circles for a three-punch knockout of Scott Norton in a Japanese bar years ago when both were regulars with New Japan Pro Wrestling, although there are reports it was a sucker punch knockout. The other confirmed entrant is Steve Graham, who all we know about is that he's big and strong.

However, for the top quality names to work in the United States, SEG may wind up being the only place to go because if EFC is gone, the remaining competition is largely of the fly-by-night variety with fighters having no capability of making a serious name outside of the most hardcore of fans.

ECW, which went in with only an estimated 16 million homes cleared due to Viewers Choice deciding not to carry its 4/13 PPV because of a combination of perceived violent content and what it considered an unacceptable storyline (The Tyler Fullington angle, which ECW has since dropped) took another hit from Cablevision Systems Corporation, which is strongest in the Northeast, particularly in theoretical ECW strongholds such as Connecticut, Boston and Long Island. Exactly how many homes this entails isn't clear because some of the Cablevision systems were already not carrying the events due to relying on Viewers Choice for their PPV channels. This comes on the heels of a few Inter Media Systems that use Request as its PPV carrier including Nashville, TN also deciding not to air the ECW PPV.

Although NHB and ECW are two entirely different animals, one being a somewhat dangerous and sometimes brutal sport, although both aspects are highly exaggerated by its opponents and in the media; the other being a sometimes violent and dangerous form of theater, the censorship issues involving both are similar.

While cable companies are publicly-owned businesses that due to that fact should have the right to make decisions on what they will and won't carry, they are somewhat unique, like the power companies, in that they are basic monopolies within their franchise area. Consumers don't have a choice if they don't agree with the decisions of their cable company to switch to another company. Their only choice is to switch to buying a satellite dish.

However, the inconsistencies in regard to both animals and the attempts to eliminate them from PPV raises serious questions. Unlike over-the-air television, PPV is something consumers have to subscribe to. The argument that these shows are harmful to children is somewhat questionable in that they have to be specifically ordered and paid for, no different from the adult movies that most of the systems that are banning these programs still air.

In addition, to single these out creates some terrible inconsistencies because movies with themes far more controversial than any ECW angle or violent content that makes ECW look pale by comparison aren't singled out. In addition, numerous Cablevision systems that won't air ECW on PPV, do air ECW on broadcast television, some in decent time slots. We have yet to hear of a cable system blacking out individual programs of any type on stations due to perceived content, let alone ECW, yet the same product, on PPV, which consumers have to subscribe to rather than children can witness simply by channel surfing, is being blacked out.

Even though ECW, with all the high-risk stunts and more frequent stiff shots is more dangerous than WWF or WCW wrestling, both of the latter promotions contain most of the same types of content as ECW, just in smaller doses. In addition, is there any call to ban movies in which stunt men, who on occasion suffer very serious injuries, attempt things far more dangerous than anything done on an ECW show?

The inconsistencies in regard to violence and danger involving UFC have been stated here numerous times. While networks can show pro boxing, which has a much higher injury and mortality rate; or auto racing, which regularly produces deaths; on weekend mornings and afternoons; UFC, which for the most part isn't available on broadcast television, is being banned by cable companies. The irony is that the November MARS PPV show was later sold to Mexican television and then broadcast on a Saturday afternoon on an over-the-air Spanish language network nationally in the U.S. and was the source of no censorship or even controversy.

Chapter Twelve

WCW vs. ECW

APRIL 7

Lots of rumors regarding Van Dam leaving for WCW. Supposedly when asked about his martial arts background, Van Dam told someone over the weekend, wait a few weeks and you'll hear about it from Mike Tenay on Nitro.

APRIL 21

Lots of concern in ECW since WCW had Nitro the next night and many of its people were in town. Nick Patrick and one of the members of Harlem Heat came to the building about 30 minutes before the show started. The dressing room reaction from actually several of the guys was to start a fight but it was quelled down pretty quick (it's amazing that Heyman has now become the level-headed guy).

Dean Malenko and Ted Petty came to the building but left before the show started, and Kevin Sullivan, Hugh Morrus and Dave Penzer came after the show ended and were cordial with everyone. Gary Juster came to the building to buy a ticket but it was sold out and he wasn't let in.

The only ECW performer who came to Nitro was Bill Alfonso. There were people in WCW joking about how the same fans who do those anti-Bischoff and anti-WCW chants on ECW shows were noticeable on television at Nitro right in front of the camera marking out for WCW bigger than they do at ECW.

APRIL 28

WCW has made major plays for several of the wrestlers within ECW over the past week. In response, Paul Heyman has either signed or extended the contracts of Shane Douglas, Francine, Eliminators, Sabu, Taz, Joey Styles, the Dudleys, Stevie Richards and Tommy Dreamer all in the last few days and will take steps to do the same by the end of the week with Sandman, the Pit Bulls and Chris Candido.

WCW apparently offered Raven a three-year deal at six figures per annum to join the NWO. Raven has a meeting with Heyman later this week to discuss the situation. WCW wanted to bring him in immediately, but he's apparently under contract to ECW through August and under a non-compete clause when it comes to appearing on PPV shows through 10/13. It's expected that Heyman at the very least would insist Raven stay through the 8/17 PPV show in order to finally put over Dreamer and that Heyman has already contacted Kevin Sullivan to claim WCW is tampering with ECW contracts.

Heyman's attorneys also contacted WCW claiming by using the terms "The Extreme Team" (for Ace Darling & Devon Storm, who did a job on the 4/14 show in Philadelphia) and by using the name Kimona, they were violating ECW intellectual property. ECW claims they've used the term The Extreme Team since August 1995.

MAY 5

Raven (Scott Levy) officially informed Paul Heyman on 4/23 that he was accepting a three-year contract at $225,000 per year from WCW. The belief is that because of the money figures and because he was welcomed into the company by Diamond Dallas Page, Eric Bischoff and Kevin Nash, that he'll politically be protected and not used in the manner that a lot of the talented wrestlers are used—basically as television cannon fodder to get over the protected group.

WCW wanted him to start on the July PPV show in Daytona Beach but his ECW contract prohibits him from appearing on a rival PPV until 10/13. Heyman is attempting to work out a deal with Bischoff where ECW would get some compensation from WCW for using The Extreme Team in Philadelphia, using Kimona's name in Philadelphia and to let Raven out of his contract ahead of time.

On the other hand, at this point it appears the whole Rob Van Dam deal has turned into a total angle. Van Dam was at one point talked about by WCW officials as being close to a done deal, but nothing more has been done about it. My feeling is that the initial "You sold out" reaction was so strong to Van Dam when he was negotiating that it turned into an angle to help add to his heat. Van Dam's new gimmick being the guy who wants to work Mondays for the rival promotion has boosted him to being one of the most over heels in the group.

Officially he's only agreed to stay in ECW through the middle of June, however he has yet to give notice to All Japan, and if he was going to WCW in late June, one would think he would have done so already. Heyman said that Van Dam can do the role that he had first thought would go to Jerry Lawler as being the anti-ECW outsider, and this way he doesn't have to deal with Lawler. It would make sense for Van Dam to appear on Raw once to get his Monday night gimmick over.

There are plenty of rumors flying that The Gangstas are headed to WCW although at this point they haven't given notice to ECW and nobody in WCW is talking about it either.

The situation with Bill Alfonso and the WCW Nitro taping in Philadelphia is that Alfonso was not at Nitro, but talked with several WCW wrestlers at the hotel after the show and others heard and misinterpreted that as him being at the show. The only reason that's an important distinction is that Paul Heyman said he'd fire anyone immediately who attended the WCW show.

MAY 12

Really nothing major new to report on the situation with Raven (Scott Levy) leaving for WCW. Paul Heyman and Eric Bischoff have to negotiate some type of a deal since Heyman's got the no-compete on PPV with Raven which doesn't expire until 10/13 and WCW wants him to start on the July PPV.

Heyman claims to be pretty adamant that whatever the negotiations turn out to be, that he wants Raven to put Tommy Dreamer over on the 8/17 PPV show as his final appearance since he's planning on Raven vs. Dreamer and Taz vs. Sabu as the two main events on that show.

Not certain about anyone else, but Richards definitely has no contract here although any reports of him going to WWF or WCW at this point are premature. Apparently Raven has talked with WCW about him but it hasn't gone any farther than that. It appears pretty much a certainty at this point that Van Dam is staying and that there was little or nothing to the Gangstas rumors.

MAY 19

Got conflicting stories on Richards. One, from Heyman, is that Richards had signed a letter of intent to negotiate, thus was basically under a binding agreement, when it was reported here as such and that he has since signed a contract. The other is Richards did sign the letter of intent, which runs out in a few weeks, and has been offered a contract but has yet to sign it although he doesn't have any outside offers and this shouldn't be meant to start rumors he's going anywhere. Several wrestlers have been offered contracts but the hold up in at least a few cases is that the contracts, which call for a minimum per show guarantee, have a six month non-compete clause after the contract expires.

JUNE 2

Paul Heyman had a conversation over the past week with Eric Bischoff regarding the Raven situation. Don't know any details about it other than the belief that Raven will be in WCW in a few weeks. Heyman was trying to get make a deal where Raven would return for the 8/17 PPV show to put Dreamer over.

There is a meeting this week with Viewers Choice about carrying that PPV. People who called the Time-Warner corporate offices this week were told that Time-Warner would no longer be carrying either UFC or ECW, and Time-Warner deciding not to carry ECW would likely make VC carrying the show more difficult.

It's too early to say what is going to end up happening here but we've seen that cable companies generally don't respond well to reasoning after making decisions of this type, and with the tide in the industry from the NHB situation, you can see ECW being the next on some people's hit list. At the same time, it will be very hard to logically defend not carrying ECW for a company that carries WWF and WCW and nobody is going to drop WWF or especially WCW (which is owned by Time Warner) right now.

There are cable insiders who believe the statement a few weeks back by National Cable Television Association President Decker Anstrom where he urged cable operators to pull out of NHB and to curtail violent programming also applies to ECW. ECW isn't going to run a PPV in New York because it wants to avoid potential commission problems.

JULY 21

Richards won't be wrestling for several months so all his injuries can heal up and he'll be doing the Abbott & Costello routine with Raven every Monday until then. For whatever this was worth, since both Richards and Raven supposedly had signed contracts that wouldn't allow them to appear on a competing PPV for six months after 4/13, or mid-October, WCW wasn't sure until the last minute whether to put them on the show. Not sure exactly how everything went down but as you can see, WCW didn't take the ECW contracts (which in the case of Raven definitely did exist) seriously because they put them on without getting a release from Paul Heyman.

JULY 21

Rob Van Dam and Dory Funk were backstage at Nitro. Funk was also at the PPV. The feeling is that the last time Van Dam showed up at Nitro, it turned into an angle that made him from a mid-carder to a main eventer and with the WWF thing falling apart, he showed up to get the press and the rumor mills going. WCW had no knowledge he was coming although we'd been told in advance, but did let him backstage.

JULY 28

ECW was expected to have filed a federal lawsuit early this week against WCW regarding a number of issues including Scott Levy (Raven) and Michael Manna (Steve Richards) appearing at the Bash at the Beach PPV show on 7/13 in Daytona Beach, FL.

Steve Karel, who is handling the legal situation for ECW wouldn't comment on legal affairs or if the suit itself had been filed at press time, but did say that ECW considers the actions of both men having violated the terms of their agreements with ECW. Paul Heyman had said over the weekend and ECW had reported on its hotline that a lawsuit would be filed in Federal Court in the Southern District of New York for contract tampering, tortuous interference with contracted personnel and violation of the company's intellectual property although we have no confirmation such a lawsuit had been filed as of press time.

Heyman claimed he sent copies of Levy's contract agreement for the 4/13 Barely Legal PPV which included a six month non-compete clause in regards to appearing on a rival wrestling PPV show to Eric Bischoff but Bischoff, or Nick Lambros, or whomever in WCW made the actual call, still put the Raven and Richards segment on the show.

For whatever reason, WCW has been very careful when it comes to waiting out contracted periods before debuting WWF talent such as Kevin Nash, Scott Hall and Curt Hennig but wasn't in this case, which may or may not be based on company lawyers interpretation of the solidness of the ECW non-compete clause.

Heyman said that ECW had threatened legal action against WCW if they were to use Levy on the PPV show and there had been talks in the past between Heyman and Bischoff regarding a contract buy out where WCW would pay ECW for the rights to use Raven immediately on PPV, however WCW refused the deal. Heyman also claims WCW tampered with ECW contracted personnel by using Levy as an intermediary in trying to get James Fullington (Sandman) into WCW and is also claiming WCW has slandered ECW on its hotline.

The contractual situation with Richards is another of those disputed situations. Heyman claims Manna (Richards) signed on 5/10 an "intention to sign a contract" as opposed to an intention to negotiate deal with ECW and thus was legally under an agreement with ECW at the time he was negotiating with WCW. Manna had admitted to signing a document of that type but claimed its time period for the document had already run out and since he didn't sign an actual contract that he had no legal obligation to ECW.

Heyman claims Manna was still under the agreement but that he released him from the agreement due to him claiming that due to a broken neck, Manna was concerned he'd be unable to wrestle the ECW style although there was heat in that Heyman wasn't aware of Richards appearing on Nitro on 7/7 until the day of the show. Actually when it comes to this case, whatever deal Manna was or wasn't under is a moot point since ECW isn't claiming him as being a contracted performer when it comes to his appearing on either Nitro or the PPV show, but is claiming the intellectual rights to the characterization of Stevie Richards and not contractual rights to the person of Michael Manna.

ECW's claim is that both Raven and Richards, the characters as opposed to the individuals, and how they are being portrayed, is the intellectual property of ECW and by WCW using them in their former ECW roles it's a violation of copyright and trademark.

There have been legal precedents in wrestling in regard to similar situations. For example, WCW, after legal threats, changed the entire name and character of Ray Traylor from The Boss, doing a gimmick very similar to The Big Bossman character in WWF, to The Guardian Angel because WWF claimed the night stick, police uniform, etc. as their intellectual property.

However, numerous other wrestlers and characters have gone from company to company without changing names and/or gimmicks, but the basic premise is that to maintain a stage name or gimmick such as Randy "Macho Man" Savage, one must have established the name and character before joining the company rather than it be a gimmick established within the company.

Generally speaking, both companies have allowed wrestlers to use their gimmicked names when working independents after leaving the organization, but the problems surface when trying to use those gimmicks with the rival major promotion. Levy had claimed when establishing the Raven character, which was his idea, that he maintained the rights to the character.

AUGUST 4

On the lawsuit front in regard to the proposed suit against WCW mentioned in last week's issue, to the best of our knowledge, no lawsuit had been filed at press time.

Sources within WCW have made the following points in defense against the charges by ECW. They claim that Stevie Richards wasn't even under contract (as had been mentioned here) and his intent to negotiate a deal with ECW expired on 6/10 and he never signed a new deal. He had used the name Stevie Richards before ever wrestling in ECW so they have no right to claim the rights to that ring name. They claim Scott Levy came up with the Raven name and character with the help of Diamond Dallas Page and that Page offered him to Paul Heyman more than two years ago. Heyman at first was reluctant, figuring Levy was going to establish a new gimmick and go back to WWF, but Heyman was promised that Levy would stay a minimum of four months in ECW with the gimmick, and wound up staying closer to two-and-a-half years.

Although Levy has acknowledged several times that he did sign a non-compete on PPV contract with Heyman that expires on 10/13, he claims not to have a copy of the contract although the claim is that as part of that deal Heyman acknowledged that all intellectual and mark rights of the Raven name and character were Levy's and not ECW's which would kill that point.

Nick Lambros of WCW apparently asked Heyman to send a copy of the contract because they informed Heyman they were planning on using Levy on the 7/13 PPV show. In the letter it specifically stated that if Heyman didn't respond in ten days, they were going to put Raven on the show. Heyman never responded nor sent WCW a copy of the contract, which from a legal standpoint, because of the warning, WCW feels it was in the clear to use Levy on the show, a point agreed with by one contract lawyer I spoke with regarding that point.

Eric Bischoff in a Prodigy chat with Bob Ryder basically acknowledged the same point. It was a last minute deal on the PPV as the company was expecting Heyman to spring the contract on them at the last minute and if they felt it was binding, the Raven-Richards segment would have been scrapped from the show.

AUGUST 18

According to Steve Karel at ECW, in regard to the legal letters between ECW and WCW and the threatened lawsuit, Paul Heyman had a meeting with Eric Bischoff at a steak house in Orlando, FL and personally showed him a copy of Raven's contract with the non-compete clause. Heyman claims never to have gotten a letter from Nick Lambros asking for the contract and ECW claims that even if he had, they were under no obligation to send a copy of the contract to WCW before Raven appeared on the Bash at the Beach PPV show.

Heyman denies that he specifically was ever on the WWF payroll nor that he's ever been paid even when he appeared on television as a performer for the WWF. He said that ECW was paid for its wrestlers appearing on the various Raw shows and the wrestlers themselves were then compensated by ECW, and that WWF also paid ECW a buy-out for about six weeks when they brought in Too Cold Scorpio but that neither ECW nor he have ever gotten a regular weekly check from WWF.

SEPTEMBER 8

The major news was Perry Saturn signing with WCW. All kinds of stories have come from this including that WCW was making a major raid of ECW talent and blaming all kinds of different parties for that.

From all accounts, numerous wrestlers were contacted by WCW and it's all free enterprise and stuff, but the money WCW offered the guys is way over what one would logically believe their market value to be considering what guys with similar or a lot more talent that are already over in WCW are earning. You can read whatever you want to into that statement although Saturn actually doesn't fall into that category since the figure bandied about that he was offered was $100,000 per year.

John Kronus won't be following, as Saturn apparently has been wanting to break up the team and go as a single for more than one year and they even began the break-up angle last year, but Paul Heyman convinced the two to stay together since he'd market them as the best tag team in the world.

OCTOBER 13

Taz agreed to stay with ECW through the end of 1998 after a few conversations this past week with Eric Bischoff. Taz's deal with ECW expires at the end of this year and he and Paul Heyman were apart on a deal for next year. Taz had two conversations in mid-week with Bischoff, but no dealings with the WWF since he'd talked with them in the past and didn't like how the dealings went.

After Bischoff's initial offer to Taz, he verbally agreed to Heyman's deal for 1998. Bischoff came back with a much better offer the next day that was said to have been very tempting, but after consulting with his family and weighing the difference between working 100 or so dates per year, mostly within driving distance and close to 200 dates, few of which would be within driving distance, he decided to stay put. Bischoff on an AOL chat denied ever talking to Taz. I have no idea why.

Chapter Thirteen

ECW Arrives on Pay-Per-View

JANUARY 6

After a week of negotiations back-and-forth, it appears likely, or at least somewhat likely, that ECW will debut on PPV after all in 1997, perhaps as early as 4/13.

ECW's Paul Heyman said he was "cautiously optimistic" the deal could be put back together after several conference calls between Steve Karel of ECW and top executives from Request TV including President Hugh Panero over the past week.

The deal appeared to have fallen apart when Panero decided to cancel the ECW date on 12/20, largely over reservations about several occurrences within the promotion, in specific the fire incident in late 1995 and the 11/23 incident in Revere, MA where an underage untrained wrestler received a horrific beating and a blade wound the likes of which even some of the most hardened and callous people seeing the tape ended up being revolted by. The first PPV show would have been either 3/30 or more likely 4/13.

Panero stated on 12/30 that the two sides are in the process of talking and that the Christmas holiday slowed up the negotiations because so many people were out of the office. He said he was a little bit confused about the incident in Revere, MA because nobody had informed him of it until just over one week ago. At that point Request had approved the ECW date thinking they were just another pro wrestling promotion like the WWF or WCW, but after recognizing they are a more violent form of the genre, they had to learn what they do and insure that the company take greater safeguards against injuries as they move from a regional operation to getting national exposure. He said that he doesn't consider ECW banned from PPV but is a little concerned how a 17-year-old kid with no training got into the ring and was cut up in the manner which he was.

"As the new kid on the block they have to demonstrate they (ECW) are up to the same level of professionalism as WWF and WCW," Panero said. "My people thought they were like WWF and WCW and when we found out differently, we started to do more research. I have no intention of banning them."

Panero said that no date was on the books as of press time but if the two sides can reach agreements on the items of concern, they could still get their date in either late March or April. Heyman stated that because of the problems, he's given up the idea of 3/30, but is still hoping to put everything together by the end of the week and be a go for 4/13.

Request services about 18 million addressable households in the United States. The other major PPV carrier, Viewers Choice, which would be the sole carrier in about seven or eight million of the PPV homes along with a branch that covers most of Canada, had decided against carrying the show because of the content of the ECW television show, in particular the usage of Tyler Fullington (Sandman's son) in a wrestling angle. Even if the show goes on as planned, the loss of VC would cut out about 30% of pure profit from the show's potential. A good showing in the debut show on Request from a buy rate standpoint would probably influence Viewers Choice to carry the second show, but there is no guarantee.

Both Request and Viewers Choice in the United States carry other controversial events such as UFC, although Viewers Choice-Canada does not carry any NHB events and several cable systems in the United States, Cablevision Inc. being the most prominent, no longer carry any NHB events even though UFC is behind the major boxing and WWF and WCW events as the most profitable regular entity currently on PPV. NHB events not being carried in some cities are the result of both political and religious pressure on the cable system, which, unless ECW does a repeat of the crucifix angle which they obviously aren't going to do, doesn't figure to be a problem for ECW unless the company garners substantial national media attention. By that point the company would almost have to be incredibly successful before those types of problems would even raise their head.

The compromises being worked on have to do with ECW putting regulations and safeguards in place that would keep Request out of a major scandal and avoid a repeat of incidents such as the fire incident or the Revere, MA incident. Panero said he wasn't against blood being used on the show as long as the show is appropriately labeled with a warning at the beginning of the show that there may be graphic violence, and that the blood isn't overdone. Heyman said that they had agreed that no stabbing or puncture type of movements with sharp objects would be used on the show such as an Abdullah the Butcher type gimmick. He said that Request wanted the names and ID's of all participants in such a show ahead of time to make sure they are of age and that he has no problem with it because he wants every participant in the show to be under contract before the show before advertising them. Request wanted to be informed of any "last minute surprise" participants beforehand and Heyman said he considered all of Request's concerns to not be unreasonable. Among them was Request also demanding medical personnel be on hand as it is in boxing and NHB events, which he said the company already does on its own.

Heyman said the show itself would contain a lot of wrestling and wouldn't be a bloodfest. There will be no gimmick matches with blood connotations, at least as he has the show planned, such as cage matches, barbed wire matches, chain matches or dog collar matches. He said the show would culminate many feuds and would be the ECW product as it is today with no watering down.

Panero released a public statement on 12/31 saying that based on information garnered from staff research on ECW and the fact ECW would be taking a step up going from local events to national PPV, Request had decided to temporarily cancel the event until doing more research to better understand how ECW operates. The public statement on 12/31 was decidedly more negative concerning an imminent ECW PPV show than conversations with Panero and Heyman the previous day indicated.

"Request TV has been in on-going discussions with Extreme Championship Wrestling to carry one of its events in 1997. During these discussions we learned about specific incidents involving an underage ECW wrestler who appeared to be seriously injured during an event in Massachusetts. We were surprised that the ECW never mentioned that these public relations problems existed, and contrary to the claims made by the ECW, no tape of the incident was sent to anyone at Request TV.

"Whenever we work with a new PPV event provider we like to be thorough in investigating their ability to stage a quality event. Therefore, my staff was instructed to research these alleged incidents and discovered that they were true, and also learned that generally the ECW was theatrically more violent than other wrestling events. Based on this new information and the fact that an ECW event would be a step up from being a local event to a national PPV event, we decided it would be prudent to temporarily cancel the event while we did additional research to better understand how the ECW operates.

"We are still considering carrying the event and, as we would with any national PPV event, we are taking great precautions to ensure that when an event does air it meets all of our standards to create longevity for that particular event," Panero said in the statement.

During the week the story of the original cancellation of the PPV took on a life of its own with some ECW hardcore fans losing sight of the issues that caused the problem, as hardcore fans of anything are wanton to do, and instead blaming Wade Keller of Pro Wrestling Torch, for the show's cancellation. That had even less credibility as WWF hardcore fans in 1991 blaming the company's steroid scandal fiasco on someone like Phil Mushnick and ignoring the causes of the problems internally from the lies of Hulk Hogan, the double-talk of numerous executives at Titan Sports and the fact that 90 percent of the wrestlers in the company were on steroids and they were basically considered a necessity to be a Titan wrestler in that era.

The "fault" lies with the company for ignoring a series of warning signs and non-scripted violent acts or near-violent blow-ups both involving fans and wrestlers which date back to 1995 and culminated that night in Revere, MA—or at least hopefully culminated in Revere, MA as I'd hope that Revere, MA doesn't historically turn out to be another ignored warning sign en route to a bigger problem.

Keller's involvement was limited to questioning Panero last week about the date of the planned PPV event and his reaction to the videotape of the incident in Revere, MA that Heyman had claimed to have sent to Request to inform them ahead of time about a possible problem. Panero had not even heard of the event in Revere, MA, and upon further investigation, claimed that nobody from Request had seen such a tape nor had they as late as 12/30. Panero went so far as to in a public statement about the problem on 12/31 said that contrary to the claims made by Heyman, no tape of the incident had been sent to anyone at Request nor had ECW informed anyone in the company that these potential public relations problems existed. If anyone in ECW or any fan of ECW wants to point a finger of blame for this problem, the finger points in an obvious direction.

On the surface it was somewhat perplexing to think ECW would attempt to put a lid on the tape getting out, but voluntarily send it to the people where it could do the most potential damage, although there were people at Network One (a provider of programming for mostly low-power television stations) that claimed they had been sent a tape.

After finally receiving a copy of the tape, no previous description told to me —and I heard plenty of them from readers who were there live and even people who had seen the tape—could do it justice. Nor could anything written here do it justice to anyone reading this who hasn't seen the tape. It was the single biggest turn-off and perhaps most revolting thing I've ever seen in wrestling. I can't describe exactly why other than it was, and some wrestling personalities involved in some pretty gruesome bloodbaths in promotions far wilder than ECW that have seen the tape have had the same reaction. I've seen 17-year-olds juice. I've seen blade wounds that were as bad, maybe worse, although not many. I've seen more blood spilled although the faucet like flow of blood from a lengthy deep forehead cut was totally out of the ordinary in that regard. There was an ugly symbolism involved, and the crowd reaction to the circumstances, at least the most vocal members of the crowd, was appalling even by the worst standards of a pro wrestling audience.

It was a series of strange circumstances, the underage kid showing up with no experience and being put in a situation where he's to be juiced, taking a pretty savage beating, the cries from the father at ringside being ignored, the callousness of the audience, the botched up blade job, keeping the match going, and the post match "in character" reaction of New Jack saying he didn't care if the kid bled to death while being cheered on and the kid laying there with blood pouring out of his forehead while fans chanted taunts at him, not caring that the fun and games aspect of pro wrestling had long since left this scene. The initial reports in this publication almost down playing the incident as being a big deal were an embarrassment to the Observer.

The emotional reaction to such a tape is such that it is still difficult to find a proper perspective to put this event. Certainly nobody went out to permanently scar a 17-year-old by slicing his forehead open with an Xacto knife, although our initial reports that the length and depth of the cut were because Erich Kulas panicked from inexperienced and moved were not the case. The scene was appalling well before New Jack accidentally cut Kulas too deeply. Jerome Young (New Jack) disputed the report in the Observer that he laughed about the incident, claiming that he wasn't trying to hurt the kid and didn't laugh about it afterwards.

It got far worse after the cut as the father, Steve Kulas, ran to ringside and began screaming to stop the match and that he's only 17, while the beating continued unabated despite an incredible flow of blood. The elder Kulas' voice is evident at ringside on the tape long before the blade job as his son was being pummeled with stiff shots including breaking a crutch over his back (that in real life hurts but isn't exceedingly dangerous) to an incredible full-force shot to the head with a toaster which was where the idea that I was witnessing child abuse and a form of pornography and not professional wrestling took over.

The uneasiness about this incident is not that there was an accidentally deep blade job, but a series of things only made worse by the accident but what was done on purpose was plenty bad on a lot of levels on its own. I recognize guys show up at pro wrestling matches with their bag and if somebody no-shows, are often thrown in the ring. Many wrestlers have gotten their first lucky break in this manner. Probably on very rare occasions in juice promotions, they may even be asked to bleed.

Sometimes they are under 18. Terry Gordy's first match was when he was 14. So was Rey Misterio Jr.'s. I'm certain both had done plenty of blade jobs before they became of age. Perro Aguayo Jr. last year, at 16, was blading from time-to-time right there with his father by his side. But all those arguments that try to say it really wasn't that bad or that unusual go out the window viewing the tape.

The sad part, as much as the incident itself, was the reaction. The desensitizing of violence was such that the reaction across the board, from the wrestlers in the ring "not breaking character," to the promotion not stopping the match and "breaking the illusion," when something was decidedly wrong to the at least some members of the bloodthirsty audience itself went beyond the fact that the kid was under 18 and basically untrained when it comes to pro wrestling. It would have been just as bad if he were 19, as those in the promotion claimed he lied and told them he was, and they apparently accepted without even asking for I.D. or anyone in the promotion having ever even heard of him or knowing him.

This is not meant to downgrade everyone in the crowd in Revere, MA that night. The fact was several if not many walked out of the show, not to mention the scary sight of a fan have an epileptic seizure moments after being freaked out by the incident and the police nearly stopping the show. The incident ended later that night with Kulas in the hospital and police wanting to arrest his father for child abuse, not believing his injuries could possibly have occurred within a pro wrestling match.

A sizeable percentage of those who stayed were appalled and revolted based on the reaction we received from people who attended the show. But while watching the tape, you only hear the chants of "You fat f***" and worse while someone for all they knew could be bleeding to death in front of their eyes, which was worse than the reaction of those involved in putting on the show. It's funny, the ironic part is this description will probably sell hundreds of copies of the "banned" tape on the underground.

In the long run, hopefully this incident and near cancellation or delay, or simply scare in the debut of ECW on PPV, will be accepted for what it is. A headache for some to be sure, but in the long run the best thing for all. ECW was a powder keg, and a potential worse explosion which results in perhaps even more serious injury, could be averted by all this as a wake-up call.

It will be a whole lot better for the future of ECW for some safety guards to be put in place before the PPV, then another of those incidents occur live with the nation watching and resulting in the company never getting a second show.

MARCH 17

Paul Heyman has finalized a seven-match line-up for the 4/13 ECW "Barely Legal" PPV show.

Most of the show has already been announced, but the complete line-up will be the Eliminators defending the ECW tag team titles against Buh Buh Ray & D-Von Dudley; a singles match involving Chris Candido with an angle shot that night to determine his opponent; the Michinoku Pro wrestling match with Great Sasuke & Gran Naniwa & Gran Hamada vs. Taka Michinoku & Terry Boy (Mens Teoh in Japan) & Dick Togo; Shane Douglas defending the ECW TV title against Pit Bull #2; Sabu vs. Taz; the triangle match with Terry Funk, Stevie Richards and Sandman and the ultimate title match with Raven defending against the winner of the triangle match to end the show.

The PPV show will air in the vast majority of Request systems, and a few cable companies that carry Viewers Choice that specifically asked for the show on a stand-alone basis. There were Request systems, including Intermedia Partners and some Cablevision systems including on Long Island that don't carry NHB events that also chose not to carry this event because of the perceived violent nature.

There have been numerous so-called "third party" attempts on PPV over the years within both pro wrestling and NHB genre and some that sort of are a mix between the two like Japanese so-called and real shootwrestling. Most were unsuccessful at first. A few that showed life at the beginning were unable to sustain it. There has only been one legitimate success story.

ECW is unique in that it is well established it has a more fervent cult base of fans than any "third-party" that has attempted such an undertaking. It has more of a proven track record in regard to popularity when it comes to consistent attendance than most, but not all, that have tried, and ultimately failed previously.

The only true success to this point besides WWF and WCW on PPV is the UFC, which started in November of 1993 with a money-losing 0.35 buy rate (about 75,000 buys) and took off to the point that it was profitable on its third show. Unlike most groups that started during the same time period, its audience grew with repeated showings, peaking with the fifth and sixth shows. In 1995, its buy rates consistently topped both WWF and WCW—peaking with better than 1.0 buy rates (260,000 buys) for superfights involving Royce Gracie vs. Ken Shamrock and Shamrock vs. Dan Severn. However, its numbers declined from that point, with a noticeable decline to a new lower level of popularity over the spring and summer of 1996, settling it at doing consistent 0.4 to 0.5 buy rates, a level a little bit below what WWF and WCW are now doing.

UFC was able to be a major force on PPV, and still would be running profitable shows provided they weren't under governmental harassment, despite having no television to "create stars" and get over its storylines. What UFC has been successful in doing is getting lots of mainstream media publicity to where the UFC name is very well-known as the brand name for an illusion of a style of fighting that many would say the events themselves really can't live up (or down, depending on your viewpoint) to. UFC, and its main competitor, EFC, due to national media publicity and controversy, are a lot better known to the general public than ECW, as noted by the fact that ECW is often confused by people with being EFC, but almost never the latter.

EFC had tons of mainstream pub for the first show, particularly in New York, over being moved out of New York in the days leading to the show. This is something it's doubtful ECW will get, and enabled the first show to pop an initial buy rate of 0.3, which was either break-even or perhaps a slight profit or loss, but the two subsequent shows have done money losing ratings of less than 0.2 and the group is now in danger of closing up should this upcoming show not show some life.

NHB and pro wrestling aren't the same in that there are far more fans of pro wrestling. But there are also two established major name brands in pro wrestling that already run monthly shows. Many would say there is already a glut of PPV pro wrestling programming already out there. But pro wrestling is also undeniably the hottest its been in many years right now.

ECW has the television exposure, admittedly limited in scope, that the shoot groups don't have. TV exposure sells their stars and creates people who are huge stars to in this case a somewhat limited amount of people. In addition, the ECW exposure on Monday Night Raw has created a new awareness outside of its cult audience for the name ECW, and it's the brand name and concept of ECW that the company is selling, and not any particular individual or match, which should add curiosity buys of people who would have otherwise never heard of the group.

In a look at new groups that have attempted PPV, aside from WWF, WCW and UFC, which are the only ones to really make it big, we see the following:

> AWA/World Class/Memphis (1988) held SuperClash III from the UIC Pavilion in Chicago headlined by a so-called world title unification match with Jerry Lawler vs. Kerry Von Erich. Although generally remembered as a flop, the show was overall decent with a good main event. The buy rate was 0.5, which

would be a huge success today, but in those days was considered a flop as it amounted to about 40,000 buys which would be break-even. The groups that were working together quickly fell apart and none ever ran a PPV again, and all the groups suffered business declines in the wake of the show. This group has major exposure advantages over ECW in that all three promotions that were involved with the show had strong and in some cases very highly rated regional television and AWA had a weekly show on ESPN that drew decent ratings. None of the groups had the cult following of ECW, but all had tons more television exposure and all in those days were capable of drawing bigger crowds and had on the show wrestlers with far bigger national names than ECW does today.

Herb Abrams UWF (1991) ran Beach Brawl from Palmetto, FL headlined by Steve Williams vs. Bam Bam Bigelow. The show wasn't good, but it was a lot better than expected going in with a solid main event match. However, it totally stiffed on PPV doing about 5,000 buys. But it was well-known going in that this group didn't have a prayer and doing a PPV was simply an ill-fated ego-trip for the tragic eccentric promoter.

LPWA (1992) ran the Super Ladies Showdown in Rochester, MN. Again the wrestling quality of the show was better than expected, but with nobody on the show with a national name, or for that matter any kind of a name, and limited syndication (although probably more than ECW has at this point), it was a total stiff and the promotion folded shortly thereafter.

UWFI was the first group to run on its own from Japan (1993). This was backed by a tremendous advertising campaign which got over the slogan, "Shootfighting: It's real" (which it wasn't, but that's another story). The first show was a huge success doing an 0.48 buy rate, which was about what WCW was doing for its PPV shows at the time, and this was with no television exposure and nobody with name identity. So it shows a PPV can draw based on a new concept getting over. However, lack of follow-up and the fact the lack of punches to the face made it less appealing to Americans rooted in boxing as what a combat sport is supposed to look like, and the UFC that debuted one month later took off while this went nowhere, falling to about an 0.1 buy rate for the second show. After an excellent third show most notable for the debut of Jeff Blatnick as a color commentator, the group was done on PPV.

WCW had promoted three New Japan Super Shows, which were Tokyo Dome tapes aired months later, of shows in 1991, 1992 and 1993. The first show did an 0.6 buy rate, which was below what the regular WCW shows were doing at the time, but considered a success for a novelty event that wasn't heavily promoted and only expected to draw from the limited hardcore wrestling fan audience. The promotion of the first show was much stronger than the second and third shows, which didn't do as well. WCW tried again in 1995 with Collision in Korea, a taped show of the two cards held in front of the two largest crowds in pro wrestling history at May Day Stadium in Pyongyang, North Korea, doing less than an 0.2 buy rate. WCW also ran some unsuccessful K-1 kick boxing shows from Japan on PPV which also did less than 0.2 buy rates.

World Combat Championship (1995), a PPV event from Charlotte, NC was put on by Christopher Peters as basically the first offshoot of the successful by that point UFC. It had tremendous pre-show coverage in the martial arts magazines and was budgeted to do a first-class PPV production. When it didn't hit, it was a huge money loser, possibly to the tune of seven figures, doing less than an 0.2 buy rate, and was never heard from again.

Continental Wrestling Alliance (1996) ran one taped show from the Dallas Sportatorium, largely based around an ego trip of a prison guard named Dominic Minaldi, attempting to be a pro wrestler. Did anyone buy that show? How many of you even know it existed?

Extreme Fighting (1995) was the second UFC offshoot on PPV. It garnered far more mainstream pub than WCC, largely over scheduling its initial shot in Brooklyn, which resulted in a decent buy rate. It was basically a lower-budgeted version of UFC. That debut was considered a poor show and the follow-up show near Montreal with all the Canadian governmental intervention and post-show arrests was a total calamity. The third show was a great card, but the buy rates for shows two and three were both in the 0.14 to 0.18 range, or major losers. The group has a fourth show coming up on 3/28 which looks good on paper to martial arts hardcore fans, but realistically doesn't appear to have much of a shot at turning a profit and the group has to be considered in critical condition.

Pancrase (1996), promoted by SEG as an offshoot of UFC, ran four shows. There was virtually no hype or promotion to the events which were the closest thing to a shoot sport as the world of pro wrestling has ever seen and the style was virtually unrecognizable to American pro wrestling fans. However, it wasn't pushed as pro wrestling in the U.S., and instead pushed to the far more limited martial arts audience. The surprising draw of the first event, which did an 0.25 buy rate and 60,000 buys, may have been partially due to the $9.95 introductory price tag. The follow-up shows all did in the 0.1 range, although the final show, after the die had been cast, similar to the final UWFI show, was an excellent PPV event.

Martial Arts Reality Superfighting (1996) spent literally seven figures, particularly with a huge advertising budget, to promote a Gracie (albeit Renzo Gracie) vs. Taktarov match. There were tons of TV commercial spots, which were well produced, bought on boxing and wrestling television shows, and the Gracie name is well-known from Royce Gracie in UFC and Taktarov has name recognition although no drawing power. This was probably the single-biggest disaster ever on PPV, with seven figure losses on the show that sold about 100 tickets live and didn't even produce an 0.1 buy rate.

Which brings us to the one promotion that ran on PPV that may be the closest for comparison to ECW—the 1994 AAA When Worlds Collide PPV. Both groups were basically similar in that they were introducing a new concept of pro wrestling in the U.S. to PPV, different to what WWF and WCW were providing, that was originally popularized in foreign countries (ECW basically being an American derivative of Japan's FMW). Both had loyal fan bases but virtually no mainstream or crossover recognition when the shows were announced. ECW has gotten a few weeks of first-rate hype on WWF television. AAA got a few weeks of hype on WCW television, although nowhere close to the same degree, even though WCW actually was involved as promoters of the PPV portion of the show. Both cards, on paper, looked to be very good going in. The AAA show, in fact, was arguably one of the greatest PPV wrestling events in history. If the ECW event is anywhere close to that level, it'll be looked on as a huge success at least from that standpoint

If you compare AAA of late 1994 with ECW of early 1997, this is what you see. Both have little national recognition going in but both had tremendous cult followings. AAA in Los Angeles was far more popular than ECW is anywhere (in fact, except for WWF in the major markets during its peak you'd be hard pressed to find any American promotion that enjoyed the popularity run AAA did in Los Angeles over that 18 month period), and actually they drew more in places like Chicago, San Jose and New York than ECW has ever done anywhere in its history, so you're talking the four of the five biggest markets in the country having a real documented strong and rabid following. Of course, being a Mexican group, the following was heavily regionalized and almost exclusively ethnic with basically no crossover appeal. ECW's following is heavily regionalized based on lack of television exposure.

The AAA "When Worlds Collide" PPV show in late 1994, co-promoted by WCW, did a 0.24 buy rate, or about 44,000 buys, which was about break-even. Since AAA didn't have the negative of Viewers Choice not carrying the event and it not airing in Canada, it was available in far more homes than ECW. By all rights, with the AAA of 1994 having bigger stars with more name value (at least to its cult audience—don't kid yourself, every Mexican American at the time knew Santo, Perro Aguayo, Octagon, etc. and if you walk down the street and ask, nobody except hardcore wrestling fans know Sabu and Taz and even most average wrestling fans would be hard pressed to recognize any ECW name except Terry Funk and perhaps Shane Douglas), with more television exposure, and with a far more popular promotion and with wider distribution, ECW shouldn't be expected to do anywhere close to that figures, right?

Maybe yes. Maybe no. The difference is ECW's main strength. AAA had progressive wrestling and a hot promotion at the time, although it had already cooled in the U.S. from its peak one year earlier due to changes on Galavision cable which went from seven hours per week of AAA programming to about one hour, which actually as much as anything else was why AAA fell so fast in popularity in the U.S. because the exposure simply was no longer there and exposure is the life blood of pro wrestling.

But even at its best, AAA was totally messed up in regards to promotion, timing, deadlines, etc. It had no idea how to build or promote a PPV. It did nothing to peak angles for the PPV. As good as people remember that PPV show being, it was really no better (although the one tag team match was exceptional) than most of their major arena shows during that time period, nor did it come across to the promotion's fans as any bigger of a deal since the Los Angeles live crowd was only average for AAA in that market during that time period. AAA failed to capitalize on the aesthetic success of its first show and failed to follow up to the casual fans who may have bought the show for curiosity reasons stemming from WCW television promotion, and AAA quickly faded from those fans' memories and there was never a second show.

When it comes to hyping the importance of the show and peaking angles, there is no comparison. To the ECW audience, this is a big deal, the angles are peaking perfectly, the storylines have been geared in this direction, in some cases for more than one year. Unlike WCW, which failed to feature or put over any AAA talent on its television before the event, ECW has had its performers featured on WWF television with some strong angles, and those segments have made real mainstream impact, something AAA failed to accomplish since it was given no chance to accomplish it in hyping its PPV event. Even though WCW had a financial interest in the AAA show, there was so much of the expected interpromotional jealousy and lack of communication that kept the hype level to a bare minimum with WCW not wanting to do anything to take interest away from its own PPV event at the same time.

It's been exactly the opposite with the WWF/ECW connection. In addition, ECW already has plans for tentative dates for both a second and third show and ideas of where they are going, something AAA didn't have and when its first show was successful, everyone was scrambling about a second show, deadlines fell through, WCW really didn't care, and the second show never took place.

So how will the ECW PPV do? Realistically, they may make more profit from merchandising the event after the fact with videotape and t-shirt sales than from the event itself. With the ticket prices to the live show jacked up and revenue coming in from the Terry Funk banquet, as a singular weekend of events, the losses, if there are any, shouldn't put the company in a dangerous predicament or spell major troubles as has been the case with other companies that have banked their future and then faded away after failing on PPV. Even if there are profits, it's not like anyone at ECW will see them for 90 to 120 days.

The PPV is a cog in the wheel to build up future arena business, as with the pre-show business nowadays, it is being built to be the hottest period ever for the company. Financially, the show may prove to be a success for the company almost like a pyramid standing on its head—with the PPV itself being the loss leader rather then almost the opposite for other companies that have presented events on PPV where the events needed to be successful on a stand-alone basis and was the make-or-break for company profitability.

Of course, ECW is also the most unique perception promotion in the world. There are people ready to trumpet a failure on PPV into a success, and people ready and waiting for a failure to prove what they've believed all along. The ECW PPV story is far more interesting because so many more people are interested in how it does than all of the aforementioned companies that have tried and mostly failed over the past nine years, rather than how many people actually buy the show as compared with all those different groups.

For whatever reason, drawing 1,100 to 1,500 every three weeks in a city the size of Philadelphia is considered an overwhelming success because they pack a tiny Bingo Hall despite those being what would be considered tepid attendance figures for any promotion of any real popularity in a city of that size if it was anyone but ECW. It does have to be noted the crowd is consistent and loyal beyond belief in that it never falls below a certain figure, but it's not like there have ever been 5,000 people on any night wanting to get in, and it's not like angles have never peaked before in a manner that would be expected for a good promotion to draw a monster house with—let alone close to 26,000 that jammed traffic for miles and came to the Sports Arena the night AAA ran its debut show in the building.

ECW is able to sell out small halls in the Northeast, largely because they book small halls and rarely book buildings of any size. I can recall when AAA ran a show in Oakland, CA, a city that is largely black with very few Mexicans and with no television exposure in the city whatsoever, they drew 1,300 fans and it was considered a colossal failure—and it was. If WWF this year were to run a house show that draws 1,300 fans, it would be considered a failure and it would probably be one of the worst houses of the year. A 1,300 person house would be a bad house for any of the three different promotions that run Tijuana, a city of hardly the same population as Philadelphia. A WCW show drawing that kind of figure would be a failure. That same show would be considered by many as a great house if it was an ECW show in New York City—the largest metro area in the country.

Jim Cornette remarked that ECW is a few people who make 95% of the noise, and he's probably right in that line of thinking. But if those few people spend enough money on things like videotapes and t-shirts along with tickets so ECW can draw a profit, it doesn't matter if millions don't casually tune in on Monday night that would never even consider spending a nickel on pro wrestling and may mean something for bragging rights on Tuesdays but mean almost nothing for the company's bottom line. And if those few people make enough noise that WWF and WCW are fooled into thinking there are more than a few people and they can be a beneficial ally in a ratings war, they can turn ECW and that few into a real story and ultimately a reality of many, which may actually be the most real ECW story.

But can those few people through that same illusion convince enough people to buy a PPV show? No. That's why the WWF exposure may have been the event's saving grace. And maybe that's the real story of the PPV. On 4/13, a major question is answered and we find out if the popularity of ECW—at this particular moment—is illusion created by a few making a lot of noise or a significant reality created by a few angles on Monday Night Raw. So we'll find out how few, or how many, is a few—in a few weeks.

MARCH 24

Surprisingly, the PPV show on 4/13 at the Arena isn't sold out, which is quite a contrast to the WCW Nitro the next night at the Spectrum that has already topped 9,000 tickets in advance sales and tickets have only been on sale for five days while the ECW tickets have been on sale for a few weeks. Some ECW regulars are complaining about the high ticket prices ($40 GA) for the show. In addition, many of the suburban cable systems in the Philadelphia area aren't carrying the show because of the wrong affiliation which should have only made the early sellout that much easier.

APRIL 14

Extreme Championship Wrestling runs its first PPV show on 4/13. To some, it's the sixth of seven shows (including the much-hyped Oscar de la Hoya vs. Pernall Whitaker fight the night before that everyone else was running away from competing with) in a run of six straight weekends with major combat PPV shows. To some, it's the culmination of a dream. To some, it's the answer to some long asked questions and something of a moment where fantasy meets up with reality and a real moment of truth.

Within the industry, it is probably the most discussed PPV show of the year. Certainly this particular show is more important to this company than any show, WrestleMania included, is to WWF or WCW. Even so, even the most optimistic ECW supporters recognize this show isn't going to do business at anywhere near the level of WWF, WCW or even UFC.

Let's deal with the first and probably most important question: Will the show pull enough of a number to be successful? You can argue both ways. The debut shows of AAA, Pancrase, UFC, EFC and UWFI all garnered at least a 0.24 buy rate, which at this point I would think most in the PPV industry would be happy for this show to pull. With the exception of AAA, none at the time of their debut show had any television coverage at all in the United States, and none except AAA really had anything resembling a core following when it ran its first show, which even its most ardent detractors have to realize ECW has at least that. By that rationale, one would think ECW should be able to do at least that figure.

At the same time, we are just a few weeks removed from a WrestleMania by the WWF that delivered a 0.77 buy rate. Basically for every three households that ordered WrestleMania in the markets ECW is available, one would have to order ECW for it to do break-even type numbers. When you consider that the ECW show is being provided in numerous markets where it has no following nor television whatsoever and in most of its strongest markets (Long Island, Boston area, much of the Philadelphia metro area) it isn't available, nor are several dish providers carrying the show. By that rationale, one would think ECW doesn't have a chance.

Will ECW go over the line with this show? Hell, no. The series of wake-up calls that nearly cost them this show have been largely addressed. ECW knows exactly what it can and can't get away with, and for anyone to think at this point that Paul Heyman after all this work is going to blow it in this regard isn't paying attention. Yes, there will be blood. Yes, there will be swearing. No, nobody is going to take a knife and slice open an underage kid's forehead. No, they aren't going to set the building on fire. Yes, somebody probably will do a dive off the roof, or the ceiling, or the highest balcony they can find, through 94 tables. Yes, you'll see absolutely wicked chair shots and women with very little clothes on. Next question.

What about a second show? In many ways, this show is a test. A test to see just how much interest there is. But it's a chance for ECW to prove itself in regard to the future. If this show delivers a 0.2 buy rate in the limited availability, while the show itself would not be profitable, it could be termed, well, not a failure although it would also firmly establish them as a "C" level PPV player. There's little doubt a figure like that, barring a major catastrophe at the show, would lead to many of the carrier systems that decided to pass on this show due to the controversy to re-evaluate their thinking. And if the entire PPV universe will carry a subsequent show, ECW could conceivably break even or even make a few bucks on a 0.2.

At the same time, most, but not all promotions have a significant decrease on their second PPV show from their first. Anything less than a 0.2 on the first show is not a good sign for the future. Its oft-confused namesake, Extreme Fighting, just two weeks earlier, didn't come close to a 0.2 for show number four after debuting with a mildly successful 0.3. Pancrase started near 0.3 and was down to 0.1 on its second show. Although there are regional pockets where ECW wrestling has far more popularity than Extreme Fighting, on a national basis one would have to question whether that is the case. Certainly Extreme Fighting due to the controversy has received tons more media play and exposure, but ECW has a cult television show in some markets.

The tension in and around ECW has never been greater. It came perilously close to all-out brawls among the wrestlers due to nerves being on edge both the past two weekends backstage at the shows. Several of those involved with the show privately admit they wish it was over so things could get back to, well, abnormal. Several wrestlers that have talked of leaving had been talked into staying at times with the promise of big money once the PPV came. Few believe there will be big money now coming from this PPV, but at the same time, it's really questionable how many guys will be leaving because if you get right down to it, there isn't a lot of interest in the major promotions for most of the ECW crew.

Rob Van Dam's leaving for WCW is pretty much expected by everyone, including the ECW fans who were chanting "You sold out" at him on the house show 4/5 in Queens, NY. Van Dam has promised Heyman he would stay through a certain date (believed to be sometime in June), but Heyman believes Van Dam will likely be gone after that time. Sabu's reputation and perceived value in this business has pretty much hit the skids over the past year due to his track record but there has certainly been a lot of discussion about him elsewhere and he's floated leaving ECW to other companies, although the odds are he isn't going anywhere right now.

Occasionally the major offices bring up Stevie Richards and Raven, but it's not like either are high on anyone's want list. The so-called New York clique—Taz, Tommy Dreamer, The Dudleys and Eliminators—likely aren't going anywhere for a variety of reasons. Heyman realizes that and has worked hard to keep them all strong and make them the cornerstones of the promotion, which has led to resentment from others in the company. Sandman, while not a member of the New York clique, and arguably the most popular wrestler in the company right now, is also one who it is doubtful will be going anywhere.

The Gangstas, due to their controversial past and present, aren't exactly being wooed by the major offices either. Heyman has kept The Gangstas around, a controversial move to say the least coming on the heels of the November incident in Revere, MA that nearly cost them this entire PPV, but has taken much of the promotional focus directly away from them, trying instead to subliminally get New Jack over by leaping off higher balconies each week to get the short-term memory of fans away from New Jack as the guy who almost cost them their PPV to New Jack as the gutsiest or perhaps craziest guy in a promotion of generally very gutsy and some crazy individuals.

Shane Douglas has made his share of enemies, but at 33 and one of a few truly polished performers in the company and this being the wrestling business, those who hate him today will embrace him tomorrow if they think they can do business with him.

This will also be a moment of truth for perhaps the most underrated performer in the company in some circles, although certainly not among this newsletter's readership—Joey Styles. Styles will do most of the show solo (Tommy Dreamer is expected to come out during the ECW title match), and be placed in a position to run the gamut of styles from stiff brawling, psychotic spots, sloppy execution, worked shootfighting, Japanese lucha and climaxing with melodrama all in one three hour period. No American announcer has ever pulled all this off yet in one show, let alone someone who has never done pro wrestling live and is working his first PPV event. On Sunday night, Styles' performance, yay or nay, will be almost as talked about as most of the wrestlers.

With Chris Candido out of action for the next two months with a torn bicep (Candido opted not to have surgery which would have kept him out of action for closer to five months), the card still had one hole in it at press time. The original plan was for a night-of-the-show challenge leading to a Candido vs. Lance Storm match. It is most likely that spot will be taken by Storm vs. Rob Van Dam, which on paper sounds like a good match, although that wasn't a definite as Van Dam was said to have been mad about not being booked originally on the show and not wanting to be a fill-in guy.

Dudleys vs. Eliminators will work in the building but is more questionable how a long match between those two teams will look to the rest of the world. The Michinoku Pro match with Great Sasuke & Gran Hamada & Gran Naniwa vs. Taka Michinoku & Mens Teoh & Dick Togo, despite Sasuke being all banged up and fighting off jet lag after a match against Jushin Liger the previous night at the Tokyo Dome and Teoh banged up as well, should be the best match on the show and probably no worse than the second best match on an American PPV show so far this year. Shane Douglas vs. Pit Bull #2 will also be heated at the arena, and probably involve some booking swerves. Sabu vs. Taz will have a very difficult time living up to its hype, but will also likely involve a lot of booking swerves. Which leads us to Terry Funk.

When Heyman came up with the plan to actually do this PPV show after months and years of stalling the subject out, he already came out with the climax of the show. Twenty years after Terry Funk lost the NWA world heavyweight title in Toronto to Harley Race, at the time the almost undisputed biggest wrestling championship in the business, Funk would go on a quest for his final world title and under the most dramatic of circumstances, pull it out for a tearful emotional explosion. Heyman even wanted the PPV in early February so as to be almost 20 years to the exact date (February 6, 1977) of Funk's last run as the symbolic top man in the profession. Funk, who had largely decided he was done wrestling in the United States, was sold on the storyline of the 53-year-old hardcore legend (actually Funk turns 53 on 6/30) making a vow to his late father and battling against all odds and ending with one last stand, ending with the symbolic belt crowning him the king of the hardcores, to the extent he embarked on yet another comeback.

Much has changed since last October, although the television would lead one to believe the main focal point of the show's climax has stayed the same.

Terry Funk has had numerous last stands before. In 1983, perhaps the single most emotional scene in the history of pro wrestling saw 13,000 fans weeping in unison as he had his final match in Tokyo. At the time Funk said that he didn't want to be a pro wrestler at the age of 40 because during his career he'd witnessed too many top names hanging around too long, although part of the reason was that All Japan, his company, was losing a promotional war with New Japan due to how incredibly over Riki Choshu was and this was Funk's way of doing his part, a big farewell tour climaxing in the most emotional moment of Japanese wrestling history, to combat the opposition. By late 1984 he was back in All Japan after an angle bringing him back involving Stan Hansen and the late Bruiser Brody.

In 1987, after a serious back injury had crippled him to the point that even his friends wanted him out of the ring for good and all his cleverness in the ring wasn't enough to combat the effects of the injury, it looked like his career was going to end on a sad note. But in 1989 he came back with perhaps the most legendary run of his career against Ric Flair. When the run ended in November, Funk was again retired, this time by the company, after an I Quit match against Flair in Troy, NY which drew what was at the time the single largest viewing audience for a match in the history of cable television and was arguably the single greatest performance of his illustrious career.

But once again, he came back, and many credit him as being the foundation of the early building of ECW from just another third-rate indie to the cult phenomenon it later became, with himself as the undying legend, putting on incredible performances and putting over and in many ways making the ECW local stars into legitimate names like Public Enemy, Shane Douglas and Sabu. Not that everything was all altruistic. At one point, Funk, with basically no warning, no-showed an ECW Arena show when he was in the main event, basically walking out on the promotion. Another wrestler doing the same thing would be buried six feet deep, but with Funk it was handled delicately since Heyman had the knowledge there would come a day he'd need him again. Which happened time and time again.

Although Sabu vs. Taz has been built up for more than one year as the main event on the show, if everything goes according to the best plans, the lasting memory of ECW's first PPV show will be the climax of Funk's last (or latest) stand. The world title event is slated to go on last, once again enforcing the idea that the finish is the memory Heyman wants everyone left with. One year ago there would have been no questions and certainly no concerns about how this would all turn out. If there was anyone in the company who could be counted on in a PPV main event to deliver the goods and then some, to turn in a memorable performance that people would talk about for months that would rub off on the company itself, Funk was the person you'd give the ball to and you wouldn't worry about it for a second. Certainly Heyman was thinking like that in October when he came up with his plan to lure Funk back.

Funk's run started at the November to Remember. ECW sold out its small much-maligned and much-overly fantasized Bingo Hall farther in advance and created the most interest for any show in its history back on 11/16, with Funk climaxing his match doing a moonsault off the top rope to the floor. But in hindsight, as expertly done as this story started from November through January with the sentimental videos and tremendous television hype, people have begun picking flaws in it.

In the late 90s, when people want their heroes to be bad-asses like Steve Austin, Funk sold too much and gave too much to his foes in his comeback matches. The fans wanted the nasty old man who was tougher than shoe leather, and not the sympathetic and overly melodramatic babyface who was pounded into the ground and somehow at the end snuck by to win. This was coupled with the fact that Funk began going on the road more regularly with ECW to build up this match and how much he gives in every match, the aches appeared to have worsened.

Funk used to have this amazing knack for walking around all day looking like a beat-up old fighter, but when the bell rang, within seconds you forgot all that because he was smart enough and good enough to deliver the kind of performances that only the elite younger wrestlers in the game could touch. As he was wowing everyone in 1989 in the ring being one of the top three of four performers in the profession at the age of 45—doing a ****1/2 match on a PPV with Ric Flair three weeks after suffering a broken back in the ring, those in the WCW office, who thought they were doing the right thing out of humanity, wanted to retire him against his wishes so he wouldn't damage himself any farther. Hardcore fans, who didn't see him before and after his matches, couldn't understand the company's decision.

But between his storyline selling, and the pounding, he began looking during the matches like he looked before and after the match on this recent run. When he started this run, Funk's crowd reaction blew away that for anyone else in the company and those close to the promotion pointed to Funk being there as the difference between just barely filling the building and a show that would turn away hundreds. In some cities in recent weeks, Funk barely got a crowd reaction. By telling people he's over the hill so much, people are starting to believe it.

The storyline they were trying to tell of can the old man, the all-time legend, pull one last legendary performance out of a tired aching body, has also become something of reality. Since it's Terry Funk, and the image that name conjectures, you'd think he probably can and probably will. But if you've watched his matches this year, you couldn't say that with anything close to the certainty you could one year ago.

Funk may be a smarter and more dramatic performer than Nick Bockwinkel was at the same age when he did his legendary 60:00 draw with Curt Hennig on a New Years Eve, but physically he's taken so much more punishment during his lifetime that he is physically a much older man. A rested up Terry Funk could pull it off, no doubt. But the Terry Funk that has been at the shows the past few weeks is the one coming to Philadelphia on Sunday.

To borrow an analogy of a previous generation, there was a famous football player named George Blanda, who years after being written off, came back in his mid-40s for one improbable miraculous season where he was the MVP of the entire NFL—similar to the Funk of 1989. Funk has to carry a triangle match with Stevie Richards and Sandman, and barring a change in plans, then do a lengthy singles match with Raven with the title at stake.

Like Blanda, he not only has to quarterback the team losing by nine to a touchdown with the clock ticking down in both the game and his own personal fourth quarter, but he has to follow it up with another drive to get them within field goal range with five ticks left on the clock and the ball placed down 50 yards from the uprights and kick the win home. But a few years later, all the mystique and legendary status in the world couldn't hide the fact that his kicking leg was gone and the very idea of him going into the game as a quarterback to do the miracle comeback was a joke, and although he lasted longer than almost anyone in NFL history—more than 15 years after the first time common logic had him written off as past his prime. Even in myths, there is a finite end. And even given Blanda's Hall of Fame credentials, Funk is a far better performer in his profession than Blanda was in his.

For ECW's Barely Legal to be the show that Terry Funk and Paul Heyman have envisioned in their brains and hearts for the past several months, it'll require Funk once more staving off that finite end, a fight far harder and one hell of a lot more realistic than any pro wrestling storyline. Barely Legal is hardly the appropriate name. Almost Reality is a lot closer.

APRIL 28

The 4/13 ECW Barely Legal PPV show, besides getting a great response as a show, appears to have done better from a buy rate standpoint than the initial indications last week.

Request TV sent out a press release claiming the show would do between 50,000 and 60,000 buys in a 17 million home universe which would be a buy rate of between 0.29 and 0.35. Multi Channel News estimated the buy rate to be 0.26 and 45,000 buys, and other industry sources also estimate the buy rate at between 0.24 and 0.27 but believe the 17 million universe figure is highly inflated and the realistic number of buys as closer to 40,000.

I'm skeptical of a 17 million home universe carrying the show as well, since there is a basic rule of thumb within the industry to exaggerate that figure. Recent WWF and WCW PPV shows have had a universe of 26.2 million homes, and if you take away Canada (4 million homes), Cablevision (3 million), and half the satellite dish homes that didn't carry ECW (2 million), that already cuts it down to 17 million. That isn't even taking away the Viewers Choice homes which have to run into several million. Others who do PPV shows regularly claim that the total Request homes are more like 11 million, and if you add to that two million satellite homes and perhaps another million homes that carried the show on a stand-alone basis, that's only a 14 million total and that's not taking into consideration that a lot of the Cablevision homes and Request homes are the same and those homes weren't able to purchase the show.

The general rule within the PPV world is that the figures most companies claim publicly for their shows, not just within the pro wrestling world, are inflated by 20 percent. For example, the Oscar de la Hoya vs. Pernell Whitaker fight on 4/12 that was publicly claimed to have 1,000,000 buys really had closer to 800,000. Paul Heyman said that when he first received the press release, he thought the numbers listed were exaggerated but says he now has been led to believe the show will end up doing in excess of 50,000 buys and at that figure would be a profitable show doing a gross in excess of $400,000. Heyman estimated his expenses on the show at $320,000 to $330,000, so a break-even number would be approximately 40,000 buys.

Heyman said the only concession to get Request to carry the show was to guarantee them their share of the money the show would generate on a 0.2 buy rate, which is now a moot point. Because of it being a new player in the marketplace, there was more interest in tracking an accurate buy rate on this show throughout the industry than any show in a long time. In addition, ECW skews considerably higher to insiders (to nobody's surprise) as we received a greater number of responses to the ECW show than to most recent WWF and WCW shows, although the number of responses wasn't as many as the first show of either AAA or UWFI.

The show live drew 1,170 paid to the ECW Arena, and drew a company all-time record live gate. That figure has been given to me as either a $66,000 or $70,800 house, depending upon whether or not there were 320 or 400 ringside tickets sold at $100 as different company sources have given different numbers.

Whatever the real figure is, and really all the estimates are all fairly close, the show did along with lines of what many groups have done for their debut show so to tab the buy rate as anything like a major shock would be overstating things, especially considering that most industry estimates going in were in the 0.2 to 0.3 range. The show did about the same buy rate, perhaps a tad lower, than the debut of both Extreme Fighting and Pancrase, a little higher than the debut and only show of AAA, significantly lower than the debut of UWFI and UFC, and well above the debut shows of Martial Arts Reality Superfighting and World Combat Championships, let alone the basically forgotten debuts of the Continental Wrestling Federation, Herb Abrams UWF, LPWA and World Fighting Federation.

Of those groups, ECW, Abrams, LPWA and AAA were the only ones with any weekly television exposure. ECW is the only one that based its television for weeks around professionally building the PPV as the biggest event in the history of the company. Only one of those groups actually succeeded in PPV to the point it was consistently profitable, which was UFC. It's hard to compare different types of shows, but based on the response we've received, it appears the debut of ECW was better received than most of the above mentioned groups.

The buy rate was certainly strong enough that Viewers Choice would have no economic reason not to carry the proposed second show on 8/17, which ironically is going to be subject to enormous confusion in the marketplace because the already resurrected Extreme Fighting Championships are scheduled for 8/15. Adding those homes and maintaining a buy rate of better than 0.25 would keep the group consistently profitable in the PPV game.

And while most groups decline significantly from the first show to the second, (UFC being an exception) ECW did make the most out of its first opportunity unlike other groups that debuted by throwing a subpar show out there without any long-term purpose or direction to build it to a next show. Overall, by almost any standard, as a first show, it would have to be considered a success.

Chapter Fourteen

WWF Working with FMW

APRIL 14

WWF had expressed interest in using Atsushi Onita, however Onita had no interest in wrestling in the U.S. However, Wing Kanemura of FMW, who is a good worker, is expected to get an interview and possibly a try-out in early May.

APRIL 28

Atsushi Onita of the Frontier Martial Arts and Wrestling promotion in Japan held a press conference on 4/16 to announce that they were going to start negotiations with the World Wrestling Federation for a major show in Japan.

Full details of exactly what this entails haven't been released, but Onita got the ball rolling when he showed a letter Vince McMahon and Bruce Prichard sent in early March where the WWF attempted to open up a business relationship between the two offices.

Onita, who along with Wing Kanemura (Yukihiro Kanemura), are scheduled to come to the United States along with FMW booker Victor Quinones in early May to meet with WWF officials and perhaps Paul Heyman as well about participating in the show. The meeting is scheduled for 5/1

Although the story has already received significant play in Japan, as best we can tell the only thing definite from a WWF perspective is that they are going to meet with Onita and there have been no talks about anything other than setting up a first meeting.

In an unrelated deal, Prichard and Jim Ross met with the wrestlers from Michinoku Pro Wrestling that appeared on the ECW PPV show on 4/21 at the Titan offices in Stamford, CT about those wrestlers working in the WWF. Reports are that the chances of doing business together appear good at this point and the WWF is planning on starting a lighter weight division but is trying to work out the logistics of when the wrestlers and which wrestlers would be available at certain times.

A potential deal with the Michinoku office, provided dates could be adequately worked out, would probably make the WWF's relationship with AAA in Mexico obsolete because the Michinoku wrestlers offer the same type of action but are far more polished workers. Because of the disorganized nature of the AAA office, the WWF has been having problems getting the wrestlers they want on the dates they want, thus unable to give any of the wrestlers any kind of a push or storyline.

MAY 12

Frontier Martial Arts-Wrestling from Japan had meetings this past week with both the WWF and ECW about putting together a major joint show set for November and in addition, there is the beginning of dialogue between the WWF and EMLL in Mexico.

Atsushi Onita, Wing Kanemura, Terry Funk and Victor Quinones represented FMW in what was reported in Japan as a three-hour meeting at Titan Towers on 5/1 with Vince McMahon, Bruce Prichard and Jim Ross. According to reports in Japan, the meeting talked about a joint show which was reported in Japan as being in October (our reports indicate it was November) and the possibility of the WWF promoting an explosive bomb match later this year at Madison Square Garden, as Onita after the recent Yokohama Arena show talked about having a bomb match against Antonio Inoki on a WWF show.

Years ago there were serious negotiations for such a match at a stadium in Japan, but the match politically fell apart. It would be difficult now with New Japan's relationship with WCW, for Inoki to work on a WWF show, not to mention that the match itself would be terrible and unlike in Japan, the two aren't super over legends to be able to get away with it. It also makes no sense from a WWF standpoint to do a bomb match, if they could even do it in a place like Madison Square Garden, with wrestlers that the fans don't know.

Kanemura worked both ECW shows over this past weekend against Kevin Quinn, a former Windy City wrestler out of Chicago who most recently had worked for EMLL in Mexico. They shot an angle for Japanese consumption over the weekend where Kanemura and Terry Funk were brawling backstage when Tommy Dreamer joined in and the two Americans, who would be the heels in this angle, set Kanemura on fire, likely to build up a tag team match on a big show later this year.

FMW proposed to WWF doing a multi-promotional show on a Sunday in November which would include FMW, Michinoku Pro, Pancrase, ECW and WWF, which is quite a strange amalgamation of talent. At this point, as best we can tell, the WWF agreed to continue negotiations for such a show but that no deal had been completed. FMW also proposed to bring a crew of ECW wrestlers in for three shows during that same time period which would consist of two smaller arena shows including a Korakuen Hall date, along with the big show. FMW already has a major show set up for 9/28 at Kawasaki Baseball Stadium, but they didn't bring that date up to either WWF or ECW so it appears they already have the ideas on where they are going for that show.

Additional politics have sprung up involving the Michinoku Pro wrestlers. WCW is mad that the Michinoku wrestlers, who they believe are affiliated with New Japan since they appear on the New Japan major shows, worked the ECW PPV show and were negotiating with WWF rather than working for WCW. Don't know exactly where this all stands right now but WCW is going to pressure New Japan into pressuring Michinoku Pro on this subject and according to one report, New Japan has already told Michinoku Pro that if its wrestlers work for WWF, it'll cut-off their working relationship with New Japan.

Among other items apparently discussed at the meeting included Quinones, who is the foreign booker for FMW, booking a WWF tour to South America, and also Quinones, who books foreign talent for EMLL as well, getting involved in forging a relationship between WWF and EMLL.

At this point, the WWF relationship with Antonio Pena isn't officially dead, but it's almost certainly on life support systems. No AAA talent has been brought in for the television tapings in several weeks, nor has any been mentioned. The inability to do business with Pena due to the disorganization of the AAA office, has pretty much ended the relationship as WWF would request talent on certain dates and AAA would never get back to them about it making them unable to break one or two of the names that would be marketable in this country out of the pack of anonymity.

WWF was likely interested in booking some AAA wrestlers for the 6/28 show in Anaheim since it's a one-day war with WCW in the same market (not to mention that tentatively the Mike Tyson vs. Evander Holyfield fight is scheduled to take place the same night) but didn't even bother, and although AAA has continued to talk on television for months about big-name WWF talent coming to Mexico, aside from Razor Ramon and Diesel, who are under WWF contracts but never used in the United States because it's readily accepted in hindsight that the gimmick didn't work, and Jake Roberts, who no longer works for the WWF, no foreign wrestlers have appeared.

Paco Alonso of EMLL, who met with Eric Bischoff in late February in San Francisco, has also either met with Titan or had communication with Titan in recent weeks along those lines. It is likely that the hold-up to the proposed WCW/EMLL affiliation was WCW's dealings with Konnan and the Promo Azteca crew, which are a rival promotion in Mexico. This may result in some interesting political maneuvers behind the scenes both in the United States and in Mexico.

MAY 19

Atsushi Onita returned from his meeting with Vince McMahon, Bruce Prichard and Jim Ross and talked about wanting to do an explosive match on a WWF PPV show. He said that Mr. Gannosuke and Wing Kanemura would be wrestling in the WWF and that McMahon had asked him to help promote a WWF tour in not only Japan but also in Asia.

FMW's ideas appear to be along these lines. Run a big show on its own in September, then come back in November with a show using Michinoku Pro, WWF, ECW and Pancrase. At this point neither WWF nor Pancrase have agreed to the show. That show wouldn't have inter-promotional matches and each group would run its own matches, but it would wind up in angles where FMW would first feud with ECW, then run a larger show feuding with WWF.

JUNE 2

No WWF deals are done with EMLL, FMW or Michinoku Pro, but the odds are good that they'll eventually be consummated. The Mankind feature [on Raw] makes me think they're building up to one of those FMW style explosive electrified barbed wire matches and Atsushi Onita has been in the Japanese press talking about doing a match of that type at the September Madison Square Garden show. Onita has never wrestled Cactus Jack in a singles match although they were on opposite sides of a six-man on 4/29.

JUNE 9

The first part of the WWF/FMW tie-up appears to be an appearance by Ken Shamrock on the 9/29 show at Kawasaki Baseball Stadium. The idea is for Shamrock to do a mixed martial arts worked match which would be broadcast on television in the United States. Right now his scheduled opponent is Gregori Veritchev, a Russian who competed in judo in the 1988 Olympics (and I believe won the gold or silver although I'm not positive of that) and worked as Atsushi Onita's tag team partner with FMW several years back.

The downsides of that match are that Veritchev was a terrible worker and the match, because of Veritchev, really won't be a big money draw in Japan. However he does have the credentials and will do the job. Others who have been considered are Kimo (wants it as a shoot), Allan Goes (ditto), Yoshiaki Fujiwara (too obvious in Japan it's a work ahead of time) and someone from Pancrase (who won't work with Shamrock because of the heat between the two sides).

The main event right now is scheduled as Onita vs. Wing Kanemura, but they are contemplating shooting an angle to turn Onita heel and join Funk Masters of Wrestling (ala Bret Hart and Hulk Hogan) and feud with Masato Tanaka & Hayabusa.

JUNE 23

At this point it appears that Ken Shamrock will face Vader on FMW's 9/28 Kawasaki Baseball Stadium show. The deal wasn't finalized as of our last report, but that was where the negotiations were headed.

The feeling from Atsushi Onita and others is that Gregori Veritchev, the Soviet Olympic judo player, had been gone from Japan for so long his name would mean nothing and a match with Shamrock wouldn't sell enough tickets to justify bringing Shamrock over. They spoke with Kimo, but he wanted about $150,000 to put Shamrock over and that was out of their price range. Bam Bam Bigelow would have done it for less, but the hold up was that when Bigelow was told the match was going to be taped on a Sunday for airing the next day on Raw, he didn't want to appear on Raw doing the job.

Onita believes this is the year FMW can overtake All Japan as the No. 2 wrestling promotion in Japan which is why he's trying to work with WWF and ECW with inter-promotional feud type matches. Onita wants to bring five or six WWF stars to Japan for both November and December and do Japanese angles with them although this is all at this point in the planning stages.

They are going to do a second baseball stadium show, now in December, which as the current plans are, would consist of five WWF matches including a Shamrock vs. Vader rematch as the main event, which likely means they'll split their two matches, and a Terry Funk & Dreamer vs. Onita & Wing Kanemura explosive barbed wire bomb match, an ECW heavyweight title match, an ECW tag team title match and several FMW matches with WWF and ECW both being partners in the show.

FMW announced a show for 8/2 in Tokyo at the Shiodome with an explosive barbed wire match between Wing Kanemura vs. Masato Tanaka with the winner getting the singles match with Onita at Kawasaki Stadium. We've also heard Onita may turn heel on this show ala Hogan and Bret Hart and set up a tag team match for the Stadium main event.

OCTOBER 6

With inter-promotional help from both All Japan Pro Wrestling and the World Wrestling Federation, Frontier Martial-Arts Wrestling of Japan drew one of the largest crowds in company history on 9/28 for its annual show at the Kawasaki Baseball Stadium.

The crowd was announced as being 50,012 fans. We've had several live reports, most indicated the real number was around 40,000. However, one report said that early in the show, the 40,000 figure looked correct, but that the stadium (which should hold about 52,000 for wrestling) was almost completely filled by the time the top matches were into the ring, saying it was a late arriving crowd (not unusual at all for Japan) due to that same day in nearby Tokyo there were huge sports crowds for a baseball game and a national soccer match that ended while this show was in its early stages.

We don't have a gate figure other than FMW has done $2 million in the past in that building, and the ticket prices for this show were scaled higher than any FMW show at the stadium to date, ranging from $166 ringside down to $25. All live reports indicated it was a very good show with the interpromotional tag team match involving All Japan's Kenta Kobashi & Maunukea Mossman against FMW's Jinsei Shinzaki & Hayabusa being the highlight. The show airs on the Samurai Channel in Japan, edited down to a 90-minute format, on 10/12.

From an American standpoint, the biggest match on the show was what was billed as an Ultimate Fight rules cage match involving the WWF's Ken Shamrock and Vader. The original match plan was for Shamrock to sell the rib injury theoretically suffered in the 9/9 Muncie, IN match against Faarooq, and Vader taking advantage of that injury would lead to his upset victory in Shamrock's specialty match, largely to build for a rematch similar to the idea behind the Shawn Michaels vs. Davey Boy Smith finish in England last week.

Ultimately, that was the basic storyline of what happened, although they may have gone to the finish early. Shamrock had been out of action since coughing up a lot of blood in Muncie, suffering what was first believed to be a perforated lung, but later diagnosed as a lung infection. On his second big bump of the match, taking a power bomb from Vader, he again began coughing up blood.

According to reports, both Vader and WWF representative Bruce Prichard appeared very concerned in the ring at that point and they went right to the finish with Shamrock being unable to get up by the count of ten and the referee stopping the match at 7:17. Vader in the cage was screaming to get a doctor into the ring. Shamrock was scheduled to be examined by his doctor early in the week after returning home and his status for the 10/5 St. Louis PPV show depended upon the extent of his internal problems.

Originally when FMW and WWF agreed to send Shamrock to this show, the plan was for him to face a martial arts star in a worked match, with him going over in front of a huge crowd overseas in what would be purported as a shoot match and have the match air on Raw the next day. As it turned out, FMW was unable to get a martial arts star that would both fit the qualifications of being able to have the box office chemistry with Shamrock to make the fee FMW was paying WWF for Shamrock's services and agree to do the job for a price within their budget.

Instead they went with Vader, one of the biggest foreign attractions in Japanese wrestling history, as a package deal, believed to be a $100,000 to the WWF for both men, and again with the idea of Shamrock going over before a huge crowd to be broadcast on American television. The finish was likely changed since they had decided to instead book a rematch between the two in Japan rather than a one match series and it was felt it was better to put Vader over in the first meeting.

With Vader's face turn in the United States being decided after the agreement for this match was in place, this match doesn't make storyline sense to air in the U.S. as was the original plan and isn't likely to be aired. However, the WWF acknowledged the match and its result on Raw the next night.

NOVEMBER 17

Atsushi Onita canceled all plans for big shows in December that were to include WWF and ECW talent and won't be working with either group for anything in the future at this point. WWF is attempting to open up talent relations with All Japan. Onita wants to build the whole promotion around FMW vs. Zen, so the original NWO-like Funkmasters of Wrestling angle has been dropped and the only foreigner they are keeping is Gladiator, so it appears they won't be using Terry Funk or Head Hunters any longer.

Chapter Fifteen

Vader Arrested in Kuwait

APRIL 28

Leon White aka Vader found himself in the middle of a strange legal situation somewhat replicating the famous David Schultz/John Stossel incident from 12 years ago while appearing on the television show "Good Morning Kuwait."

White naturally was in the role of Schultz, the huge bully wrestler, while popular Kuwaiti morning show host Bassam Al Othman was in the Stossel role, actually with similar hair and moustache. White, 40, was immediately placed under house arrest at his hotel room after the incident, which took place on 4/11, and detained in Kuwait while the rest of the WWF tour returned home two days later. White had a hearing in Kuwait on 4/22 and was expected to be cleared to return to the United States the next day.

The incident very closely mirrored the Schultz/Stossel incident, which took place in December 1984 in the dressing room in Madison Square Garden and was a large factor in Schultz's wrestling career taking a turn for the worst. Many have speculated the event was a publicity stunt by the WWF to get press coverage. The fact is the incident got a lot of press coverage nationally, much of which mentioned on both its 4/20 PPV show and its 4/21 Raw television show.

The WWF did air clips of the incident on its television over the weekend, although the clips were edited, but news of the incident made newspapers and entertainment papers around the country, generally in the personality or gossip section with humorous overtones, and a clip of the incident aired on "Good Morning America" on 4/18.

The WWF first publicized the incident itself on its 900 line on 4/14, sent out press releases during the week and made Vince McMahon available for interviews regarding the story, which furthered speculation that it was a work to garner the type of gossip column mainstream publicity that WCW has been getting over the past few months with Dennis Rodman and Reggie White. The WWF was tentatively planning to hold a press conference regarding the incident on 4/25, and was working on getting White booked on "Good Morning America" on that date.

Eric Bischoff publicly called the incident a hoax, claiming Titan was doing an angle based on the Stossel/ Schultz incident that this closely mirrored. Jim Ross on the WWF hotline, in reference to that, claimed that it was very real and said those who call it a hoax don't know what they're talking about and said that when people do things that alter their minds, it messes up their thinking.

USA Today had begun working on a story, which included talking with McMahon, but because the incident may have been a publicity stunt, didn't run the story because the state department couldn't confirm the incident as legit. Nevertheless, all WWF wrestlers who were both on tour and not on tour were under the impression the incident was legitimate and front office officials are insistent the original incident itself was not an angle.

The original plan for the 5/11 PPV show was for Undertaker to headline against Vader, but apparently those plans switched to Undertaker vs. Steve Austin and Vader vs. Ken Shamrock in Shamrock's first WWF match sometime in recent weeks. Without question, since the plan is for a match on 5/11, that WWF would have wanted Vader to shoot an angle with Shamrock either on 4/20 at the PPV or on 4/21 on the Raw, and his being detained made that an impossibility. Vader was also penciled in on 4/18 as Undertaker's opponent for several house show title matches in May, taking the place of Bret Hart, who had to be pulled from those main event matches due to word getting around about his impending surgeries.

My personal feeling is that the incident, in regard to the detaining and the arrest, is very real, and the WWF decided several days after the fact to use it to gain as much mainstream publicity as possible. Even though the incident took place on 4/11, word really didn't get out about it until the wrestlers returned home from Kuwait and began telling their friends several days later rather than WWF publicizing it immediately after the arrest took place.

The situation went something like this. White and Mark Calaway (Undertaker) were guests on the live morning television show and were told ahead of time what questions were going to be asked including whether pro wrestling was fake. According to the Titan side of the story, the English speaking producer told the wrestlers to "ham it up." The question was asked, through an interpreter, to Calaway, who responded with an answer along the lines of it being entertainment, but with athleticism and that the injuries suffered are very real. White wasn't asked the question, but starting off low-key, said he wanted to answer that question and said he's not as diplomatic as his colleague.

At that point, White grabbed the host by the tie and began shaking him and said something about the question being "bullshit" and in his tirade said he was insulted by the question and shoved the terrified announcer down backward over some chairs and a table and flower plant wound up being turned over. As the show broke for a commercial, when it came back, both White and Al Othman were gone and Al Othman hasn't been back on the show since. Police were called immediately and White was arrested both for assault and for lascivious conduct because it is illegal in Kuwait to swear on television.

There was a second incident involving White, although we're not clear as to the details. It may have been on 4/21, and it was at the hotel White was being detained at, that he caused some sort of a problem that resulted in 20 police officers, people from the U.S. Embassy and his lawyer to have to calm him down. In addition, there was another situation we're not clear of details on that was said to be minor involving him and a flight attendant on the trip to Kuwait.

McMahon claimed in press reports that Al Othman had indicated that if he received a $35,000 settlement, that he would drop the assault charges. McMahon said he would have accepted the offer but than Al Othman disappeared. Complicating matters is this all occurred during Ramadan, the Muslim country's holiest holiday during which much of the country is undergoing a religious fast period and the legal system is shut down. The word among wrestlers returning from Kuwait was that the host of the show was rich and was offered a settlement by the WWF but had refused.

MAY 5

Leon White returned to the United States on 4/24 after spending ten days under house arrest in Kuwait while awaiting a hearing on charges of public aggression and public humiliation having to do with the incident on the "Good Morning Kuwait" television show.

In addition, White faces secondary charges of disorderly conduct and public drunkenness stemming from a second incident on 4/21 at the hotel he was being held at which ended up involving 20 police officers.

White, who had to promise to abide by the verdict in his trial, which is scheduled to take place in about one week before the Kuwait Court of Misdemeanors, at his hearing in order to get his passport returned and be allowed to leave Kuwait. The charges could result in a penalty of as much as one year in prison and fines, however the WWF believes ultimately the decision in all charges will only result in a fine.

After returning, the WWF attempted to use the first incident (while publicly ignoring from a television standpoint the second incident although they did acknowledge it on their hotline) to further White's heel Vader character. To this end, they held a press conference on 4/25 in Manhattan with White, in his Vader mask and somewhat in character, saying that he wasn't going to apologize for the incident and claiming that the television show's host Bassam Al Othman had initially agreed to drop charges for $25,000, but several hours later instead asked for a figure in excess of $400,000 from the WWF to drop charges, calling it a case of extortion. By this point the incident, which was a shoot in that the charges filed against White in Kuwait are real, had been incorporated into the storyline so whatever happened from that point has to be considered part of a pro wrestling storyline.

That story about the host asking for $400,000 contradicts the initial story released from the WWF saying that the host had agreed to drop charges for $35,000, a figure that Vince McMahon was willing to pay for White's release, but that the host then disappeared. The incident received substantial media play last week in the U.S., but the press conference was only covered strong locally in the New York media, although the television show "Xtra" was scheduled to do a piece on the entire incident on 4/30. The WWF's attempts to book White on "Good Morning America" on 4/25, a show which aired the incident from Kuwait on its 4/18 show, were unsuccessful.

While in the press, McMahon and Titan expressed sympathies toward White's situation claiming his actions were because a producer of the show told him to ham it up, but apparently never told the host. Mark Calaway (Undertaker) was in the studio just a few feet away while the incident took place and never appeared to be alarmed by it and never even got up or attempted to calm White down. On television they portrayed it as an angle and he as a heel who had embarrassed the company by his behavior.

White was given the weekend off WWF house shows since he hadn't been home to see his family in weeks, and returned on the 4/28 Raw taping in Omaha, NE. On that show, they teased a reprise of the angle with Jim Ross, acknowledging the "Is wrestling fake?" question, saying that every wrestler has been asked that question a million times and he should have known better than to do what he did. Vader knocked off Ross' cowboy hat and grabbed his glasses and grabbed him by the throat and teased that he was going to attack him when Ken Shamrock did a run-in and gave Vader a belly-to-belly suplex and Vader fled the scene.

MAY 12

More on the trials of Leon White in Kuwait. Dave Hebner, a WWF road agent, and an English speaking producer of "Good Morning Kuwait" arranged all the questions that would be asked of Undertaker and Vader ahead of time. Supposedly Hebner at no point agreed to a question about wrestling being fake. When Undertaker and Vader got there, they received ahead of time a list of questions they would be asked, in order, and the fake question was listed ninth. Instead, it was asked first.

White was told by the English speaking producer to be in character and act menacing, so between that, and because the Kuwait tour wasn't doing well, he figured he would do something on the TV show to try and build up the house for the rest of the tour and he knocked over the table and plants and grabbed the host. So he thought what he was doing was a work, but the host hadn't been clued in and did call the police and the arrest and charges weren't a work. At the police station, the English speaking producer told the police that it was all a work but they still pressed charges because the host didn't know.

Several days later while not allowed to leave the country, White went to the U.S. Embassy to try and get out of the situation and had a few drinks and got sick. He was looking for something to take because he was sick and went to a doctor, who smelled the alcohol on his breath and that was the situation where he was arrested for being drunk in public and more than 20 police officers came and took him down to the station although nothing further is expected to happen on the public drunk charges. The aggravated assault charges figure to wind up with White paying a decent-sized fine but no prison time.

JANUARY 12

Vader was fined 50 dinor ($166) for the deal in Kuwait where he roughed up the Good Morning Kuwait TV show host. He's still facing possible civil action in that country where the host is asking for 120,000 dinor ($398,000). He was on the KUSA news in Denver on 1/2 with tears rolling down his face saying that he was just doing what he was told, that he's not the character he plays on television and his TV persona is all an act and he thought the host was in on the angle. He was referred to in the newscast as Big Van Vader, and all the clips shown were of him in WCW.

Chapter Sixteen

Bret Hart vs. Shawn Michaels

JUNE 2

If you turn the clock back 14 months, it appeared the future of the World Wrestling Federation was based around the two men nearly everyone would consider its two top performers, Bret Hart and Shawn Michaels. The two were expected to have a classic WrestleMania match with Michaels getting the title. Hart would take a few months off and they would re-start their feud and eventually build up to another WrestleMania main event.

Long-term planning is virtually impossible in a business built around trying to get attention and ratings points on Monday nights and Tuesday mornings. But even so, if one would have figured that Hart was going to return to the WWF last fall, few would have thought it would be possible that the two would have yet to meet in the ring, and the long-awaited rematch between the two is now nowhere in sight.

Officially, the participants have been told the Bret vs. Shawn match which wasn't being pushed as the main event, but was easily the most anticipated match on the 6/8 King of the Ring show, will not be taking place. It will be replaced by Michaels vs. Steve Austin, which one would think would stem from an angle that will take place on the 6/2 Raw is War tapings from Huntington, WV. There are other changes on the card as well, which weren't clear as of press time but would include a six-man tag with Owen Hart & Davey Boy Smith & Jim Neidhart against the Legion of Doom and someone else, and that Brian Pillman wouldn't be wrestling on the show. The main reason is that Hart's recovery from knee surgery has come a lot slower than expected and he isn't expected to be ready to wrestle until sometime in July. However, the plan last week for the 10:00 match was based on the idea Bret wasn't ready to work and they would turn the match into a short angle with Michaels getting screwed in the end. But there is far more, and was far more, to the story of both men, a story that seemingly changed several times over the past week.

As everyone knows, the jealousy and dislike between the two is strong. Nobody knows where the work ends and the reality begins. At times, it seems the two who can't draw the line when it comes to the difference the most aren't the fans or the other wrestlers, but the two protagonists themselves. Keep in mind that in the current wrestling environment, the post Pillman-Sullivan angle era so to speak, that we have companies that spend an incredible amount of effort in an attempt to work a small amount of people, oftentimes neglecting the fact that the masses watching don't have a clue of the wool they're trying to have pulled over their eyes.

At the same time, with live television every Monday night, guys have the opportunity to say what they want and do a lot of what they want and the script writers have to make changes as they go along. Mankind messes up a fire spot twice while a PPV is running, and the entire angle has to be changed when Undertaker improvises on the spot. And on and on it goes.

Bret and Michaels have blurred the line between shooting and working on their interviews going back to the build-up of their 1996 WrestleMania match, through Bret's comments during his hiatus, and the comments of both after Bret returned.

The original office plan was for Bret to return around SummerSlam, and put Shawn over in a series of ladder matches. This was when the plan was to build the entire company around Shawn, and Bret would be one in a long list of challengers to headline a classic series of main events. Bret felt that the ladder match was his gimmick, an invention of the old Calgary Stampede Wrestling territory that his father ran and that he participated in several early in his career. He brought the idea to the WWF and demonstrated it in a few dark matches and made-for-video bouts, before the idea was debuted for the mass audience at the famous WrestleMania X—a match with Shawn Michaels against Razor Ramon.

Ramon won the bout, but it was Shawn who turned the ladder match into the hottest new gimmick (a short-lived identity as it turned out none of the copiers were able to do ladder matches anywhere near as well as Michaels) in wrestling. So Bret vetoed the idea of putting Michaels over again and lengthened his time off, and when he returned it was with the proviso that he'd be getting the title from Michaels at WrestleMania. Of course, a lot changed before that never happened.

It's been blurred to the point that the issue of which one will put the other over has become a heated point. Once Shawn's days as being the guy the company was going to be built around for the foreseeable future had ended—about the same time that Bret on the sidelines became the new savior and the hottest commodity in wrestling, so now it was Shawn's turn since Bret did the first one.

To this day Bret hasn't forgiven Hulk Hogan for what he perceives, and there is a lot of truth to this, that Hogan bailed out on the WWF rather than put Bret, his promotion picked successor, over clean at SummerSlam in 1993, voluntarily dropping the title to "big" Yokozuna on a fluke rather than putting "little" Bret over clean since Hogan came from the period where size ruled and even when standards in the business change, the guys whose heyday were under previous standards, can almost never change with the times.

Of course Hogan's problems with Vince McMahon at that time were likely a lot deeper than just being asked to drop the strap to Bret Hart. Naturally Michaels' knee injury, which the vast majority of those within wrestling believe was more a personality collapse and a business move for Michaels to avoid doing two key jobs in a row, the second would have been to his most hated rival, only made Bret feel the same way, if not more strongly.

On Raw on 5/12, Bret babbled on and on at the end of the show leaving Michaels standing there like an idiot to the point the show went off the air before Michaels got his comeback, the superkick spot which people had to wait five days to see. While most WWF officials seem to believe that it was simply Bret missing his time cue, Michaels, and his friends who are in his ear, believe Bret was double-crossing him on live television to make him look stupid.

On 5/19, Michaels showed up at the Raw taping in Mobile, AL and appeared to be in no condition to perform. When he was on television, he was slurring his words badly and made a remark that Bret was having some Sunny days, a remark that naturally sent the rumor mills buzzing all week.

The unfortunate thing in the age of the Internet is that wrestling stars have now become like television stars in the tabloids, and because of that, the work feud can carry over into real life because the public at large doesn't differentiate between the fantasy world and the reality world. It isn't as if Bret's family wasn't well aware of what Shawn was supposed to be saying and for every rumor, whether real or otherwise of that type, there will be plenty of people ready to make up confirmation of such, and you can imagine how someone's wife and young kids will react.

But the situation with Michaels over the past weeks has gone far deeper than making shoot comments after being told not to, slurring his words on live television, wearing a bandanna on his head on television to signify to the world he's still best friends with Kevin Nash, complaining backstage about having to do an interview putting Ken Shamrock over, or even walking out on the company the day he was supposed to drop his title, and not returning until after the WrestleMania that he was supposed to return the favor from the biggest victory of his career, thereby screwing up nearly one year of promotion and being a key factor in the show during a poor buy rate and the company being down literally millions of dollars in revenue from its biggest show of the year.

The enigma of being arguably the most talented performer in American rings and seemingly being ill-equipped emotionally to handle the spot his talent has gotten him, came out again in recent weeks.

Michaels became at odds with Vince McMahon by demanding a new contract, one that would put his pay at the same level as his rival, who fell into a bidding war and came out of it with the most lucrative guaranteed money contract in the history of the WWF. When McMahon turned down his demands, he gave his notice, wanting to join his "real friends" in WCW. With four years remaining on his contract, McMahon refused, and the general attitude during the week was that they had no idea where Michaels' head was and contingency plans were being made both for television and the PPV and house shows if Michaels wasn't going to appear.

There are reports that Michaels had a contract clause that was to guarantee him the status of being the highest paid wrestler in the company. What exactly happened, and how the contract with Hart was structured, is unknown in regard to how this has all and will all play out. In WCW, Scott Hall and Kevin Nash have contracts guaranteeing them to be the second-highest paid (behind Hogan) in the company, but were both willing to waive that clause in order for WCW to sign Bret.

The feeling during the week seemed to be that if Michaels were to quit the promotion, that they would do everything they could to enforce the contract and make him sit out the next four years rather than go to WCW. Michaels had signed a five-year contract shortly after getting the title with a downside guarantee believed to be in the $750,000 per year range and having the top spot during a period where house shows are doing well and the merchandising that goes with the top spot, he figured to earn significantly more than that.

At the time Michaels, figuring he was going to be the long-term king of the promotion, seemed more than happy to sign the deal and was outwardly bragging when the subject of his buddies leaving for WCW about how the opposition couldn't afford to pay him what he was making. Michaels was a huge success in some ways as champion. His PPV matches for the most part were excellent, with a few exceptions. House show business was very good. Of course, television ratings plummeted and he regularly seemed on the verge of self destruction, freaking out way more than he should have over bad time cues, heckling crowds, a timing problem on a high spot, or even musical screw-ups.

His dropping the title the first time was more an angle to build up a monster house in San Antonio, which ultimately proved successful. But the reality of the WrestleMania screw-up was a decision as much by McMahon as Michaels—the idea that the match the company spent a year building would be a non-title co-feature and that he was going back to the big guys, Sid and Undertaker for the main event title match. So while Michaels walking out destroyed the biggest match on the supposed biggest show of the year in the United States, it was a corporate decision that destroyed it being the biggest match to begin with.

In hindsight, one would think if Vince McMahon had a crystal ball, he may have reacted a lot differently when it comes to matching offers that WCW had made for both Nash and Scott Hall, although I've always been told that is likely the case with Hall, but not Nash, who the feeling was that the company felt was more trouble than he was worth after being a failure as champion.

There were complaints about the WWF not competing when it comes to negotiations with top talent on a level playing field because WCW can offer the top stars more money and at the same time have them work less dates and certainly the industry belief is that WCW has a less-restrictive if non-existent or unenforced drug policy.

On the first two points, the field in any entertainment field is never level and the situation isn't all that different from a decade earlier when the roles were reversed. The idea of a less restrictive drug policy being a means to lure talent is a sad commentary if there is truth to it, and the fact of the matter is that everyone inside the business knows full well there was some truth to that belief, whether outwardly expressed or just understood. However, it isn't as if the WWF hasn't all but eliminated drug testing and if drug problems are singular to any one company or not prevalent in every major company in this industry.

The match with Hart was already pretty well being scrapped, largely because Hart himself wasn't going to be able to make it back in time. That situation was explained in storyline fashion on the 5/26 Raw when after Michaels & Steve Austin beat Owen Hart & Davey Boy Smith in a excellent tag title change, Austin attacked Bret's injured knee.

Several people close to Bret are saying that Bret is actually, when he gets the chance, going to punch Michaels out, and although he is saying that to friends, nobody knows how much of that is bluster or a work, although the emotion behind it most feel is clearly a shoot after Michaels went "too far" with that remark. Or is that all a carefully designed work as well?

The decision for Michaels & Austin to win the tag team titles was apparently made at a booking meeting on 5/23, although at the time the decision was made, the future of Michaels wasn't clear. Michaels showed up on 5/26, wrestled his first match since early February, and showed no signs of injury or ring-rust, and could very reasonably be described after his performance in the tag title match as being the best performer in the United States.

He stood out in a match that included Austin, the hottest wrestler in the company and a top-notch worker, and the inconsistent former tag champs, who are as talented as they come when they have their working shoes on and decidedly did have them on in the television match. On 6/2, Michaels & Austin defend the belts against the Legion of Doom, who were initially promised to win the tag belts on the 6/8 PPV. Don't take that as a sign the belts are going to change hands again, just because logic seems to indicate a title change and break-up situation.

JUNE 9

The photo of Michaels wearing an Outsiders t-shirt appears in the July issue of one of the Napolitano magazines, which should further endear Michaels to the WWF. One more note regarding Michaels and his contract. If he did have a written clause saying he was guaranteed to be the highest paid guy in the company and McMahon didn't renegotiate his contract when Bret got the better deal, then that's a contract breach and he could leave anytime he wants. The fact that he can't leave tells me there is more to the story.

JUNE 23

Heat from fantasy feuds and storylines in this attempted shoot environment spilled out into real life dressing room problems on 6/9. The end result was no serious injuries, but Michaels' future with the WWF is questionable.

The incident took place at approximate 7:20 p.m. in Michaels' dressing room resulting in both Hart and Michaels not appearing on the live show from Hartford, CT that they were originally both supposed to play a prominent role in.

The problems had been brewing for a long time, for well over one year as has been well documented in these pages. Although skeptics could try and label the incident, since it involved wrestlers who have a bitter feud in the storyline as promotions and wrestlers attempting to work the boys in doing angles for the hardcores ala the Brian Pillman-Kevin Sullivan angle which in many ways changed the entire face of pro wrestling and not necessarily for the better, that was absolutely not the case.

The problems between Hart and Michaels, bad seemingly forever based on professional jealousy based on who would be the top star and highest paid wrestler in the company and who would put the other over in their next meeting and if they ever would have a next meeting, some of which has become ironic since in their personal battle, Steve Austin and probably Undertaker as well passed them both by when it comes to being the top star although not the highest paid.

They got hot in recent weeks when Michaels believed that Hart stalled out a live interview on Raw to where the show went off the air before Michaels could do his superkick comeback, which was shown on tape later in the week. As revenge of sorts, Michaels said that Bret had been seeing "Sunny days" on the next week's television show despite both Michaels and Hart supposedly having been told by management to quit doing insider references that the majority of the viewing audience doesn't understand.

That remark, combined with a remark made months ago by Michaels on television saying that Bret professes to be a role model but he's seen him on the road and he's no role model, apparently caused friction in Bret's personal life to the point that Hart had been telling friends for weeks that he was going to at some point soon punch Michaels out.

Nobody, including Michaels, would debate that should Hart have chosen to start a fight with Michaels that Michaels would come out of it unscathed. But a lot of people didn't believe he'd do it since Hart has the reputation for being such a professional, not to mention that with his knee in the shape it's in, this would be a foolish time for him to do so. Nevertheless the rumors throughout the WWF locker room were that if Hart got the chance, he'd take a poke at Michaels.

Apparently the problems escalated before the show on 6/9 as both were meeting in long personal conversations with Vince McMahon, to the point that McMahon was having little time to converse with anyone else regarding details and attention to the ensuing live television show.

Hart wound up going into Michaels dressing room and the two began arguing. There were eye witnesses to this which basically said they argued and started fighting, and it was rather quickly broken up. Most versions have it that Hart was screaming about how Michaels comments affected his personal life and he crossed the line and that Michaels was a smart-ass back. The two went at it, with most versions having it that Hart started it but that Michaels was every bit as guilty in precipitating it. It was believed to have been a one-sided short tussle which resulted in a few punches thrown and a large clump of Michaels' hair being pulled out of his head to the point it was described that Michaels was given a major bald spot. Michaels face was all puffed up from the punches and he was bleeding from the elbow, apparently from being thrown on the floor. Hart apparently aggravated his recently repaired knee, but none of the injuries were serious.

Agents Jerry Brisco and Pat Patterson and some other wrestlers quickly broke it up with Hart on top of Michaels pounding on him, and Brisco and Hart argued loudly back-and-forth in another room for a long time before Hart finally left the arena at about 8:30 p.m. without appearing on the television show. Michaels was blown up from the fight and a little worse for wear, but not injured to the point he couldn't have appeared on the television show.

Michaels was scheduled to wrestle Brian Pillman in the television main event, doing the run-in after the Hart Foundation were all scheduled to jump Austin as he was coming down the aisle for the match. The Austin vs. Pillman match that had been hyped all week was canceled because Austin injured his right knee (the good one) by landing wrong on it coming off the top rope during a spot in the previous night's match with Michaels. The knee was swollen badly to the point they decided to keep him out of the ring on 6/9 although he was willing to gut out doing the match, because they didn't want him being hurt any worse and with all the other problems, add Austin to the list of guys who would be missing the upcoming weekend's major shows in Montreal and Toronto.

Michaels was going crazy after the predicament and said that he would never work against anyone in the Hart Foundation because he couldn't trust them. He ended up walking out of the building claiming that he couldn't work or stay in this kind of an environment just before the show was scheduled to go on the air at 7:57 p.m.

Other performers claim as he left the building that he was screaming about how he was quitting and that if he could make it to Boston (where Nitro was being done live) on time he'd just as soon go there. At that point the entire television show had to be scrapped and a new show put together literally minutes before it went on the air.

The main changes involved doing three angles with Ken Shamrock to put him into the mix as Shamrock will be put in Michaels' spot in the ten man tag team main event at the next PPV on 7/6, the Canadian Stampede. Shamrock teams with Sid, Austin and the Legion of Doom against Bret, Owen, Davey Boy Smith, Jim Neidhart and Pillman. Mankind was then made the replacement for Austin in Pillman's first major television match, but the match totally fell flat because there wasn't much to it. It was a major letdown with all the hype of Austin vs. Pillman both on television all week and throughout the live television show airing clips of the ankle breaking angle, the breaking into Pillman's house angle and Austin sticking Pillman's head in the toilet bowl the previous night. In addition, Mankind isn't over as a babyface at this point the way everyone expected he would be and Pillman is limited in what he can do in the ring with his ankle still in tremendous pain.

Exactly how this affects other schedule matches is unclear, although almost all of Michaels scheduled house show matches involved members of the Hart Foundation including a first meeting with Bret in a triangle match scheduled for the 6/28 head-to-head showdown in Anaheim/Los Angeles which at press time barring a reconciliation will now be changed. If Michaels won't work with the Hart Foundation, it'll make it extremely difficult to use him in an effective manner since they are the lead heels and his most natural program is with Bret.

On the live show, Vince McMahon did address the situation saying late in the show that both men had been sent home from the arena due to conduct unbecoming unprofessional. Jim Ross acknowledged the incident on the WWF hotline calling it a fistfight and not going into anymore details other than making it clear it was not an angle, that Michaels had walked out of the WWF, that he didn't know what the results of it would be but acted like he wasn't sure of the future of the WWF tag team championship with Michaels & Austin as a team and that a decision about it would be made this week.

On 6/10, McMahon sent an internal memo out to WWF executives saying, "Last night in Hartford, Shawn Michaels breached his contract by refusing to perform. We are hopeful Shawn will reconsider his position and return to work. Shawn has four years to go on his five-year contract. The door is open for Shawn to return under the terms of his contract."

By virtue of that memo, at press time it would have to be concluded that unless a reconciliation takes place, that for the time being Michaels won't be appearing on the house shows advertised or future television shows but there are no official replacements matches aside from the change in Calgary since the incident had just taken place.

What happens next should Michaels not return is a really tricky situation. If he doesn't perform, Michaels could and likely would be suspended without pay. The question becomes can Titan theoretically if things don't work out, suspend him for four years without pay. Would they continue to pay him his downside guarantee, believed to be close to $15,000 per week, for not working to keep them from breaching his contract and enabling him to go to WCW? Would they give him a limited release allowing him to work elsewhere in the world besides WCW, which is where he says he wants to go? Or could Michaels use the fight and other incidents in the past such as when he was given a scare by the Harris Brothers (who were on their way out at the time but eventually brought back) in the dressing room at Madison Square Garden and try to claim an unsafe working environment as a way to claim he should be legally let out of his contract to go to WCW, where he claims he wants to be.

Michaels and his father had a meeting at McMahon's request on 5/18 to air out their problems, at which time Michaels told McMahon that he wanted out of his contract to go to WCW and McMahon claimed Michaels told him that if he went to WCW, "I could be set for life." McMahon refused to let him out of his contract.

That statement about being set for life brings yet another question to mind, that of potential contractual interference by WCW, a charge that has been made whenever major stars under contract to either ECW or WWF have jumped to WCW and has been claimed by WWF in the Curt Hennig case. Reports that Michaels had a clause in his contract that guaranteed him being the highest paid wrestler in the company turned out to not be true, however Michaels has claimed he and McMahon had a verbal deal on such when he signed his contract.

Since that time Hart signed a far more lucrative 20-year deal with McMahon since he was the subject of a bidding war. Michaels also claimed to friends that McMahon told him that if he was ever unhappy in the WWF that he would be free to go. McMahon did make that promise to Ric Flair years ago and allowed Flair to return to WCW in 1993 despite having time left on his contract, but the situations were far different then as compared with now and others close to the situation are skeptical of the latter story if only because the whole reason McMahon has broken his longstanding business practices by signing every major wrestler in the company to guaranteed money long-term contracts is so he can keep them from going to WCW.

JUNE 30

After a week in which it appeared the future of Shawn Michaels in the World Wrestling Federation was uncertain in the wake of a legitimate backstage fight with Bret Hart, it now appears Michaels will be returning in a few weeks.

Michaels, 31, had cussed out Vince McMahon, reportedly saying something to the effect of "I'll never work for your f***in ass again" while leaving the Hartford Civic Center about a half hour before the live Raw television show was to begin on 6/9. This came after a fight with Hart which was quickly broken up, but not before he had a large clump of hair pulled from his head.

Supposedly Hart and Michaels began a heated discussion largely about Michaels now infamous "Sunny days" remark on television saying he'd gone over the line. Supposedly Michaels responded with a cocky "What are you going to do about it?" type of remark which set Hart off and started the fight. The general feeling was that Michaels was provoking an incident with his retort, although Hart wasn't considered blameless since he was the one who threw the first punch.

Michaels was telling people on Tuesday that he was done with the WWF and would sit out the next four years of his contract rather then return. Logically that wasn't going to happen and the question was more when he'd return, although Michaels could have sat out a long period of time since he received a seven-figure inheritance from a wrestling fan of his that passed away and has made a lot of money in the WWF over the past five years as a singles headliner.

The WWF claimed Michaels had breached his contract by walking out in Hartford and he didn't appear on the weekend shows in Montreal and Toronto where he was scheduled in singles matches against Davey Boy Smith for the European title. The contract breach basically meant that the WWF wasn't going to have to pay him his estimated $15,000 per week guarantee until he agreed to return. As the week went on, Michaels disconnected his telephone making it impossible for WWF officials to attempt to smooth things over with him.

However, by the end of the week, his feelings seemingly changed. Michaels' attorney sent the WWF a letter saying that Michaels hadn't breached his contract, but that he was injured in the fight with Hart, claiming both knee and neck injuries and that he would be unable to wrestle for four to six weeks. He requested a meeting with McMahon in San Antonio on 6/19 for both sides to settle their differences and the WWF is making plans now with the idea that Michaels will start back around the latter part of July.

Plans seem to be from a storyline standpoint to keep Michaels and Hart apart so it isn't like they'll turn this into an angle for a SummerSlam match due to problems, as obviously it's a match that people are interested in seeing. On the weekend Live Wire and Superstars cable shows, they read a statement from Jim Ross talking about the situation, saying that Michaels was in a contract breach and had seemingly left the WWF and that neither man was injured in the fight.

On Raw on 6/16, after hearing from Michaels attorney over the weekend, they opened the show saying that neither of those statements on the weekend television turned out to be true, that Michaels would return to the WWF, and perhaps be on television the following week, that Hart was expected on television the following week.

Hart wanted to do a live interview on the 6/16 Raw to turn his fight into a wrestling angle and give his side of the situation in his typical semi-shooting work fashion but for whatever reason, likely to avoid antagonizing Michaels, it was decided against using Hart on the live show for fear he might say something Michaels would take the wrong way on a live interview.

It was also said on television that both men were injured in the fight, citing Michaels' aforementioned injuries and that Hart re-aggravated his knee injury (he's expected back on 6/28 for the Anaheim house show), using that as the reason he wasn't at Raw although they did show a tape of him doing an interview from 6/14 in Toronto.

The situation with the tag team championship was announced as them having a tournament on Raw, which began on 6/16, with the tournament winners facing Austin and a partner of his choosing in a title match. This idea was formulated when it appeared Michaels wasn't going to be around, but since the tournament was already put on paper, with the idea Michaels will be around, they decided to go with it and Michaels may or may not be

Austin's partner when that match rolls around.

With just three weeks to go until the Calgary PPV, the line-up for that show is very much in the air. The only match officially announced is the main event, which is now scheduled as Bret & Owen Hart & Jim Neidhart & Brian Pillman & Davey Boy Smith vs. Goldust & Ken Shamrock & Steve Austin & Legion of Doom. Goldust was put in Sid's original spot in a change that was made before the auto accident. Don't know why that change was made—perhaps Goldust was put in to do the job since they may not have wanted to beat Sid again—perhaps they just felt it would be a more attractive show with a Sid vs. Vader match underneath.

Since we don't know the extent of Sid's injuries, the match with Vader has yet to be announced nor do we know at press time if it will happen. Vader himself has not returned after surgery on his nose and he was originally scheduled back for the Canadian shows over the weekend.

They shot the angle to lead to the Undertaker vs. Ahmed Johnson WWF title match on the 6/16 Raw. The other scheduled match that should be etched in stone is Mankind vs. Hunter Hearst Helmsley. In Japan it was announced that Great Sasuke would face Taka Michinoku on the Calgary PPV, and that is also planned to happen, although the final details on that match hadn't been solidified at last word.

SEPTEMBER 22

Probably the biggest news of the past week revolved around Shawn Michaels' behavior at the Raw taping on 9/9 in Muncie, IN. Neither Vince McMahon nor Undertaker were at the taping, and Michaels did an interview where he came out in tight biker shorts with a sock or socks stuffed in his crotch for whatever reason and proceeded to make some very lewd gyrations like acting as if he was humping Jim Ross, swearing during his interview and called out Undertaker who was on a tape on the video wall. Everything was able to be edited off the show, and if you didn't know about the incident, you wouldn't even know the interview was heavily edited.

Since Undertaker wasn't there, but since he was on a tape on the wall people thought he was, when Michaels kept insulting him, calling him a big chickenshit, and begging him to come out and call him more names when he didn't come out, it made Undertaker look bad in the city, not to mention it being totally unprofessional. Whether Michaels was doing it in another attempt to get fired so he could go to WCW or he had other ideas up his sleeve, it's definitely brought a lot more negativity toward him in a lot of circles.

Chapter Seventeen

NJPW vs. AJPW

JUNE 16

All Japan and New Japan had a wrestling war of sorts with consecutive nights at Budokan Hall on 6/5 and 6/6.

From an attendance standpoint, All Japan, which traditionally runs its major shows in that building, won out. All Japan announced its crowd as a sellout 16,300 on 6/6. New Japan announced its crowd on 6/5 at 14,000. Reports from people who attended both nights said that All Japan's show was totally full, while New Japan was almost, but not completely full.

All Japan, which always announces a sellout 16,300 at Budokan even though most of the time the crowds are closer to 14,000, ran its biggest singles match of the year on top with the annual Mitsuharu Misawa vs. Toshiaki Kawada Budokan Hall classic. Apparently this match lived up to that billing as it was reported to us as the single best match of the year with Misawa scoring a pin with a German suplex in 31:22 to retain the Triple Crown. Kawada destroyed Misawa with moves such as a power bomb on the floor and a long stretch plum with Misawa getting to the ropes. Kawada dropped him on his head four times in a row, but Misawa got up and hit a desperation forearm. Misawa then used forearm after forearm to knock Kawada out, although he did a few dramatic kick outs before the German suplex finish.

It was the 15th time the two had wrestled in singles matches during their careers, dating back to 1982. Misawa won the first four meetings in 1982-83 when they were both undercard green wrestlers. They never met again in singles until October 21, 1992 at Budokan Hall, by which time Misawa was Triple Crown champion and made his first title defense by pinning Kawada in 29:52. All in all, Misawa has ten wins and there have been four 30:00 time limit draws. Kawada's lone win came as part of the triangle match in the Champion Carnival finals on 4/19 at Budokan Hall which set up this match.

New Japan had a deeper show, headlining with the return of Keiji Muto after the NWO angle in the United States, challenging Shinya Hashimoto for the IWGP heavyweight title. The match was said to have been very good, although not nearly on the level of the match the next night. The big surprise is that Muto wrestled a total babyface style and Muto didn't act as if he was part of the NWO. The intrigue in how Muto would behave was one of the major selling points of the match. Apparently the storyline is that Keiji Muto is a New Japan babyface, but Great Muta is an NWO heel. Hashimoto ended up winning the match after two DDT's in 26:01.

Also on the show was the finals of the Top of the Super Junior tournament where El Samurai pinned Koji Kanemoto in 23:51. Kanemoto unmasked Samurai at 17:00 and Samurai wrestled the remainder of the match with his face totally exposed. He won the match after hitting three reverse DDT's (slop drop) to capture his first ever junior tournament championship. In the other title match on the show, Satoshi Kojima & Manabu Nakanishi retained the IWGP tag team titles beating NWO Sting & Masahiro Chono in 14:15 when Kojima pinned Sting after a lariat.

There were three other key matches on the show. The legendary Satoru Sayama vs. Kuniaki Kobayashi feud from 1982-83 was revisited with Sayama wrestling as Tiger King and winning with a cross armbreaker in what was said to have been a so-so match. An eight-man junior heavyweight tag team match saw Gran Naniwa & Dr. Wagner Jr. & Chris Jericho & Jushin Liger beat Tatsuhito Takaiwa & Yoshihiro Tajiri & Hanzo Nakajima & Shinjiro Otani in 13:45 when Liger pinned Takaiwa with an inside cradle as Takaiwa was doing his series of power bomb finishes, cradling him after the fourth power bomb. The other interesting match saw Big Japan tag team champions Takashi Ishikawa & Kengo Kimura, who won the tournament two days earlier to become the first champions, come out wearing the belts on a New Japan show and beat Riki Choshu & Osamu Kido when Kimura pinned Kido in 10:55.

The Misawa-Kawada match was more like a monster movie than a wrestling match in that both competitors continually rose from the dead time-after-time. At the finish, both men collapsed and were taken to the dressing room. The traditional end of a Budokan show is the presentation of the title belt and trophy to the winner after the match, but Misawa never came back out for the presentation to sell just how physically taxing the match was supposed to have been.

The other important match on the All Japan show was the semifinal, where Kenta Kobashi & Johnny Ace & The Patriot beat Steve Williams & Gary Albright & The Lacrosse (real name Jim Roche). Kobashi & Ace & Patriot announced before the match their new team name at "GET" which stands for Global, Energisch (?), Tough. The finish of this match came at 22:00 when Williams was given a triple team power bomb and pinned clean by Ace after a cobra suplex. It was a huge surprise for the finish since Ace has never pinned Williams during his career and basically is another step in the attempt to position Ace at the same level as Williams and Stan Hansen when it comes to foreign stars.

It's really surprising to see Patriot get this kind of a push because he has signed his multi-year WWF contract and is expected to debut toward the latter part of the summer and it's believed his next All Japan tour, which ends 7/25, will be his last tour with the company. Besides Patriot, both Sabu and Rob Van Dam have also quit All Japan which actually led to a heated situation on the final night of the show.

Sabu quit the promotion because he was mad about how he was positioned as an undercard wrestler who put over the top names when he was in the ring with them. The straw that broke the camel's back apparently was him having to put Giant Kimala II over on 6/4 in Takasaka and both Sabu and Van Dam quit that night effective the end of the tour two days later. Sabu's lengthy All Japan deal wound up lasting all of three tours.

Van Dam had been considering leaving for quite a while so chose Sabu's leaving to be his time to leave as well. Despite Van Dam's stature in the U.S. going way up based on ECW, and on the verge of going up even more with the WWF feud, his stature in Japan hasn't changed much since he started going to All Japan and really never has done anything big with the group since his memorable junior heavyweight title match against Dan Kroffat (Phil LaFon). On this tour he put over PWF jr. champion Yoshinari Ogawa in a singles title match.

Due to Sabu's reputation from other groups in Japan, the promotion, which usually pays the wrestlers for the tour the afternoon of the Budokan show, refused to pay them until after Budokan, apparently trying to make sure they wouldn't no-show the big show. At this show they, even though it was their final show, were put over Yoshinari Ogawa & Tsuyoshi Kikuchi when Van Dam pinned Ogawa in 8:48. However Sabu wasn't allowed to do any of his gimmick spots during the match and apparently the wrestlers stationed around the ring were given orders to make sure the match went according to plans.

This makes the fifth promotion that Sabu has left in Japan over the past few years, including both majors. It's expected that both Sabu and Van Dam will return to Japan as part of the ECW contingent when ECW makes deals to work with whatever promotion it ends up working with, which is expected at this point to be either WAR or FMW with the belief being the former is the more likely.

CHAPTER EIGHTEEN

RIKI CHOSHU RETIRES

JUNE 30

The announcement of the retirement of Riki Choshu at a press conference in Tokyo on 6/19 was surprising, but only for the humorous candor.

Choshu, real name Mitsuo Yoshida, 45, announced that he would only wrestle eight more matches before retiring on the January 4, 1998 show at the Tokyo Dome to conclude a pro career of more than 23 years. He also announced an added show to the New Japan schedule, which would have a retirement ceremony for him, on 8/31 at the Yokohama Arena.

Choshu cited an injury to his right shoulder which makes it impossible to lift his famous lariat arm, as the main reason for the retirement. He strongly suggested and it was widely believed that unlike nearly every pro wrestling retirement of a major star, this one is legitimate.

Choshu has been hinting and talking retirement for nearly two years, first in late 1995 after exhaustion had taken its toll on him after an incredible last three-weeks of a promotion of the October 9, 1995 Tokyo Dome show with UWFI that resulted in what still is the largest live gate in pro wrestling in history, $6.1 million, and biggest crowd ever to attend an indoor sporting event in Japan, 67,000. A few days after that event, with Choshu claiming he hadn't gotten much sleep over the previous several weeks, he strongly hinted he'd be out of the ring by early 1996.

However, he never officially announced a retirement and used 1996 as his final run for glory, capturing the G-1 tournament in a week where he secretly screwed up his knee on the first night and struggled through the week to complete his planned comeback story after he had announced beforehand would be his final G-1 tournament, in highly dramatic fashion.

This set up his final world title challenge at the 1/4 Tokyo Dome, which even with the weakest undercard for a Dome show in years, his challenge to Shinya Hashimoto's IWGP heavyweight title resulted in a sellout of 62,500 fans—the fifth time in his career he headlined a show that drew more than 50,000 fans, a figure that only two or three men in history can claim. But even last year the general feeling was that Choshu's final push of himself in the G-1 tournament and challenging Hashimoto in the Dome main event was his final hurrah, and that he would be out of the ring by the end of 1997.

The humor in the press conference was Choshu after being asked if he would ever make a comeback from his retirement and he responded something to the effect of, "Never. Unless New Japan becomes a poor company (business hits the skids)."

Choshu will concentrate on his primary duties of the past several years as being the head booker for New Japan and the most powerful force in its front office and would also like to help train new wrestlers for the company. While Choshu's career resume as a wrestler firmly establishes himself as a Hall of Famer in this industry, his records set while being a booker actually blow away his credentials in the ring.

As a wrestler, he came from an amateur background which included winning the Japanese collegiate championships at Senshu College, placing highly in American tournaments in the early 70s while with the vaunted New York Athletic Club, and going to the 1972 Olympics in Greco-roman wrestling representing South Korea (something that was largely kept secretive for most of his career due to the racial problems between Japanese and Koreans).

He left amateur wrestling with a decent amount of fanfare in late 1973 for New Japan, which heavily publicized his signing, and debuted on August 8, 1974 in Tokyo beating El Bello Greco of Mexico under his real name. He was rechristened Riki Choshu in April 1977, having to do with the most famous name ever in Japanese wrestling being Rikidozan.

After returning from Mexico where he held the UWA world heavyweight title, he very much changed the entire face and course of Japanese wrestling with his 1982 angle where he turned on Tatsumi Fujinami and formed the Ishingun group, the single most successful predecessor to the current WCW/NWO booking concept. This led to one of the most successful years when it came to house show business of any wrestling company in history.

New Japan in 1983 sold out 90 percent of its house show dates and earned a profit that year of $9 million. Before that angle, Japanese wrestling generally revolved around a patterned Japanese natives vs. Gaijins, or foreigners, as the top attractions. But when Choshu and his group "pulled out" of New Japan to form their own company but still worked within the New Japan company, which included the likes of Yoshiaki Yatsu, Masa Saito, Animal Hamaguchi, Killer Khan, Kuniaki Kobayashi and numerous others began doing basically an NWO against the traditional group of Antonio Inoki, Tatsumi Fujinami, Kengo Kimura, Seiji Sakaguchi and Akira Maeda, the box office success couldn't be denied and its success directly carries over to the main angle that changed American wrestling 14 years later. It led to a greatly lessened importance on American talent in the Japanese marketplace, and resulted in a boom period where record gates were set by Japanese vs. Japanese in angles that were worked to appear to be inter-promotional.

Choshu and company, in one of the biggest stories in the history of Japanese wrestling, changed the entire power balance of the business in Japan in late 1984 when they quit New Japan to join All Japan, leading All Japan to a year of incredible business and television ratings. But in 1987, Choshu, and most of the rest of his group, jumped back to New Japan, which ultimately changed the balance of power back to where it has largely stayed the past decade.

This was strongly against Japanese culture at the time where a worker, once he left college, would join a company and stay with the company for life. The public accepted Choshu's first jump because of all the problems in New Japan with an embezzlement scandal that rocked the company. But many soured on Choshu and the wrestling industry by late 1987 when he jumped back, because there were no allegations of improprieties when it came to All Japan, and his behavior was seen as like a greedy American athlete as opposed to a pure sportsman as Japanese in those days liked to consider their national hero athletes to be, and many blamed Choshu's actions for a short-term decline in wrestling's popularity.

But upon his return, Choshu picked up a power base within New Japan, and with Antonio Inoki leaving the company to become a senator, by 1989, he became the most powerful entity in the front office and the group's lead booker (although he was not officially given the title until 1991). His first major show that he booked was the very first wrestling show ever at the Tokyo Dome on April 24, 1989 which drew what at the time was a Japanese record crowd of 53,800 fans and an all-time pro wrestling record of a $2.8 million gate, records that have been shattered many times since then.

The Choshu booking philosophy was apparent on that show as Inoki lost his first ever mixed match to

Russian judo champion Shota Chochyashivili, and Choshu, the odds-on-favorite, lost in the first round of a one-night tournament for the vacant IWGP heavyweight title to unheralded 23-year-old Hashimoto. The creation of Hashimoto as a major star dates back to this match, which in the long run created his atypical long-time world champion and one of the biggest drawing major show headliners in history. He also established Big Van Vader, already a long-time headliner, as the monster foreign superstar as he beat Hashimoto in the finals to win the title on what at the time was the biggest show ever.

It was approximately from this period that Choshu instituted the almost all clean finish philosophy, largely following in the steps of the highly successful UWF office, and eliminated the famous Japanese double count out finish that was in vogue in many if not most of the main events between big names during the 70s and most of the 80s in Japan.

Choshu's loss to Hashimoto became symbolic of New Japan booking, later spreading to assistant bookers Hiroshi Hase and Keiichi Yamada (Jushin Liger) in that the bookers themselves set the example for rest of the company by putting people over in the cleanest fashion possible, often to lesser level stars and lesser workers to create new stars and new programs.

This was probably best exemplified in the very first G-1 tournament in the summer of 1991, where Choshu put Hashimoto, Bam Bam Bigelow and Masahiro Chono over clean in going 0-3, setting the stage for New Japan's big run with Hashimoto, Keiji Muto and Chono as the top stars and he more in the shadows, and the shocking story of the top star in the group doing three jobs, along with career performances by most of the talent, in one week created one of the biggest tournaments in the industry that is now in its seventh year. The memories of that paid major dividends five summers later when Choshu, who had never won a G-1, announced just before the 1996 tournament that it would be his final one.

In addition, strong style, or more believable wrestling, became the core of the New Japan philosophy, which led to a run of popularity among hardcore fans and gates the likes of which had never been seen before in pro wrestling history.

There was a downside. In the long run that hurt it as a television entity as the work became more technical and the characters became less outlandish. Since that time, Choshu has produced and booked 16 shows that have drawn in excess of 50,000 fans and drawn live gates that no other booker in pro wrestling history has ever approached. However, there have been signs, particularly in recent months, of the Choshu booking philosophy going stale as New Japan has been in a rut of late with no fresh storylines.

In addition, New Japan had to cancel a Tokyo Dome show in October of 1996 because of its inability to do business with Royce Gracie, who the show was to be built around, and nearly found themselves in the same situation this past April after adding another Dome show when they believed they had put together a Hashimoto vs. Ken Shamrock match that fell through when Shamrock went to WWF and resulted in the company having to heavily paper this past April's show.

In addition, even though the angle to set up the October 9, 1995 Tokyo Dome show was among the greatest and most important angles in history, the follow-up of the New Japan vs. UWFI feud, with New Japan basically destroying the financially strapped smaller office, served only to cut the legs out of what could have been a far stronger program when it came to longevity. Still, even with the flaws, mistakes and current staleness, any listing of the great bookers in the history of the industry that wouldn't have Choshu in or near the top spot for his eight-year run would have to be laughable for its ignorance.

Although Choshu was able to pull out a classic dramatic match with Hashimoto in the first round of the G-1 tournament last August, and an excellent Dome world title match main event in January, for the most part he has been very limited in the ring for the past year. Even in his heyday, he was really a guy who built a match around a few signature spots. The Saito suplex, a move popularized by its namesake and one of Choshu's pro wrestling mentors. The lariat, popularized already in Japan by Stan Hansen. And the sasorigatamae (scorpion deathlock). The latter move Choshu didn't invent, but he was the one who popularized the move worldwide it and made in the in vogue move in wrestling in the mid-80s which led to Sting and Bret Hart making it their trademark move later in the decade.

But he got by through having tag team partners who were incredible workers, a great sense of timing and drama, and a level of charisma matched by only a few performers in the history of the business.

In the Hashimoto series, the real storyline was a shoot. You had a legend, whose body was aching from two decades plus in the ring mainly as a headliner, who was going to suck it up and take as much brutality as possible to deliver a few memorable moments on the way out. While it paled in comparison to what Terry Funk has done many times over, Choshu will go out with fan's final remembrances of his wrestling career as the week in August where he won the G-1 setting up his last world title shot, where he put Hashimoto over one more time and not with the memory of someone who stuck around years too long to where they were a shadow of their former legend.

Besides the UWA heavyweight title, Choshu also held the PWF heavyweight title (one of the belts part of the current All Japan Triple Crown), and International tag team titles (part of today's Double tag team title with All Japan) during his tenure in All Japan. With New Japan, he held basically every heavyweight title in the company including three reigns as IWGP heavyweight champion, although none since 1992.

Chapter Nineteen

WWF vs. WCW:
The Battle of Los Angeles

JUNE 9

Sending the likes of Ric Flair, Sting, Eric Bischoff and Bobby Heenan to Los Angeles on 5/30 for the biggest first-day promotion in WCW history resulted in what would have to be called a solid but not spectacular first day of sales for WCW's show on 6/28 at the Great Western Forum in Los Angeles.

The show, billed as "Saturday Nitro" in which the WCW announcing team will all appear for a non-televised card, that goes head-to-head with a WWF event the same night at the Anaheim Pond, sold just under 4,000 tickets for $98,000 the first day and as of 6/2 the numbers had increased to 5,054 tickets and $120,651. The WWF show, which has had tickets on sale for several weeks, had sold around 3,000 tickets as of 6/2. Although the WWF line-up for the show would have to be considered as somewhat loaded, this appears to be more of a war from the WCW side as opposed to WWF, which aside from the bikini tanning contest with Sable, Marlena, Sunny and Chyna, is running the same card for Anaheim that it is doing all weekend.

The WCW house show has a stronger line-up than virtually any PPV it has run in recent months, climaxing with a non-match confrontation at the end of the show with Hulk Hogan and Sting. The revised card consists of Scott Hall & Kevin Nash defending the WCW tag team titles against The Giant & Lex Luger, Ric Flair vs. Roddy Piper, Diamond Dallas Page vs. Randy Savage, Syxx vs. Rey Misterio Jr. for the cruiserweight title, Hector Garza & Lizmark Jr. & Juventud Guerrera vs. Konnan & La Parka & Villano IV, Dean Malenko vs. Eddie Guerrero, Rick & Scott Steiner vs. Scott Norton & Masahiro Chono and Ultimo Dragon vs. Psicosis.

The WWF show is headlined by a triangle match for the WWF title, which at last word would be the return of Bret Hart although that isn't a definite. The last line-up we had for the show was the triangle match for the WWF title with Undertaker, Bret Hart and Shawn Michaels (I'd suspect that Steve Austin would replace Hart in the triangle match should Hart not be ready by that date), Steve Austin vs. Brian Pillman in a no DQ match, Davey Boy Smith vs. Sid for the European title, Owen Hart vs. Goldust for the IC title, Legion of Doom vs. Godwinns, Rocky Maivia vs. Hunter Hearst Helmsley, Vader & Mankind vs. Faarooq & Crush, Flash Funk vs. Rockabilly, Blackjacks vs. Doug Furnas & Phil LaFon and the tanning contest. The only major change from the originally planned line-up is eliminating the Ken Shamrock vs. Vader match.

WCW did even better the same day in Detroit for promotion of its 8/4 Monday Nitro date at the Piston Palace in Auburn Hills, MI with sales as of 6/2 topping 6,200 tickets and $144,000, which already beat the 5,088 tickets and $103,749 that the WWF ended up doing for its 5/23 house show in the same building.

Yet another head-to-head confrontation will be taking place even sooner, with WWF running its King of the Ring PPV in Providence, RI on 6/8 and a Raw taping on 6/9 in Hartford, CT, while WCW debuts at the Fleet Center in Boston with a Nitro taping. King of the Ring, with the card somewhat revised this past week, had sold 6,650 tickets for $159,132 as of 6/2, so the show isn't expected to sellout the 16,000-seat Civic Center even though it had been advertised until 6/2 that the card would feature the first return match between Bret Hart and Shawn Michaels since their WrestleMania main event more than one year ago.

With Hart's knee not recovered enough to put him back even in a short gimmick match and Brian Pillman's ankle not 100% and the feeling would be not have him overextend himself in a match that would have to carry the show, both were pulled from the card. As announced on the 6/2 Raw show, Michaels vs. Austin will be the match to carry the show while the other non-tournament matches will be Undertaker defending the WWF title against Faarooq, Legion of Doom & Sid vs. Jim Neidhart & Owen Hart & Smith and Crush vs. Goldust. King of the Ring matches will be Jerry Lawler vs. Mankind and Ahmed Johnson vs. Helmsley with the winners meeting for the KOR championship. Pillman vs. Austin will headline the Raw taping in Hartford, CT where there won't be as much pressure on the two to have a match to carry the show, and more importantly, won't have to do a 20 minute match.

WCW will break company records for both attendance and live gate on 6/9. As of 6/2, there were 15,350 tickets sold for $231,946, the latter breaking the company's all-time gate record set last October for the Hulk Hogan vs. Randy Savage match in Las Vegas. The company record for tickets is 15,834 set for the January Nitro in Chicago.

As of 6/2, there were no tickets available, however they are going to open up hundreds or perhaps thousands of killed off seats this week in those curious problems as how every week they can't get the building ticketing situation straight and after announcing a sellout locally and pulling ticket sales off the market, they almost routinely have several hundred seats to fill at the last minute. However, when it comes to dollars, the biggest upcoming advance of all belongs to the WWF, not WCW, for the 8/2 SummerSlam PPV show at the Meadowlands which has sold 9,298 tickets for more than $321,000.

JUNE 30

The battle of Los Angeles is just days away and how it's going depends upon who you choose to ask.

WWF officials claim to be thrilled because according to ticket outlets as of 6/23—five days before the two shows—they were only 190 tickets behind WCW—and they play the market regularly while WCW is running its first show in the market in two years, and hyping it huge on television as "The show Eric Bischoff doesn't want you to see", now claiming Bischoff is keeping the show from being on PPV and doing a live Internet audio commentary. WCW officials claim the ticket counts aren't even close, with them well ahead. Both sides claim the other is papering the market heavily.

The WCW card officially changed on 6/24 after they finally got around to doing the Ric Flair-Roddy Piper angle the previous night on Nitro, with Flair vs. Piper added to the show, and the Kevin Nash & Scott Hall tag team title defense changed to Lex Luger & The Giant, as has been reported here from the start. The headline event is actually not a match, but promising the first elusive Hulk Hogan vs. Sting confrontation. The WWF card will be headlined by the first wrestling appearance of Bret Hart since knee surgery, in a triangle match for the WWF title with Steve Austin and Undertaker.

WWF officials claimed 5,643 tickets sold and $107,433 as of 6/23, and claimed WCW had sold 5,833 tickets and $135,257. WCW claimed they had sold 8,660 tickets and expect that another 1,000 to 1,500 more season ticket holders to all Forum events will show up with the Forum adding $44 per season ticket holder to the gross, which puts the gross at theoretically more than $200,000 with only $12 and $10 tickets remaining which they expect most of the late sales, if they are significant, to be Mexican mat fans.

Both groups have tons of last minute promotion with WWF sending Sunny to Los Angeles all week to promote the Anaheim show, and sending Ken Shamrock (who was added to the show in a singles match against Jim Neidhart) and Chyna to Venice Beach, a nearly two hour drive to the Anaheim Pond, the afternoon of the show, to push late buys. WCW is heavily promoting late buys at the Mexican market, which traditionally buys tickets the night of the show, but also has phone-in radio appearances by Hogan and has Randy Savage in town during the week.

Traditionally the Mexican wrestling fans haven't supported promotions where the Mexicans work in supporting roles rather than as the top stars when it comes to Los Angeles mat history. In San Jose last year, which AAA drew big houses in during the heyday of that promotion, when WCW came to town, the Mexican audience was virtually non-existent despite a lot of promotion designed in that direction. There was a noticeable, but not overwhelming Mexican audience at the SuperBrawl PPV at the San Francisco Cow Palace.

The other major battleground for this week was Detroit. WWF ran Raw at Cobo Arena on 6/23, packing 10,863 fans into the building, however it was heavily papered with the paid attendance being 6,370 paying $113,858. WCW has already sold 8,093 tickets for $177,083 for the 8/4 Nitro at the Palace in Auburn Hills, MI and the expectations are that the company will break its all-time gate record set on 6/9 in Boston at this show.

However, WWF, despite the common perception of it being No. 2, still on a consistent basis is outdrawing WCW at arena events and its Meadowlands advance for SummerSlam on 8/3 is more money than WCW has ever done for any show in its history. WWF officials also claim WCW spends more money to promote its major shows that are doing the big houses in the major markets while WCW counters that claim.

JULY 7

After a few months of planning, the "Battle of Los Angeles" took place on the same night as the Tyson-Holyfield rematch. The winner? One would have to call it shrouded in controversy.

World Championship Wrestling, running 6/28 at the Great Western Forum in Los Angeles claimed a total attendance of 10,948, with a paid of 9,705 and a $189,940 gate, figures confirmed by the Forum box office, in a building that seats about 18,000. The WWF, citing Ticketron as its source, claimed that their information was that WCW did a crowd of 11,629 fans, but with only 7,699 paid and a gate of $158,716.

Part of the dispute over the money figures and total paid attendance may be in regard to season ticket holders at the Forum. WCW made a deal with the building to get paid by the building a certain amount for each season ticket holder who attended the event and thus in the Forum box office figures they would be considered paid attendance, which is a highly unusual deal at arenas of this type in that usually season ticket holders aren't figured into the paid attendance nor do the event promoters receive money from their attendance, although from a mathematical standpoint, that wouldn't add up the numbers correctly either to explain a discrepancy between the two figures.

There were also according to Forum figures 780 ticket holders, virtually all comp ticket holders, that had tickets but didn't attend the show which would explain part of the reason the Ticketron figures listed a higher actual attendance than the Forum figures, although as you can see, those numbers don't add up perfectly throwing that in either.

The figures are by far its best showing from a gate perspective ever in Southern California, a market that neither WCW nor its predecessor, Jim Crockett Promotions, were ever able to sustain consistent business in although there have been a few solid crowds in the past.

Crockett's debut show in the market in the mid-80s in the same building drew about 8,500 fans, and that was with a company that didn't have a microscopic fraction of the promotional ability or promotional budget of today's WCW and theoretically wasn't nearly as over on a national basis although live wrestling attendance overall nationally was stronger in those days. However the history since then has been spotty, with the last paid show in the market being a 1994 Hulk Hogan vs. Ric Flair main event in Anaheim which drew less than 3,000 paid and $40,000, and a free 1995 PPV show at Huntington Beach which drew approximately 9,500.

However, given the intense marketing push and loaded show, the numbers have to be a disappointment, particularly since there was virtually no walk-up with lots of last week promotion aimed at the Hispanic community, and one would question how profitable the show was given the huge advertising budget, costs for all the production special effects given the "Saturday Nitro" theme, the live appearance of Hulk Hogan and the fact the Forum is among the most costly buildings in the country to run. Throwing in the merchandise figure of $82,000 would be the only way to make the difference between profitability and red ink for the show as a whole.

Although WCW has the more depth and thus had the stronger undercard, the WWF was able to counter, even with all the injuries and what seemed like weekly line-up changes, with a main event that put its three biggest stars in the ring against each other with the world title at stake. WCW instead had to push its biggest stars, Hulk Hogan and Sting, as appearing in a "face-off," which sounds more like a debate than a match, since Hogan opted not to wrestle on the show wanting to save the first Sting match for PPV later in the year.

Since WCW has been able to pack crowds most Mondays promising nothing but personal appearances and advertising no matches, in most markets that would have been enough. New York and Los Angeles are both different from most markets in that in both cases, the WWF is the decided "home team" because of history, and that people who live in those cities expect only the very best from an entertainment standpoint not just in wrestling but across the board entertainment wise since they are the media capitals and something perceived as anything but the best product possible isn't going to pack the building.

The World Wrestling Federation, which runs the market regularly and has dominated Southern California live wrestling business since the early 80s with the exception of a brief period where AAA was doing off the chart numbers, ran the same night at the Arrowhead Pond in Anaheim drawing 9,469 fans, of which 8,449 were paid with a $150,447 gate in a building that seats a little less than 16,000. The WWF also did $72,000 in merchandise business at the show. Those figures have to be considered successful even though the dollar figures are lower than the WCW figures.

It was going against the biggest money boxing match in history and with a rival show in the same basic market (in some ways Anaheim and Los Angeles, although within driving distance of one another, are also different markets) and still drew, with the exception of the 1996 WrestleMania, the largest paid attendance and gate for a WWF show in the market in more than two years, although it also was given a far bigger promotional push than a typical house show.

WCW considered it a victory because it drew the larger crowd and gross. WWF considered it a victory claiming their show was the more profitable because less money was spent on advertising, which is also the case since WCW spent slightly more than $100,000 just on advertising alone for the show.

Both sides pushed the show heavily with lots of public appearances. The WWF's final promotional stop was a public workout by Ken Shamrock, Hunter Hearst Helmsley, Chyna and Sunny at Venice Beach (about a 90 minute drive from Anaheim) the afternoon of the show. Kevin Nash, Scott Hall and Syxx came to Venice Beach to hang out with Helmsley and were there as well.

The WCW show, billed in some circles as "The show Eric Bischoff doesn't want you to see," was described as a good but not great show, with a very strong undercard and weak work in the main matches, similar to the typical WCW pattern. It was a heavy heel crowd, with the only main event faces to get major cheers being Roddy Piper and Sting, and described as being 25 to 30 percent Mexican.

There has been a lot of controversy about WCW being unable to draw Mexican fans in markets like San Jose and Los Angeles that these same former AAA wrestlers drew on their own years back, but that is going to be the case because those wrestlers have no Spanish language television as opposed to about seven hours per week when AAA was doing over $200,000 per show over a two-year period.

In addition, when promoting to ethnics, the ethnic stars in order for the promotions to be successful have to be the headliners, and in WCW's case, the former AAA superstars are generally prelim wrestlers, which gives the former AAA fans no great incentive to follow them in WCW. This has probably greatly hurt their drawing potential for the future in the U.S. even if WCW follows through on its plan to develop a WCW Latino television show to focus on Mexican wrestling and develop anywhere from quarterly to monthly Lucha Libre style PPV shows for the U.S. to hit the growing Spanish language market.

WCW geared much of its advertising over the last week to the Spanish language market and pushed the six-man tag team match, which turned out to be the opening match on the card, as the main event in the advertising and also focused on Rey Misterio Jr. and Eddie Guerrero, and downplayed Hogan, Sting and the rest, and the result was no walk-up at all.

The show opened with them introducing all the announcers, with Lee Marshall, a long-time Los Angeles DJ, being booed heavily. The other announcers all received smatterings of boos with the exception of Bobby Heenan, who was cheered wildly by this largely heel crowd.

1. Juventud Guerrera, Lizmark Jr. & Damian beat Konnan, La Parka & Villano IV in 10:18 when Guerrera pinned Villano turning a power bomb into a huracanrana. This was said to have been a great fast-paced match, with Guerrera doing a Liger dive over the head of announcer Mike Tenay at ringside. Guerrera slipped on the planned finish, some sort of a springboard move, likely that somersault into a dropkick, but Villano did a great job of covering his mistake. ***1/2

2. Ultimo Dragon pinned Psicosis in 12:28 after a spinning huracanrana off the top rope and a tap out to a dragon sleeper submission. Dragon was said to have been really over with the crowd. Psicosis did a running springboard into a moonsault block off the top rope to the floor as the highlight. ***1/2

3. Eddie Guerrero pinned Dean Malenko in 16:31 with his feet on the ropes. Guerrero was mainly doing the Art Barr heel routine and was tremendous in his new role. This was largely considered the best match on the show and from reports from the previous night in Fresno, totally stole the show there as well. ***3/4

4. Steiners beat Marcus Bagwell & Masahiro Chono in 16:20. Most of the entertainment was provided by Bagwell's antics. Rick pinned Bagwell with a belly-to-belly suplex while Chono's back was turned and he was fighting with Scott outside the ring. After the match, Bagwell tried to explain to Chono that he was the one who had pinned Rick and that they had won the match. *3/4

Before the next match, Gene Okerlund did a live interview with Ric Flair. Flair was out there to turn himself heel for the match with Roddy Piper. Flair got a huge babyface reaction coming out, but then started insulting the fans, the Lakers and the women in Los Angeles with the typical old-style Flair heel promo. Even when it was over, he still got at best 50% of the fans turned against him.

5. The next match was scheduled as a cruiserweight title match with Syxx defending against Rey Misterio Jr. Before the match, Chris Jericho came out and challenged the winner to defend the title against him later in the card. Jericho wasn't over a lick. Misterio Jr. accepted and then Syxx, to a huge face pop said something to the effect of nobody in this building even gives a rats ass about you and talked about having beaten him before on television, which was true since they largely didn't. The two had a good match, although not as good as some of their previous bouts, ending in 11:33 with the buzzkiller submission. Highlight was Misterio Jr. doing the Liger flip dive springboarding off the back of the referee and Syxx doing the Michinoku driver II on Misterio Jr. for a near fall. ***

6. Jericho was challenged to get in the ring, and he came in, hit a leg lariat and pinned Syxx in :32 to capture the cruiserweight title. Jericho was booed out of the building for winning.

The entire NWO, including Hogan, came out for an interview to a total face reaction. The crowd totally cheered Hogan. Hogan challenged Sting to come out then and there, but nothing materialized.

7. Roddy Piper beat Ric Flair with the sleeper in 8:10. Match didn't have much heat but when Flair's arm went down the third time there was a big pop. The only other big pop was Piper pulling Flair's trunks down. Told it was watchable live but it would be a bad match if it were on a PPV. Since much of the crowd had already learned of the Tyson result, Piper started biting Flair's ear to try and get heat. *1/2.

8. Diamond Dallas Page pinned Randy Savage in 5:16 after two Diamond cutters. Big early pop but told the match was a major disappointment as they appeared to both be phoning in the performance. 1/2*

9. Lex Luger & The Giant beat Kevin Nash & Scott Hall via DQ in 12:01 in a WCW tag team title match. Unlike Flair, who tried to get the crowd not to cheer him, Hall & Nash were doing everything to encourage the crowd to cheer for them. There were lots of chants of "Diesel" and "Razor" which is something that hadn't been heard at arenas for months. Typical not good match with these four ending with Luger having Hall in the rack in the ring and Giant fighting Nash outside the ring. Hogan did a run-in and hit Luger with a pathetic shot with the title belt for the DQ. *1/4

The NWO beat on Luger and Giant until Sting came down from the ceiling for the save. Sting ended up putting Hogan in the scorpion deathlock with Hogan tapping out to make sure everyone registered it until Syxx broke it up by hitting Sting with a lead pipe. Sting ended up getting the pipe from Syxx and along with Luger and Giant, cleaned house momentarily. At this point Hogan went back to the dressing room. Hall, Nash and Syxx ended up going back to the ring. Sting gave Hall the scorpion death drop (slop drop), Luger racked Nash and Giant choke-slammed Syxx. While the other two continued to sell, Nash got up and went after Sting, but Sting destroyed him with a baseball bat shot. The faces left while the heels sold in the ring for a very long time until they finally got up and said that everyone knows Los Angeles is NWO country. Even though Hall, Nash and Syxx were the faces for the most part, the fans pelted the ring with garbage at the end, seemingly this has become the thing to do because people copy what they see on television. Nash actually caught a cup and drank from it, which considering what they sometimes put in the cups they throw in Los Angeles, isn't necessarily the wisest idea.

We don't have as much detail on the WWF Anaheim show.

1. Rockabilly pinned Flash Funk with a DDT off the ropes. Funk got a bloody nose in the match.

2. Faarooq & Kama beat The Blackjacks when Kama pinned Windham.

3. Ken Shamrock, who got the biggest pop on the show except for Austin and Undertaker, beat Jim Neidhart.

4. The tanning contest went a too-long 22:00. It turned into a strip show atmosphere with fans throwing money, which Sunny was only glad to collect. Similar to the Slammys, Sable worse the least and got the biggest pop to win. After it was over, Honky Tonk Man began insulting what Chyna was wearing and she bodyslammed him.

5. A Triple Threat match billed as to determine the No. 1 contenders for the tag team titles saw Owen Hart & Davey Boy Smith win over Godwinns and Legion of Doom when Hart pinned Phineas in what was described as a bad match.

6. Vader pinned Goldust due to distraction from the Hart Foundation.

7. Mankind beat Hunter Hearst Helmsley via DQ due to interference from Chyna. After the match, Mankind put the mandible claw on Chyna to a big pop.

8. Undertaker retained the WWF title in the Triple Threat match over Bret Hart and Steve Austin. Bret was said to be about 50% of his usual effectiveness as he's not fully recovered from knee surgery. Said to have been the best match on the show ending when Undertaker pinned Bret with a choke slam. After the match, Paul Bearer came out and talked about revealing the surprise on Monday and Undertaker knocked him out of the ring.

Chapter Twenty

Wrestling's Drug Problem

JULY 14

The arrest of Gary Wolf and Anthony Durante, ECW's Pit Bulls, by federal authorities on 7/2 on three counts of steroid and marijuana trafficking just adds to the list of arrests of pro wrestlers this year predominately on drug charges.

It once again points to an industry that, while in many ways is thriving on the outside, seems to be in other ways a ticking time bomb that may be setting itself up for the same collapse that befell it only five years earlier.

In recent months, we've seen nine arrests and a few trips to rehab or drug suspensions of wrestlers, which may not sound like that huge a total, but it is when you consider it's only a six month period we're talking about and it's an industry that really only has about 200 or so wrestlers in it. It's a problem that goes far deeper than any individual promotion and problems have taken place internally in most major promotions in the world.

Pro wrestling and drug problems is hardly a new story. In the mid-80s, the problems were cocaine and downers and to a lesser extent steroids, which led to several major deaths of wrestlers that quite frankly had they lived would have changed the entire landscape of the industry, and a no-show problem of major stars. Ironically, even with the body count, that drug story didn't hurt the industry's growth since the media never picked up on it.

But in 1991, when Dr. George Zahorian was convicted of illegally distributing steroids to a number of WWF wrestlers, it set the stage for a scandal that got a good deal of media coverage and greatly damaged the WWF, not that it was alone in having a drug problem but the fact is it was a company at the time built on the back of steroids. Its top stars, marketed to fans as clean-living anti-drug super heroes were people like Ultimate Warrior and Hulk Hogan. Hogan painted the bullseye on both himself and Vince McMahon by lying under pressure, and there are circumstances remarkably similar in the profession today, including more media attention than ever before, right down to a few doctors known in the industry as being handy men with the prescription pad (although none with the visibility and name recognition inside the profession like Zahorian had during the 80s and with the laws on steroids changing and use decreasing, those are no longer the drugs in question), that may set the stage for history repeating itself, particularly if a major star either gets busted or collapses in public.

The world has changed and where five years ago everyone in the industry did whatever they could to unsuccessfully deny or hide the problem, today, particularly in WCW, certain wrestlers have at times come close to almost flaunting the fact they are loaded and can get away with it every Monday night. In a business that appears to be more star-driven than ever before, the feeling is a big name can flagrantly do anything these days and get away with it, and that goes a whole lot deeper than the drug issue.

Can you imagine a situation currently if an NFL team had a publicized quarterback controversy which affected the two guys fighting over the spot so much that they both got into a fight backstage where one pulled the others' hair out and both wound up aggravating already injured knees to the point both had to miss several key games what the reaction of the team, the league and the media would be? Certainly it wouldn't be to be somewhat embarrassed and pass it off as boys being boys.

Realistically, the situation the same night in WCW with Kevin Nash and Roddy Piper, had it happened in another sport, likely would not have resulted in any major disciplinary problems and would have been viewed as boys being boys because nobody got hurt, but I don't see in any other sport if the Bret Hart/Shawn Michaels situation had happened where the organization would have reacted the way the WWF did.

In recent months, there have been publicized arrests of Doug Gilbert, Tommy Rich, Steve Williams, Gary Wolf, Anthony Durante, Alex Rizzo (Big Dick Dudley), Leon "Vader" White (twice no less in a two week period in Kuwait) and Billy Travis, not to mention Scott Hall checking himself into rehab and a suspension of Brian "Jesse" James. Those names cut across every promotion and include major superstars and journeyman wrestlers. They don't include the alarming frequency where major stars have showed up on Monday nights in condition where they are barely making it through their interviews because they are so loaded.

The aforementioned arrests are all isolated incidents in their own way, some quite minor, some having absolutely nothing to do with drugs, some are almost in their own strange way black comedies, and all can be explained away as isolated incidents except that there are too many of them happening too frequently in a profession where too few people are employed.

Ever since Hall checked into rehab, combined with WCW continuing to advertise him for shows that they full well knew he wasn't going to appear on, that company, particularly due to its high visibility with usage of top pro athletes on its major shows, opened itself up for the same potential bullseye of bad publicity that ECW did with the Erich Kulas incident. We may be one incident by a major star away, and perhaps not even that, from one influential reporter playing connect the dots of this story and we'll be back to a situation where, like 1992, the profession starts lying for cover, and digging itself into a deeper hole.

In some of the aforementioned cases, wrestlers have lost their jobs or a secondary job. In other cases, nothing of the sort. Probably in a lot of cases the wrestlers shouldn't have lost their jobs over the incidents. During this same period, drug testing has for all real purposes been dropped in both WWF and WCW although both theoretically still have policies in effect. But even when there was drug testing, virtually nobody in the industry believed the policies were indiscriminately enforced or that if top stars were to fail a test that they would actually be punished unless it was an extenuating circumstance such as Hall's showing up positive in a test on the same day he gave notice.

You can't be realistic and be all pristine about the drug issue in wrestling at the same time. The nature of this industry breeds drug problems. The physical punishment, self inflicted in most cases, can be brutal among the wrestlers with the most internal drive to get over and it's no surprise that many of the hardest working wrestlers are going to wind up hooked on downers.

While steroid use is still around, it is nothing close to rampant nor on the level of just five years ago due to the change in the fans tastes for workrate over a stationary cosmetic package. While there are a handful of wrestlers due to their prescribed roles that still almost need to take steroids for their specific role just as virtually every woman in this profession needs a boob job to get over, that number today is exceedingly few.

But you can't defend the industry because for those that play those roles because there are certain characters who by their gimmick are pretty well forced to use steroids. Unlike in the 80s where the mentality was you needed the physique to get a good job, the majority of the wrestlers using steroids today really are doing so making their own personal choice, but not all.

Many said that in the 80s, even under oath, but when you consider probably 80% or more of the major wrestlers were using steroids just six years ago and today that figure is so much lower among the basic group of people in the industry tells me the decision making process wasn't internal by the wrestlers, even among those who believed their own decisions were, but coming from external pressures as those same wrestlers who recognize that steroids today aren't going to be much of a factor in them getting a better job, seem not to be taking steroids today and don't tell me they are suddenly concerned with their health or the law or had no idea there were negative side effects six years ago.

The road schedule, while tough, is far easier then in the past when wrestlers really did work 300 matches a year so the need for uppers to keep going while doing seven nights a week isn't there like in the previous incarnation of drug problems. But while some of the nearly inhuman working conditions of the past in pro wrestling have been alleviated and pressures to juice up have been greatly lessened, there is a problem that is being ignored—that a series of so-called isolated incidents are signs of a dangerous pattern.

Wolf, 30, and Durante, 29, were arrested on 7/2 at their respective homes in South Philadelphia after a grand jury came up with three indictments against the two for trafficking in 1995 in their home area. They were released on bail and are awaiting trial. At least at the present time, it's unlikely they'll be used in ECW, just as Williams was no longer used after his recent arrest.

Chapter Twenty One

Maurice Smith Upsets Mark Coleman

AUGUST 4

In the most stunning upset in the history of the Ultimate Fighting Championships, Maurice Smith combined tremendous defense on the ground with superior conditioning to win a unanimous decision over previously unbeaten and some thought unbeatable UFC heavyweight champion Mark Coleman on 7/27 in Birmingham, AL.

Smith, 36, added the UFC title to his numerous major kick boxing championships including currently holding the ISKA heavyweight title. He's also done pro wrestling in Japan with organizations such as UWF, PWFG, Pancrase and currently RINGS and actually has lost numerous matches, some shoots, others works, via submission in Japan. His lengthy kick boxing career saw him at one point considered as the best heavyweight in his sport in the world. He survived the first several minutes on his back and largely took control over a completely exhausted Coleman at the 9:00 mark and used his stand-up skill to score points, mainly with leg kicks, while a totally spent Coleman held on for dear life. It probably ranked just behind the 1995 Oleg Taktarov vs. Tank Abbott match as the most dramatic match in UFC history.

Many, particularly within the world of martial arts magazine, will call this victory of a kick boxer over a wrestler as proof that UFC's dominance by ground fighters was only because no world class kick boxer has entered, similar to how many magazines tried to trumpet Smith's win over Marcus Silviera to win the EFC title.

There couldn't be more of a wrong statement. It wasn't kick boxing that beat Coleman, it was scouting, game plan, ground defense and cardiovascular conditioning. No doubt Coleman's running out of gas so badly after 7:00 will bring up all kinds of whispers, or whether he simply trained for a fast sprint and never believed Smith was going to last on the bottom, which was the prevailing wisdom of how the fight would go going in. Coleman's conditioning problem is very likely linked to a chemical imbalance from an improper working thyroid that kept him out of Ultimate Ultimate last December. It was believed in this case, as was the belief going into the Dan Severn match, that in a long match, Coleman would lose, but in this case, nobody gave it much of a chance that it would be a long match.

The main event saved what turned out to be the most one-sided series of fights in UFC history underneath.

As expected, world-class freestyle wrestlers Kevin Jackson and Mark Kerr, both from Coleman's "Hammer House" team, dominated their respective under and over-200 weight divisions enroute to victory. If anything, their easy wins paved the way for the drama that was to unfold making the show's climax that much stronger and a very one-sided thumbs up ratio. Coleman, the heavy favorite, appeared likely to use the same vaunted "ground and pound" tactics that his teammates used on a fighter with considerable stand-up skill but not believed to be a serious threat on the ground.

Smith held the heavyweight title with the Extreme Fighting Championship company when it went out of business a few months ago and in some circles this was promoted as something of an interpromotional title unification type of match. While Smith was 2-0 in NHB, he hadn't faced anyone believed to be close to the level of a Coleman, who came into the match with a 6-0 record and having never been seriously challenged in any of his matches. Smith, on the other hand, had lost many mixed matches by submission in Japan to competitors not believed to be anywhere the capabilities of Coleman.

It is also interesting to note just how strong the connection between working and shooting and pro wrestling and UFC has become when it comes to the top stars of UFC. Of the major champions produced in UFC, only Royce Gracie and Mark Coleman had no connection to pro style wrestling and working. Ken Shamrock was a pro wrestler before UFC and worked with Pancrase during UFC, and is back as a pro wrestler after UFC. Dan Severn was a pro wrestler before, during and will be after UFC. Don Frye did a few pro wrestling matches on small Arizona independents many years ago, but is now with New Japan Pro Wrestling. And now Smith.

The match started the same way most of the fast and one-sided matches underneath had started, with the powerful world-class wrestler taking down his foe quickly. Smith, who in hindsight beat Coleman more in a mental game than a physical one, made a remark that Coleman punched like a girl (actually that statement was stolen from Tank Abbott's remarks about Dan Severn before their match which ended up with Abbott on his back almost the entire match). Coleman took the remark seriously and came into the cage looking to quickly tear Smith's head from his shoulders. Smith came in looking far more concerned than he had made it appear he'd be going into the fight. Smith, for the match by Frank Shamrock, had spent the past several weeks training at the Lions Den. They had clearly done his homework in scouting Coleman and weeks ago were very confident of a game plan that would work against the fighter they considered and in some ways exposed as one-dimensional.

After taking some punches and head-butts early from Coleman, he was able to, while on his back, neutralize much of the damage with both a Jiu-Jitsu guard and an ability to block the telegraphed roundhouse blows Coleman attempted to throw in. Coleman's bread-and-butter submission hold, the strangulating headlock that put away Dan Severn and that purportedly in practice he was tapping out Kerr and Jackson with, was blocked and wiggled away from by Smith every time Coleman came close to getting it on. It had been said by numerous people who had viewed Coleman's matches in the past, that the first person to be able to survive against Coleman early would be the first person to beat him. After a few minutes, it was clear Coleman was tiring out. While people had said it, just how true it turned out to be ended up being the shock of the show.

After the 6:00 mark, Coleman's offense slowed down to simply keeping his position on top of Smith. By 7:30, the live crowd 4,800, a near sellout of the Boutwell Auditorium in Birmingham, began chanting "Maurice," sensing what was about to unfold. Finally at the 9:10 mark, Smith escaped Coleman's top position, a clear indication Coleman was running on empty. But when both were on their feet it was clear Smith's face had been marked and he was tired, looking like he'd been in a war. But Coleman was shockingly even more spent than anyone could imagine. He appeared to be out of breath and cramping, bending over, to a degree the likes of which you almost never see in a combat sports situation, and certainly never see anyone survive with for more than a minute or two longer. Smith's strategy at this point was to using leg kicks and a few jabs and mainly stay away.

Those who talked with Smith after the fight said Smith said he never went to the all-out attack even though it appeared Coleman was ready to go out because of fear Coleman's superior weight would result in them going down with Coleman on top and even though Coleman couldn't damage him from that position, he didn't want the judges to see him on his back after spending so much time on his back early in the fight. Coleman did get another take-down at 10:15 in, but Smith was the more aggressive from the bottom throwing elbows. Coleman actually came close at this point to getting his headlock, but Smith threw a few knees to the head from the bottom. Smith escaped and tagged Coleman with some punches before the 12:00 regulation time expired.

The two overtime periods were all Smith, mainly using leg licks. At one point Smith went for a big roundhouse and whiffed badly, lost his footing and went down, but Coleman was so exhausted he couldn't even move to capitalize on it. Coleman's attempts at take-down were incredibly slow at this point and not even a threat and at this point the only battle for him was to survive. Smith kept backpedaling and taunting Coleman, telling him to ground and pound him, while Coleman was trying to find out how much time was left, seemingly hanging on with as the living embodiment of the famous Vince Lombardi saying of how fatigue makes cowards of the toughest of us all. Just as the second overtime expired, Smith appeared to go in for the kill, but time ran out and he was awarded the easy decision and the championship. The next day, Coleman's face was described as looking like he had been on the losing side of a war.

"Everything he did we had practiced to a t," said Frank Shamrock, who has trained Smith in ground fighting the past few years. "It was pretty much textbook in how to pick apart a wrestler. It was just a matter of how well he'd last for two or three minutes."

Shamrock said that they knew Coleman couldn't knock Smith out so the only danger was getting caught Coleman's one submission headlock choke maneuver. Even though virtually nobody within the NHB world gave Smith much of a chance in the fight, both Smith and Shamrock were talking very confidently about winning well before the fight. And Shamrock was talking equally confident about a possible match with Vitor Belfort.

"I think Vitor would be an even easier match," he said. "Don't get me wrong, this was a hard fight. Vitor would be more dangerous early on but the match would get easier as it went on."

The strategy in that case is that Smith's usage of leg kicks in a standing fight, over time, would take out Belfort's leg strength and quickness and eliminate the full body power he brings to those punches.

Although SEG had been planning its year around a Coleman vs. Vitor Belfort ultimate match in December, officials couldn't have been more thrilled. They liked Smith, who is a true professional fighter in the sense he knows how to conduct himself, is a great talker and knows how to hype a fight and they believe him to be marketable. The feeling beforehand was that they would have been thrilled even if Smith won and ruined their long-term plans, but just didn't think it was likely to happen.

So there's a new champion. But is Smith now going to become the champion of two consecutive organizations that go out of business? While throughout the broadcast there was hype for a 10/17 show, built around a Belfort main event with no opponent mentioned (there were hints at either Randy Couture or Dan Severn), no location was announced. Economically, these shows can't be profitable unless more cable systems carry them then carried this show and the previous one and there is no political climate for a turnaround on that issue.

When promoter Bob Meyrowitz congratulated Kerr and Jackson on their tournament wins and talked about the future, there was trepidation in his voice. Unlike most sports and businesses that fail due to economic conditions, UFC is fighting what at this point appears to be a losing battle against political conditions with no signs of change.

Perhaps the most interesting note when it comes to the buy rate is that numerous Time-Warner systems around the country actually did carry the event after saying that they wouldn't. There were at least a few systems that we are aware of that reversed their positions in the past week due to numerous complaints from subscribers. That also means in those systems the event was never advertised and thus the buy rate was likely microscopic with no advance pub in those systems that an event was even taking place.

In other words it was likely to get almost an 0.0 buy rate which will kill the national average. That may end up making it easier for the cable industry to finish serving up UFC as it sacrificial lamb, or more likely was one of those strange lack of communications in a big business that those of us who follow pro wrestling are familiar with. Promoter David Isaacs acknowledged the numbers weren't going to be impressive, but that they were thrilled with the main event and were now beginning plans for a follow-up show.

As a show itself, due to the shortness of the undercard, there were numerous features plugged into the show. Some, talking about the whereabouts of former UFC stars that seemingly had disappeared, were interesting. But there was far too much dead time and the quality of the fights overall was a disappointment. It turned out okay because of how the show-long storyline developed into the main event, but had the main event gone the way of the rest of the show, it would have been the weakest UFC show to date. Some of the one-sidedness was simply things you can't plan out, such as Johnston just being unable to cope with Bobish and conversely, Bobish being unable to hang with Kerr, as on paper even though the expected favorite won, they shouldn't have been expected to win so easily. But the squash match nature of several of the matches was expected.

If Belfort wins his match and don't think SEG is going to risk putting him in against anyone they think has a decent chance of beating him like Kerr, it sets up the obvious match with Smith for December. This would be interesting because it would be the first main event featuring two fighters with both world-class striking ability and considerable ground experience in one package.

The local publicity in the Birmingham media was all favorable and there were no last minute attempts to get the show moved out of town. One major area politician who attended the show was interviewed on the local news saying not only that he enjoyed it but that there was nothing to the stories about brutality. It was certainly among the least brutal shows in UFC history with a few bumps being raised but no significant blood spilled. The most serious catastrophe didn't take place in the ring, but in the stands where the wife of Joe Moreiera went into premature labor while watching her husband's fight and gave birth almost on the spot.

Chapter Twenty Two

Steve Austin Injured at SummerSlam

AUGUST 11

There was an injury that appeared to be major at the time involving the WWF's hottest star, Steve Austin, which wound up with Austin hospitalized after his arms and legs went numb in the middle of his match with Owen Hart where he was scheduled to win the IC title.

The two did an impromptu and totally unconvincing finish after Austin feared his neck was broken and was paralyzed from the waist down for several seconds and whispered to Hart that he couldn't move after taking a tombstone piledriver with his head too low. Hart stalled for as long as he could, trying to get a "USA" chant going to chanting Canada and with major concern all over his face, tried to stall waiting for Austin to recover. Austin managed to roll toward him, using almost only his stomach muscles and got his arms up for a weak schoolboy finish, ending the match some six to eight minutes early. Apparently the original finish was for Austin to win using his stone cold stunner. The weak finish was explained on television as Hart having sympathy for a beaten opponent and that's why he was stalling so long after Austin was obviously injured.

Austin could barely get up after the match, limped with his left leg dangling out of the ring where he almost collapsed after getting backstage, and was rushed to the emergency room at Meadowlands Hospital where he was released at about 1 a.m., having apparently suffered a "stinger" in his neck, an injury more common in football. Austin had been having some legitimate neck problems earlier in the week stemming from the constant aggravation his neck has taken from wrestling. Austin appeared at Raw the next night but clearly wasn't walking well, with his activity limited to doing an interview and interfering in the Dude Love vs. Owen Hart main event by hitting Hart with a Slammy Award leading to Love's victory.

We haven't heard any long-term prognosis when it comes to Austin other than we're told that it's possible he could be back in action this coming weekend but the most likely situation is he'll be out for a few weeks. The original plan for the Raw main event was for Shawn Michaels to solidify his heel turn by costing Austin & Love the tag team titles which would revert back to Owen & Davey Boy Smith. Instead Michaels solidified his turn by doing a total heel interview.

AUGUST 18

Steve Austin went in for an MRI on 8/8 and was told by one of the leading neck specialists in the country that he should retire and that he'd be risking paralysis to continue.

The MRI showed what's known in football as a stinger, trauma to the C-4 and C-5 vertebrae. Since he's not going to retire, he's going to get a second opinion from a Philadelphia doctor who is reputed to be the leading neck specialist in the United States.

Those who have talked with Austin say he really doesn't feel that bad now. He has some pain, but he's ready to go back to work. When the injury happened, he was scared out of his mind, fearing not only the end of his career but paralysis since he couldn't move for a few seconds.

He will likely attend the weekend house shows but it's questionable if he'll wrestle on them. WWF is going on the assumption he'll be back for the PPV. Until he comes back, the plan is for the triangle main events of Bret Hart, Austin and Undertaker to be singles title matches with Bret vs. Undertaker.

AUGUST 25

The latest on Steve Austin is that, as said on television, he had an appointment with one of the leading neck specialists in the country on 8/19 in Philadelphia. At press time we don't have any details on what the doctor recommended.

Everything regarding Austin is up in the air right now so this is all what would be tabbed semi-educated speculation. He won't be wrestling for sure until 9/7. He may work that PPV show but the odds may also be against that happening. At that point the tag titles will go to the winner of the four-way match. He probably will return to the ring but have to modify his style to where he doesn't take any moves that would be dangerous to his neck such as high angle suplexes on the back, DDTs, piledrivers or power bombs.

The neck injury is expected to completely heal, although it was clear from the television interview it was far from healed at this point, but he'll always be susceptible to re-injury which is why he'll likely have to modify his style.

SEPTEMBER 1

After his exam by noted Philadelphia neck specialist Dr. Joseph Torg, the current prognosis on Steve Austin is that he'll be out of action for a minimum of two months. Austin aggravated an already injured neck when his head was too low when Owen Hart gave him a tombstone piledriver at SummerSlam on 8/3 in the match where Austin was given the IC title.

Among other injuries, Austin, 32, suffered a bruise of the spine along with his fairly significant neck problems that were a combination of both the recent jar and the cumulative effect of the wear-and-tear of his wrestling career. The injury has resulted in continual tingling in his shoulders, similar to if one sleeps wrong on their shoulders and wakes up with their limb asleep.

The feeling was that Austin would eventually be able to wrestle although the first doctor he saw in Texas recommended he retire and warned him that suffering another serious injury of the type would put him at risk of paralysis. Due to that, he'll likely have to modify his style in the ring and not take certain bumps that could potentially aggravate the injury. The basic prognosis was that after laying off and doing rehab for the next two months, he'd be re-examined and at that time he'd have a better idea of when he could return to the ring.

When it comes to WWF current plans, Austin will have to relinquish both the tag team and probably the IC title belts. The original plan was for Austin & Dude Love to drop the tag titles to Owen Hart & Davey Boy Smith on the 8/4 Raw show due to outside interference from Shawn Michaels, but Austin's injury thwarted those plans.

The tag title will now go to the winner of the "Fatal Four Way" a four corners tag team match on the 9/7 Ground Zero PPV from Louisville, KY. With Austin out of the match, the advertised four teams will be Hart & Smith, Godwinns, Legion of Doom and Head Bangers. However, I've got a suspicion that the day of the show that they'll shoot an angle to get the Head Bangers out and put Dude Love back in the match and given him a new partner, with the best bet being Vader, although that is all speculation and officially Head Bangers are the fourth team.

As of press time, no decision has been made regarding the IC title. Since the WWF hadn't advertised any major matches nor made long-term plans regarding the belt, there is no hurry to make a decision. The position seems to be to wait about two weeks to see how Austin is progressing and have a better idea when he could return, and make a decision at that point.

On the WWF One Night Only England PPV from Birmingham, England on 9/20, Austin was scheduled to challenge for the WWF title against Bret Hart. That match has been changed to Hart defending against Undertaker (whose undercard match with Ahmed Johnson was also going to have to be dropped since Johnson won't be back from his knee injury by that time of that show). The only other change on the England PPV show is that the Owen Hart vs. Hunter Hearst Helmsley match has been changed to Hart vs. Ken Shamrock. This means that both Shamrock and Vader (who is working a dark match in England) will have the unenviable schedule of working within a one week period in England, Madison Square Garden, Albany, NY and Kawasaki Baseball Stadium in Japan.

The Austin injury has spooked a lot of wrestlers in both WWF and WCW as to the dangers in the current style of wrestling. With the American style being harder hitting, faster paced and with more high risk maneuvers than ever before, the injury rate has skyrocketed. Austin's injury, while just another one on the list, seems to carry more weight because it was so visually scary, it came on such a high profile card, it was from a maneuver that is delivered regularly in pro wrestling where the person taking the bump wasn't at fault and because Austin was one of the highest profile wrestlers and arguably the hottest wrestler in the entire business at the time. Not to mention that the wrestler delivering the move has a reputation for being one of the most competent people in the business to work with.

In many ways the U.S. is experiencing what Japan did several years ago when it started down the similar stiffer and more fast-paced style path. Eventually, because the wear and tear on the wrestlers was such that top stars were literally risking premature ends to their career not from any move but just from the accumulation of daily pounding, that submissions were put over strong to enable to holds to mean something. WCW, and to a far lesser extent WWF, have also started down that road which may be a necessity for a combination of maintaining the now expected intensity level of the matches while at the same time preserving the species.

Chapter Twenty Three

First Three Hour WCW Nitro

AUGUST 11

The results of the first experiment are in and it looks as though we are in for a lot of three-hour long Nitros.

The 100th edition of Nitro, on 8/4 from Auburn Hills, MI, headlined by Lex Luger winning the WCW title from Hulk Hogan by submission with the torture rack in 11:25, drew a record setting 4.34 rating (4.13 first hour, 4.25 second hour, 4.65 third hour) and 7.39 share. It's generally expected that Hogan will regain the title on the 8/9 PPV show, since the promotion is being built around a Hogan vs. Sting title match at Starrcade after a Hogan vs. Roddy Piper cage title match at Halloween Havoc. The old Nitro record was set August 26, 1996 from Palmetto, FL for an unopposed show when Raw was pre-empted that did a 4.3 rating and 7.2 share with Sting & Lex Luger vs. Chris Benoit & Steve McMichael as the main event.

As a live show, the total crowd of 17,616 fans at the Palace would have been the second largest in company history (trailing the record setting 18,003 fans at the Fleet Center in Boston on 6/9), as was the live gate of $240,519 (the Boston set company record is $243,946). It was basically a sellout, in that all the tickets originally planned to be sold were gone a few days ahead of time, but on the day of the show they opened up obstructed view seating, some of which went unsold so it wasn't a turnaway crowd. The only reason the gate record wasn't broken is because the show had 4,258 comp tickets so the paid attendance was 13,356 (Boston record was 16,025), which would somewhere near the top in company history as well.

As would be expected, with the replay now starting immediately after the live show ends, it also set a record doing a 2.31 rating and an incredible 6.58 share for a replay show. Since a two-hour show would have the replay start at a more favorable 10 p.m. time slot, that rating record likely won't last more than a week or two although the share record is going to be tough to beat.

Nitro's first hour whipped the debuting "Walker: Texas Ranger" series on USA, which did a 2.3, by nearly two full points. Raw, moved back one hour, did slightly higher than it had been averaging in the old slot, with a 2.66 rating (2.60 first hour; 2.73 second hour) and 4.36 share, although whatever minuscule gain from the average it would have been is likely more due to curiosity stemming from angles at SummerSlam than the new time slot being a positive.

For Raw and Nitro combined between 9 p.m. and 11 p.m., the total rating was 7.11 and an 11.86 share meaning a total of 5,065,000 total homes. That share figure is phenomenal because it shows just how mainstream pro wrestling really is at this point. It's the first time the five million homes barrier had even been broken when it comes to viewing pro wrestling at one time in the history of cable television (virtually all the NBC specials in the WWF's heyday drew far larger audiences than the combined audience of both these shows).

That destroyed—by a full 13 percent—the all-time record combined rating of 6.27 (4,470,000 homes) set the previous week. However, the Hogan-Luger match (3,614,000 homes) fell short of the Hogan-Flair record set on the August 24, 1994 Clash of the Champions (4,126,000 homes) as the most watched match in the history of cable television.

From a show quality standpoint, WCW easily won the week, although largely by default as WWF offered little more than Sgt. Slaughter, an explanation as to the physical condition of Steve Austin and the mental condition of Shawn Michaels. The WWF's matches, with the exception of Brian Christopher vs. Taka Michinoku, ranged from bad to baaaaad. Granted, the three hours of WCW seemed at times like an endurance test more than a wrestling show, but the viewer patterns with the ratings generally growing throughout the three hours tells the important story.

Viewers stayed with the show and grew with it, through the teases for the Steiners surprise, Sting being offered a contract, and the Hogan-Luger match with Luger guaranteeing victory (the general pro wrestling rule is if a babyface either guarantees victory or swears to God that he's going to win, than he's either going to win or he's going to turn heel). The overall wrestling in WCW ranged from very good short matches (Jarrett & Malenko vs. Chavo & Hector Guerrero and Chris Benoit vs. Syxx); a heated world title change that offered little in regard to wrestling but had been built up great and featured an awesome post-match textbook example of how to get a title belt back over, average wrestling with big names (Flair vs. Page); solid wrestling with no names (Villanos vs. Garza & Lizmark);and bad wrestling regardless of names (Public Enemy vs. Voltage, Barbarian vs. Wrath, Silver King & Damian vs. Ernest Miller & Glacier).

WCW, with no first hour opposition, started strong at 4.0 for the Hogan interview with Curt Hennig vs. Mortis match and stayed in the 4.1/4.2 until 9:45 p.m. when a combination of Silver King & Damian vs. Glacier & Ernest Miller and a J.J. Dillon-Eric Bischoff confrontation drew a 4.6. WWF started at 2.6 for the Hart Foundation opening interview and introduction of Sgt. Slaughter, stayed that way with Ken Shamrock vs. Kama Mustafa, and grew to 2.8 for Michinoku vs. Christopher and Helmsley vs. Vader. While WCW grew to 4.6 at 9:45-10 p.m., WWF fell to 2.4 for Patriot vs. Sultan and Patriot/Bret Hart angle. WWF's one surge was the 3.2 for the Michaels interview, while WCW actually dropped down to a 4.2 for Flair vs. Page. The Hogan-Luger title switch did 4.9 (which also included the angle where Sting was offered the contract by Dillon) and 5.2 quarters respectively while WWF consistently fell in the second hour after the Michaels interview, with a 2.5 (Godwinns vs. Head Bangers and Pillman in a dress) and 2.4 (Owen Hart vs. Dude Love) closing the show.

On the replay Nitro still held up to a 2.15 rating and 8.95 share between 1:30 and 2 a.m. for the replay of the Hogan-Luger match. The WWF pulled something of a bait and switch, which may have hurt it from a letdown factor in the final half hour, since they did the show opening angle building toward an Owen vs. Steve Austin match, and plugged it as the main event throughout the show, before making the switch to Dude Love in the last half hour citing Austin's legit injury.

Chapter Twenty Four

Sabu Captures ECW Title

AUGUST 18

In what apparently was among the most gruesome matches in the recent history of American wrestling, Sabu captured the ECW heavyweight title for the first time beating Terry Funk in a barbed wire match on 8/9 at the ECW Arena before a packed house of about 1,400 fans.

The last-minute change was apparently to shake things up for the 8/17 Hardcore Heaven PPV show, which will now be headlined by Sabu, Funk and Shane Douglas in a three-way dance for the title in a rematch of one of the most famous matches in ECW history. With Sandman out of action, although he will be at the PPV and likely will participate in some sort of an angle, it left Sabu without an opponent so he was inserted into the match before the title change took place, although the title change will likely be the public explanation as to why he was put in the match.

Both wrestlers along with manager Bill Alfonso were covered with blood by the finish of the match. Most of the cuts were blade induced, including it being obvious that ref John "Pee Wee" Moore was slicing up Sabu's back after it would hit the barbed wire. The most serious looking of the injuries was Sabu going for his leap off the chair into the spinning hip into the corner and Funk moved and Sabu's arm was ripped to shreds in a sickening manner. He reportedly received 75 stitches after the match backstage but didn't go to the hospital afterwards. Sabu quickly screamed for Alfonso to get some tape and Alfonso ran to the back and brought back tape. Sabu was actually taping up the wound while selling for Funk's offense.

At another point, Sabu crotched himself on the barbed wire. The finish saw both wrestlers tied up together in the barbed wire after Sabu had legdropped Funk through a table, due to outside help from Rob Van Dam, and scored the pin. Tommy Dreamer also got involved hitting Van Dam with a garbage can lid. Both men were so wrapped up in the barbed wire with each other that officials needed wire cutters to get both of them out of it after the match ended.

Virtually the entire dressing room emptied to watch the title change from the stage area, reminiscent of the old days in wrestling when a super worker like a Harley Race, Jack Brisco, Dory Funk or Lou Thesz type would come to a territory and all the wrestlers would stay and watch the main event which was considered within the profession the ultimate show of respect to a top wrestler.

The match was so bloody that only the finish, which apparently was shot in a manner where the blood didn't look that bad, will air on television although it'll be pushed hard for videotapes sales.

Besides the change in the main event, there are a few other minor changes in the PPV line-up which is tentatively scheduled as a six-match show. The other matches listed last week, Taz vs. Chris Candido for the TV title, Tommy Dreamer vs. Jerry Lawler, the Dudleys defending the tag team titles against PG-13 and Spike Dudley vs. Bam Bam Bigelow (set up at the ECW Arena where Dudley scored a pin on Bigelow without outside interference) all remain. In the tag title match, the match itself is likely an angle to set up a feud with Dudleys vs. New Jack & John Kronus. The Rob Van Dam vs. Balls Mahoney match has been switched to Van Dam vs. Al Snow, who is expected to start with ECW as a regular even though he will remain under WWF contract as part of the two company's new working agreement. If any of the matches go short, another match may be added at the last minute to the show but it will most likely be a six-match plus angles stemming from the six matches show.

Approximately 1,000 tickets had been sold to the 1,800-seat Fort Lauderdale War Memorial Auditorium as of press time which has to be considered somewhat disappointing since ECW hasn't been in Florida in years and this is a PPV show. With much of the crew going down early for promotional work, the building still should wound up being packed.

While there doesn't appear to be the anticipation of this show as compared with ECW's first PPV show on 4/13, most likely the show will do similar business. ECW was buoyed by last minute plugs on WWF's Raw on 8/11 in return for Rick Rude starting up as the new "bodyguard" manager for Shawn Michaels, and its arena and overall business along with the ECW name is stronger now than it was before the first PPV show.

The first PPV show was generally considered very good, so it's doubtful many first-time buyers were turned off by the show itself, at least when it came to the in-ring product itself. Some wrestling fans who were looking primarily at the glitz aspects and wowed by things like production values and the major league atmosphere they've seen on WWF and WCW may have considered it second rate but those into harder violence and blood likely would have enjoyed it more.

However, the hoped for new clearances for this show for the most part didn't take place. Request TV is claiming a universe of 17.6 million for this show (they claimed 17 million for the first show), although those numbers have to be considered with a grain of salt (Multi Channel News in an article this week on the last UFC show said the universe was 21 million when the real figure was just under 15 million). The only real major difference is that DirecTV is carrying this show, which didn't carry the first show, and Time Warner, which carried the first show, isn't carrying this show.

Paul Heyman before the first PPV show said that the show wasn't about drawing a good buy rate, but about putting on the kind of the show which would increase the universe for subsequent shows. By that standard, even though the first show did an acceptable and profitable buy rate and had to be considered a success from a product standpoint, it didn't accomplish its objectives because for the most part the people who passed on show No. 1, are still on the pass list although there are negotiations ongoing that could change that for the third show.

The 7/27 UFC show, at less than 15 million homes, was carried by the larger servicing Viewers Choice and not Request, (ECW is being carried by Request and not Viewers Choice), and had all the satellite services cleared while ECW has most but not all. Most companies that decided against carrying UFC also aren't carrying ECW (TCI being the most notable exception as they are carrying ECW in their systems that subscribe to Request).

Heyman also instituted a number of new company rules at the Arena show. The main ones were there can be no wrestling or fighting over the guard rail unless specifically authorized; There can be no fighting near tables or using tables unless specifically authorized; There can be no using the house mic during the show unless specifically authorized; There can be no crotch shots of any kind unless specifically authorized; And there can be no touching of fans under any circumstance.

There are several likely reasons for the changes. One is that ECW has come close on several occasions to fan problems that were one step from becoming incidents that could have threatened their future. ECW is under major pressure from Request to not have any incidents garner negative publicity for the company or Request's deal to carry the PPV would be in jeopardy. In addition, in the case of the tables and crotch shots, Heyman will continue to use those spots but lessen usage of them to attempt to make the spots mean more. Wrestlers in all U.S. promotions use not only low blows, but crotch shots on the ropes because they are the one move almost guaranteed to get a response from any crowd, but then that leads to wrestlers relying on them and they lose their value when it comes from using then in angles and finishes.

Heyman's own background from Memphis in 1987 where they drew several huge houses based on one crotch shot angle, and used Dreamer in several of those in recent weeks, plus used it for a finish where Spike Dudley beat Bigelow at the Arena, wants to protect the spot. Ditto the tables. The fighting in the crowd and touching fans is more a response to problems of late that needed to be addressed because they were happening too frequently again, rather than changes made for booking reasons.

Chapter Twenty Five

The Death of Plum Mariko

AUGUST 25

When you actually think about all the risks wrestlers take in the ring, the injuries that do happen and the accidents that can happen, it's actually almost an unbelievable statistic when it comes to the mortality rate in the profession from in-ring injuries.

The death of Japanese woman wrestler Plum Mariko (real name Mariko Umeda) on 8/16 stemming from an in-ring accident in a match the night before was actually the first death stemming from an incident inside the ring in the history of pro wrestling in Japan. It is the first death stemming from an incident in the ring at least in a major promotion since the Mexican wrestler Oro passed away on October 26, 1993 of a brain aneurysm suffered after taking a routine bump off a chop in the middle of a match.

While there have been a few heart attack deaths in the locker room after a match over the past several decades, with names like Larry Cameron, Killer Mal Kirk (who I believe actually died of his heart attack in the ring), Ray Gunkel, Luis Hernandez, Jay Youngblood and Mike DiBiase coming to mind, deaths from actual in-ring injuries are astonishingly rare. This is not to lessen the tragedy when such a rare occurrence does take place, particularly in a case where many in hindsight seem to feel it was preventable.

Mariko, 29, was working a tag match on the JWP card on 8/15 at the Hiroshima Astell Plaza teaming with Boirshoi Kid against Mayumi Ozaki & Rieko Amano. Ozaki delivered Liger bomb on Mariko, who landed higher on her back and on the back of her head, which is not unusual for such a power bomb landing, but what was rare was she was knocked completely out and the match had to be ended at that point.

She never woke up again, and was rushed to the hospital in an ambulance for an emergency brain operation that night. She officially died at 6:25 p.m. the next day, with the cause of death believed to have been from an abscess in the brain and a fractured skull, a condition she may have gone into the ring with since she had been complaining of for some time—and company officials after the fact admitted—she had been unusually tired as well of late, although she had refused to miss any matches. The belief is the injury was the final blow in a cumulative group of injuries resulting in brain trauma, such as repeated moves such as piledrivers, suplexes landing on the back and head and power bombs as opposed to a singular injury during her career.

The death has resulted in a lot of introspection within the Japanese wrestling world both from inside and outside. There are questions, both from the amount of punishment that the women pro wrestlers with their smaller size and frames, and for that matter, even the men, are expected to endure, combined with the fact that Japanese wrestling isn't regulated. In fact, despite the physical nature of most of the major offices, only New Japan Pro Wrestling has a doctor at its shows who checks out the wrestlers before putting them in the ring and can administer to them in case of an accident.

Since this story is a major mainstream media story in Japan, there has become a lot of talk about some form of regulation of wrestling such as the commission system in some states in the United States (although most commissions when it comes to governing the actions and safeguarding the participants within pro wrestling are a joke), and of mandating a doctor at ringside both for immediate attention to injuries and for checking out participants ahead of time.

Mariko, who had suffered numerous serious injuries over the past three years wrestling a style not really designed to allow for long careers, was wrestling despite numerous concussions that made it impossible for her to remember complicated finishes and thus kept her out of the main events. And despite having what after the fact became known that she was working with tremendous head pain in recent weeks, continued to wrestle because that's the mentality within the Japanese wrestling world. The police in Hiroshima wanted to investigate the death but her parents asked them not to do so because she loved pro wrestling and it was her decision to continue on despite suffering constant injuries.

Mariko's death came just one day before the 11th year anniversary of her pro wrestling debut which was on the inaugural card of the first JWP promotion on August 17, 1986 at Korakuen Hall. Her debut was the same night as the pro debut of Dynamite Kansai, Ozaki, Shinobu Kandori, Harley Saito and Rumi Kazama among others with the formation of the group that originally was considered opposition to All Japan women forming in the wake of a peak in womens wrestling popularity from the Crush Gals. JWP had scheduled two Korakuen Hall shows on 8/17, an afternoon and evening show as the anniversary of both the start of the promotion but also of the debuts of Kansai, Ozaki and Mariko, but the shows turned out to be more tragic then celebratory. At the show, they held a 10 count memorial announcing her death. Her funeral took place on 8/19 in Tokyo.

All the women from the initial JWP wrestling class, which also included Cuty Suzuki and Eagle Sawai, were trained by former New Japan wrestler Kotetsu Yamamoto (at the time between stints working for that company in the front office), Atsushi Onita and Gran Hamada, the latter two of whom were unemployed as pro wrestlers during that time period.

That first JWP folded five years later, and basically splintered into two different promotions, one of which is today's LLPW and the other being the second incarnation of JWP which re-started in 1992. During her career she held both the JWP and UWA jr. championships, and during the early 90s was considered a second-tier star with the group and a good undercard worker with a submission expert gimmick. With her training in sambo, the shooter gimmick was based in reality as despite her small size (5'2", 132 pounds) and pretty looks, she was at one point considered the "policewoman" in JWP to protect Ozaki and mainly Cutie Suzuki outside the ring as they hung out together publicly. Suzuki at the time was the big draw for the company for her early run as something of a mainstream popular picture book model who eventually did what would be considered softcore porn videos.

She suffered several major injuries that kept her out of action for long periods of time before coming back to the ring on October 13, 1996, although she didn't get any kind of a push on her most recent comeback. Her first major injury was on April 10, 1994 in a match at Korakuen Hall against Hikari Fukuoka, where she suffered a broken nose and broken left collarbone and was out of action for 16 months. Shortly after her return, on December 9, 1995, she broke her right collarbone and was out another ten months. Her most recent return was on JWP's biggest show of 1996 at Sumo Hall, and blew an important spot in the match which ended her chance of getting a push. She worked only on-and-off since that point without any kind of a push, with reports being that she was unable to memorize the complicated series of spots worked in matches within the current style.

When the Japanese women wrestlers were taking the standard of pro wrestling to the next level that many of the top male workers have reached since that time, during the 1992 to 1994 period, there was some discussion behind-the-scenes and even articles written in Japan about the potential of a death or major injury because of all the high risk moves, particularly the alarming frequency in which women wrestlers suffered injuries serious enough in the ring that it was commonplace for them to have to be carried out of the ring after a match because of an inability to leave under their own power. It became a non-issue publicly over the past three years because nothing as serious as was feared ever occurred.

While this was the first death from a ring injury from a match in Japanese wrestling history, in the past decade there had been two other deaths of trainees who had never had a professional match in the dojos, one with New Japan of a national champion amateur under circumstances so suspicious that it was largely responsible for Hiroshi Hase, the mentor of the young wrestler, leaving the company, and the other in the dojo of the old UWF.

SEPTEMBER 1

A few more notes on the death of Plum Mariko. The death is now thought to have not been related to the Liger-bomb from Mayumi Ozaki or landing wrong, although she was knocked out from the move, but from injuries she went into the ring with. She died the next day on the operating table from a combination fractured skull, brain hemorrhage, aneurysm and was also believed to have been suffering from post-concussion syndrome. Reportedly there were 50,000 bouquets of flowers sent to her funeral, which was attended by about 500 people.

After the anniversary shows at Korakuen Hall the next day, JWP went back on tour on 8/20 to Fukui where it drew a much larger than usual crowd with tons of press and Ozaki, in the first minute of her singles match with Kanako Motoya, symbolically used the Liger bomb. She said to the press after that she believed that Mariko would have wanted her to continue using the move.

According to wrestling historian Gary Will, there have been approximately 36 deaths since 1950 of pro wrestlers either in the ring or the dressing room or hospital immediately after a match, but only five this decade, one each in England, South Africa, Mexico (Oro), Germany (Larry Cameron) and Japan (Mariko). Virtually all of the deaths were heart attacks and only two conclusively appear to be from injuries.

The last recorded death due to a ring injury (and in hindsight Mariko's death doesn't neatly fit into that category either anymore than Malcolm Kirk's 1987 death of a heart attack at the time Big Daddy gave him a big splash does) was Sangre India in a match in Mexico City on December 25, 1979 after hitting his head on the floor missing a tope. The other injury related death appears to have been a wrestler named Curtis Peterson in 1951 in Richland Center, WI from a broken neck.

Chapter Twenty Six

Arn Anderson Retires

SEPTEMBER 1

Perhaps it was only fitting that the official announcement on 8/25 of the end of the wrestling career of Arn Anderson was largely an angle to get someone else—in this case Curt Hennig—over. Because in many ways that was the story of his career.

Anderson, born Martin Lunde, in one of the best interviews of this or any other year, announced on the live WCW Nitro show from Columbia, SC that he recognized he had nothing left to give due to neck injuries and he wouldn't be coming back. This announcement was confirmation of what nearly everyone had speculated since he had major neck surgery a few months back which resulted in the strength in one of his hands being so weak he couldn't even button his own shirt.

Anderson received an incredible standing ovation, that overwhelmed even the reaction to Sting earlier in the show, when he showed up on camera for the first time since his operation before fans in one of his old stomping grounds. And the fans who reacted that way had no idea of what he was there for, while long-time partner Ric Flair was in the background fighting hard to hold back tears.

Anderson labeled himself an average wrestler, with average size, skill and speed, who achieved success through a lot of hard work. Although at his peak Anderson was considered among the best workers in the world, he always low-keyed his talents and would refer to himself as a solid journeyman wrestler.

In looking back over the nearly 15-year career of Lunde, 39, asks the question of whether he was one of the luckiest or unluckiest wrestlers when it comes to his level of success. On one hand, while a solid worker, he was unspectacular, not the slightest bit glamorous or muscular in an era where that meant a lot more than ability, so you could say he came along in the wrong era for his strengths.

But he was still a prominent star everywhere he went due to the respect most in the profession had for him. He was one of the best interviewers in history. But the real truth is, his break in wrestling came due to his looks, his uncanny facial resemblance to Ole Anderson. The other truth is without a great deal of ability that "luck" would have only taken him so far before the business spit him out like virtually all his contemporaries. It was his non-glamorous look that made him almost a "meat and potatoes" wrestler, a wrestler with tremendous charisma based on the fact that he looked, based on the standards of his era, like he shouldn't have any charisma.

But due to his ability, respect the fans—particularly in the Southeast—had for him, his long-time affiliation with Flair and perhaps most importantly, the Four Horseman name, Anderson lasted longer as a major player in this profession despite being written off numerous times than 90 percent of the pretty boys lavished with major pushes and in many cases bigger money contracts that he spent his career putting over. His career was made putting over a collection of stars of the past and "Where are they nows?" and then getting on television the next Saturday and doing such a strong interview that after a few years fans actually forgot he made his mark while almost always putting people over.

Lunde, who played football, wrestled and powerlifted in Rome, GA while growing up, broke in under his real name in 1982. Due to his resemblance to Ole Anderson, he was re-named Arn Anderson after about one year in the business, and billed from Minneapolis, MN, since Ole & Gene Anderson had made the Minnesota Wrecking Crew legendary heels in the Southeast.

After being a headliner in the small Alabama promotion teaming with and later feuding with Jerry "Mr. Olympia" Stubbs, he was brought into the Carolinas to continue the Anderson family dynasty. He was billed as a nephew, cousin or brother, depending on the week, of Ole's before the fictitious world seemed to settle on him being cousins of both Ole and Ric Flair. Put together with Ole, Flair and Tully Blanchard, they became the original pro wrestling Four Horseman in 1985, in many ways a forerunner to nearly everything that goes on in pro wrestling today, and a name that has remained in existence on-and-off in wrestling to this day.

With Flair as the perennial world champion, Anderson, known as "The Enforcer," was generally the fourth banana on the four-man team which had later incarnations with the likes of Lex Luger and Barry Windham during its glory days after Ole phased out of active wrestling. Arn usually feuded over the tag team and TV titles holding tag titles with partners such as Stubbs, Ole Anderson, Blanchard, Larry Zbyszko, Bobby Eaton and Paul Roma. He and Blanchard are one of only four teams in history to have held both the NWA (or WCW) and WWF tag titles, and was TV champion on five occasions. Anderson was often times high on the Observer balloting for tag team of the year and best on interviews, capturing the 1990 award in the latter.

Although the run that solidified his reputation came from a push from booker Dusty Rhodes, by 1988, with Jim Crockett Promotions on the verge of bankruptcy which many blame on Rhodes' booking patterns, Anderson and Blanchard, fed up with how things were going, quit JCP to join the WWF, where in a land of the Giants, they became the undersized tag team known as The BrainBusters with Bobby Heenan as manager and had classic matches against The Rockers, Shawn Michaels and Marty Jannetty.

The other irony of Anderson's career is that he was considered too small to be pushed to the top during his heyday, yet by today's standards he'd be considered a large wrestler. But in his heyday he was considered one of the best workers in the business, but by today's standards his work, while solid, would be hard pressed to get him past the middle of the shows.

After the demise of Rhodes, and Ric Flair obtaining power in what was now WCW, Flair was able to lure both Anderson and Blanchard back in late 1989, although Blanchard never did return as after giving notice and dropping the tag team titles back to Demolition, he failed a WWF drug test, was suspended by the WWF and WCW pulled its $250,000 per year offer off the table.

Alternating between face and heel, Anderson had another strong run for a few years before it was believed that he had run his course. There were periods his career was virtually iced out. There were periods he was doing fast jobs for the likes of Erik Watts, Van Hammer or The Renegade, the next generation of supposed superstars of the future that he, and most of the fans as well realized—even though promoters at the time couldn't see it—couldn't even carry his jock.

At one time, when Bill Watts was brought back in control of WCW, after jobbing Anderson to his son, he basically cut Anderson loose figuring there was nothing left to get out of him. But in every case, both being jobbed out to the future nobodies of wrestling, after a herniated disc in a 1992 match against the Steiners that threatened his career and after an overseas incident where he was stabbed silly in a hotel room brawl with Sid Eudy after both had apparently had too much to drink, he came back, not quite to superstardom, but to that level one notch below where he seemed to fit perfectly.

The most recent neck injury, suffered nearly one year ago, was far more serious, and he didn't come through surgery with flying colors. It had largely been acknowledged for a few months that Anderson wouldn't be able to return to the ring, and every now and then ideas were thrown out, either of being a color commentator or as the late 90s version of the J.J. Dillon of the 80s with the Horseman to take advantage of his interview skills although the last word we'd heard was that the powers that be nixed the idea when Flair pushed for it.

He currently and has been working behind-the-scenes with the WCW booking department. He wasn't supposed to steal the show on Nitro on 8/25. That was for today's glamour boys who are just toooo sweet. But unlike the glamour boys from ten years earlier in the same position, this time Arn Anderson won't be still around in a prominent role while they become "Whatever happened to?" trivia questions.

SEPTEMBER 8

This week's major controversy revolves around the skit that Kevin Nash (as Arn Anderson), Syxx (as Ric Flair), Marcus Bagwell (as Curt Hennig) and Konnan (as Steve McMichael) did on Nitro doing their imitation of the now famous Arn Anderson interview from one week earlier.

As the story goes, the deal was played out ahead of time where they would dedicate the show to Anderson, and then the NWO would make so much fun of him with the combination of the two things theoretically building up tremendous heat. Which is what happened. We got more reaction, some very positive thinking it was hilarious and some very negative thinking it was in terrible taste, largely depending upon what part of the country people were from and who they grew up watching.

Originally the finish of the skit was going to have the Horseman run out and totally clean house on the NWO, with Anderson watching from the stage area with his arms folded and a big smile on his face. Before the show started, Terry Taylor was told by Eric Bischoff to nix the Horseman comeback and not let them do the run-in, which it is believed came at the suggestion of Nash. Later in the show, Flair was supposed to instead do an interview, but by this time Flair was so mad he refused to go on because he felt that by not coming out during the skit it made the Horseman look so bad that there was nothing he could do to salvage the situation.

Anderson wasn't as mad immediately after the skit, but was said to be furious later that night including winding up in a confrontation with booker Kevin Sullivan after calling home and finding out how mad and upset his wife and 12-year-old son were. Flair wasn't so mad about the portrayal of him, but of the portrayal of his best friend who he's protective of and the mockery of the very serious retirement interview he did the week before. There were even reports Anderson wound up so mad he was thinking of quitting the company.

Flair's contract expires in February and he hasn't signed an extension, although WWF due to the lawsuit against WCW is very leery about doing anything that would look like they were interested in WCW talent right now even though you know they'd like to have Flair, if only as primarily a goodwill ambassador more than a full-time wrestler.

There are also reports that some or all of this behind the scenes controversy was simply a Kevin Sullivan/ Brian Pillman angle although my impression is that isn't the case. Of course this only make sense if the War Games were to turn out to be Horseman vs. NWO, which isn't going to be the case.

The skit itself was absolutely hilarious in spots, particularly Waltman with the fake oversized nose, the clothes, the tears and the dancing, and Nash was incredible, but it went on way too long and realistically was so inside and biting, since Anderson's mother died very young due to alcoholism, that one could see if the former scenario is the real one that it was designed that way by Nash to stick it to Anderson.

The heat between the Horseman and NWO is legit to a point that's silly because at the Clash on 8/21, there was a bomb threat called in Nashville on the Flair match, and Nash was joking after the show that Anderson must have called it in because they wanted management to think somebody actually cared about Flair. And there is a major level of discomfort of late in the dressing room regarding people trying to take all the credit for the recent success.

The funny part is, the TV ratings are still slightly lower for the year as compared to the same period the previous year before there was a such thing as the NWO. Buy rates aren't all that different, and that's with hotshotting guys like Kevin Greene, Reggie White and Dennis Rodman all over the place. House business is way up, but the most valuable person when it comes to that is Zane Bresloff and the fact that the television show

Nitro, and not any of the individuals, has become super hot as the rank-and-file house shows aren't put together with strong line-ups to draw big houses to begin with, and tickets are being sold mainly for the name brand as opposed to any singular individual.

Not that the wrestlers and angles aren't overall hotter this year when it comes to drawing because they are, but WCW is at a point right now where any individual, whether it be Savage, Hogan, Flair, Sting, Hall or Nash could leave tomorrow and it would make no serious difference in ratings, buy rates or arena grosses.

SEPTEMBER 15

The aftermath of the NWO skit where they did a parody of the Arn Anderson retirement interview is another interesting piece of curiosity.

The angle and much of what was said and done was known ahead of time to all the particular parties being mocked. However, from all accounts after the show in Pensacola, the heat was really bad between the two sides, supposedly because Kevin Nash in particular had gone too far or hit too close to home on certain subjects, in particular drinking, when mocking Anderson.

There was also supposedly a lot of heat from the Horsemen side as originally the parody was supposed to end with the Horsemen hitting the ring and cleaning house while Arn Anderson, who never appeared before the cameras on a show designed as a tribute to him, stood on the ramp and watched with a smile on his face. However, just before the show went on the air, Terry Taylor told Ric Flair that was being nixed and instead Flair was supposed to do an interview as his comeback later in the show. As is well known, Flair, after the segment aired, refused to do the interview and there was a lot of concern because of the heat with Flair, and Anderson after he called home, based on the parody hitting home. How much of that was a work and how much was a New Japan style shoot angle becomes a question, particularly in the current wrestling environment.

If Flair and Anderson's reactions were an angle, done in conjunction with Kevin Sullivan and kept between those three with virtually nobody else knowing about it, everyone else in the company was being worked. We know for certain that the NWO and none of the other wrestlers were in on the angle. If it was a work, it was more a work on the wrestlers involved in the skit than it was on anyone else, but Sullivan likes doing those things such as attempting to work the boys in his angle with Pillman and in his wife having an affair with Chris Benoit and the two even having a fake bar fight in front of nobody but the boys after a Nitro in New Orleans.

In fact, the heat from the other side because of what they believed was heat from the Horseman side reached what could be termed scary proportions later that night to the point there were people thinking another Arn Anderson-Sid Vicious situation, not as severe but that basic situation, could take place. Even as late as after the 9/8 Nitro in Milwaukee, there continued to be what several close to the situation called legitimate heat between the two sides although the situation was no longer considered dangerous.

We've learned in so many cases that Sullivan and Eric Bischoff, stemming from last year's Pillman angle, get off on working the boys on their angles even if it never pays off in traditional wrestling storyline fashion and in the long run only leads to even more mistrust then the natural wrestling day-to-day business produces naturally among the employees. In addition, sources close to the situation claim that Flair and Anderson's acting was too good and emotions too real for it not to have been legit. Flair's comeback angle on the 9/8 Nitro was his best interview in a long time and nothing short of yet another in a three week string of classic memorable stuff stemming from this angle.

This brings two other questions to mind. If Flair's actions in not doing the interview on 9/1 were legit, how come there was no disciplinary action taken against him for refusing to perform on a live television show (oh yeah, because there is no discipline when it comes to behavior of any top star in wrestling, not that if Flair was truly as upset as he appeared to be with the manner of mocking the injury-forced retirement of his best friend that his actions weren't somewhat understandable)? And how come the main event was changed for the 9/14 Winston-Salem PPV to Horseman vs. NWO to fit perfectly into this storyline?

This change was supposedly made mid-week at a WCW booking meeting stemming from the reaction so strong both positively and negatively to the parody that the main event change was an obvious business decision.

The fact it wasn't something planned out in advance could be confirmed by the fact that Benoit was booked into Japan starting 9/11 for the New Japan tour, and neither he nor New Japan were informed his debut would have to be delayed a week until the end of this past week because WCW was going to need him to stay for the PPV show.

However, if there was really internal fear about problems occurring, changing the main event wouldn't take place. In a situation that was legit, like the Bret Hart-Shawn Michaels backstage problem at Raw, because of those problems the WWF was forced to keep the two apart for several months rather than book them against each other as had been planned and had already been built up in the storyline.

Speaking of Benoit, in the angle the NWO was supposed to bring a mannequin out to play the part of Benoit. Several reasons were given that day as excuses as to why that was nixed, although it's pretty clear from Nitro on 9/8 that the real reason was because Hogan and Bischoff were going to use a mannequin in a skit the next week.

SEPTEMBER 29

I don't know if anything is certain in regard to the Four Horsemen. We've heard talk about the entire group disbanding with Flair going on his own as a single, and the group being put together again with Dean Malenko as the fourth member. There were complaints by certain headliners regarding Malenko's size and having to sell for him that have the potential to stand in the way of the latter. The political problems between the Hall/Nash faction and Flair continue to be pretty heated. They're cordial to each other, but the underlying animosity continues to exist.

Chapter Twenty Seven

AJW Goes Bankrupt

SEPTEMBER 1

The future of the 29-year-old All Japan Womens wrestling promotion, the third oldest major wrestling promotion in the world, has come into serious question over the past week with word that the company may be one step from bankruptcy.

The company, run by the same Matsunaga Brothers who formed it in 1968, hasn't paid its talent and office staff since the end of March which has caused several of its top stars and many key members of the office staff to leave of late including wrestlers Aja Kong, Kyoko Inoue and Toshiyo Yamada along with undercard wrestlers Yumi Fukawa and Rie Tamada. The company's long-time headquarters, a combination business office, restaurant, dormitory type apartments and wrestling gymnasium, is up for sale. And all four Matsunaga brothers have had to sell their houses and move into apartments to keep the company going.

Exactly what the true story is as far as the financial picture and how things got to this stage are somewhat clouded and unclear. The general belief is that the problem is more stemming from non-wrestling business interests of the Matsunaga brothers than the wrestling company itself being a big money loser, although nobody can dispute the popularity of the company and the future of the company have hit the skids over the past year or two.

During the boom periods of the company, both in the mid-80s with the Crush Gals, and the early 90s behind Kong, Bull Nakano, Manami Toyota and Akira Hokuto, the company was tremendously profitable. The Matsunaga brothers at that point got heavily into real estate and a failed attempt at franchising a health food style Ramen house restaurant chain. When the real estate market in Japan took a nosedive, the company took out heavy bank loans to keep up with its obligations in that business, and in recent times were having a hard time simply keeping up on paying the bank interest on the loans, let alone paying the principle owed.

Still, there is little question the wrestling side had hit the skids. With the exception of groups in Mexico, no company in the world ran more house shows that AJW, to the tune of about 250 shows per year. Attendance had dropped considerably since Japanese wrestling when it comes to drawing at spot shows is based on fans watching new stars grow up to the next level, and AJW had failed to find a new star that fans cared about in years.

Womens wrestling even more so, has in its history been based on teenage sensations who would draw fans only a few years younger than the stars themselves, but AJW was no longer a big deal to that age group since it's TV was moved from weekly on Saturday afternoon delivering huge ratings to maybe a few specials per year, which aired well past midnight to tiny audiences.

In many ways, up until a year or two ago when the company was still doing well, it was living off the success of the Crush Gals era since so many young girls wanted to be pro wrestlers having grown up watching the heyday that they had a great pool of athletes to pick from. Even though all the Crush Gals attendance records were broken in the latest hot period from 1993-95, the promotion didn't have the television visibility and it was more driven by traditional hardcore wrestling fans rather than teenage girls, so the pool of those wanting to become wrestlers with the group dwindled.

When the likes of Toyota and Kong debuted, AJW literally would get thousands of applications from teenagers wanting to be wrestlers and weed them down into try-outs where only a few would survive, and those that did were trained by Jaguar Yokota, whose departure has also resulted in a lowering of the quality of work of the newer women wrestlers. This past year, there were maybe 15 women who attended the try-outs, so the pool to get superior athletes for the future isn't there and both Yokota and Chigusa Nagayo of Gaea were doing a better job of training the teenagers for the future.

As spot show attendance fell, it became harder to sell shows to local promoters (in its heyday, the group would sell its spot shows usually for $20,000 to $25,000 to local promoters and do the big shows on its own). To keep up the 250-show schedule, they began promoting more and more of the shows on their own and without being local and knowing the localities, that became an overall financial drain. In addition, many of the local promoters if crowds were poor had stiffed the office on its guarantee, causing more of a drain.

Still, those who remember the groups history aren't nearly so negative about the future, citing that there were occasions in both the 70s and the 80s (before the Crush Gals) that the company was in every bit as bad a financial position and near closing, and in both cases ended up rebounding stronger than ever.

Word of the problems reached the public this past week after one of the company's traditional biggest show of the year on 8/20 at Budokan Hall, where then-champion Kyoko Inoue, Fukawa and Tamada joined Kong, who had made the announcement several weeks back, in announcing they were leaving the promotion. There was tremendous heat on Inoue, who held the WWWA championship at the time, because she made the announcement unbeknownst to anyone in the company over the p.a. just as the show was getting started.

As all the wrestlers before the show were introduced, Inoue said something to the effect that she would be leaving the promotion after finishing up her current commitments, which apparently majorly upset her long-time rival both in and out of the ring for the top spot, Manami Toyota (who have had something of a Bret Hart/Shawn Michaels rivalry behind-the-scenes since their situations and positions in the company are actually remarkably similar) and Yumiko Hotta, who was scheduled to challenge her for the title that night.

The crowd, announced at 9,100 but estimated to us at around 6,000, was comprised of largely smart fans who have something of a knowledge of the business and Inoue's announcement told everyone that there would be a title change in the main event and largely killed the heat during the match and the expected surprise reaction to the switch when Hotta got the submission with the armbreaker in 18:33. It was clear that Inoue was doing this on purpose since logic would say her own announcement would have carried far more weight and emotion had she done it after losing the title, not to mention would have made for a better match.

Kong, who wrestled to a 30:00 time limit draw with Toyota in her final major match with the company, is expected to fare well outside the company. Virtually all the women promotions in Japan are interested in using her as a freelancer on major shows, and several of the smaller mens groups including Big Japan and Social Pro Wrestling Federation are interested in booking tag matches involving well-known Kong and Kyoko Inoue on their shows. The big fight in her case is which company can get her to do the first job in cleanly putting over one of their own.

Kong this past week did an angle in FMW for a match with Shark Tsuchiya, and has a prominent match on 9/20 for Gaea against Chigusa Nagayo. In addition, because of her unique look, Kong has a measure of celebrity status and is expected to fare well doing appearances, television shows and television commercials outside of wrestling. Inoue and the other women really can only be celebrities within the wrestling world.

It appears that Toyota, Hotta, Tomoko Watanabe, Kaoru Ito, Kumiko Maekawa and heels Etsuko Mita and Mima Shimoda will remain with the company and try to rebuild it, although from all accounts the company isn't going to be able to run the kind of scheduled it has in the past nor remain on the level it had with the depleted office staff.

SEPTEMBER 22

Etsuko Mita, Mima Shimoda, Chaparita Asari, Saya Endo and Yuka Shiina will all officially leave AJW as rumored after the company's big show on 9/21 in Kawasaki. The loss of Mita & Shimoda is a big one since the company had been almost everything around them as the top heels. In addition, the group after this week will be down to a skeleton crew with only 11 women on the roster, one of whom, Tomoko Watanabe, is currently out of action after an operation on 9/4 after suffering a broken rib although she was expected to return on 9/21.

Largely due to losses in real estate as opposed to pro wrestling, the AJW company is $22,000,000 in debt and none of the employees have been paid in nearly five months. The Matsunaga Brothers, who have owned the company since its inception in 1968, have gotten so deep in debt with bank loans that they've been no longer able to even handle the interest on the debt, let alone the principle. If they declare bankruptcy as a protection against the debt, by Japanese law they won't be able to start up the business again for three years.

The women who have left the company, those mentioned along with the likes of Aja Kong and Kyoko Inoue, are attempting to get a sponsor to open up on their own, with a January target date. Until that point they will attempt to get booked with other companies, but at this point only Kong and Inoue have gotten any bookings.

OCTOBER 27

The 29-year-old All Japan Womens wrestling promotion officially filed for bankruptcy on 10/21 and held a press conference later that afternoon in their Tokyo offices.

The bankruptcy documents filed listed the company as being 1.6 billion yen in debt (approximately $13.6 million) and they've bounced some checks of late with the banks they were doing business with canceling their line of credit. The news came just days after the company's traditional Wrestlemarinpiad show on 10/18 at the Yokohama Bunka Gym drew a poor crowd (it was announced as 2,350 but the real number was closer to 1,000 to 1,500) and canceling its planned biggest card of the year on 11/2 at Tokyo Sumo Hall due to virtually no advance sales.

The Sumo Hall cancellation was covered as a pretty major story in the Japanese press as tickets had been on sale for the show since 8/31. The company was down to 13 wrestlers, most of whom hadn't gotten paid in several months.

Exactly what this means was unclear at press time whether the group would be able to continue its schedule as at the press conference they indicated they would continue to try and keep the promotion going and run more than 200 house shows in 1998, but the feeling is strong that this really signals the end of the promotion.

The AJW office, founded in 1968 by the four Matsunaga Brothers, would be the third oldest continuing wrestling promotion in the world, trailing only the EMLL in Mexico (founded in the 1930s) and the World Wrestling Federation (which as a WWWF name dates back to 1963 but was founded as Capital Sports by Vince McMahon Sr. in the 50s). The group ran between 200 and 250 house shows per year and had occasional specials, which had been running monthly of late, on the Fuji Network, the top network in Japan, but airing past midnight.

Over the years the promotion, which from the early 70s to the present was generally considered the top womens wrestling promotion in the world, has had its ups and downs, with the ups for the most part built around young rock idol type headliners that would burn out quickly. By the late 70s, the workrate among their best wrestlers was close to the level of the top men from the same era.

During the 80s, with headliners like Jaguar Yokota, Chigusa Nagayo, Lioness Asuka, Devil Masami and later Manami Toyota, Kyoko Inoue and Akira Hokuto, it presented a quality of matches unsurpassed anywhere in the world. From a business standpoint, it peaked in the mid-80s behind the Crush Gals phenomenon, and then broke all of the Crush Gals attendance records during a big run of inter-promotional matches from 1992-94.

In recent years, due largely to the lack of new talent replenishing the promotion, the interest level has gone way down and the parent corporation itself, largely due to real estate debts, has been in bad financial straits for a few years.

NOVEMBER 24

Two new women promotions that had been rumored to be ready to begin made their official announcements this past week. Kyoko Inoue announced that her new promotion, no name given, would debut on 1/9 at Korakuen Hall and that Inoue would have Etsuko Mita, Mima Shimoda, Yuka Shiina, Yoshiko Tamura, Misae Genki, Saya Endo and Tiny Mouse, all former AJW wrestlers who left when they weren't getting paid. In addition, Aja Kong and Hiroshi "Rossy" Ogawa, the latter a long-time publicist and booker for AJW before leaving when the money ran out, announced they would be starting up in February a promotion called "Arsion." Former AJW wrestler Sakie Hasegawa will work in the front office, while Kong will be the President and the booker. The only names announced for this group as wrestlers were former AJW wrestlers Mariko Yoshida, Rie Tamada and Yumi Fukawa.

DECEMBER 1

Of all the new womens wrestling offices being created in Japan in the aftermath of the economic collapse of the All Japan Womens office, it appears the most ambitious is going to be the Arsion promotion headed by Hiroshi "Rossy" Ogawa, a key member of the AJW front office for years and booker Aja Kong.

At a press conference on 11/19, besides former AJW wrestles Rie Tamada, Yumi Fukawa and Mariko Yoshida, Ogawa said that his promotion would steal JWP champion Hikari Fukuoka and its best younger wrestler, Tomoko Kuzumi, and also take Mikiko Futagami and Michiko Omukai from LLPW. Arsion also announced that it would set up a U.S. office and have Reggie Bennett run it and become the top foreign star for the group and also use former AJW star Sakie Hasegawa in the front office. Bennett had become a top star with AJW as a full-time regular until about one year ago when she became the first casualty of the AJW economic woes.

As the week went on, JWP President Masatoshi Yamamoto said that Fukuoka and Kuzumi would be staying with his group. JWP is now working closely with both LLPW and AJW to the point that Yamamoto in response to Ogawa's press conference, appeared at the AJW house show at Korakuen Hall on 11/21 and announced the two groups would work together for a combined major house show in early 1998 and stated the two wrestlers wouldn't be leaving his group. However, Rumi Saito (Rumi Kazama), the LLPW President admitted that Futagami and Omukai would be leaving her company for Arsion.

Chapter Twenty Eight

Shinya Hashimoto's Reign Comes to an End

SEPTEMBER 8

Shinya Hashimoto's run as the longest reigning heavyweight champion in a major league promotion came to an end on the same day that Akira Maeda stepped foot in a New Japan ring for the first time in more than ten years.

Kensuke Sasaki captured the IWGP title from Hashimoto before an overflow crowd of 18,000 fans on 8/31 at the Yokohama Arena. Maeda, who started his career in New Japan before being fired from the promotion in 1987 for his infamous shoot-kick on Riki Choshu that in some ways contributed to making him one of the more enduring lasting legends in Japanese pro wrestling history, showed up unannounced in the ring to congratulate Choshu in his retirement ceremony and got a huge reaction from the crowd.

Obviously that was another lifetime ago in the careers of both wrestlers, as Maeda, in a shoot, kicked Choshu hard in the eye, breaking his orbital bone, during a six-man tag match while Choshu was basically defenseless as he was holding a wrestler in a scorpion deathlock. Maeda was fired from New Japan, not exactly from that incident which caused both wrestlers to have to miss the important tag team tournament that year, but for refusal to accept the punishment (a fine, a tour of Mexico and having to return and put Choshu over clean) handed down by New Japan.

Instead, Maeda got the financial backing to start his own promotion, the UWF, which became the hottest wrestling promotion in the world for a short time and in many ways was revolutionary in paving the way for groups such as K-1, UFC, RINGS and Pancrase which all catered and garnered interest in Japan from a fan base originally created by Maeda's UWF, which split into several promotions a few years later. On 7/6, Maeda, who himself will be retiring next year, surprisingly showed up at a major WAR show, his first time at a traditional pro wrestling event since 1987, to congratulate Genichiro Tenryu, who was celebrating his 20th year as an active pro wrestler.

Sasaki, who in August won both the IWGP title, the IWGP tag team title (with Kazuo Yamazaki on 8/10 at the Nagoya Dome) and the G-1 Climax tournament (beating Hiroyoshi Tenzan in the finals on 8/3 at Tokyo Sumo Hall), is being given the biggest push in a long time within the New Japan organization. He was also put over in a tournament in September of 1996 involving the top names from both New Japan and WCW.

Sasaki captured the IWGP title for the first time in his career on a show honoring his mentor, who will be retiring on 1/4 at the Tokyo Dome. After winning the title, Sasaki immediately challenged Choshu for what will almost surely be the Tokyo Dome main event and be a sure sellout. Sasaki, who is generally considered the worst worker and least over of the big four who are programmed by Choshu to dominate the New Japan singles scene (Hashimoto, Sasaki, Great Muta and Masahiro Chono), has never beaten Choshu in a singles match. Originally he was supposed to get his first career win over Choshu in the 1996 G-1 tournament, but an injury to Junji Hirata screwed up the plans and made it necessary for Choshu to beat Sasaki to get the necessary points to reach the finals, since the end result of that tournament was for Choshu to go over.

Hashimoto had held the IWGP title, New Japan's belt which was created in 1983 as being a championship considered one step in stature above a world heavyweight title, since April 29, 1996 when he defeated Nobuhiko Takada at the Tokyo Dome before 65,000 fans and $5.9 million, the second largest crowd in Japanese wrestling history and second largest gate in all of pro wrestling history.

While the title change, described as a good match, ending in 16:54 when Sasaki got the pin with his wife's patented finisher, the Northern Lights bomb, was the main event, there is little doubt it was Choshu who drew the house. The match took place just one week after a well reported tragedy in the Hashimoto family where his mother-in-law died being hit by a car in protecting the life of his two-year-old daughter.

The crowd went crazy for Choshu, as it has in all his matches since he announced his farewell series. All Choshu merchandise sold out in record time at the show, which likely drew the biggest non-Dome or outdoor stadium show gate ever in Japanese wrestling history. Choshu was put in an old generation superstars vs. NWO six-man tag, teaming with Tenryu and long-time rival Tatsumi Fujinami against Muta & Tenzan & Hiro Saito (taking the place of an injured Chono). Muta's face was painted with black lettering that said "Bye Bye Choshu."

After Choshu pinned Saito after his lariat in 8:56, they had a retirement ceremony in the ring. Among those honoring Choshu were Tenryu, Fujinami, Maeda, long-time tag team partner Animal Hamaguchi and his daughter, current world champion in womens freestyle wrestling Kyoko Hamaguchi, along with Antonio Inoki.

During the ceremony, Choshu said emphatically that unlike virtually every wrestler who announces his retirement and then comes back, he will never wrestle again after 1/4, to the point that most believed him. It is generally expected that after retiring in January, that Choshu will when it comes to duties, will take over as President (maybe not in name right away, but eventually in name as well) of the company from Seiji Sakaguchi.

Chapter Twenty Nine

Tod Gordon Leaves ECW

MAY 26

Tod Gordon got attention that he likely didn't want this past week. His family business, Carver W. Reed Jewelers, was a hot commodity when it was revealed that murder suspect Craig Rabinowitz allegedly hocked the engagement ring of his wife that he's suspected of murdering with Gordon. Several TV stations along with "Good Morning America" and People Magazine were wanting to talk with Gordon, who was ducking everyone saying his loans are all confidential. One TV station showed up at the 5/11 ECW show but Gordon ducked that reporter as well. All of the hocked jewelry is now in police hands. According to a short item in the Philadelphia Daily News on 5/14, Rabinowitz took out a $1,250 loan in 1994 and had been paying interest, and returned on 5/2—after he was under suspicion for his wife's death—for a second $1,000 loan.

SEPTEMBER 15

For numerous reasons, the biggest one being that this is the pro wrestling industry, it was almost a given that ECW Founder Tod Gordon and the prime decision maker, Paul Heyman, would eventually split. Like most business separations of the type, it probably wouldn't be pleasant.

Still, the circumstances surrounding the split wound up being strange, even by pro wrestling standards, complete with alleged backstabbing, intrigue, secrets, leaks and all the elements of a good wrestling angle.

The split officially and somewhat quietly as far as the company went appeared to take place over the weekend, although many insiders knew it was coming for more than one week and reportedly Heyman had informed the WWF of the goings on and probable end result at least two weeks earlier. It was no secret to anyone at the ECW shows this weekend that Gordon was out, allegedly for failing in an attempt to get numerous ECW wrestlers to join him in jumping to WCW to do a new version of the NWO angle using the ECW wrestlers as the outsiders. Such a scenario may very well have been discussed.

There is little doubt that two things did occur. One, that Gordon and WCW booker Terry Taylor had a conversation or more regarding the availability of ECW talent as WCW is looking to expand its talent roster in 1998 because of its more ambitious schedule, and that Taylor contacted at least one (Shane Douglas) if not more ECW wrestlers after the conversation with Gordon.

Douglas claimed to have been offered $300,000 per year to sign (which begs the logical question that if that was true, what kept him from signing although Douglas has in part blamed his failed WWF stint on heat from Scott Hall and Kevin Nash). Supposedly Scott Levy (Raven) contacted Tommy Dreamer who was given an indication he could get a $200,000 per year contract should he want it, although there have been denials of that story as well with people close to Levy claiming that Heyman and Kevin Sullivan were spreading the story about Levy contacting ECW wrestlers.

The other is that a few ECW wrestlers over the past two weeks told Heyman that Gordon approached them regarding a similar plan and storyline. As it turned out, none of them accepted the deal at this point, although Bill Alfonso appears to have been a party to the situation and his ECW tenure looked bleak as he was buried at house shows over the weekend. Perry Saturn's leaving last week was a different set of circumstances unrelated to the Gordon-Heyman split.

It is difficult to buy such a scenario as the story is out and may have been discussed actually being able to take place in WCW. What Gordon and Taylor were supposedly putting together begs the question as to whether Hulk Hogan, Kevin Nash and Scott Hall would allow a group of wrestlers, none with any name value to mainstream fans, do what is basically their own angle within the same promotion at a time when their angle is still, based on TV ratings and house show attendance, in its ascension rather than its decline? And even if it was on the decline, we've seen how they guard their positions and their angle.

A source within WCW claimed that Gordon approached Taylor with the idea of being a manager of two or three ECW wrestlers that he would bring along, but that they nixed the idea because they didn't think Gordon would make a good manager.

There are other pieces of the puzzle that are somewhat curious and don't appear to add up, Gordon's being surprisingly quiet in the wake of his departure from the company that he had founded, particularly since he wasn't a behind-the-scenes anonymous type money man (although Heyman had been controlling the company finances for some time now and Gordon was more a figurehead television personality with some behind-the-scenes duties) but instead seemed to relish in the kissing up from the hangers on, outside favorable publicity given to himself as the so-called promoter of a cult favorite wrestling company, the "Tod is God" chants from the fans and his own on-air role as commissioner and his frequent bumps.

The other is that given the opportunity to go to a major league company that is far more stable when it comes to long-term, particularly after several parties expressed dissatisfaction with PPV payoffs, to earn more money and at the same time work a less dangerous style, that at least a few of the wrestlers wouldn't have taken offers if they were serious.

From a public standpoint, Heyman has tried to portray the situation as simply a business split and wouldn't say anything negative publicly about Gordon, although his comments behind the scenes to wrestlers, friends, ECW personnel and others close to the company haven't been nearly as kind. When Gordon was contacted for comments, he said he didn't want to discuss the situation but appeared from those who spoke with him to be curiously pleased that he was coming off as a major heel to the ECW fans, almost as if this was an elaborate wrestling angle. His only comments were that it was a personal situation between himself and Heyman and that he didn't want to talk about it. Gordon is rumored to be divorcing himself not only from ECW, but from the wrestling business.

When the story became somewhat public knowledge toward the latter stages of this past week, Gordon canceled going to the two ECW shows in Waltham, MA and Revere, MA while the word spread among the boys. Earlier in the week, on several wrestling hotlines including ECW's own (which was later quickly changed), a story about a mole within ECW looking to steal its wrestlers and bring them to WCW had surfaced, spread to at least some degree by Heyman and/or others in his inner circle.

It was not a secret to anyone close to the situation that the identity of the so-called mole was going to be Gordon. Heyman had the ECW ticket office, which is part of Gordon's long-time family business, Carver W. Reed Jewelry Store in Philadelphia, cleaned out on 9/5 after word began surfacing about the story and with Gordon's name connected, in lieu of setting up a new business office in New York. To show that this was hardly a smooth and well planned out transition, the new business office is something in the talking stages rather than one already set up.

Heyman toward the end of the week was attempting to get his ducks in a row so to speak on other ECW business that Gordon was involved with, most notably the booking of the ECW Arena, which Gordon has handled and had the relationship with the building owners. Besides Heyman, it appears the most powerful forces in ECW are now all the inner circle of wrestlers sometimes known as the New York Clique—Tommy Dreamer, Taz, Chris Candido and Buh Buh Ray Dudley although Douglas and Sabu also have input.

Gordon founded ECW as Eastern Championship Wrestling in 1992 after Joel Goodhart's Tri-State Wrestling Alliance, the forerunner of ECW which Gordon was a business partner in, folded. The company was drawing small houses playing in area night clubs and schools using mostly local wrestlers and a few ex-WWF and WCW mid-level stars before Gordon brought in Eddie Gilbert as booker and started producing a local television show.

Dating back to Goodhart, who was a big fan of Memphis wrestling and put together the kind of shows that he as a fan wanted to see, the company was built largely around the brawling with objects and blood, angles and turns in nearly every match, and what later became known worldwide as either FMW or now ECW style although in both cases (since Atsushi Onita learned the style in the early 80s when he wrestled in Memphis) it really dates back to old-time Southern style booking.

ECW was spilling a lot of blood in the ring, but it was bleeding to death money-wise and on the verge of folding when Heyman, who Gilbert himself actually brought into the company, maneuvered himself into the booking position in 1993. Building around Terry Funk, Shane Douglas and giving Sabu his first significant exposure in the United States, by early the next year began expanding on the company's very small cult base of fans and through his amazing talents in media relations, wrestler characterizations and public manipulation and changing the company name to a more hip and catchy Extreme Championship Wrestling, survived and grew largely through its merchandising and videotape sales.

During a period where both WWF and WCW were at times limited in vision when it came to the present and the future, he was able to introduce new great workers, most of whom were small, that had already been established in either Mexico or Japan to the U.S. audience and is, along with many others, responsible for the break down in the size barrier and the accompanying increase in overall workrate industry wide.

In addition, many of Heyman's booking patterns from the wildness to more of a product that appeals primarily to males in their late teens and early 20s, have been copied by WCW and WWF and have helped the resurgence of interest in both groups over the past year-and-a-half.

ECW presented some of the best wrestling matches in the world in 1995 and early 1996 with the likes of Dean Malenko, Eddie Guerrero, Chris Benoit, Rey Misterio Jr., Juventud Guerrera and Psicosis among others, all of whom wound up as the backbone in WCW's in-ring product taking major steps forward, and few of whom (actually Benoit would be the only exception) would have, despite success elsewhere, been pushed in WWF or WCW due to lack of size.

But Heyman's manipulations when it came to others were so good that by the end of 1995, both WWF and WCW were making major pitches toward his top act at the time, the tag team of Public Enemy, with neither group even recognizing PE's actual lack of wrestling ability. ECW became almost an unofficial stepping stone to WWF and WCW for a lot of mid-level and international talent due to Heyman's ability to create characters and get a variety of types of wrestlers over, and the fact that so many people pay attention to ECW as the only real alternative in U.S. wrestling.

Heyman, who eventually bought out the financial control of the company from Gordon, was able to get the group into a loose almost unspoken working arrangement first with WCW briefly (to obtain the services of Brian Pillman) and later a more public relationship currently with WWF, not to mention presenting two PPV shows, all the while building the company around a storyline of being the independent politically incorrect alternative to the big two.

Exactly what the true story as to what Gordon really did and why isn't clear. In particular, since at least some of the wrestlers Gordon allegedly spoke with allegedly had contracts with ECW which one would think he would have known about. Who is said to be under contract with ECW and what those contracts actually stipulate is always questionable given claims about contracts with Raven, Stevie Richards and Saturn and WCW's ability to use all of them with no problem with the exception of the questionable use of Raven on the Bash at the Beach PPV show because of a PPV non-compete clause in a singular event (as opposed to a long term) contract Raven definitely had signed.

Heyman apparently informed the WWF of all this weeks ago with the idea that WCW was involved in contract tampering with his company, which he had already claimed in regard to a lawsuit that he publicized on his own television show and hotline but hasn't been filed at press time. Heyman claimed as well he told Taylor specifically he was tampering with ECW contracted personnel.

That charge would be similar to a charge in WWF's lawsuit against WCW that they tampered with Nash and Hall while the two were still under WWF contracts and prior to them giving notice and jumping. In other words, that the two companies could work together in their respective legal claims to try and establish a pattern of behavior by their mutual business enemy.

SEPTEMBER 22

All that was said on television about the Tod Gordon situation is that Paul Heyman was on and announced that Gordon was no longer commissioner due to time constraints from having to raise a family and run a family business. After the break-up the two made an agreement not to say anything bad publicly about the other largely because mud-slinging back-and-forth would wind up with both covered in dirt.

From what we've been able to ascertain, when the change in ownership went from Gordon to Heyman, the deal was that Heyman would assume the outstanding ECW debts which Heyman believed was in the $140,000 range but turned out to be closer to $400,000 due to some outstanding lawsuits. Heyman had about four months remaining on paying off Gordon.

Chapter Thirty

Mark Hall Throws Fight

OCTOBER 13

The biggest behind-the-scenes controversy in the history of the Ultimate Fighting Championship unfolded with the claim by Mark Hall that he threw his fight at the 1996 Ultimate Ultimate to eventual tournament winner Don Frye.

The strange scenario of the fight on 12/7 in Birmingham, AL had been a subject of discussion by many since it had taken place. Frye, coming off a grueling victory over Gary Goodridge in the first round, fought Hall, a stablemate, who replaced an exhausted and dehydrated Kimo, who had to drop out after his first round win over Paul Varelans. Hall won impressively won an alternate match against Felix Lee Mitchell. Frye and Hall had two previous matches, with Frye winning both times, once in a UFC and the other in Japan. Frye won the third fight, the one in question, in 20 seconds with a ankle lock.

In the 12/16/96 issue of the Observer, the suspicions were noted as it read: "Between Frye's post-match interview where he praised Hall as one of the greatest fighters in the world, the ease of the victory at a time where Frye badly needed to conserve energy, the fact that both men have the same business manager and the fact that Hall's first match corner woman, Becky Levy, was in this match Frye's corner woman, brought out a major air of suspicion in some circles with this match and finish. Despite the suspicion, the reality was that it wasn't suspicious in the least and Hall actually tapped too late and Frye did some serious damage to Hall's ankle with the finisher."

From being there, and just a few feet away while all this was going on, my immediate reaction to the finish is that it was a work. Same business manager. Such an easy fight when Frye was clearly exhausted. The strange post-match interview. My opinion changed viewing the reaction largely of Hall's fiance, who, unless she was a top-flight actress, couldn't have pulled off her reactions of concern at Hall's apparent injury so convincingly. The suspicion from a major pro wrestling type was that they simply were working the fiance as well. Hall was limping for the rest of the night.

Still, there had been behind-the-scenes suspicions of the fight, which may have been among the reasons Hall, like Anthony Macias, who lost a suspicious (but in a totally different way) match to Oleg Taktarov in 1995, had never been invited back to a UFC. Since the match, both have become involved in pro wrestling, Frye as a big-show regular with New Japan, and Hall working one show with Kingdom. The story resurfaced after Hall did an interview in Brazil on 9/14 stating that at the Vale Tudo tournament he had done that night, losing in the semifinals, all the matches were real and that some day the truth would come out about his match with Frye. Frye responded by threatening Hall with a lawsuit and also challenging him to a $10,000 winner-take-all match to prove he didn't need to fix a match to beat him.

In response to that, Hall wrote a letter which was posted on the Internet on 10/1, written almost like a pro wrestling interview. He claimed Frye came into his dressing room and begged him to throw the match. Hall claimed that both his fiance and two of his students heard the conversation, and that Frye sounded nervous and desperate trying to talk low to conceal the conversation. He said there were also other people's in Frye's corner involved in setting this up but refused to mention their names.

Hall said the decision he made was the wrong one but said he was given an ultimatum and that he believed it would be the end of his fighting career if he didn't take a dive. He said Frye also tried to make him feel guilty about costing him the championship at UFC X. In that tournament, Frye, who went into the show somewhat ill, exhausted himself in the first round against Hall in winning, barely hung on but still beat Brian Johnston in the semifinals before losing to a relatively fresh Mark Coleman in the finals, taking a horrific beating in the process. Hall also claimed Frye had promised him 20% of his eventual earnings that night for losing the match and then never paid him. Hall said that Frye had given all he had and suffered a broken hand in the first match with Goodridge. He went on to call Frye overrated, a fake and a fraud as Ultimate Ultimate champion and said he's dodged fights with Marco Ruas, Vitor Belfort and Mark Coleman.

Hall mocked Frye's finishing hold saying, "You made me look like an idiot in UU 96 with one of your so-called predator leglocks when you finally got it somewhat in and I did my little acting routine, most people could see the fight was fixed. I thought you knew how to do a leglock. You lied to me. I should have rolled up out of it and broke your damn nose like I did in Japan. I broke my ribs four weeks before our fight in Japan. But I kept that quiet and still showed up to fight. I still wore your butt out and even broke your nose. It was hard to train and get in proper condition because of my ribs. If I would have been in better condition, I think I would have beaten you in Japan." He then issued his own weird challenge.

"I can't even dignify those remarks with a reply," Frye said in response. "Look at the tape of the fight. It speaks for itself. I had fought him and beaten him two other times. Why didn't I just pay off Gary Goodridge?"

Frye claims that since the Ultimate Ultimate, Hall came to Arizona to train with him for a match in Brazil but left after two or three days complaining about the heat and, after getting food poisoning from a restaurant sandwich, started blaming him for the weather and the sandwich. Hall claimed Frye brought him out to Arizona and was going to pay him his cut for taking the dive, but after a few days Frye told him money was tight and he had a big tax bill coming and didn't pay him and Hall left furious.

Later Frye did a seminar for Hall in California, and before the seminar, Hall asked to borrow $800 for advertising. Frye said he sent it to him under the guise he'd be given it back from the money from the seminar. The seminar was a financial flop and Frye said he felt so badly for Hall, who lives in his gym, that he didn't ask him for his $800 and just wrote it, and the money he spent to travel to the seminar and for his hotel, off as business losses.

The fighting world, and for that matter, any one-on-one sport is subject to potential strange goings on. There are works, like pro wrestling. Then there are things like Sumo, Pancrase, K-1 and RINGS which can be a weird mixture of shooting and working and even shooting but with professional agreements made ahead of time about what won't be done even though those agreements could affect the outcome.

Tanking matches is commonplace in tennis, but it's not considered a worked sport. Fixed matches in boxing, usually with the fix known to only the promoter and the guy taking the dive (often the winner of the fight doesn't even know he didn't win legitimately) are more common than most people realize (although less common than most within the pro wrestling industry believe). There are matches fixed by the promoters, but there can also be fixed matches where the competitors themselves make a deal unbeknownst to the promoters, which if Hall's charges are true, this would fall into the category of. Mark Hall Throws Fight

However, these charges are very serious when it comes to UFC. Not as serious when it comes to its future because its future depends more on cable companies than any internal problems with the events credibility. But even though UFC has a crossover audience with pro wrestling, and UFC competitors on a weekly basis seem to drift into pro wrestling, UFC is not traditional style pro wrestling and thus its credibility has to be well protected. In addition, the fact is, news travels very fast these days and UFC has numerous enemies inside and outside the martial arts world, who would love to attack them for looking the other way when someone claimed one of their fights, one that in a large part affected the outcome of their biggest tournament of the year, was fixed.

To an extent, many in UFC recognize this, and they have become very leery of booking two fighters in any tournament from the same team or with the same manager stemming from the suspicions coming out of Ultimate Ultimate with so many fighters managed by Robert DePersia—Varelans, Frye, Hall, Goodridge and Johnston.

However, SEG needs to look at this situation rather than ignore it, because the credibility of its biggest show of 1996 is now in question. Hall's future with the group has to be done, because either he fixed a fight, which should be grounds for never being brought back, or he lied in public and claimed his loss was a fix, which should also be grounds. However, if Hall's statements are true, and his description went into a lot of detail, then Frye also can't be brought back, and more importantly, questions need to be asked about who these other parties were that Hall was talking about involved in pressuring him, and they also have to be expelled from having any part in the promotion.

At this point, it is still one person's word against another, but an investigation needs to be done to find out if there is validity to the story and if that's the case, the whole story needs to be brought to light and all the parties involved can't be part of UFC any longer.

Chapter Thirty One

The Life and Death of Brian Pillman

OCTOBER 13

Even though this is the first thing you are reading, this is actually the last thing I'm writing. As you all know, a very good friend of mine passed away a few days ago. You all knew of him. Some of you knew him. This is not the first person that I've known fairly well in this business that died at a young age. Friend is a word that I'm not very liberal with, particularly when it comes to wrestling because in many cases it depends on the last word you've written about someone. But it is one that I'd use in this instance without reservation. The shock that I personally felt when Vince McMahon went on the free-for-all segment with that cut-in was like a knife going through me. But the shock was nothing compared to the sadness when the reality set in the next day. The sadness is largely for those who loved him and needed him in their daily lives and have to do without him. From a selfish standpoint, he was one of the funniest people I knew and someone, almost no matter how bad his or my situation was, he would find a way to be both humorous and entertaining. We had a lot of strange similarities, particularly when it comes to sense of humor and being students of the wrestling business and the insanity that surrounds it, yet in other ways we were complete opposites. His insanity reminded me of my high school days. We were at different ends of the business with different pressures. The business contributed to his craziness. Dealing with the craziness of this business forced me into the other direction. Whenever one of those weird things that somehow always happens in wrestling, and can only happen in wrestling, he'd say about how if we were in baseball, football or basketball, that none of this could ever happen and we'd never have all these entertaining stories to joke about. There are a lot of people who knew him and were very sad this weekend that had to perform, and a lot of decisions that had to be made under a lot of pressure. If things seemed strange or if people seemed distracted while performing, I hope everyone understands. I expect there will be a lot of criticism of several people and decisions that were made, and under other circumstances I'd probably agree with a lot of them and can't say I disagree with them now. There will be a lot of people very critical of themselves and their own decisions. Usually in life if you make a mistake, you have the chance to rectify it. But sometimes mistakes have absolute results that can't be rectified. Those are the ones hardest to deal with. I've been doing this for 15 years, and this was the hardest issue I've ever had to write.

It would be convenient to label the death of Brian Pillman from an apparent heart attack at the age of 35 as another in the unfortunately long line of tragedies within the industry and then go on to the next chapter.

The death, at first believed to be from an accidental overdose of prescription pain killers, was after further examination believed to be from a heart attack while he was sleeping with a theory that the pain killers he had taken may have kept him from awakening which resulted in him dying in his sleep. Medical examiners found heart damage, some of which was congenital. He had a family history of heart problems including his father dying from a heart attack at the age of 50 when he was only three months old. Police Sgt. Jim Ryan said an overdose of the prescription drugs is one possibility as to the cause of the heart attack but no official determination can be made until toxicology reports are completed, which was expected to be later in the week.

It's a death, more than any other at least since the almost unavoidable Von Erich family tribulations, that is going to cause a lot of people to go through a lot of unpleasant introspection.

There is the industry itself. After all, this isn't the first and won't be the last death of a young man leaving behind a family of young children. There is the World Wrestling Federation, the company that employed him learning of the tragedy literally minutes before going on the air live and a group of wrestlers and office personnel were forced to try to postpone their collective grief for a few hours and try put on an entertaining show with a happy face on. The death of any star wrestler is a tragedy. Finding out about it in regards to the timing only made a terrible situation that much worse.

And there are his friends. Their grief itself had to be multiplied many times over because of feeling, whether justified or not, that this didn't really come out of the blue and there were scary warning signs known best to those closest to him. It isn't as if any of his problems were ignored, or anyone attempted to have them swept under the rug because of his star status. There is a question that is bound to be asked questioning how everything was handled based on the end result. Perhaps if the situation was handled perfectly, the end result could have been different, and perhaps, based on the cause of death, that isn't the case.

It also could be easy and convenient to blame the industry and even the company, but it also wouldn't be fair. When Melanie Pillman stated on television that he gave his life for this profession, that would be a fair assessment. The reality is this isn't a movie, or a pro wrestling angle, or escapist entertainment and there is simply no way to really know. And the situation is no less of a shock just because there were eerie premonitions by some close to him afraid of exactly what ended up taking place.

Pillman was found at 1:09 p.m. Central time on 10/6 dead on his bed at the Budget-tel Motel in Bloomington, MN. There were several bottles of pills, muscle relaxers and pain killers, all prescription medication along with one empty beer bottle, all found near his body when the police opened the door to try and find him. Unlike in other similar situations where well-known wrestlers would clean up a victim's room before calling police to protect the business, nobody had seen Pillman since 10:45 p.m. the previous night and the entire crew was already in St. Louis before anyone knew anything was amiss. There were no illegal drugs found in the room, and the bottles were not empty, nor was there a note, basically eliminating the possibility of it being a suicide. Even though Pillman had his own personal demons, those closest to him, remembering his reactions to a former girlfriend who was the biological mother of one of his children that later committed suicide, believe that the last thing he would ever do would do anything that would harm his children or their future.

He had relied on pain killers heavily, particularly in the wake of his April 1996 humvee wreck that destroyed his ankle and subsequent September 1996 reconstructive operation when the ankle failed to heal properly. While everyone in the industry knew about the severity of the injury and it was apparent watching him wrestle on his recent comeback just how much it affected him athletically, Pillman really tried to hide from nearly everyone just how severe his daily pain was. The truth is, let alone compete at a high level athletically in pro wrestling, Pillman couldn't even play the field with his local softball team, the "Loose Cannons," and would be in tremendous pain, which he'd largely keep to himself, just running the bases.

This was a double frustration, because he prided himself on his athletic ability in the ring for most of his career and he took his level of performance professionally as seriously as anyone in the profession. He was the prototypical student of pro wrestling. He liked to read whatever he could, and reacted passionately to it. He watched tapes of old-timers, and loved to talk with them, to learn little forgotten tricks of the trade. When he first went heel, he wanted to see tapes of Buddy Rogers. He read, in fact, memorized the Lou Thesz book Hooker in one weekend and went crazy trying to verify all the anecdotes and went crazy when some of them turned out not to be historically accurate. When he and Steve Austin were put together as a tag team, he wanted to see tapes of Pat Patterson & Ray Stevens. Secondarily and most importantly, he was in constant severe pain to the point just getting through airports was difficult, let alone the pain from wrestling even though the promotion understood his limitations and kept his non-television matches short.

He had wrestled the previous night at the St. Paul Civic Center and was scheduled for a major series of angles continuing his saga with Goldust and Marlena on a PPV that afternoon in St. Louis, and continuing at television tapings the next two nights. According to the story that ran nationally, ref Ed Sharkey at the matches in St. Paul noted that Pillman was sleeping on the floor in the dressing room during the card, which is very unusual and said he had a real strange look to him. He had a few drinks after the matches with some of the wrestlers and was described as being "tipsy" when he declined invitations to go out with other wrestlers to dinner, and went back to his room at about 10:45 p.m. that night and left a message at home to his wife on his answering machine which is the last anyone heard from him.

The next afternoon, neither Pillman nor Bret Hart had arrived at the Kiel Center in St. Louis as of the mid-afternoon for the evening Badd Blood PPV show. The feeling was they probably were going to take the last flight out of the Twin Cities, but when Bret arrived and Pillman wasn't with him, they became concerned since the show was scheduled to start in less than two hours. Pillman had missed two house show in recent months, one of which was due to suffering an auto accident on the way to a show in early August. His behavior stemming from the pain killers had plenty of people in the company worried. When they called his house in St. Louis about 30 minutes before the free-for-all was to begin, his wife Melanie didn't know anything. Just minutes later, the police came to her door and upon hearing the news she fainted. At about the same time, a WWF official called the hotel in Bloomington that he was staying at and was given the news that the police had come and found him dead in his room.

He was in the middle of an angle that was taking advantage of his greatest strength as a performer, his acting ability and his ability to play as convincing a real-life as opposed to a cartoon version of borderline psychotic, with Goldust and Marlena. It was an angle that after the two sets of tapings this week was to result in Marlena leaving Goldust for him. The angle appears to have been completely dropped, as the proposed renewing of the vows angle hyped for weeks to take place at the Kansas City Raw taping was dropped without any sort of explanation, nor were the names Goldust nor Marlena ever mentioned during the show.

Since coming up with his "loose cannon" character in late 1995, a character that made him the single most talked about performer in the industry in early 1996, it was a characterization that he took with him almost all the time. His lasting contribution to pro wrestling unfortunately was nothing short of changing the industry in many ways with his angle that blurred the line between work and shoot to the point that not only did the wrestlers have no idea where the work ended, but even the scattered few in on the angle from the start that thought they knew really didn't.

If anything, the bizarre interplay the next night in Kansas City between Bret Hart and Shawn Michaels, and the interview that Ric Flair did on Nitro in Minneapolis, were the most fitting tributes to him even though that was hardly the idea in either case. It's not unfortunate because of the evolutionary path the angle (and the influence of ECW and Japan shoot angles) have taken the industry, but unfortunate because if there is a lasting contribution Pillman has made to pro wrestling it should be, as in other similar situations, in the lessons learned from his death.

There is the simple version of that lesson, and the more complicated one. The simple version is that the problem with pain pills, despite how comedic or entertaining some might find people's behavior when loaded, is no laughing matter. Mixing somas with alcohol, which is a part of day-to-day living for so many in the industry on almost a daily basis, can be a Russian Roulette cocktail.

The more complicated version is real life. Being passive in this situation is easier then being confrontational, but it enables the situation to continue. And when it comes to these problems, confrontational usually doesn't work either. It isn't as if, internally within the business, the problems are a secret or the potential end result and repercussions to them wasn't perhaps the single greatest fear of those in charge of the respective companies.

So live, on a PPV, Vince McMahon had to go on with the show moments after one of his greatest fears had become reality, a major star dying on his watch, so to speak, possibly from drugs. After the scare on the airplane where Road Warrior Hawk passed out, combined with the warning article at about the same time in these pages, there was no secret within the WWF that something could happen and wrestlers were told that drug tests would be re-implemented based on suspicion.

McMahon taped a short cut-in which aired during the pre-game show, and a few times during the broadcast, mentioned the death again, in most somber tones. He brought up, which was the presumption at the time it was from an overdose. As the owner of a company that has had a long and storied history of drug problems and repercussions, that had to be as great a living nightmare as could be possible and it was almost as if while talking about abuse of drugs being a problem in both sports and entertainment, he was asking for mercy himself.

Whatever nightmare he and the company was going through while trying to entertain an audience was minuscule compared to the nightmare of the family left behind. He had a family with five children, with another on the way, which, making the tragedy even more pronounced, his wife found out just a few days before his death and had yet to tell him about. His wife Melanie had two daughters from a prior marriage, he had two daughters from previous relationships and they had a four-year-old son named Brian, with a knack for jumping off tables and counters and telling people, "Look, I'm Flyin Brian."

Pillman had an eight-year-old daughter named Brittany from a previous relationship whose mother, his girlfriend from years back, had killed herself two years earlier. She was just beginning to recover from that shock when she learned about her father dying, and she let out a horrific scream for 15 minutes straight like a wounded animal. Pillman took his ex-girlfriend's suicide very hard. After a life destroyed from drug problems herself, it appeared she wanted to shoot herself in the head while on the phone with him for the most dramatic ending.

Unfortunately, Pillman was on the road when she decided to make her grand exit, and after a lengthy conversation with Melanie, trying to counsel her out of it, she then called up her mother, who Pillman thought the world of, and while on the phone with her, blew her brains out. Whether rightly or wrongly, many close to her blamed her downfall on losing a very bitter child-custody fight with Brian over Brittany, a fight that left everyone involved with very bitter internal scars. Her family's reaction after the death to Pillman was yet another in a very long line of internal hardships life dealt him.

That was just another of what in many ways was a lifetime of tragedies, defying odds, athletic accomplishments, wild times and occasional lunacy that told the story of his life.

Brian Pillman was born May 22, 1962, growing up in Norwood, OH, a working-class suburb of Cincinnati, where the Cincinnati Gardens is located. He was raised mainly by his mother since his father died fairly young, who worked as a waitress. He was born with throat cancer and underwent 31 different operations before the age of three, leaving him with a raspy voice that he was teased about incessantly in childhood. The voice became his trademark when he began to make his mark in pro wrestling.

He wound up being a local high school football hero, but because of his size, wasn't thought to have any potential to play in college. He went to Miami of Ohio as a walk-on, and not only made the team, but wound up by his senior year in 1983 as a second-team all-American noseguard. As a 5'9" defensive lineman, a combination of weight training and heavy use of steroids bulked him up to nearly 250 pounds, and he was bench pressing close to 450 and squatting more than 600 pounds. Still, there wasn't much demand in the NFL for 5'9" defensive linemen and he went undrafted.

He went to the Cincinnati Bengals as a free agent, and made the team in 1984, being converted to linebacker but mainly playing on the special teams. Although he was not a star, he had a lot of local popularity for being a local product who defied the odds and gained a reputation for being one of the physically and mentally toughest players on the team. As a rookie, he was voted the winner of the Ed Bloch Courage award. He ended up being traded to the Buffalo Bills prior to the 1985 season, but was cut in training camp.

Although Pillman himself may have never been aware of this, the Bills staff had already decided Pillman made the team. But shortly before the final cuts, an assistant coach found his steroids at camp and the team realized he was a little guy all juiced up and during the final cut it was enough to sway the decision. He wound up signing with the Calgary Stampeders of the Canadian Football League in 1986, and after playing the first three games of the season, broke his ankle, the same ankle that eventually was destroyed in the humvee wreck, which ended his football career.

Kim Wood, who was and still is the strength coach with the Bengals and has had a long-time knowledge of the inner-working of pro wrestling, recommended to Pillman, who had watched some of The Sheik's pro wrestling as a kid in Cincinnati, that he hook up with the Hart Family and try to break into pro wrestling. After making contact, Bruce Hart, the Stampede wrestling booker, Hart used Pillman's stature as a former Stampede, however limited his actual tenure with the team was because of his wild personality at the time, he was very popular with most of the players, to jump-start his pro wrestling training and rush him into the ring. It wasn't long before he was an instructor rather than a student at the camp.

He started his career with Stampede Wrestling after doing an angle the previous week, in the main event of a November 5, 1986 show at the Calgary Stampede Pavilion. With numerous Stampeders in the babyface corner rooting him on, Pillman teamed with Owen & Keith Hart to beat Makhan Singh & Great Gama & Vladimir Krupov. At the time Stampede Wrestling was developing some of what would turn out to be the biggest stars in the world including the likes of Owen Hart, Chris Benoit, Jushin Liger and Hiroshi Hase.

Another almost unknown piece of wrestling trivia was that during his early Stampede stay, an angle was done where heels attacked his supposed sister Teresa to build to a big match the next week. Teresa, real name Teresa Hays, resurfaced many years later as ECW's Beulah McGillicuddy. Bruce Hart & Pillman as the tag team called "Bad Company," clad in sunglasses and leather jackets in the final and most memorable run of Bruce's career, were the territory's top babyface tag team for most of the next two years.

He was the 1987 Rookie of the Year in the Wrestling Observer poll. He survived the craziness of Calgary wrestling, including suffering a severe shoulder injury that nearly ended his career, and a tricep tear in a backstage fight where he was ambushed by a much larger Brick Bronsky, then after being knocked to the deck, got up and tore him to shreds. Although he remained good friends with Bruce and Owen Hart, that fight was a wake-up call to him that it was time to leave Stampede Wrestling.

Largely through making a contact with Jim Ross, he was brought into World Championship Wrestling in the spring of 1989. He was supposed to start a few months earlier, with the original idea for him to be a heel managed by Paul E. Dangerously and team with Dennis Condrey as a new version of the Midnight Express. However, his job was nixed when new booker George Scott didn't want to bring in a wrestler that he had never heard of. Shortly after Scott was let go, Pillman's name resurfaced and he was brought in as a babyface with numerous musical videos.

Pillman wrestled several television dark matches, but was very nervous and didn't perform well, and gained a reputation immediately for being far more green and inexperienced than he really was. But it probably worked in his favor, because once the butterflies wore off and he got his confidence back up, he started having good matches, and the belief was that he was improving at an amazing rate. His first major match with the company would have been at the 1989 Halloween Havoc PPV show from Philadelphia, where he had one of the best matches on the card, more impressive since it was with Lex Luger, which surprised most since the feeling going into the match was that Luger was going to have a hard time carrying Pillman in his first major match.

Pillman's seven-year WCW tenure, largely as a mid-card babyface who was generally considered among the best athletic workers in the company, saw several different rebirths. He was "Flyin Brian," the heartthrob pretty boy babyface with Tom Zenk, a role he was never comfortable with. He was the personal protege of Ric Flair, including a famous match on WCW Saturday Night that drew what is still to this day the largest audience ever to watch that program in early 1990. He was the high flying lightheavyweight champion having the best matches in the country against Jushin Liger highlighted by a Christmas week house show run in 1991, and a match-of-the-year candidate on the February 29, 1992 SuperBrawl PPV show in Milwaukee.

Based on the Liger matches and his performances as champion, he signed a three-year $225,000 per annum base with numerous incentive bonuses contract with Kip Frey, who was at the time running WCW. When Bill Watts came aboard, Pillman's contract, unusually high for his position given the industry standards at that time, particularly as a lightheavyweight, caused an immediate dispute. Just before that time, Pillman's potential really began to show for the first time as he turned heel, which was his true calling. Watts gave Pillman an ultimatum, either re-sign a lower priced contract, or be jobbed out, Pillman refused.

After a short period of being jobbed in the opener nearly every night despite being among the company's hottest workers at the time, with lots of internal pressure on him to cave in to Watts, he stood firm claiming he was going to become the highest paid opening match jobber in pro wrestling history until the situation of his jobbing and the reasons for it became an embarrassment for the company and both sides settled their problems in a solution that was largely face saving for both sides. In the wake of all the problems, Watts decided to drop the lightheavyweight division.

Pillman's career was back in limbo until he was put together as The Hollywood Blonds tag team with Steve Austin in 1993. Ironically, Austin complained against the idea at the time, not wanting to be a tag team wrestler, but the two ended up becoming good friends and even better partners, and were voted in the Observer poll, tag team of the year for that year. At the time people thought they could become the great tag team of this decade.

The two captured the WCW tag belts from Ricky Steamboat & Shane Douglas on March 3, 1993 in Macon, GA. However, business went into the toilet during that summer, and when Ric Flair was signed back into WCW after leaving the WWF, a feud was put together with Pillman & Austin as the obnoxious young heels against Flair & Arn Anderson, building up to Flair's first match in WCW on a Clash of the Champions. When that Clash drew only a 2.6 rating, still the lowest Clash rating in history, the booking committee put the blame on Pillman & Austin being a failure as a heel team, a conclusion that almost nobody watching at the time would agree with, and broke them up, with Pillman being put back in a babyface role sans any push. By this point, Pillman suffered a serious back injury and did very little wrestling for months.

Outside the ring, his personal life, which he largely kept quiet about, had major ups and downs. He had a reputation, well deserved, of being a wildman with an apparently endless supply of beautiful women. He had one girlfriend of many years, Rochelle, who he knew from Cincinnati and lived with in Atlanta who was viciously stabbed in a break-in while he was on the road. Their break-up years later wound up in one tragedy after another. The two of them had a daughter, and he also had another daughter from another woman. Rochelle developed a major drug problem and Pillman was far from perfect himself which turned into a child custody battle that turned his and his new family's life into a one-year-long nightmare.

By this time Pillman had married a former Penthouse Pet, Melanie, who ironically had her own background around wrestling as being the one-time girlfriend in a stormy relationship with Jim Hellwig when he was riding high as one of the two biggest stars in the WWF. After a whirlwind romance, Pillman proposed to her at the Grand Canyon. It was typical Pillman apparent insanity, as he saw her photo in a magazine and immediately decided this was the woman he was going to marry. In 1993, in the middle of the child custody fight, Rochelle was supposed to pick up Brittany and never showed up. She had disappeared, and nobody, not her family nor friends could find her. While this was going on, Pillman was literally scared to death feeling he was about to become the white O.J. as he became the obvious lead suspect.

Pillman, drinking heavily based on fear he was about to be arrested for something he didn't do, decided to play amateur detective to clear himself and went traveling in the worst section of Cincinnati, carrying a photo of her and talking to the corner drug dealers. While he was there, the police were riding by and saw a fairly well-known local celebrity hanging with drug dealers in the worst part of town. They thought he had swallowed something and arrested him. As it turned out, he had one or two pain killers, without carrying the prescription, on him. He ended up plea bargaining down to a drunk driving offense once he proved he had a prescription for the pills on him and no other drugs were found. He was still under suspicion in his girlfriend's disappearance, until a few weeks later she was found in Florida, totally messed up, when the car she and a few men she was with was pulled over.

In late 1995, knowing his contract had only a few months remaining and with him still not receiving much of a push and fear, which was totally well founded at the time, that his high price tag would be cut, he decided to take his career into his own hands. In Wood's kitchen, the two devised one of the more unique approaches in wrestling history largely as an attempt to emulate the late Bruiser Brody and make his own break into superstardom.

He became, both in the ring and often out of the ring as well, the "loose cannon." Someone who could and would do anything at any given time. He became a reactionary right-winger on a Cincinnati radio station to get the gimmick over. He continually would do things and say things on live Nitro to seemingly put his position in jeopardy, and his behavior outside the ring around the wrestlers was all part of his work in convincing everyone that he had lost his mind. He had seriously talked with friends, most notably Terry Funk who became something of a secret mentor to him, about doing a publicity stunt where he'd run on the field and chain himself to the goal posts during the 1996 Super Bowl game.

Within the company, only Eric Bischoff and Kevin Sullivan were aware that what he was doing on Nitro and outside the ring with the boys was a work, which is why he stayed on television even though Bischoff continually threatened to both publicly and privately say he was on loose ice and on the verge of being fired. The work continued to the point that Pillman had an on-air confrontation with Sullivan, the booker, which they worked to look like a match had gotten out of control. The angle was so well done that people believed Sullivan was attempting to rip out Pillman's eye in a fake shoot angle, however Sullivan blew the credibility of the shoot part of the angle, much to Pillman's chagrin who wanted to fool everyone all the time, the next week on television by using the incident as part of his interview to build up a rematch on a PPV.

So Pillman took his fantasy reality one step farther, in what was billed as a "respect" match on February 11, 1996 in St. Petersburg, where the loser would have to say he respected the winner, against Sullivan, Pillman took a few shots, sarcastically said the famous line "I respect you, booker man," and walked out of the ring, out of the building and out of the promotion. But where Bischoff and Sullivan, who thought they devised the angle with Pillman, thought the angle ended, it really had only begun.

Pillman had talked them into actually firing him, to work everyone in the company and the business, getting TBS to send out the termination notice and everything. At the same time they had worked out a deal with ECW, which was supposed to be the renegade independent group, to slide Pillman over (Pillman largely worked out the deal himself with Paul Heyman and WCW approved it) and his appearing on ECW would theoretically give credibility to the fact Pillman really was fired from WCW for whenever his surprise return would take place.

Although he never wrestled one match for ECW, nearly every angle and video he did during his brief tenure was memorable. At the same time, Pillman had to undergo another throat operation which would keep him out of action a few weeks. Desperate for ratings in the Monday Night war, WCW ordered Pillman to show up in the audience just a few weeks later, and Hulk Hogan, seeing the pop Pillman got, attempted to get Pillman booked onto the heel team in an infamous 2-on-8 match on the Uncensored PPV show on March 24, 1996 in Tupelo, MS.

Due to Pillman's throat surgery, his doctor sent a note to WCW saying that he couldn't perform that soon. Pillman probably shouldn't have wrestled, but under normal circumstances, he probably would have, balking more because his not-so-amazing clairvoyant powers told him the match, which included Tom "Zeus" Lister as Ze Gangsta and the late Jeep Swenson, would near the top of every list of the worst matches in the history of the industry, and he didn't want to be a part of it. WCW continued to advertise Pillman and pressure him to perform and even during the pre-game show were saying he was going to be there even though he had firmly told them several days earlier he wouldn't.

Pillman was technically fired from WCW, a worked firing with only Sullivan and Bischoff in on it, although by this time the fact it had almost all been an angle (about the only "memorable" thing during that run that was truly a shoot was when Pillman was grabbing Bobby Heenan during a Clash match against Eddie Guerrero, and Heenan freaked out because he was afraid Pillman was going to accidentally hurt his bad neck, swore on the air and walked off) was pretty well established. This made him the most talked about wrestler on the inside of the business, and a free agent at the same time.

He began negotiating with Vince McMahon, who initially was leery of dealing with him because Pillman, acting completely out of his mind, approached McMahon at the NATPE convention in Las Vegas. After assuring McMahon that everything he'd done was a work, and after Ross and Jim Cornette went to bat for Pillman since McMahon and everyone in wrestling had reservations about him because he was living his gimmick to a scary degree, McMahon decided to start serious negotiations.

The original plan was to use the WWF, which at the time wasn't offering guaranteed money, to up his price to Bischoff, figuring Bischoff and Sullivan didn't want to lose the character they helped create. At the same time, there was the consideration, with him just weeks away from his 34th birthday, that this next contract signing would be the prime years of his career for business and he knew the top of the mountain at WCW was blocked with the Hogan clique and with Kevin Nash and Scott Hall arriving, while the field in WWF was more wide-open.

The basic WCW plan was for him to form his own Four Horseman with Chris Benoit and two others, and feud with Flair and Anderson once again. It was a good spot, but at that point, he was looking for a shot at the top spot. With a babyface Shawn Michaels being groomed to be the long-term WWF champion, size wasn't going to be a major issue in being the top heel in that company.

McMahon offered a guaranteed deal, believed to be only the third or fourth time in history he'd done such a thing (although it soon become commonplace given the realities of the wrestling war), which caused Bischoff, who had low-balled earlier negotiations, to up his offer to the $400,000 range.

While Pillman was in the catbird seat, just a few days from becoming a real-life hot commodity free agent in the midst of a competitive Monday Night wrestling war, he was still going out of his mind, staying up all night, calling everyone and doing everything at all hours trying to get advice on how to play the game to make the most money.

Soon after purchasing a humvee, he apparently fell asleep at the wheel on 4/15, went off the road, and got thrown 40 feet into a field where he was lying in a pool of his own blood. His face was so swollen that his friends who visited him in the hospital really couldn't even recognize him. By the end of the week, after surgery which included taking bone from his hip to reconstruct his ankle, he was released from the hospital. Since Pillman had been orchestrating works on the entire world to keep himself the most talked about name inside the industry, many within wrestling thought this was simply the latest chapter of a bizarre work. But this was real.

Even though the future of his career in the ring looked questionable, neither Bischoff nor McMahon let up on the offer. Pillman claimed he'd been told he'd recover 100% from the injuries in a few months, although secretly he feared the worst. Eventually Pillman chose McMahon's offer largely because internally he thought there was no choice in the matter since Bischoff wouldn't eliminate the 90-day termination cycles from the contract, and Pillman, fearing the possibility of not being able to return to the ring, didn't want to risk his family's future on what was he believed could have turned into a short-term deal.

WWF tried to make a big deal of Pillman's signing, rushing him onto television in a failed attempt to close the ratings gap. Although months from being able to wrestle, Pillman was running around the country constantly on airplanes trying to keep his gimmick strong while being unable to wrestle. Doing so caused his ankle to not heal properly, and a few months later they had to re-break the ankle, do another reconstructive surgery, and start the procedure from scratch, with the end result being an ankle fused into a walking position.

WWF created an angle with its top heel at the time, Steve Austin, which positioned Pillman as strongly as possible to explain the injury and an absence while he truly rested and recovered this time, for his return. Just a few days after surgery, in a controversial desperate attempt to establish a new Raw time slot, the WWF did the infamous gun angle where Austin broke into Pillman's house where Pillman was with his "bereaved" wife, was held off by a shotgun, and the satellite lost transmission as they teased that shots had been fired. Pillman was largely kept home for the next several months, until resurfacing doing the announcing on Shotgun to build for his in-ring return after WrestleMania.

His return as an active competitor is probably going to be the most criticized and second-guessed decision, hindsight being 20/20, stemming from this entire situation. Hindsight being 20/20, his death unfortunately may not have been a freak occurrence, but as a simple end result to an emotional mathematical problem, just as 1+1+1+1+1=5.

You had a person who spent his life doing things athletically people told him he couldn't do. He did them not only to stick it to those who doubted him, but to prove things to his toughest critic of all—himself. Although he did defy the odds and numerous medical authorities by even coming back, and his acting ability was likely to keep him in the forefront as a star for years, his physical limitations had to be mentally driving him crazy and the constant pain didn't help. Everyone goes through bad periods in life that leave certain scars, and he went through far more than most people and the scars were very deep.

The fact he couldn't perform physically up to the level he could mentally, because he literally lived for nothing but his family and the wrestling business, took its toll on him. The fact was, unlike many who seem to take advantage of injuries while on a guaranteed contract, Pillman had guilt feelings that he wasn't earning his money during the entire period he was out and felt he had to do whatever the company wanted to feel in his own mind that he was earning his big contract.

WWF officials and some of his business associates were extremely worried about his behavior. Wrestlers who liked him were afraid to travel with him. There was an argument while he was on an airplane telephone where he was shouting and cursing loudly out of control which further fueled the worrying of both WWF road agents and other wrestlers. About five weeks before his death, Ross, who had remained close friends with him and had been counseling him several times per week regarding his problems, ordered him to undergo a drug test. He was furious about being singled out, since he had never gone on television so loaded he couldn't perform in or out of the ring as it is believed another top star had done one or two times in the recent weeks.

Melanie was also worried about the level of pain medication he'd been taking and her own knowledge of being close to and around wrestlers on-and-off for ten years that the wrestlers shared their prescription drugs back-and-forth and wanted him to undergo rehab, but he had a saying that he even wore on a t-shirt that rehab was for losers. He refused and blamed being singled out to take the drug test on wreaking havoc with his marriage, and felt that when a wrestling company affects his marriage that he had to get out of the wrestling company. He requested a release from the WWF, feeling he could go back to WCW and slide back into the final slot in the Four Horseman.

His personal situation was rocky for a short period of time, which included him violating a restraining order and Melanie filing for a divorce. After a brief separation, he had returned home. He was pulled from the 10/3 house show in Winnipeg and from all Friday night house shows for the next few weeks because of a court-mandated Anger Management Class he had to take for violating the restraining order for four straight Saturday mornings, and went back on the road after the class for the matches in St. Paul for the final match of his career against Goldust.

The drug test came back a few weeks ago showing nothing in his system except for the prescription pain medication it was well-known he was using, and also showed a small amount of decadurabolin, an anabolic steroid that was very popular among bodybuilders and wrestlers in the 80s. Decadurabolin can stay in the system literally for several months and there have been medical cases of it showing up on a drug test even one year after use had stopped although cases like that are extremely rare. Pillman had apparently used it as almost a desperate attempt to speed up the healing process for his ankle before his return to the ring. Because it was a small amount and the drug has such a long half-life in the system, he wasn't suspended.

Pillman had suffered internal side effects many years ago from his steroid use from football and early in his wrestling career, not to mention suffering many muscle pulls and tears which he attributed to his use. This caused him to get off the drugs before it became a major issue in the industry, and actually he was fairly vocal about their potential problems and the effect they were having on the wrestling business. In fact, when Frey started doing anti-steroid public service announcements when the industry was under the steroid cloud, Pillman was the first to go on television, admit to use and warn others against it.

The PPV show went on, although not as scheduled. About 25 to 30 minutes of the show had been blocked off for Pillman matches with Dude Love and Goldust. With very little warning, the Mexican minis were rushed onto the show and did not have a good match. With the show running way short, an eight man tag was added, again with very little notice. It was a show that was under a dark cloud from the beginning, and the matches certainly reflected that. And then, seemingly oblivious to everything that had gone on, Shawn Michaels and Undertaker put on one of the greatest cage matches in the history of wrestling to save the show.

The next night, both WCW and WWF opened their Monday night live shows with mentions of Pillman's death. WCW had a brief graphic and it was never mentioned the rest of the show. WWF opened the show with virtually all the wrestlers in attendance coming out for a ten-bell salute. During the show they constantly promoted an interview with Melanie Pillman, live from the family home in Walton, KY. During the show they showed large framed photos in the family den, a photo of Brian holding his baby son, a photo of Brian & Melanie together and a photo Pillman & Austin as WCW tag team champions as teases to build to Melanie's interview.

Melanie Pillman had reservations about going on live, but eventually consented due to her own loyalty to the company that employed her husband. The only thing I'd like to say in defense of everyone involved, is that under the emotional state everyone was under, it would be cruel and heartless to be critical of the segment because it wasn't smooth flowing perfect television. But the segment left a lot of people very uneasy for many different reasons, not the least of which were all the teases and holding it off until late that made it come across as a way to build up ratings.

She had a very heartfelt message, a warning for mainly those within the industry as to not let her husband's death, and for that matter similar deaths within the profession be in vain and use this as a lesson to be learned from everyone. She wanted her husband to best be remembered as the greatest father in the world and as a warm and compassionate person.

We all knew abuse of pain killers among some wrestlers is out of control and the stories of erratic behavior that some find funny just aren't very funny today. It is impossible to have pro wrestling, or for that matter pro football, pro basketball or anything of the type as we know it today without some form of pain killers. But there comes a line that everyone has to draw, and that's when the pain killers take over the body and simply aren't medication to heal the body. This was going to happen to someone in the business, and whomever it would be, the odds were that it would be somebody's husband and somebody's father. As it turned out, it was Melanie Pillman's husband and the father of their five, soon to be six, children. And to them, and to his friends, the story doesn't end this week as the rest of the industry goes on to its next chapter.

Mark Madden of WCW, who had known Pillman for many years, wrote an article for the WCW website and asked if we could have it printed here. I never imagined anything written by Mark Madden at this point to be in the Observer, but it is a great piece:

It's one o'clock in the morning, and I'm waiting for a phone call.

It's a phone call that's never, ever going to come.

It's from my friend Brian. You knew him as Flyin Brian, as the Loose Cannon, as the Ticking Time Bomb, as one-half of the Hollywood Blonds, as a member of the Hart Foundation, as a member of the Four Horsemen, as the Rouge Horseman, as one-half of Badd Company, as Brian F'n Pillman. But to me, he was just Brian.

He drove me absolutely, totally insane.

I never knew when I was going to hear from him. Sometimes he wouldn't call for weeks. Sometimes he'd call five times in one day. He'd usually call me at home, but sometimes at work. Once he called me when I was on my radio sports talk show. And got on the air.

Thank God for seven-second delay. Hey, you know what he was like.

Brian was a good friend. Not many give a damn about friendship these days. Most see friendship as a means to a self-serving end. But Brian valued friendship and so do I.

And now I sit by the phone.

Sit waiting for a call that will never come.

Because it's the only way I can make myself feel like he's still around.

Those most affected by Brian's death are his wife, Melanie, and their five children. But anyone who knew him was touched by him. Wrestling is a backstabbing kind of business on a good day. But I don't know anyone that disliked Brian. He got along with wrestlers in both major companies, with management in both major companies. He was a great guy. A great husband. A great father. A great friend.

And a great performer. Brian loved wrestling. He had an old-school style respect for the business but a 90s sensibilities about what would work. I believe he would have wound up running one of the major companies someday.

Brian wrestled in WCW from 1989-96. He had two hot runs. The first was in 1993, when he partnered with Steve Austin as the Hollywood Blonds. By my reckoning, they were the best tag team of the 90s. Brian shed his pretty-boy babyface image to become a sadistic, psychopathic heel. He was as easy to hate in the ring as he was to like outside it.

He got torrid again in 1995, when he was a member of the Four Horsemen. That was an exciting time for him. He really looked up to Flair, fashioned his persona after both Flair and Terry Funk. To team with Flair was like a dream come true.

In 1996, he had a pseudo-shoot feud with "booker man" Kevin Sullivan. It had everyone in wrestling, from the boys to casual fans to dirt-sheet readers wondering if it was legit or if it was pro wrestling.

It was easy to wonder that about Brian himself. In the ring, he was half-crazed. Away from it, he was sometimes totally crazed. He could even be scary. But just when you thought he was about to go completely off the edge, he'd smile and say, "It's all a work, you know," and then laugh.

Brian was in a bad wreck in April 1996. He flipped his humvee, mangling one of his ankles. The ankle was eventually fused into a walking position. He never regained his mobility. It frustrated him.

By the time he recovered and started with the World Wrestling Federation, he had his character down pat. His interviews were so strong, his psychology was so good, that he didn't even have to wrestle at all to get over. And when he did wrestle, he was fine. It hurt. But he did well. Brian would have been an all-time great. He was like Terry Funk on acid, and that was without doing acid. And now he's gone.

Wrestling makes strange friendships, and there haven't been many stranger than ours. A wrestling star and dirt-sheet alumnus. An ex-NFL player married to a Penthouse Pet and an overweight sportswriter.

Now that I've worked for WCW for four years, it's kind of fashionable to be my buddy. But when I wrote for the dirt sheets, even though I talked to a lot of wrestlers, very few would acknowledge me in front of other wrestles. Kayfabe, you know. But Brian would introduce me to other guys, as only he could. "Hey, do you know Mark Madden? No? Well you should, because he buried you in the Pro Wrestling Torch this week." Thanks.

I have some regrets. I regret that I never tried very hard to help him curb his inner demons. For the rest of my life, I'll wonder if Brian might still be with us if someone had gone the extra mile to help him. I doubt it, because there was no telling Brian what to do.
I regret we didn't spend much time together in person, although we did talk on the phone constantly. By the time I started going on the road to work at WCW, he was already in the WWF.

But the regrets are few. And the memories are many

Brian often called late at night, one, two or three in the morning. He always had a crazy plan, a way to get over, a way to make money, a way for us to work together. He made me laugh. I trusted him. His friendship meant a lot to me. I hope he knew that. I've shed a few tears over this, but I've found a way to beat that.

Every time I feel like crying, I think of Brian laughing his maniacal laugh. Of him talking about Melanie and his kids. Of him trying to work me during his feud with Kevin Sullivan. Of one of his schemes and plots. Or anecdotes. Or one of his booking ideas. Of his advice to long-suffering WCW wrestler Joey Maggs. Of his dealings with his seemingly luckless lawyer Elliot Pollock.

It was a pleasure knowing Brian. He was a lot of fun. I miss him. I think I'm going to bed. It's two a.m. The phone isn't going to ring. No thought and no memory can stop the tears from flowing now. Good bye, Brian.

OCTOBER 20

So this was the week the corpse of Brian Pillman was being used by everyone for their own personal vendettas. At least, that's what everyone was saying about their enemies.

Whether it was Eric Bischoff saying how disgusted he was about the WWF and the USA Network using the death and rushing on the Melanie Pillman interview the very next day to draw a rating on 10/6, something that was the prevailing view from virtually everyone within the industry we spoke with as the week went on; to the complaints not only about having teased the interview through most of the show but of the nature of the interview itself; or Jim Cornette claiming Phil Mushnick was using the death to further a personal vendetta against the WWF in his editorial on the 10/13 Raw; or the belief that the WWF put Cornette up to doing the promo, which was delivered better than probably any pro wrestling interview all year, to use the corpse of Pillman to cut a promo on Mushnick based out of fear of what someone from the outside looking into this situation would discover; to the tremendous amount of second-guessing in hindsight about how everyone in and out of the business handled the touchy situation. Brian Pillman lived for being the center of controversy. And in death, the situation turned out to be no different.

After reflecting back one week, without question the Melanie Pillman interview in hindsight was a bad idea. While I haven't spoken with anyone in the WWF on the subject, I'd be shocked if in hindsight they at this point haven't come to the same conclusion and there are people who have given me that impression. It was too soon. It shouldn't have been done live. Some questions appeared to be asked attempting to garner a close-up of her crying. Given certain realities of the situation, it put Mrs. Pillman, already in an incredibly emotionally trying situation for both obvious and not so obvious reasons, under a microscope that she didn't deserve to be put under.

My impression is that the interview stemmed from a conversation that Vince McMahon had with her the previous night, where she spoke about wanting to warn other wrestlers and their families about pain killers and for them to try and avoid a repeat of this situation. McMahon said that he wanted to put her on television to say that, but the point didn't get across as well for a variety of reasons. The fact the interview was teased throughout the show and they showed the photos from his basement did come off as ratings-driven. I'd hate to think so but recognize the realities of this business and know that it is a possibility and it isn't as if the record companies that promote rock & roll stars don't have business plans of making money off deaths considering that's the one industry where the per capita mortality rate seems to be worse than pro wrestling.

In the video that aired after the interview, I was uncomfortable with them claiming that his 1996 car wreck was the result of a drunk driver when it was actually him losing control of the vehicle and running off the road and being thrown from it when it rolled. Personally I'm willing to cut McMahon and the WWF a lot of slack for how it handled 10/6 if only because if there were numerous errors in judgment in how things were handled, everyone making those decisions was also under a tremendous amount of emotional stress.

There was criticism of the promotion not announcing the death to the fans in St. Louis for fear it would dampen the enthusiasm of the live crowd at the PPV. Certainly it put a shadow on the PPV portion of the event. Just as the show was going on the air, the WWF told Elliot Pollack, Pillman's business agent (not to mention USWA commissioner), that they had decided not to mention the death at all during the show, but then minutes later changed their mind.

Mushnick wrote only a few lines during the week, basically pointing out that if this had been another sport, it would have been page one news and there would be investigations because of the frequency of deaths of wrestlers, and also called Pillman "an admitted steroid user." That line got a lot of people hot. It's a term that isn't incorrect, and there is a very slim chance it's applicable to the situation since the preliminary diagnosis of his death was a heart attack and apparently he had used decadurabolin somewhat recently as a desperation attempt to strengthen his lower leg, but most of Pillman's steroid use was during his football days and the early part of his wrestling career which was many years back. The WWF, which was scared to death from the moment it learned about the death about how Mushnick would write about it, apparently had Cornette go on television to attack Mushnick about taking advantage of the death to wage his personal attack against the WWF and his crusade against steroids in pro wrestling.

This is a situation where I can see both sides of the story from their respective positions to a point. The idea of abolishing this industry is ludicrous and I don't agree with how strongly Mushnick comes against the industry but for the most part can't argue that most of the points he makes have validity. And for all of Cornette's protesting about the Bill of Rights, Mushnick has not only the right but his job and the reasons he's won awards from his job is because he pulls no punches and doesn't go halfway with his opinions, in many ways no different than Cornette.

There are legitimate problems with the industry, and the number of deaths is one of the major ones, and many of its stereotypical portrayals of various ethnics and women to children, that Mushnick has pointed out. In the long run, had it not been for Mushnick probably more than any other person and his enemies can deny this until they are blue in the face, but if they do they are lying to themselves, the steroid situation within pro wrestling today may be just as rampant as it was in 1991 and the number of injuries and even tragedies stemming from it would be greater to go along with it. Not to mention that the style of wrestling in the ring would be totally different.

At the same time, his categorization of pro wrestling fans as a group I'm not comfortable with and Cornette made some valid points in his commentary. The pro wrestling fans Mushnick deals with on the Internet validate his belief about most or all wrestling fans, and it's a belief grounded in some cases, but I think it's unfair to paint all of them with the same brush. But a lot of the anti-Mushnick backlash comes from wrestling fans who want to blame the messenger because they are hiding from or aren't able to deal with the message.

This latest chapter of the story goes back a few weeks. Mushnick has written a few columns of late, mainly anti-WCW, about wrestling. In one of them, he criticized the management of Madison Square Garden for firing

Marv Albert for a sex crime but not canceling WWF shows at Madison Square Garden when it was proven in court that the WWF was built on steroids, or words to that effect as I don't have the column in front of me and the fact is a slight semantic difference in the wording could make a big difference in the points either side could make on whether or not the statement was fair.

WWF was furious, using the 1994 U.S. Government v. McMahon not guilty verdict as saying the exact opposite was true. Cornette made that point in his interview. As far as the decision making process at Madison Square Garden regarding either Marv Albert or pro wrestling, that's another issue and I don't think the two things are comparable to begin with. But to use the not guilty verdict (Cornette's saying the McMahon was declared "totally innocent" of all charges was technically incorrect, as the verdict was not guilty, although that may be nothing but a semantic argument) as a defense when virtually all the testimony in that trial confirmed everything Mushnick had written and that Titan had denied years earlier on the quantity of the steroid use in the company (Hulk Hogan testified to 75, 80 percent maybe more of the WWF wrestlers as steroid users, Jim Hellwig testified to 90 percent) is a bad can of worms for Titan Sports to try and re-open, let alone to try and defend themselves against Mushnick with.

Titan has attempted to use the trial verdict as proof that there was never a steroid problem, but the trial was only about two points—did Vince McMahon distribute steroids to Hulk Hogan, and did Vince McMahon and George Zahorian enter into a legal conspiracy to distribute steroids to the wrestlers. The first issue was thrown out because it was being tried in the incorrect venue (and truthfully, given the evidence at the trial there is no way there could have been a conviction) and McMahon was declared not guilty on the second point. If the trial was to decide whether the WWF had a steroid problem, or were most of the WWF wrestlers on steroids, or even was the WWF itself built on the back of steroids, based on virtually all the testimony, the result would have been different.

Additionally, it was PROVEN, in court, that the WWF had many top wrestlers on steroids. Dr. George Zahorian III was declared guilty and spent a few years in jail for, among other things, illegally distributing steroids to several WWF wrestlers. The fact is, for the WWF to try and argue about the past and the steroid subject with Mushnick is an argument they have little logic and only a misinterpretation of the end result of a trial and not the testimony of the trial to stand on. It's an old story. The business has changed tremendous since that time.

But there were three basic viewpoints that people had within the industry who called here on Monday and Tuesday had on the Cornette interview. One, that Cornette was right in almost everything he said. Another, was that it was a great delivery and a fantastic promo, but in the long run would explode in the WWF's face. I believe, in fact know, Cornette was every bit if not more sincere in what he said than in his promo the previous week on Hall and Nash because of his delivery.

However, my gut reaction, basically shared by many who called since the promo, was that it was a preemptive strike by the WWF to attempt to turn the focus of a potential story that could be negative to the company in regard to the death of Brian Pillman into a personal issue against Mushnick and get the personal vendetta angle out to the public and its fans, to try and rally wrestling fans to their side and make the company the babyface against the heel Mushnick, for fear of what a close examination into the Pillman death could reveal.

In hindsight, people who want to point a finger of blame at WWF have a lot of points to draw on. Should he have been put back on the road full-time in his condition? Well, in hindsight, No, but remember that Pillman tried to publicly downplay the level of pain he was in because it was very important to him to earn his keep and not be someone who is under contract and sits around and collects his money with a dubious injury as some have done, not to mention that even though there were aspects of wrestling that he hated, he did live for other aspects of the business.

Should the WWF have tried to put him in rehab? Well, in hindsight, Yes. But he probably would have quit the promotion before going. It's easy today to say he should have been a heel manager, or a heel commentator rather than put in a position to wrestle several times per week. Unfortunately, hindsight is 20/20, and some of the people in decision making positions knew his past history too well, of being someone who athletically had defied the odds, literally from childbirth. While people may not have known all the details, they knew the basic story and wanted to give him another chance to beat the odds again—or, as some critics might say, extract their pound of flesh from him.

Pillman's life was well documented from newspaper clippings that covered his athletic accomplishments from his youth. He should have died at the age of two, and again at the age of four when his heart stopped both times due to complications from cancer. He played the defensive line in high school as a 5-foot-7, 147 pound junior and regularly blew by the 200 pound offensive lineman. He led the city in tackles and sacks as a senior, yet was the only member of the All-City team to not get even one college offer because the idea of a 5'9", 180 pound defensive lineman in college ball is on the surface ludicrous.

When he was a teenager, he was actually even better at ice hockey than he was at football, starting as a 15-year-old on mens teams every Saturday. He walked on and was placed on the seventh team as cannon fodder at Miami of Ohio and told since his attitude was so good that if he played his cards right for four years, by the time he was a senior he could get a jersey and make the traveling squad. He wound up as the back-up nose guard midway through his freshman year and was actually by all accounts at the time a better player than the starting senior.

He probably discovered steroids between his sophomore and junior year, as he went from, according to local newspaper reports, in one summer from a 195 pounder with no muscle definition, although by this point he was already a starter and a good player as a defensive lineman, to a 225-pounder described as having the physique of the Incredible Hulk, and bench pressing 425 pounds and squatting 600, attributed to palling around with a local contest winning bodybuilder.

During his junior year in 1982, he was a Division I-AA first team All-American middle guard. As a senior, he was the Mid-American conference defensive player of the year, leading the conference in both sacks and tackles, and the only member of the 1983 AP All-American team to not be drafted by the pros, yet still made the Bengals despite his size. He came back from a shoulder injury suffered early in his wrestling career that was at first considered to be a career ender.

I probably know the situation better than all but a few people, and I can't in any good conscience point fingers at the WWF when it comes to blame or culpability in the death nor did I sense others equally close or closer to the situation coming to a different conclusion. I could also see where an outsider investigating but not truly understanding the situation could come up with a lot of evidence to come to a different conclusion.

On 10/7, the WWF's General Counsel sent letters out to several doctors known to both management and the wrestlers as being so-called mark doctors that the boys go to. The basic letter was to reiterate company policy, which has been largely not enforced, banning physicians backstage with the wrestlers except in the case of an emergency. The only physicians allowed backstage under other circumstances would be those assigned by state athletic commissions (ironically the most famous mark doctor, the famed Dr. Zahorian, fell under this umbrella) or those sent by the WWF itself to compile medical information needed by the company. The WWF also said that any writing of prescriptions or dispensing of medicine to wrestlers should only be performed through an individual appointment at the physician's office in a traditional doctor/patient relationship.

Listing all Pillman's past accomplishments isn't meant to forget that his practical jokes were legendary or to ignore that there was a dark side to him, largely the drugs and wild behavior, that caused good friends to become estranged from him and put his marriage in jeopardy and may have played a role in his death.

The stories from college and his early days in Calgary were incredible. Pillman at one time was the hero of Mark Coleman, who was a freshman at Miami of Ohio when Pillman was a senior and the star of the football team, for an incident in the dorms where he had sex with a woman, who was hanging upside down from a pull-up bar wearing gravity boots, while the other jocks watched. The joke before people who knew Pillman knew him, is that they figured the letters in Penthouse were all a work. But once they knew him, they knew they were real and that Pillman wrote most of them from personal experience.

Another time in Calgary, Pillman and Bill Kazmaier, who Pillman nicknamed "Quagmire," who at the time was probably not only the strongest man in the world but probably the strongest man who ever lived, who

Pillman routinely would torture unmercifully to the amusement of all the other wrestlers on the circuit, were about to get into a fight once the bus was about to stop. By the time Pillman was done telling made-up stories, about how he beat up Lawrence Taylor, Mike Webster and Mike Tyson in street fights, and Kazmaier heard and evidently believed them, Kazmaier ran away from Pillman, which was a hilarious sight seeing the world's strongest man running from fight against a guy half his size.

As far as the cause itself, the toxicology reports had not been completed at press time so his death certificate at this point still doesn't list a cause of death.

Pillman's funeral took place on 10/10 in Walton, KY, a suburb of Cincinnati. There were about 150 people there. Most were family and friends, only a few from the industry, basically limited to Bruce Hart, his original trainer, Joey Maggs, the WCW jobber who was like his little brother, Pollack, WCW Executive Vice President Eric Bischoff, former area wrestler Les Thatcher and a few of his students.

There was speeches by his high school football coach, who thought someone was playing a rib on him when he first saw 147-pound Pillman as a junior going out for the defensive line; by local radio talk personality Bill Cunningham who frequently had Pillman as a guest; by Bruce Hart, who was so moved he couldn't continue his speech several times; to his college football roommate who noted that Pillman was a genius as a student in college ("He could get a book and within 20 minutes know everything in the book") and related how they both nearly got kicked out of college when he was about to fail a class which would have made him ineligible for football, and Brian, who was a great student, let him copy off him except they ended up getting caught; his best friend from high school and a few others. Vince McMahon and Jim Ross attended a private wake the previous evening limited to family and a few close friends.

NOVEMBER 10

The official cause of death of Brian Pillman will apparently be listed as a heart attack due to natural causes. At press time, the Hennepin County Medical Examiners Office had not released an official press statement on Pillman, but family sources said such a statement would be released later in the week.

Pillman was found dead at the age of 35 in a Bloomington, MN motel room at 1:09 p.m. on 10/5, the night after wrestling his final match at the St. Paul Civic Center and just hours before the WWF was about to go on the air with a PPV show.

Reports from those close to the situation indicate that after nearly one month of tests, the coroners reported on 11/3 that they were stumped for a cause of the heart attack, although his heart showed an unusual amount of damage for someone of his age. This could have been partially hereditary given his family history, and also due to the amount of stress he had placed on his heart. Either steroids and/or cocaine have been known to cause heart damage which over the years can have a cumulative effect. It was no secret Pillman had used steroids dating back to his college and pro football days and through the early part of his wrestling career for obvious reasons, being that in all the aforementioned professions use was plentiful during the 80s and his own lack of natural body size was really the only thing holding him back from stardom.

Toxicology reports did not reveal any intake of drugs that could have caused the death. The reports revealed the expected prescription pain killers, although not at dangerous levels. There were no traces of steroids or any other illegal drug found in his system. The steroid decadurabolin was the only illegal drug found in his system when he was drug tested by the WWF on 8/28, although the low levels and the fact that drug can stay in the system and show up in tests longer after usage than any other steroid, in rare occasions for more than one year after its last usage (although usually it won't longer than a few months), was the reason he wasn't suspended for what could have technically been ruled a failed drug test. There wasn't even any trace of alcohol in his system. There was an empty beer bottle found in his room along with several bottles, none empty, of prescription pain pills, when the police opened the door. Later reports indicated that while the bottle of beer was empty, the cap was still on the bottle and this it had broken and the contents of the bottle apparently spilled onto his clothes so it appeared he had never even drank the beer.

The only strange drug found in his system, a prescription drug that he apparently did not have a prescription for was medication used to combat high blood pressure. This would not have been something he would have been taking medication for. Later reports have indicated that when he went on the road trip to Minneapolis for his first match of the weekend, he had run out of a certain pain killer and theoretically he had either asked for one from another wrestler or a hanger-on, and was given something that was actually not a pain killer. However, the amount in his system wasn't ruled dangerous and that was also ruled out as being a potential cause of death.

The toxicology report showing no traces of cocaine put tremendous heat on Gene Okerlund in WCW who had claimed to have the inside scoop directly from the doctor that Pillman died of a cocaine overdose. On 10/27, on a WCW Internet audio show with Mark Madden, Okerlund discussed this fact as his lead scoop. This naturally led to rumors running rampant as the week went on of that being the actual cause of death. Okerlund had all along privately claimed to have inside connections with the police and the doctors since Pillman's death occurred in the Twin Cities, where Okerlund lived for decades and regaled people with sordid tales, which apparently greatly differed at least from police reports of the scene at the motel room, and of what would be the final report from the corner. Okerlund nor any other WCW personnel never discussed this information publicly anywhere except on the audio show and not on the hotline.

Chapter Thirty Two

Randy Couture Beats Vitor Belfort

OCTOBER 27

Vitor Belfort, the reputed 20-year-old (as in some circles it's believed he's actually older than what he's claiming) Brazilian sensation that many pegged as the young, charismatic and scarily effective performer that would become the superstar that the Ultimate Fighting Championship would be built around for years to come, was derailed in brutal fashion by U.S. national Greco-roman champion Randy Couture as just one of the feature events of the latest UFC PPV on 10/17 from Bay St. Louis, MS.

The win by Couture, generally regarded as a stunning upset, puts him in the title picture, earning a shot at UFC heavyweight champion Maurice Smith, who retained his title with a win over last-week replacement David "Tank" Abbott in the main event, on the "Ultimate Japan" PPV show on 12/21 from the 17,000-seat Yokohama Arena.

In both superfights, the Belfort vs. Couture and Smith vs. Abbott, it was conditioning more than skill or overall strength and toughness that was the deciding factor. Both matches went just past the 8:00 mark, and in each case, the loser was totally out of gas and either being, or about to be, hammered unmercifully. Belfort took a terrible beating and was hospitalized for several hours after the show, likely as much from exhaustion as from the punishment Couture dished out. Abbott simply quit when he ran out of gas, again putting his future in UFC's in question. He attempted after the match to get his heat back by doing a f--- this and f--- that interview, saying that he didn't care about winning or losing and that he didn't train at all for the fight.

The show itself, before a sellout crowd estimated at around 1,500 in the small Casino Magic tent, had to be considered above all as the night where American amateur wrestling stars once again took the spotlight over from the Brazilians.

Not only was Belfort, who the feeling from most ahead of time would be able to hammer Couture early as he had all his four previous NHB opponents, upset, but so was Carlson Gracie stablemate Carlao "Carlos" Barreto, the 6-4, 253-pound Brazilian who came into the match undefeated with victories over top American wrestles like Daniel Bobish and Kevin Randelman. Barreto lost a very close fight, although the decision was unanimous, to David Beneteau in one of the most evenly-fought and exciting matches in UFC history. Barreto, who didn't protest the decision after the match, said that he came into the fight overtrained and couldn't get his body to do anything he wanted it to.

However, Beneteau, like Abbott in the main event, came off of the biggest win of his NHB career with something of a negative aura since he refused to go out for his tournament championship match against Mark Kerr. Beneteau, who had a grueling 15:00 first round match with Barreto, hinted in his interview after the win that he wouldn't be coming out for his match with Kerr, who won his first round match in just 22 seconds. Later in the show he officially stated he'd made the decision to leave on a positive note after his upset win, and not ruin the night, saying he thought even-up he could beat Kerr, but, basically said the difference in energy expenditure in each's first round match resulted in his decision.

Instead, Kerr faced alternate Dwane Cason, a natural light heavyweight wrestler who had to eat his way up to 205-210 pounds just to be a heavyweight, and Kerr won the third NHB tournament (two UFC's and another in Brazil) of his career with very little competition. Beneteau's decision was weird since he's probably done amateur wrestling for around 15 years and in that period must have done countless tournaments. I doubt if he'd ever withdrawn from a tournament without being injured simply because his opponent had an easier draw. While some gave him points for honesty, in not making up an injury as a reason to withdraw, the truth nowadays in UFC always gets out because they do extensive post-fight medical examinations and if there is no legitimate injury, the word would get out anyway so lying would be of no benefit.

In many ways, this pointed out the big problem nowadays with doing tournaments. Tournaments, which put the UFC on the map in its early days, may be passe now because the expected climactic matches for some reason, whether they be injuries or upsets, never take place no matter how tournaments are "stacked." In addition, it is hard to get good quality fighters willing to risk their reputation in a tough tournament, so often easy matches are given in the first round, which defeats the very purpose of having a four-man tournament.

Even though the expected Kerr vs. Barreto battle of undefeated top-ten ranked fighters didn't occur in the tournament and Kerr breezed through, the show was considered by virtually everyone as one of the best UFC's in a long time with the upsets, several evenly matched fights, and a competitive championship match with a weird finish.

Abbott, who officially got the word on Tuesday afternoon (although he had gone on a television show in Los Angeles on Monday night when the word was out there was a very good chance Dan Severn was out and he talked about the match with Smith), managed to tag Smith with his trademark hard punch and mount and pound him and did at one point have him in very legitimate trouble. However, like Mark Coleman before him, as the minutes went on, even though Abbott had Smith in the top position, it was Smith who was scoring more, generally elbows to the top of Abbott's head. Smith, who is by no means a submission expert, but has been training with Frank Shamrock on-and-off for a few years, tried a few arm submissions but Abbott was strong enough to get out of them.

However, when ref John McCarthy stood them up due to lack of action with Abbott simply laying on Smith, it was evident that Abbott was done. He really didn't even want to come out of his corner, but was convinced to do so, took two hard whipping leg kicks, the second of which was quite brutal and told McCarthy that he had enough. While the leg kicks were brutal (Ken Shamrock, who has fought both of them, has told people that Smith's leg kicks are a lot stronger than the more flashy looking leg kicks of Bas Rutten) and he was totally out of gas, the simply quitting at that point did a number on his aura that he'd managed to manufacture about his toughness and fighting ability.

It was the first time anyone in a UFC had ever quit a fight based simply on leg kicks, and in many ways it was a logical decision in that he had nothing left and staying out there was only going to result in a lot of punishment. However, his manufactured image was such that a Tank Abbott wouldn't quit a fight.

So after all UFC shows, the question is now, what happens next. The most important factor again is that there has been no movement from the cable industry, even though rule changes have been put in place largely to satisfy the people who have made UFC a sacrificial lamb. The show was available in around 15 million or so homes. For whatever reason, even though the line-up was more attractive and they were coming off a good show, based on our limited areas of response, we don't have an impression the show did as well on buys as the previous one.

The reality is, until there is movement from cable, the short-term future of UFC is in jeopardy. Based on so many organizations world wide and fighters who have built up names (largely through UFC), NHB will continue in some form, although political realities in the U.S. seem to make it so Japan and Brazil may be the prime sites and not North America.

The plan is for the 12/21 show in Japan to be the biggest show of the year, because the idea is they'll have a big live gate to play with in Japan, with two tournaments and two or three superfights. The plan originally was to hold off Mark Coleman vs. Vitor Belfort for that show, but we know that happened there. So then the dream match became Smith vs. Belfort, and that isn't going to happen either. Belfort vs. Kerr would make a great semifinal to a Smith vs. Couture main event, however putting Belfort against such a tough opponent, who at this point would be favored against him, would put him at risk of suffering a second straight devastating loss and I'm sure there's the theory now to rebuild Belfort's image if possible rather than throw him in their with one of the biggest lions in the NHB jungle.

Quite frankly, even with how impressive Couture came out of this show, there are a lot of questions about the marketability of that match both on American PPV and in Japan. It's also going to be quite a difficult match for Smith, whose 4-0 record in NHB and world championships in both EFC and UFC on paper make him undisputedly the No. 1 star in the sport, but the reality is his unbeaten record has been built on three wins against stronger men that ran out of gas and one win against an overmatched opponent.

There had been serious talk of Kevin Jackson vs. Frank Shamrock to crown an under-200 world champion, although with Shamrock having an 11/29 match in Japan against Ensen Inoue on the Shooto Vale Tudo card in Tokyo, there is now the feeling that using the Shamrock-Inoue winner (Inoue, the world heavyweight champion in shooto, was also considered as a potential foe for Jackson) may be a risk due to an injury just a few weeks before the fight, and the name Murillo Bustamante (who defeated former UFC under-200 tournament champ Jerry Bohlander recently in Brazil) has surfaced as another possible foe for Jackson.

For Japan, names like Frank Shamrock, Kimo, Dan Severn, Bas Rutten and perhaps still Abbott would mean something, particularly as foreign draws against a top name from Japan, as they have already established their names in Japan, and because the early UFC shows did very well in Japanese video stores and received far more publicity both in pro wrestling and martial arts magazines, but the recent shows where guys like Couture have made their names haven't been nearly as well publicized.

But without question, due to the somewhat unpredictable nature of what happens when top guys square off due to various ways styles match up, it appears now than building a match for months, like is done in boxing and pro wrestling, may not be feasible. Coleman vs. Belfort and Smith vs. Belfort were both circumvented by upsets as well as injuries. Smith vs. Severn didn't even wind up taking place.

The other lesson that is becoming painfully obvious is that when it comes to the top level of competition, steroids, the big controversial subject, haven't appeared to have been a positive because they work against the stamina of the fighter and it doesn't matter how fast, or strong, or skilled someone is, when they're out of gas, they're done. We've seen it before and we saw it again.

Because of the various cable outlets not carrying the event, this show was also broadcast on the Internet for $20. As a test market without a lot of publicity, it drew about 1,000 orders. If the Internet can be viable as a distributor of the shows in the long run, it may mean survival of UFC even without a turnaround within the cable industry. But there is no guarantee of enough people willing to spend money to buy the signal through their computer or how long it'll take before such technology becomes viable to the masses.

Chapter Thirty Three

The Battle for Mexico

FEBRUARY 10

In Mexico, it was announced that Antonio Pena is now the President of WWF Latino. This is kind of their own oneupmanship between Pena and Konnan, since Konnan had been having discussions with Eric Bischoff about starting an American television show called WCW Latino which he'd book and run. Pena really ran down not only Eric Bischoff, but also Kevin and Nancy Sullivan in the local press. He said Bischoff was just a second-rate television announcer who didn't know anything about pro wrestling, but because of his budget is able to buy talent and doesn't use it right. He called Kevin an old man who has no business wrestling and is only on television because he's the booker, and said that Nancy was a no-talent who is only in wrestling because she's the wife of the booker.

FEBRUARY 10

The WWF aired a Perro Aguayo Jr. vs. Abismo Negro match on Superstars. Match wasn't bad and Jim Ross and Jim Cornette as announcers did a better job with these guys than the WCW crew does after six months of having the guys on every week. However, the fans were leaving for the concession stands in droves right in front of the camera.

FEBRUARY 24

AAA will be running the first major show of 1997 in Mexico on 2/21 in Ciudad Madero in which the tentative plan is for Vince McMahon and Bruce Prichard to attend representing the WWF to start what is expected to wind up with more WWF talent working AAA shows, in particular the upcoming TripleManias, and the potential of doing a second AAA PPV show in the United States this year in conjunction with the WWF.

The show, entitled "El Rey de Reyes," will be based around what is known in Mexico as "Relevos Tijuanes" matches which is basically the same four corners match as the Final Four match on the recent WWF PPV. There will be four different four corners matches with the four winners meeting in a championship Final Four match, the winner being crowned "The King of Kings" of AAA. That wrestler will then in March or April face a WWF representative, which may be Bret Hart but that isn't a definite, on AAA's final major show which would lead into the AAA vs. WWF feud at the TripleManias.

MARCH 3

Francisco "Paco" Alonso, the President of Empresa Mexicana de Lucha Libre (EMLL), the oldest wrestling promotion in the world, was at SuperBrawl in San Francisco and put together some sort of a deal with Bischoff and Onoo. This meeting had been planned for several weeks as when Alonso was in Japan a few weeks back for the EMLL tour, he spoke of having a meeting planned in San Francisco to start a business relationship with WCW.

This gives WCW access to any wrestlers of its choosing from two of the three major wrestling offices in Mexico. With EMLL and Promo Azteca both working together at times but also being business rivals (since Promo Azteca recently raided Lizmark Jr. from EMLL and Black Warrior is expected as well and there is a longstanding bitterness from the past between Alonso and Konnan), it brings up yet another set of political implications and how, if at all, this will affect the current Konnan/Promo Azteca deal which had formerly been their exclusive booker of Mexican talent.

Konnan had used his connections with WCW, which pays wrestlers quite a bit more than they can earn in Mexico, as a way to lure several wrestlers to join with him in going to upstart Promo Azteca from either AAA or EMLL. With Alonso having the same connections, it makes using that connection no longer as effective a chip in Konnan's favor in trying to bring new talent in.

It's unknown at press time what EMLL wrestlers would be coming to WCW (aside from Ultimo Dragon, who recently returned to EMLL and was already a WCW regular) or when, but I'd suspect people like Mr. Niebla, Felino, Rey Bucanero, Negro Casas, El Hijo del Santo and Silver King will be in WCW before long.

MARCH 10

WCW has made a talent trading agreement with EMLL as reported here last week. This was not without some trepidation from the Promo Azteca contingent. Apparently both EMLL and Azteca considered they were being slapped in the face over last weekend because of the other being around. The Azteca guys were mad because Bischoff was openly negotiating with their rival promoter in Mexico, Paco Alonso, right in front of everyone, similar to if when Bischoff went to New Japan next month if New Japan also invited and signed a deal at the same time with Vince McMahon.

Alonso felt he was being slapped in the face because Kevin Nash & Scott Hall wore Azteca t-shirts on the PPV, as if they were rubbing the rival company in his face. Bischoff assured the Azteca wrestlers that none of them would lose their jobs if a deal was made with EMLL. Alonso then went home from San Francisco and immediately went to the press talking about signing the talent exchange deal with WCW which Azteca was again mad about because it made them come off as second rate as if they had somehow screwed up their deal. No word on who from EMLL or when this deal will get off the ground.

MARCH 24

The war heated up once again with Antonio Pena filing lawsuits this past week against Konnan, Rey Misterio Jr., Psicosis and Juventud Guerrera for breach of contract for leaving AAA for Promo Azteca and WCW. The lawsuit not only calls for dissolvement of the group's connection with Azteca, but also with WCW.

When Pena made the deal with Vince McMahon, Eric Bischoff immediately put the pressure on to make sure all the Mexican talent in WCW was signed to WCW contracts. WCW received a legal letter from AAA saying those contracts should be voided since most of the wrestlers who had signed them already had existing deals with AAA. WWF may be involved in this since one would figure if AAA were to win the suit and control the bookings of these wrestlers, they may be forced to work for WWF, although all of that happening seems at this point to be a remote possibility.

The same group has counter-sued Pena asking for back union dues that they are supposed to receive upon leaving the company and for moneys owed to them for appearing on television and merchandising that they have yet to receive.

Pena had previously filed a suit against La Parka several weeks back to try and keep Parka from using the name (Pena is using two wrestlers with similar costumes, La Calaca and La Parka Jr., neither of whom is getting over because they are bad copies). There are several other lawsuits out there, but a lawsuit from a ways back involving the former AAA minis (Mascarita Sagrada, Octagoncito, Jerrito Estrada, etc.) should be coming to court in about two weeks and a lot of people see the result of that suit as a barometer for future suits in that whichever side wins will be favored in the future.

APRIL 14

Antonio Pena has filed suit against WCW claiming that the Mexican wrestlers they signed to contracts were done so illegally since they were all under contract originally to him. As mentioned before, one of the bargaining chips Pena used in starting a deal with WWF was that all the Mexicans in WCW that were doing so well in the ratings he had under contract so he could send to WWF. Who knows how this will end up being sorted out. The funny thing about the suit is that the wrestlers Pena claimed under contract that WCW had used included several people WCW had never used, but shockingly didn't include in the suit, Misterio Jr., who is the wrestler that no doubt WWF wanted the most of all.

MAY 26

Antonio Pena lost a lawsuit in Mexico regarding breach of contract where he claimed the rights to La Parka, Super Calo, Juventud Guerrera and Psicosis because he had them under contract and then they signed WCW contracts. Pena and Parka are still in a legal fight over who owns the rights to the La Parka name.

MAY 26

The biggest news appears to be the jump of Hector Garza from AAA to Promo Azteca. Garza, who began a heel turn with AAA, which apparently was something he didn't want to do, was in Asheville, NC on 5/19 for Nitro (he didn't work the show but was at the show) which pretty much signifies a jump to this office. Garza had jumped from EMLL to AAA largely due to the promises he was given that by jumping he would end up with a WWF contract. When that didn't materialize, he jumped here since it came with a WCW contract offer.

JUNE 16

Paco Alonso has had recent talks with both WWF and WCW regarding a talent hook-up. Alonso knows he needs to make a deal because his wrestlers are leaving for Promo Azteca because it's the connection to getting WCW contracts. For WCW, making the deal with Alonso will cut down on Konnan's internal power over the Mexicans in the company and more importantly, largely eliminate WWF from getting major Mexican talent, because it's readily acknowledged that nobody can deal with the disorganization of AAA. Bischoff has talked with Alonso about ideas for promoting Mexico and even South America, and doing two or three Lucha Libre PPV shows per year that would air both in the U.S. and Mexico since Televisa and Turner Broadcasting are beginning a programming relationship having nothing to do with pro wrestling.

JUNE 23

EMLL promoter Paco Alonso had no idea that Silver King was in WCW this past week. What happened was that Ciclope was supposed to work the TV on 6/9 and 6/11, but he was stopped at the border as he didn't have the correct paperwork. Since EMLL had a tour in Monterrey, which is a Northern Mexico city, they desperately searched for someone to take his place and they talked Silver King into coming with the idea that if he came in, he could get a WCW contract.

However, since Eric Bischoff is trying to work out an agreement with Alonso, so he would have another ally in Mexico for obvious reasons and also to freeze Titan out of the Mexican market since that's the country which right now is producing the best good new talent, what may end up happening is that Silver King will have to stay with EMLL rather than join Promo Azteca as was the original agreement, since Bischoff doesn't want Konnan stealing Alonso's talent while they are negotiating a deal.

It's still too early to tell how this will all end up. Bischoff was at a company meeting this past week and said that WCW would be doing two or three Lucha Libre PPV shows per year and that he would be traveling to Mexico sometime next week to try and finalize the deal with Alonso and Televisa.

There are a lot of political ramifications in Mexico regarding this. Bischoff has either gotten signed or gotten the agreements from all the key Lucha Libre wrestlers in WCW for WCW to own their worldwide rights. Initially WCW only had their rights for the United States and I believe Japanese markets and they dealt for themselves in Mexico. The problems were that since WCW never gets its booking done far ahead of time, and Mexico always does things at the last minute, that guys would get booked in Mexico for dates and then WCW would want them on the same dates.

There have also been lots of problems with guys arriving late to arena shows forcing changes in the house show cards and cancellation of matches due to transportation problems in Mexico so they want the wrestlers to leave a day early rather than the day of, which would mean them giving up a potential previous night booking in Mexico.

If Bischoff makes a deal with Televisa and Alonso, it could result in the group being forced out of Promo Azteca and doing an NWO angle in Mexico against the EMLL crew, or even not being able to work Mexico at all if that's what Bischoff wants although obviously by getting their rights to Mexico it wasn't to keep them from working Mexico but to make him a major power broker in the Mexican marketplace.

JUNE 30

Most of the major news regards Eric Bischoff's planned trip to visit with Paco Alonso and the political repercussions. As is well known, WWF has also had talks with Alonso through Victor Quinones. Bischoff, who has talked internally about doing as frequent as monthly Lucha Libre PPVs starting as early as late this year, needs to add Luchadores to the roster.

Alonso talked in the local press about being able to get 15 of his wrestlers under contract to WCW, which has caused strife with the Promo Azteca wrestlers under contract since in Mexico they are rival offices. In addition, it dilutes the control Konnan has over the Lucha product.

The other internal story how it relates here is that Azteca has been very aggressive of late when it comes to raiding talent, but Bischoff wants the two groups to work together and do a promotion vs. promotion angle in Mexico that will be the focus of the PPV shows and theoretically the big feud at Arena Mexico as well.

At the time same, Silver King & El Texano have jumped, Silver King for the second time. What apparently happened is that Silver King was supposed to work in WCW again but Alonso told WCW that he had Silver King under contract in response to Silver King working Boston without his knowledge. Silver King claimed he didn't have a contract (very few EMLL wrestlers are under contract which is why raiding isn't nearly as difficult as it would be in the U.S. or Japan) and quit EMLL to join Promo Azteca in response, making it the second time he's made the jump in two weeks.

Due to the Bischoff attempts to make a truce between the groups, Azteca had Silver King return to EMLL, but this week it appears the truce is gone again with King and his uncle coming in and rumors that other top EMLL stars are ready to quit the promotion as well. Technically speaking, King and Texano announced in the press that they were free agents and had left EMLL, so when they go to Azteca, it isn't as if they were raided but as if they were free agents signing a new deal. Quinones is also recruiting wrestlers to sign WWF contracts although we haven't heard any names officially signed.

JULY 7

Paco Alonso had a meeting with most of his top wrestlers on 6/26 telling them that he's got 15 contracts that he's in charge of filling with WCW which repeated what he's already said in the press. This has caused further heat with the Promo Azteca wrestlers with the feeling that they worked hard with no contracts or guarantees to get American fans into a foreign product and now they're being shoved aside from a rival promotion. At the meeting, Alonso claimed that Konnan would be working for him when it comes to the power in the U.S. and that he'd be the main decision maker.

Eric Bischoff still hasn't gone to Mexico, although again that is supposed to take place shortly, at which time some sort of a deal is expected to be finalized. One would suspect, given what has been successful both for WCW and in Japan, that Bischoff would try and work the EMLL crew against the Azteca crew as the top feud for PPV. Although the "When Worlds Collide" show was marginally successful, at about the same level as the first ECW show, the popularity and exposure levels of Lucha Libre in the United States are way down so a Lucha Libre PPV show today wouldn't do anywhere close to as good business, particularly when so many of the top stars have been badly hurt in the U.S. marketplace by their jobber roles.

At the meeting were Apolo Dantes, El Satanico, Black Warrior, La Fiera, Lizmark, Rey Bucanero, Violencia, El Hijo del Santo, Negro Casas, Mr. Niebla, Emilio Charles Jr., and Rayo de Jalisco Jr. Warrior, Bucanero and Niebla are all young and good workers and would, with experience in learning the new style, eventually do well in the U.S. Santo, Charles and Casas are all very good workers but since they're older, they'll have more trouble adapting to a new style and since their name gets them over and they aren't as spectacular as the guys people have seen, they'll have a harder time breaking out of the pack. Guys like Fiera, Lizmark and Rayo are too far past their prime to even be brought in.

JULY 14

Bischoff was in Mexico this past week negotiating with Paco Alonso. Not sure of what came out of it but they met on 7/2. Alonso, who had also been negotiating with WWF, told WWF that Bischoff offered him $750,000 in exchange for 15 wrestlers under contract. Others are denying that story is correct although when Vince McMahon was given the story, his recommendation was for Alonso to sign with Bischoff because he wasn't about to match that deal. He also met with Promo Azteca and gave his ideas for doing the promotion vs. promotion feud and taping big shows in Mexico for U.S. PPV.

AUGUST 25

Lots of rumors regarding wrestlers now jumping from Promo Azteca back to EMLL. Nothing is official. Vampiro told friends this week that he would be leaving on 8/20 to work a program in EMLL with Dr. Wagner Jr. and that most of the top names for this promotion that don't have WCW contracts would be leaving as well since EMLL hired Ricardo Reyes to work with Negro Casas in the booking.

Reyes was the booker here when most of the non-WCW wrestlers joined the group, but lost out in a bitter power struggle over direction with Konnan and the guys who aren't considered as "Konnan's guys" may go to EMLL with Reyes in power. However, at a house show later in the week, Vampiro told Konnan, who he has just started a program with that should draw very well, that he was staying.

It is believed that Los Hermanos Dinamita are almost surely at the top of the list when it comes to those leaving, and that the original Mascara Sagrada, Super Elektra, Mariachi, Zapatista and Angel Azteca are likely candidates and Vampiro is certainly a strong possibility.

Of those names, the Dinamitas are a mixed blessing. They are the biggest name main event heel trio in the promotion, but they are all past their prime in a company building around young wrestlers. Sagrada has a name but he's also 38 years old. Vampiro has a name and is hot again and his potential feud with Konnan should do business, while the other losses really have no business effect.

AUGUST 25

There is a meeting scheduled for the end of the month with Paco Alonso, Konnan and Eric Bischoff where Bischoff is going to explain exactly what he wants and probably pressure both sides into a truce when it comes to not raiding talent from each other. Anyone want to bet on the over-and-under when it comes to how long that one will last?

SEPTEMBER 1

Most of the news we have regards things outside the ring. The meeting with Eric Bischoff, Konnan (Promo Azteca) and Paco Alonso (EMLL) to discuss working together in Mexico, getting a weekly television show on in the United States and doing PPV shows is scheduled for 8/27 in Marina del Rey, CA. However, Konnan and Alonso and their companies remain at war.

As expected, Los Hermanos Dinamita jumped from Azteca to EMLL and debuted at Arena Mexico on 8/22 as retribution for Konnan's recent signings of the likes of Silver King, Mr. Aguila and Black Warrior. The war between the two groups has gotten deeper as Alonso was attempting to get the independent promoters to no longer book Promo Azteca talent on their shows, thus attempting to bring the group to its knees and force the wrestlers without WCW contracts to work for him.

There was yet another hearing last week in regard to getting Konnan deported for his frequent fights with fans and the like, but the end result of the hearing was he was fined $1,000 but not deported.

Alonso also sent letters to independent promoters saying he wouldn't allow any of his talent to work on any shows where Lizmark Jr., Super Calo, Damian or Halloween appeared because he claimed they were all attempting to talk his wrestlers into jumping to Azteca. At the same time, Antonio Pena registered the names, costumes and gimmicks of Juventud Guerrera and Psicosis and is attempting to get them banned from using their names and outfits.

SEPTEMBER 8

In the wake of an unsuccessful meeting between Eric Bischoff, Konnan and Paco Alonso which was an attempt to put together Lucha Libre style PPV shows in 1998, the war between Promo Azteca and EMLL heated up again over the weekend with CMLL heavyweight champion Steele (Sean Couples aka Sean Morley), The Head Hunters and Kevin Quinn no-showing the 8/29 show at Arena Mexico and instead doing a run-in on the Promo Azteca show in nearby Naucalpan.

The report from the meeting held on 8/28 in Marina del Rey, CA are that Konnan and Alonso were cordial at the beginning, but there ended up being a disagreement and things got worse and they were yelling and swearing by the time the meeting ended on the sour note.

The run-ins were the public confirmation that Victor Quinones, the FMW booker and WWF foreign talent liaison, and Konnan had put together a deal in which Quinones would sent his talent to Azteca instead of working with Alonso and EMLL, and in exchange Azteca talent not booked with WCW would be made available for Quinones to send to the WWF.

With Konnan and Quinones working together, it solidifies both of their power base since they are supplying the cheaper working foreign talent for both WWF and WCW. In addition, all the Lucha style wrestlers that the WWF were to sign to contracts would likely wind up working for Azteca instead of EMLL, which would mean that Histeria will be jumping to Azteca from AAA.

SEPTEMBER 15

The basic reason for the split between Victor Quinones and Paco Alonso and Quinones sending his talent on 8/29 to Promo Azteca when they were originally booked for EMLL at Arena Mexico stemmed from international politics.

It's a long involved story that started with a meeting Quinones set up with Alonso and Vince McMahon in Connecticut in April where Alonso agreed to supply talent for the WWF's proposed light heavyweight division. The deal fell through in June when Eric Bischoff and Alonso spoke and Alonso decided to work with WCW. A few weeks later when the Bischoff deal wasn't concluded, Alonso gave Quinones the green light to book EMLL talent himself for WWF.

One of, if not the prime reason WWF still hasn't done its light heavyweight title tournament is because of problems in getting the expected talent from both Japan and Mexico they were expecting to be the backbone of the division. Quinones claimed he was going to send Dr. Wagner Jr. and Shocker to WWF for the TV tapings on 9/8 and 9/9 and Alonso agreed to it, but after the meeting with Alonso, Konnan and Bischoff in California, Alonso pulled Wagner and Shocker from going to WWF and said he was going to send them on 9/8 to Nitro instead. In retaliation, Quinones pulled his four wrestlers, The Head Hunters, Steele and Kevin Quinn, from the EMLL show on 8/29, telling Alonso about it at 2 p.m. the day of the show, and had them do a run-in on the Promo Azteca television tapings that night instead.

His feeling is that Alonso was using both he and the WWF to get Bischoff back interested in a working arrangement. He also agreed to a business truce with Konnan and the Azteca promotion and sent Pantera of Azteca along with Histeria (who was scheduled to wrestle under his former name of Super Crazy) to the WWF tapings this week along with four minis. Wagner and Shocker were supposed to debut on the 9/8 Nitro and we're not sure what happened except that they weren't there.

OCTOBER 20

The Head Hunters and Steele have been suspended from wrestling in the Distrito Federal, which is going to force Promo Azteca to do all its television tapings when those three are around to be outside the D.F. (Mexico City metropolitan area). The Box y Lucha commission issued the suspension after Paco Alonso of EMLL accused them of no-showing his major card without any warning and showing up the same night on the Azteca show.

The Azteca group claims that Alonso was called at 2 p.m. that day and told that they weren't going to appear due to Victor Quinones, their business manager, and Alonso having the falling out when Alonso canceled Dr. Wagner Jr.'s bookings with WWF because he wanted to work with WCW. The funny thing now is that WCW has decided against using any new Mexican wrestlers so Wagner Jr. never did even make it to WCW, and now is scheduled to debut, probably under another name, with WWF at the 10/20 tapings in Oklahoma City.

Giving credence to the Azteca story, aside from it being consistent with what we've known all along, is that Alonso was frantically the afternoon trying to contact big-name independent wrestlers to work the show which he wouldn't have done unless he had knowledge that big names were canceling out of the show. The climate is expected to change because a new commission comes in on 12/5, because the PRI party, which has controlled Mexican elections forever, lost the last election and the PRD party is coming in, and commission posts are generally awarded in exchange for political favors and the new group is thought to be more favorable to Azteca.

NOVEMBER 3

There seems to be a movement by Bischoff to totally neutralize any power or leverage Konnan has regarding the Mexicans. There was an order given to take all references of Konnan out of the Lucha Libre documentary, despite him being probably the biggest drawing card of the past ten years in that country. In addition, as the Glacier-La Parka match is an indication of, with the exception of Misterio Jr., none of the Mexicans are getting any kind of a push and they are no longer doing the six-man tag matches on PPVs and Nitros.

WCW is attempting to either get all the Mexican wrestlers to sign contracts giving WCW exclusive worldwide rights (in other words, they would no longer be allowed to wrestle in Mexico which would take much of the headline talent away from the Promo Azteca promotion, which Konnan is part owner of, nor tour Japan unless the tour was booked through WCW). In exchange for their worldwide rights, all the wrestlers who sign were to get raises although for the most part they earn far less than comparable (and even far less comparable) American wrestlers.

NOVEMBER 10

All of the Mexican wrestlers signed two-year contracts this week, and were all drug tested (given the nature and climate of the industry this week you can probably read into that) with the exception of Misterio Jr., who is still negotiating a new price. Not sure exactly what the deal is regarding them working in Mexico. They are all definitely not allowed to work indie dates in the U.S. It appears WCW doesn't want Konnan or Misterio Jr. to work Mexico at all, but that may not be finalized and they may be interested in working maybe two television tapings per month just to keep their names on top in the market. My belief is the others are all able to continue working in Mexico provided WCW gets first priority on the dates and that WCW gets a commission on their Mexican bookings.

CHAPTER THIRTY FOUR

THE MONTREAL SCREWJOB

NOVEMBER 10

Bret Hart gave notice over the weekend that he was leaving the World Wrestling Federation and his 20-year contract and officially agreed to terms for a two-year deal with World Championship Wrestling.

The 40-year-old Hart, who had along with The Undertaker been the face of the WWF promotion after the end of the Hulk Hogan era, had reportedly been more and more unhappy with the new cruder direction of the WWF and that, far more than money, played a part in his decision according to some close to the situation. Others have categorized it as simply a money deal and that any other explanation as to the main reason would be misleading.

Both Hart and the World Wrestling Federation were attempting to keep the story under lids, so to speak, until after the Survivor Series PPV show in Montreal on 11/9, at which time Hart would have likely given an interview at the taping the next night in Ottawa, or an announcement would have been made by the WWF on that show or at least teased for hotline fodder. On the same night, on the Nitro from Memphis, Eric Bischoff would have also made an announcement about Hart coming to WCW.

After the story got out on 11/4, the WWF did release a statement saying they were giving Hart the opportunity to explore other options. On the 11/3 Nitro, Bischoff teased a big surprise on next week's show which was to be the announcement of Hart coming to the NWO, although no doubt the NWO aspect would be a swerve similar to the introductions of people like Curt Hennig and Jeff Jarrett.

The plan at press time was for Hart to continue with the WWF working all his scheduled house shows through the end of November, and then return for one final show on the 12/7 PPV show from Springfield, MA and he would start with WCW shortly thereafter. However, all plans could change since the story got out everywhere on 11/3.

Negotiations between Hart and Eric Bischoff went back about six weeks, known to only a few people, almost all of whom were sworn to secrecy. The two met three weeks ago in Los Angeles, at which time WCW officials seemed about 80 percent sure Hart was going to make the move, but Hart didn't make his final decision until the weekend. The top WWF officials were aware of the negotiations at least over the past two weeks, if not longer, as those aware of the story as it was breaking could see in the past two weeks certain phrases said on television that wouldn't have been said had they not been aware, although the finality of his leaving the company wasn't known until the weekend.

As mentioned in last week's Observer, Hart had a clause in his contract that would have allowed him to get out of his contract with the WWF if he was unhappy by giving the company just a 30 day notice. Hart negotiated both that clause, and another clause giving him creative control of his character during those final 30 days, last year in negotiations that literally went right down to the wire as Hart was deciding between huge offers from both WWF and WCW. At that point he decided on the WWF offer more because of how he always felt the "story" of his career that he wanted to write was going to end with him riding off in the sunset as a hero in the WWF, something Hulk Hogan never did, legitimately out of loyalty to the company that made him a celebrity and the WWF fans, and also to avoid what he felt were potential pitfalls of going to a company where long-time rival Hulk Hogan was the biggest star.

His "story" had to be amended to a "story" where he left the company that made him famous because he could no longer put up with the direction of the racial angles and antics of his most-hated rival and the company's pick to replace him as champion, Shawn Michaels, that had made him so embarrassed as to no longer allow his children to watch the WWF television.

Hart agreed to his 20-year-deal with the WWF on October 21, 996, with the plan at the time, which didn't quite materialize as promised, that he would be getting the title long-term beating Michaels at WrestleMania. As the story played out, Michaels didn't last until WrestleMania as champion, or until WrestleMania where he was to put Hart over.

Exact contract terms weren't known, but it is known that Hart was earning well over $1 million per year guaranteed on his Titan deal and the total worth of the contract between guaranteed money and other considerations over time was probably in the $10 million range. Hart chose the deal over a WCW contract that offered him a $2.8 million guaranteed figure over three years, figures that were $800,000 in wrestling income and another $2 million guaranteed for starring roles in two movies per year over the terms of the contract, at a time when Hart was contemplating easing out of wrestling and into being a full-time actor. The structure also allowed the huge wrestling contract to be picked up on the Turner movie studio books, making the wrestling company appear to be more profitable at a time when corporate restructuring with the Time Warner purchase was going on. That figure that didn't include potential merchandising revenue and bonuses for PPV appearances so it would in all likelihood also have been worth well in excess of $9 million.

All that is known about the WCW deal he agreed to is that it is similar to the original deal Bischoff offered last year, although the money is scaled down because Hart insisted on working fewer dates, believed to be in the 125 to 140 range, than in the original deal because of his injuries, in particular his knee that has never fully recovered from an injury earlier in the year and a chronic bad wrist from numerous breaks and no time off to allow for proper healing. There may be modifications or changes in the movie role aspect of the deal as well. In addition, the contract is for two years rather than three, with an option for a third year.

When Hart arrives, he'll immediately be inserted into the top of the mix within the promotion and used to get the new Thursday night live show on TBS over, as well as help the company's presence in Canada, where he is the country's most popular wrestler. Nitro just began airing weekly on TSN in Canada, and TBS just became a regular as opposed to a premium cable station throughout the country, giving WCW tremendously improved exposure in a country they've never really done a lot of business historically in. Even before Hart's signing, the company was making plans to run shows more frequently and market its product stronger in Canada in 1998. Although Hart would also help internationally, particularly in Europe, WCW doesn't appear to have any interest in cultivating that market after a series of largely unsuccessful tours in that part of the world over the years.

Hart, in one of the most memorable live pro wrestling interviews of all-time, announced literally hours after making up his decision, live in Fort Wayne, IN on Raw, his acceptance of the WWF offer while Vince McMahon feigned concern over a decision that he actually already knew. However, it didn't take long before Hart started getting disgruntled with the new direction of the WWF.

After a few months, Hart devised his own angle starting with a double turn in his WrestleMania match with Steve Austin, which would result in he, along with brother Owen and brother-in-law Davey Boy Smith, being the top babyface internationally, particularly in Canada, but as strong anti-American heels in the United States.

During the summer, particularly in the wake of the WWF PPV show in Calgary which was the single most well received PPV show in company history, the angle appeared to be red hot. It had cooled and the focus of the company had shifted from Hart as the top heel to his long-time rival, Shawn Michaels, who he had a legitimate dressing room fight with earlier in the year due to a Michaels television interview referring to Bret having "Sunny days" which affected Bret's personal life, a line that he thought was unprofessional to cross.

The problems between the two went back farther, dating back to Bret putting Michaels over at WrestleMania in 1996, and then deciding to sit out to watch Michaels flop with the spotlight on him. With Bret gone and Michaels on top, things both did and didn't go exactly as Hart had surmised. WWF house show business flourished. At the same time, with Michaels as the focal point, television ratings hit company all-time record lows. Although a tremendous performer in the ring, Michaels was seemingly on a path of self destruction, as a perfectionist throwing unprofessional fits when the show didn't go exactly perfectly or if a few hecklers would get on his case.

Michaels, claiming a career ending knee injury, walked out on the promotion just before he was scheduled to have to put over Sycho Sid for the WWF title on a live USA network special, and getting out of his scheduled match where he was going to have to put Bret over at WrestleMania to boot. Many within the company blamed WrestleMania's poor buy rate on the fact they had spent one year building up to one match, and then just a few weeks before the show, that match was pulled and they had to start building into a different direction. When it became apparent Michaels' knee injury, while legit, was nowhere near as serious as he intimated, he was scheduled to return. But before another scheduled match with Bret that he was supposed to lose on 6/8, this time it was Bret whose knee gave out and he underwent surgery. After some classic verbal battles on television, no match took place—in the ring.

With Bret still recovering from his knee surgery, he and Michaels had a backstage brawl on 6/9 in Hartford, CT, resulting in Bret aggravating his knee and keeping him out of action even longer, and Michaels, claiming knee and neck injuries, walked out on the company claiming an unsafe working environment, just weeks after he attempted and failed to get out of his own five-year contract with the WWF so he could join WCW. Neither Hart, who by all accounts threw the first blow, nor Michaels, who taunted him into doing so by sarcastically responding to Bret's complaints by saying something along the lines of "so what are you going to do about it," were punished for the fight, and instead officials seemed to beg Michaels to return, creating the sense of anarchy that has resulted in what some categorize as the beginning of the fall of a once great promotional power.

Eventually the two agreed to peacefully co-exist, agreeing to keep families and personal lives out of their interviews. Bret felt Michaels violated that when in a recent interview he brought up Bret's 83-year-old father Stu, claiming that he was walking around Calgary dead, only his brain and his body didn't know it yet, although Michaels did apologize afterwards claiming that he simply got carried away performing for the crowd.

Michaels antics in recent weeks, which even though his television persona pretends otherwise, were obviously encouraged and allowed by Vince McMahon, turned Hart off worse because his vision of pro wrestling dating back to his childhood was of something that a father could watch with his kids and not have to turn off the television set in embarrassment. Perhaps the final blow was when Titan made the decision to go with Michaels as champion over Bret in the Survivor Series, a decision that asks even more questions.

Of course that decision could simply by the latest in the line of short-term business decisions by a company that seemingly changes its direction by reacting every other Monday. Michaels had become such an effective heel that he literally had turned his rival, the anti-American foreigner, almost into a babyface in the U.S. At the same time, there were thoughts within the company that the Hart contract was a 19-year debt that in hindsight many were questioning, with the feeling being McMahon made the decision out of wanting to win a momentary battle that he and others hyped into the immediate priority in a bitter wrestling war and not necessarily a contract that made economic sense given the financial structure of the company.

Certainly those in charge had to know how Hart would feel if asked to put Michaels over for the title, which leads to the speculation that all of these actions by both Michaels and Hart to an extent were actually an expert marionette pulling strings of his two strongest puppets. Michaels' track record of finding a way numerous times to not drop titles (besides walking out earlier this year instead of dropping the title to Sid, he also quit the WWF in 1993 rather than drop the Intercontinental title, he was injured and failed to drop the IC title in 1995, and earlier this year walked out on the company at a time he and Steve Austin held the tag team title) and the fact he's refused to work more than once a week made any decision giving him back the major title to be one somewhat perplexing. Even more so to his most hated rival who valued the title belt to a degree that outsiders would find almost incredulous.

Most of Michaels' juvenile television behavior that fans see were part of his new character orchestrated by McMahon where he continually does things "to try and get fired" based on the idea that "everyone" knows that earlier this year that is exactly what he wanted to do. Still, as noted below, it clearly rubbed Hart the wrong way, particularly when he jumped up and down and showed his bare butt on television, which over the past week many have given as the reason for an incredible 26% turn-off ratio of the Raw audience after that segment aired on 10/27, although Raw's 2.63 rating on 11/3 was right at its usual average. Michaels had already been put over British Bulldog for the European title in a match that was originally booked for Michaels to do a clean job in.

Exactly what is going to happen in Montreal is unclear. With Hart leaving, everyone will expect him to lose to Michaels for logical common sense business reasons. With wrestling the way it is today, the title switch shouldn't be taken as a lock, although obviously he will be dropping the title at some point very quickly.

WCW scored a second major coup with word that Bischoff and Ric Flair had basically agreed to terms this past week and that it was expected Flair would be signing a contract extension very shortly. Flair, whose contract expired in a few months, was someone WWF officials were highly interested in going after and who at least strongly considered the idea of such a move back.

The next obvious questions concerns the future of Owen Hart and Davey Boy Smith. The belief is that both, who signed five-year contracts each over the past 14 months, will remain with similar roles as at present in the WWF and the situation with Bret has nothing to do with their futures.

Just a few days before Hart made his final decision to leave, he wrote a column in the Calgary Sun. Obviously much of the column was typical pro wrestling attempting to hype his next big match in the new in vogue more realistic insider fashion, but in hindsight, you can see where his head was at in other ways just before making his decision. The column was written as a letter to Michaels:

> *Shawn Michaels, you are a disgrace to professional wrestling. It amazes me that there was a time I actually thought you'd be the guy who could come up behind me and carry the ball when my time comes to retire. Now when you're behind me, I have to make sure I don't bend over. I am a second generation wrestler. Like a lot of second generation wrestler, I've paid my dues. The way you are degrading the business makes me sick and breaks my heart. That's not what Heartbreak Kid was supposed to mean. I told you, and Vince told you, to leave our families out of this. So you got on RAW and said that my father is dead. This time you're so far over the line that there's no coming back. Every so often, after you shoot off your mouth, you come to me backstage with a lame apology and a limp handshake. "Oh Bret, my mouth always gets me in trouble when I get goin' out there. You know I didn't mean nothin' by it."*
>
> *Don't bother this time, I'm not buying it. I would not embarrass my father—who is not only very much alive but is still tougher today at 83 and more of a man than you will ever be—as you have embarrassed your father with your degenerate behavior. How humiliating for your poor father to have to explain your lewd gestures to her friends. You don't respect anybody, do you? What does Jose Lothario think of how you've made pornography out of what he taught you? Shawn Michaels, you are nothing more than a whore for this business.*
>
> *You called me a paper champion because it bothers you that my contract is worth more than you and the whole Degeneration X put together. You said I wrestle because I need the money, but you wrestle because this business needs you. You are a festering cancerous tumor in this business. After WrestleMania*

XII, I went home for a while to give you the chance to become "the man" because as long as I'm around you'll never be "the man." You were so bad at being "the man" that the WWF and WCW had the biggest bidding war in wrestling history to get me to come back. You'd have the World championship belt. But you don't. What do you have, besides a big mouth and a bad attitude?

Shawn Michaels, you said that beating the Undertaker makes you an icon. Not taking anything away from `Taker, but you weren't the first guy to beat him, you just did it too late. You said you're the only icon that can still go, not like the fossils. You're so beat up from taking completely overdone bumps like a Mexican jumping bean that you can't even work a full schedule like the older guys. You only wrestle about once a month and you're proud of that? Then people who think they know more about this business than they actually do, write about what a hard worker you are. Anyone can work hard once a month. You've barebacked your way to main event matches and they give you the best guys in the business to make you look good.

So you and your boyfriend, Hunter, think I'm told. Hunter said he's bigger than me in more ways than one, and then you pointed at Hunter's crotch and said he could put an eye out with that thing. Thanks for admitting that you know what Hunter has in his pants. So how come I have four kids and all you two have is each other? I'm not the one shooting blanks. By the way, you both looked very comfortable eating bananas together on Raw. Lots of parents tell me they won't let their kids watch the shows anymore because of you and they don't watch either because you're such an asshole. People are shutting the show off because of you! It took so long to make wrestling into family entertainment. Thanks for setting the business back 50 years! You are the one who is confusing expansion and destruction, not me. You, Shawn, are the destruction of this business. You make me sick. You said you're the best sports entertainer in the world. Don't even think about saying you're a wrestler. What I do is an art form and what you do is...what do you do, anyway, cause it's not pro wrestling anymore?

You called the WWF world championship a "tin title" but you're only saying that because you don't have the belt. When you did have it, you treated it like garbage and then threw it away! So now you want to try to win the title at Survivor Series? You'd better reconsider that because when I get my hands on you it's going to make the beating I gave you in the locker room last June look like a warm up. After that little scuffle, you went running to Vince, complaining that the work conditions in the WWF are unsafe. The only thing unsafe about the working conditions in the WWF is you, Shawn. You've gotten in the ring so "pilled up" lately that you can't even talk straight on TV. You'd better shake the cob webs free before you get in the ring with me at SS. This business has been my mistress for my whole life and I love her. You ar raping her and taking her dignity away. Don't count on my reputation for professionalism saving your ass at SS. You're the one who threw the rule book out the window. The 17 stitches you got at Hell in the Cell are nothing compared to what's coming at Misery in Montreal.

NOVEMBER 17

It will go down in history as the single most famous finish of a pro wrestling match in the modern era. Twenty or 30 years from now this story, more than any famous wrestler jumping promotions, more than any prominent death, and more than any record setting house, will be remembered vividly by all who watched it live, and remembered as legendary from all who hear about it later. Through the magic of videotape, the last minute of this match will live forever, and be replayed literally millions of times by tens of thousands of people all looking for the most minute pieces of detail to this strange puzzle. But the story of what led to those few seconds starts more than one year ago, far more reminiscent of the dirty con man past of the industry than the current attempted facade of a multi-million dollar corporate above board image those in the industry like to portray outwardly that it has evolved into.

(October 20, 1996) Bret Hart was in a hotel room in San Jose, CA, hours from making the biggest decision of his life—who would win the biggest bidding war in the history of pro wrestling. He had pretty well leaned toward staying with the World Wrestling Federation despite a much larger offer from World Championship Wrestling, but had changed his mind a few times over the previous two weeks as each side presented new offers.

In the waning hours, Eric Bischoff and Kevin Nash were trying to convince him to change his mind and how great life was with an easier schedule. Bischoff was offering big money and a shot at becoming a movie star, a goal Hart had been pursuing while on a semi-retirement from wrestling since dropping the title to Shawn Michaels a few months earlier at WrestleMania. Vince McMahon was offering him, in the now immortal words of Arn Anderson, not just a spot, but the top spot in the company, the chance to be a major part of deciding the future direction of the company, and almost literally, to be WWF 4 life.

Many close advisers of Hart's tried to tell him going to WCW was the best move for his present, and more importantly, his future after wrestling. But largely out of loyalty, and that obviously wasn't the only factor involved, he declined the offer.

McMahon, determined not to lose a very public fight, offered him the famous 20-year contract where he'd, after retirement in about three years, become almost a first lieutenant when it came to the booking process. Hart would earn somewhere in the neighborhood of $1.5 million per year as an active wrestler, and a healthy but far lesser figure working the front office for the 17 years after retirement as an active wrestler. As part of McMahon's offer, he also was going to allow Hart to explain live on television his decision making process should be sign with WCW.

Hart flew to Fort Wayne, IN, where the WWF was holding its live Raw taping after having already verbally agreed to the deal, signed the contract, and gave the interview saying basically that he would be in the WWF forever, figuring to be positioned as the top babyface and perennial champion until he finished his active career riding off in the sunset in a blaze of glory, like Hogan, Savage, and the rest of the superstars before him didn't.

As is the case in wrestling, not all the promised scenarios that everyone believed were going to happen transpire as originally planned. And just over one year later, the feelings between McMahon and Hart had taken a 180 degree turn, to the degree nobody would have ever believed.

(March 10, 1997) Top babyface didn't last long as McMahon asked him to turn heel. At first Hart balked at the idea but after three days, McMahon presented him with two lists. One list was his prospective opponents as a babyface—Vader, Mankind and Steve Austin. The other list was his prospective opponents as a heel, Undertaker, Michaels and Austin. Hart agreed for drawing money, his opponents as a heel made up a better list, and he and McMahon agreed that he would turn back babyface over the last few months of his contract and end his career on a positive note. He and Steve Austin did the double-turn at WrestleMania. Hart himself then came up with the Anti-American angle, where he would remain a babyface in Canada and Europe and do interviews that would for the most part speak the truth, so he could when the time came to turn back in the U.S., have a reasonable explanation.

(September 8, 1997) Vince McMahon and Bret Hart had their first meeting where McMahon seriously approached Hart about his contract. About three months earlier, McMahon had told Hart that the company was in bad financial straits and that they might have to defer some of the money until later in the contract. This time his approach was more point blank. He wanted to cut Hart's regular salary, around $30,000 per week, more than in half and defer the rest of the money until later in the contract period when hopefully the company would be in better shape financially. Hart declined the suggestion, because he didn't want to risk not getting the money in the future after he was through taking all the bumps.

(September 20, 1997) About one hour before the beginning of the PPV show in Birmingham, England, McMahon approached Davey Boy Smith and asked him to put over Shawn Michaels that night for the European title. Smith was apparently shocked, having been told all along in the build-up of the show, that Michaels was going to do a job for him, since Europe was promised to be "his territory."

The explanation, which made and still makes logical business sense, is that they wanted to build for a bigger show, a second PPV from Smith's former home town of Manchester, England, where Smith would regain the title—the same scenario the WWF did to draw 60,000 fans in San Antonio with Michaels in the other role working a program with Sycho Sid. So while it all made sense, it was rather strange he wasn't approached with this idea until just before the start of the show.

At around this same time period, McMahon approached Hart about working with Michaels. Hart said that he had a problem with that since Michaels had still never really apologized to him for the Sunny days comment, and said it would be hard to trust somebody like that in the ring and due to their past, and told McMahon that he would figure that Michaels would have the same concerns, since a few weeks earlier after first making it clear he would never work with anyone in the Hart Foundation, Michaels had finally agreed to work only with Smith, saying he couldn't trust Bret or Owen.

(September 22, 1997) On the day of the Raw taping at Madison Square Garden, McMahon told Bret Hart flat out that they were going to intentionally breach his contract because they couldn't afford the deal. He told a shocked Hart that he should go to World Championship Wrestling and make whatever deal he could with that group.

"I didn't feel comfortable doing it," Hart said of the suggestion. "I felt like an old prisoner in a prison where I know all the guards and all the inmates and I have the best cell. Why would I want to move to a new prison where I don't know the guards and the inmates and I no longer have the best cell? I felt really bad after all the years of working for the WWF."

Hart had an escape clause built into his contract since he had so much negotiating leverage when making his WWF deal 11 months earlier, in that he could leave the company giving 30 days notice, and that he would have what the contract called "reasonable creative control" of his character during that lame duck period so that he couldn't be unreasonably buried on the way out.

There was a window period for giving that notice and negotiating elsewhere that hadn't begun, so McMahon, showing he was serious, gave Hart written permission to begin negotiating with WCW and Hart contacted Eric Bischoff. The same day, during a meeting with Hart, Michaels and McMahon, Michaels told both of them point blank that he wouldn't do any jobs for anyone in the territory, word that when it got out made most of the other top wrestlers feel even more warmly than usual toward Michaels.

Michaels later reiterated that statement to Hart on 10/4 in St. Paul when the two had agreed that for the good of the business that they'd work together. At the meeting, McMahon proposed a scenario where the two would have their first singles match in Montreal, where Undertaker would interfere causing a non-finish. This would lead to Hart wrestling Undertaker on the 12/7 PPV in Springfield, MA, where Michaels would interfere causing Hart to lose the title, as poetic justice since his interference caused Bret to win the title in the first place, and that Royal Rumble on 1/18 in San Jose would be headlined by Undertaker vs. Michaels.

During the meeting, Hart told Michaels that he'd be happy to put him over at the end of the run, but Michaels told Hart flat out that he wouldn't return the favor to him. Michaels and Hart spoke again on the subject on 10/12 in San Jose, where once again Michaels told Hart that he wasn't going to do a job for him.

(October 21, 1997) McMahon approached Hart with the idea of losing the title to Michaels in Montreal, but promised that he would win it back on 12/7. Hart, remembering his conversations where Michaels was adamant about not doing any more jobs in the territory, was reluctant, saying after the way the angle had been done with him representing Canada and it becoming a big patriotic deal, that he didn't want to lose the title in Canada.

He was then asked to lose to Michaels on 12/7 in Springfield, MA. Hart told McMahon that since Michaels had told both of them that he wasn't doing anymore jobs, that he had a problem doing a job for someone who wouldn't do a job back. He told McMahon that he didn't want to drop the title in Montreal.

Later, McMahon, Pat Patterson, Michaels and Hart had another meeting where Michaels, teary eyed, told

Hart that he was looking forward to returning the favor to Bret and once again talked about his mouth saying the stupidest things (in regard to saying he'd never do another job in the territory). Hart still refused to lose the title in Montreal.

The night before he had been asked to put Hunter Hearst Helmsley over in Oklahoma City via pinfall due to Michaels' interference, but changed the finish to a count out. On this night he was asked to tap out to Ken Shamrock before the DQ ending involving Michaels, which he had no problem doing because he liked and respected Shamrock and wanted to help elevate him.

The personal problems with himself and Michaels, which had become legendary in the business, resurfaced once again when the two and McMahon made an agreement to work together but to leave their respective families out of their interviews. It took just one week before Michaels did the interview talking about Stu Hart being dead but walking around Calgary because his body and brain hadn't figured it out yet. By this point, Hart had already stopped watching Raw because he had problems with the content of the show because he had four children that were wrestling fans that he didn't want seeing the direction it was going, so he was reacting to the remark based on the fact that his father and brother Owen heard the remarks and were upset about them.

(October 24, 1997) McMahon, before the show at the Nassau Coliseum, told Hart that the money situation in the company had changed and they would have no problems paying him everything promised in his contract. Hart told McMahon that WCW really hadn't made him a serious offer and that he really didn't want to leave but that he was still uncomfortable doing the job for Michaels in that situation. He left the country for the tour of Bahrain and Oman with the idea that he was staying with the WWF, but knowing due to his window in his contract, he had to make the decision to give notice by midnight on 11/1.

(October 31, 1997) Never one to work without a flair for the dramatics, Bischoff finally caught up with Hart who was basically incommunicado in a foreign land most of the week. Just one day before Hart had to either give notice or stay for another year, Bischoff made a huge concrete offer. We don't know the exact terms of the offer, only that Hart said of the $3 million per year figure that both Jim Ross and Jerry Lawler talked about on the 11/10 Raw, that "they don't have any idea what I was offered," but others close to the situation say that figure is "close enough that you couldn't call it wrong." Hart neither agreed nor turned down the deal, but gave the impression to WCW that they had a great shot at getting him.

(November 1, 1997) Hart had until midnight to make up his mind. He called McMahon and told him about the WCW offer and said that he wasn't asking for any more money to stay, but that he wanted to know what his future in the WWF would be over his next two years as an active wrestler and that at this point he was leaning toward accepting the WCW offer. McMahon said he'd think about it and call him back in one hour with some scenarios.

Before McMahon called back, Bischoff called again trying to solidify the deal. McMahon ended up calling back four hours later from his barber shop in Manhattan and told Hart that he didn't know what he was going to do with him but to trust his judgment because of their past relationship, that he had made him into a superstar and that he wanted him to stay and that he should trust him and asked Hart to give him ideas of where he wanted to go.

During the conversation, McMahon still brought up the scenario of wanting Hart to drop the title in Montreal, but promised that he would get it back in Springfield. "I realized he had given the top heel spot to Shawn, but to turn back babyface, it was too soon," Hart said.

Like in the negotiations one year earlier, it was going down to the wire and he had until midnight to make up his mind. When he was talking to McMahon, McMahon told him he could extend his deadline for giving notice. Hart asked for the permission in writing but McMahon told him that he was going out to a movie that night with his wife and said that he was verbally giving permission to extend it and to get written permission from the company's Chief Financial Officer. When Hart called to get the written notice, he wasn't given it because he was told he couldn't get it in writing on such short notice.

At 7 p.m. Bischoff called again and presented a deal that, according to Hart, "would have been insane not to be taken." At that point Hart was really having mixed emotions. He somehow felt bad about leaving the WWF and was just hoping McMahon would lay out a good set of scenarios for him and convince him to stay. At 9 p.m., McMahon called and, reversing fields once again, urged him to take the WCW offer.

Hart told him that his heart was with the company and it would break is heart to leave, and that he appreciated everything McMahon and the company had done for him. McMahon told Hart that he wanted him back as a babyface, and had been wanting him to turn babyface for two or three months but just hadn't brought it up until this point.

He then presented a scenario to Hart, presenting it as a way to get Hart to stay, but obviously designed to get Hart to take the WCW offer. He wanted Michaels to win the title in Montreal. For Springfield, they would do a Final Four match with he, Michaels, Undertaker and Ken Shamrock, that Michaels would again win. At the Royal Rumble, the two would have a ladder match, which Michaels would win. On Raw on 1/19 in Fresno, CA, Hart would open the show and say that if he couldn't beat Michaels and win the title that night, that he would retire from wrestling, and in that match he would regain the title. And then in Boston at WrestleMania, he'd drop the title to Austin.

Hart looked at that scenario of four major losses with only one win and before his midnight deadline, gave official notice to the WWF and signed the contract WCW had sent over, with the agreement from all three parties that the word wouldn't leak out until 11/10 to protect the Survivor Series PPV. Hart went so far as to have his few confidants sign written confidentiality letters to make sure the word of his negotiations and signing with WCW didn't get out until 11/10.

(November 2, 1997) Hart and McMahon started a very amicable conversation with the pressure finally off and the decision for Hart to leave having been made. He again suggested that Michaels win the title in Montreal, and in what will go down as perhaps the ultimate irony, said they could do a screw-job ending to steal the title from him, and that the next night on Raw, McMahon suggested the two get into a mock argument where Hart would punch him, blaming him for the screw job. McMahon even suggested to hardway him (give him a hard punch that would either open him up or at least give him a noticeable black eye) to make it look legit.

Hart again refused to do the job in Montreal, saying that he had never refused to do a job but he wasn't going to lose on Sunday or Monday (at the Raw tapings in Ottawa). He agreed to put Michaels over in Madison Square Garden on 11/15, Springfield, or anywhere else, and said he'd put over Vader, Shamrock, Mankind, Undertaker or even Steve Lombardi (who earned a title shot at MSG by winning a Battle Royal at the last show, but they dropped that idea almost immediately but there had been talk of giving Lombardi the match after all).

McMahon then made legal threats to Hart if he wouldn't lose in Montreal. Hart talked about the clause in his contract giving him "reasonable" creative control, but McMahon claimed that refusing to drop the title in Montreal wasn't reasonable. The two argued about the finish in Montreal and the legalities of their respective positions all day Sunday and well into the night before finally agreeing to do a DQ finish in Montreal.

Then in Springfield, in the final four match, Michaels would win the title. Bret would then go out on Raw on 12/8 in Portland, ME and give a farewell interview as a babyface to WWF fans and put the company and McMahon over as big as possible. He would apologize to the American fans and try to reasonably explain his actions as a way to end his 14-year association with the WWF on the highest note possible, something largely unheard of in pro wrestling, so that all parties and the fans could come out of it and his legacy with the company with a good feeling. Technically there was a problem, in that his WCW contract began on 12/1, so Hart called Bischoff, who when presented the scenario, agreed to allow him to work through 12/8 with Titan.

Hart asked an associate who monitors news for him if he thought it was possible to keep the secret from the public until 11/10. Hart specifically asked about being able to keep it secret from one person until after the show, and the associate laughed and said they would bet a million dollars that person already knew.

(November 4, 1997) McMahon called Hart and said that he had changed his mind. He suggested now that Michaels should lose clean in Montreal, then he'd "steal" the title with a controversial finish in Springfield and Hart would get to do his farewell speech in Portland. He said he was going to call Michaels and present the scenario to him.

By this point, word that Hart had signed with WCW had actually been reported the previous night on the Observer and Torch hotlines, and it was only about one hour later before the folks who call those hotlines for much of their news started breaking the latest "biggest story in the history of wrestling" as their "exclusives." In response, WWF Canada released a press statement originally totally denying the story, claiming it was simply propaganda being spread by WCW. However, as the word got out, Titan Sports in Connecticut a few hours later contradicted that story saying simply that Bret Hart was exploring all his options, but not going any farther, with the feeling that they wanted to protect the PPV show. Hart wouldn't publicly talk to anyone.

(November 5, 1997) The Internet had paved the way for stories in the Calgary Sun, the Toronto Sun and one line in the Montreal Gazette in a PPV preview story about Steve Austin, a line which resulted in the paper getting an incredible switchboard-blowing response of phone calls.

McMahon called Hart and said that Michaels had agreed to the previous days' scenario, but that now he had changed his mind. He said the news was out everywhere and that Bret had to drop the belt before Monday because he couldn't have Bischoff go on television on 11/10 and announce the signing of his world champion while he still had the belt. Hart said that he would get Bischoff to postpone the announcement, but with Bischoff on a hunting trip all week in Wyoming, Hart couldn't get a hold of him.

McMahon then asked Hart to drop the title on 11/8 at the house show in Detroit. Hart again refused, feeling the way everything had been built up, he wanted the match with Michaels, which in the wake of all the insider publicity was building up a life of its own like no match in the recent history of wrestling, to not come off as anti-climactic and for that to happen he needed to go into Montreal as the champion. He said that he would drop the title any time after 11/12, suggesting he'd do it at the house shows in Youngstown, OH on 11/13, Pittsburgh on 11/14 or in Madison Square Garden if they wanted it that soon rather than waiting for 12/7.

Jim Ross, on the company's 900 line, acknowledged the statement that Hart was exploring other options, said that nobody knows the real story, and in hyping the big match, tossed in the phrase they'd be pushing in the final days leading up to the match—it will be their first meeting in 18 months, and most likely the final match between the two ever.

(November 6, 1997) In a story in the Toronto Sun, Tiger Ali Singh, at a press conference promoting the WWF house show the next night in Toronto said of Hart's leaving, "It's very disheartening. He's not only been a mentor, but I've been a great admirer of him since I was a kid. And if he leaves, you're going to see a whole bunch of other people leaving. And I'm not going to mention any names but WCW has been approaching a lot of people."

(November 7, 1997) There is no question that the power of online services when it comes to influence of pro wrestling was established this past week. It was generally portrayed that it was a power struggle between Hart and Michaels, that Michaels had won out, and to a lesser extent Hart was leaving over the direction of the product. While there was some truth to all of this, probably the greatest truth of all is it was simply a manipulation by McMahon to get out of a contract that in hindsight he wished he'd never offered.

Whether Michaels, who the wrestlers feel has McMahon's ear right now and has convinced him that what turned around WCW is Kevin Nash and Scott Hall, and not Hulk Hogan and Roddy Piper, and that he should and the company should do what they did to get WCW over. There is also feeling among WWF wrestlers that Michaels pushed McMahon in that direction to rid the company of his hated rival who had apparently one-upped him when signing the new deal that made him so much higher paid. Maybe it was simply economic because the company is in financial straights. Hart did have a lot of problems over the direction of the company and his own decision was partially made based on that, but it's clear, in hindsight, that McMahon had a strong hand in manipulating Hart's decision to get out of the contract.

In the vast majority opinion on-line from people who really had no clue as to what was really going on, Titan, McMahon and Michaels were coming off as major heels. The WWF's own online site, said to be the domain of young kids with no clue about wrestling, was besieged with the reports about Hart leaving and the so-called marks were reacting very negatively toward Titan to the point Titan pulled all its folders by the early afternoon, which caused another outcry of censorship of opinions from wrestling fans. Finally, McMahon responded publicly online with a letter of his own, stating:

> *Over the past few days I have read certain comments on the Internet concerning Bret Hart and his "alleged" reasons for wanting to pursue other avenues than the World Wrestling Federation to earn his livelihood. While I respect the "opinions" of others, as owner of the World Wrestling Federation I felt that it was time to set the record straight.*
>
> *As it has been reported recently online, part of Bret Hart's decision to pursue other options is "allegedly due to his concern with the "direction" of the World Wrestling Federation. Whereby each and every individual is entitles to his, or her, opinion, I take great offense when the issue of the direction of the World Wrestling Federation is raised.*
>
> *In this age of sports-entertainment, the World Wrestling Federation REFUSES to insult its audience in terms of "Baby Faces" and "Heels." In 1997, how many people do you truly know who are strictly "good" guys or "bad" guys? World Wrestling Federation programming reflects more of a reality-based product in which life, as well as World Wrestling Federation superstars, are portrayed as they truly are—in shades of gray...not black or white.*
> *From what I am reading, it has been reported that Bret may be concerned about the morality issues in the World Wrestling Federation. Questionable language. Questionable gestures. Questionable sexuality. Questionable racial issues. Questionable? All of the issues mentioned above are issues that every human being must deal with every day of their lives.*
>
> *Also, with that in mind, please be aware that Bret Hart had been cautioned—on "numerous" occasions—to alter his language, by not using expletives or God's name in vain. He was also told—on numerous occasions—not to use certain hand gestures some might find offensive.*
>
> *My point is: regardless of what some are reporting, Bet's decision to pursue other career options IS NOT genuinely a Shawn Michaels direction issue, as they would like you to believe! In the personification of DeGeneration X, Shawn Michaels' character is EXPECTED to be living on the edge—which, I might add, Mr. Michaels portrays extremely well.*
>
> *The issue here is that the "direction" of the World Wrestling Federation is not determined by Shawn Michaels, OR Bret Hart for that matter. It is determined by you—the fans of the World Wrestling Federation! You DEMAND a more sophisticated approach! You DEMAND to be intellectually challenged! You DEMAND a product with ATTITUDE, and as owner of this company—it is my responsibility to give you exactly what you want!*
>
> *Personally, I regret the animosity that has built up between Shawn Michaels and Bret Hart, but in the end, it is the World Wrestling Federation that is solely responsible for the content of this product—NOT Bret Hart—NOT Shawn Michaels—NOT Vince McMahon, for that matter. May the best man win at the Survivor Series! .*

That only made the situation worse in regard to how fans were viewing McMahon and the company even worse. "You demand to be intellectually challenged?" By doing racial angles. The fans chose that direction? They asked to see Michaels pull his pants down and jump up and down on television?

Hart was booked for his first public appearance before the house show that night at the Sky Dome in Toronto. It was on a half-hour TSN (The Sports Network, the Canadian version of ESPN) talk show called "Off The Record." Host Michael Landsberg opened the show saying the show had received more than 1,000 calls to ask Hart if he was leaving for WCW. Despite the word being out everywhere by this point, Hart would only go so far as to say that he had given his 30 day notice to the WWF, that he's reviewing offers from both groups and is strongly leaning going one way. "I'd like to really come more clean on it than I can, you know, than I have, but I have to do this thing by the book kind of thing."

Hart categorized the split as not being a money issue but said that he and the WWF had "reached kind of a crisis or we've reached professional differences as to what direction that the wrestling shows are taking. You know, I'm not saying I'm always right, but I feel that some of the content of the shows goes against my belief in what wrestling should be, and can be." Later in the show he criticized Michaels, and then stated that "wrestling is often scoffed at as a form of entertainment sometimes, or it used to be. I believe it came way up, and I was very proud in the direction, which has a lot to do with where I am right now today. Wrestling was cleaned up, and it became something families could watch..."

He talked about inner workings of the business, having to trust the guy you are working with because you give them your body and said the real animosities and hatred that exists have to be set aside. He said that everything he has said about Shawn Michaels is about the Shawn Michaels character, but said that Michaels has said things that have hit a raw nerve with him to the point it's unprofessional.

The show aired the footage of the Shawn Michaels interview where he blamed the Hart Foundation for trashing the NOD dressing room and insinuating that Hart was a racist. Hart said that he doesn't blame Michaels for that. "That's obviously a promotional direction, and that's a poor concept. I think that racial tension is something to be very, very careful with. When you start messing around with racial things, that I don't like."

Hart said that he stopped watching Raw about five weeks earlier because he didn't like the direction, and agreed when the host brought up Michaels calling him the Grand Wizard (a KKK reference, not a reference to a famous wrestling manager of the 70s), and then brought up what Michaels said about his father that he didn't see. "You know, I don't mind if someone pokes fun at my dad. Jerry Lawler's made a living the last two or three years saying comments about my mom and dad, but he's always fairly humorous about it. Actually I used to get offended at some of the things he used to say about my mother...until I realized that my mother thought they were humorous, and then it was kind of OK with me." He then spoke at length about Brian Pillman.

By this point, in certain circles and particularly within the industry, interest in the match on Sunday due to all the uncertainty, some of which was known and most of which actually wasn't, had reached a level not seen in years. For all of Hart and McMahon's wanting to keep the story quiet, word getting out was the greatest thing for the buy rate. There were 14,374 fans paying $296,674 at Sky Dome that night for the show. To credit the huge house to the interest in Canada since Hart leaving had been reported in the local newspapers would be incorrect, as WWF officials a week before the event had figured on a crowd of 15,000. Obviously some fans knew, and there were chants of "You sold out" directed at Hart. Although this should have been expected, and Hart has been a pro wrestler for 21 years and been around the business a lot longer than that, the chants in his home country knowing what he was going through did get to him.

The main event was a six-man tag with Undertaker & Mankind & Austin vs. Bret & Smith & Neidhart, subbing for brother Owen who was supposed to start back but still wasn't ready to return after a severe concussion from a few weeks earlier. Bret was asked to do the job for the stone cold stunner, debated the question for a while, then refused, figuring he was the only Canadian in the main event in the U.S. vs. Canada type match with the big nationalistic angle, and Austin ended up using the stunner on Neidhart instead.

(November 8, 1997) The WWF ran a house show in Detroit at Cobo Arena for what would turn out to be Bret

Hart's final match in the United States as a wrestler for the World Wrestling Federation. Tensions were really high and the prospects of a double-cross were looming by this time in many of the more paranoid types.

But really, this was 1997, and this was the World Wrestling Federation. That's stuff from the 20s when the real bad guy lowlives were running the business. The days of making Lou Thesz world champion because you needed someone who could handle himself in the case of a double-cross had been over for more than three decades.

That day, Hart went to the one member of the front office he knew he could trust, Earl Hebner. While there are what you call a lot of good acquaintances in the business, Hart and Hebner were genuine close friends for years. Hart said he'd use his influence to get Hebner to referee the match because he wanted someone in the ring that he could trust. Hebner said he understood the situation, and told Hart, "I swear on my kids lives that I'd quit my job before double-crossing you." On a personal basis a little more than 24 hours later, remembrance of that conversation crushed him more than anything.

At about the same time, the WWF braintrust was in Montreal one day early. Vince McMahon held a meeting at the hotel with Jim Ross, Jim Cornette, Pat Patterson and Michaels. Reports are that at least two of the aforementioned names looked extremely uncomfortable leaving the meeting.

Ross, on the WWF 900 line, filed a report saying due to the tension between Hart and Michaels that there would be armed security backstage and the two would dress as far apart from each other as possible. That was a total work since Michaels and Hart actually dressed together and were on professional terms the next afternoon. He also said that McMahon was not going to announce the show, and instead would be handling any last minute problems backstage. Ross also hinted that it could be Hart's final match in the World Wrestling Federation, something Hart at that point wasn't aware of.

(November 9, 1997) Imagine going into the most anticipated match on the inside of pro wrestling in years and on the day of the show, not having any semblance of a finish? McMahon and Hart met that afternoon and McMahon said something to the effect of, "What do you want to do? You've got me by the balls." Hart said that he just wants to leave the building with his head up. Hart said to McMahon, "Let me hand you the belt on Raw (the next night in Ottawa). Everyone knows I'm leaving. I'd like to tell the truth on Raw Monday."

At this point the "truth" wouldn't include talking about finances, contract breaches, arguments about finishes or anything that would make McMahon or the company look bad publicly. McMahon said he agreed, that it was the right thing to do and the two shook hands on it.

Hart and Michaels were dressing together putting together a match. Both were professional with one another and talking about putting on the best match possible in Hart's last hurrah, agreeing to a DQ finish in about 17:00 after a lengthy brawl before the bell wound even sound to start the match. As they were putting their spots together, Patterson came in. He had a suggestion for a high spot in the match as a false finish. There would be a referee bump. Michaels would put Hart in his own sharpshooter. Hart would reverse the hold. Hebner would still be down at this point and not see Michaels tap out. Hart would release the hold to revive Hebner. Michaels would hit him when he turned around with the sweet chin music. A second ref, Mike Chioda, would haul ass to the ring and begin the count. A few paces behind, Owen Hart and Smith, and possibly Neidhart as well, would run down to the ring. Chioda would count 1-2, and whomever got to the ring first, likely Owen, would drag Chioda out of the ring. While they think they've saved the day on the pin on Bret, suddenly Hebner would recover, 1-2, and Bret would kick out. That would set the pace for about five more minutes of near falls before it would end up in a disqualification ending.

Before the show started, both Vader, with his Japanese experience, and Smith, told Hart to watch himself. He was warned not to lay down and not to allow himself to be put in a compromising position. He was told to kick out at one, not two, and not to allow himself into any submission holds. Hart recognized the possibility of the situation, but his thoughts regarding a double-cross were more along with lines of always protecting himself in case Michaels tried to hit him with a sucker punch when he left himself open. The idea that being put in a submission or one of the near falls while working spots would be dangerous for him would be something to worry about normally, but he put it out of his mind because he had Hebner in the ring as the referee.

People on the inside were watching this as close as on the outside. Would Bret do the job? Would Shawn do the job? Would Bret give Shawn a real beating before putting him over? The Molson Center was packed with more than 20,000 rabid fans, who up to that point had seen a largely lackluster undercard. While the fear going in about the word getting out of Hart leaving hurting the PPV most likely turned out to be just the opposite, the sellout was not indicative of that either as it was well known by the advance that the show was going to sellout one or two days early. It appeared that about 10 to 20 percent of the crowd knew Hart was leaving, and there were negative signs regarding his decision, and negative signs toward the promotion for picking Michaels above him or the direction that seemingly forced him to leave.

Some things were also strange, and not just the absence of McMahon from the broadcast. Hart, the champion in the main event, wasn't scheduled for an interview building up the match. When his name was announced early in the show, there were many boos from fans who knew he signed with the opposition. Once he got in the ring for the introductions, Michaels wiped his butt, blew his nose and then picked his nose with the Canadian flag. He then put the flag on the ground and began humping it. Hart was immediately established as the babyface.

The two began the match as a brawl all around ringside and into the stands. The crowd was so rabid that it appeared there was genuine danger they'd attack Michaels. At one point, they were brawling near the entrance, knocking down refs as planned, knocking down Patterson, as planned, and as planned, Hart and McMahon had an argument almost teasing the idea of a spot later in the match where Hart would deck McMahon. But it was also clear that everything going on was 100% professional and the only curiosity left at that point was how good the match was going to be (it appeared to be very good) and how would they get "out" of the match (with something nobody will ever forget).

But one thing was strange. Why were so many agents circling the ring, and why was McMahon right there, and acting so intense? About eight minutes before the show was "supposed" to end, Bruce Prichard, in the "Gorilla" position (kind of the on-deck circle for the wrestlers) was screaming in his headset that we need more security at the ring. Why? They had already done the brawl in the crowd. The finish was going to be a DQ and it was still several minutes away. Hart climbed the top rope for a double sledge on Michaels. Michaels pulled Hebner in the way and Hart crashed on him. Just as planned. Michaels for a split second, looked at McMahon and put Hart in the sharpshooter, just as planned.

The next split seconds were the story. Chioda, listening to his headpiece for his cue to run-in, heard the backstage director scream to Hebner that it was time to get up. Hebner, listening himself, immediately got up. Chioda started screaming that he wasn't supposed to get up. Owen Hart and Smith, readying their run in, were equally perplexed seeing him get up. Prichard was freaking out backstage saying that wasn't supposed to happen. Bret, still not realizing anything was wrong, laid in the hold for a only a few seconds to build up some heat before doing the reversal. Michaels cinched down hard on the hold, glanced at Hebner and then looked away, which more than one wrestler in the promotion upon viewing the tape saw as the proof he was in on it, but then fed Bret his leg for the reversal. Hebner quickly looked at the timekeeper and screamed "ring the bell." At the same moment, McMahon, sitting next to the timekeeper, elbowed him hard and screamed "ring the f***in bell." The bell rang at about the same moment Bret grabbed the leg for the reversal and Michaels fell down on his face on the mat.

Michaels' music played immediately and was immediately announced as the winner and new champion. Hebner sprinted out of the ring on the other side, into the dressing room, through the dressing room, and into an awaiting car in the parking lot that already had the motor running and was going to take him to the hotel, where he'd be rushed out of town with his ticket home, instead of staying to work the two Raw tapings. Michaels and Hart both leaped to their feet looking equally mad, cursing in McMahon's direction and glaring at him. Hart spit right in McMahon's face. The cameras immediately pulled away from Hart and to Michaels. Vince screamed at Michaels to "pick the f***in belt up and get the f*** out of there." Michaels, still looking mad, was ordered to the back by Jerry Brisco who told him to hold the belt up high and get to the back. The show abruptly went off the air about four minutes early.

The officials left the ring immediately. McMahon went into his private office in the building with Patterson and a few others, and locked the door behind him. Hart, in the ring, flipped out on the realization of what happened, and began smashing the television monitors left behind until Owen, Smith and Neidhart hit the ring to calm him down. The four had an animated discussion in the ring, all looking perturbed. Finally, Hart thanked the fans, who for the most part left with the air let out of their sails, gave the "I love you" sign to the fans, and finger painted "WCW" to all four corners of the ring, which got a surprisingly big pop, and went back to the dressing room.

He first confronted Michaels, who swore that he had nothing to do with it. Michaels, obviously afraid Hart would punch him out right there, told Hart that he gets heat for everything that happens but this time it wasn't his fault and he was as mad as Hart about the finish. He said he didn't want to win the belt that way, was disgusted by what happened, and to prove it, would refuse to bring the belt out or say anything bad about Hart on Raw the next night. Hart said that Michaels could prove whether he was in on it or not by his actions on television the next night.

The entire dressing room was furious at McMahon by this point. The feeling was that if Hart, having worked for the company for 14 years and not missing shots due to injuries the entire time, and having made McMahon millions of dollars throughout the years, could get double-crossed this bad, then how could any of them trust anything he would say or do? People were saying that how could anyone trust anyone ever again, and that it was an unsafe working environment.

For three years, after the steroid trial and all the bad publicity, McMahon had worked feverishly to change his legacy in the industry as not the man who ran all the other promoters out of business, not the man who marketed pro wrestling to young children while pushing steroid freaks, not the man who tried to destroy wrestling history and create his own, not his worked Harvard MBA, worked billion dollar company, a man who was so vain as to give himself a huge award in Madison Square Garden as "the genius who created WrestleMania," not the man who at one time tried to monopolize every aspect of the business for himself, but instead as a working man's hero, coming from humble beginnings, fighting those ruthless rich regional promoters and through nothing but guts, guile and vision, became the dominant force in the industry and taking it to a new level. And now, against all odds, the generous friend trying to help all the small regional promoters, acknowledging the past history of the business, fighting against Billionaire Ted, the man who was stealing all his self-made creations while wasting his stockholders money because of some alleged petty vendetta because the WWF would never be for sale, stealing his patented idea of Monday night wrestling, was hanging in there and would outlast his enemy again and somehow in the end come out on top.

Three years of a facade, that was largely working to a new generation of wrestling fans who saw him as their underdog hero. The man who to a generation that didn't know better, created pro wrestling, Hulk Hogan and localized interviews and rose this grimy little industry from carnival tents to major non-smoking arenas and who was the friendly face in the Father Flanagan collar who every Monday night epitomized the world of pro wrestling, was flushed down the commode. Even though he was so good at hiding who the old Vince McMahon was to the point only those who had dealt with him for many years remembered about not letting your guard down, when the pressure was on, the old Vince returned. Only this time, it was in a situation where those who didn't "know" him were truly "introduced" to him for the first time.

Undertaker was furious, pounding on his locked door, and when he came out to talk with him, Undertaker told him in no uncertain terms that he needed to apologize to Hart. He went to Hart's dressing room, where Hart had just come out of the shower. Smith answered the door and Hart said he didn't want to see him. Vince and son Shane McMahon came in with Sgt. Slaughter and Brisco anyway. Vince started to apologize, saying that he had to do it because he couldn't take the chance of Hart going to WCW without giving back the belt and he couldn't let Bischoff go on television the next night and announce Hart was coming while he was still his champion and said how it would kill his business.

Hart shot back that he had no problem losing the belt and told McMahon that he was going to dry off and get his clothes on and told McMahon, "If you're still here, I'm going to punch you out." Hart called McMahon a liar and a piece of shit, and talked about having worked for him for 14 years, only missing two shots the entire time, and being a role model for the company and the industry and this was his payback. McMahon tried to say that in 14 years, this was the first time he'd ever lied to him and Hart rattled off 15 lies over the last year alone without even thinking about it. Those in the dressing room watching were stunned listening to Hart rattle them off, and McMahon not offering a comeback.

Hart got dressed and twice told McMahon to get out. Hart got up, and a scuffle started, with them locking up like in a wrestling match, Hart breaking free, and throwing a punch to the jaw that would have knocked down a rhino. One punch KO in 40 seconds. McMahon growled like he was going to get up, but he had no legs. Shane McMahon jumped on Hart's back, and Smith jumped on Shane's back pulling him off. Not realizing there would be trouble, Smith had already taken off his knee brace, and hyperextended his knee in the process of pulling Shane off. Hart nearly broke his hand from the punch. McMahon's jaw was thought to be fractured or broken.

Hart asked Vince if he was now going to screw him on all the money he owes him and a groggy Vince said "No." He told Shane and Brisco to get that "piece of shit" out of here and glaring at both of them, told them if they tried anything, they'd suffer the same result. In dragging McMahon out, someone accidentally stepped on his ankle injuring it as well.

Hebner, at the hotel and on his way out of town, was confronted by one of the wrestlers who asked how he could do that to one of his best friends. Hebner claimed ignorance and swore that he knew nothing about it and was so mad about it he was going to quit. Jack Lanza, likely as part of another facade, was begging him not to. Patterson, Michaels and Prichard all denied any knowledge to the boys. Everyone denied it, but it was clear everyone had to know, from the production truck to go off the air several minutes early, to the director to get the shot perfect of the sharpshooter where you couldn't see Bret's face not quit, to Hebner in particular, to the ring announcer to get the announcement so quickly, to the man handling the music to have Michaels music all cued up, to all the agents, who were surrounding the ring knowing the possibility of something unpredictable happening.

When Hart got back to his hotel room in a total daze, he was furious at McMahon because he knew he was screaming at the timekeeper to ring the bell but almost recognizing it as a reality of a business that he should have known better than anyone. But when he had a tape of the finish played to him, he clearly heard that it was Hebner's voice screaming "ring the bell" and at that point was personally crushed.

Phone lines were ringing off the hook around wrestling-land that night. People closest to the inside of the business were thinking double-cross, although the big question was whether Michaels, since he looked so pissed at the finish, was in on it. Some more skeptical types, remembering Brian Pillman and Kevin Sullivan, thought it because of the prominence of the match and the interest, that it had to be a very well acted work. Virtually all the wrestlers backstage thought it was a double-cross, but a few, not wanting to be marks, were wary of fully committing to the idea.

Some people who were close to inside thought it was the greatest worked finish in the history of wrestling, because it got everyone talking. Others, particularly people who had casual fans watching with them, or those attending the show live, saw how the finish to a casual fan came off looking so badly, thought it was either a poorly conceived angle that was well acted by a company trying too hard to fool smart fans; or maybe a double-cross. But by the morning the true story had become obvious.

(November 10, 1997) When the wrestlers fully realized what had happened, Hart turned into almost a cult hero, and McMahon's image took an incredible tumble. Hart himself remarked that while he had his problems with McMahon in the late 80s, that when Phil Mushnick wrote all those scathing articles about him during the 90s, he defended McMahon, even though he deep down knew most of what was written about him to be true.

According to two WWF wrestlers, roughly 95 percent of the wrestlers in the company were planning on boycotting the Raw taping later that night over what happened. But as the day went on, the talk simmered down, Hart told those who asked him that since they had children and mortgages, that they shouldn't risk breaching their contract and should go. However, Owen Hart, Smith, Neidhart and Mick Foley were so upset they all flew home, missing the tapings both this night and also in Cornwall, ONT the next night. Many were saying they could no longer work for someone who would do something like that.

While rumors abounded about Hart, Smith and Foley all quitting, at press time it appeared none of the three truly knew their future but that they all had a bitter taste in their mouth for the company. They weren't the only ones. Most of the wrestlers were there and with none of the Hart family around, McMahon gave his side of the story. He portrayed it as if Hart had agreed to drop the title in Montreal, but when he got to the building, he said he was a Canadian hero and an icon and refused to drop the title and said Hart said he would give the belt to McMahon on Raw the next night and refused to ever drop it.

Reports were that by this time few if anyone in the dressing room believed a word of it. Most of the wrestlers by this time knew Hart was more forced out than voluntarily leaving over money, although knowing he had signed a great money deal. Most of the heat was on Michaels, with the belief that Michaels was younger and more in Vince's ear and there was a lot of bitterness because it wasn't a secret by this point that Michaels had told people on several occasions that he would never do a job in the territory.

The show went on in Ottawa, but not before Bischoff had already announced on Nitro one hour earlier, in what was the same angle he's done so many times to tease and deliver the opposite, that Bret Hart had signed with the NWO. Bischoff opened the show with the entire NWO holding Canadian flags, and badly mockingly singing "Oh Canada." WCW announcers Tony Schiavone, Mike Tenay and Larry Zbyszko talked for most of the first hour about the announcement, with Schiavone and Tenay, likely on orders from Bischoff, acting stunned, describing Hart as a second generation wrestler who stands for tradition, in other words positioning him as another Curt Hennig or Jeff Jarrett, rather than the level of a Hulk Hogan to justify a nearly $3 million per year salary. Zbyszko was the one who acted as if he didn't believe it.

In the first commercial break, Gene Okerlund did a 900 line tease saying how Bret Hart punched out a prominent official and he'd have the story on his hotline, which did huge business. During the hotline, because of fear of legal repercussions, the story wasn't told until late in the report, only a sketchy version told, and McMahon's name was never mentioned.

With more curiosity than anything in recent memory, the WWF drew its strongest Raw rating since the early days of the Monday Night War—a 3.39 rating and 5.16 share—largely due to curiosity stemming from the publicity, the match, and from the announcement about Hart earlier in the event on WCW—and amidst all the chaos and confusion, presented one of its all-time worst shows. Nitro did a phenomenal 4.33 rating and 6.39 share.

Michaels opened the show. Yes, he was carrying the belt. And what did he say about Hart? He said he beat the man in his own country with his own hold and that he ran him out of the WWF to be with all the other dinosaurs down South. And said that the few down there who weren't dinosaurs are his good friends and some day they'd kick his ass too. Those who were on the fence on the Michaels issue waiting for his interview to prove himself were given their final answer.

McMahon never showed his face on camera. The fight with Hart was never acknowledged in the commentary, although Michaels couldn't resist in his interview saying how Hart beat up a 52-year-old man after the show. In the commentary, nobody tried to bury Hart, but Ross, who had never used this figure before, on both Sunday and Monday used the phrase 21-year-veteran, perhaps as subtle acknowledgment of Hart's age, and Lawler did bring up the $3 million per year figure, as a way to encourage the mindless "You sold out" chants. It was acknowledged that it was Hart's final match in the WWF although the reasons for it being the case were never even hinted at. The replay was pushed harder than ever, and why not, since it was the most bizarre finish in modern wrestling history, complete with a commercial clearly showing Hart spitting in McMahon's face, and destroying the monitors which took place after the show itself had gone off the air.

The show dragged on, and the efforts to push the new stars, Mero as a heel, Goldust back as a heel, Interrogator, Blackjack Bradshaw and Road Dog & Billy Gunn, all came off lame. You could almost hear the crowd groan when it was Rocky Maivia positioned as the next challenger for Steve Austin's IC title. With all the special effects, the Kane gimmick still came across as a sure winner. And Ken Shamrock was thrust into the spotlight as Michaels' first challenger on 12/7 after all. However, there was another screw up. Shamrock's main event with Helmsley was supposed to end with Michaels interfering and then Shamrock pinning him and the ref counting to three, perhaps to take heat off Michaels rep for not doing jobs, and perhaps as a way to convince Shamrock to return the favor for such an unpopular wrestler on PPV. However, the show went off the air with Shamrock down apparently being pinned after Michaels nailed him with the briefcase, however he kicked out just as the show went off the air.

The crowd in Ottawa, largely pro-Hart, finally figured out about 15 minutes before the show was going off the air, that none of the Hart Foundation was there, and that the Bret Hart situation was no angle. The Shamrock-Helmsley main event heat was non-existent, drowned out by vehement chants of "We Want Bret." Ross went on his hotline and did nothing but praise Hart for all his work, even to the point of saying that he himself, being right there, never heard a submission but that the referee claimed that he heard it.

(November 11, 1997) The Calgary Sun ran an article about the double-cross, reporting that Hart's leaving for WCW was actually requested by the WWF due to the WWF claiming financial hardships. And where does it go from here: It's hard to make sense out of all that happened.

While Hart's contract with the WWF was much higher than anyone else's, to dismiss him as being paid above market value is missing a potential valuable point. What is the Canadian wresting market worth? Far more than $1.5 million per year. At the Calgary Stampede PPV show alone, the market was worth about $400,000 on PPV and another $200,000 in live gate, granted those are Canadian money and he was being paid in American money, but you get the drift. While WWF had lost its foothold in the United States to WCW, it owned Canada.

WCW, with TBS getting moved from premium cable to basic cable nationwide, and with TSN picking up Nitro every week, was for the first time getting strong television exposure in the country. No matter what he did or didn't mean elsewhere, and there is no denying he was a major draw in the United States, and probably more so in Europe, Germany in particular, he was the wrestling star in Canada. Handing him to the opposition will mean from a Canadian standpoint, every bit as much as Hulk Hogan joining with WCW, and we've all seen what the long-term effects of that turned out to be.

It's hard to ascertain fan reaction. Fans are more loyal these days to brand names than ever before, more than to wrestlers themselves. When, in a similar situation only he didn't get into the ring and was fired before "not" doing the job, Ric Flair came out of a situation with Jim Herd in 1991 recognized by most fans as the real world champion, the WCW belt became largely meaningless, Flair went to WWF and did big business in what were never called unification matches but many thought of them as such against Hulk Hogan. For nearly two years, before Flair returned as the cult hero, the small crowds attending WCW matches never stopped the "We Want Flair" chants. There are similarities here, and if anything, times being different mean more people than ever will be aware of it, making similar chants perhaps more likely. But a lot of the newer fans also for the most part have less respect for the wrestlers as people and more as animals to perform stunts to entertain them, like in other sports, have more loyalties to the "home team" than its players who come and go for the biggest buck.

And while everyone will put their different spin on what happened, and like with Hogan, and Bruno, and nearly every other superstar of the WWF beforehand, Bret Hart failed one of the things he wanted most out of his career, and that was to walk away from the company without the bitterness and with mainly good memories. Both Bret Hart and Vince McMahon wanted their legacies to be tied together and represent all that can be good about pro wrestling. But the fact it is, no matter how great the match with Smith at Wembley Stadium or at the In Your House in Hershey were, or the WrestleMania match and SummerSlam matches with Owen were, or the SummerSlam match with Hennig, or the Survivor Series match with Michaels, or any of the rest, his legacy, and Vince McMahon's legacy will forever be tied together in wrestling history.

The defining moment of both a Hall of Fame wrestler and the man who for a decade was the dominant promoter in the industry will be the moment that the world realized, right in front of their eyes, with no apologies, and with no turning back to re-write history, just how truly deceitful, to the core this business can be, and just how much 14 years of being one of the great performers in the history of the industry truly meant on the inside to the company that benefited from it.

Only the future can determine whether this was a defining moment in the balance of business when it comes to pro wrestling. Did McMahon really hand over the keys to Canada to WCW? Will fans really hate McMahon four weeks later when Michaels headlines a PPV show with a four star match? Will Hart be a huge success keeping WCW at its current level, or even taking them to an even higher level by having main events on PPV shows that can live up to the quality of the preliminary matches? Or are his best years really behind him and McMahon will have the last laugh at how much Bischoff paid for him? How long will Hart remain a cult hero to the wrestlers for doing what none of them had the guts to do and all at one time want to do? Will McMahon file criminal charges for assault? And will, someday, and stranger things have happened although in this case it would be hard today to believe it as possible, will the two get back together in a few years for a final triumphant run?

One of the first major moves when Vince McMahon Jr. took over the World Wrestling Federation from his father was on December 26, 1983, when the Iron Sheik captured the WWF title from Bob Backlund. The title switch was basically a prelude for Hulk Hogan winning the title a few weeks later. The finish of the match saw Sheik have Backlund in a camel clutch, and Arnold Skaaland, a former part-owner of the company who worked as Backlund's manager, threw in the towel signifying submission. Backlund remained with the company for the next eight months, largely buried in the middle of the card despite being the face of the company for six years. After all the big gates he'd headlined, just a few months later, in August, McMahon, who was starting on the road to changing the entire face of wrestling and Backlund represented the old, asked him to die his hair and turn heel. He refused and was fired. Backlund spent the next several years claiming that he didn't know the finish of the match and was double-crossed on it when Skaaland threw in the towel. Everyone in wrestling heard the story but really very few took it seriously, figuring Backlund was just clinging onto a worked story to protect his image claiming he never really submitted and was robbed of the title.

On November 25, 1985, before a match in Madison Square Garden, Victoria "Wendi" Richter, literally minutes before going into the ring for a match with Spider Lady in Madison Square Garden, was given a contract by McMahon and asked to sign off on all her merchandising rights. She actually didn't refuse to sign the contract, but said she wanted to read it before signing it because she was literally on her way to the ring. McMahon told her, actually she has claimed, demanded to her, to sign the deal. She told him to wait until after the match so she could read the contract and then maybe sign it.

As it turns out, Spider Lady wasn't the wrestler who had been Spider Lady in the past, but was instead Lillian Ellison, better known as Fabulous Moolah. Although Lillian was probably closing in on 60 by that point, she maneuvered Richter into a position, and the unsuspecting Richter was held in position and had her shoulders counted out for the pin, and never worked in the WWF again. After the match and to this day, Moolah had always maintained to Richter, like Michaels to Hart, that she wasn't aware of the set-up either and the three count came as just as big a surprise to her.

It brings to mind a few old sayings. History repeats itself. Leopards don't change their spots. Perhaps as much as we would all like to believe otherwise, deep down to its core, the wrestling industry really doesn't change either.

Famous Pro Wrestling World Title Double Crosses

1911 - Frank Gotch vs. George Hackenschmidt

One of history's most famous pro wrestling matches ever. Gotch, who became recognized almost universally as world champion with a win over Hackenschmidt three years earlier, was defending his title in the first ever rematch of the century. Before the match ever took place, Ad Santel, a noted "hooker" (an old term for submission expert or bonebreaker), a sparring partner of Hackenschmidt who as it later came out, was paid $5,000 by Gotch's people to do so, tore out Hackenschmidt's knee. Because a record breaking gate was expected and achieved ($87,000 in those days would probably be like $8 million today), the show had to go on and the promoters kept the injury a secret from the public. Gotch, knowing about the injury, reached an agreement with Hackenschmidt, who wanted to pull out of the match due to his injury, to give him one fall in the best-of-three and carry him to a match where he looked credible. But once the match started, Gotch double-crossed him, winning easily and quickly in two straight falls.

1920 - Earl Caddock vs. Joe Malciewicz

Caddock, the champion, had already agreed to drop the title to Joe Stecher just a few weeks later in New York, but in this match Malciewicz shot on him and hammered him the entire match and was given the decision. The press, largely controlled in those days by the wrestling promoters, hushed up the match and the title change was never recognized.

1925 - Wayne Munn vs. Stanislaus Zbyszko

Munn was a 6'8" giant, especially for his time, and a college football hero, but he actually couldn't wrestle but he could draw football fans, so I guess that made him decades ahead of his time. Seeing box office, Strangler Lewis, who controlled the world title with promoter Billy Sandow as the Hulk Hogan and Vince McMahon of their eras, dropped the title to Munn to build up a successful run leading to it being returned in due time. Rival promoter Tony Stecher, whose brother Joe was a legendary wrestler and rival of Lewis at the time for who really was the best wrestler around, put Zbyszko up to stealing the title. Two months earlier, to prove his loyalty to Sandow, Zbyszko put Munn over cleanly and professionally so they had no fear in giving him a title match. Once this match started, Zbyszko, one of the great true wrestlers of his era, although nearing 60 by this point, shot and beat him so badly the referee, one of Sandow's most loyal employees, had no choice but to stop the match and award the title to him to save Munn from more of a beating and prevent the Philadelphia fans from rioting from the farce of any other decision. Sandow got the commissions in Michigan and Illinois to erase this match and still bill Munn as champion, and as quickly as they could arranged for him to drop it to Lewis, creating two champions, while Zbyszko, on the same night as Lewis beat Munn, put over Joe Stecher as planned.

1926 - Joe Stecher vs. John Pesek

This match was at the Olympic Auditorium in Los Angeles. The two worked the first two falls of a title match with Stecher defending. In the third fall, Pesek, another wrestler who most experts of the time would rank as among the greatest wrestlers ever, double-crossed Stecher and beat the hell out of him, putting him in a double wristlock. But this was all for naught because the referee at that moment ruined the double-cross by disqualifying Pesek for no apparent reason. There was a major investigation by the athletic commission, but as was likely during that time period, the promotion probably bought off the commission and Stecher retained the title.

1931 - Ed Don George vs. Strangler Lewis

At this point, Lewis and Sandow had been in business with Northeast promoter Paul Bowser and all were making big money with Gus Sonnenberg, another football hero who couldn't wrestle, as champion. After Sonnenberg was beaten up on the street by a middleweight wrestler in a situation set up by their rival promoters, Bowser, without consulting Sandow and Lewis, had Sonnenberg drop the title to George, who had just come out of the Olympics and was another great wrestler. Lewis was waiting for his revenge, but did jobs for Bowser's wrestlers to show his loyalty, and a title match was set up for Los Angeles. As they got into the ring for a match George was supposed to win, Lewis came out and casually said that he was going to take the title and they could do it the hard way or the easy way. Since George knew he couldn't beat Lewis, he chose the easy way.

1931 - Strangler Lewis vs. Henri DeGlane

It took only three weeks before Bowser signed Lewis to defend the title in Montreal against Henri

DeGlane, the 1924 Olympic gold medalist who had become a big draw. This was the famous battle of the bite we wrote about after the Tyson-Holyfield fiasco. Lewis went into the ring knowing he was going to win in three falls. After the second fall (in those days wrestlers returned to the dressing room between falls so they could have intermissions and sell concessions), DeGlane bit himself in the arm near the armpit until he drew blood. He kept the arm covered, went out for the fall, immediately started screaming like Holyfield did, Lewis backed off having no idea what was happening. The ref saw the blood and teeth marks and disqualified Lewis awarding the title to DeGlane. Lewis was so furious about the double-cross that he went backstage to do to Bowser what Hart did to McMahon, however Bowser was a little more ready, having six bodyguards all armed with baseball bats covering him, and Lewis, trying to play it cool, said he was quitting anyway and left for Europe.

1933 - Jim Londos vs. Joe Savoldi

In the history of American wrestling, Londos ranks with Hulk Hogan and Andre the Giant as the biggest drawing card ever. However, he had made enemies at this time with the promoters in New York, who had their own world champion in Jim Browning. The New York promoters set up the double-cross in Chicago by buying off both Savoldi and referee Bob Managoff (whose son was a champion wrestler of the next generation). Savoldi put on a submission and as planned, Londos made the ropes, but Savoldi then put real pressure on, the ref pretended he didn't see Londos touch the ropes, called for the submission and awarded Savoldi the title. Savoldi then brought the title to New York and lost a unification match to Browning, giving the New York promoters a champion with even more credibility. The irony of all this is that over the next year, the crowds in New York started falling and they begged Londos to come back, and gave him the world title from Browning to get him back to save their business. The moral of this story is obvious.

1936 - Danno O'Mahoney vs. Dick Shikat

O'Mahoney, an Irish star who wasn't much of a wrestler, had turned into a monster draw in Boston for Paul Bowser, drawing several stadium crowds of around 30,000, and also drew well in New York for Jack Curley, and throughout the Northeast. In a match in Madison Square Garden, Shikat, considered one of the legitimately toughest men in the business at the time, was put up by rival promoters Jack Pfeffer and Al Haft, who were at war with Curley, to shoot on O'Mahoney and he destroyed him. The ref had no idea what to do about it. Shikat won the title, but then his promoters had him drop it just a few weeks later. Bowser in Boston continued to bill O'Mahoney as champion until he lost it a year later in Montreal to Yvon Robert. Many point to this match as the match, because it was a shoot, that exposed wrestling and killed the business in New York that it wasn't until the advent of Argentina Rocca some 15 years later that wrestling became lucrative at the Garden.

1950 - Don Eagle vs. Gorgeous George

Eagle was recognized primarily in Boston as world champion, and was defending his version of the title outside the territory in Chicago. This was in many ways the most similar to Hart-Michaels as ref Earl Mollohan double-crossed Eagle and counted him down when Eagle kicked out, then bailed out of the ring as quickly as he could with an enraged Eagle chasing him down the aisle. We've also heard disputes on this one saying that was actually planned as a controversial finish but the general feeling from those viewing the tape is that it was remarkably similar to Hart-Michaels.

1979 - Antonio Inoki vs. Bob Backlund

The previous week in Japan, Backlund dropped the WWF title to Inoki with the agreement that he'd win it back in their rematch and return to the U.S., with no title change ever being acknowledged in the U.S.

The match is completely worked, and as planned, in the finish Tiger Jeet Singh interferes causing Inoki to lose the title back. Inoki gives the title back to Backlund. However, in the double-cross, after the match WWF President Hisashi Shinma ruled the match a no contest and said that Inoki was still the champion. This was a set-up by Inoki and Shinma, primarily because New Japan was scheduled to do a television taping about seven weeks later in Madison Square Garden on a WWF show and they wanted for their own TV purposes and ratings, for Inoki to main event the Garden, where he'd drop the title to Backlund. Vince McMahon Sr. was already building up Bobby Duncum as the big man of the month to work with Backlund. McMahon basically ignored everything, and as a face saving gesture, brought in Inoki to wrestle Iron Sheik and billed his match as for the WWF World Martial Arts championship, a title Inoki would continue to use for many years in the future both in Japan and the U.S. For Japanese television, neither Backlund nor Duncum entered the ring for the belt, nor was Backlund introduced as champion, and he was then given the belt after beating Duncum. However, all the pre-match hype in the U.S. for the match had Backlund defending against Duncum.

1983 - Bob Backlund vs. Iron Sheik
(See above)

1985 - Wendi Richter vs. Spider Lady
(See above)

1991 - Nobuhiko Takada vs. Trevor Berbick
While technically not a world title match, this was one of two mixed matches on a UWFI show in Sumo Hall. This match, featuring a former boxing heavyweight champion, and another featuring James Warring, at the time recognized by the IBF as the world cruiserweight champion, against pro wrestler Billy Scott were expected by the Americans to be worked. However, once the bell sounded, Takada shot on Berbick, laying in a few hard leg kicks. Berbick freaked out, left the ring at 2:52 of the first round, and refused to come back out. Scott and Warring had worked out a match, and Scott was working with Warring early. When it came time for Warring to make his comeback and win, Scott shot on him, took him down and controlled him on the ground for the rest of the fight, which turned into a shoot, and Scott won the match via decision.

1994 - NWA Title Tournament
While also not at the time a major league world title, the NWA name was being resurrected by a number of small promoters, who had Tod Gordon's Eastern Championship Wrestling, ostensibly and really controlled by booker Paul Heyman, host a tournament to crown a champion. There was no double-cross in the ring, as it was agreed ahead of time, although reluctantly by some, for ECW's champion, Shane Douglas to win the tournament. It was after the match that Heyman, Gordon and Douglas double-crossed the rest of the NWA, throwing down the title belt and grabbing his own title while a shocked NWA President Dennis Coraluzzo was in the ring watching. Coraluzzo was tricked after the speech into doing a promo for ECW television stripping Douglas of the title, allowing Gordon to announce they were splitting from the NWA and forming a new company, Extreme Championship Wrestling, and recognizing Douglas as their first champion. Coraluzzo and ECW had been territorial enemies in the past, had mended fences for this show, and have remained enemies ever since with the exception of a peace truce between the two sides in 1997 that lasted for about 15 seconds before both sides claimed the other had double-crossed them again.

NOVEMBER 24

After a week of both private and public comments in the aftermath of the double-cross finish in the Shawn

Michaels vs. Bret Hart match at Survivor Series and Hart's subsequent leaving the WWF about one month earlier than originally planned, the basic gist of the story was covered here last week.

But any more discussion of the decision making processes involved by Hart and McMahon as it related to the double-cross finish, there are a number of points both relating to this story and how it was presented in last week's issue, and to the historical nature of last week's piece that need to be clarified and discussed:

Bret Hart's heel turn in March was Vince McMahon's idea, that McMahon sold Hart on as mentioned in the story. It was Hart's idea to remain a babyface in Canada and internationally while being an Anti-American heel in the United States. However, it was Hart's idea all along to do a heel turn. In the original plan formulated by McMahon and Hart in July 1996, when McMahon flew to Calgary to woo Hart, who was sitting out and attempting to break into acting, was for Hart to beat Michaels in a babyface match and win the title at the 1997 WrestleMania, and then make a slow heel turn. As that was going on, they'd avoid a third match for a long time until the heel turn was complete making Michaels that much stronger of a babyface. At that point the agreement was that Hart would put Michaels over in the third meeting. That scenario changed when McMahon decided to take the title from Michaels to Sid, make Sid vs. Undertaker for the title the WrestleMania main event, and then make Hart vs. Michaels as the semifinal. Seeing that he would have to do two major jobs in a row, Michaels showed up the night he was supposed to drop the title to Sid, claimed he had a career ending knee injury, and later that night on television handed the belt back.

The decision by McMahon to pave the way for Hart to leave, largely stemming from Hart's huge salary and his refusal to renegotiate the terms, started the natural rumors about what the actual financial condition of Titan Sports is and why McMahon, in the middle of a wrestling war with only four true superstars, one of whom was mentally unstable and another of whom physical future was questionable, would want to hand one of the remaining two to his opposition. Stories have come out in regard to Titan Sports wanting to make its bottom line look better for the company to go public, or to sell a percentage of the company to outsiders, thus infusing new money into the company, while the McMahon family would retain the majority interest. Having in the last week talked with four different high-level executives in the company, all claim there is nothing to either scenario nor has there been any discussions at any time of either scenario.

The idea that Hart's salary was dumped as a way to open the door for a return of Hulk Hogan was discounted as a theory worthy of Oliver Stone. McMahon, in a controlled Internet discussion after the 11/17 Raw, responded to a similar question saying, "Yes, one day the WWF might go public but there are no current plans for that to happen." From all accounts, the WWF has been operating deeply in the red for most of the past four years. According to one source, at the time McMahon offered Hart the huge contract last year, the company was losing about $135,000 per week. Theoretically if a piece of talent in any sports or entertainment business such as this isn't worth the price he is asking, you don't pay him that price and if someone else will, you let them. McMahon offered Hart the 20-year deal, at about $30,000 per week for the first three years as an active wrestler. Since his company was losing so much money, one would think he, when making the deal, felt that Hart was worth more to his company than what he was offering to pay him at the time he made the offer to him.

The interesting thing about all this is that now, from all accounts, Titan Sports has turned the financial corner and is operating in the black. In other words, during the same time period that McMahon brought Hart back and was paying him the huge money and the period he told him he was going to breach his contract because he felt he wasn't worth the money, Titan's financial situation had greatly improved, not gotten worse. One could argue that is proof Hart was worth more than what he was being paid, although that isn't necessarily the case. The biggest reason for the financial turnaround was from increasing the price of the In Your House PPV shows from $19.95 to $29.95 while maintaining (and in some cases even increasing) the number of buys, which over the course of a full year would add between $5 million and $6 million to company revenue, or almost by itself, wiping out that huge weekly deficit incurred throughout most of 1996. This is not a judgment on Hart's value to the company financially, just a factual statement that from all accounts, the company could afford his salary today a whole lot more than it could at the time it made the deal in the first place.

In examining whether Hart was worth the money, there are many ways to look at it. Based on the salary structure at Titan Sports right now, the answer would be no. Did Hart generate twice the revenue of Austin, Undertaker and Michaels? Probably not. Based on our new phrase for the week, time honored traditions of the business, he was greatly underpaid. If you figure Titan Sports will gross $80 million this year (that's a rough estimate), well, in the old days of NWA champions, the champion's cut was eight percent of the gross, which would mean by traditions of the business Hart would be worth $6.4 million.

If you go by McMahon's fathers' standards with Bruno Sammartino, Sammartino earned six percent of the gross at house shows with the exception of Madison Square Garden, where he was to earn five percent. In the great traditions of the business, Sammartino never actually was paid nearly that much and ended up in court over being screwed on money, and McMahon Jr. settled out of court with him, but that's another story that will be repeated in the future as well. But even at five percent, that's still $4 million per year. If you argue with all the front office personnel that they didn't have in the past, overhead, travel expenses, etc., and that the champion doesn't stand alone above the competition as the NWA champs or Sammartino did in their day, even at two percent, which would always be considered a real bad payoff for a main eventer in the past, you are still talking about more money than Hart was earning.

If you determine what somebody is worth as to be what his value is on the open market (how one values what a home being sold is worth in a free enterprise economy), then that figure was already established as the $2.8 million per year by WCW making the offer. But all those hypotheticals mean nothing. The fact is, he had a contract and the company is now operating in the black. They were not under any duress financially to remove the contract from the books at this point in time even if the company would like to claim otherwise. They wanted to remove him, or his contract, for other reasons. The contract did cause a salary structure argument internally, because no doubt people like Undertaker, Austin and Michaels, realizing what Hart was making, might feel in comparison they were underpaid and have a valid argument. One of the reasons Michaels himself wanted out earlier this year was because McMahon wouldn't pay him what Hart made and what his buddies in Atlanta were making and what he felt his position in the business today was worth.

I can understand a few months back Titan wanting to restructure Hart's deal because the company wasn't doing well at the time and his salary was huge. But right now, things had started to change and the problems now from an economic position make far less sense. One Titan official said that McMahon knew ultimately that either Hart or Michaels would have to go, perhaps even that Michaels demanded it as a condition for him to return after he walked out over the fight.

When Hart returned from his knee injury, they felt his career was on its downslide and maybe he wasn't the same performer and given the decision, Hart was 40, Michaels was 32 and Michaels was costing half as much money and not a threat to the salary structure in regards to the other headliners pointing at his salary and thinking they were underpaid, and that Hart had 19 years left to be paid and maybe only one good year left in the ring. Supposedly Hart himself had told other officials he thought he only had about 200 good matches left in his career, which may also have precipitated the decision in that direction.

Michaels, in the Charleston Post and Courier before the PPV stated, "The world should know this—this is not Bret Hart leaving. This is Vince McMahon asking him to leave. For me, it's only a good day in that people who are really somewhat intelligent will see who is really the guy behind the scenes who is causing Vince McMahon trouble. Vince asked him to leave, but he allowed him to take care of things here, and I think that says a lot for Vince McMahon. He simply didn't feel Bret was giving what he was getting."

Exactly what was offered to Hart financially in regard to renegotiations is contradictory depending upon the source. Jim Ross, on the WWF hotline, claimed the WWF wanted to lessen his huge weekly guarantee, but increase the money he would earn from PPV events so that he would actually wind up earning basically the same amount of money per year, just that it would come in lump sums after Titan would get the cash flow influx from a PPV rather than every week when Titan's cash flow was from house shows, or far less money coming in on those weeks. Hart's claim is that they wanted to cut his weekly salary more than in half, but were going to make it up by increasing his salary in the latter 17 years of his contract when he was to earn far less since at that point he'd be retired from the ring. Another source said they wanted to spread the big money aspect of the contract over five years instead of three, thus cutting the weekly salary from $30,000 to $20,000 per week but extending it two more years.

Probably more than one of these scenarios and possibly all were discussed at one time or another. Hart and his financial advisers turned that down, not wanting to risk getting screwed, another of pro wrestling's time honored traditions, after he was no longer an active performer and had no leverage anywhere. McMahon on television portrayed Hart as not being worth what they were paying him and wanting to get rid of him for that reason, a story that contradicts the other versions.

McMahon, on the 11/17 Raw, without actually using the words, tried to imply that Hart was unprofessional because he had refused to drop the title in the ring. The wording McMahon used is that Hart failed to honor a time-honored tradition of the business (you do jobs on the way out of a territory). For those with memories longer than two or three years, the realization is that any discussion of McMahon and time-honored traditions of the wrestling industry is worthy of not a chapter, but an entire book. The only true time honored tradition of this business is that everyone in power lies and manipulates to get people to do things that are often against their best interest, or top talent with leverage agrees to do jobs, then holds up promoters at the last minute to squeeze money or promises out on that end. And then everyone pretends to like each other, and that's not a digression from the actual issue.

Indeed, one could argue the core of the wrestling industry more than anything else was epitomized by this double-crossing on a finish that everyone involved had supposedly agreed upon. How many jobs did Hulk Hogan, Junkyard Dog, Jesse Ventura and all the rest do on the way out when they were leaving their territories in 1983-84? Zero. They cut interviews for one promotion and showed up the next day with the WWF, with the promoter lucky if he got a telegram of resignation after the fact. Just as people like Lex Luger, Curt Hennig and Rick Rude when they got the leverage, couldn't wait to screw Vince McMahon, so did the wrestlers of the past feel about people like Verne Gagne and Bill Watts.

But the reality is, Bret Hart got a finish changed on a television match to Hunter Hearst Helmsley from a pin to a count out; refused to do a job in a six-man tag in Toronto and instead had his brother-in-law Jim Neidhart do it; never refused to do a job in Detroit in the six-man although did refuse to put Michaels over for the title at that show as McMahon suggested as a compromise so Hart could lose the title to Michaels but not on Canadian soil before 11/10. To add to the problems, the front office believed he had also refused to do a job in the six-man in Detroit (in reality he was never asked because the agents running the show didn't convey the plans made at a booking meeting two days earlier to him to avoid heat from him after he turned it down in Toronto, but then to avoid heat from the office, claimed he had once again been asked and refused, which unjustly intensified the heat between McMahon and Hart, going into Montreal the next day).

During the 11/2 conversation between Hart and McMahon where he agreed to put anyone over as long as it was after 11/13, unlike what was reported here last week, "anyone" at that point did not include Michaels but did include basically everyone else and he even mentioned Steve Lombardi since he had a match scheduled against him on the 11/15 Madison Square Garden show. However, on 11/5, he finally agreed to put Michaels over as long as it occurred after 11/13 and thus not in Canada.

McMahon's portrayal to the fans, to the wrestlers, and to his own front office that Hart refused to drop the title in the ring has been vehemently denied by Hart and is also contradicted completely in documentation from Hart's legal representatives to McMahon sent the day before the show. But it is true that Hart, all along, refused to do the job for Michaels on that specific night. It is also true that McMahon agreed to several different finishes for that match that didn't involve a title switch during the week, would change them, and in the end on the last day supposedly everyone was on the same page with a finish, the same finish that was discussed at the production meeting the night before.

This is not to justify the position of Bret Hart at all, because these are two items unrelated to Bret Hart, but related to Vince McMahon, and also to Shawn Michaels. If McMahon felt dropping the title in the ring was of such importance to the future of his company, why was the decision made to go to Michaels? No questioning his talent at all and not taking seriously his asshole television personality as anything more than a contrived work.

Let's even for the sake of the argument throw out that he won't work full-time anymore and thus for house show business wouldn't be as valuable as a champion as a wrestler on the road every night. He refused to drop not only the WWF title in the ring earlier this year which many in the company point directly to killing the buy rate at WrestleMania, but several other titles on numerous different occasions since 1993, one of which he had legitimate medical reasons for and three other times because he simply walked out while holding a belt, whether it be a WWF belt, an IC belt or a tag team title belt. He also had refused to do any jobs for anyone in the territory on numerous occasions, including to Davey Boy Smith in Birmingham, England.

How was Michaels' behavior, which certainly was not a romantic "time-honored tradition" of the business handled? By changing the finish in England and giving him the title to avoid a conflict. And a few weeks after that, by making the decision to give the WWF title belt to him once again. In 1993, when Hulk Hogan was WWF champion, McMahon wanted him to drop the belt to Bret Hart. Hogan, with the big guy mentality from the 80s, refused to lose to "little" Bret, basically hand-picked "big" Yokozuna to drop the belt to and quit the promotion over it, which for the most part created the heat with Hogan and McMahon and also for years between Hogan and Hart. Both Hogan and Hart have made statements in recent weeks about looking forward to working with one another, despite their heat from the past. WCW's plan at present is for Hart's first major match to likely be against Ric Flair, setting the stage for possible matches against Hogan or Sting.

It appears the tension between McMahon and Hart grew a lot worse in the week leading to the event for a number of reasons. When the word got out, Hart was positioning his leaving as having something to do with the direction the WWF was going. While he was unhappy with the direction and with Shawn Michaels, neither was the prime reason for his decision. McMahon and others in the office were unhappy about that, and Ross on the 900 line, said that to say the prospective (since nobody was willing to publicly admit to the departure until after the show) departure was due to anything but financial reasons was ludicrous.

Since Hart was leaving, the decision was made before the weekend shows in Toronto and Detroit that he should do the job for Austin in the six-mans, since it wasn't for the title, that Austin was one of their top wrestlers and that Austin had put Hart over at WrestleMania and Hart had never given one back clean. Hart refused in Toronto, for reasons outlined last week. He was never asked in Detroit, and the agents told the office he had turned it down again, putting more heat into the fire.

Bret Hart did not so much ask Earl Hebner to referee the match as much as know in advance that Hebner would be the referee when they had their conversation in Detroit the night before the show. Referees for the main event on PPV are assigned based on who the company considers to be their top official, and Hebner has been the referee in the main event virtually every show. If Hebner wasn't the referee, it would have been a tip-off to Hart that something fishy was going down and he wouldn't have allowed himself to be put into a compromising position. Hart was aware of the possibility of a double-cross the night before but when Hebner swore he'd quit first, somewhat relaxed his guard in regard to allowing compromising spots in the match. Officially, the referee assignments were made at the production meeting that was going on in Montreal at the same time Hart and Hebner were in Detroit, and as expected, Hebner was given the assignment for the title match.

It has been insinuated here and portrayed elsewhere that the double-cross decision came at a meeting at the Montreal Marriott the night before the show. Such a meeting did take place as it does on Saturdays before every PPV show or Sundays before every Monday-Tuesday set of tapings. McMahon, Jim Ross, Jim Cornette, Pat Patterson and Michaels were all at the meeting as were several others including Bruce Prichard, Sgt. Slaughter and production people. The finish of the match and future scenarios in regard to the title belt were discussed at the meeting.

What was discussed was not a double-cross on Hart. The scenario discussed at the meeting and fine-tuned was the scenario McMahon, Hart and Michaels had all theoretically agreed upon. In Montreal, the finish would be that Hart would have the sharpshooter on Michaels when Rick Rude, Chyna and Hunter Hearst Helmsley would hit the ring. Rude would never get into the ring but his briefcase would be thrown into the ring. Hart would win on a DQ for the outside interference. They were trying to create an ending for one big pop at the end by the fans in Montreal, since the outside interference DQ would be a weak "groan" finish for such a highly anticipated PPV match. They appeared to have settled on Hart getting the briefcase in a struggle, and knocking out Chyna, who had yet to sell anything big in the WWF up to that point, and were debating the pros and cons of that finish.

The next night on Raw, Jim Ross would interview Hart and point-blank ask him the question about him leaving, using the Canadian newspaper clippings on the screen, and Hart would reluctantly, or maybe not reluctantly, admit that he was going to WCW. Hart would say that he was going to remain in the WWF until the end of the month and work his final shows in the various arenas, and his final match would be the 12/7 PPV show in Springfield. They would push that fact as a way to build up a big buy rate for the traditionally weak December PPV show. Hart would say on his interview that he would defend the title against anyone in Springfield and wanted to leave the WWF with his head up and still the champion, since he would be doing the interview in Ottawa where he was the top babyface. At that point Slaughter would announce the final four match, with Hart, Undertaker, Ken Shamrock and Michaels and Hart would react as if double-crossed by the Americans again and put in a situation where he didn't have to lose the fall to not retain the title.

I've heard two versions of what was discussed as rules of this match, one that it would be the first pinfall scenario in that the man who scored the first pin would become the champion. The other is the final survivor, as with the Final Four match earlier this year on a PPV, after eliminations going over the top rope, would be the winner. In either case, the basic gist would be that either Undertaker or Shamrock would put Michaels over in the end. This was a scenario created by the WWF, discussed and agreed upon at a meeting that Hart wasn't involved in, to give Hart an out in the storyline world to say that the WWF in his final match put three guys, instead of one, in the ring against him and that he actually was never beaten by Michaels since the two had their personal issue with one another.

Part of the reason it was booked like this is because as of 12/1, Hart was under contract to WCW. For Hart to work in Springfield and Portland, ME, Eric Bischoff had to okay the scenarios and he had agreed to allow that basic scenario to take place, which actually is where the story gets even more interesting. Hart would then do the interview in Portland, where he'd apologize to the American fans, thank the organization for 14 great years (actually Hart started with the WWF in late 1984, so it's really 13 but everyone has been using the number 14 for so long I guess it'll always be 14), and leave on a high note. Supposedly as of that point, McMahon wasn't even considering the double-cross and nothing of the sort was brought up at that meeting.

That does leave two questions: Why did McMahon decide not to announce the show, as that decision was definitely discussed at the meeting, and why did Ross go on the hotline and hint that the match could be Hart's final match in the World Wrestling Federation?

By all accounts, everything else was just fuel for a fire that would explode just six hours later when Hart arrived in Montreal at about 4 p.m. after coming in from Detroit. Hart and McMahon had the discussion. Where Saturday's scenario fell apart was in that discussion. Supposedly McMahon suggested he had another change in plans, and that he wanted Hart to lose the title to Michaels in a singles match instead of a Final Four match in Springfield. Hart supposedly balked, because that wasn't the scenario he had sold Bischoff on, which is where Hart brought up the scenario of just handing the belt back to McMahon in Ottawa that according to Hart, McMahon at the time agreed to but later McMahon portrayed to the wrestlers two days later as that being Hart's demand and not suggestion.

Hart was still going to finish out his contract by working all the house shows through the end of the month. This could be confirmed because he had people contact friends in various cities to meet him after matches for the remainder of the month for his final hurrah in the promotion. Hart at this point said he was still amenable to dropping the title to anyone after 11/13, including Michaels. Supposedly Hart didn't turn down McMahon's proposal, only say he'd have to get Bischoff's permission since he'd be under contract to Bischoff at that point.

Clearly you can see the position McMahon felt he had been put in with the idea that his most hated enemy actually could have decision making power over his championship belt and this may be what caused the decision, perhaps an overreaction to that fact. But at the same time, all these time frames were created and known by McMahon and in hindsight, he should have gotten the belt off Hart long before telling him they wanted to cut his contract, let alone before asking him to negotiate with WCW. As it was, they were suggesting to restructure his contract informally at least, even before putting the belt on him in the first place at SummerSlam. No doubt with visions of Madusa throwing the title belt in the garbage can at Nitro, this is where those close to McMahon claim he later said where he came up with the double-cross idea.

Only two people were involved in this, ultimately, the most important of all the conversations that supposedly led to the ultimate finish. McMahon portrayed it to his staff and later to the wrestlers that Hart told him this would be his final match with the company, that he wouldn't drop the title, and that he wanted to hand McMahon the title the next night on Raw, and McMahon felt this was his last chance to get his title back. "The only thing I asked for and after 14 years, I thought it was a fair request, is that they didn't beat me in Canada."

Hart said he turned down the request to put Michaels over for the title in an unannounced match in Detroit the night before the PPV because it would defeat the whole purpose of what the match had been built up for if he showed up for that match without the belt. "He knew full well I'd be happy to drop the belt at the Garden. I even suggested to him taping the show at MSG and airing the match (as a special event) on Monday and show everyone the title change. Vince shot that down because it would cost too much to film there (Madison Square Garden charges around $40,000 for rights if a television event is filmed there). I really told Vince I'd even put over Lombardi. It was a problem between Sunday and Wednesday in putting Shawn over, but as long as I could get out of Canada, I'd put Shawn over anywhere he wanted."

McMahon told his staff after the fact that he did it because he couldn't allow the WWF champion to show up the next night on Nitro (the Madusa vision, even though it is exceedingly difficult to believe this would actually happen), or be announced on Nitro, as coming to WCW. However, the WWF was at the meeting the night before planning on using that very information as a way to build its December PPV show.

"He gave Bret a lot of options, all of which Bret turned down," said one of the members of the inner circle. "Bret said he wouldn't do it (the job). Vince said his back was against the wall. Vince wasn't happy with the decision he had to make and takes full responsibility for the decision. It was Vince's decision. Nobody else had input. It was to protect the business from his standpoint. He had to protect his title. Bret wouldn't do business (the job). We were told (by McMahon) he was going to show up in Memphis (the Nitro on 11/10, the day after Survivors) with the belt. Vince claimed Bret didn't want to make the December PPV. Bret took away every opportunity to get the belt back. The only people who really know the whole story are Bret and Vince."

Yet another person close to the situation said that McMahon really didn't believe Hart would be on Nitro but was more worried since he'd agreed that afternoon to allow Hart to relinquish the belt on Raw in Ottawa and afterwards was worried about what Hart would say in his last interview about why he was leaving, given what he had said in the newspaper and on the TSN television show over the previous week and since it was live TV, or talk in positive terms about where he was going. McMahon could call for a commercial in the middle of the interview, but that also would make the company look like they were hiding something and the word of what he said would get out everywhere anyway. "Vince was desperate because he didn't want Bret to put over WCW on (his) television." He also told supposedly told the staff that Hart never offered to lose the belt in Madison Square Garden or anywhere else and that Montreal would be his last chance to get it back.

The Madusa story is another that wrestling history seems to have distorted. The prevailing view appears to be that Bischoff offered Madusa big money to walk out on the WWF, show up with the belt, and drop it in the garbage. The actual story is that McMahon fired Madusa without having her drop the belt five days earlier. Bischoff, who clearly loves nothing more than rubbing McMahon's face in it at every chance possible, saw his opportunity and the end result was the end result. This is not to say Madusa was right, or McMahon was wrong (in hindsight once again he should have gotten his belt back if it meant so much, and if the belt is just a prop, than everyone in the industry on both sides certainly overreacted to the Madusa incident), just that since the Madusa story was brought up by so many people, including high-ranking WWF officials, in the days following the double-cross, the actual story needed to be clarified.

I guess for curiosity and historical reasons, people want to know how many were involved in the double-cross. It is in the WWF's best interest to keep the number low, because all those involved will be viewed warily by the wrestlers, and the already low trust level in a business that to be successful has to be built around trust, would be even worse when any of those parties are involved. The circle admitted to were McMahon, obviously, Gerald Brisco, Hebner and perhaps Michaels. Michaels has since told his friends in WCW, if his actions on Raw the next night didn't prove it, that he was involved in it, despite his reactions that night trying to prove to the world that he wasn't, I guess figuring that had he acted differently, Hart might have slugged him in the ring right at his moment of realization. Clearly more knew. Pat Patterson was the one who suggested the spot. The guy who cued the music had to know, because Michaels music played immediately and Hart was the one scheduled to go over. The production people in the truck had to know. They pulled away from Hart almost immediately once he spit at McMahon. If they didn't know, they should have assumed that was part of the angle and would have kept the camera on him and McMahon. They also had to know to abruptly end the television show, which actually ended seven minutes, not five, ahead of the theoretical schedule.

We incorrectly reported last week that the ring announcer made the announcement of the title change immediately, as in fact, the show went off the air without such an announcement being made. Hebner did run "faster than Donovan Bailey" according to a ringside fan out of the ring and through the dressing room into the awaiting car, but did not fly home, nor as reported did he miss both Raw tapings. One could assume the double-cross had a back-up plan when you think about the spot Patterson offered in the match. If Hart had reversed the sharpshooter before Hebner and Vince could get the bell rung, Hebner still would have been able to fast count him from the superkick, which he probably should have done because at that point the finish wouldn't have come off to the public as smelling so bad.

We've talked with four eye witnesses to "the fight." Two had similar stories, basically exactly how it was reported on last week. Clearly, Hart threw one punch. It hit McMahon's left temple and not his jaw. McMahon went down and on television on 11/17 claimed to one week later still have blurred vision and suffered a concussion from the punch and had a nasty black eye most of the week, which on television was somewhat covered up by make-up.

The others had very different stories, saying there was no fight, just a punch. That McMahon was never helped out, but walked out on his own power, although McMahon definitely did suffer an ankle injury after the punch that wasn't as a result of Hart but in his either leaving or being helped out and someone stepping on it. One even confirmed the story McMahon had on television and that two days later he tried to get across to the wrestlers, basically that McMahon let him punch him, and as he portrayed to the wrestlers, he was taking the punch for "all the boys" since Hart wouldn't do the right thing on the way out and he had to make the right thing happen for the boys and the future of the company.

There have been denials that Shane McMahon ever jumped on Hart, or that Davey Boy Smith ever jumped on Shane McMahon and that neither was involved at all. On 11/13 Smith's attorney faxed a letter to McMahon saying that he had injured his knee in breaking up the fight and might need surgery. One eye witness maintained there was no fight, only one punch, and Smith was never involved to have gotten hurt.

For whatever reason, and I guess this involves the machismo nature of the business, because the fight was an unfortunate after-effect of the double-cross, but that people on the WWF side, and even McMahon himself, are trying to give people the impression that had it been a fair fight, whatever that constitutes, that McMahon would have won, and/or that Hart backed down after the altercation from Shane McMahon and not visa versa. Almost as if somehow the end result of the fight was more of a figurative instead of a literal black eye on Vince McMahon and the powers that be in the WWF, because he was the one with the concussion, than the double-cross.

The weirdest part of McMahon's speech on Raw on 11/17 was his broaching that subject, almost like a kid in a schoolyard who got decked and claiming it was a sucker-punch, and maybe it was, one week later after replaying it in his mind, decided that really he could kick the other guys butt. It really shouldn't matter. Clearly when it comes to the fight, both men were in the wrong. McMahon to precipitate the situation after what happened and not walk away from trouble when he had good reason to expect it would happen. Hart because he threw the first and only punch, even though he had warned McMahon earlier that he would.

Yes, it made Bret Hart a cult hero to the wrestlers, and the next night McMahon's former employees in WCW were all smiles, not just in the ring. It was described as the climactic moment from the movie "One Flew Over the Cuckoo's Nest" when Nurse Ratchett finally got it, and that somewhere in Pittsburgh, Bruno Sammartino was going to have a big smile on his face. Hart wasn't apologetic about it and McMahon on television described him as "crowing" about it. Many wrestlers, who in their dreams would have liked to have done it, were celebratory.

It was the right thing to do in the fantasy wrestling world, where the babyface gets screwed for so long that he finally decks the heel that screwed him. But the cameras were off and this was the real world, and the real world doesn't operate that way. With all the pressures and paranoia on both sides, a lot of it justified, one could see how things ended up as they did, but you are talking about a 40-year-old and a 52-year-old, both of whom are very intelligent, albeit very stubborn, and everything up to that point was business. Bad business to be sure, but business.

The end result was two nine-year-olds, and the one who got the black eye going on television and crying about it. It was so weird to see McMahon, on television, try and get over the idea that if they were to fight again, that even though he's 52-years-old, the result might be different. Whether he believes it to be true, or because he's trying to somehow save face with the boys as a kid on the schoolyard does in the same situation, or even if true makes an issue of professional differences turn into nothing more than "my daddy can beat up your daddy" on the Kindergarten playground.

To the millions of wrestling fans watching, what does it say for the business McMahon was so intent on protecting when the television announcer and company owner says publicly that he thinks he could kick butt on the supposed five-time champion of the world? Earlier in the week many in the company were thinking McMahon wouldn't say anything that negative about Hart and certainly not from that perspective, because they knew it would come off badly. Let alone focus on the fight in that vain because even though most fans know pro wrestling is worked, they like in their own imaginations to believe that the wrestlers, particularly the main event wrestlers, really are tough guys, whether true or not, and not violating that is another of pro wrestling's time honored traditions. Why, in Syracuse, NY a few years back, when Michaels was beaten up or whatever actually happened, that the WWF tried to put the word out it was by eight or nine people, rather than by one person who had three friends with him who were largely run off the scene by Davey Boy Smith?

Anyway, on 11/17, Ross, on the 900 line, said that Smith injured his knee in breaking up the altercation after the show in Montreal. As far as the tapings themselves and the supposed boycott, we were contacted throughout 11/10 as to what was going on. Nearly all the wrestlers didn't feel like going to television in Ottawa. Upper management was literally on the phone all night long after the show trying to pacify an upset crew of wrestlers who felt that they had all been double crossed. Many wrestlers talked of quitting the promotion. According to Hart, eight wrestlers called his room the morning of the show and he told all of them not to breach their contracts and to do what was best for their families and to attend the show. One of those who called was Rick Rude.

As it was, only Owen Hart, Smith and Mick Foley flew home rather than worked the TV in Ottawa. Neidhart was there, although he didn't work since his appearing would call too much attention to the fact the other members of the Hart Foundation weren't there and would likely get the Canadian crowd more up in arms on a live television shoot. Foley, after one day, flew back and worked in the second night in Cornwall. Clearly, Hart and Smith were furious about what happened and for family reasons were wanting to leave the promotion. McMahon had made it clear that he isn't going to let either out of their respective contracts, which in both cases have a little less than four years left. Reports that one or both had an out clause in their contracts similar to Bret were untrue, as Bret, due to his negotiating leverage at the time he worked out the deal, was the only Titan wrestler under contract who had such a provision.

Smith hasn't returned, with his only communication to Titan being the fax that his lawyer sent about his knee injury. Owen Hart was talked into working on 11/12 in Barrie, ONT, en route to a meeting in Connecticut the next day with McMahon. Hart wanted some sort of an apology, and as McMahon later showed on Raw a few days later, he has in his own mind worked out that all the problems were Bret's fault and wouldn't do so. Hart left the meeting and went home, and was removed from all of his house show bookings. McMahon and Owen had a second meeting on 11/16, again not reaching a satisfactory ending. The Titan position on the matter is that Hart is taking a hiatus to work everything out due to the family situation. Others portray it as Owen being given a deadline, either 12/1 or 1/1 depending on the source, to return to work but he has until that time off to work everything out since the company realizes that he is in a bad position and that in no way is he at fault. The bottom line is that both Owen Hart and Smith have families and can't work anywhere else, and whether they would like to leave or not, ultimately they don't seem to have much of a choice.

Yet another scenario to convince Bret to do the job in Montreal was proposed on 11/5. In this one, proposed by Neidhart, Bret would have Michaels beaten in the middle. The Hart Foundation would come out and attack Bret and put Michaels on top leading to the title change. This was proposed to Bret as a way to put a lot of heel heat on his family after he left, to where he didn't lose clean, and his family could explain it on television as being mad at Bret for deserting them and going to the other promotion. Bret nixed that one saying, "I'm not dragging my family through that crap again."

McMahon addressed the wrestlers in a meeting on 11/11 in Cornwall. His story line was that it was Bret who changed his mind on an agreed upon finish on Sunday and wasn't willing to do anything but hand over the title belt on Raw when he announced he was leaving the WWF. McMahon tried to portray Hart as someone who actually believed he really was a legend in Canada to make fun of his not doing the job in that country. He brought up the idea of if Hart didn't do the job, that it would be a break in the historical legacy of the belt (forgetting that the belt's historical legacy already had a break earlier this year when Michaels handed it to McMahon rather than put over Sid). McMahon claimed to have taken the punch for all the boys. It's unclear exactly who believed what depending upon who one listens to. It appeared even after the speech that most wrestlers poked holes through the explanation and most realized that Hart was never unwilling to do a job before leaving the company as it was portrayed, but some also bought McMahon's story.

The Bob Backlund vs. Iron Sheik finish on December 26, 1983 at Madison Square Garden was not a double-cross even though many throughout the years have claimed it to be, although most put no credence in that story. The question as to whether it was or wasn't was resurrected after the Hart-Michaels finish. It was a finish negotiated to where Backlund could save face and claim never to have legitimately lost the title, but that they could get the title to Hulk Hogan who had been promised it to jump from the AWA a few days earlier. The Wendi Richter vs. Fabulous Moolah finish was a double-cross exactly as described last week.

The 1933 Jim Londos vs. Joe Savoldi finish was actually a pinfall, where Londos was under the ropes but the referee in Chicago, who was bought off before the match by rival promoters in New York wanting to discredit Londos as a world champion, counted to three anyway. Before Savoldi went to New York to "unify" the title with their champion, Jim Browning, he first did a job for Strangler Lewis. The reason for that was if any state athletic commission ordered a match between Londos and Savoldi to settle the controversy from Chicago, the belief was Londos, who was considered a very good legitimate wrestler, would win a legitimate match between the two of them easily. So Lewis, who was one of the toughest wrestlers in history, was put in the Savoldi position, and there was little question that Lewis was out of Londos' league. Londos in that era had a long history of avoiding Lewis since Lewis would never put him over and was a threat to shoot and embarrass him if they were ever to wrestle.

A generation later the situation with Buddy Rogers, one of the biggest drawing cards of his era and the first truly great worker in the business, and Lou Thesz, the perennial champion, was somewhat like Hart and Michaels in that Thesz would never put Rogers over for personal reasons, and Rogers would never have a good match with Thesz when Thesz went over, and would only work to make the match good if they did a DQ or time limit draw finish. Although McMahon would like to portray things differently and maybe old-timers would as well, there are numerous historical precedents for what happened here. And one more note is significant in that story.

Finally, in 1935, Lewis' camp and Londos' camp made peace and a match was arranged, advertised as "The last shooting match in history," (and you thought using insider terms was something that had just come up this year) between the two biggest superstars of the era, who hadn't worked together in years, probably because by that point Lewis realized his heyday was over and it was time to make the last big payday. It worked met because everyone knew they hated each other and "wouldn't" work together, and maybe more than any other match would be the historical precedent for all the New Japan matches like Muto-Takada. The show drew 35,000 fans and $95,000—both at that point in time all-time records for wrestling. It was not a shoot, and Londos went over. The U.S. attendance record stood until Rogers vs. Pat O'Connor in 1961, and the gate record stood until Thesz vs. Baron Leone in 1952.

So the battle lines were drawn for the next Monday night ratings war. WWF had been promoting, "Why Bret Why?" a candid interview with Vince McMahon, plus promising McMahon would discuss the situation further after the show on AOL. Bischoff beat him to the punch with an even bigger coup. In the Nitro open, out came the newest NWO member, Rick Rude, who 24 hours earlier (and since Raw was a taped show, one hour later, still sporting a beard he had shaved off to further embarrass McMahon) was a member of Degeneration X. Before getting into storyline matters, Rude stated that "Shawn Michaels never beat Bret Hart. Vince McMahon told the referee to ring the bell and rob Bret Hart of the title."

Rude, in the truest time honored traditions of the business, a day or two after debuting with the WWF on 8/4 in Atlantic City and appearing without signing a contract, called Bischoff up and the two opened dialogue. Whether they agreed at that point and held it off for the opportune moment, or whether Rude, one of the very few WWF television personalities to have not signed a contract, contacted Bischoff again this past week, figuring the timing wouldn't ever be so perfect for his leverage, is unknown. He was among the group really upset with how McMahon handled things although it would probably be incorrect to describe this as anything more than a monetary deal that had been in some form in the works for three months. By mid-week the two had struck an agreement to appear on Nitro before McMahon could give his speech, but still had to work out the legal issues with Turner because Rude had sued the company after his career ending injury in 1994.

"Rude was in the room when it (the fight) happened," Hart said. "He didn't know what was going on (in regards to the finish) and was waiting to hit the ring (for the planned finish). I got the impression that he, like a lot of people, had problems with the ethical side. I knew he had a problem. He called me Monday and asked me if I thought he should go to TV. I told him, like everyone else who called, to go."

One thing can be said: Even though this wasn't an angle, as an angle, it was more successful than any the WWF has run in a long time. According to WWF sources, the Survivor Series is projected to do 250,000 buys, which would be an 0.89 buy rate—the best the company would have done since the Hart-Michaels match at the 1996 WrestleMania. Other U.S. sources weren't as positive in their projections, as Request and Viewers Choice early returns projected an 0.55 buy rate, which would be absolutely miserable if true.

The difference could be Canada, which would be really scary for the WWF if that was the case. A buy rate through the roof in Canada, where the stories of Hart leaving made mainstream press the entire last week, and where the national angle and Michaels picking his nose with the flag should have fueled the patriotic fervor, which would be logically expected, could explain the difference. Most WWF PPV events usually do better in Canada than the U.S. even without an angle geared toward the Canadian market as this match clearly was, and one of the reasons for the big drop in UFC buy rates was when they lost Canada.

McMahon's interview did strong quarter hour ratings although the end result was the typical Nitro win. Nitro did a 4.11 rating (4.33 first hour; 3.94 second hour) and 6.18 share. Raw did a 3.15 rating (2.95 first hour; 3.15 second hour) and 4.89 share. McMahon's first interview segment went head-to-head with Guerrero vs. Malenko with WCW holding a 3.5 to 3.4 edge. His second interview segment went unopposed and drew a 3.5 rating.

McMahon was unapologetic, some would say almost vindictive in spots, but also probably was persuasive on the surface to some who only half understood. One has to think his cryptic remarks about Bret refusing to do the job came off as out of place as the Melanie Pillman interview (which also drew great ratings for a quarter hour) about Brian being a loving husband to fans who follow the storylines and watch as two hours of weekly escapist entertainment and saw him supposedly sleeping with Marlena the week before. "Some would say I screwed Bret Hart. The referee didn't screw Bret Hart. Shawn Michaels didn't screw Bret Hart. I believe

Bret Hart screwed Bret Hart." Later he went on to say "There is a time honored tradition in this business that if someone is leaving, they show the proper respect for the organization and its superstars. Bret didn't want to honor that tradition."

McMahon explained that Hart's leaving was a joint decision between the two of them and said together they put together an idea to "orchestrate the opportunity for Turner to steal Bret." He said that he felt Hart's salary was too high and that Hart felt he'd lost his spot to Michaels. He claimed Hart had signed a three year contract at $3 million per year for 125 dates per year. McMahon said that he is still contemplating legal action against Hart for the punch, saying it's up to how Hart reacts, apparently meant as a scare tactic for Hart not to knock McMahon publicly. "I have no sympathy for Bret whatsoever. No sympathy for a guy not doing the right thing for the business and the fans that made him. Bret made a selfish decision and he has to live with it for the rest of his life."

McMahon came back later in the show and said wrestling was a strange business and he'd take Bret Hart back in the future, but he'd have to apologize and know if there was a problem in the future, he wouldn't let Hart throw another punch at him, describing the punch as him giving Hart "a free shot." "Bret sold out but it's okay that Bret sold out. I helped Bret sell out. It's not a big deal because I helped him do it." He claimed Hart loses credibility every time he says he didn't make the decision for the money. "I regret I was forced into making the decision. I regret Bret didn't do the right thing. I regret that his fans are upset. I regret that his family had to endure his tirade. I regret that my son had to witness this. It was the right decision for the fans and the superstars that remained here[...] I felt I had to do what I had to do. I'm unwavering from that point of view. Perhaps he's unwavering from his point of view."

McMahon said that Bret had a chance to prove he was the best there was, the best there is and the best there ever will be. "It's just too damn bad that in the end Bret really wasn't the best there was, the best there is and the best there ever will be. He had the opportunity to live up to that and he failed." McMahon after the show went on AOL, where he said almost nothing and from all accounts, was shielded from all probing questions. He claimed the vast majority of WWF wrestlers supported his decision (from all accounts that isn't the case although some did buy his explanation).

Bret Hart, who actually didn't watch Raw because TSN pre-empted the show on 11/17, but heard a tape on the phone, said he thought McMahon's arguments were pretty lame to anyone that knew the story and was actually disappointed in his comeback. "Isn't there more of a time honored tradition to tell the truth to your top stars? I don't know how anyone could expect me to apologize for what they did to me [...] Money was not a part of my decision. It was an afterthought of my decision. I'll always be thankful for the deal I got (from WCW). But even on Saturday (11/1), I never asked McMahon about how much money he would offer me. I asked him what (ideas) he had for me. In my mind, I didn't do it for the money. If it was for the money, I'd have left last year. This was all about legacy, retiring to be a company spokesman and leaving the organization with a lot of pride."

In regard to a possible return, he said, "I don't believe I could ever work with Vince McMahon, Jerry Brisco or Pat Patterson again. I'm very stubborn when it comes to my pride. I don't think I can forget the finish. I put so much pride into my ring work. (Returning) would be like selling out my ethics to them."

And finally, Hart was scheduled for a return appearance on 11/19 on the TSN Sports talk show "Off The Record" that he first appeared on 11/7. However, when McMahon got himself booked on the show on 11/20 to do counter whatever Hart was going to say and do Canadian damage control, Hart canceled. Hart scheduled an on-line chat for 11/21, and then wants to get on with his career, think about getting acquainted with the WCW product which he really doesn't know well, and leave this story for the history books.

DECEMBER 1

When you look up the term "bait and switch" in your dictionary, there should be a synonym to it—"World Wrestling Federation."

In a decision to forfeit potential PPV money, the biggest revenue stream in the company, in favor of television ratings and probably short-term at that, the 11/24 live Raw from Fayetteville, NC was built around Bret Hart. The same Bret Hart who wasn't there and based on his own words, will never be there again. Nevertheless, the WWF had drawn two of its strongest ratings of the year basically due to the wrestler the company has now tried to label as not being worth what they were paying him in the wake of the double-cross finish at the Survivor Series.

There can be little doubt based on the quarter hours, and logic itself, that the first week's rating came from a combination of the curiosity over the finish the night before and a gift from WCW in making the Bret Hart announcement before Raw started, and even though WCW drew a better rating in the process, they also created curiosity as to what was going to be said on the WWF show later that night. Based on quarter-hours, there is no question that the strength of the 11/17 Raw rating was based on curiosity regarding the Vince McMahon interview about Bret Hart, an interview that the plan was originally done to put "closure" to the Bret Hart issue. Of course it only fueled the fire among some, but more importantly, it became obvious that after trying a million hotshot ideas and failing almost every time, that the WWF has finally found something that can move the ratings.

So, for the 11/24 Raw, in newspapers around the country including USA Today, they listed the main event on that show as being Bret Hart vs. Shawn Michaels. That was the hook. To make sure when the show started that people didn't wise up to the hook, they opened the show with Michaels doing an interview claiming he had a secret conversation with Hart, unbeknown to everyone including McMahon and using the term "As God is my witness," even using terms like Internet and underground dirt sheet, and doing the interview out of character to make people believe he was shooting and not working in the new blurred environment the WWF is working under. He said that Hart was going to be there, and a white limo was shown several times for the remainder of the hour with announcers Jim Ross and Jim Cornette trying for all they were worth to sell the idea that it was Hart in the limo.

Of course, you all know the rest of the story. Instead of Hart, they dressed a mini up in a leather jacket and sunglasses and called him Hart, had Michaels put him in a sharpshooter and Helmsley stick the mic in his face where the mini said that he submitted and that Michaels was the icon and the show stopper, put a "WCW" sign on his butt, kicked him in the butt out of the ring and said to go there with the rest of the garbage. Then WWF can hide behind the idea that it wasn't the company doing a bait-and-switch but Michaels, the heel, who was lying to the fans, which is what a heel should do.

Granted, the humiliating a big star with a skit like that is a standard wrestling gag, but in the past it has always been done to set up a big grudge match. Usually when it is done otherwise to bury talent that has left, such as in the Billionaire Ted skits in 1996, it has backfired in the face of the promotion doing so. No doubt, if this entire Hart-McMahon-Michaels thing had been an angle, it was the best one McMahon has done in years, and there would be tons of money to be made when the Hart-Michaels rematches were to take place.

Only one problem: There are no rematches. The match they need to hype people for seeing is Michaels vs. Ken Shamrock, and how did anything on that television show result in that feeling in your gut that you can't wait to see Shamrock beat Michaels? No, you wanted to see a match the company can't deliver. In this case the skit was done with the idea of humiliating someone who has signed with the opposition, but if anything, it backfired, only making Hart even more of the focal point of the WWF than when he actually held the title. Whatever the company was theoretically trying to accomplish by doing the double-cross in regard to the so-called protection of the company has been made far worse. The focal point of the company, a bigger deal to the company when he held the belt itself and now a bigger deal than the belt itself, is about to debut on their rivals' television show.

How much time did Michaels spend during the show talking about Ken Shamrock, his opponent on the next PPV, the revenue stream where the big money is generated? How much time did the announcers spend hyping that and the other matches on the next PPV? Let's face it. Aside from Slaughter vs. HHH and Butterbean vs. Mero, can you name a match on that PPV based on watching the television show? How much time was spent trying to humiliate Hart, Rick Rude (because he had left the company and actually the skit with Harvey Wippleman playing Rude was hilarious had they dropped it at that point rather than try to run the same gag twice and it being not funny and really pathetic the second time) and Jim Neidhart (because of fear he was going to leave the company and because it was another way where the WWF thought it could get under Bret Hart's skin)?

The show itself is weird enough, like watching the last years of the AWA but with much super production values, where the emphasis is on burying the wrestlers who had left the company rather than building up what was left. The burials only made the wrestlers bigger and the promotion itself look like it was going down in those days, and it looks no different from the outside today. The legitimate bitterness the company appears to have toward Hart, which delivered another strong rating, appears to be taking it away from its job of promoting wrestling. And the weirdness of the attempts at other symbolism during the show, in particular Jeff Jarrett complaining about McMahon not fulfilling his contract to the letter trying to create the idea to the fans that people who take Hart's side because of the valid point about not living up to contracts by the WWF are nothing but whining crybabies.

As it was, against the weakest Nitro show in a long-time but with the marquee Hogan vs. Giant title match on top, Nitro drew a 3.88 rating (4.15 first hour; 3.66 second hour) and 5.82 share. Raw did a 3.05 rating (2.80 first hour; 3.30 second hour) and 4.66 share. In the average of the five head-to-head segments, Nitro beat Raw 3.66 to 2.88. In the quarters head-to-head, WCW drew a 3.5 (Iaukea vs. Wright and Savage vs. Disco) to WWF's 2.7 (Rude spoof and Michaels interview regarding Hart), WCW drew another 3.5 (Malenko vs. Brad Armstrong) to WWF's 2.7 (LOD losing tag titles to Gunn & Jammes), WCW did another 3.5 (McMichael interview and Bagwell vs. Jericho) to WWF's 3.1 (Goldust introduces Luna, lengthy Slaughter interview but probably the teasing of the limo and saying Hart was in the limo is more of what peaked the rating), WCW did a 3.8 (Hennig vs. Traylor) to WWF's 2.7 (Christopher vs. Flanagan and finally WCW did a 4.0 (Hogan vs. Giant) to WWF's 3.2 (Bret Hart skit). The WCW peak was a 4.5 for Benoit vs. Sick Boy and the rating inexplicably dropped to a 4.2 for the Zbyszko-Bischoff challenge before the top of the hour where the expected 9 p.m. drop took place. WWF peaked after Nitro went off the air with a 3.4 for Shamrock vs. Vega, and the rating held for the Maivia-Austin angle, Jarrett gimmick and the Kane run-in on Crush. The Nitro replay did a 1.82 rating and 3.70 share.

As far as the Hart situation itself from a news value goes, it largely has run its course. During the week, Hart canceled scheduled interviews on the TSN show "Off the Record" due to Vince McMahon booking himself on the show the next day. McMahon then canceled as well. Hart canceled a Prodigy chat on advice from his lawyer since he is still under contract to WWF through the end of the month and it was believed WWF has an exclusive deal with AOL, agreeing to do it the first week of December. However, the AOL exclusive must not be as exclusive as thought since Jim Ross is going to do a chat on Prodigy after Hart to give the WWF side of things. Virtually every significant aspect of the story was covered the past two weeks in these pages and there is little from an informational standpoint that can be added.

Titan Sports has been strongly hinting that McMahon will pursue legal recourse, either criminal and/or civil against Hart for decking him. The WWF is now saying McMahon suffered a broken ankle in the fracas along with the blurred vision and the black eye. Hart suffered a cracked bone in the hand a few inches up from the wrist and a few fractured knuckles which are giving him a lot of pain although at this point his hand hasn't been put in a cast. He was told by his doctors that he shouldn't train or wrestle for six weeks although there are no plans for him to wrestle in WCW until January at the earliest and his first major match could be on the WCW SuperBrawl PPV show. If one goes with the idea that Scott Hall, by winning the Battle Royal, will face Sting (and don't bet the mortgage on that yet because Hogan will play that one for all its worth) in the title match, that leaves a Hogan vs. Hart match as a possibility for that show.

As far as who is right and who is wrong. Everyone has an opinion. Most of the facts in great detail are out there and readily available for those who want to know them. The general consensus has been decidedly pro-Hart. Based on a WWF hotline report, McMahon is very upset about the fan reaction and has already taped another interview which will likely air on the 12/1 Raw addressing his feelings about the reaction, in which he'll likely attack, among others, the Canadian media which has been sympathetic to Hart from the start.

The reality is that the real world doesn't consist of black-and-white babyfaces and heels. Both have their sides. Because one is wrong doesn't make the other one right or visa versa. If this was a simple issue, either double-crossing a guy in the ring for no logical reason; or a guy refusing to do a job or drop the belt in the ring while leaving for a new territory, maybe you could make a black-and-white distinction. Many, attempting to use either point as the key to this story and use that point to say the other was the one in the right are using an argument that is emotional rather than logical.

Simplifying what is a very complicated story into someone who refused to do a job or someone who changed a finish is missing most of the story. The portrayal of Hart as someone who refused to drop the belt in the ring, which is how McMahon has attempted to portray him both in his cryptic interview and to the rest of the WWF wrestlers and his front office as his reason for justifying to them what he did is simply incorrect and totally misleading. The argument that the WWF needed to get the belt off Hart that weekend because of the WCW announcement on Nitro coming misses several points.

My big question to that is simply, looking at the big picture. Why? Of the two scenarios, can you logically say that the one McMahon picked, a Michaels vs. Shamrock main event (made worse since the company decided to built itself around Bret Hart during the hype period) or a Final Four match as proposed and everyone had agreed to, using the fact Hart was leaving as part of the hype for the match with the "smart" fans knowing the title would switch but not knowing which of the other three was going to get it, was the one that would have drawn the most money.

It could have been played out at the arenas all November with Hart in the lame duck role having matches against Michaels, Shamrock, Undertaker, Vader, Austin and whomever else at different arenas, as fans would attend the house show "knowing" a title change was imminent, just not knowing when and to whom. The idea of seeing an arena title match where there was an actual possibility of a title change, particularly in a city like New York or Boston where the belt means more, would have done what for the gate in those cities?

Fact is, if the lame duck deal was a killer to the company, the buy rate in Canada for Survivor Series, where it was mainstream news that Hart was leaving, by that logic should have been horrible and the exact opposite was true. Fact is, any fan with the slightest access to inside knowledge knew before Survivor Series that Hart was going to WCW. Those who complain about the lame duck aspect of Hart as champion are forgetting the point that he already was before the match with Michaels. It wasn't an announcement by Bischoff that made him such. Among that group that knew, a decent percentage of fans in Canada and the insiders in the U.S., was the interest in Survivor Series heightened or lessened by that knowledge? The answer to that is obvious. A lame duck champion angle done correctly in this day and time would have been huge at the arenas at a time when business traditionally flourishes, and done well for the traditionally weak December PPV show.

A legitimate argument, one that has been expressed to me from those in Titan, is the fear that Hart would have shown up the next night on the Nitro in Memphis with the belt. McMahon could have taken the physical belt from him in the dressing room and told him he'd get it back when he showed up for TV the next night in Ottawa. I don't believe it was going to happen but due to things that have occurred in the past and probably will in the future as well, he has a strong argument that there is justification for that fear. One could argue that he would still be under contract through 11/30, but by this point who is to say there wasn't a minor breach that could be used as a loophole?

Lame duck scenarios have occurred in the past. In early 1992, Lex Luger, who had a valid long-term pro wrestling contract with WCW, along with Vince McMahon, found a loophole in that McMahon signed him to join the World Bodybuilding Federation, a McMahon company that wasn't a pro wrestling company and thus wouldn't be violating the terms of his pro wrestling contract. Luger sat out the remainder of his WCW wrestling contract while being employed by the WBF, and then when the time limit of his WCW wrestling contract ended, he had his contract switched from the WBF to the WWF. He was a lame duck champion but had no problem doing the job for his best friend Sting on the way out, but wouldn't work any house shows or put anyone else over in the interim.

If you accept the premise that it would have killed the WWF or the WWF belt had Bischoff made the announcement about Hart while he still had the belt, then yes, it was McMahon's last chance to get the belt back and Hart had refused to put Michaels over on that night, or for that matter, before that night either. In this case, given the potential of the respective paths for business following the match, the path with Hart as champion until the last night in or the path where they are today, my feeling is that premise in this specific case holds absolutely no water. This path, doing a double-cross and executing the double-cross so pathetically that everyone knew and making the guy you're trying to bury larger than life and using his name as the focal point of television even though he's about to work for the opposition, did probably turn out to be the best one for television ratings, which if nothing else, shows just how strange a world pro wrestling has become.

The Toronto Sun did a readers poll in which 55% of the readers responding said they would be watching more WCW wrestling than WWF wrestling due to Bret Hart being with the group. 12% said they would watch more WWF wrestling than WCW. 8% said they would watch less pro wrestling overall. And 23% said they wouldn't change the amount of wrestling or the group they were watching due to Bret Hart leaving WWF. Keep in mind the wording of the questions, the time frame in which they were asked (basically right after the double-cross hit the news) and the nature of the people most likely to respond will skew things in the direction the poll turned out to be. I don't believe 55% of the wrestling fans in Toronto will now become more WCW fans than WWF fans due to Hart switching sides, but the poll does indicate Hart's name value in Toronto is exceedingly strong.

In McMahon's defense, waiting until 12/7 to take the title back was risky. You have a main eventer on a PPV who would be already under contract and working for your main competitor. The timing was awfully precarious. Losing the title at MSG, or in Boston, or on the 11/24 Raw, would have made sense because it would have eliminated the risk of relying on Eric Bischoff not to change his mind to screw with someone that he obviously gets great joy in screwing with. There are a lot of things that should have been handled differently, probably dating back many months in letting the Michaels/Hart rivalry turned into dislike grow into unprofessional levels. If McMahon, for whatever reason, wanted out of the contract and was willing to breach it, he should have at least waited until he had created a scenario where Hart would drop the title to someone other than the one person, for reasons good or bad is another issue, that dropping the title to would become a personal issue with.

Whether Hart or Michaels were the one in the "right" in their personal problems over the past year plus, how could anyone have been so blind after what had already happened and what was continuing to happen between the two to believe Hart wouldn't have a problem putting over a guy who had steadfastly refused to ever put him over? Even if you believe Hart was "wrong" in refusing to lose to Michaels on that night, the fact is McMahon should have known ahead of time it would be a problem because everyone halfway close to the situation knew, and with that knowledge, why did he go in that direction?

The argument that Hart is an actor and should follow the script of the director misses the point about him being given reasonable creative control over his scenarios over his last 30 days of the contract. The point was, there was a script. Supposedly all knew ahead of time and agreed to the script. It wasn't Hart who didn't follow the script. It was the director in the middle of a scene, right in front of the audience, changing a script out of fear, spite, desperation, wanting to show he could, or whatever series of reasons he had.

An argument can be made Hart was unprofessional in refusing to lose to Michaels in Canada. But no argument can be made that McMahon wasn't unprofessional in the way he handled the situation in the ring that night. The ambiguous interpretation of the word "reasonable" is a key point in the argument. Was it reasonable for Hart to agree to drop the belt one week later rather than on a certain night? I'd agree it was unreasonable for him to refuse to drop it, period. I'd agree it was unreasonable for McMahon to ask him to drop it to Steve Lombardi, which McMahon never suggested, although Hart was apparently willing. Interpreting that Hart was within bounds of reasonable creative control by wanting to drop the title a week later instead of that night can't be used to justify anyone's behavior after the double-cross. At that point, all reasonableness on both sides was long gone and what happened was very unfortunate.

To this day, neither Hart nor McMahon are apologetic and you can see both would feel that they had wronged. Hart was clearly double-crossed and the company he'd worked being a top star for tried, in what will be a failed effort, to destroy his legacy, reputation and dignity for a situation that the company clearly started.

McMahon was clearly punched in the temple very hard. Even if you think his behavior was so dishonest that he just got what he had coming, it still shouldn't have happened. If the WWF title is nothing more than a prop that shouldn't be taken seriously and Hart is such a mark for taking it seriously (missing the point that his exit to him was supposed to be the symbolic last scene of a 13-plus year long story and will always be the thing his wrestling career is most remembered for, and that, not the belt, is what McMahon really did steal from him), then so is McMahon going to the lengths he did to get it back.

And so is this industry in reality, because the double-cross, a fixed ending of a match in a sport where every single ending of a match is fixed, became arguably the biggest news story of the year. And the fixed ending of a fixed match was a bigger part of the story than some very real major aspects in the same story. A real, not fixed, attempted breach of a contract. A real, not fixed, jump of one of the biggest names in the business. A real, not fixed, locker room assault. A real, not fixed, morale problem. A real, not fixed, problem with fan reaction that the company may be overreacting to. And a real, not fake situation where two of the biggest stars in the company went home in disgust over the incident.

On television, the WWF portrayed Owen Hart as having severe mental strain due to the pressure of what happened and he's on hiatus. In reality, he was on vacation in Disneyland. His contract is such that it is pretty much accepted across the board that against his wishes, he's going to return. His deal is believed to be so one-sided that if the WWF terminates him for failing to return to work, he still wouldn't be able to work anywhere else in wrestling for the next nearly four years.

Davey Boy Smith is expected to have knee surgery later this week. On television, Michaels referred to it as the old fake knee injury deal which he knows full well. This, among other things, will buy him time until he returns although he also has been adamant in some circles about not wanting to return, although he doesn't appear to have much in the way of options either as Titan has apparently made it clear it won't release either of them from their deals. Bret, Owen and Smith are all still receiving their weekly paychecks from the WWF although there are other monies that supposedly the WWF is behind in paying Bret.

Jim Neidhart was not under a WWF contract and could leave at anytime. Unlike the other two, he's not someone who would be guaranteed a job with WCW should McMahon get rid of him. The belief is that the angle where he agreed to join DX, only to have them turn on him at the end, was a way to bury him in case he were to show up on WCW television the next week (although it also buried him when it comes to real future value in WWF as well), and at the same time, continue to send a message back to Calgary about who is really in (or not in) control. Neidhart could have refused the angle and lost his job, but there are no guarantees WCW would take him. Had he lost his job under those circumstances, WCW probably would have taken him, but for a 42-year-old wrestler who is lucky to be in the mainstream, a job in the hand is far more valuable than one that might not be there.

Whatever people were clinging to the argument that this whole scenario from start to finish was the most well orchestrated scam in wrestling history ended on 11/24. If it had been a scam, everything was teased for Hart's returning big pop to show up and confront Michaels. But he was in Calgary, not Fayetteville. And was still in Calgary on 11/25, which was the last television taping by the WWF before his contract expires on 11/30. Eventually, this reality will turn into a pro wrestling angle if or when Owen Hart returns, perhaps with Smith, and goes for revenge against Michaels, and perhaps Helmsley. It wouldn't even surprise me for McMahon to try and use the negative reaction to himself and do a heel turn himself. And the fact this caused so much commotion, I'd say it's a lock that companies for years will try copycat scenarios, which will be complete works.

DECEMBER 8

It was not true that Earl Hebner found out about the finish just as he was going through the curtain. Earl and Dave Hebner were both told by McMahon well ahead of time and told not to let anyone in on it. Hebner theoretically had plenty of time to warn Hart although he obviously chose not to. Nobody in the WWF hierarchy knew that Hebner and Hart were good friends (actually, I guess this proved they were right, although friends of Hart do corroborate that Hart believed Hebner to be one of his best friends in the company before this happened). Earl had all his gear packed in the car well before the match started and Dave was in the car with the motor running in the parking lot for most of the match readying for the getaway.

The basic argument points within the WWF (and for that matter in a lot of the wrestling industry and among fans) in debating who was right (you know, there has to be one side right and the other wrong because it's a simple black-and-white world we live in) depends on who you believe in the most simplified form. Those who believe Hart had refused to drop the title believe McMahon was right, as I guess you have to accept Hart refusing to drop the title to justify McMahon's actions and a lot of people for a lot of reason need to find some justification. Those close to McMahon insist Hart isn't telling the truth when he said he was willing to do a job later in the week. Hart, of course, insists he was.

In that simplified question of the whole big deal, it all depends upon who one believes and who has more credibility, McMahon or Hart. There is documentation that indicates Hart is the one telling the truth, however those defending McMahon say Hart changed his mind at the last minute and wouldn't do business, hence things turned out as they did. With Hart not around to defend himself in the WWF locker room, there are many of the boys who now believe he did refuse to put anyone over at any time to the point when Michaels did the deal on 11/24 with the mini, he asked several of the wrestlers around in a group whether he should do the right thing for business and ignore Bret and build up the PPV, or stick it to Bret, and the guys there told him he should stick it to Bret.

The WWF claimed it was USA Today that made the mistake in the 11/24 listings of a Bret Hart vs. Shawn Michaels match on Raw, and that their P.R. department simply wrote that Shawn Michaels would challenge Bret Hart, and that was the storyline theme of the show, but never indicated there would be a match. However, we've received several newspaper TV listings that weren't USA Today that also had listed for Raw in that time slot a Bret Hart vs. Shawn Michaels match.

The other story is that, whether this is to save Patterson's credibility with the boys or whatever, is that Patterson really didn't know, and when he suggested the key spot to Hart, it was unknowingly relaying a message from McMahon and that he felt McMahon set him up as well. Of course Patterson and McMahon have both been around this business their entire lives and understand manipulation as well as anyone.

Michaels, in an article in the 11/23 Charleston Post-Courier stated about Hart:

At one time Bret was a fantastic wrestler. But I've been in the ring with a lot of people. He ranks up there with exceptionally average. His brother Owen is ten times the talent he is.

The man's very different. He sees the wrestling business very differently. He really believes he's a hero in Canada. We all love the feeling you get when you have the adulation of the fans, but you have to learn to control that. This is the wrestling business. This isn't real life. My God. Get a grip.

I've never had a problem with Bret Hart. He mostly had a problem with me. There's nothing I can really do about that. I'm just having fun and trying to be entertaining and controversial. Bret is from the old school, which is fine, but obviously it doesn't mix. He takes it much more seriously than I do. You should be able to have fun at your job. I don't take things that seriously.

I didn't even have a problem when he attacked me in the dressing room. I just defended myself and that was it, I left. The situation got out of hand. At that time I needed to stay away—my good old fake knee injury. Bret was harboring a lot of bitter, bitter feelings that were really his problems. He's the guy who has to work through them. Not us.

The world should know this was not Bret Hart leaving, this was Vince McMahon asking him to leave. He simply didn't feel Bret was giving what he was getting. He was always late. He only did personal appearances in Canada when he felt like it. As WWF champion, I did everything. The Undertaker still does everything. Steve Austin does everything. There's a lot of legwork that comes with working in the WWF. Bret didn't want to do any of it. It wasn't convenient for him. He wanted, he wanted, he wanted but he wasn't willing to give.

DECEMBER 15

The never-ending saga of the Survivor Series finish has now become both the catalyst and focal point for both new angles and instances that aren't angles at all in the WWF, and perhaps even an angle in WCW.

Among them, Vince McMahon's going from babyface television announcer to almost a dictatorial heel owner role as a television persona, stemming from such a strong negative backlash to him from the Hart-Michaels finish; Owen Hart's getting a huge raise to return to feud with Shawn Michaels; Jim Neidhart's leaving and the possible departure of Davey Boy Smith; McMahon threatening Bret Hart with a lawsuit; and yet another angle spoof where Steve Austin voluntarily "gave up" the Intercontinental title rather than wrestle (i.e. "do a job" for Rocky Maivia).

McMahon showed up on yet another in the almost monthly "new-look" Monday Night Raws on 12/8 from Portland, ME, an even more harder edged, strange insider type show designed to throw out constant "shocks" ala ECW, complete with Marc Mero doing an interview before a match with Salvatore Sincere calling Sincere a "jobber" and a "jabroni" and explaining those were terms used for a guy who is paid to lose, and saying that Sincere was just a silly marketing gimmick and that he was really Tom Brandi; Shawn Michaels playing strip poker for about 30 minutes, including drinking Jack Daniels and smoking a cigar and finally getting down to his BVD's, and actually putting his hand on and shaking whatever it was that he had in there right in front of the camera (and pulling down his underwear and mooning the live crowd during a commercial break); Goldust "flashing" Vader and Sable, wearing ultra high heels, taking off a potato sack to reveal as skimpy a swimsuit as possible. All in all, it was almost like the joke of "I went to the fights and a hockey game broke out," in this case, I went to the variety show and they did some wrestling matches as there was a total of 14 minutes of wrestling on the two hour show.

McMahon, who was heavily booed coming out based on the response to his "Why Bret Why?" interview, came out and began a heel turn in confronting Austin, making it clear he expected Austin to do as he said since he was his boss. McMahon, with the ring surrounded by agents ala the Hart scenario, claimed Austin "endangered the lives of the fans" by driving the truck (which they are giving away in a Royal Rumble marketing gimmick) into the arena and claimed he used the truck as a weapon in his match.

During the show they showed McMahon talked with agents, Gerald Brisco in particular, trying to give the impression they were plotting to screw Austin out of the title since earlier in the show McMahon called Rocky Maivia "the people's champion." Then at the end, with McMahon in the ring and the ring once again surrounded by agents, Austin, in fantasy to "foil" the double-cross (and in reality to avoid doing a job on television while getting the belt to Maivia), voluntarily handed the belt to Maivia. He then gave Maivia a stone cold stunner after congratulating him on being the new champion, grabbed the belt and walked off and, actually using the term ratings ploy, said that next week on the show he'd show everyone what he was going to do with the belt. Before leaving, while bouncing off the ropes, he "accidentally" knocked into the ropes that McMahon, who was standing on the apron, was holding onto, resulting in McMahon taking a pratfall on the floor and getting up, just as the show was going off the air, spewing a string of expletives at Austin that were edited off the broadcast in the seven second delay mode. The one thing getting old is weekly opening the show promising a wrestling match with Austin as the headline event (or last week with Hart vs. Michaels), and always finding a way not to deliver it.

The show basically held the same ratings level as the previous shows since Survivor Series, doing a 2.99 rating (2.78 first hour; 3.20 second hour) and 4.59 share. Monday Nitro on 12/8, a lackluster show before a sellout crowd of 16,848—15,101 paying $251,698 in the Marine Midland Arena in Buffalo, NY, did a 4.24 rating and 6.42 share. It was the third largest gate in the history of WCW and largest ever for a Nitro, trailing only PPV gates the past two months in Las Vegas and Auburn Hills, MI. The Nitro replay did a 1.70 rating and 3.18 share.

Quarter-hours told an interesting story as there was more switching back-and-forth than ever before. Nitro did huge unopposed, then took an unusually large drop from its 5.0 peak for Chris Benoit vs. Lodi, to a 3.7, when football and Raw began despite having the "star power" of Ric Flair, who has delivered the strongest ratings boosts of any wrestler in the business thus far this season, and Randy Savage in the first quarter. Both shows stayed steady in the first opposed 60 minutes with WCW having a 3.80 to 2.78 cumulative lead. Then at the 10-10:15 p.m. mark, WCW grew to a 4.6 while Raw fell to a 2.4—WCW having Scott Hall vs. Diamond Dallas Page and more likely the draw was that everyone knew they were doing a big Sting angle to close the show since it was teased twice earlier in the show. WWF had the strip poker game in mid-ring. It was more likely this big difference was a positive reaction to WCW than a negative reaction to the strip poker angle because once WCW went off the air with the live show, the Raw audience grew nearly a point even though the strip poker angle was still going on.

As noted many times, when WCW ends, Raw has often not grown at all, and usually only grows slightly, but this week it went up nearly a full point to a 3.3 and ended up peaking at a 3.7 for the teased but not delivered Austin vs. Maivia IC title match. This says that the WCW audience is remaining at a very strong level, and the WWF base audience really hasn't grown to a great degree in the past five weeks, but that the WCW audience is more curious than before in watching WWF as long as WCW isn't on the air opposing them. To counter this, expect WCW to "go long" on Nitros once again to keep from providing WWF with too much "unopposed" time once Nitro goes off the air.

For 12/1, Nitro did a 3.80 rating (3.90 first hour; 3.72 second hour) and 5.66 share to Raw's 3.01 rating (2.75 first hour; 3.28 second hour) and 4.53 share and the Nitro replay did a 1.70 rating and 3.08 share.

Another new-look of the show was yet another in the almost weekly change in the announcers situation. McMahon has gone from his interviewer role to a television role as the heel owner of the company, seemingly replacing Sgt. Slaughter's commissioner role that looks to have been dropped since his character was too cartoonish for the more serious direction the company is going. The Jim Ross/Jim Cornette first hour announcing team became Ross along with Michael Cole and Kevin Kelly, with Cole and Kelly almost dominating the announcing to the point Ross was strangely quiet to the point he could be compared with Bruno Sammartino's role in his last days with the company. However, Ross was as lively as usual in the second hour doing the announcing with Jerry Lawler.

The situation with the remainder of the Hart Foundation was largely squared away during the week. McMahon, to soothe the hard feelings, offered Owen Hart a huge raise to return in a more prominent role as a singles headliner to work against Shawn Michaels. He offered Davey Boy Smith some form of a release opportunity after Smith came through arthroscopic knee surgery on 12/4. At the same time Jim Neidhart, who wasn't under contract to the WWF, followed Bret as expected in making the move to WCW.

This led to even more problems with McMahon and Bret Hart, with McMahon at one point personally and at another point lawyer-to-lawyer threatening to sue Bret Hart for tortuous interference with contracted personnel because Bret had voiced his opinion to Owen that he thought it would be in bad taste to try and exploit the reality and trivialize it by making it a wrestling angle. Bret Hart had previously stated something, I believe on the TSN "Off the Record" show earlier in the week, to the effect of that he wondered if McMahon were to at this point give all his contracted wrestlers freedom to negotiate elsewhere that how many on their own volition would choose to stay.

McMahon and Hart, in their first discussion, described as not cordial in the least, since the Survivor Series, largely regarding the subject of Owen returning and doing the angle, saw Bret Hart say he should give Owen the opportunity to negotiate elsewhere and McMahon said that he wouldn't, although the words on both sides may have been a lot stronger than that and the conversation ended on a bad note with the lawsuit threat.

Bret Hart had decided ahead of time not to bring up the subject of his last day in the WWF ever again after doing three interviews this week (a TSN "Off the Record" interview on 12/3, a taped 10:00 feature on Headline Sports in Canada which aired on 12/8, and a Prodigy Internet interview on 12/7). Although advised against it by lawyers due to the threats made by McMahon over the weekend, Hart blistered McMahon and the WWF for what went down in his final day with the company in the Prodigy interview. McMahon had this past week offered Smith some sort of an escape clause allowing him to negotiate elsewhere, and indications were that WCW would be seriously interested in him.

There has been some thought given in the WWF to the idea of not wanting unhappy wrestlers around and even if they are under contract, to give them the opportunity to leave. Of the two, it appeared there was more heat with Smith and the office over suspicions of the timing of his knee surgery whereas Owen Hart was largely seen by everyone on both sides as being someone put in a bad position through things that he had no control over.

The belief is the McMahon/Bret conversation originally was agreed to for both sides to take pressure off Owen for being caught in the middle of wanting to do the right thing for making as much money for his company (doing the angle) and removing the stress on his family and letting the memory of what happened die out (not doing the angle).

Smith's knee surgery turned out not to be as serious as some had feared, and he'd likely be able to return to wrestling within the next two months.

Among the highlights of Hart's Prodigy interview were:

- Saying he thought Jim Neidhart made mistake in judgement in going along with the angles in his final two weeks in the WWF, and said he thought the WWF humiliated Neidhart out of spite against him which he claimed was a bad reflection more on the WWF than anyone else.
- He thanked Mick Foley for his show of defiance in missing the Ottawa show and said that he received calls from nearly every wrestler in the WWF with the exception of only a handful who felt the same way he did about the situation.
- He claimed that when he swore on TV before WrestleMania that he was misled by the referee and thought they were off the air. He said McMahon didn't set up the situation where he swore, that he explained to McMahon afterwards that he thought they were off the air and was never reprimanded by McMahon for it. McMahon had noted when Hart complained about the direction of the company that Hart had done things on his own that contradicted that viewpoint, and WWF officials had noted that the incident where Hart swore on the air got them more heat from the USA network than anything they did in 1997.
- He called Dory Funk Jr., "conceivably the greatest worker of all-time."
- He claimed that Roddy Piper, Curt Hennig, Davey Boy Smith, Owen Hart, Shawn Michaels, Diesel, Razor Ramon, Yokozuna, Bam Bam Bigelow, Isaac Yankem and Hakushi among others all had the greatest matches of their career against him. He said his pick as his best match ever was the 1992 Wembley Stadium match against Smith.
- He claimed that Michaels was crying and weeping like a baby in the dressing room after the match and sat in the corner biting his nails. Michaels and Helmsley did get out of the dressing room in Montreal as quick as possible, both showing up at the hotel still in their wrestling outfits.
- Said that he knew he'd sound like a hypocrite now, but called Ric Flair one of the greatest performers in history. He said he's regretted for a long time some of the comments that he's made about him in the past, and said all he really ever meant is that Flair wasn't the greatest wrestler he ever worked with and that he may not have been in the top five, but was in the top 20. He said he never met a wrestler, particularly at his age, who could wrestle the pace Flair could and has been wanting to apologize to him for a long time (on a radio show about one year ago Hart did echo these same comments in regards to Flair, who Hart could empathize a lot more with once he turned 40 and was working nightly while banged up). "I know that sounds like crap, but it's all true."
- Blamed his previous problems with Hulk Hogan on Vince McMahon putting thoughts and words into his head and that after realizing the kind of person McMahon was, wanted to talk with Hogan to find out the real story of what happened when Hogan left the WWF in 1993.
- He said he would not attend a WWF Hall of Fame banquet if he were invited to be an inductee.
- He said he wasn't proud of his actions in the dressing room after the match (hitting McMahon) although

he thought he handled himself pretty cooly under the circumstances.

- On Earl Hebner: "I know that people think that Earl Hebner was just doing his job. Maybe he was. But all he had to do was tell me that the day before as a friend and a man of his word. I told him if he was uncomfortable with me to just say so and that I wouldn't hold it against him, because I suspected something like this was being drawn up. He got tears in his eyes and told me he could never do something like that, and he swore on his children that he would never let it happen and he'd quit his job first. We talked for over a half-hour and I left that room, the bathroom in Detroit, feeling in my heart that he was a close friend and no matter what pressure Vince McMahon put to bear on him, he would never be a part of or be involved in a conspiracy to tear down a guy with the reputation as good as mine. When I finally saw the match back, when I came home, nothing broke my heart more than seeing Earl Hebner sell me out without even any hesitation. It's one thing to get screwed over by my enemies. I already sensed who they were and what they had in mind. But it's a much more hurtful thing when you get screwed over by a very good friend. I hear Earl Hebner is drinking himself into oblivion racked with guilt for the role he played, and all I can say is, "Have another drink on me, Earl, keep biting your nails like your buddy Shawn and keep looking over your shoulder because sooner or later what goes around comes around."
- He claimed he wouldn't let his kids watch Raw ever since the McMahon interview with Melanie Pillman the day after Brian's death.
- Compared the WWF having his brother Owen do an angle based on his final match in the WWF to "a pimp forcing someone into prostitution."

JANUARY 5

Davey Boy Smith officially agreed to a deal with WCW on either 12/24 or 12/25 after paying the WWF $150,000 to buy out the final 32 months of his original five-year contract. He may debut for an interview or an angle on the 1/8 Thunder show, although he probably won't be able to wrestle in the ring due to recovering from arthroscopic knee surgery for two or three weeks.

He had the surgery on 12/4, and his recovery slowed by getting a staph infection which ended up in both legs. He began training on 12/25. When his knee was examined, they found he did have a torn anterior cruciate ligament along with the other damage and he was told he needed reconstructive surgery which would have meant six to eight months on the shelf, but he decided against the surgery because he didn't want to be out of action for that long. The rest of the damage besides the ACL tear was repaired in the scope.

The story we have from sources close to Smith is that he was on the phone with Vince McMahon and somehow the direction of the WWF television came up and he, who is one of the bigger wrestling fans among the wrestlers since his son Harry, who is training to be a wrestler, is such a huge fan. Anyway, he apparently complained that the shows weren't suitable for his son to watch and one thing led to another and McMahon offered him the opportunity to negotiate with WCW for ten days and if he couldn't cut a deal, he could return to WWF. Supposedly two days later was when he got word about the $150,000 buy-out before he could get permission to negotiate with WCW or Japan, which held up the official leaving by a few weeks.

His leaving is largely due to knowing too much about the Hart-Michaels situation, from being ready to do the run-in for the finish and seeing all the pretending that went down there, to seeing Michaels throw the belt down and almost shatter it in the dressing room as he went through the curtain because he was so "mad" about the finish, to being in the dressing room for the actual post-match conversation between Hart and Michaels where Michaels promised not to bring the belt to television the next night or to act as if he had won the match, and actually physically involved in the fight (and injuring his knee in the process) dragging Bret Hart and Shane McMahon off, to witnessing the hotel charade for the boys between Jack Lanza and Earl Hebner where Hebner, in front of an audience of a few wrestlers since there was so much heat on everyone involved in the double-cross that night in Montreal, was claiming to know nothing about the finish and that he was double-crossed as well.

I don't know how much details we've gone into about that aspect of the story, but after Earl Hebner sprinted from the ring into the awaiting car driven by Dave to get to the hotel room so there were no problems involving him in the dressing room, when he was in the lobby later in the night with several wrestlers, he and Lanza had a discussion loud enough for the wrestlers to hear. In the discussion, Hebner claimed he had been double-crossed on the finish, that he had no idea why the bell rang, and that he was flying home and quitting the promotion. Lanza talked him into staying in front of an audience of wrestlers claiming that everyone knew he wasn't involved.

After all that, he felt it would be impossible to trust anyone in decision making power. WWF was pretty much aware of how vehement his feelings were and it's most likely that had he stayed, he wouldn't have been given any kind of a push and thus would have been unhappy and it was a situation bad for everyone.

Chapter Thirty Five

WCW's Record Breaking Year

JANUARY 27

Just one day after WWF drew the second largest paid crowd for pro wrestling ever in the United States, World Championship Wrestling set the company all-time attendance record drawing a sellout of just over 17,000 fans paying $189,206 to the United Center for the 1/20 Monday Night tapings in Chicago. In addition, the company's all-time single event merchandise record was devastated with nearly $107,000.

The gate was the fourth largest in company history, trailing the record mark of $224,660 set for last year's Halloween Havoc in Las Vegas, which also set the merchandise record with $69,000. The largest paid attendance ever for a WCW house show would have been 14,082 for the 6/7 Ilio DiPaolo show in Buffalo, NY. Even dating back to the company that preceded WCW, Jim Crockett Promotions, you'd probably have to go back a good ten years to one of the successful baseball stadium shows in Charlotte to find a crowd of this size.

APRIL 21

The Nitro show in Philadelphia drew the second largest crowd and gate in the history of the WCW promotion and devastated the all-time merchandise record. The sellout crowd of 16,256 at the Core States Spectrum, which was largely sold out a week in advance although due to the typical weekly seating screw ups from the earlier site surveys, several hundred tickets were put on sale at the last minute. Paid attendance was 15,132—a few hundred shy of the company record 15,834 paid at the Nitro on 1/20 in Chicago. The gate of $219,816 fell just below the company record of $224,660 set for last year's Halloween Havoc PPV show with Hulk Hogan vs. Randy Savage on top. Total merchandise sales was $143,000, which broke the record of $107,000 set at the aforementioned Chicago Nitro.

Some, if not all of those records, will be broken for the Nitro tapings on 6/9 in Boston at the Fleet Center. Buoyed by a tremendous job of local promotion including working with the Cam Neely Foundation and sending Ric Flair, The Giant and Gene Okerlund into town for a press conference, public and media appearances, WCW set its all-time company record for first day sales on 4/10 selling approximately 10,000 tickets for in excess of $170,000. As of the close of business on 4/14, the advance was 13,789 tickets sold for $217,242. The way they have the Fleet Center set up for the Nitro leaves only 800 tickets left unsold, however, they may change the set-up and could probably get as many as 4,500 more seats which would no doubt sell easily being that they have nearly eight weeks left to sell them.

While a lot of the turnaround in WCW when it comes to house show business has to be credited with the success of Nitro making it the hot promotion in the country, and also to several angles that got people back into going to matches (and as mentioned here many times, and it's largely been not given its proper due, but you can trace the house show turnaround to the Ric Flair-Randy Savage angle involving Elizabeth in January 1996 and the Hogan-Hall-Nash NWO took it to the next level).

It also can't be emphasized enough what a great job WCW has done of local promotion, something the company in the past had a tradition of doing poorly, most of which is headed by Zane Bresloff's Awesome Promotions out of Denver. In the list of people that WCW got from WWF when it comes to importance to the company, with the exception of Hogan, Bresloff has been as—if not more—important than any of them when it comes to the turnaround in house show business.

OCTOBER 27

World Championship Wrestling once again broke its all-time gate record this past week. But the amazing thing is, it's a show that is more than one month away.

WCW puts tickets on sale for its 11/23 World War III at the Palace in Auburn Hills, MI, announcing nothing locally except a 60-man three-ring Battle Royal and that WCW, the NWO, "exciting cruiserweights" and "high flying Mexicans" would appear, sending Larry Zbyszko and Bobby Heenan to do local promo work. By the end of the first day of ticket sales on 10/17, they had already sold 7,268 tickets for $247,671. The company all-time record house was set for the 6/9 Nitro in Boston which was $243,946. As of the end of business on 10/20, the Detroit totals were 9,153 tickets sold for $306,971, making it the first show in WCW history ever to break the $300,000 mark.

In the 80s, Jim Crockett Promotions, which was the predecessor to today's WCW, did break the $300,000 mark on a few major occasions such as Starrcades in Greensboro and Atlanta. WCW will actually break the $300,000 barrier for the first time at the Halloween Havoc PPV on 10/26 in Las Vegas, as they are expecting a gate in the $315,000 to $325,000 range with 2,200 tickets still left unsold as of press time. One of the reasons these gate records are falling is because the ticket prices for WCW have been raised considerably as the live events, and in particular the Nitros and PPV dates, have become so much more of an in-demand ticket.

It's become a really weird psychology when it comes to wrestling fans, in that there is a huge demand for high-price tickets in particularly the major markets, but lower priced tickets are difficult to sell, and the frequent Monday sellouts have been done simply by raising ticket prices across the board. On the surface, it makes no sense, but it again proves that pro wrestling tickets are an impulse rather than a rational buy, and thus normal economic factors in regard to pricing don't apply.

NOVEMBER 24

To the surprise of virtually nobody, World Championship Wrestling broke its all-time gate record once again on the first day tickets went on sale for the Hulk Hogan vs. Sting WCW title match headlining Starrcade' 97 on 12/28 at the new MCI Arena in Washington, DC.

First day sales on 11/15 were 11,036 tickets for $389,910. All of the expensive tickets went almost immediately, leaving only $15 tickets remaining in the building which at this point is being set up right now for an 18,975-seat capacity, although that number usually changes slightly once they set up the PPV and open up more seating. As of the end of business on 11/17, those numbers had increased to 12,501 tickets sold for $423,431. Since the show is still six weeks away, a sellout is a virtual lock and the gate is projected to be in the neighborhood of $537,000, which would be the largest live wrestling gate ever in the United States by a company other than the World Wrestling Federation.

The WCW all-time record will be set on 11/24 in Detroit, which will be the company's first show ever to top $300,000. As of the end of business on 11/17, the numbers for World War III were 13,882 tickets sold for $393,520 with 2,200 tickets left remaining. Up until the recent Halloween Havoc show on 10/27, no WCW event had ever topped $250,000.

The all-time record for Jim Crockett Promotions, the predecessor to the current WCW, was for Starrcade '86 at the Omni in Atlanta headlined by Ric Flair vs. Nikita Koloff which drew about $380,000, and the Starrcade at the Omni main event the previous year of Flair vs. Dusty Rhodes did nearly the same similar figure. The famous Ric Flair vs. Kerry Von Erich match at Texas Stadium in 1984 drew $402,000, while all of the $500,000 plus gates in North American history, of which there have been in the neighborhood of 15, were for major WWF events, mostly WrestleManias.

While the WWF has definitely sold more than 11,000 tickets on the first day for a few major events in the past (the record is believed to be 22,000 tickets on the first day for the 1990 WrestleMania match headlined by Hulk Hogan vs. Ultimate Warrior), the first day gate figure is certainly among the two or three biggest in North American history.

For world pro wrestling history, the SummerSlam on August 29, 1992 at Wembley Stadium in London sold more than 55,000 tickets (perhaps far more than 55,000 tickets as there have been claims as high as 80,000 although tickets actually were on sale for months after the big first day and the live estimate was a crowd in the 75,000 range) the first day which is believed to be the all-time record.

The biggest Tokyo Dome shows (the 1989 UWF's Akira Maeda vs. Willie Wilhelm and New Japan's 1995 Keiji Muto vs. Nobuhiko Takada matches) that have sold in the 30,000 to 40,000 range of tickets on the first day, all of which would be first day sales in the several million dollar range. The 11/9 K-1 event at the Tokyo Dome sold out all 54,500 tickets the first hour tickets were on sale for a gate that probably topped $5 million.

Chapter Thirty Six

WWF Controversy

DECEMBER 1

Bischoff in a Prodigy chat ripped WWF for the degree of sexual content and racial overtones that play during children's programming in the morning:

> *I read a copy of his [Vince McMahon] online chat where he compared the sexual content and racial content of his program, and he said he isn't doing things that haven't been done before and he singled out NYPD Blue. That's the kind of poor judgment that if he does go out of business, he has nobody to blame but himself. While NYPD Blue has exposed derrieres and sexual content, one only has to look at the advertisers that ABC includes in that programming and you'll see that clearly that program is targeted toward adults, while McMahon's programming is clearly targeted to children, in many cases children under 12 years old. For the USA Network and Vince McMahon to suggest that it's OK to produce programming with the degree of sexual content, racial overtones and in my opinion general bad taste while obviously selling their program to advertisers that are targeting children's toys and candy, I think it's nothing short of professional and social irresponsibility on the part of McMahon and the people who work with him, and the USA Network.*

On the subject of creative control by wrestlers:

> *Given the circumstances that we unfortunately all witnessed, or at least have knowledge of, with regards to the Bret Hart situation, it's clear to see why wrestlers would want creative control. If you can't trust the people you work with and for, it's very difficult to put your career in the hands of people who if given half a chance would attempt to ruin your career. Actors have an opportunity to look at a script before they accept a role, and then decide whether they want to risk their career with a specific script or director. Wrestling isn't like that, as we all know. There is a big difference. I think violation of trust is one of the things that has created the kind of atmosphere that I have heard exists in the WWF locker room.*

DECEMBER 22

After getting past the turmoil regarding the ending of Bret Hart's tenure and the finish of the Survivor Series match, the World Wrestling Federation is now facing even more controversy coming from three different fronts, all of which in some ways are related to Shawn Michaels.

The WWF's more risqué edge set a new standard for being gross on the 12/8 Raw show from Portland, ME. On the show, Michaels did an interview going on in descriptive detail about "a big smelly turd," describing Owen Hart as being a small piece of the turd that keeps coming back up no matter how many times he flushes the toilet.

Later in the show after doing an angle where he'd removed all his clothes with the exception of his underwear, he looked right at the camera and grabbed and shook whatever was in his pants. This has raised some issues about the direction of the company when talking about its past marketing and some of its current marketing toward young children. The recent characterizations of Goldust and Luna with the illusions of having an S&M bondage relationship have also come under the same criticism.

There is talk within the industry that the Los Angeles Times will be running a major story in the Entertainment section in approximately one week regarding the contradiction of WWF running adult-oriented programming and storylines while having its television shows viewed by a young audience which includes a sizable children under 12 audience, and the shows are even being sponsored by products aimed directly at a very young audience.

Phil Mushnick of the New York Post is also expected to run some sort of a short item regarding the Michaels interview, although it's expected he'll be an equal opportunity critic and also bringing up WCW in regard to the Raven's cult angle and ECW for using porn star Jenna Jameson.

With reports in the industry of the Los Angeles article being on its way and faced with some severe criticism of the 12/8 show, the WWF fired its own preemptive strike on the 12/15 Raw in a short taped interview by Vince McMahon that appeared to have been done earlier in the day.

McMahon stated that the WWF was changing because they want to entertain the wrestling fans in what he described as a "more contemporary manner." He categorized the new direction as more broad-based entertainment and tried to compare the programming with music videos, soap operas, Jerry Springer, Seinfeld and King of the Hill. He attempted to get pro wrestling, with the sports entertainment term used, as positioned as more entertainment, which because it is accepted as not being real, has a wider latitude toward what is acceptable than in a sporting event, saying they use the term sports entertainment even though they are entertainment simply because there are great athletes and great athleticism involved.

He said the public was tired of the same old good guys against bad guys, using those terms in a very condescending manner, and said the days of superheros telling kids to say their prayers and take their vitamins are passe. McMahon tried to come off as a nice guy, toning down some of the self righteous arrogance that made him such a big heel in his televised comments on Bret Hart.

Without exactly saying so, he gave the impression that they would tone down the first hour of Raw, that the second hour would be more risqué saying it was geared toward a more mature audience, and that most of the objectionable material from this point forward would be edited from the morning shows. He talked about the new direction causing a "huge increase" in the Raw ratings, which is an overstatement to a few week trend caused mainly from curiosity over a unique finish to a well-hyped match and every week attempting to keep that story alive.

A combination of Nitro going three hours with the debut of Bret Hart and one of the hottest football games in years featuring the attempted miracle of the Jerry Rice return and the Joe Montana retirement ceremony put the Raw ratings back to its old level with a 2.71 rating (2.85 first hour; 2.58 second hour) and a 4.14 share. Nitro, probably somewhat due to Hart, did far better than expected going in against such strong football competition doing a 4.11 rating (4.38 first hour; 3.88 second hour; 4.08 third hour) and 6.30 share while the Nitro replay did a 1.55 rating and 4.19 share.

On the 12/15 show, which was taped before word of these articles surfaced, but the commentary was done live, Kevin Kelly and Michael Cole referred to Billy Gunn as B.A. Billy Gunn, without saying the words "bad ass" in the first hour. During the second hour, Owen Hart went on an obscenity-laced tirade worked shoot style interview with all the questionable language edited out. Plenty of questionable language in interviews by Steve Austin on the bridge and tapes involving Austin and Vince McMahon and their incident the previous week was readily visible through even a cursory reading of lips.

The fact is that things are only going farther in that direction, as on the 12/11 Raw show taped in Lowell, MA for airing on 12/22, there is a segment where Michaels and Hunter Hearst Helmsley both remove all their clothing with the exception of t-back speedos, revealing the words "Merry" and "Christmas" written on their respective butt cheeks. And there remain weekly attempts to get Sable into as little clothing as possible, the end result making Sable on tour this weekend in at least some of the cities actually get a bigger pop than Undertaker.

There is no question the WWF has been trying, actually for more than one year although it's gone farther in this direction over the past several weeks, to change from being a kiddie-oriented show to appeal more to early 20s males, the group most likely to buy tickets to arena events and the group most likely to create a heated atmosphere in the buildings. It is an obvious reaction toward losing the Monday night ratings war to WCW, which actually popularized the "bad attitude" wrestlers with the NWO spray painting, pointing to their crotch and saying "Bite me." Due to fear of potential sponsor backlash, WCW has attempted of late to differentiate itself from WWF and Eric Bischoff has ordered some of that behavior when it comes to gestures, language and phraseology to be toned down.

The Raw show airs from 9 p.m. to 11 p.m. on the USA Network, and there is nothing more sexual or for that matter more violent on the Raw program than USA regularly runs during those hours on other nights of the week. There are arguments, such as were expressed during the Brian Pillman/Steve Austin gun angle, that pro wrestling looks too real to get away with the same things that occur with regularity of a violent drama or a t&a tease show, as much of the USA network's late night programming is combination of.

However, much of the Raw show is also repeated on both Saturday and Sunday mornings, and very little has been edited out. If the WWF is going to put most of the more risqué material in the second hour War Zone show, that was a recent decision in face of the heat as the Michaels/Helmsley deal wearing nothing but their jocks was taped for the start of the first hour on 12/22. It is believed that material, along with the Goldust/Luna interviews and angles, will largely be edited off the weekend morning television shows. In different countries where television broadcast standards are different, lots of things going on Raw don't make it to the airwaves.

This of course brings up the question of standards in pro wrestling. Please. Pro wrestling has no standards. It will exploit deaths in a war to get its top babyfaces over. It will exploit deaths of its personnel to draw a television rating the next night. It will regularly advertise matches and talent knowing full well it isn't going to appear. To say it'll exploit the physical health of its competitors and then chew them up and spit them out is an understatement, although in that aspect it is in no way any better or worse than any sport with any kind of an injury rate. It will exploit almost any situation if there is a possibility it'll mean ratings or dollars.

Every business, including this one, should have standards. It just so happens in this one the standards are very low. The economic standards are that if it goes too far, its audience will constrict. In wrestling's past, this has happened numerous times with numerous promotions, although the nature of the desensitized audience today makes it less likely than in the past. A niche group like ECW can go very far since it's not drawing a general audience to begin with. A more mainstream group like WWF has an audience that it may turn off by going too far off the deep end.

But at this point there are no signs that is happening, even though people express the fear this direction will end up with that result. Television ratings are up. That probably can be credited in most part due to the curiosity over the Survivor Series finish and the aftermath regarding Bret Hart, but there is no evidence any of these risqué angles have resulted in any measurable number of people turning off their television sets in disgust either. Arena attendance hasn't shown any decline, in fact overall, it is on the rise.

And the decline in the buy rate of the 12/7 PPV from the one the month before is more attributable to the television more being focused on burying a guy who wasn't there and less on pushing the main event challenger combined with the unusual circumstances leading up to making the November main event a hot ticket, and not due to a turn-off because of the controversial nature of the angles or television behavior of some of the top stars (other than in the case of Michaels, having him spend more time getting over his past opponent than his future one in his television interviews leading to the PPV).

My feeling on parents who have kids watching is simple. When the WWF started down this path, there were parents probably caught in a squeeze with them watching something with their kids that they didn't realize was coming. That day is over. The direction is clear, although I think the Raw show, and the second hour for sure, would best be served having a TV-M rating as opposed to TV-PG since that's what those ratings were designed for in the first place.

I personally had a lot of qualms regarding pro wrestling when it was aimed to young children in the 80s, particularly the idea that Hulk Hogan's name was used as a vitamin pitchman for vitamins aimed at young children when he himself attained his stardom in wrestling largely through using excessive amounts of steroids and he was hardly alone in that contradiction as the entire business was marketed to young children filled with performers where steroids had become a staple of their diet.

Then again, there are plenty of NBA players with dolls sold at Christmas and people who are close to the NBA can point out similar contradictions between public perception and reality. By the way, because somebody else does the same thing doesn't make it any less of a contradiction. At this point if parents have a problem with the content, they need to know and after a week or two of viewing should know what it is and where it is going, and they should act appropriately. Don't blame the producers of the movie "Scream 2" if you take your young children to the movie and they end up being scared during some of the scenes. At the same time, don't blame the media for investigation and criticizing when standards of practice reach new lows, the shows air on weekend mornings and still have a sizable young childrens audience, and where many of the sponsors themselves aim their products toward children.

The WWF has not only opened itself up for criticism but is asking for it. They can either modify the product or decide to attempt to weather the storm, although the latter approach does have its risks. There has been no audience backlash nor any sponsor backlash at this point. But for anyone to predict what the long-term of this will or won't bring would be foolish.

The WWF was hit hard on many fronts in the early 90s and the problems did not immediately affect the business side. But in the long term, its business and for that matter the entire industry, took a major tumble and the result was several years of multi-million dollar losses for both WWF and WCW (although WCW was going to lose money at that point in time no matter what the economic climate was).

The entire industry started rebounding in 1996 and this past year has been one of the most profitable in this country in many years. If the lessons of what took it down in the past are ignored, the probability is that it'll eventually in some form go down again for the same ignoring of warning signs.

Yet, that is hardly the only controversy related to the product. Over the past week, coming in the wake of the Bret Hart fiasco in the Survivor Series finish, two of the WWF's three remaining top stars, Steve Austin and Shawn Michaels, dropped their respective singles championships (Michaels losing the European belt and not the WWF belt) without either doing a job.

In the case of Austin, the original plan was for him to lose the title at the 12/7 PPV to Rocky Maivia. When he balked, a compromise was worked out where instead he got over his defiant anti-establishment role, Maivia got the title although the reasons clearly made no sense and Austin didn't have to do a job. As best we can tell, there was no heat regarding what ended up happening as everyone involved in the decision making process was comfortable with the compromise, although the end result was a storyline that made no logical sense in regard to Maivia ending up with the title.

The approach Austin took, basically since the current plan is for him to win the WWF title at WrestleMania from Michaels, is that since he's headlining Mania, he didn't think it would be good for him to do a high-profile job to a heel who is just getting established as a top name like Maivia, even though no doubt the finish would have involved tons of outside interference. Not to mention that unlike in his past, his physical limitations wouldn't allow him to put on a great match in a losing effort.

Whether one agrees with the logic or his side of things, and it isn't believed that he has creative control clause in his deal with Vince McMahon like Hart did, there is a logical argument that can be made if you want to take that side. Austin shouldn't be the IC champion today. He's unable to work lengthy singles matches and that title belt won't make him any more of a star than not having it. The title belt will be a big help in elevating Maivia, although he would be helped that much more as a new superstar if he actually won the belt from Austin.

At the same time, the argument could be made that Austin should be protected from doing a job since he is going to headline Mania not to mention that he's currently the hottest star in the industry. Should he wrestle Maivia with his limitations, unless they had a truck parked in the aisle again as a gimmick and had D-Lo Brown going through the windshield, they would be hard pressed to have a good match. But that line of logic hardly makes sense for the second scenario.

At the 12/11 tapings in Lowell, MA, Michaels dropped the European belt to Helmsley. It started out with the aforementioned interview where they ended up in nothing but their jocks. Sgt. Slaughter then came out and said that since Michaels hadn't defended the European title in more than 60 days, that he was ordering a title match to be held later in the show and that Michaels' opponent would be Helmsley. At one point, which will likely be during the first segment of the second hour, the match begins, however Owen Hart did a run-in before it ever got off the ground.

The match was then teased until the end of the show, and the two did a mock slow-motion match (imagine this, an overtly fake pro wrestling match) ending with Michaels literally laying down for Helmsley and getting up and crying mockingly about how sad he was for losing the title, and Slaughter, vowing to not be made a fool of, ordering Helmsley to defend the title against Hart on the ensuing Raw, which will air live on 12/29 from the Nassau Coliseum.

Since this scenario hasn't completely unfolded, we'll just look at the logic defying in it. With Michaels holding the European title (which he originally was given since he wouldn't job for Davey Boy Smith in England but was then given it presumably to set up doing a later job in April for Smith on the second England PPV show, which obviously also is never going to happen), it created the perfect opportunity for the WWF to create a new world title contender and someone who could be put in the position vacated by Bret Hart, whether it be Dude Love, Owen Hart, Ken Shamrock, Vader or someone else. That wrestler could pin Michaels cleanly and win a title, albeit a secondary title, which would logically spin off in the wrestler holding the clean win in a title match over the WWF champion but with the WWF belt not at stake, getting a WWF title run either on PPV or at the house shows in the early part of 1998.

Instead, Michaels, to avoid doing the logical job and a time when the job would have helped business and done nothing to hurt him since he's maintaining the theoretical top spot in the company as WWF champion, instead got the belt moved over to Helmsley, whose dropping it to any of the aforementioned wrestlers or anyone else wouldn't carry anywhere close to the boost of them to the next level. We aren't clear whether it was Michaels suggestion to give the belt to Helmsley so he could avoid doing the job when asked to drop it, or the promotion simply recognizing all the problems inherent in asking Michaels to do a job (when the real job they need without any compromise is the one to Austin) and coming up with the scenario as a way to get the belt onto somebody else without ruffling Michaels' feathers at this point coming in the wake of Austin not doing a job when he was originally asked isn't clear.

For those keeping score, that makes of Michaels' nine championship reigns in his WWF tenure (three WWF titles, three IC titles, two tag team and one European) he's done exactly two jobs to drop them, both in situations where it was a short known turnaround (WWF title to Sid, IC title to Marty Jannetty) until he got the respective belts back.

In the excuse category, there was one career ending knee injury, there was one walking out after a fight claiming unsafe working conditions, there was a break-up of a team rather than dropping a tag title, there was one quitting the promotion, there was one stemming from a concussion in an out of the ring skirmish and there was this most creative one of all. That makes him either the most clever or the least professional champion of our era, not to mention arguably the most talented to keep getting titles with his track record.

Even though the end result is the same, there is an obvious huge distinction in where the problems lie in the process that led to the end result of this specific instance. Not to mention the environment all these things is leading to, and the four DQ endings on the last PPV for a promotion that for most of this year has attempted to run mainly clean finishes but in recent months has become nothing but run-in DQs in the top matches, seems to indicate that problem is getting even more out of hand.

Chapter Thirty Seven

WWF and UFC Working Together

DECEMBER 15

The world of NHB and traditional style pro wrestling again came closer together with a working agreement between the UFC and WWF that resulted in the announcement by the former of a Ken Shamrock vs. Nobuhiko Takada match, the first NHB match-up between huge name pro wrestlers, on its 12/21 PPV show from the Yokohama Arena.

And even stranger than the alliance between reality fighting and the historical masters of fiction is whether or not this match will actually take place. Shamrock, with the approval of the WWF, signed for the match on 12/4, and SEG officially released it on its web site the next day. However, this news was strangely never announced by the Japanese group that is running the local promotion for the show, nor did the WWF say anything about the match either on the 12/7 PPV show, in which Shamrock was in the main event, or its live Raw show the next night, despite an apparent agreement with SEG to push the match.

The word is that WWF is planning to tape a feature of Shamrock training for the Takada match and insert it into the 12/15 Raw show, and use it to plug the UFC PPV on 12/21, although by ignoring the match completely on 12/7 and 12/8, it shows that the WWF is at best going to mention the match but not make a big deal of the match. The WWF will also have the rights to use the match after the fact on its television should it desire to do so. And the weirdest of all was at the Kingdom house show on 12/8, reporters there talked with Takada, who once again claimed, as he has publicly in the past, that he is suffering from a variety of injuries and wouldn't even be able to start training until the new year and claimed that he had never agreed nor would he be doing the UFC show.

As of press time, the situation regarding whether that match will take place or if Shamrock will appear on the show, perhaps against another opponent, are unclear.

The deal to get Shamrock to appear actually started several weeks back. SEG made the WWF an offer believed to be in the $100,000 range for Shamrock to appear on the show, and WWF turned it down flat because they had major plans for Shamrock and didn't want to risk either his health or his reputation in an environment where they weren't in complete control.

After that point, there were negotiations between SEG and WWF to secure Leon White (Vader) for the show, being that Vader was a huge drawing card in Japan as a pro wrestler with New Japan and UWFI (a worked shoot group) and a lot of wrestling fans believe he's tougher due to his size than people who train specifically for real fighting. WWF may have considered White, but eventually turned down that proposal with the feeling that due to their own roster being depleted with injuries, they didn't want to risk White's health since he was in their plans as well.

Although there were reports elsewhere putting the fact there were talks involving these two together and that their first match in Japan for FMW was booked in the manner it was specifically to build up a rematch, at no point was it ever considered having a shoot or a worked match with Shamrock vs. Vader on the UFC PPV show. Also, it has been made clear that at no point was SEG interested in having any pro wrestlers, no matter how big their names, do the show in any kind of a worked situation.

The talks largely were dormant until word came from Japan that Takada would only do the show if his opponent would be Shamrock. With ticket sales for the live event slow due to not having a big name Japanese draw, it was felt imperative to get Takada to do the show. SEG more than doubled the offer to the WWF for Shamrock at that point, at which point the WWF became very interested. It is believed the money offer is actually largely coming from SEG's Japanese partners, a group headed by a Mr. Sakata with money backing from Tsutya Video, a Blockbuster-like chain in Japan.

After a few days of negotiating and the price changing upwards once again to where it would be by far the biggest payoff in the history of UFC, and among the biggest for a pro wrestler or NHB fighter for one match in history (Rickson Gracie reportedly earned more for his Tokyo Dome match with Takada, and it isn't in the range of Hogan's major PPV payoffs), Shamrock signed the deal. The contract terms it is believed give Shamrock veto power over choice of a new opponent in the event of a late substitution. In the past, Shamrock had expressed interest in fighting either Vitor Belfort (who doesn't have a signed opponent at press time for the show) or Tank Abbott (who is scheduled at press time to appear in a tournament), but whether he'd want to do so with only one week of training is another question.

From a business standpoint, if correctly promoted, Takada-Shamrock should have a lot of curiosity and some box office impact in Japan, although with it going in "cold" (no storyline build-up) and not much time to get the pub out, not to mention no major office with weekly television to promote the match, it is by no means enough to guarantee a huge crowd at Yokohama Arena by itself.

For the U.S., Takada's name means nothing and UFC has no television so for it to mean anything from a business standpoint, it would have to be largely through whatever hype the WWF would give the match in hyping Shamrock, which at this point doesn't look like all that much if any. It is also interesting that Shamrock will be doing the show along with several people he's had a hand in training, his brother Frank, who faces Kevin Jackson in the under-200 title match, Maurice Smith, who faces Randy Couture in the heavyweight title match, and Telligman, who is an alternate in the heavyweight tournament.

Why Takada, 35, whose only true shoot match was his one-sided loss to Rickson Gracie (although he's been victorious in double-cross situations with Koji Kitao and former heavyweight champion boxer Trevor Berbick and was a world champion pro wrestler and a tremendous drawing card with UWFI before being one of the greatest workers in the world in the late 80s with New Japan but working credentials mean nothing in the octagon), would insist on Shamrock raises several questions.

It could be that since Shamrock, a former UFC heavyweight champion and the first King of Pancrase champion, who has a NHB record of 6-2-2 (although both draws would have likely win wins had their been judges), is already a major star in Japan with a tremendous shooter reputation, that Takada could risk a loss to him without devouring whatever is left of his falling reputation. It also could be that Takada feels it would be okay from a reputation standpoint, not to mention not as punishing, to lose to a mat submission expert as opposed to slugging it out with someone who would be more likely to deliver a knockout blow. Or it could be that Takada recognizes that Shamrock, 33, is on the road with the WWF in a very brutal road schedule, and that he can't possibly be in top fighting shape and maybe he can catch him at less than his best and a victory would totally rehabilitate his reputation after the relatively easy Gracie win.

But even with only one week of serious fighting training, Shamrock would be considered a heavy favorite in this situation and of the reasons, the first would seem to have the most validity. The risk Shamrock is taking by going into this match is probably more of a risk of injury, as he's suffered numerous injuries in his fighting career, than a risk of losing.

Takada's main weapon is that he can kick extremely hard, although he's not experienced in using that in legitimate competition and certainly not against a fighter with Shamrock's experience in mixed matches. Shamrock has fought and beaten both Maurice Smith and Bas Rutten in legitimate Pancrase matches and Don Nakaya Neilsen (a former WKA World cruiserweight kickboxing champion) in a mixed shoot match at a Tokyo Dome pro wrestling card, all of whom one would think kick as hard or in some cases quite a bit harder.

While in Pancrase, Shamrock only lost one legitimate kick/submission rules match (he lost a kickboxing match to a trained kickboxer from The Netherlands), to Masakatsu Funaki and that was largely to avoid any kind of an injury since the match was only a few days before the second Gracie match in UFC. His other loss, his Pancrase championship loss to Minoru Suzuki, was a Pancrase business decision before the first match with Dan Severn in that Pancrase didn't want to risk having their world champion lose to a world champion in the world of pro wrestling, even though Shamrock beat Severn in that match.

Shamrock, after signing for the match, did a WWF house show in Providence, RI on 12/6 but only did about a 30 second squash match to avoid getting banged up. He followed it up working a hard 18:29 on PPV against Shawn Michaels in the main event of the PPV, before flying to Dallas and missing the television tapings to begin training with Guy Mezger, Tra Telligman and Peter Williams for only about one week before leaving for Japan. But at press time, Takada's statements make everything questionable.

Which makes two major NHB main events that are unclear as the rival KRS promotions announced for its Pride Two show on 1/18 at the same Yokohama Arena, a main event of Royce Gracie vs. Mark Kerr. Kerr has a contract with SEG which prohibits him from appearing in any televised fights (this show will be taped for television) and from doing any NHB shows 30 days before or after an SEG show and a court date is set for 12/19 to determine whether Kerr has the legal right to do the show.

A secondary question is whether or not a court in New York has legal jurisdiction over stopping a fight in Japan even though the contract was signed in New York. Nothing was officially announced as far as the rules of the fight although that has been a sticking point. Obviously Gracie would want no time limit and no stand-ups for lack of action and eliminating head-butts, which would theoretically be one of Kerr's most valuable lessons while on top caught in the guard. Kerr wants as close to no rules as possible (i.e. head-butting legal) and since it will be fought in a ring rather than an octagon, netting under the bottom ropes so Gracie can't roll out of the ring.

The Japanese promoters will likely insist of some sort of a time limit (Kerr may agree to the stipulations that if Gracie lasts the time limit, than rather than having judges, that Gracie be awarded the victory just for hanging on because of the expected 75 pound weight differential) and make wearing grappling gloves mandatory, but Gracie is against wearing gloves. Gracie also wants the referee to not have the power to stop the match.

The first Pride One Event, on 10/9 at the Tokyo Dome, was the first PPV event ever in Japan and drew an 8.0 buy rate, although with the limited universe that is actually 12,000 buys out of a universe of only 150,000 homes. Even so, that was considered a phenomenal success even though the number of homes makes it likely not profitable nor was profit ever considered any kind of realistic proposition from the PPV at this stage of the game. The buy rate does show the potential in Japan for NHB (and even more so pro wrestling) when PPV technology reaches the U.S. level. Even with the Japanese debut of Royce Gracie, the second event is not going to be put on PPV.

On paper, Gracie vs. Kerr looks to be among the most intriguing NHB fights in years, and also perhaps one of the most boring. Gracie, 11-0-1, who hasn't fought since going to a 36:00 draw with Shamrock in 1995 in a match that had their been judges, he would have likely lost via decision.

Kerr, a world class amateur wrestler who weighed 255 pounds in his most recent UFC appearance, 7-0, has been victorious in three consecutive tournaments, two in UFC and another in Brazil, without every being on the defensive. Kerr has won almost all of his matches in rapid order with the exception of a one-sided and brutal 30:00 decision against Fabio Gurgel, a Brazilian Jiu Jitsu expert with a similar style and considered to have similar level of abilities to Gracie.

Unless Kerr makes a quick mistake, the match figures to go to the ground with Gracie hanging onto the guard. Gracie figures to take the most punishment, and if he can catch Kerr unaware in a submission, he can beat him, but if he can't, it's largely going to be the defensive posture and trying to avoid serious blows and wait out the time for Kerr to make a mistake since points aren't awarded for aggressiveness.

Also announced for Pride Two are Renzo Gracie (4-0-2) vs. karate expert Sanae Kikuta, Juan Mott (MARS; 1-1) vs. Akira Shoji (1-1-2; best known for his 30:00 draw with Renzo Gracie at the Tokyo Dome), Branko Cikatic (the 42-year-old former K-1 champion) vs. Ralph White, another kickboxer in a rematch of their Tokyo Dome no contest match and Marco Ruas (6-1-1) against TBA, who is rumored to be Brazilian Roberto Traven (4-0).

DECEMBER 22

The proposed Ken Shamrock vs. Nobuhiko Takada UFC match on the 12/21 PPV show from Yokohama fell apart during the week with Shamrock's appearance on the show being canceled. In addition, over the weekend Vitor Belfort's fighting on the show was in question although now appears to be back on, but against what almost appears to be a hand-picked opponent.

Shamrock and the World Wrestling Federation agreed to terms, which Shamrock signed on 12/4 for a payoff which would have been in the range of double UFC's previous record single-event payoff of $150,000 for the Takada match. However, as noted last week, on 12/8, Takada when asked about the match at the Kingdom house show, said that he had no intention of fighting on the UFC show and was suffering from several injuries that would make it impossible for him to even begin training until early next year.

Semaphore Entertainment Group, which signed Shamrock after being given the word that Takada, whose drawing power was considered almost a must given slow ticket sales for the live event at the 17,100-seat Yokohama Arena, would only do the show if Shamrock was his opponent, must have fallen victim to a communication breakdown somewhere along the chain regarding its Japanese partners doing the house show promotion and Takada himself.

Those close to the situation claim Takada had never agreed to do the show in the first place, although SEG had spoken of his participation as a possibility ever since its press conference in Japan, and how things got to the situation they did are perplexing to say the least. Kingdom had its first televised card on 12/14 with Takada doing the color commentary, and during the show Takada was asked about when he'd return to the ring and Takada didn't give a definitive answer, saying only that he would begin training early next year.

To make things even more muddy, Shamrock's contract reportedly guaranteed him the money once it was signed even if the fight was canceled, which it ended up being. The WWF was also to get a sizeable booking fee as their end of the deal. However, the group on the hook, so to speak, for providing the big payoff in the contract was not SEG, but its Japanese co-promoters, who are attempting to get out of paying it claiming a contract loophole.

The contract provided, in the case of the opponent backing out, for Shamrock to have veto power if a substitute match was suggested. Since the deal to use Shamrock and pay the big money was not primarily due to whatever drawing power he'd bring to the U.S. PPV, although that was considered a helpful part of the deal, but more because it was the only way they believed to get Takada into the show, the decision was made that rather than offer Shamrock a new opponent, that his price tag was such that they decided his appearance would be scrapped to save themselves the big payoff.

Shamrock and the WWF officially got the word from SEG on 12/10, and Shamrock left what was reportedly a brutal high-intensity training camp in Dallas where he was trying to basically cram one months worth of training and conditioning into one week, and returned to the WWF for the television taping on 12/11 in Lowell,

MA and worked the weekend house shows in Tennessee and Arkansas.

The WWF never mentioned Shamrock's match on the 12/8 Raw show even though the contract was signed and they were at the time completely unaware of the problems regarding the match that had surfaced in Japan. However, they did plug the UFC PPV in a 30 second plugs, hyping in specific that it was coming from Japan and the appearance of Frank Shamrock challenging for the middleweight title on both weekend USA network shows and twice on the 12/15 Raw. Supposedly the WWF was going to give the UFC show and in particular the Ken Shamrock match with Takada a huge promotional push all weekend, and in particular on Raw.

There have been hints thrown that UFC will try and reach a compromise in that they'll book Shamrock on the May PPV when they are tentatively scheduled to return to Japan, in which case he'll get more advance notice and UFC and WWF will both have more time to use his name in promotion of the event and in conjunction with WWF storylines as well.

The fact that the March show will be in the U.S., and its proximity time-wise to WrestleMania make it highly unlikely WWF would even consider allowing him on the show nor that UFC would want to pay that kind of money without a Japanese partner footing the bill for what it would cost to get him on the show. But doing the second proposed May show in Japan is largely dependent upon the first show doing well, and that has many questions of its own.

Chapter Thirty Eight

Fan Riots

OCTOBER 6

The first loss by a Gracie since NHB became popularized in the United States with the advent of UFC in 1993, was averted by a riot on 9/27 at Rio de Janiero's Tijuca Tennis Club that turned into a real-life war zone and adds Rio to the places where the entire future of NHB is threatened.

Renzo Gracie (4-0-1) was facing Eugenio Tadeau, a famous Luta Livre fighter from Brazil, in the main event of a show called Pentagon Combat put on by Nelson Montiero when the Jiu Jitsu and Luta Livre practitioners at ringside began arguing and brawling and a full scale riot broke out and the match and show had to be stopped. Based on reports from Brazil, the fighting started in the stands early in the match when Gracie got the first take down and held the early advantage.

An estimated 150 to 200 Luta Livre practitioners, including many students of Tadeau, rushed the ring as their mentor was on the receiving end. One of Tadeau's students and seconds was kicking Gracie through the fence from ringside throughout the fight, and Gracie managed to deck him as he stuck his head over the cage throwing a punch that knocked him off the fence. At this point another second started trying to climb the fence, and Renzo's brother Ryan began fighting him.

However, even Gracie himself admitted that he blew up during the match, which he attributed to over training. He claimed to have "beaten the shit" out of Tadeau, who was bleeding from the lip, nose and underneath the eyes and had to be hospitalized after the match, but most reports felt the match was even overall. Most reports also indicated Tadeau, who needed 11 stitches to close one of the cuts, had taken control of the match when the riot got out of hand including reports of several gun shots fired in the air but luckily no one was hit by a shot.

At one point Gracie went down from a leg kick, which appeared to be out of exhaustion, and he stayed on the ground rather than standing back up, which was about 13:00 into the match which had been scheduled for three rounds of 15:00 each in duration. By this time the riot outside the ring had gotten even more out of control with the Jiu Jitsu and Luta Libre students fighting each other with chairs throwing. When chairs hit the ceiling lights and broke them as they fell into the ring, the place went dark and the match had to be stopped without a decision being rendered.

The brawl was said to have been the worst in recent memory at a Vale Tudo match in Brazil, and having seen tapes of some of the fights in the stands at those shows which go far beyond anything you'd ever see in the U.S., that is quite a statement, although reports were that nobody was seriously injured in the brawl. There was talk the next day that Vale Tudo may be banned completely from the city of Rio de Janiero because of the fan violence. Both the Mayor of the city and Governor of the state said they wanted NHB events banned because of the unruliness of the fans.

Tadeau gained fame in Brazil many years ago battling Royler Gracie to a 40:00 draw, in which according to some reports, he held the upper hand. He was scheduled to face Ralph Gracie at the final EFC PPV show, but a few weeks before the show the match was canceled under strange circumstances. The public report was that there were problems getting a visa for Tadeau, but Ralph Gracie also claimed before hand to have suffered an injury, a report others were dubious of.

The belief going in was that Renzo, who bulked up to 182 pounds for the fight, would be the larger of the two, since Eugenio fought years ago at 150-160 pounds, however he weighed in at 185 and Renzo Gracie told Vale Tudo News that he looked "juiced" and claimed he wasn't able to finish him by submission because he had oil all over his body which allowed him to slip out of his holds.

Gracie, who has another fight scheduled on 10/11 at the Pride One Japanese PPV show at the Tokyo Dome against Akira Shoji, considered an easy opponent, challenged Tadeau to a rematch but said he wanted the match in a closed gymnasium with nobody there except for one second for each fighter and someone to videotape the fight with the winner gets the rights to sell the tape.

NOVEMBER 10

It would make a good story, considering what the lead story was in last week's Observer, to try and tie in the stupid angle WCW did on its Halloween Havoc PPV with the fake fan getting beaten up with the subsequent two near riots that took place days later.

However, even though the timing of WCW's angle couldn't have been worse, as fan violence and a general lack of respect by fans to the product has become more of a problem largely as fans imitate their so-called heroes television behavior, the near riots may have had nothing to do with imitation being in this case, the stupidest form of flattery. In the first incident, it certainly didn't due to the location where it took place. In the second, it may or may not have, although the ECW situation on 10/30 was clearly an example of a group of fans going to matches with the specific intention of causing a disturbance and starting a fight with wrestlers.

The first such incident took place on 10/29 in Tijuana, the Mexican border city across from San Diego, where WCW PPV shows don't even air although the show did take place just two days after the WCW Nitro taping not all that many miles away in San Diego. The second took place the next night in Plymouth Meeting, PA at an ECW house show, although that incident from all accounts was a group of five fans going to the matches with the specific intention of getting into a fight.

The Tijuana situation at a Promo Azteca show came during a post-match angle after the main event—a 16 man elimination tag match with Konnan & El Hijo del Santo & La Parka & Rey Misterio & Dandy & Lizmark Jr. & Super Calo & Hector Garza beating Psicosis & Juventud Guerrera & Los Villanos IV & V & Damian & Halloween & Silver King & Zandokan. It came down to Lizmark Jr. and Psicosis, with Lizmark Jr. scoring a clean pin to win the match before about 3,500 fans at Auditorio Municipal, which between the match itself and the post match lasted 82 minutes making it probably the longest combination match and angle on a major league wrestling show probably in years.

At that point Psicosis began complaining about the officiating when Santo, who Psicosis had eliminated next to last in the match, hit the ring and jumped Psicosis. At this point Rey Misterio Jr., who didn't work on the show but was in attendance, hit the ring and jumped on Psicosis, but then also attacked Santo. The idea appeared to be to set up a triangle match between the three, tentatively on 11/14 in the same building, although that depends on several outside forces such as possible commission suspensions based on the riot and potential WCW intervention since the match involves Misterio Jr. and WCW doesn't want him wrestling in Mexico anymore.

Earlier this year Misterio Jr. and Santo had a classic match in Tijuana which resulted in Santo capturing the WWA middleweight title from Misterio Jr., and at the last Tijuana show, Psicosis scored a clean win over Santo in a match for a title belt that Psicosis was defending, not to mention Misterio Jr. and Psicosis' rivalry in that city dating back many years. However, since Santo has been put over big as a face in Tijuana, the crowd turned on Misterio Jr. when he attacked Santo. In their singles match earlier in the year, even though it was a total face vs. face style and Misterio Jr. definitely had his fans, it was Santo that was the more popular by a small degree.

Misterio Jr. and Santo exchanged words, and eventually Rey Misterio hit the ring, and first attacked Psicosis, but then also attacked Santo. Damian and Halloween then hit the ring and began fighting with Santo, who had no allies, and also helping Psicosis against the Misterios, at which point the crowd began chanting for Konnan to make the save, apparently they believed, for Santo. Konnan started attacking the rudos, but then also joined in with the other faces in attacking Santo, which caused the crowd to go nuts since it appeared Santo was alone against everyone.

A fan hit the ring and gave Misterio a dropkick. Another fan went to hit Misterio with a chair, but he ended up taking the chair from the fan which caused more fans to begin throwing chairs at the ring. Supposedly it wound up with more than 200 fans throwing chairs, and much of the rest of the audience, seeing that a riot was breaking out, leaving the building while this was all going on, before everything was calmed down. The idea they were apparently trying to portray is it being everyone for themselves for the triangle match, but with nobody helping Santo, it came off to the crowd that their long-time local heroes like Konnan and the Misterios had turned heel on Santo.

The next night at the ECW show at the National Guard Armory in Plymouth Meeting, PA saw a very different type of crowd disturbance. According to several witnesses, a group of three or five (the police claimed three people but some ringsiders said it was actually five) big tough-looking guys were at ringside at the ECW show looking for trouble from the start of the night. It was more likely coincidental the timing of this disturbance and the WCW angle, although there is always a possibility that the WCW angle glorifying fans fighting wrestlers may have put the idea into someone's head and that this is another example, and this may have been one harder to avoid than most, of problems that are happening with far too much frequency at ECW events.

The ring-leader, wearing a shirt that said "Fite Me" on the front and "Antichrist 3:16" on the back, were harassing the wrestlers throughout the show. One person close to the situation all night described those few as the worst group of wrestling fans ever to attend an ECW show. During the first match on the card, ECW security asked them to quit leaning over the rail and spitting and they shouted down security. The feeling was they should have been removed then and there, although Paul Heyman, defending his security team (which many fans close to the situation were critical of for not doing anything when it became apparent something bad was going to go down), claimed they were misbehaving but not doing anything that would warrant being thrown out. Others close to the situation said security realized to throw them out would end up starting a big fight and perhaps they were trying to avoid that.

The fans did cause some minor changes regarding working the matches in that the wrestlers were all avoiding where the fans were, and even Taz, whose gimmick is to stand up to fans, was avoiding doing anything near them. With just a few matches left in the show, with Axl Rotten & Balls Mahoney vs. New Jack & John Kronus wrestling in the ring, and time running out on Mr. Fite Me and his group, trouble started.

According to reports filed by two Plymouth, PA detectives who happened to be at the matches, Richard Lefler, 26, and Mark Cheskey, 23 of Conshohocken, were spitting on wrestler Jon Rechner (Mahoney). According to the report, when Rechner was outside the ring in their vicinity, Lefler punched him in the back. When Rechner turned around to see who hit him, Lefler punched him in the face. At that point Lefler grabbed his hair allowing Cheskey to get in a shot on him. At this point Rechner started covering his face and throwing wild blows to protect himself.

The ECW dressing room emptied at this point and it was ten to 20 minutes before the situation started getting back to order, with Mahoney, Axl Rotten, John Kronus, Shane Douglas, Tommy Dreamer and Buh Buh Ray and Big Dick Dudley among others joining in the fray. Reports are the Dudleys were going through the crowd like buzzsaws and that Big Dick seemed impervious to anything thrown at him almost like his pro wrestling gimmick.

By the time the incident was over, about half the crowd of 800 fans were outside the building either trying to get away from the near riot or some trying to get close to it as the five fans and the wrestlers fought. There were fans injured being too close to the wild swinging wrestlers and fans, although there were no reports of serious injuries although ambulance units were on the scene.

Just as the situation was calming down, approximately 40 police officers from several different neighboring municipalities including East Norristown, Norristown, Whitemarsh, Conshohocken, West Conshohocken and Whitpain, several dressed in riot gear and one with a police dog, arrived on the scene. Various reports from the scene claim that the wrestlers, who were trying to protect their own and whose actions were defended in the police report, in their exuberance, made things worse as far as getting the crowd all panicked, and that when the police arrived, the situation was calming down and their arrival made them worse again.

Others said it was simply a bad situation. There was additional heat since ECW, according to a local newspaper story, had failed to get a permit to hold the wrestling show in the city, which was expressly specified in the contract they signed with the building.

The incident made a lot of local press, both in the newspapers and was carried as a top local news item on most of the area radio stations.

Wrestlers Rechner and Jerome Young (New Jack) went to the police station for questioning, largely to have complaints filed against the two fans, who were expected to be arrested on charges of assault, disorderly conduct and harassment and the two fans were taken to jail that night. Paul Heyman said that he was going to order Rechner to testify against the fans to get them put away, even if it meant him missing a major show. Just as the dressing room emptied, Heyman grabbed New Jack to keep him from joining in on the fight, largely because any problems with New Jack could reflect badly on the company at this point with the Erich Kulas legal and civil situations still pending.

There were reports that the police wanted the show stopped at that point, however Paul Heyman denied that being a problem. After everything got under a little bit of control, Dreamer got on the p.a. and got the fans who had remained in the building back into the show by saying that they didn't want to let the action of three people ruin the night for everyone else, and they went through with the three-way dance main event with Sabu going over Douglas and Dreamer.

Not to be outdone, the WWF on its live Raw show on 11/3 did its own fan out of the audience angle with similar results, in this case glorifying it even more allowing the fan (former Stampede wrestling performer Steve Blackman, a one-time roommate of Brian Pillman in Calgary in 1988, who for the past decade has been living in Pennsylvania teaching martial arts), obviously a wrestler doing a martial arts gimmick the way the heels sold for him, who it appeared would wind up being the fourth member of the Team USA replacing Del Wilkes in the Survivor Series.

Fan out of the audience angles are as old as carnival wrestling itself, in fact the mark who isn't really a mark out of the audience was one of the classic carnival wrestling cons, but in this day and age with real fan violence becoming such a serious problem, encouraging and glorifying it in any company at this point in time, and to an extent all three major U.S. companies have, is irresponsible almost to mind-boggling levels.

Just as an example over the past week of something we know happened specifically due to the incident in Las Vegas. The very next night, at the WCW taping in San Diego, during the commercial break, a fan threw something and nailed Johnny Grunge and security did throw him out. But those sitting near the fan reported that the fan had been talking the entire show about doing a run-in for self-publicity, talking over-and-over again about how the fan who did the same thing the night before really didn't get hurt or didn't appear to get in trouble.

DECEMBER 22

More problems occurred at WWF house shows on 12/14 in Memphis and 12/15 in Little Rock, when, due to actions and decisions that appeared at least to people at the show to be by Michaels, the main event didn't take place at either show, resulting in a near riot in Memphis and a full-blown riot in Little Rock. In Memphis, the scheduled main event of Jerry Lawler & Jeff Jarrett vs. Michaels & Helmsley never took place.

Before a crowd of 5,078 fans at the Pyramid, Michaels, came out for his once per week scheduled arena match and was met with so much garbage thrown his way that he simply refused to wrestle and the show ended without the match ever taking place. As it was described to us, the show itself was poor and the crowd, many of whom had been drinking heavily, were getting unruly even before the main event. Michaels was hit with a few cokes, and a large wad of tobacco juice nailed Helmsley in the face, at which point Michaels grabbed the house mic and said, "Well, that just cost you your main event," and walked out of the ring with Helmsley and Chyna.

When the crowd realized what had happened, they got even more unruly. There was an attempt by Dude Love, who was at the event but couldn't wrestle due to fractured ribs, to get the crowd to chant "HBK" to get Michaels to change his mind and wrestle but he refused to come back out. Finally Lawler tried to apologize to the crowd, but the crowd pelted the home town hero with debris after chanting for Lawler and Jarrett to wrestle each other and Lawler responding by saying that since he didn't have a contract to wrestle Jarrett that match "couldn't" take place. That combined with no refunds being offered when some fans began demanding them at the box office made the mood of the fans even worse with the general feeling leaving the building among many fans according to our reports is the WWF had killed the city for themselves and fans swearing that they'd stick with WCW.

Of course with the big promotions running so infrequently in specific markets, usually the fans forget a bad show by the time the next show comes to town. However, WBII, the Memphis area television station that broadcasts the syndicated show in the market, received more than 130 complaining phone calls from fans that attended the house show by early the next morning due to the main event fiasco, and in addition that morning, another group of fans who attended the show were picketing the television station from the start of business until noon, claiming to be in protest against the tactics of the WWF.

Based on the report we had of the incident, the fans actions could not be blamed strictly or even largely on Michaels inciting them as much as a few fans being drunk and out of control. However, this situation came close to happening in other cities where Michaels' gimmick is to incite the audience into throwing things at him, including in at least a one recent case by saying things like he's heard the fans in (insert city) have terrible aim, thereby making himself the target for every object every idiot has nearby. It was Michaels who decided to walk out when the fans were so unruly.

The WWF backed Michaels up in Memphis claiming WWF officials were the ones who decided to end the show early for the safety of all concerned, although that decision actually made the arena even more unsafe because it only made the fans behavior worse.

They blamed the problem on local security that didn't search fans as they entered the arena as they routinely had done for other wrestling events in the city, and that allowed fans to bring bottles of alcohol into the building with them resulting in several drunk and unruly fans who had empty bottles in their possession.

The reports the WWF received from the agents on the road were the fans were throwing empty bottles, and there were Internet reports saying Michaels was hit with a bottle or with flying ice, although several live sources have denied Michaels was hit with either a bottle or ice.

The throwing of things began to get out of hand in the previous match between Shamrock and Phineas Godwinn, with Henry Godwinns' antics at ringside starting fans in the mood to pelt the ring, and when Michaels and Helmsley came out for their main event, they might as well had painted bullseyes on their faces.

Little Rock was even worse. According to several reports, the undercard for the show at the Barton Coliseum was terrible and even the densest marks were getting restless about the poor quality of the matches, in particular a terrible match with Kane vs. Chainz and an Undertaker vs. Rocky Maivia casket match that only lasted two minutes due to Undertaker being injured and having high blood pressure. In addition, fans were upset because the card that was taking place was completely different than the line-up that was advertised with no explanations given.

The scheduled main event was to be Shamrock, with Danny Hodge, one of the greatest real wrestlers who ever lived and was also the top pro wrestler in the area during the 60s and 70s as the perennial NWA world junior heavyweight champion, as his manager for one night only, against Helmsley, with Michaels in his corner, which drew 6,449 fans. We're not clear if that was going to happen as we received a report that Helmsley was going to face Dude Love in the main event, although that may not have been correct since Dude has fractured ribs and was supposed to only make appearances and not wrestle this week.

Since fans had no idea what was going to take place because everything had been changed, my impression is that the show was stopped when Michaels and the rest of DX walked out, and that neither Shamrock nor Hodge actually came out for the main event match before the show ended. Michaels and Helmsley came to the ring and began riling up the crowd that was already mad about the poor undercard.

Naturally they became target practice again, and when a piece of paper hit Michaels, he told the crowd that they had just lost their main event and walked out with Helmsley and Chyna. Fans, thinking it was just part of the act, didn't react right away. After several minutes, DX failed to come back in the ring, no opponent for Helmsley appeared, and the ring announcer said that they had refused to come out and the show was over.

At this point, a real riot started, with chairs and whiskey bottles being thrown everywhere including at police trying to get the crowd out of the building. The situation got so bad that the police had to spray the building with tear gas to get the fans outside. Several fans tried to get refunds and were unsuccessful and at that point a second riot took place in the parking lot before the police broke it up. At least one fan was rushed to the hospital but there didn't appear to be any serious injuries to fans either night.

This incident was so out of hand it was reported on the news later that night with at least one report giving the impression that the WWF wouldn't be allowed back in the city although with this all happening at deadline it is really too soon to figure out how this is going to unfold locally. The reports from this event live pointed the finger directly at Michaels for the problem starting, although the behavior of the fans was the actual real problem but unlike in Memphis, the real problems didn't occur until the fans realized that they weren't going to see the main event and that DX walking out wasn't simply part of the show to get heat.

Crowds pelting Michaels with garbage have become commonplace since he made his latest heel turn, but these were the first situations where a show ended abruptly and a main event never took place, although situations beforehand with Michaels and at some WCW house shows on the West Coast a few months ago threatened to get to this level and ECW was having fan problems on almost a regular basis of late and came close on a few occasions from nearly having a show stopped on them before the main event.

The actions of the wrestlers have encouraged fans throwing objects so even though it is a minority of fans, some if not most drunk and engaged in mob mentality, that are ruining things and making conditions dangerous for the rest of the fans and the wrestlers. The fact is Michaels' act encourages it, and in Little Rock, basically caused the riot by walking out.

Supposedly the difference between a professional top heel is they can rile the crowd up to a certain point, but calm them down before things get out of control. That fine line is easier to write about than totally control, but if the WWF hasn't gotten the message that the DX act at least on the road shows needs to be toned down, then whatever happens is being asked for at this point because Memphis was a warning. Actually there were many warnings before Memphis that clearly have been ignored by the WWF. Little Rock was no longer a warning. Little Rock was caused by ignoring warnings.

Hopefully 12/15 can be a wake up call for both WWF and WCW, because on the live Nitro that night in Charlotte, about a half-dozen fans at different points in the show hopped the guard rail and security was having a field day trying to stop them before hitting the ring, and at least three made it into the ring, one stomped on by Randy Savage, another pulled out by security and another snatched by ref Randy Anderson. It was described as the single most unruly crowd in the history of Charlotte wrestling, blamed in some part by being a three hour show with fans drinking for the entire three hours and lots of incidents of fans throwing things at the wrestlers.

As mentioned before, some day the drunk fan or fan looking to impress his friends on television isn't going to be smaller than Randy Anderson and the situation is going to get worse than it already has. In Charlotte, the main angle to end the show was totally botched up because so many fans were hitting the ring, ruining the built-up climax to the show.

WCW only has itself to blame. After the idiotic angle they ran to glorify fans hitting the ring at Havoc in Las Vegas, it was inevitable what would happen and the fiascoes in both Charlotte and Little Rock on 12/15 were not isolated instances, but the result of fans reacting as the promotions on television have "educated" them to act. If they don't get "educated" differently, this industry is going to blow its current level success, not due to risque programming or gutless booking of talent that thinks it is above the business, but due to an unforeseen tragedy taking place at one of its live events.

WCW officials after the Charlotte event said that they were going to institute a policy similar to the NFL, NHL and many concert acts in that drinking will be banned after the mid-point of the show at all their arena events. In addition, they are going to beef up security at the shows.

DECEMBER 29

After major problems screwed up shows over the past week in Charlotte, Memphis and Little Rock, it is apparent that changes have to be made given the current climate among wrestling fans and the direction of the promotions.

The World Wrestling Federation was forced into making a "damned if you do and damned if you don't" decision when crowds, apparently fueled by alcohol, became unruly throwing things at the wrestlers and creating a dangerous environment in both Memphis and Little Rock. The end damning result in both cities was the main event in each city being canceled, which in both cases made the crowds that much more upset and resulted in significant problems both nights among fans after the call to end the show.

The other call, given the behavior of the crowd throwing things could have meant serious injury from an errant or on target bottle, to either fans at ringside or wrestlers in the ring, although the call that was made almost guaranteed fairly serious problems, just not to the wrestlers.

In Charlotte, WCW at a live Nitro had so many problems with fans hitting the ring while the lights were being turned off for the climactic angle of the show involving Sting, that the angle never made it to the ring and ended up being botched to the point that there was an audible voice, which may have been Eric Bischoff's, in the ring swearing over a live mic about the angle.

The problems wouldn't be front page news if they were isolated incidents, or if one could truly say that it wasn't the result of problems that have been festering not only in WWF and WCW, but also in ECW for more than the past year.

The wrestling audience has in many cases changed from being a family mainstream suburbia crowd, if it truly ever was that, to a crowd largely consisting of the old stereotype white trash fans from another era. The fact is, and don't let anyone fool you about this, this new direction is working. WCW and ECW are doing record business for those companies and WWF is the most profitable the company has been since its business took a nosedive in the wake of the 1991-92 scandals. In November the WWF averaged 7,440 fans per show and over the month grossed $2.4 million in 20 house shows.

That's the best month for business since we started keeping a monthly tab on things in 1992, and without question, the $123,455 per show average would be the best average over a one month period in the history of the promotion and rank just behind WCW's September mark of this year as the best month, money-wise on a per show basis, in the history of the business. That is in some sense a misleading statement because prices for tickets are higher than ever but nonetheless is hardly misleading in showing that the popularity of pro wrestling at this point is on the rise.

Interest is the highest it has been since it lost semi-regular network television in this country nearly seven years ago. Merchandise is selling like never before, which shows the level of loyalties either to companies or to the top talent in that companies to be at a level that surpasses even the mid-80s peak period. While there are exceptions, generally the crowds at the arenas are hot. Everything should be great, but the direction that has made things hot is the same direction that has caused all the problems.

The current direction of wrestling, best exemplified by its coolest star in its universe, Steve Austin, is one of glorifying, among many things, defiance of authority. The crowds that go to see the top stars, whether they be Austin, Hulk Hogan, Kevin Nash & Scott Hall, Shawn Michaels or whomever else, are going to see their heroes that have been popularized in both companies by doing weekly anti-social behavior and getting away with it. No rules and no limits. Fans who rally behind those wrestling cultural symbols, whether they be young kids, or more violent prone older teens and early 20s males, are going to emulate that behavior.

And the problems aren't limited to the characterizations of the top stars. WCW glorified fans throwing things by capturing it on camera, starting with the Hulk Hogan turn in Daytona Beach. Fans at ringside, not to mention the NWO wrestlers, were getting hit by whatever fans had at their disposal to throw. Fans were taught, from television, as they always are and probably always will be, that the people who are important to pay attention to are the ones who get all the interview time, what holds are important and what holds aren't, and more importantly when it comes to these problems, that with your purchase price of a ticket to a pro wrestling event comes with it the right to use the heel wrestlers (that in many cases those same fans cheer for) as target practice at the end of the show.

Not that in recent weeks the WWF, with Degeneration X basically copying the NWO gimmick and trying to take it to the next step, hasn't taken over in giving its audience that feeling. Both companies as well have glorified fans hitting the ring. Nitro is a live television show and it's no secret that it draws big ratings to the point that a lot of fans believe the most important result of the week is not the winner or loser of the PPV match on Sunday, but the result of the ratings on Monday. Any drunk punk who wants to impress his friends knows he can hit the ring on Nitro, and the worst that will happen to him is he might take a few worked punches from Hulk Hogan, or get snatched by a 150-pound referee, neither of which on television looks to be all that awful a fate for a story you can brag about to your friends for weeks.

Both groups in recent months, WCW with the Vegas fan angle and WWF with the original Steve Blackman angle before Survivor Series, have glorified fans hitting the ring to attack heel wrestlers. ECW, which has actually had more crowd problems then both the other groups put together over the past year, took crowd participation one step farther by encouraging fans to bring weapons to hand to their favorite wrestlers to use in the matches. It is no wonder that in their trips into small town grungy suburbs of Philadelphia that local toughs would think a ticket to ECW wrestling enables them to bully fans and try to start a fight with the local scrub wrestlers who they believe to not really be big-time and don't respect as stars. The company is almost lucky situations haven't been worse, because there have been numerous situations where they came one step from being full-scale riots.

Which brings us to Little Rock. We have a lot more details on what took place on 12/15. It was a strange show, headlined by Ken Shamrock, with Danny Hodge in his corner, against Hunter Hearst Helmsley, with Michaels and Chyna in his. Earlier in the show they were going to do a special presentation to Hodge.

For reasons that make absolutely no sense other than he simply wanted to do it and has the juice to do what he wants, Michaels asked to present the award to Hodge as the top star of the WWF today. Forgetting that Michaels as a heel has been on television every week and even though Hodge was probably the biggest wrestling star in the area at one point, it's been more than 20 years since he was regularly featured on television. And forget the storyline that they were on opposite sides in the main event later in the show and the presentation was planned, nor did it lead to an angle to heat up the main event, but simply something Michaels talked agent Jack Lanza into doing out of respect for Hodge and ignoring the storyline itself.

Michaels felt his ability with words and to control the crowd would result in it being a dignified presentation. It ended up being target practice, which made everyone associated with the show that grew up watching Hodge totally embarrassed with the fans' treatment of the 65-year-old two-sport Hall of Famer. It probably did wonders for Michaels temperament for later in the show. As DX went out for the main event, it was more target practice.

From later reports, we understand that Helmsley got something thrown that hit him in the eye hard enough that his eye started swelling badly. Chyna was also hit with something in either her back or her neck hard enough that she was hurt. Although Michaels didn't get nailed with anything worse than paper, when Helmsley got nailed, he took it upon himself to call off the show. Shamrock never even made an appearance. And Michaels never got to work his angle where he would put Hodge over, and where Hodge's participation would lead to Shamrock winning at the end.

Problems were made worse when fans went to the box office demanding refunds since the main event never took place and basically the entire show was changed from what was advertised and by all accounts was a poor show. As detailed last week, a riot took place afterwards, first in the building, and then outside the building.

At one point when leaving the arena, rowdy fans began pounding on the rental car driven by Charles Skaggs (Flash Funk) and Charles Wright (Kama Mustafa). They got out of their cars which nearly started an incident that would have benefited nobody, but as it turned out, were talked by other wrestlers into getting back in and leaving the area. Michaels and company needed a police escort to get out of the parking lot. All in all there were about 13 arrests, mainly for misdemeanor alcohol charges including several who were underage, and another for disorderly conduct.

Historically in wrestling, situations with top heels carrying that kind of heat, or near riots aren't that unusual. In the past, they usually resulted from screw-job finishes rather than simply public appearances and it is so rare I couldn't even remember the last time it happened that a major league promotion canceled its main event because the crowd was so unruly, let alone it happening on two consecutive nights.

But I can remember seeing it every three weeks at the Cow Palace growing up with situations that could have gotten as bad as the worst situations of today, with trashier and more violent fans, some of whom were carrying knives which were regularly pulled out in the parking lot as fans argued leaving the arena. The difference seemed to be that the numbers of security in those days was much larger than today, and when there were even hints of problems, they reacted far more quickly and FAR more aggressively.

I'm not sure if it's better for all concerned to see a hoard of security guards crack open the head of someone who threw a cup at the ring which was a routine occurrence at the Cow Palace in the 70s, but that usually quelled any problems when it came to people throwing things at wrestlers in a hurry. Fans never hit the ring in those days, because they were stopped and pounded on long before crossing the demilitarized zone. I'm not advocating security being as overly aggressive as it was in those days, but that did keep people in line at a time when the heel wrestlers aggravated fans to a greater degree than the heels of today usually do.

There is a problem. Hopefully this past week was just a series of weird coincidences resulting from a full moon, but deep down anyone who believes that is fooling themselves. Solutions aren't as easy.

Alcohol isn't the problem, but alcohol fuels the problem. I've been to numerous sports and entertainment events in this area where alcohol sales are cut off about halfway through the show. This won't eliminate problems, but at least might cut down on a percentage of them when fans are completely out of control after three straight hours of unbridled drinking.

Fans hate to be searched at the door. It gives them the feeling going in that this isn't a safe environment to take their kids. But this also happens routinely at concerts and sporting events. In Memphis, WWF officials blamed fans not being searched, which had been routine policy at the WCW matches at the Mid South Coliseum, which allowed them to smuggle bottles into the building that they later used for their target practice.

Problems cited by fans in both Memphis and Little Rock included fans becoming impatient and unruly due to poor action and bad matches. As wrestling gets more and more spectacular on television and PPV, the physical toll it takes makes it impossible for a regular house show to be of the quality fans are used to seeing weekly on television. In addition, fans in those cities grew up on a wilder style of wrestling and a tame house show after seeing all that wildness on television doesn't cut it.

But that's a catch-22 that can't be answered. The injury rate in this business is already alarming. The idea that wrestlers should take the risks they do on PPV at the nightly house shows is unreasonable, especially when there are very few wrestlers in their early 20s in the major league promotions whose bodies can recover fast enough from that kind of punishment, even if the road schedule itself isn't anywhere near as taxing as it was during the "good old days."

So then we move to television. Do we change back to the 80s style of television where evil are slapstick villains that are made to look like fools by superheroes, standing in a chorus line taking bionic elbows or having their biggest moves not sold by babyfaces who then put them away like impotent refuse? That wouldn't play today, particularly with long-term contracts, little new talent being developed and little movement between two groups, so the idea of heels being fed to babyfaces and moved out for new heels just is no longer feasible.

If the Steve Austins, NWOs and Shawn Michaels types weren't drawing money, you could say to lighten up the product. But they are, so that isn't the answer. However, once people pay their money at the arena show and are rowdy to the point things can be out of control, the wrestlers need to know to immediately tone the show down rather than antagonize the crowd and make it worse. If the crowd is already out of control, the monologue spots insulting the members of the audience can be dropped in favor of starting the wrestling match.

But there are changes that should be implemented yesterday. If fans start throwing things, particularly at television tapings because that's where all the behavior is learned, it needs to be stopped before it's raining debris. Go to a commercial. Announce in the building the show will be stopped if the fans can't police themselves.

I was at an ECW show in 1996 in New York where the fans were throwing more stuff that at nearly any Nitro and where it was bad enough that the commission wanted to stop the show, which no doubt would have created New York's version of the Little Rock massacre. Paul Heyman got in the ring and told the fans that if they can't police themselves, the show is going to be over. The problem stopped immediately. If it doesn't stop and it's a live shoot, go to the talking heads, keep the stars out of the ring and keep the cameras away from the "action" until it's over. It'll make for boring television. Once.

Sure, some fans will take it as empowering them to shut down a national broadcast, but those dozen fans will soon be discouraged by the 10,000 others whose neighbors aren't getting to see them hold up their posters with the cameras on. And it discourages it as being acceptable behavior. It won't stop it completely, because doing unacceptable behavior is what fans want their wrestling heroes of today to do so it's a catch-22 unless one changes the product to a product that would be less successful financially, and in a business like this, that isn't going to happen, particularly during a period where there is no company that has a true monopolistic hold.

NEVER run angles where fans come out of the stands to be part of the show. Maybe when fans respect the product again. But not today when fans have no respect and see that as a license showing it's okay to follow. There are plenty of swerves to fool the marks that can be done without spots which encourage dangerous follow-ups by the audience.

Chapter Thirty Nine

The Demise of the USWA

JANUARY 6

The story about Jerry Jarrett selling his 50 percent of the company to Jerry Lawler is confirmed. Lawler appears to be running the business end of USWA along with Larry Burton, who is General Manager of the promotion, and Elliott Pollock, a legitimate sports agent, who is USWA commissioner. Jarrett has been devoting almost all his time to business other than pro wrestling so his selling really isn't as big a deal other than symbolically in that he was the last of the mohicans so to speak, the last remaining promoter from the late 70s early 80s era of regional wrestling to finally be out of the ownership end of the business.

JANUARY 27

Lots of turmoil behind the scenes largely revolving around Larry Burton, who is Jerry Lawler's friend who has been running a lot of the business and some think may have put up some if not most of the money Lawler bought out Jerry Jarrett with. Burton has had heat among the wrestlers because they see him as a Hollywood mark outsider telling them how to run Tennessee wrestling business for a while, but apparently the heat really got a lot worse over the past week with lots of wrestlers talking about quitting although I'm not sure of anyone who has actually left.

FEBRUARY 3

After more than 30-years of being one of the most popular wrestling television announcing institutions ever on a regional basis, Dave Brown abruptly called it quits on 1/23 after a blow-up with USWA General Manager Larry Burton.

Brown, the long-time sidekick to Lance Russell, was the single longest running pro wrestling announcer on any single show still active. His career in Memphis television wrestling dated back as far as anyone can remember, to at least 1970. The two were without question, from a general public perspective, the most well-known pairing to host local wrestling television anywhere in the country during the modern era. Brown is even more famous locally for being the most popular television weatherman and perhaps the most famous local news personality in the Memphis market for the past two decades.

Brown and Russell hosted Championship Wrestling during its peak in the late 70s and early 80s when it was often the highest rated show of any kind in the Memphis market. At its peak in the early 80s during the days of the Fabulous Ones, the Saturday morning live television show on Ch. 5 in Memphis drew a 23 rating and an incredible Super Bowl like 70 share, beating out every prime time network show in the market for total viewing audience. It also got high ratings in the markets it was syndicated to on a week delay.

Brown starting working with Russell, whose legacy in Memphis wrestling dates to the 50s, on WHBQ, Ch. 13, where he served as the weatherman on the news. In the late 70s, the television wrestling show moved from Ch. 13 to Ch. 5 with Russell as host, and a short time later, strings were pulled to lure Brown from Ch. 13 to Ch. 5 to be both the weatherman and wrestling announcer. Brown became the singular host of the show in 1989 when Russell moved on to WCW.

Apparently there was some sort of a remark from Burton, who has heat with just about everyone in the Memphis territory except owner Jerry Lawler, that led to Brown abruptly calling it quits. Several other wrestlers have either quit or threatened to quit or are looking to quit for similar reasons.

The feeling was that after investing nearly 30 years of Saturday mornings, the combination of heat with Burton and it just being time to take his Saturday mornings back led to his leaving. Apparently Lawler spoke to Brown after his quitting, under the impression Brown would finish up on the 1/25 show, saying not to mention that he was leaving or say goodbye to avoid a maudlin feeling to the show. Brown told Lawler it wouldn't be a problem because he had no intention of doing the show. Lawler and others in USWA attempted to contact Russell about doing the show, but he had prior commitments so Lawler and Cory Maclin hosted the show.

During the show, there was no mention of Brown made whatsoever. Previously when Brown would miss a week due to vacation, it would always be acknowledged at the beginning of the show that he was on vacation and would be back next week. Russell, who hasn't done the show in months, was contacted about coming back but there is no word whether he'll do so or not at press time although it is believed he won't come back full-time.

FEBRUARY 10

Add long-time general manager Randy Hales and announcer Cory Maclin to the list of those who have left over problems with new general manager Larry Burton. Maclin left because he wanted a raise since his position with Brown leaving would be upgraded from second banana to regular host, and was turned down by Burton. Burton's ideas of changing the way things have been done and attempts to upgrade but also his knack for getting under people's skin and not showing them respect they believe they are deserved has led to the mass exodus.

With both announcers, Maclin and Dave Brown having left, and Lance Russell, who has been asked to return, still on vacation in Florida over the weekend, they called up local sports talk radio hosts John Rainey and another guy who I believe is named Brad Shapiro to do the show. The two have experience as Rainey did an angle some time back with Downtown Bruno and even did some matches with him, and also has done radio play-by-play of the Memphis matches. At the beginning of the show, the two said that Dave and Cory weren't available, giving the impression that the two were on vacation. The previous week when Brown wasn't on, his name was never mentioned.

This is the second time Hales has quit the promotion in recent months and this time appears to be for good as he's said to be frustrated at being 35-years-old and having spent his life working long weeks and traveling 100,000 miles a year in his car to cities and having nothing to show for it. There is a lot of bitterness among those who left that Jerry Lawler turned his back on several people who kept the promotion going when all the other regionals folded.

FEBRUARY 17

Lance Russell returned as announcer on the 2/8 television show which also featured an appearance by Brian Pillman. Russell has agreed to do the show every week until the end of the month and will do it fairly often after that point but refused to commit to a weekly regular deal because he's largely retired and spends a lot of time vacationing. Pillman showed up and played total heel, including one reference to Russell having Alzheimer's and claiming his personal friend Dr. Jack Kevorkian can take care of Russell's problems. On the show, Russell acknowledged Dave Brown's leaving saying that Brown had done the show for 30 years and it appeared almost that he and Jerry Lawler were trying to convince Brown to change his mind and return.

MARCH 24

Business is way down across the board and there is a lot of talk about impending doom, particularly since the 3/12 show in Memphis drew something like 250 fans and a $1,300 house with the loser leaves town match. The main on that show was Lawler vs. Reggie B. Fine and if Lawler won, he'd get five minutes with Queen Nikki (who is apparently the girlfriend of area indie wrestler Crazy Luke Graham Jr., who I believe is no relation to the original). Lawler won, but Reginald piledrove him and Nikki started on him for a few minutes. Lawler made his comeback, and finished doing the Tommy Dreamer piledriver spot where the dress falls down. Nikki got into it later with ref Downtown Bruno and they are now feuding.

APRIL 21

All kinds of behind-the-scenes turmoil. Mike Samples quit as booker and the new booker will be Dutch Mantel. Larry Burton, who has been running the company for the past several months, at press time was expected to be leaving and moving back home to California as well. Samples and Jerry Lawler had a disagreement when Samples wanted to stop booking Bill Dundee, feeling that at the age of 57, it was time for Dundee to get out of the ring. Lawler overruled him and put Dundee back on the cards feeling they needed to use more talent known in the area rather than fill the slots with young wrestles.

JUNE 2

Update on the business situation here. The situation doesn't appear to be as bleak as some have made it out to be. In regard to the reports of them losing television in Nashville and Louisville, that doesn't appear to be the case. In the case of Nashville, the television situation is going to stay the same (on both local Ch. 30 and Ch. 58). In Louisville, they are dropping the station they were on because the company felt it couldn't afford the $1,000 per week fee, and are moving to a new station. They haven't run Memphis in several weeks, but the plan as we can tell is that they will go back to Memphis in a few more weeks, although most likely not run the city on a weekly basis as in the past, and they may move to a new location since they were only doing 200 to 300 fans for night shows at the Big One Flea Market.

JULY 7

Christine Jarrett, Jerry's mother, was fired by the promotion. She's worked the box office in Louisville literally since the beginning of time. That fed all kinds of rumors that Jerry Jarrett would come back to run opposition, but Jarrett really doesn't follow wrestling very closely anymore and has his own land development business to run.

JULY 21

Lots of news both in and out of the ring here. The promotion has reorganized and there has been a lot said and speculated about it. Exactly who owns the group isn't clear but the new President of the promotion is Michael Selnick of Cleveland. The wrestlers were brought to a meeting on 7/10 and told that new money would be put into the company, that they would be expanding operations and that Jerry Lawler would no longer be running things.

Although it has been reported that Lawler has no more ownership in the company, I've been told that isn't the case, although Lawler is not going to be involved in day-to-day running operations because of his commitments particularly in the WWF. Lawler's title is Vice President in charge of Public Relations.

They are going to change the way they do business hoping to expand syndication in getting on new cable stations that are opening up and desperate for programming, but without paying for programming which killed Paul Alperstein's AWF when he tried to do something similar. They are also talking about expanding into new markets, with both New Orleans and St. Louis having been discussed and with the former more likely than the latter because it already has a TV clearance.

Dutch Mantel was officially announced as booker. The wrestlers were told it would no longer be a nickel-and-dime promotion with the influx of new capital. There were several new officers announced, but only one with any previous background in pro wrestling, being long-time Texas referee and Japanese booker James Beard.

SEPTEMBER 8

The final live television show on WMC-TV took place on 8/30 after a 21-year-run (actually more than 30 years since the show was on WHBQ in Memphis live on Saturday mornings for many years before going to Ch. 5). The show is moving to a one hour (it had been 90 minutes) taped version which will air at midnight on Saturdays and be replayed on Sunday afternoons. Tony Friedman and Bill Behrens handled the announcing since Michael St. John wasn't there. Lance Russell did a telephone interview late in the show thanking fans for their cards and flowers and sounded great and said that he hoped he could return to the show at some point. They also did a video montage showing clips of among others, Lou Thesz, Tommy Gilbert, Eddie Gilbert, Jeff Jarrett, Miss Texas, Andy Kaufman, Bill Dundee and Jimmy Hart. They dropped balloons from the ceiling as the show went off the air. Dundee returned as referee for the Dutch Mantel vs. Tommy Dreamer main event the next day in Memphis.

SEPTEMBER 8

There is some serious discontent among members of the current ownership group since lots of money is being spent on things like a new set, but no real money is coming in. Nothing at this point has happened but some sort of a shake-up is expected and many of the stockholders are tense. USWA survived for years under Jerry Jarrett basically by never spending any money while everyone else went out of business. Many of the wrestlers already believe there is an ownership change and the rumor is flying around everywhere.

SEPTEMBER 15

There continues to be all sorts of chaos behind the scenes. Although it has been reported that the USWA has been sold to a Texas group, we're again told by people in the company that the same three person ownership group from Cleveland is still in control. The only person from Texas in a management position is James Beard, who along with Bert Prentice is in charge of booking and promoting spot shows, and his hiring came at the recommendation of Bruce Prichard of the WWF.

There is in-fighting among that ownership group because very little money is coming in after a lot of money was spent on cosmetic changes to give the promotion and the television show a more modern look, and General Manager Larry Burton was again talking about leaving this week.

I believe they went eight days without running any house shows, and with nobody under a guaranteed contract except the people sent here by the WWF, the wrestlers have to survive on their either $40 or $100 (depending on the wrestler) per shot, which doesn't add up to much when you multiply $100 times zero shows.

In addition, the company has eliminated the babyfaces picking up extra money working the gimmick table, as it has wanted to take over concessions in a more professional manner, but as of yet that really hasn't started happening either.

SEPTEMBER 22

Mark Selker, one of the three Cleveland-based part-owners of the USWA filed a lawsuit on 9/11 against Jerry Lawler and Larry Burton, the latter of whom controls the other 50% of the ownership, charging fraud in the sale of the company. Lawler was served with the lawsuit papers by an armed guard at the television tapings two days later.

Selker sent a memo to the wrestlers at the 9/14 house show in Memphis stating that this wasn't a USWA Inc. card and he wasn't responsible for paying them. The show went on as scheduled before a crowd of 207 fans with Larry Burton agreeing to pay the wrestlers. A subsequent show was scheduled for 9/16 in Louisville headlined by Lawler vs. Tommy Dreamer with Burton saying he'd pay the wrestlers for both that show and a casino show later in the week, which, if canceled, would violate an important company contract for a regular guaranteed money casino date.

Lawler was scheduled to fly into Louisville for that show after doing voice-overs for Raw the day before. Earlier on 9/16, Eugene Selker, the father and attorney for Mark Selker, attempted and was turned down in Federal Court in Cleveland in an attempt to get a temporary restraining order to keep Lawler and Burton from doing any business within the company until the resolution of the lawsuit.

Selker attempted to cancel the Louisville show and every other show on the books has already been canceled. At this point, television is still scheduled to be taped on 9/20 in Memphis but there is discontent at WMC-TV in Memphis and with poor ratings in the movie to midnight combined with all the problems such as an armed guard coming to television and serving Lawler which nearly turned into a physical altercation, police being involved as a shoot on recent television shows and the latest problems, it wouldn't shock people to see the station finally wash its hands of its long-time powerhouse wrestling show.

The lawsuit against Lawler and Burton alleges mail fraud, theft by fraud, fraudulent business practices and fraud as it relates to the sale of the company. The claim in the suit is that Lawler and Burton doctored the books to inflate the value of the company, syndication profits and potential were inflated, expenses were understated and the defendants withheld important information from them including the knowledge of the expected time slot move on WMC. There have been rumors of criminal charges being filed as well but at press time that hadn't happened.

Lawler claimed that it was just a case of people buying a business, then losing money in the business and then suing the previous owners. Both Lawler and Burton claimed that the Selkers had done this same scenario with two previous businesses in an attempt to gain complete control of the company and remove Burton from the company.

The Selkers idea is to shut the company down temporarily except for continuing to produce television, but the question is with the company shut down, who would stay in the area to work television. This has, among the wrestlers, put Burton in the babyface role since he's the one who is now paying them. Eugene Selker, the attorney listed as filing the lawsuit, was the same attorney who wrote the contract in the initial sale of the company, a point Lawler and Burton have been quick to point out.

It has been expected that if/when this ownership group bails out, and them doing so wasn't unexpected, that the WWF would attempt to take over the territory and use it as a grooming ground for inexperienced wrestlers they have under contract, but control the booking of that talent which they didn't do in previous incarnations of attempting to use USWA to train wrestlers. At this point, until everything it settled, the WWF isn't expected to send any new talent to Memphis.

SEPTEMBER 29

The prospective legal fight over the future of the USWA got messier during the week, resulting in no television show taped on 9/20 in Memphis.

As the week went on, the scorecard stood as follows. The 50% ownership group, an investment group headed by Mark Selker, had filed suit in Federal Court in Cleveland against the other 50% owner, Larry Burton, along with former owner Jerry Lawler, who had sold them their shares for $1 million, claiming fraud. They had claimed they had such a strong open-and-shut case that during the week they would get a temporary restraining order to keep Burton and Lawler from doing any business within the company. However, a Cleveland judge turned down their request. There was also talk they'd have criminal charges for fraud pressed against Lawler and Burton, but by the end of the week, no such charges were filed.

Lawler was publicly claiming he was going to file a countersuit because the Selkers had stopped paying him on his $125,000 per year salaried front office position within the company he was contracted to when he sold them his stock, that he and Burton would attempt to get the other case moved to Memphis, and that they would attempt to disqualify Eugene Selker, father of Mark, from being the attorney in the case because of the conflict of interest since he was both the attorney who drew up the papers for the sale of the company and the attorney who filed the lawsuit papers.

Mark Selker attempted and failed to get a USWA house show on 9/16 in Louisville canceled, headlined by Lawler vs. Tommy Dreamer, which drew a $4,000 house, about double what the company usually draws in that city. However, several other spot shows during the week were canceled, as was the television taping. The belief at press time is that Lawler and Burton would continue to run shows in Nashville and Louisville every week and there are no plans announced for a return date in Memphis.

During the week there had been talk that Lawler and Burton would bring in a crew of wrestlers for the scheduled Saturday morning taping at WMC-TV studios in Memphis for airing at midnight, and that James Beard, a representative of the Selkers, would also bring in a crew of Dallas-based wrestlers and nobody knew which group of wrestlers would end up appearing on the show. As late as the day before, it was believed that a wrestling show would be taped and a show had been scripted out.

As it turned out, the Selkers managed to lock up the company's editing equipment, making it impossible for a show to be taped, and the program that aired on WMC-TV had Beard in a studio doing lead-ins for random clips from USWA's past that had nothing to do with today's storylines. About the only comment, other than it being a totally dead show with no plugs or mentions about any future house show dates or talk of current angles, is that it appeared from the clips to be kissing up to Jerry Jarrett. They aired clips of Jarrett's mother Christine, who was fired by the Burton group, being honored and of Jerry Jarrett accepting an award for his late partner Tojo Yamamoto, along with favorable clips of Jeff Jarrett as a babyface.

It was a seven-hour deposition that the Selkers had with Jarrett just prior to filing the suit that gave them the information about how much Lawler had purchased the other 50% of the company for and how much money the company had taken in when Jarrett was co-owner, and the huge profit Lawler had made in selling the company. Burton and his booker, Dutch Mantel, were going to attempt this week to get their own restraining order so they could stop the video equipment from being locked up so they could tape a television show this weekend. If that restraining order fails to come through, it is expected that the show this weekend would be another old-time highlight show with Beard in the studio.

Absolutely nobody seems to have a clue what is going to happen next week, but the show certainly put the television future of the promotion in jeopardy. There were several reports that WMC-TV was unhappy about all the goings on surrounding the wrestling show, and now with it airing Saturday nights at midnight, the ratings are way down and patience with trying to salvage what had for years been the most popular local television show in the market was wearing thin within the station due to the problems with the power struggle and the idea that an armed guard came to the studio the previous week and a confrontation took place when Lawler and Burton were originally served.

In addition, the syndication contract that USWA has with its generally weak line-up of UHF stations around the country calls for first-run programming 50 weeks per year (they are allowed recap shows during December for the holiday season), and this show was a clear violation of the contract. Even Lawler himself during the week called the time shift in Memphis as the "kiss of death" to the group in the market, particularly on the heels of the 9/14 house show drawing just 207 fans, to the Wrestling Observer Hotline.

The Selkers filed a suit asking for $1.5 million plus punitive damages from Lawler and Burton in Federal Court claiming the two made false representation of facts when selling he and his investors the company. Apparently Selker claimed in the lawsuit to be the head of the group that controls 55% of the stock in the company although most reports that have come out list the Selker group and Burton as each controlling 50%

The crux of the situation is that Lawler and Jarrett each owned 50% of the company dating back to the early 80s. In December, Lawler purchased Jarrett's 50% for either $250,000 or $262,000, of which Jarrett himself received, depending upon the source, somewhere between $175,000 and $187,000 with the remaining $75,000 supposedly going to Burton for being the intermediary in the deal. Jarrett at the time was seriously thinking about folding the company, which was no longer profitable and had openly said that receiving any money at that time for his stock in USWA he saw as a gift from above.

The Selkers, who had raised $1.5 million to buy the company outright, were then told that Burton had purchased Lawler's 100% of the company for $2 million, $500,000 of which was paid immediately and the remaining $1.5 would be forthcoming in six payments of $250,000 apiece. The Selkers began making payments to Burton for 50% of the company based on half the company being worth $1 million.

If all of that is correct, then Lawler came out of it with money eventually promised to total $2 million for his original stock and the 50% that Jarrett owned, for which he paid theoretically Jarrett $250,000 or $262,000. The other key points are whether Burton actually paid Lawler the $500,000 and payments on the other $1.5 million at that price before selling half the company to the Selkers and whether Lawler really paid Burton the $75,000. Where this gets even more intriguing is that the Selkers were given paperwork to show that Burton was working for USWA on a $750,000 per year salary plus performance bonuses.

In other words, if all these allegations are correct and one were to put all the pieces together, it would appear that Lawler, the 100% owner of the company, was on paper paying Burton this ridiculous amount of money (the entire company grossed less than $500,000 from all sources in 1996), which then got kicked back to him as a huge purchase price for his shares. Plus Lawler theoretically paid Burton $75,000 as the intermediary on the Jarrett deal, so there may be a paper trail of Lawler and Burton paying each other huge sums of money as salary and a brokering fee in one direction, and as the purchase price for the company in the other direction, with them using the same money to pay each other and thus little or no actual money changing hands, but making it on paper appearing to greatly inflate the actual value of the company.

Lawler wouldn't confirm the $750,000 figure when asked but has admitted to Pro Wrestling Torch that Burton was hired for a huge salary because he believed with the money from the Selkers being put into the company that USWA was going to greatly increase in business, although he has changed his spin on the latter point 180 degrees over the past week, claiming the Selkers were people who got into a business they knew nothing about and were losing money hand over fist.

It has been a common wrestling scheme of the past to use the money of outside "money marks" to fund wrestling companies. Another scheme, generally credited to former promoter Ron Fuller (Ronald Welch) although he assuredly wasn't the first to do it, was to sell his territory to outsiders who didn't understand the wrestling industry, who would then lose money like it was going out of style, and then after not making a go of it, sell the company back to Fuller at a much smaller price. Fuller would then buy it, build the territory back up, and sell it again to a new money mark for a higher price. He did this until he felt running territorial wrestling could no longer be profitable due to the changes in the industry as a whole caused largely by Vince McMahon, and is now a minor league ice hockey owner.

It is believed the Selkers, who Lawler claimed raised $1.5 million from a group of investors to buy half the company but only paid $1 million for it, attempting to muddy the waters against the parties that have sued him, thought they'd make their money back largely from new revenue streams, mainly television syndicated ad sales, along with merchandising based on how WWF, ECW, and WCW were raking in money on that end and not predominately from live event business.

This would be in total contrast to the policies of Lawler and Jarrett as owners that kept USWA alive and profitable when all other regional offices had failed—basically spending almost no money at all and paying the guys $40 per night and $25 for television because there are always people around who are willing to almost pay to be television stars, or see it as paying dues with the hopes of being discovered by the big-time offices, and virtually all the money coming in came from selling tickets to live shows with the babyfaces able to add extra money to hustling their own gimmicks to fans.

The payment structure had changed with the new ownership in that experienced wrestlers were getting $100 per night with the younger undercard guys getting $40, however the promotion was now controlling the merchandising, although little money was coming in from that direction.

The new group went to the other extreme, with the idea of expanding into more bordering states along with spending money to theoretically make money from new revenue streams. They hired non-wrestling industry people as company executives at high salaries, some in excess of six-figures, and rented a $3,000 per month office in Memphis, bought a new television set for $20,000 and were quickly realizing a lot of money was being spent and no money was coming in.

The basic problem, the same that has faced everyone (remember AWF, POWW, GLOW, Global, et al) with the idea they'd make their money from national advertising sales as opposed to selling tickets is that it just doesn't work. Few advertisers generally look at spending big money on pro wrestling, even if it gets good ratings. Those that do are already with WWF and/or WCW.

If television syndication was such a cash cow, why was Titan Sports, at the time it was the leading company in the industry, at one point contemplating getting out of the syndication business because it was no longer cost effective? If the brand name leader wasn't making a profit in syndication, how could a far smaller group expect to do so? Pro wrestling gets pennies on the dollar in advertising as compared with other shows that would do similar ratings with similar national penetration, which is one of the reasons USA Network preempts Raw with the U.S. Open, despite it drawing only half the viewing audience, every September.

Despite hiring someone to sell national advertising at a six-figure salary, the USWA had yet to sell one national ad spot, still had only one revenue stream, which was the house shows which were bringing in virtually no money compared with the new overhead, was no longer being paid $1,500 per week by WMC-TV to pay for production of the show with the move to midnight, and it has been questioned who knew and how far in advance it was known about the move of TV time in the flagship city on the circuit. If this all winds up as nothing more than a power struggle between the Selker group and Burton over control of the company, the natural question becomes is the winner the real loser, or is the loser the real winner?

OCTOBER 6

Things remained largely status quo this week. Larry Burton failed to get his injunction to get the video equipment away from the Selker group, which had it locked up. In addition, the main house show of the week scheduled for 9/23 in Louisville was canceled by the Kentucky State Athletic Commission because nobody had a promoters license. The 9/16 show was saved when they used Jerry Lawler's license, however with Lawler having to be in Albany, NY for WWF tapings, he wasn't there. The commission shutting down the show garnered some local publicity, particularly since the wrestlers picketed the building.

The television this week was another highlights from the past with them doing no hints or angles or storylines or building up to anything for the future. The featured stuff on the show was showing some angles leading up to and the match where Lawler beat Curt Hennig in Memphis to win the AWA title back in 1988. Ironically, the 9/20 television show which was a taped highlights show from the past did a five rating, which is better than some of the poorer rated Saturday morning live shows had done. However, reports are that WMC-TV isn't going to take sides in the current dispute and won't let either tape a show until their differences are settled, and there are people who believe if they aren't settled within a week or two, that the station will simply cancel the wrestling show and it would leave the company without its by far most valuable station.

OCTOBER 13

The latest on the trials and tribulations from what was once the United States Wrestling Association saw cancellation of its flagship wrestling show and the opening of a new promotion in its territory.

WMC-TV in Memphis, the local NBC affiliate, which had run pro wrestling since 1977, announced this past week that its final wrestling television show would be on 10/4. The decision, which came as no surprise to anyone following the story, made by WMC General Manager Mason Granger was based on a lawsuit for control of USWA that wasn't going to be settled, and until it was, the company was largely no longer in operation. The USWA canceled all its house shows this week and there are no more cards scheduled. The final television show was another highlight show, although the highlights were more current than in the previous two weeks.

Also on 10/4, Bert Prentice, who had run opposition to USWA for several years before joining the group just prior to it falling apart, opened up a new promotion with a show in Lebanon, TN before about 200 fans using Wolfie D vs. Billy Travis as the main event. The show was a television taping, using mostly the same wrestlers Prentice used in his old North American All-Star Wrestling office (some of which aren't doing this group and are instead working for yet another rival group run by former Prentice wrestler Farren Foxx).

The big news with the new promotion, called Music City Wrestling, is the surprising involvement of Jerry Jarrett. Jarrett is providing some funding for the group and is trying to downplay his involvement with the group although has admitted to an involvement, which will be largely run by Prentice.

The belief is that this group will wind up taking over the USWA syndication network due to the fact USWA isn't providing any new programming and the contract with the syndicator and the station only allows for two highlight shows per year, a quota of which they topped with the third highlight show this past week. In addition, with the WMC cancellation, it is questionable if USWA will even tape new highlight shows.

NOVEMBER 3

For all real purposes, it appears that we can officially signal the death of the United States Wrestling Association.

The group, which was the latest of numerous names throughout the years of the promotion owned by Jerry Jarrett, and later Jarrett and Jerry Lawler dating back to the late 70s when Jarrett gained control of the territory from Nick Gulas, at this point doesn't exist except as a name on a lawsuit.

Mason Granger, the General Manager of WMC-TV in Memphis, which had been the flagship station for the promotion since before Jarrett even owned it, officially canceled pro wrestling a few weeks back. Contrary to stories circulating within the industry, Granger has made it clear that he isn't interested in adding a new wrestling show on his station having turned down a number of promotions.

There had been an attempt at a deal worked out between the two sides involved in the USWA lawsuit, the Larry Burton/Jerry Lawler side and the Mark Selker side, to attempt to save the company's most valuable asset, the WMC-TV slot, by having a neutral party, namely former USWA General Manager Randy Hales, produce a weekly television show before the court decides who controls USWA, but that deal fell apart before it ever started.

Most of the existing stations and the syndicated network, generally weak UHF stations that use the program as something of a "C" program distributed by the World Wrestling Federation (which gained control of syndicating the show away from World Championship Wrestling as a way to improve in comparison in the highly misleading weekly syndicated ratings standings) will wind up carrying Bert Prentice's Music City Wrestling promotion after a deal struck between Prentice, former USWA syndicator Bill Behrens and WWF officials on 10/21.

Michael St. John and Prentice will handle the announcing of the television show, with the first major taping to be on 10/30 in Nashville at the Fairgrounds, the long-time home of USWA. The idea on the boards is for Music City to use a Country Music backdrop on the show since the tapings will be coming from Nashville, and use Doug Gilbert, Billy Travis and Flash Flanagan as the top stars. Jerry Jarrett was offered ownership in the Music City group, but turned it down, but is working with the group in an advisor role, and his mother, Christine, will be the promoter for matches in the Nashville area.

Jerry Jarrett, along with Eddie Marlin and Frank Morrell were at a show last week at the Nashville Fairgrounds which drew about 150 fans. In addition, they are hoping to use wrestlers under WWF developmental contracts. The group will also get television in Memphis on WLMT-TV at the old USWA time slot of 11 a.m. on Saturdays.

For legal reasons, largely due to a non-compete clause he has in his old USWA contract, Jerry Lawler won't be used by the new promotion even though his name still means something in Memphis, nor, at this point, will Brian Christopher for other reasons.

Music City won't be running the Louisville market, as the old USWA time slot on WBNA on Saturday afternoons, was taken over by a new company called Kentuckiana Championship Wrestling run by Mike Samples and Jerry Faith out of Campbellsville, KY that has had a small-time television presence in the latter market for a few weeks, and using the two co-owners along with Flanagan and Steven Dunn as the top stars, and they will probably fight with Ian Rotten's IWA for control of the grass roots of the Louisville market.

Larry Burton—or at least the person who goes by the name Larry Burton, as it has since come out in discovery in the lawsuit that no such person exists under the name Larry Burton—has been talking about starting his own wrestling company out of Cleveland. Those close to the situation believe now that the lawsuits will simply disappear because there is nothing to gain anymore from winning, and the company will never return, and friends of Lawler claim he's resigned himself to the fact that the company he built is really kaput.

At this point, with the syndication gone, the only thing that the winner of the legal battle would get for winning is a large debt as there are tens of thousands of dollars in unpaid bills to arenas and television stations throughout the old USWA territory. In addition, there may be IRS problems to deal with as well as apparently the company never paid payroll taxes on those inflated salaries they were paying to those in management positions.

NOVEMBER 10

In the battle for the old USWA territory, here's the latest on the scoreboard. USWA no longer exists, however Jerry Lawler is continuing to run one show per week at a casino in Mississippi to hold onto that deal for himself using himself (despite a no compete clause in his USWA contract), Brian Christopher and Spellbinder as the top stars. In Louisville, the battleground is between Kentuckiana—a group run by Mike Samples and Jerry Faith—and Ian Rotten's IWA.

Both will be running on Tuesdays and Rotten will be putting together television for local promotion for the first time using Les Thatcher as his announcer. Samples' group will start running the traditional weekly shows at the Louisville Gardens and has the old USWA time slot. Between the weekly Gardens rent and time slot costs, that's an $1,800 nut per week.

In Nashville, Bert Prentice's Music City Wrestling—which through a deal with former USWA syndicator Bill Behrens and the World Wrestling Federation, is taking over the old USWA syndication—is battling with a group called New South Wrestling headed by former Prentice wrestler Farren Foxx and local mainstay Tony Falk.

Prentice taped television on 10/30 with a three-camera shoot for syndication, drawing 400 fans to the old Nashville Fairgrounds, about 200 paying $3 a head and the other 200 from about 1,000 freebies passed out around town. PG-13 are in for that group and Doug Gilbert returns this week after Japan. They drew 337 fans to a house show in Nashville two nights later. There is talk of using both Tommy Rich and Adrian Street this month and they are going to attempt to use the Harris Twins (Skull & Eight Ball in WWF) when they are home in Nashville for the holidays provided WWF gives the okay.

This group debuts on 11/15 on WLMT, Ch. 30 in Memphis at 11 a.m., the traditional time slot of USWA, and will run its first show in the Memphis market at the Big One Expo on 11/28, and plans to run once or twice per month in Memphis.

DECEMBER 1

Mark Selker dropped his lawsuit against Jerry Lawler and Larry Burton on 11/14. No reason was given for dropping the suit. There wasn't much left to win anyway. The most valuable assets the company had were the syndicated clearances, which are long gone, and the WMC-TV slot, which is also gone. So to win control, you have the rights to run a promotion with no television in markets where there is now one or two opposition groups in most cities, that were all big money losers to begin with, and you can inherit the past due bills in several of the markets to arenas and television stations just to restart under the USWA name.

DECEMBER 22

The investors in the now-defunct XL Sports (USWA Selker group) have filed an individual $1.4 million lawsuit against Jerry Lawler in Memphis, claiming he conspired to con the investment group out of money by misrepresenting the value of the company, and claiming he misrepresented to them the price he paid to acquire the other 50% of the company from Jerry Jarrett.

Lawler paid approximately $250,000 to Jarrett for 50% of the USWA, of which Jarrett received about $175,000 and Larry Burton, or Bergman or Bertman or whatever name he's going by this week, received the difference as a brokering fee for putting the deal together. Lawler and Burton then sold the Selker group 55% of the USWA for $1.1 million. There are also hints of the Selkers filing an individual suit against Burton and filing criminal fraud charges, although those threats were also out there a few months back and nothing materialized.

This was the second similar lawsuit filed by the group, the first against Lawler & Burton was looking to obtain control of the promotion, but it was dropped and the promotion officially declared bankruptcy. The investment group then filed suit to get its money back.

JANAURY 5

The old USWA territory has turned into something of a hotbed of news outside the ring. The lawsuit between XL Sports, Limited (The Mark Selker group of investors) and Jerry Lawler was filed in bankruptcy court where the degree of proof is generally considered easier than a regular civil suit. XL Sports is suing Lawler to recover $1.11 million (the price they paid for their USWA purchase) and $300,000 in expenses claimed as a result of a fraudulent transfer.

The dropping of the original suit and subsequent filing of bankruptcy appeared to be measures to get the suit into what would be an easier court to recover money since the idea is no longer to gain control of the dead company (because all you would win was liability to pay owed money to television stations and arenas and the most valuable asset the company actually had, the television deals, have all been lost) but to recover the money spent.

The basic claim in the suit is that Lawler and Lawrence Bertman (Larry Burton) "conspired, colluded, aided and abetted one with the other and with others as yet not named as defendants to concoct a scheme and device by which to trick, cheat and deceive debtor by lies, tricks, misrepresentations by material omissions, conversion and other forms of theft designed to victimize persons later to become principals of and/or lenders, vendors, employees and other creditors of and to debtor into delivering to Lawler and/or Bertman/Burton approximately $1,110,000."

The suit itself has a lot of wording but no documentation to back it up and not a lot of specifics as to what happened, other then the factual prices, that Lawler and Bertman bought Jerry Jarrett's 50% of the USWA for $187,000 (the actual sale price would have been $262,000 but Bertman received $75,000 of that as a brokering fee for putting together the sale between Lawler and Jarrett) and immediately sold that 50% plus another 5% to XL Sports for $1,110,000.

The suit claims Lawler and Bertman misrepresented to both sides aspects of the sale. The suit claims that the maximum value of the entire company in which Lawler & Bertman sold 55% of would be $500,000. The suit also claims Lawler and Bertman conspired to deplete the assets of the company basically to run it down. It is rumored that the other person not named as defendants in the lawsuit is a very prominent current major wrestling official.

Lawler has always maintained that he simply made a big profit on a transfer of stock and that the Selkers had no idea how to run a wrestling company and after buying it, immediately ran it into the ground. The only action involving the suit is that Lawler's attorney asked for a continuance until January.

Bertman and Mike Samples and Jerry Faith of Kentuckiana Championship Wrestling had been working together in a small way and Bertman, as Larry Burton, even appeared on the KCW television show introduced as the new General Manager of the company (a figurehead Jack Tunney role).

Bertman and Samples then had a falling out as Bertman is making noises of re-starting a promotion along with Lawler and Elliot Pollock. Lawler and Brian Christopher have been working regular casino shows in the Northern Mississippi area promoted by one of the Nunnery Brothers, who are long-time friends with Lawler.

Chapter Forty

Bits and Pieces

WWF Shotgun Saturday Night

(January 13) The debut of Shotgun Saturday Night on 1/4 was largely a flop content and reaction-wise. The show didn't air in this market but the reaction was 100% negative by those who called and faxed and strongly negative for that matter.

First show was from the Mirage, a New York night club, and drew 350 fans and a $6,000 house (they had talked about a 3,000 capacity for the show) as they charged $20 to get in the door for a risqué comedic show that wasn't funny according to the reports we received. With all the hype nationally over the week before the show about the debut taping at the Mirage, that kind of a turnout was pathetic. Next week at the All-Star Cafe the show is going to be free admission and because it's in a theme restaurant as opposed to a bar, the show will be less risqué. The third show on 1/18 will be done live at 9 p.m. Central time in San Antonio from a bar there.

The show was apparently like watching a poorly-lit minor league promotional cross between Incredibly Strange Wrestling and "Grunt: The Wrestling Movie" but with bigger name stars. It opened with The Flying Nuns (Glen Ruth & Chaz Warrington, formerly the Head Bangers) wearing nun outfits managed by Brother Love, using the ring names Mother Smucker and Sister Angelica, beating Godwinns when Brother Love hit Phineas with a loaded bible to lead to the pin.

Goldust beat Sultan. Sultan had the camel clutch on when Marlena jumped on the apron, pulled down the top of her dress (the camera shot her from the back, she was actually wearing pasties over her nipples) and Sultan, supposedly a celibate man under the tutelage of Bob Backlund, freaked out, and dropped the hold and Goldust won.

Ahmed Johnson beat Crush via DQ in a match which saw them brawl into the street. The NOD members (not Faarooq since he was in California) interfered and it wound up with Johnson doing the Pearl River plunge on former SMW wrestler D-Lo Brown on the roof of a car, which was said to have been the highlight of the show.

Final match saw Mini Vader lose to Mascarita Sagrada (the wrestler billed as Mascarita Sagrada Jr. in Mexico, not the original who appeared on Nitro a few days earlier although the WWF wrestler is the more spectacular of the two). Before the match Cornette picked up Mini Vader at a bus depot from Mexico and he had the runs and Cornette had to take him to the bathroom. Sunny (who did the announcing with Vince McMahon and they were said to have come off as unprepared) got in the ring and did the Macarena with Mascarita, but they called it the Mascarita and changed the words to what was termed a bunch of unfunny semi-racist Mexican lyrics. Match was said to have been good, but contextually is couldn't be taken seriously. After the match Cornette got pants'd by Mascarita and was running down the streets of New York as the show was going off the air in his underwear.

Next week has Mero vs. Razor plus Furnas & LaFon appearing. There were ECW and BWO chants. A lot of the stations carrying Shotgun were stations that had been carrying AWF. Titan is paying for many, if not most, of the time slots to get back into syndication, but because they are only looking for late night time slots and the majority of stations are UHF's, the costs aren't what they were last season.

(January 20) My impressions of the first Shotgun show: It looked like a public access wrestling TV show, which I don't think is the intention. Bob Backlund was a riot but he wasn't enough to carry an entire show. Most of the skits didn't work. The deal where Todd Pettengill changed the words to Macarena to do the Mascarita wasn't the slightest bit racist as I'd been led to believe, but it also didn't work. Mascarita did debut the corkscrew plancha on American TV but it was in a setting and done at a time (just back from a commercial break) where it meant nothing.

The second Shotgun Saturday Night got mixed reports although most were strongly negative saying the only improvement was the lighting. The show was from the All-Star Cafe with free admission. I've heard various reports of the crowd but one person there live said that the number of people there for the wrestling was only about 150 and the rest were people who just happened to be there and casually watched the wrestling while eating.

Diesel beat Marc Mero in a match where Honky Tonk Man and Razor both interfered and Mero lost because he was saving Sable from them as he had the bout won. Afterwards Mero yelled at Sable and walked out on her, and she cried. Honky tried to console her but she kept crying. Then Rocky Maivia came out to console her, Mero came out and saw them together and they began brawling.

Faarooq beat Savio Vega. Maivia beat Razor. Lots of ECW and Rocky sux chants. Actually since the numbers there for the wrestling were so small, they cheered the heels in every match. Phil LaFon & Doug Furnas wrestled Head Bangers to a match which went off the air in progress (LaFon & Furnas won afterwards). Head Bangers didn't use the Flying Nuns or Sisters of Love gimmick as WWF has already dropped that because of outside pressure. LaFon had beaten Thrasher of the Bangers in the pre-show dark match. They announced the Flying Nuns had been arrested during the show and that's why they weren't there.

Among the lame skits were Honky and Pettengill singing and Honky was really bad. They went out to talk to homeless people and when they saw a guy in a box, it was Nikolai Volkoff in the same Russian hat and suit he's been wearing for the last 20 years. By the way, the Baltimore newspaper did a story on Volkoff getting a $25,000 a year government inspector job with the story saying that a series of bad investments left Volkoff with nothing from his wrestling days.

They announced Goldust was pregnant and showed a photo of him supposedly pregnant and announced he would give birth live next Saturday night. Maybe Pena will bring them a Mini-Goldust they can debut on the show. Or maybe the idea will be even more lame. The Sunny supposed sex video was apparently really lame with a Fondle Me Elmo doll and a bunch of moaning and no picture.

1/18 will be from a night club in San Antonio, 1/25 will be back at The Mirage (which is really scary that they're already repeating locations especially when Mirage looked so bad the first time), no word on 2/1 and 2/8 is at Webster Hall in Manhattan.

AJPW Working with FMW

(January 20) AJPW seem to be building up an inter-promotional angle working with FMW. The storyline is that Atsushi Onita wanted to meet with Giant Baba to put together a match where Hayabusa would challenge Kenta Kobashi for the Triple Crown later this year. Onita was going to attend either the 1/2 or 1/3 Korakuen Hall shows to meet with Baba but the storyline was that Baba sent out word he wasn't interested in meeting with Onita and didn't want him at his show. Baba then got mad that the magazines were reporting on this inter-promotional angle and said he hasn't talked with Onita. Rumor has it that the two will officially meet sometime this week and begin talks to set up that match.

(January 27) Major news stems from rumors concerning a meeting between Giant Baba and Atsushi Onita in Tokyo for 40 minutes on 1/16. The two met and agreed to work together, but exactly what capacity isn't certain, although Onita was trying to put together a Kenta Kobashi vs. Hayabusa match for his 4/29 show at the Yokohama Arena.

When asked by press about the meeting and future of working together, Baba did his typical pretending not to know anything but what he reads in the newspaper act; Mitsuharu Misawa said it's okay if FMW wrestlers come to All Japan but he has no interest in going to FMW and pretty much stated he didn't think the FMW wrestlers were of the caliber of All Japan wrestlers; Kobashi made no comment while Toshiaki Kawada said he was against working with FMW basically saying why should they work with Onita who he called "Mr. Tell a Lie" in reference to Onita building up gates for one year with his retirement gimmick and then trying to come back very quickly and the only reason it took so long is because of public and media pressure.

Billy Jack Haynes vs Matt Borne

(January 20) This sounds like a 90s shoot angle but from all accounts it isn't an angle. Billy Jack Haynes has switched personas once again.

On his 12/28 radio show, Haynes said he was ashamed of himself for jumping on the bandwagon to get rid of local commissioner Bruce Anderson, who has had a long-running feud with local promoter Sandy Barr, who is banned from promoting in Oregon and has to run his shows in the state of Washington instead. He said Anderson was doing nothing but trying to help the wrestlers. He than said that Barr, who has been at war with Anderson for years, was his friend but wasn't crap when it comes to being a businessman.

He also went on the air and embraced the local wrestling newsletter Ring Around the Northwest that he had knocked hard numerous times on his show, saying that he now realizes the public knows more about wrestling than ever before and that times have changed.

He also said he had changed his opinion in regard to Buddy Rose and Moondog Moretti, two local wrestlers that have publicly supported Anderson. Haynes also talked about blading on the show. He's also contacted a local sportswriter about doing a tell-all book on pro wrestling in the 80s.

Barr then had Matt Borne and father Tony Borne (one of that area's biggest wrestling legends in the 50s and 60s) come on and bury Haynes with Tony calling Haynes a loose cannon, saying he burned every bridge in his career, talked about Haynes using steroids and they claimed to have no idea what he was talking about when he talked about blading. Matt Borne than challenged Haynes to a fight.

Haynes then came back on his 1/3 radio show challenging Matt Borne to a boxing match with $10,000 winner-take-all (based on each man's past athletic experience, one would expect Haynes, now 43, to hammer Borne in a boxing match while Borne, 39, should tear Haynes up in a wrestling match).

Haynes went so far as to say he lied under oath to the state police in his previous effort to destroy Anderson, and apologized for everything he had said in the past about Moretti. Haynes said he didn't want a wrestling match with Borne because he didn't want a promoter to ask him to take a dive but wanted to fight him for real, and then claimed during his career that he bladed himself probably 500 times.

Barr's next show tried to blow Haynes off by calling him a has-been and when asked about the boxing challenge, dismissed it by saying Haynes didn't have $10,000 to put up.

(February 17) The Billy Jack Haynes-Matt Borne feud continued on the radio in Portland this past month. Haynes, who is now claiming pro wrestling is a work on his radio show, has challenged Borne to a $10,000 winner-take-all shoot match. On Haynes' radio show, former wrestler Scott Ferris called up and also admitted pro wrestling was a work. Haynes than called up Sandy Barr and Borne's radio show and issued the challenge and called Borne a liar. Borne said he hadn't told one lie all day. The conversation turned unintentionally hilarious at this point:

> Haynes: Have you ever used a razor blade on your head?
> Borne: I haven't told a lie all day.
> Haynes: Have you ever used a razor blade on your head in the pros?
> Borne: I haven't said a lie all day.
> Haynes: Have you or haven't you?
> Borne: Listen, I didn't mean to get under your skin.
> Haynes: Point blank question Matt, have you ever used a razor blade on your head to induce blood?
> Borne: Say what you got to say, and then I'll speak my mind.
> Haynes: Yes or No, have you ever used a razor blade on your head to force blood out of your head to make more money for the promoter?
> Borne: Have I ever used a razor blade? I used one this morning.

It wound up with Haynes challenging Borne to fight again, and Borne telling Haynes to come down to the local wrestling matches and they'll fight. After Haynes hung up, Borne said that he could whip Haynes because he's only a boxer. The next week Borne called up Haynes show and told him to come down to the matches the next night. Haynes said if Borne put up $10,000 he'd fight him.

The two argued again until Haynes accused Borne of being on cocaine. Borne than called Haynes a liar because he said he had been propositioned by homosexuals when he was in the WWF. Haynes then asked Borne whatever happened to Doink the Clown. "You failed your piss test, didn't you. That's what you told me. Did you fail your piss test, Matt, Doink, whatever your name is? Borne then responded, "Tell me about being propositioned by homosexuals." That was about the end of it.

Rick Rude

(January 20) A surprise appearance from a masked Rick Rude highlighted the first ECW Arena show of 1997 on 1/11, which, for a show with only four matches announced on television, still drew a packed house estimated at 1,400 fans with another 300 turned away at the door.

Rude wore the mask the entire time he was backstage and never admitted to anyone in the back who he was. The vast majority of the wrestlers figured it out before he went out, and virtually all the fans recognized him even before he began his distinctive interview pattern, which upset promotional plans to keep his identity a secret for the time being.

Before the scheduled main event, where Shane Douglas was to defend the TV title against Tommy Dreamer (who was stretchered out earlier in the show), Rude under the mask came out and said that his New Years Resolution was to f*** up the life of Douglas. When Douglas asked why he wouldn't show his face, he said that if he took his mask off, Douglas would shit all over himself and he and all the fans would have to deal with the smell.

Rude said he had brought someone there to take on Douglas, which turned out to be Gary Wolfe, Pit Bull #1, who has been out of action for several months after legitimately breaking his neck in an accidental spot when he landed wrong as Douglas gave him a DDT, which has been heavily pushed ever since. A short brawl erupted with Douglas and the heels taking a powder, with Rude throwing forearms as part of the brawl.

Rude, now 38, has been rumored to be headed to the WWF when his disability insurance deal with Lloyd's runs out, for some time, with the rumors within the WWF saying it would be late spring. However, WWF officials have continually denied these rumors. Those close to Rude insist that Rude will never wrestle again, due to broken back suffered in a match at the Fukuoka Dome against Sting on May 1, 1994 coming on the heels of a herniated disc in his neck which destroyed his once impressive workrate.

Paul Heyman said that the masked wrestler wouldn't ever wrestle in ECW but would be making more appearances as a regular performer leading up to the proposed PPV show. There may be an attempt to bring in another person under the mask in future shows to attempt to make it not a certainty in people's eyes that it is Rick Rude under the mask. Rude had claimed his injuries were career ending in a lawsuit filed against WCW subsequent to the Fukuoka Dome match.

(August 18) Rick Rude was brought into the WWF as part of the working agreement with Paul Heyman. Rude appeared and in exchange, Ross plugged the ECW PPV show and the Lawler-Dreamer match several times on Raw. The original deal was for it to be a one-time only thing, but judging from the TV, Rude will be Michaels' bodyguard on TV for the time being (since Michaels isn't going on the road soon). He'll likely still work some ECW as well. As of press time, all Rude had committed to in the future is the ECW PPV show this Sunday and the Raw in Atlantic City on Monday. Rude has no contract with ECW (although ECW did do an angle where Rude claimed to have signed a long-term contract) and it's likely he'll be offered a deal by WWF that would allow him to still work ECW. Heyman thinks Rude's character is unique enough to where he'd be fine with him working both places. It appears bringing back Rude and Sgt. Slaughter is to bring back the famous names from the 80s to combat WCW using all the 80s big names that are drawing the 30+ age bracket fans that are killing WWF in the Monday ratings.

(September 22) On the 9/8 Raw in the triangle match (Hunter Hearst Helmsley vs. Savio Vega vs. The Patriot), originally the British Bulldog was supposed to do the match and win the match when Rick Rude would interfere helping Bulldog beat Helmsley, showing that Rude works for whomever pays the premium, but Michaels got the entire deal nixed.

(December 1) According to Paul Heyman, he only received word about Rick Rude showing up on Nitro one hour before the show, and that the WWF didn't know about it until five minutes before the show went on the air. Rude had a lawsuit pending against both WCW and against Sting personally for negligence in his career ending back and neck injuries. There was a lot of personal heat between Sting and Rude over how Sting's deposition in the case went. With the contract with WCW, Rude settled the lawsuit.

Mitsuharu Misawa Threepeats

(January 27) Mitsuharu Misawa captured the Triple Crown championship for the third time on 1/20 in Osaka by pinning Kenta Kobashi in 42:06. It was the third title change in five days for the normally conservative All Japan promotion, coming on the heels of Yoshinari Ogawa winning the PWF junior heavyweight title from Tsuyoshi Kikuchi on 1/15 at Tokyo Korakuen Hall and Toshiaki Kawada & Akira Taue capturing the Double tag team championship (PWF World & International) from Steve Williams & Johnny Ace on 1/17 in Matsumoto.

The Triple Crown change got a major publicity boost when on Nippon Television's nightly network 11 p.m. newscast, Misawa appeared live in studio as the guest and they broadcast the final two minutes of the title change, which will air within the next few weeks on the regular All Japan 30 television show.

Misawa was working with an "injured" elbow from missing an elbow and hitting the post and Kobashi using armlock submissions. Kobashi went for a piledriver or power bomb on the apron but Misawa reversed it into a huracanrana off the apron the floor. Misawa used a Tiger driver where he dropped Kobashi on his head in the ring, and then used his regular Tiger driver followed by his running forearm smash to KO Kobashi and get the three count.

The title switch, which drew 5,500 (about 900 shy of a sellout) in the Osaka Furitsu Gym, was expected for a number of reasons, not the least of which is that Kobashi has never beaten Misawa in a singles match. All Japan is currently planning on running a 25th anniversary Tokyo Dome show in October, and Misawa, 34, who is the group's top drawing card, has to be in the main event and probably as champion to headline the show.

The tag title switch took place three days earlier before 3,550 fans. Kawada & Taue captured the belts for the fourth time, coming on the heels of winning the tag team tournament in December for the first time, in a match that went 26:12 and ended with Taue pinning Ace after two nodowas (choke slams). That match aired two nights later on the group's television show. Taue scoring the pin set the stage for the match three nights later where Jun Akiyama scored the biggest singles win of his career by pinning Taue in just 4:48 with his exploder suplex.

KEVIN SULLIVAN

(JANUARY 27) Sullivan and Benoit are taking their angle to the extreme so to speak. After the Nitro on 1/13, there was a brawl where Sullivan punched Benoit twice at about 12:30 a.m. at Hightoppers, a bar near the Superdome, and they had a major pull-apart after Benoit was making out with Nancy. This is similar to the Pillman deal in that the only ones in on it are probably Kevin, Nancy, Chris, Bischoff and a few others and they are trying to pass it off to the boys as legit since most of the wrestlers were there. Because of the Pillman deal, almost none of the wrestlers buy it but there are a few who thought it was legit. There were only a few people at the bar that weren't WCW personnel.

(APRIL 24) There is tons of behind-the-scenes heat in regard to the different factions. There is the Kevin Sullivan faction and the Hulk Hogan faction, of which Kevin Nash seems to be the most vocal member. The interview Nash did ending the show on 3/31 was totally not what it was supposed to be. Sullivan wanted him to do a promo running down Hogan and Bischoff for not being there and going to the Rodman thing instead (which he did) as an idea for a one-week storyline to build up this week's ratings, which it did. But Sullivan also asked him to run down Scott Hall, which he refused to do apparently believing it was some kind of a trick and instead praised Hall and did the rest of his interview talking about Little Napoleon (Sullivan) backstage giving orders. All this shoot stuff makes for fascinating television for some people, but it's one thing if it's Bret Hart and Shawn Michaels using it as ammo to sell tickets for an eventual match, but to do it in that way and waste TV time airing real stuff on a fake TV show is kind of unprofessional.

(APRIL 21) In the continuing saga of Sullivan vs. Nash, the Nash contingent is working to get Sullivan out of the ring. As many of you are aware, nearly one year ago Eric Bischoff told Sullivan that when the current program with Chris Benoit runs its course, that he has to get out of the ring. So Sullivan has done basically a brilliant job of keeping the feud going by using his wife, his son, Jacquelyn, etc., and to give the devil his due, in the process it has been a hot feud and has taken Benoit to superstardom. But if you've noticed, the angle where Kevin's son hit him with a chair in Baltimore hasn't been acknowledged and the pressure has been on from the other side to get Sullivan out of the ring and end the feud.

(MAY 19) The main topic of Eric Bischoff's speech to the wrestlers before Nitro on 5/12 was that Kevin Sullivan was taking a hiatus as booker of four to eight weeks due to burnout and all the pressure of the job and outside personal pressures as well. Bischoff emphasized Sullivan wasn't being replaced, although naturally that denial started all kinds of rumors that he was, and that he wanted him to come back fresh and was very adamant about how all the backstage dissension stories being public in the "sheets" are hurting the company (they should worry about the backstage dissension and bookers plans constantly being ignored winding up in angles not making sense before worrying about people reporting on it to a microcosm of the audience, but this is the wrestling industry we're talking about).

Sullivan is taking a leave of absence so he isn't expected to be around for a while as a wrestler either which also puts the Jacquelyn angle on hold. The Jacquelyn angle in Palmetto, FL last week wasn't taped, it was just done to gauge crowd reaction to it which was said to be strong, but it was scheduled to eventually take place and lead to Sullivan putting Jacquelyn over in a match.

On the Saturday TBS show, Sullivan did a bizarre interview talking about having a shoot in the bar with Benoit (the angle on the boys from New Orleans in January that nobody in the general public would have a clue about) and Meng talked English and said he broke the nerve hold on Benoit because Nancy said so because Nancy was still family. Sullivan started the Jacquelyn turn by saying she forgot where she came from and that he's the man and told her not to come to Slamboree. They've given her a new wig and are dressing her to look softer and more feminine for her babyface turn.

Chris Benoit's scheduled house show matches against Sullivan have been changed to Meng. In Baltimore, the dark match main event was supposed to be Benoit vs. Sullivan in a death match, but no announcement was made in the building regarding the match and neither Benoit or Sullivan appeared on the entire show. Bischoff, J.J. Dillon and Terry Taylor will be handling the booking temporarily.

(May 26) There appeared to be even more of a feeling this week that the booking change was something more than temporary although only a few know for sure. Terry Taylor appears to be doing much of the detail work along with J.J. Dillon, although most seem to think Kevin Nash is a very strong influence on much of what is going on and it's Nash who was Sullivan's biggest critic. Those close to Sullivan say that he fully expects to be back as booker when he returns.

(June 9) There are people who expect Kevin Sullivan to make a surprise appearance on 6/9 because the Boston show is such a big deal to him since it's where he grew up. Supposedly he's still not due back for a few more weeks. Most of the feeling now is that he'll be back as booker on his return, although there are wrestlers with clout who have complained to Eric Bischoff and want to have Terry Taylor stay in the spot.

Jacques Rougeau

(February 17) Jacques Rougeau's press conference for his 4/11 show in Montreal got more media publicity than any show anyone can remember ever in the city. All three newspapers covered the press conference along with every TV and radio station, attributed to a combination of Rougeau's aggressive promotion and the appearance of Hulk Hogan. There was tape on every evening newscast and a photo of The Giant and Pierre Carl Ouelett in a shoving match while "promoter" Cookie Lazarus was laughing (the irony of the promoter laughing while a serious situation was going on is why the photo made front center top) made the front page of the Montreal Gazette.

The complete show besides Hogan vs. Jacques and Pierre vs. Giant in a pirate match (Giant must wear an eye patch) has Flair vs. Luger, Heat vs. Faces of Fear, Malenko vs. Guerrero, a midget match with local midgets and Mike Payette & Ron Trottier & Eric Shelley vs. Serge & Martin Rolland & Richard Charland and Nelson Veilleux vs. Sunny War Cloud, who are local area wrestlers that worked for Rougeau's defunct promotion.

Most notable line was Rougeau asking Hogan how old he was, and Hogan said 43, and Rougeau's reply to a lot of laughing was that he asked him how old he was, not how many years he'd been wrestling.

Local sports columnist Jack Todd wrote a story about the proceedings. Todd, who is 6'6", appeared to be two inches taller than Hogan, which didn't go unnoticed by anyone including Hogan, who refused to take a photo with Todd unless Todd scrunched down because it would ruin the gimmick of his size. Todd said that Hogan was 6'4" and 250 pounds. He also wrote Giant was nowhere near 7'4" and 450, but he was one of the biggest humans he'd ever seen.

The French newspapers brought up Andre the Giant, or Jean Ferre, as he was known in Montreal, who lived in Montreal for many years before becoming an international superstar, when talking about the new Giant and talking about him being billed as Andre's son.

Rougeau at the press conference said he'd sell the 24,000-seat Molson Center out, which would break the all-time city indoor attendance mark set by Jean Ferre vs. Don Leo Jonathan in 1972.

(April 21) Hulk Hogan did a rare clean job for promoter Jacques Rougeau Jr. on the 4/11 WCW show at the Molson Center in Montreal which drew an estimated 9,000 fans and $209,000 Canadian.

Rougeau, the last active member of the family which has been a fixture on the Quebec wrestling scene for something like 40 years, was supposed to be the home town hero in what was promoted as a battle of the legends. However, the crowd was mixed with our reports indicating Rougeau had about 60% of the fans cheering for him and Hogan had about 40%.

Hogan lost clean to a small package with no outside interference in what was never advertised beforehand as either a title match or a non-title match although the assumption all along was that it was a title match, but made clear after the finish it was a non-title match. The finish enables them to book a rematch for the title when WCW returns to Montreal although no return date was announced in the building. It is the first pinfall job with no outside interference that Hogan has done since losing the WWF title to Ultimate Warrior at the 1990 WrestleMania in Toronto (the Piper match at Starrcade wasn't a 1-2-3 finish) and probably the last one until this coming year's Starrcade against Sting.

In the semifinal, The Giant was disqualified in a Pirate match (having to wear a pirate's patch during the match) against Carl Pierre Oulett. In the other top match, billed as a battle of football players, Lex Luger, who was a starter a lifetime ago with the Montreal Alouettes of the Canadian Football League and played on a championship team there, beat McMichael via DQ. After the match, Ric Flair did a run-in and was racked by Luger.

Hogan vs. Rougeau was said to be a decent match, but overall the card was said to have been a major disappointment with the only above average match on the show a prelim match with Jeff Jarrett beating Chris Jericho.

(June 9) The Rougeau Brothers, Jacques and Raymond, who hadn't talked in more than two years, were back talking. It was supposedly Raymond who initiated things as he followed Jacques home and they talked in Jacques' garage. With Jacques and Pierre's WCW contract up at the end of July and with WCW supposedly considering not renewing it, this mending fences may be a way to get them back into WWF, particularly since WWF is running Survivor Series this year in Montreal. Although those close to the situation said not to discount the idea Raymond was feeling Jacques out about going to WCW.

Ted Turner on Nitro

(February 24) It's not exactly the best kept secret that Ted Turner is supposed to appear at the 3/3 Nitro to fire Eric Bischoff. In fact, the story was not only released on WCW's own hotline, much to the chagrin of Kevin Sullivan (who was also thrilled with Mark Madden reporting on Wednesday that he never had a conversation with Paul E.—he did—and that his angle with Nancy and Benoit was all a work), but two days later was in a planted story in the New York Daily News page six gossip column. The item was slanted toward WWF, saying how Turner is frustrated because he's been unable to overtake Vince McMahon and the WWF in house show attendance and PPV buys and the only category he wins is cable television ratings.

(March 17) Ted Turner wasn't at the 3/3 Nitro in Atlanta because 1) An office assistant died and he was attending her funeral; 2) He was out of town on business and canceled at the last minute; or 3) He didn't want to do it and sent Harvey Schiller in his place. They are keeping the possibilities of doing something with Turner alive in the storyline.

Mark Madden vs Jerry McDevitt

(March 3) The Pittsburgh Post-Gazette on 2/23 ran a lengthy story about Mark Madden's position in the WWF lawsuit against WCW. The story is that Madden invoked a journalists shield law to avoid having to give up his sources in discovery by Jerry McDevitt. However, during the same deposition, Madden admitted that WCW has veto power over what he says on the hotline and that he could be fired if he didn't make script changes when WCW requests them. McDevitt claims that makes him no more than a shill for WCW and thus should have no journalistic privileges to maintain confidential sources and is attempting to get U.S. District Judge Donald Lee to force Madden to reveal his sources.

John Houston Pope, who is defending WCW and Madden, says that it is WWF that is having trouble with truth vs. fiction and not Madden and WCW. He said that on one hand, Titan argues Madden shouldn't be treated as a journalist because he admitted his hotline commentaries are entertainment and not journalism:

"If Titan is correct in that proposition, (the lawsuit) should be dismissed, because neither defamation nor unfair competition can be based on statements the audience knows to be unreal. On the other hand, Titan has sued alleging that Madden's commentaries are treated as serious journalism by the public—and if that's true, he's entitled to 'shield' (his sources)."

McDevitt said that Madden claiming to be a journalist is against evidentiary records which established he deliberately passed false information to the public at the insistence of his employer to promote PPV events.

(March 17) Latest Jerry McDevitt quotes on Mark Madden. McDevitt said that Madden is to journalism what Heidi Fleiss is to dating and said, "What does it have to do with journalism when you are deliberately lying" in regard to Madden using the Pennsylvania reports shield law to protect his sources in the WWF lawsuit against WCW.

(April 21) In the WWF vs. WCW lawsuit, a Pittsburgh judge ruled that Mark Madden was a journalist and thus isn't required to reveal his sources, however the judge also ruled that if Madden was told by his higher-ups in the company information to report that he knew was false, that his sources for that information can't be protected. Madden was also suspended by Nick Lambros from the WCW hotline for one week for using the phrase "Say hello to the Bad Guy" which resulted in another nasty letter from Jerry McDevitt to WCW.

Yokozuna

(March 3) Yokozuna hasn't had liposuction yet but has already lost more than 200 pounds through an amazing loss of fluid retention, which amounted to an immediate 100 pound drop. They are hopeful after lipo that he can return at a manageable weight in the fall.

(May 5) Yokozuna was contacted about coming back with all the injuries but he's on blood thinning medication so if he were to suffer an accidental cut, the blood wouldn't clot and it could be really disastrous. No word on when he'll get clearance to return.

(August 25) Yokozuna is still under contract but they want him to get down to 400 pounds and it just isn't happening. He had a recent heart scare but his heart recovered after changing his medication.

(October 20) Yokozuna, who is said to be down to 500 pounds, starts back on the road in November. The preliminary plan is for him to be a heel and he may work a program with Vader.

(November 3) Yokozuna won't be returning after all. He was scheduled to start back originally this past weekend, but underwent tests to get a license in New York and failed the physical due to obesity and an irregular heartbeat. He was said to still weigh in excess of 600 pounds. Because commissions honor other commission suspensions in the United States, because his license was pulled in New York, that means he'd be unable to wrestle in about 20-22 states that are left still regulating pro wrestling and coming on the heels of the Pillman situation, it's doubtful if even that wasn't the case, that WWF would want to risk putting someone in the ring with any kind of heart problems.

(December 8) Hogan is trying to get Yokozuna into WCW. Remember, he still has a win he needs to get back. Problem is with New York revoking his license, he wouldn't be able to wrestle in about 20 states.

Dan Severn

(March 3) Dan Severn had a meeting with Titan on 2/20. Titan liked him but both sides pretty much agreed not to do a full-time exclusive deal. It's expected Severn will work some shows for Titan around his schedule but how much or when hasn't been decided.

(April 21) Dan Severn was backstage at the ECW PPV show. He talked with Paul Heyman who was enthusiastic about bringing him in, likely to work a program with Taz. You can imagine the fireworks that would cause regarding the NWA title. Severn was asked to drop the title to Dory Funk on 4/12 at basically the last minute and refused, with the two doing a double count out, claiming he wasn't given notice in advance and that since he didn't have a deal with anyone else he didn't want to drop it. Rumors of any kind of a done deal with he and WWF are premature at this point. Sabu was the intermediary in this deal. Severn hasn't done a job in a pro wrestling ring since hitting it big in UFC in late 1994.

(November 17) Dan Severn had a weird altercation with Dory Funk after a show on 11/8 in Gainesville, FL. Believe it or not, it was in no way a work and I can say that 100% even though I'm sure most won't believe it. Marti Funk threw a drink on Severn, who got upset, and Dory was having to defend his wife. They ended up in the ring with about 50-75 onlookers and didn't fight, but did wrestle each other with reports being that Severn was too quick and technical but they mainly tried to stretch each other before a furious Severn walked out of the ring and went to his hotel room. The local police hearing about the disturbance came to arrest people just as it was breaking up.

(November 24) More on the Dan Severn-Dory Funk incident after the show on 11/7 in Gainesville, FL. The two had been booked together a few times on indie shows and worked well together in the past. The problem initially seems to stem from a match scheduled a few months back. On the day of the show, Severn was asked by NWA President Dennis Coraluzzo to drop the NWA title to Funk, and refused to do so. Severn, among other things, felt it wasn't right that he was asked at the last minute. Coraluzzo asked because he was afraid that Severn was going to work a program in ECW with Taz, which was being talked about, and Coraluzzo wanted to get the belt off Severn before he left. Since Severn never left for ECW, the issue for the most part was dropped.

Apparently Funk refused to dress in the same dressing room as Severn in Gainesville over the incident a few months earlier. There was enough concern that promoter Howard Brody switched the order of the matches so that instead of Funk's match with Steve Keirn coming before Severn's, that Funk's match was moved to just before intermission. Funk stuck around for the rest of the show since his wife Marti, a photographer, was shooting the card for the Japanese press.

After Severn won his main event over Typhoon, subbing for Greg Valentine, he was signing autographs. Marti Funk was packing her equipment and talking with some friends. Marti poured some bottled water on Brody as kind of a joke, but he didn't take too kindly to it. She then did the same to Severn, who didn't appear happy about it and she said something about having a sense of humor.

It wound up with Severn saying something to Marti and Dory getting involved to ask what was wrong and it ended up with words being exchanged. Since there were still 35 to 50 people around and Severn was embarrassed so many were watching, he asked to continue the discussion in private, but people seeing something was amiss followed them. Before long Dory starts saying how Severn thinks he's above the wrestling business and Marti calls him names, and Dory challenges him to get in the ring. Severn said that he respected Dory, but had nothing to prove to him, and then got mad at Brody feeling it was a set-up like the night Coraluzzo asked him to drop the title to Dory.

They talked for about 15 minutes before Severn finally agreed to get in the ring. Apparently Severn was trying to avoid it but by that point with so many people watching felt backed against the wall. When they got in the ring, they basically wrestled, it wasn't like a fight or anything but it definitely wasn't a worked angle.

While this was going on, the Alachua County Sheriff's Department showed up with six or eight officers and were about to go into the ring and break the "fight" up. When the officers asked if the "fight" was real, the promoter, figuring if he said yes they'd be arrested, said no, and instead the police then wanted to arrest Brody for attempting to incite a riot.

As they wrestled each other with Severn, according to reports, being too fast and too technically advanced,

Severn rolled out of the ring saying he had nothing to prove and left the building without showering and being very upset at the entire situation and feeling like he didn't understand the wrestling business at all.

Joe Higuchi Retires

(March 10) One of the most enduring behind-the-scene figures in the history of pro wrestling nearly quietly ended his career over the weekend.

In a surprise to almost everyone, just prior to the Mitsuharu Misawa vs. Steve Williams Triple Crown championship main event on the 3/1 show at Tokyo's Budokan Hall, it was announced that it would be the final match of the career of referee Joe Higuchi. With the possible exception of Johnny "Red Shoes" Dugan, a Los Angeles based referee who worked all over the world including Japan, Higuchi would probably be the most famous pro wrestling traditional referee ever. Although other referees achieved more short-term fame doing either gimmicks or being heel refs such as Danny Davis for a stint in the WWF or Tirantes in Mexico, Higuchi often received some of the biggest pops of the entire show when he'd ref a prelim match in recent years at the All Japan big shows at Budokan.

Now 68, Higuchi, real name Kanji Higuchi, along with the late Dory Funk Sr. were the prime movers in helping Shohei Baba start the All Japan Pro Wrestling company in 1972 after all left the JWA promotion as it fell into financial difficulties. In addition, he served a function very similar to what we'd call in the U.S. as a road agent since the beginning of the promotion, as he'd travel with the foreign wrestlers and help them in translations, understanding the culture and getting everyone to the bus on time to make the shows.

Higuchi, before getting involved with pro wrestling, worked with American servicemen in Japan and spoke fluent English, and in the early days of All Japan was important as a referee in the ring because he understood both English and Japanese, and helped carry Baba's finishes to the foreign wrestlers in the dressing room. Higuchi also occasionally refereed in St. Louis for NWA title matches, including for a famous Jack Brisco vs. Dory Funk Jr. match at Kiel Auditorium in the early 70s.

One of the few remaining players who can date back to the days of Rikidozan and the infancy of Japanese pro wrestling, Higuchi, a former bodybuilder, started as a pro wrestler for Rikidozan's JWA promotion in the 50s. After a short career in the ring, he wound up working behind the scenes taking care of the foreign wrestlers while on tour, and became a referee, which he became most famous for, with the old JWA in 1969.

The simple announcement before the main event saw many fans cry recognizing it as the end of a lengthy tradition of the grandfather-like bald-headed referee who was a fixture on the Baba shows and on network television in an anonymous role going back more than a generation.

During the last five minutes or so of the main event, where Misawa ended up pinning Williams in 27:52 after three Tiger suplex '91s (basically a half nelson taken over into a German suplex), Baba, who was at ringside doing the color commentary, had tears streaming down his face which again caused many in the audience to break down as well.

It is not known whether or not Higuchi will remain in his long-time road-agent like role with All Japan.

WWF on the MSG Network

(March 10) The 3/16 Madison Square Garden card has Sid vs. Bret Hart in a cage match for the title, Undertaker vs. Vader in a casket match, Johnson vs. Savio Vega, Goldust vs. Faarooq, Owen Hart & Smith vs. Doug Furnas & Phil LaFon, Maivia vs. Helmsley for the IC title, Godwinns vs. Blackjacks, Bob Holly vs. Crush and Aldo Montoya & Bart Gunn vs. Head Bangers. That card will air live on the MSG cable network.

The show actually for the most part goes head-to-head with the Uncensored PPV show, but neither WWF or WCW are seeing it as competition since WWF is starting the show at 7:30 p.m. rather than moving it up to compete with the same starting time, nor is WWF advertising on its own television shows that the card is on free cable, trying to protect the live gate.

Only about 4,300 tickets had been sold for the show which is way below normal for an MSG show. The belief is that they'd built up the Michaels-Sid cage match for a blow-off at the Garden since the angle started there with Sid winning the title, but with Michaels out, even though Hart has an issue, it's not registering at this point at the ticket window.

MSG cable used to broadcast the Garden house shows dating back from the mid-70s until the early 90s when the decision was made to drop it when crowds were falling and the WWF made the decision not to televise its arena shows on local cable. MSG cable and WWF agreed for this as a one-time try-out deal.

Disco Inferno

(March 17) Disco Inferno (Glen Gilbertti) was fired on 3/4 when he refused to do a program which would have ended with him putting over Jacquelyn in the singles match at Uncensored. The vast majority of the wrestlers were totally in support of Disco on that one and felt that putting over a woman in a singles match was a career killer.

(March 31) Supposedly as a parting shot on the way to being fired, Bischoff told Disco Inferno that for the rest of his life he'd never get another job making $80,000 a year. There is a non-compete clause in his contract so he can't go to Titan for at least three or four months, so my feeling is the rumors of him being Honky Tonk Man's secret protege won't be the case.

(April 28) Disco Inferno (Glen Gilbertti) said that reports here and elsewhere that he wasn't taking any indie bookings after 7/1 and that he was going to WWF are false. He said that he's never talked with anyone from WWF about going there nor indicated at anytime to anyone that he was going to WWF.

(May 12) Since we wrote the deal in the 4/28 issue about Disco Inferno never telling anyone he was WWF bound, we've received calls from several different wrestling personalities and two promoters independently who claim he's told them he's WWF-bound after his no-compete with WCW runs out so who knows what's up. My feeling on this is that IF he's Titan bound, due to the no compete and the fact Titan is constantly hassling WCW about tampering with contracted personnel (Curt Hennig, etc.) that both he and Titan are going out of their way to say they haven't talked at all until he's free and clear of his WCW contract. IF he doesn't wind up there, then they probably haven't talked and who knows why so many people are saying he's saying he's going.

(August 4) There have been rumors about Disco Inferno returning to WCW, but it appears the only way he can come back right now is to agree to do the job for Jacquelyn.

Hulk Hogan

(March 17) The 3/3 St. Paul Pioneer Press ran an update about the situation involving Hulk Hogan's lawsuit and counter-suit involving an alleged sexual encounter after the first Nitro on September 4, 1995. The woman involved, Kate Kennedy, claims she helped Hogan sell his merchandise at the Nitro at the Mall of America, and when she delivered merchandise to his hotel room, Hogan forced her to have oral sex with him. Hogan claimed the story was false and as a preemptive strike against a lawsuit, sued her for extortion. Kennedy's attorneys are now filing a counter-suit against Terry Bollea. In the suit, Kennedy says she arrived at Hogan's room after midnight to deliver merchandise, at which point Hogan lifted her off the floor and carried her to his bed where he forced her to perform oral sex.

(September 22) Hogan's contract expires at the end of the year and he's already sent feelers to Titan Sports about returning for a big run. The general belief is that Hogan has no intention of returning to Titan, but is using it as leverage to get a better deal. Hogan has incredible leverage right now as the execs at Turner probably feel the company turnaround and staying in the position is more due to Hogan, not that he isn't a strong part of it, than it really is. In addition, his contract is due about the same time as he's scheduled to drop the title to Sting at Starrcade, so he can use doing that job as even more leverage because if Hogan doesn't put Sting over at Starrcade, it'll flatten out Sting big-time and make this entire year of him not being on the road be almost a waste. Hogan is also back attempting to get Ed Leslie back in.

(December 1) As far as Hogan is concerned, with all the new money coming in with the Thursday show and considering his value with the movie ratings and the buy rate for the Piper match, he's going to be able to command huge money and so he probably will and should play all avenues out but it's hard to believe he'll end up anywhere else. The idea that WWF would cut Hart to "make room" for Hogan's salary misses the entire point of Hogan and why the big stars are paid so much in the entertainment world. Much as people will hate to admit this because he's out for himself and he's so bad in the ring, he is worth every penny he makes and then some because he draws that and more. WWF wouldn't have to cut people loose to make room for his salary, because Hogan, one would think, would draw in revenue every bit as much and more than he gets paid in the first place. If he couldn't and they thought he was asking more then he could draw, he's not worth it to begin with and cutting other people's contracts wouldn't make him then worth more.

As far as the top players in this industry are concerned, whether it be Hogan, Savage, Hart, Austin, or whomever, the idea that there is a finite budget for talent they need to fit into like an NFL salary cap is ridiculous, because the companies are carried by the big names. It's the mid-card guys that budgeting works with because they are generally replaceable. If, using Savage as an example, WCW loses him and his estimated $1 million per year salary, does that mean there is $1 million extra to pay the other boys. No, it actually may mean there is less to pay the other boys because Savage is worth more than $1 million per year to the company (largely due to the Slim Jim ads and exposure he gives them as much as his drawing power and name recognition to the product) and actually losing him would be a bigger cut in company revenue than the amount saved by not paying his contract.

New Jack

(March 24) There was another incident with New Jack backstage at the ECW Arena. New Jack was on the balcony with someone who was apparently either a promoter or booker for Soul City Wrestling, a local indie that uses mainly African-American wrestlers. Next thing anyone knows, it appeared New Jack tried to throw the guy off the balcony. The guy escaped and ran down the stairs and tried to run away. New Jack did another balcony jump (this time one he wasn't getting paid for) and kind of bulldogged the guy and got two punches in before the guy got away and began running for his life. Apparently Sabu pretty much saved the guy's life as he helped him escape while about ten other wrestlers, seeing one of the wrestlers in a fight, were about to join in and kill the guy.

(March 31) New Jack was at the Waltham show but never came out and wasn't at the Revere show. Paul Heyman said in regard to the incident on the 3/15 ECW Arena show, that it was a wrestler from Soul City Wrestling, an nearly All-Black indie group in Philadelphia, who was talking with New Jack and used the dreaded "N" word. He said New Jack chased him out of the dressing room but never caught him but admitted they were both running pretty fast, although others said New Jack did catch him but the guy got away.

Curt Hennig

(March 31) The latest chapter in the Hennig saga started at the Cauliflower Alley Club banquet in Studio City, CA on 3/15, and ended, or at least appears to have ended on 3/24 when Nitro opened with the appearance of Larry Hennig in the front row in Duluth.

At the CAC, Larry Hennig introduced his son, who was being awarded, as a future WWF champion, and the two talked highly about Vince McMahon. The reports we received is that Hennig, whose Titan contract expires in a few weeks (he's been sitting out until the contract expires when he's legally able to sign his new WCW deal) and was expected to join WCW immediately as a full-time wrestler at that point, was in Titan Towers on 3/18.

According to WWF sources, Hennig was expected to make a surprise appearance at WrestleMania, largely to return the Lex Luger favor from the original Nitro. When Eric Bischoff got the word about the CAC banquet and the Titan rumors, he contacted Hennig, which I believe was on 3/21, who told him something to the effect of it being him just screwing with McMahon, which Hennig has probably now done as much if not more than any wrestler alive.

Of course, nobody was sure, being this is pro wrestling and there were those in WCW worried until Mania ended that he still might make a surprise appearance since he's still under contract to Titan. WCW wanted to put it back in Titan's face by opening Nitro with Curt Hennig, however, due to the WWF contract, they are still legally unable to do so, so they did what they figured was the next best thing and put Larry Hennig there to open the show and make it clear that Curt was on his way to their side.

(April 7) Based on several different versions of the same story, Vince McMahon and Bruce Prichard had a meeting on the Tuesday before 'Mania with Curt and Larry Hennig. According to the version the Hennigs were telling at Nitro the next week, McMahon and Prichard were one hour late and they were just about ready to walk out when they came.

The sides were talking about a return to the WWF and the Hennigs pulled out the letter Prichard wrote to Lloyd's of London which resulted in Lloyd's not paying Hennig his reported $350,000 lump sum disability deal. It was basically a deal where Hennig was talking to WWF at the same time about returning and WWF needed to get the legal situation straightened out with Lloyd's as to what their situation was, and it wound up as the blow up which ended with Hennig walking out and agreeing to go to WCW.

The meeting really didn't go positively for WWF after that although the idea at that point that it was made clear that business between the two sides was done doesn't appear to be the case either and there was talk all week of potentially getting Hennig back. The Hennigs claimed at Nitro that Prichard backpedaled from the point they pulled out the letter with his signature and he claimed he knew nothing about it, but WCW was afraid as late as while 'Mania was going on that even though the Hennigs had assured them they weren't going, that it was pro wrestling and anything was possible. WCW put Larry Hennig on TV specifically to show Titan that they had Curt. People in both companies noted that Curt was extremely large, much bigger than in the past.

(May 19) Curt Hennig is now expected to start with WCW in June. There are all sorts of legal claims on Hennig that have to be sorted out. Even though Hennig's WWF contract expires right around now, the WWF is claiming they still have him under contract using the same logic Pancrase used for Ken Shamrock after the date on his contract expired. WWF claims WCW tampered with contracted personnel and since Hennig no-showed a PPV that the WWF booked him on, he was technically suspended and they believe him being suspended means his contract doesn't expire until he comes back from the suspension and fulfills the remainder of the term of the contract. Without seeing the contract, WWF would have an argument if Hennig had agreed to perform a minimum of dates within the contract (that was the Pancrase position with Ken Shamrock since it was a nine show, one year contract and their position was Shamrock hadn't done the nine shows when the one year was over) and it's doubtful that was in the contract but who knows. WCW is planning on using him in a few weeks anyway no matter what WWF claims.

(August 4) There were reports that Hennig's matches last week at Universal were so bad that they couldn't even air them, but actually the matches were never taped. Hennig was working to get the ring rust out and there were no plans for his matches to be on television to begin with. There are several different ideas on what to eventually do with him and it goes back-and-forth. He may be a Horseman, although the original plans were for that not to happen.

Scott Hall

(March 31) We have little in the way of details at press time, but Scott Hall, 37, voluntarily checked himself into rehab this past week, missing his WCW house show main event booking in Minneapolis, MN on 3/22 and his

Nitro booking on 3/24 in Duluth, MN.

On the live Nitro, it was acknowledged that Hall wasn't there, with no reason given, although it was strongly hinted during the show that it was due to transportation problems as there was a legitimate snowstorm going on in Duluth, which was a very poor way to handle the situation because they gave no hints he wouldn't be at upcoming shows where he's the scheduled main eventer.

There doesn't seem to be a definite timetable known as to when he'll return to action. On the show there were no announcements as to a change in the 4/6 Spring Stampede PPV, where the Hall & Kevin Nash tag team title defense against Rick & Scott Steiner was realistically the top drawing match on the show, nor a change in the card for 3/27 in Baltimore, where Hall is in the main event, the latter of which it is virtually a lock that Hall won't appear on. At press time, we don't have any word on how either of those shows will or won't be changed.

In Minneapolis, and most likely in Baltimore as well, Hall was replaced by Syxx in the main event, which was no longer a tag team title match, teaming with Nash against Lex Luger and The Giant.

Kingdom

(April 7) A new Japanese promotion which will basically be a reformation of the old UWFI, but apparently with a style change to being worked UFC-style matches, called "Kingdom" will be debuting with a show on 5/4.

Takeshi "Ken" Suzuki, the long-time business manager of Nobuhiko Takada, announced the new promotion, which had been rumored for several weeks and reported on in the past both in Japanese newspapers and here, in a press conference on 3/30 in Tokyo. They announced that unlike UWFI, which Suzuki basically ran from a business standpoint, although it was Takada's name as President, and went out of business at the end of 1996, that Takada would not have an executive or behind-the-scenes role in the new group, although he would remain the group's top star.

The first show will be 5/4 in Tokyo at the Yoyogi Gym. The matches will differ from the traditional UWF style, that was popularized in a big way in Japan in 1988-90 and largely continues in RINGS. This group will allow punches to the face and allow fighters to wear gloves, and also allow both punching and using elbows down from the mount position on the ground. The only difference between the rules of this and UFC rules are banning of blows to the base of the spine. In initial reports regarding the formation of this promotion, the belief was that it was largely being done to set up for a Tokyo Dome match later this year with Takada vs. Rickson Gracie, although nothing of the sort was even hinted about in the press conference.

Besides Takada, other former UWFI wrestlers signed with the group are Yoji Anjyo, Yoshihiro Takayama, Yuhi Sano, Masahito Kakihara, Kazushi Sakuraba, Hiromitsu Kanehara, Kenichi Yamamoto, Ryuki Kamiyamato and Shunsuke Matsui. With the exception of Takayama, who worked for All Japan at Budokan on 3/1, and Sano, who worked the All Japan show in Nagoya on 3/30, all the aforementioned wrestlers have been inactive this year after UWFI closed up shop in December. Anjyo, Takayama and Yamamoto worked numerous indie shows in 1996 for a number of promotions as the Golden Cups.

Apparently the group was put together by Anjyo's older brother who got the money together, largely through major financing from Nishin Kensetsu, a real estate development company.

Jim Cornette

(April 7) Jim Cornette will be managing again soon. He was replaced by Raymond Rougeau on the Challenge tapes this past week because he was suffering from a bad flu and had no voice. That's probably why when he did the angle where he offered a contract to the Blackjacks and they ripped up the contract, that the entire angle was pantomimed rather than vocal. What I expect to happen is Cornette will end up managing a heel Doug Furnas & Phil LaFon who will feud with Blackjacks, and that mix doesn't sound like it's going to get either team over. Furnas & LaFon at first were going to be managed by Bob Backlund, but Cornette is a lot better fit.

(September 8) Regarding all the rumors of Jim Cornette as a manager, Cornette has so much office work which includes writing the television shows and announcing on Shotgun and perhaps on Raw for the new season that he doesn't have time to go on the road so he can't get involved in any kind of a major program so that's been holding up his going back to managing.

Real Life Fights in ECW

(April 7) There was a backstage near fight after the 3/30 ECW show. Shane Douglas was the promoter of the two Pittsburgh area events (a lot of the ECW spot shows are promoted by the wrestlers—Buh Buh Ray Dudley does the Long Island shows, Chris Candido will be promoting the New Jersey shows).

During the show, Brian Lee suplexed Pit Bull #2 through the concessions table. Several weeks back there was a brawl that broke the concession table that resulted in a lot of merchandise stolen, and the same thing happened this time and Douglas was hot at the wrestlers. Douglas wound up arguing with Tracy Smothers until Rich pulled Smothers out of there.

There has been tremendous backstage stress of late over the situation with Van Dam possibly leaving, WCW coming into Philadelphia, and more than anything else, all the pressure because the PPV show is really about to happen and nobody really knows how well it'll do.

Heyman gave a 75 minute long speech after the show saying that this is the time everyone needed to pull together as a group. Apparently during the speech he talked about Sabu and everything Sabu has been through, apparently trying to put Sabu over, and had Sabu in tears and Sabu is now talking about staying for the long haul and even promoting ECW shows in Michigan and Indiana.

Heyman also said that if anyone from the company went to the WCW show on 4/14, not to ever talk to him again and that any relationships, business or friendship, would be over. He said that if anyone wanted to leave the promotion, contract or no contract, to tell him now and he'd get anyone who wanted one a meeting with McMahon or give them a release to talk to WCW. Nobody said anything about officially leaving although Van Dam did tell Heyman he's considering going to WCW and gave the impression he'd be staying through at least June at this point.

(April 14) There was actually quite a bit more going on behind the scenes than in the ring over the weekend. Shane Douglas and Sandman nearly got into another fight, with the heat stemming from last week. Let's just say that every version of the story I get from eye witnesses differs from the other, but the basic consensus is that last week when Brian Lee and Pit Bull #2 broke a table, Douglas, who was the promoter of the show backstage said they should be fired.

The word got to Lee, and when Douglas found out he was screaming about the stooge who told him and how the dressing room had stooges and that's what's so bad about the WWF, etc. Anyway, when it came out that Sandman told him, the two pretty much started to fight and the guys broke them up. Douglas and Tracy Smothers also nearly got into a fight stemming from all that.

This week in Scranton, PA on 4/4, they did an angle to "injure" Sandman, who wasn't going to work because of his cracked ribs, and in the angle, Douglas used Sandman's cane on him. Sandman was mad because somebody else was using his gimmick and backstage the two were about to go at it.

At this point, the different versions of the story differ, and it was that they were first held apart, and for whatever reason, some of the guys acting at peacemakers said screw it and wanted to see them fight. Tod Gordon and/or Sabu or Pit Bull #2 were the ones who pretty much broke the thing up when it looked like it was going to happen, depending on which version you hear.

Neither guy backed down, although with one week to go before a PPV show, the intelligent thing in this situation would have been to avoid the fight since it would be stupid to risk an injury before the most important show in company history, especially for Sandman who has never been on a show this big and is already going in with cracked ribs.

Paul Heyman spoke to both (he was elsewhere in the building when all this was going on) and got them in a room together for a long time and they talked everything out.

(July 21) From a news standpoint, the most talked about thing in ECW was an incident in Allentown on 7/12. We've heard about five different versions of what happened including by eye witnesses.

It started with a fan taking a swing at Douglas as he was leaving the ring. Douglas went after the fan and before he got to him, was jumped on by a second fan. At this point Gabe Sapolsky, who works behind the scenes at ECW went backstage and was basically right there as it was going on (which was only 10-15 feet away) said that there was a problem with Douglas in the crowd. At this point, the dressing room emptied.

Of all people, Perry Saturn, tackled one of the guys who was on Douglas and held him down and Dreamer and Buh Buh Ray Dudley were out there trying to keep other fans from getting involved and to keep it from getting more out of hand. The whole thing was over in about three minutes, although it became a black eye to a point for ECW on the Internet with claims from people there that the wrestlers were fighting the fans and how unprofessional it was. Others said the incident was blown out of proportion although there was an incident, but not as bad as wrestlers fighting fans incidents that happened a few times before the April PPV show.

Earlier in the show there was an incident where a fan threw a drink at Rob Van Dam, and Van Dam snatched him and in doing so ripped the fans' shirt off. Heyman claimed that Douglas was going to press assault charges against the first fan, that he heard rumors that the fan would press charges against Douglas but didn't know if it had happened, and has threatened to pull out of the building in Allentown unless he can bring his own security to the shows instead of using the local security which he blamed the problems on for not quelling bad situations before they happened.

Reggie White

(April 14) Future NFL Hall of Famer Reggie White of the Super Bowl champion Green Bay Packers signed to appear on the 5/18 WCW Slamboree PPV show in Charlotte, NC to face Steve McMichael in the semi-main event on the show. WCW had been negotiating with White on-and-off probably since January, when Kevin Greene suggested to White they form a tag team. The plan for a long time was for the two to work as a tag team with Jeff Jarrett to face Ric Flair & Roddy Piper & McMichael in the main event in Charlotte. The logic of that apparently felled that one as they realized Flair, Piper and Greene in Charlotte needed to be teammates since all would be huge babyfaces in Charlotte.

At one time it appeared the deal for White looked to be dead since White's asking price was $500,000, but WCW is generating huge money these days and a star of White's caliber guarantees lots of mainstream publicity, particularly in May when sports news is at a slow period.

Eric Bischoff put the deal together to get White to appear at Slamboree last week, and the news broke on 4/10, and it was carried on 4/14 nationally through the AP wire. White debuted that night at the live Nitro from Philadelphia, the city he played most of his career in as a member of the Eagles before joining the Packers after going through free agency and making a multi-million dollar contract.

White is a long-time wrestling fan, having followed the old NWA shows at the Philadelphia Arena in the days of Dusty Rhodes and the Four Horseman, and has been considered at various times in the past of doing something in pro wrestling. He has also been friends with Doug Furnas for probably 15 years since the two were college teammates at the University of Tennessee.

White joins Greene, an NFL star with the Carolina Panthers, and Dennis Rodman of the NBA's Chicago Bulls as superstar pro athletes who will work in the ring for WCW over the next three months.

It was announced during the show that White had signed for Slamboree, and White was at ringside for most of the show. After his match, McMichael actually began heavily praising White, but said he'd beat him in their match and it wound up with White hopping the guard rail, charging the ring and tackling McMichael before the two were pulled apart.

WWF and WCW Auto Accidents

(April 14) There was a nasty auto accident before the WCW PPV on 4/6. Regal, Benoit and Nancy Sullivan (yes, they do their angle ALL the time) were coming from the gym to the hotel when an apparent drunk driver hit Regal's four-wheel drive car that rolled over twice. Nancy was banged up a little and Benoit was bleeding from the hand (that opened up again during the Malenko match) but all were basically fine.

(June 23) Four WWF wrestlers were involved in an auto accident on the late afternoon of 6/15 which left them all hospitalized, but as luck would turn out, with none suffering serious injuries and all but one checked themselves out of the hospital that night.

The wrestlers involved were Sycho Sid (Sid Eudy), Doug Furnas (who suffered the most serious injuries), Phil LaFon and Flash Funk (Charles Skaggs). The accident occurred on the way to Ottawa, where the four were scheduled to wrestle that night, from Montreal, where the wrestlers were stationed after working the previous night in Toronto.

Sid was driving a rented Lincoln Continental at a speed described as being around 100 MPH and apparently was adjusting the sun roof and the car went out of control, hit the shoulder of the road and rolled four times about a mile from the Ontario border on the way from Montreal to Ottawa near Pointe-Fortune, Quebec. The car was destroyed to the point of being unrecognizable and all four wrestlers were taken to Hawkesbury, ONT General Hospital in an ambulance.

The original fears were that Sid was badly injured in the accident but as it turned out he suffered some facial cuts and was suffering from a major headache from a concussion and experienced some numbness in his arms and legs as he apparently re-aggravated his bad back.

Furnas was the most seriously injured, suffering a separated and broken shoulder and underwent surgery on 6/17 in San Diego to find out the extent of the damage. LaFon suffered a concussion and numerous cuts and bruises all over his body. They had to shave a lot of his head in the hospital to get out the glass that got in his forehead. Funk came out of it the most unscathed, just shaken up. The incident wasn't acknowledged on television the next night.

Funk is expected back in action for the house shows this weekend but the rest will be out of action for a few weeks, and in the case of Furnas, likely longer than that.

Sycho Sid

(April 21) The story on Sid is that he supposedly has a herniated disc in his back caused by straining the back while working out in the gym. The reason it was handled so clumsily on the 4/7 Raw is because they literally didn't know about it as the show was going and didn't know if he'd be there or not. Apparently Sid left a message at the office over the weekend, but since nobody was there and since Raw was taped on a Sunday night, nobody knew, and he didn't think to call the building to let anyone know he was hurt. He finally talked to Vince McMahon late in the week. No word on how long he'll be gone. There is also a lot of skepticism not limited to just the skeptical wrestlers as to the legitimacy of this, in that people seem to be following the Shawn Michaels lead. We don't know if Sid was going to have to put Mankind over in their match although it would make sense given Mankind was in the main event on the next PPV. Sid was definitely supposed to put Bret over on the 4/20 PPV since Bret had put him over three times in a row and it was time for Bret to get the push. You can figure the skepticism out from there.

(June 2) Sid was supposed to return on 5/30 in San Jose but now claims to have the flu and won't be back until 6/28 in Los Angeles. I know what you're thinking and so is everyone else. Guess the softball team must have made the playoffs or something. It'll be real interesting to see: 1) How large he is. If he really had a bad back and the flu, he'd be way down in muscle size and why do I think he'll show up bigger than ever? 2) How the company will use him if he shows up so large because that'll be an indication the back injury and flu couldn't have been all that bad. My feeling is they'll push him hard again and a few months down the line history will repeat itself. And if it does, if any of you feel sorry for the WWF's bad luck, you should feel more sorry for bad judgment of people who ignore the lessons the past should teach them.

(July 21) Sid collapsed backstage due to his back problems and was rushed to the hospital. They never showed a close-up of him and showed him in clothes because the auto accident injuries are legit (as opposed to the questionable nature of previous injuries) and he's dropped a lot of weight and clearly hasn't been able to weight train and he no longer has that Sid look. The belief right now is that his match with Vader is almost surely off SummerSlam. It hasn't been announced, but I believe Goldust vs. Pillman will be taken from the free-for-all and put on the main card in its place.

(July 28) The actual situation last week with Sid was that he is believed to have suffered an anxiety attack at the tapings. Sid told friends that he thought he was having a heart attack. He wasn't taken to the hospital, although WWF officials wanted to take him to the hospital, but he refused to go and instead went back to his hotel room and they had Downtown Bruno stay with him to make sure everything was okay. Sid has lost a ton of weight since he hasn't been able to train due to the back injury, and also from the flu has had no appetite. He was to get another MRI this week with problems with both a pinched nerve in his neck and the bad back which sometimes causes one of his legs to go numb.

(August 4) Sid was officially fired by the WWF. It's almost mind-boggling that a star of that magnitude in this kind of a wartime situation would be fired, but WWF officials apparently felt they had no alternative citing their inability to get any straight answers from him concerning his condition and injuries and when he'd be available. Under normal circumstances, WCW would try to bring a guy in with the illusion it's another major jump, but Sid has a lot of heat with a lot of people in Atlanta, not to mention quite a track record in this industry.

(August 11) Sid is scheduled to undergo surgery this week where they'll take bone from his hip to fuse his neck. The surgery would have kept him out of action another three months had he not been fired. He's contesting his termination and has hired a lawyer and threatened to sue the WWF for breach of contract. He's told friends that he thinks because of the legal threat that the WWF now wants him back but he doesn't want to go back. Based on what we hear, WCW would be interested in him, but only on a per-show deal and not a long-term guaranteed deal because of his track record, and then only if people like Arn Anderson approve of him coming in.

(August 18) The situation with Sid is that he wasn't immediately fired. There was some sort of clause in his right about $400,000 per year guaranteed contract, which may have been an injury clause, that WWF felt they had the right to cancel it. He was then offered a new deal which was a nightly deal which basically had he worked a complete schedule would have earned him the same $400,000 per annum, so something along with lines of $2,000 to $2,500 per shot and maybe more for PPVs, which he turned down, feeling his existing contract shouldn't have been canceled. At that point he was fired and is threatening legal action back.

(September 29) The latest on Sid Eudy is that he's back training. His neck is almost completely healed from his surgery but his hip is still giving him problems (they took bone from his hip to reconstruct his neck, which was injured both in the ring and from the auto accident). He won't be able to wrestle until January and is hoping to go to WCW at that time. The lawyers are still fighting over his WWF status. What we've gathered from WCW is that they'd be interested in him if too many of the wrestlers didn't complain (he had heat in the past not only with the Nash faction, but also with the Flair/Anderson faction and Hogan has never been fond of him either) and try and stand in the way, and even then, only on a per-night deal and not a guaranteed contract due to his track record.

(January 5) Despite all kinds of rumors to the contrary, there have been no discussions with WWF and Sid Eudy since he was told he was going to be released. Titan has made no inquiries about bringing him back. Eudy has told friends that when he's able to return to wrestling, he has no intention of working for the WWF as he's bitter about the situations leading to his dismissal. This is wrestling so never say never, just that there is nothing to any of the rumors about him coming in or him being considered to come in as part of the DX PPV show.

WCW Women's Division

(April 28) To almost no fanfare, the WCW women's cruiserweight tournament ended on 4/7 in Huntsville, AL with Toshie Uematsu winning the finals over Malia Hosaka in a match that took place before Nitro went on the air. The womens cruiserweight title hasn't been mentioned on Nitro or WCW Saturday Night since the first womens cruiser match bombed on the 3/31 Nitro.

(May 12) It was announced over the weekend on the Main Event and the Pro show that Madusa beat Akira Hokuto on 5/2 in Japan to win the womens title and would defend the belt against Luna Vachon at Slamboree. The match actually never took place, but at least they saved money in the transportation budget by doing the fictitious match. Apparently they forgot to tell Madusa she won the title as apparently when she got to Nitro, she had no clue and was telling people who asked that she hadn't won the title.

(May 19) Here's this week's storyline on the womens title. It was announced on television that the title was in dispute because of a legal dispute in the match (which never took place) between Madusa and Akira Hokuto. Not only was Madusa when she showed up at Nitro last week unaware that she had won the title, but mid-week in Japan when the news hit that Hokuto was no longer the champion, when the reporters asked Hokuto about it, she had no idea because nobody had clued her in on the angle either.

Tommy Rich and Doug Gilbert Arrested

(May 5) Tommy Rich and Doug Gilbert spent a night in prison on 4/20 after being arrested on charges of taking money under false pretenses and possession of less than 15 grams of marijuana. Rich, real named Thomas Richardson, 40, and Gilbert, 28, were released the next afternoon after pleading guilty to misdemeanor charges of taking money under false pretenses and each were fined along with being ordered to return the $500 cash they received the previous night for headlining a show that they apparently walked out on. The two were scheduled to headline against each other on a River City Wrestling show in Sisterville, WV. According to Sisterville Police Chief Robert Haught, Rich and Gilbert, seeing the crowd was about 100 fans and with each promised $250 to make the shot, asked to be paid up front. The two then drove off with the money and were stopped near St. Marys, WV, where the two were found with a small amount of marijuana. The two were held on $2,000 bond at the Tyler County Jail, and since they were unable to post bond, they spent one night in jail. Rich worked this past weekend for ECW as a manager at their two shows in Massachusetts. His status with the company wasn't affected by this incident.

Invader vs Trompetilla

(May 12) The biggest angle in a long time involved Invader #1 with the top comedian on the Island of Puerto Rico named Trompetilla (real name Raymond Arrieta) doing their 90s version of Jerry Lawler/Andy Kaufman.

It started a few weeks back with Invader as a guest of "Hello Wapa!" the local lunch-time talk show on the same TV station that airs WWC, so they were doing some cross-promotion. Trompetilla does a comedy segment on the show. They started doing the angle on the wrestling show saying that Colon and Invader would be on the show to receive achievement awards for their careers.

On the talk show, Trompetilla began insulting Invader saying that he was old, not useful anymore and that pro wrestling is all fake. Invader challenged him to get into the ring. Trompetilla threw a bucket of water on Invader and ran away. Invader then did a promo challenging Trompetilla to come to the house show that weekend in Cayey, but Trompetilla didn't come.

They had a second television confrontation on 4/22. Trompetilla brought out a guest who wasn't Invader, but a guy wearing an Invader mask and a "Just Say No" t-shirt. Trompetilla threw water on the guy. At that point the real Invader showed up and challenged him again to show up at the 4/26 house show in Humacao and said that he would put the sleeper on Trompetilla and put his hand in water so he'd urinate all over himself in the ring. Trompetilla acted afraid, but accepted the challenge.

On the 4/26 house show, Trompetilla did an interview before the match and got in the ring and did a comedy bit running away and throwing a pathetic looking dropkick. Invader chased him around the ring with Trompetilla running away. After about 90 seconds, Trompetilla got in front of Invader and did the Ric Flair begging on his hands and knees.

Rico Suave then ran-in and held Invader and Trompetilla went for the water bucket, but naturally Invader broke away and Suave got hit with the water. Invader put the sleeper on Trompetilla but several of his bodyguards hit the ring and broke it up and held Invader for Trompetilla to start paint-brushing his face which was the end of that part of the angle, but sounds like there is more to come.

(May 26) The Invader #1-Trompetilla (Raymond Arrieta) angle came to its conclusion on Arrieta's television show on 5/6. Invader said he was going to teach Trompetilla not to throw water at his guests on his TV show. The whole television angle was done in comedy, with WWC television announcers El Profe and Eluid Gonzalez at ringside with a ring acting as if it was a match. Trompetilla, who wears a clown outfit, came out wearing a mask, and was obviously not the original character. They did the match with heel manager Rico Suave (Julio Estrada) managing Trompetilla, who was unmasked, revealing WWC prelim heel Chuck Singer. The real Trompetilla came out with a role and began choking Suave and Singer and threw water on Suave. He claimed he was betrayed by Suave and that's why he saved Invader, and promised that he would never throw water on his guests anymore on his television show.

Alex Wright vs Hard Body Harrison

(May 12) Perhaps the biggest news backstage at the WCW tapings was a fight between Alex Wright and jobber Hard Body Harrison. It started when they were arguing about who would get to play heel, since both wanted to. Finally ref Randy Anderson came out and said that Wright was the heel. Harrison then started getting mad about Wright going to the office or something to that effect. Harrison had some sort of a warm-up exercise apparatus and apparently Wright thought Harrison was going to clock him with it and threw the first punch, right in the eye and split his eye open. Harrison grabbed a front face lock and they went at it until it was broken up. By most accounts, Wright was getting the better of it which surprised some people since apparently Harrison has done tough man contests and is supposed to be a really tough guy. To make matters worse, since he's not a star, Harrison pretty much got most of the blame put on him.

Leif Cassidy

(May 19) Leif Cassidy (Allan Sarven) gave notice but that was more an attempt to get the WWF to do something with him than a sign he's quitting. His contract is up at the end of July. They had talked with him about doing a gimmick as The Worlds Greatest Mexican Wrestler wearing a mask and spoofing Mexicans, but with the AAA deal falling apart, they never got it off the ground. Since he doesn't have a guaranteed contract and is only on the road as a fill-in, he isn't making all that much money and you can imagine the frustration with not getting a push when far less talented wrestlers who aren't getting over have angles. At the same time, he's been a disappointment in the ring in his big matches.

(June 2) Leif Cassidy attempted to give notice, but he didn't understand his contract. He signed a two-year contract with a one-year WWF option. The WWF picked up his option for the third year so he can't give notice until next year. They are doing a gimmick where he loses match after match on television until he snaps like a postal worker.

The Ultimate Warrior

(May 19) Jim Hellwig is apparently booked for Ultimate Championship Wrestling on 5/24 in Deer Park, NY against Chris Chavis (Tatanka), which would be his first match since leaving the WWF last summer. Kind of strange since the building only holds about 800 people. UCW usually draws about 200 per show and you figure Hellwig's price demands are exorbitant.

(June 23) Jim Hellwig appeared at the Licensing Fair in New York this past week pushing his Ultimate Warrior comic books. He said that under no circumstances would he ever return to pro wrestling.

Michinoku Pro Wrestling

(May 26) Although no deal has been completed, there is a strong probability a deal is going to be worked out with Michinoku Pro Wrestling including being a strong part of the WWF's light heavyweight division. There is nothing new on the Mexican front other than continuation of relations with AAA don't look good and there is more interest in EMLL, although no deal there as of yet. There is nothing when it comes to a deal as far as we can tell regarding Silver King coming in at present, although if a deal is made with EMLL, he's likely to be among the first in.

(June 9) Another of the most accomplished light heavyweight wrestlers in modern times, Great Sasuke, signed a six-month contract with the WWF where it is believed he'll become the focal point of that promotion's new division.

Sasuke (Masanori Murakawa), 27, held a press conference on 5/28 in Tokyo to announce the signing. He said the WWF offered him a one-year contract, but that he would only agree to a six-month deal since he is President of his own Michinoku Pro Wrestling promotion. Sasuke will finish up with the next Michinoku tour which ends on 6/22, and debuts with the WWF on the 6/30 Raw is War show facing Independent jr. champion Taka Michinoku, which will probably be something of the kick-off to the new division.

The WWF is making a new set of championship belts and a lighter weight belt is among them, and it is believed the division in its inception will be built around Sasuke, who would likely defend his crown against other wrestlers from the Michinoku and possibly FMW promotion, along with Americans and potentially wrestlers from EMLL as well.

One of Sasuke's rivals of a few years back, Jinsei Shinzaki, wrestled in the WWF as Hakushi. The WWF needed an international star to jump start the division, lest it be built around inexperienced Americans or wrestlers that the company has already established as jobbers. However, in doing so, it does look like WWF is copying WCW since WCW has been successful in building a cruiserweight division.

Sasuke signing with WWF is a bigger deal than just the President and top star of a smaller Japanese office leaving his company for six months. After Sasuke and five others from his promotion appeared on ECW shows in February and again on the 4/13 PPV show, WCW and New Japan attempted to pressure Sasuke into not wrestling with either ECW or WWF. Through WCW, New Japan told the Michinoku office that if their wrestlers appeared on future WWF or ECW shows that the promotion ties between New Japan and Michinoku would be severed, which means the Michinoku wrestlers couldn't appear on the several upcoming lucrative Dome shots and it would kill the already set up angle of Sasuke & Liger as a tag team against Kaientai Deluxe and New Japan juniors Otani & Kanemoto.

Sasuke was asked about the problem at the press conference and pretty well acknowledged New Japan had made that ultimatum and indicated by his signing what his answer to the ultimatum was. One would suspect Sasuke would return to Japan for a few major shows with his promotion this year but not appear as a regular on any of the tours. He said at the press conference that he had a dream of presenting his six-man tag team main event on a Madison Square Garden house show in the year 2000.

It's funny how Japanese think based on the past. Sasuke was a huge wrestling mark growing up and a mark for major promotion belts so the idea of being WWF light heavyweight champion and being a Japanese wrestler who is successful in the United States which was the elusive Japanese dream in previous decades is a big deal. As is the case in almost every instance, people who grew up as wrestling fans have something in their blood that tend to make them take those extra chances, work extra hard and ignore the injuries and become the top caliber of worker which Sasuke has made himself in just seven years as a pro.

But the idea of appearing in Madison Square Garden, which when he was growing up was portrayed in the Japanese wrestling magazines as the ultimate, is more important to him than appearing on a major PPV show, which today really is the ultimate in the United States.

(June 16) WWF officials claim Great Sasuke was never offered a one-year contract as he claimed in Japan, nor has he signed a six-month contract, nor was he promised the light heavyweight title belt to come in. However, it is 95% certain he'll be coming in for six months. Sasuke had another press conference this week in Japan talking about wanting the WWF jr. heavyweight title because the old WWF jr. heavyweight belt was the historical foundation of the junior heavyweight division in Japanese wrestling from 1978-83 when it gained popularity in New Japan (when New Japan and WWF were business partners) under Tatsumi Fujinami and the original Tiger Mask.

(June 30) There was a really weird incident at the Michinoku Pro show on 6/22 in Namia, which was Great Sasuke's final appearance with the promotion before leaving for the WWF. Sasuke & Tiger Mask lost their dream tag match to Jinsei Shinzaki & Gran Hamada. After the match Shinzaki said he was going to go on tour to work with other companies, which fans believed to mean FMW.

The main event was a singles match with Dick Togo vs. Super Delfin, however it was a weird match where Delfin stalled outside the ring nearly the entire match before losing. While he was out there he was doing the Zbyszko yelling and swearing at the crowd stall. Let's just say it didn't work. He may have been injured, or he may have been doing some sort of a protest in the ring or it may have been a really strange angle. Whatever it was didn't turn out as expected, as the fans began a mini-riot throwing garbage at the ring. While this happens frequently at Nitro, it's a rarity in Japan and when it does, it's not a sign of "good" heat if you get my drift.

Sasuke came out to calm the crowd down, but they were really upset and started screaming at him for leaving the promotion and abandoning his fans for the WWF. Fans were so hot that when they finally got the wrestlers out of the ring, the fans waited at the dressing room and were ready to continue to throw things and fight for one hour until they finally were able to break up the mob and people went home.

(July 14) Lots of strange goings on within Michinoku Pro Wrestling, which appears to be falling apart at the seams with Great Sasuke possibly leaving for WWF. Sasuke's WWF deal isn't finalized, or at least wasn't as of the weekend, as to anything other than doing the dates this past week. Michinoku Pro is now advertising Sasuke's match on 7/19 as his final match in Japan before going full-time with WWF. Shiryu has left MPW and is now in Mexico. Jinsei Shinzaki has left and is working for FMW. The situation with Super Delfin isn't clear either although he is booked on the 7/19 show, but at a press conference this past week Sasuke said that Delfin had also quit the promotion. Vampiro Canadiense from Mexico was fired since he missed a recent tour claiming an injury but the office found out he was working regularly in Mexico.

(October 13) Just six days before its biggest show of the year, the Michinoku Pro Wrestling office in Japan announced that they would be suspending operations effective early next year.

Great Sasuke (Masanori Murakawa) held a press conference in Tokyo on 10/4 and announced that the company, which has been operating heavily in the red, would suspend operations in January. At the same time, Sasuke said that he would be undergoing reconstructive surgery on his right knee which would keep him out of action for most of 1998. The belief is that Sasuke would restart the promotion when he's able to return to the ring. In the interim, the heel group within the promotion called Kaientai DX led by Dick Togo, would probably promote some of their own shows, while wrestlers like Gran Hamada and Tiger Mask would wrestle full-time in Mexico.

Michinoku Pro wrestling was formed in 1993 as a regional promotion in the Northeast part of Japan based in Aomori. Their trademark was running small school shows in gyms, usually before 200 to 400 fans with fans sitting on the floor rather than in chairs enjoying the Lucha Libre style action.

Sasuke put the company on the map largely through a promotional affiliation with New Japan, an affiliation that fell apart when Sasuke started negotiating this year with the WWF. Those dealings largely fell through with the exception of the end result of Taka Michinoku joining the WWF. The group has a major show on 10/10 at Sumo Hall in Tokyo with a double main event of Sasuke vs. Michinoku in a street fight and Undertaker vs. Jinsei Shinzaki

(October 20) Michinoku Pro Wrestling ran its biggest show of the year on 10/10 at Sumo Hall in Tokyo before 6,000 fans with some help from the WWF. Appearing on the show booked through WWF were Undertaker, who was managed on this show by Bruce Prichard, and Sunny, along with Chris Candido from ECW and Taka Michinoku and Victor Quinones as well.

Show opened with Yone Genjin, managed by Miss Mongol from FMW, beating Magic Man in 1:53. Magic Man did his juggling and magic act before the show which was really good, but his wrestling was poor. Tiger Mask & Gran Hamada beat Chris Candido & The Convict (Super Boy from Los Angeles) in a match described as so-so because of the style conflict. Sunny was at ringside taking photos of this match. Satoru Sayama made El Satanico submit in 6:38 with a cross armbreaker. The story behind this match is that this was the first meeting between the two since March 28, 1980 when Satanico beat Sayama to win the NWA middleweight title in Mexico City. Undertaker pinned Jinsei Shinzaki, who for this match used his old WWF ring name of Hakushi in 12:08 with the tombstone, and then put him in a coffin after the match. Fans enjoyed the basic Undertaker gimmick show with the lights and everything. Then came the basic Michinoku style six-man with Super Delfin & Naohiro Hoshikawa & Masato Yakushiji beating Dick Togo & Mens Teioh & Shoichi Funaki in 18:44 when Delfin used the Delfin clutch on Togo. Main event was a street fight with Sunny serving as the ring announcer with Great Sasuke vs. Michinoku. She introduced Michinoku as being from the WWF and she sat at ringside in his corner but never interfered. The match was a high-flying spectacular ending in 28:21 when Sasuke got the pin with a German suplex. After the match Sasuke vowed to keep the promotion alive. The show aired over the weekend on the Samurai Channel.

Strange IFC Main Event

(May 26) One of the strangest, in a number of ways, situations involving an NHB show in the United States took place on Buddy Albin's IFC show on 5/15 in Metairie, LA. The show drew a whopping 4,000 fans into the New Orleans suburb for a show sanctioned and allowed by the Louisiana Boxing Commission. The bad news is that after the fiasco of a main event, it may have killed NHB from returning to Louisiana.

The main event was actually two pro wrestlers, doing a pro wrestling cage match in an octagon. Rod Price, billed as a former NFL football player (he was in a training camp although never made a team) against Dikembe Oluwanide of South Africa. The South African wound up being Perry "Action" Jackson, who was well known by some of the audience as an area pro wrestler. Fans began loud booing since they did a worked match, throwing junk and beer and chanting it was fake, which it was, although it appeared to be the only fake match on the show. The commission was so upset they held up the gate receipts from the show.

The promoters claimed they had not booked a worked match, although they did agree that it was a bad match, but what do they expect when they put two pro wrestlers who have been working together for years in a shootfight, not to mention that neither has ever done this before, and that they fraudulently billed Jackson as being from South Africa with a fake name.

Two other pro wrestlers worked the undercard, with local wrestler Kevin Northcutt (who also works in the area as The Sandman, not to be confused with the ECW wrestler) winning a preliminary fight, and Carl Greco, who has experience with Pro Wrestling Fujiwara Gumi, lost a first round match in the over-200 tournament. Anthony Macias, an experienced NHB journeyman, won the under-200 tournament, while Gary Myers, who is 1-1-1 in EFC, (who did pro wrestling in Indiana indies many years ago) destroyed two opponents in a total time of 1:36 to win the heavyweights, just nine days before his Japanese pro wrestling debut with Pancrase against KOP champion Yuki Kondo on 5/24 in Kobe.

Kevin Nash vs Roddy Piper

(June 16) An incident took place after the conclusion of the Nitro show, in Roddy Piper's dressing room, when Kevin Nash came in to complain, blaming Piper for perhaps the single worst match thus far in 1997 when he and Scott Hall faced Piper and Ric Flair in the Boston main event before the largest crowd and gate in WCW history.

It was actually a worked match in the ring that precipitated the real problems. Flair & Piper were wrestling Hall & Nash in a non-title match. The early part of the match consisted of Flair and Hall brawling in one corner and Piper and Nash in the other. Nash claimed that Piper wasn't doing what they agreed on doing, although Nash also didn't appear to want to sell much for Piper.

The match storyline was that Piper would work and sell the match, leading to Flair's hot tag. However Piper looked horrible and even with the star power, the match was killed and was well into the negative stars. Piper also called for the finish way early, about 6:00 into a match scheduled for 12:00, which meant the post-match brawl to end the show literally lasted forever. After the show went off the air, it was Hogan and Savage, and not Hall and Nash, who remained in the ring to brawl with Flair and Piper and for Flair and Piper to clean house on, and Piper ended up in the ring holding the WCW heavyweight, tag team and cruiserweight belts up in the air while Flair finished the fight.

After the show, Nash went to Piper's private dressing room and knocked on the door, very hard apparently. Finally Craig Malley, Piper's bodyguard (the guy who did the boxer gimmick in the famous Piper team skit) opened the door. Nash basically pie-faced Piper, which is throwing something of a palm blow and shoving him into the wall. Piper tried a kick to Nash's bad knee before Malley and Ric Flair, who was there with Piper, acted as the peacemakers and quickly broke it up before anything serious took place, but also leaving the heat between the two unresolved.

According to two versions of the story, Nash and Malley did nearly go at it as well but Malley, who is obviously much smaller, backed down. Most of the internal heat within WCW was on Piper for not doing what they had agreed to do in the ring and then calling for the finish early and making the show-ending brawl go so long it totally lost its focus as well. There have been problems with the Wolf Pack and Flair and Piper stemming from the beginning of the hype for the six-man tag in Charlotte, where Flair and Piper didn't want Syxx in the match feeling he wasn't a big enough star, and where Kevin Greene didn't want to turn on Flair as the company wanted.

At one point the entire match was in jeopardy because Piper didn't want his team to lose, which was the original plan, and since he has creative control of his programs, asked to do a singles match with Syxx who he liked personally and thought he could prove he could still work and felt he needed to prove it to some of the wrestlers who saw him as someone existing totally off his past made name, by having a good match with him. The compromised was reached where the NWO team agreed to not only do the job, but not have Syxx do it because that would be the predictable finish, but instead have all three basically do the job at the same time to show that they were the more professional of the two teams.

The company feeling in WCW seems to be that hopefully everyone will be professional and the match on the 6/15 PPV show won't be ruined. After that point, they'll all be programmed in a different direction and Piper will be feuding with Flair and kept apart from Hall & Nash so those problems in the ring regarding selling and the like won't be an issue.

Billy Travis

(July 14) The angle last week involving Billy Travis being arrested on live USWA television was only partly an angle. Apparently Travis' daughter was flipping the dial on 6/21 and saw her father on the wrestling show. Apparently the ex-wife and daughter had no idea he was back working in wrestling, which is really scary, since he's been pushed there for months. They called the police since he allegedly owes child support and alimony and the police showed up at the studio on 6/28. Jerry Lawler, who apparently knew the officers, asked them to wait until the show was over to take him but they said they had a job to do. Lawler then talked it over with them to try and make it an angle, apparently saying they could take him while he was on TV and he'd fight them off as a work in exchange for them agreeing not to try and add resisting arrest charges which all agreed to and that was what happened. On television to explain the situation they had Brian Christopher claim he pressed charges against Travis for vandalizing his truck to make it part of their feud. Apparently to make matters worse, Travis' daughter was watching TV on 6/28 and seeing the police fighting with her father and arresting him and she went hysterical to the point she had to be taken to the hospital.

One Night Only Changes

(August 4) The current plan, and this isn't totally finalized but is almost a certainty, is to add a PPV show just for the United Kingdom on 9/20 from NEC Arena in Birmingham, England headlined by Bret Hart vs. Davey Boy Smith, in a rematch of their famous SummerSlam match in 1992 at Wembley Stadium.

(August 25) The "One Night Only" PPV from Birmingham, England was officially announced by Sky as a two-hour show starting at 8 p.m. on 9/20. No price has been officially announced for the show. As of 8/18, there were only about 200 tickets remaining in the 12,000 seat NEC Arena. The current plan for the PPV show is Bret Hart vs. Austin for the WWF title, Bulldog vs. Michaels for the European title, Undertaker vs. Ahmed Johnson (which will likely be changed since Johnson likely won't be ready by then), Owen Hart vs. Helmsley and LOD vs. Godwinns. Vader vs. Tiger Ali Singh, Rockabilly vs. Flash Funk and Head Bangers vs. Savio Vega & Miguel Perez will likely be dark matches.

WCW Backstage

(August 4) At a meeting with the wrestlers last week, Eric Bischoff specifically said he doesn't want any bad words, vulgar or distasteful gestures on the television shows. There were complaints from the higher-ups about these things. Among the new words banned for use on television is hosebag. Bischoff told the wrestlers to leave the dirty words and vulgar gestures to Vince McMahon.

(October 27) Bischoff had a meeting with all the wrestlers before the 10/13 Nitro in Tampa. He talked about attending Brian Pillman's funeral and then said that he wasn't naive enough to think that there's no drug problem in WCW but that he hasn't personally seen any examples of major abuse. He asked any wrestler that if they have a problem to go to him and the company would take care of the wrestler and treat the problem like it was an injury and brought up that wrestlers that have been hurt on the job have been paid while injured.

Actually there is a historical problem some had with that statement remembering both Steve Austin and Ricky Steamboat, particularly in the case of Steamboat, who may have been the most unselfish worker in the company's history, who were both fired by the company after suffering injuries.

He said that on the 10/6 Raw that they used the word "ass" 17 times (on 10/20 it seemed like they used the word 117 times) and said that WCW is going in the opposite direction of WWF. He said that Syxx could no longer do the bronco ride spot and that the NWO guys would no longer point to their crotch because he wanted a clear differential between the two products.

His explanation was that there are very few national advertisers that touch pro wrestling to begin with and he was afraid the more lewd harder edge direction of the WWF would erode the advertising base for both companies. He claimed that some of the advertisers are already on the verge of pulling out of WWF and that the direction WWF was going was going to hurt the entire business. He claimed WWF would be out of business within six months, actually I believe he used the word that he guaranteed, which I guess was his way of trying to scare people from jumping. (Don't hold your breath waiting for that one)

He said he was tired of all the whining among the wrestlers saying that they'll look back at this period in the future as one of the greatest periods in their careers. He brought up that the schedule would be increasing next year. He also said something to the effect that there are only three wrestlers in the room that have ever put asses in the seats and said they were Hogan, Piper and Savage and said he was willing to debate anyone if they disagreed with that assessment.

The description is that there was steam coming out of Ric Flair's ears and several others were fuming on the inside as well. The belief is he dissed Flair since the two are in a major contract negotiation period and he was trying to sent the hint to Flair that the company doesn't need him. As far as Flair's future is concerned, there is no question he is considering a WWF jump, but to call it a sure thing at this point is way premature. No doubt Flair knows how the game is played and he'll get word out to get the best offer.

Bischoff's deal with Jeff Jarrett was his own way to try and avert the leverage of negotiating publicly with both sides since Jarrett was far more expendable to make an example out of than Flair.

(NOVEMBER 17) WCW is thinking seriously about doing a cruiserweight tournament over several weeks with round-robin rules similar to the Japanese tour-long tournaments. The winner would be No. 1 contender for Eddie Guerrero's title. Dean Malenko came up with the idea and would be in charge of booking it Japanese style where the results stay fairly even. WCW is also going to do a Tough Man division with the likes of Benoit, Finlay, Goldberg, McMichael, Meng and others, including creating a World championship in the division.

(JANUARY 5) On 12/22 before the Nitro show, Bischoff had a meeting with the wrestlers where he emphasized that he didn't want any low blows, lewd gestures or any kind of swearing on the show. He emphasized it was important to differentiate the product from the WWF's because of what he felt would be bad publicity and a potential sponsorship problem if both companies get painted with the same brush. However, at Starrcade, Sting did "crotch chop" ala Hall, Syxx and DX. Bischoff also made a point to say how Craig Leathers, Annette Yother and Kevin Sullivan had written a great television show.

STEVEN REGAL

(AUGUST 11) The status of Steven Regal is questionable at press time. Regal was allegedly involved in some sort of disturbance on an airplane coming from to the United States from Japan for the G-1. We don't have details, but Regal allegedly caused a major disturbance in first class which caused the plane to make an emergency landing in Anchorage. A felony charge stemming from this could affect his working visa and cause him to be deported which would cost him his job. Even if he's not deported, there was considerable internal speculation that his job was in jeopardy because of the incident as the airlines don't react well to problems in the air that cause emergency landings.

(AUGUST 18) Still not totally clear about the Steven Regal situation. What we know is that Regal, Scott Norton and Marcus Bagwell were on a flight back from Japan from the G-1 tournament. Regal was acting up to the point the plane made an unscheduled landing in Anchorage and all three wrestlers were made to leave the plane. Norton and Bagwell claim it was guilt by association although there were news reports that claimed they were rambunctious on the plane. Regal was supposedly worse with reports that he urinated not in the bathroom in first class. Supposedly WCW officials don't even have the straight story of exactly what happened and aren't clear as to what Regal's future is. He was not at any of the shows this weekend.

(SEPTEMBER 1) Update on Steven Regal is that he was charged with a misdemeanor over the incident on the airplane. The belief now is that he accidentally urinated on the flight attendant which caused them to have an emergency landing of the flight from Tokyo to Detroit in Alaska and boot Regal, Norton and Bagwell off. He won't be deported, but he may not be allowed to fly for one year which would mean WCW couldn't very well use him so his status is very much up in the air to pardon the pun.

NJPW Sets Records in Nagoya

(August 18) Shinya Hashimoto solidified his unique all-time drawing power record with his headlining a sellout crowd of 43,500 at New Japan's first show ever at the Nagoya Dome on 8/10.

The show, entitled "The Four Heaven in Nagoya Dome," set the all-time attendance record for any event in the new building that opened earlier this year, and easily was the largest crowd and gate ever for pro wrestling in Nagoya. It was the eighth time that Hashimoto has main evented a major show that has drawn in excess of 40,000 fans (actually he's headlined nine shows that have drawn more than 40,000) and more than $3 million live, both figures that are likely unsurpassed in pro wrestling history (the latter figure is unquestionably the case and the former is most likely).

This isn't to label Hashimoto as the all-time greatest drawing card in pro wrestling history although that record alone has to put him on at least the list as "one of the" most successful when it comes to drawing money on big shows in that he's been the man on top while New Japan Pro Wrestling has drawn the most consistent big houses in the history of the industry. It also beat the crowd that K-1, which right now is a more popular promotion than New Japan, drew in the same building three weeks earlier for its first-ever Dome show.

Hashimoto retained the IWGP heavyweight title from Hiroyoshi Tenzan, who replaced an injured Masahiro Chono in an announcement made just one week before the show, in the main event of a show that featured two title changes. Kensuke Sasaki & Kazuo Yamazaki won the IWGP tag team titles from Manabu Nakanishi & Satoshi Kojima, and Shinjiro Otani captured the seven belt J Crown title for the first time in an upset win over El Samurai.

The show was reported to us as being very good, with only two of the nine matches not being at least good matches. No gate figure was released at press time, but it was almost surely more than $3.5 million and merchandise sales looked to be huge as well. K-1, with a similar pricing structure, drew $3.75 million on 36,500 paid. New Japan drew the crowd without any major foreign pro wrestling stars, as the only non-New Japan full-time regulars on the show were former UFC star Don Frye, and his opponent, Cal Worsham.

Reports from this week are that Chono got a third medical opinion that he wasn't going to need ankle surgery, which would have put him out of action for probably the rest of the year. Both an American doctor in Florida and New Japan's doctors suggested surgery. Chono elected not to have surgery due to his having the pro wrestlers mentality about taking time off, particularly when he's the focal point of the top feud in his promotion. Chono has been officially taken off New Japan's next big show on 8/31 at Yokohama Arena and will be replaced by Hiro Saito in the six-man main event. The belief now is that he'll be back in the ring for the September major shows.

WWF Discontent

(August 25) WWF is bringing back drug testing for a combination of reasons, largely to nip problems in the bud (a poor choice of phrases) before they become real problems. There was a scare on an airplane with a wrestler passing out coming at about the same time as the warning article in the Observer and the drug references in Phil Mushnick's column and after past history, they made what is the best choice for long-term.

(September 15) Among the topics of seemingly consensus discontent among the WWF wrestlers seem to be:

1) A negative reaction to Sid being fired after being in a serious auto accident. WWF contractually in most contracts can let wrestlers go, as can WCW, with 90 days notice even on long-term deals if the wrestler is unable to perform. WWF has never exercised that option in the past and wrestlers are thinking if they start with Sid, they'll make a habit of using it to get rid of highly paid guys when money is short. Of course the Sid situation is totally different. From a Titan standpoint, because he's always injured and there is little doubt the auto accident injuries were legit, but people question some of the seriousness of other injuries, they didn't fire him but wanted to change his deal where he'd get paid per date worked rather than guaranteed weekly paycheck. Since he just signed his old deal, he didn't want to re-negotiate and then they used their clause to drop him. There is also a

dispute over when his 90 days runs out as Titan is trying to make it three months from the auto accident but Sid claims it should be three months from the night in San Antonio where he showed up the last time.

2) The continuing push of Helmsley, which everyone believes is due to his friendship with Michaels, since with all his push, he's still not over even when put together with Chyna who should make it easy for anyone to get over and he's in line for an even bigger push.

3) Drug testing. Right now Titan has indicated it will test individuals but it's not random testing as much as testing based on rumors and/or supposed behavior. Only one wrestler has been tested thus far. The fear is if there's a problem that the testing would become regular and widespread and the wrestlers who partake in pot would have to give it up again. It has been confirmed and reported elsewhere that Hawk was the wrestler who passed out on an airplane several weeks ago, although he wound up being okay, it was the scare combined with the remembrance of the drug repercussions from the early 90s that along with a few other incidents and no-shows caused testing to be considered again.

WCW CLASH OF THE CHAMPIONS FINISHED

(SEPTEMBER 1) With TBS officially adding a new weekly live prime time wrestling shows on Thursday nights beginning on January 7, 1998, the future of the "Clash of the Champions" series becomes a question mark. Currently we've heard no official word that the show on 8/21, the 35th Clash in a history dating back more than nine years, would be the last one. But with Nitro, a two-hour live weekly show almost making the Clash obsolete, doing a second live show should finish the deal because if WCW goes through with its plans of two Clash specials in 1998, it would mean during those weeks it would have three night of prime time live wrestling.

If the 8/21 turns out to be the final Clash, it'll probably best be remembered by one of those unfortunate screwed up angles that seem to only happen at Clashes (remember when the Shock Master fell through the wall?). After the main event, they built to the Sting appearance. The angle was built up on Monday that Sting would have to speak to J.J. Dillon about what he wanted or WCW was going to break off negotiations with him. As it turned out, Dillon wasn't even part of the planned angle. Sting was on the rafters while the NWO was celebrating a victory in the main event. With him was a buzzard. The idea was that when they would ask Sting what he wanted, the buzzard would fly from the rafters to the ring as the lights in the building were turned off with a note that said, "Hogan's soul." Well, somewhere on the buzzard's trek, the note fell out of his clutches and he wound up on the ropes, with a group of NWO guys in the ring trying to avoid outwardly laughing and crying at the screw up with several minutes left to kill and nothing to do on a live television show. Actually even if the angle had gone as planned it would have been a stupid finish to the show.

Just to show how Clash is a name and concept from the 80s and considered passé, WCW, which has been packing them in for regular house shows and Nitros, drew a disappointing crowd of 4,122 paying $75,089 to the Nashville Municipal Auditorium despite a heavy local promotional push. The show drew a 3.64 rating and 6.36 share, which is a healthy number, although lower than they've been drawing with head-to-head competition on Monday nights for regular weekly television shows.

There isn't much to say about the ratings. It started with a 2.6 and continuously built, peaking with a 4.5 rating for the Savage & Hall vs Luger & Page main event. The overrun segment with the Sting/NWO angle with the bird fell to a 4.3. As a show, it had two title changes, one of which was a surprise (Steve McMichael winning the U.S. title from Jeff Jarrett) and the other which was expected (Alex Wright winning the TV title from Ultimo Dragon). It had three good matches out of seven, but in typical Clash fashion, the good matches were somewhat rushed. And it featured a show-long silly angle where two TBS movie hosts played fantasy wrestlers, doing a heel turn during the show and ending up with one of them getting a Diamond cutter from Diamond Dallas Page.

WWF VS NJPW

(SEPTEMBER 22) WWF has threatened New Japan with a lawsuit over the company having the old WWF light heavyweight title belt as part of the J Crown since WWF is introducing a new light heavyweight title shortly.

Once word got out, then Hisashi and Hisatsune Shinma got into the same act and threatened New Japan over the UWA belt that is part of the J Crown. The WWF went to Japanese reporters and asked if it would be better to file the suit or simply to get word to New Japan of the threat and not make a public spectacle out of it to allow New Japan to simply drop the belt on its own.

Jeff Jarrett

(October 13) Jeff Jarrett's WCW contract expired on 10/7. He was offered $300,000 per year to stay but turned it down, and the general feeling is that he's gone. Jerry Jarrett, who is handling his negotiations, smartly used media avenues to play up the contract expiring and get the word out he was negotiating with Titan to play all the leverage. He was still being advertised on Nitro and they even did an angle to build up a match with Steve McMichael where if Steve won, Debra would have to get out of the wrestling business, even though he wasn't signed nor had he agreed to work the show without a contract.

(October 20) Jeff Jarrett's WCW contract expired on 10/7 and he's through with the promotion. There is a lot of speculation he's WWF-bound, particularly with Jesse Jammes changing his ring name back to The Roadie and turning heel, and when he made the turn, they acknowledged his former partnership with Jarrett. Jerry Jarrett had been handling the negotiations with Eric Bischoff and had been, at least in Bischoff's opinion (and I'd concur on this) negotiating in the media. Bischoff then went public and told the same people that he was pulling his $300,000 offer off the table because of that.

Bischoff, who clearly sees himself in a powerful, perhaps omnipotent position because of just how far the company has turned around, is playing lots of hardball in negotiations which naturally leads to ruffled feathers. Terry Taylor asked for a raise but was turned down. Bischoff put his foot down in regard to Konnan, canceling the bookings at the Universal studio tapings this past week of all the Mexican wrestlers scheduled to come in from Promo Azteca that weren't already under contract and said he won't bring in any new Mexican wrestlers until 1998.

In addition, they are going to take the mask off Rey Misterio Jr. in a mask vs. title match against Eddie Guerrero at Halloween Havoc. The Mexicans had been strongly against Misterio Jr. losing his mask. There had been office sentiment that the mask was keeping him from fully getting over in the U.S., and because he's got a good look, it would help him, although many feel he looks so young without the mask on that he'll look like a teenager and nobody will take him seriously. Either way, it's probably 18 months to two years too early to remove his mask because it could be built into something incredible if it's done correctly over time but nobody has any care or patience unless it's the top of the card.

Survivor Series Changes

(October 27) The complete Survivor Series card as of a few days before press time was listed as Bret vs. Shawn Michaels, Owen vs. Austin, Mankind vs. Kane and a series of eight-man elimination matches—Ken Shamrock & Ahmed Johnson & LOD vs. NOD, DOA vs. Truth Commission, Vader & Patriot & Goldust & Marc Mero vs. Davey Boy Smith & Jim Neidhart & Glenn Kulka (a former Canadian football league player who has been under a WWF developmental contract for some time and was trained by Bret Hart and Leo Burke and worked a few weeks in Eastern Canada where reports were he was exceedingly green but showed potential) and TBA, and Head Bangers & Blackjacks vs. Godwinns & Billy Gunn & Jesse Jammes. After this line-up was released, there were words that Jim Ross was going to give the card a minor revision but we have no idea if or what that means. There had been some talk of bringing in a womens match using Aja Kong and Kyoko Inoue but I guess that must have fallen through.

(November 3) Updates on Survivor Series. Everything is the same as listed here last week except the Team USA vs. Team Canada match has some changes. The Patriot (Del Wilkes) suffered a torn tricep on 10/21 in Tulsa, apparently it tore upon impact delivering a shoulderblock to Jim Neidhart in a match taped for this weekend's

Shotgun show and surgery has been recommended and he's expected to undergo the surgery in Columbia, SC sometime this week. If he has the surgery, he should be out of action about three months. Wilkes has a history of tricep tears dating back the last few years in Japan. His replacement on the U.S. team with Vader & Marc Mero & Goldust wasn't going to be finalized until meetings later in the week, although Jeff Jarrett has been considered. Team Canada will be Neidhart & British Bulldog & Phil LaFon & Doug Furnas, so Glenn Kulka is out for now. Plan, at least for now, is for Furnas & LaFon simply to be part of Team Canada for this match but not for them to join the Hart Foundation, although that has been considered at various points. The funny part of Team Canada is that none of the four were originally from Canada and two of the four don't even live in Canada. Neidhart is of course from Los Angeles (at one point he lived in Reno) and now lives in Tampa. Bulldog is originally from Manchester, England although he now lives in Calgary. LaFon was born in France, although he grew up in Montreal and now lives in Calgary. And Furnas grew up in Oklahoma, but now lives in San Diego. There was consideration about doing a womens match at Survivor Series and bringing in Aja Kong. There is still talk of doing that for house shows although nothing is definite as to either if or when.

SPORTATORIUM

(OCTOBER 27) Another weekly wrestling tradition will be biting the dust in a few weeks. The Dallas Sportatorium, which has hosted wrestling dating back several decades, will be torn down in a few weeks and there will be a drive-through liquor store built on the property. The last pro wrestling event in the building will be the CWA show on 11/14. Negotiations to buy the land and put up the liquor store have been rumored for some time, and there was even an attempt to keep the building from being torn down by making it a local institution (insert your own joke). The Sportatorium housed weekly wrestling in Texas during its early 70s glory period on Tuesday nights, and then in the 80s moved to the Friday nights that became its new tradition during the heyday of the Von Erichs and the Freebirds. Since the folding of the World Class promotion, one new group after another has booked Friday night shows in the building, but none have had anything that could be labeled success in many years. The CWA, which was being run by wrestler Mike "Buster" Blackheart, had been drawing between 75 and 150 for the recent shows.

(NOVEMBER 10) The Dallas Sportatorium appears to have gotten at least a temporary reprieve. After news reports of its imminent demise, promoter Mike Blackheart on 10/24 told fans it wasn't a done deal and if enough noise was made, they may save the building. Even though the shows draw between 75 and 150 fans weekly, the remaining die-hards made enough noise and the building lease to wrestling was extended and the building won't be torn down.

(NOVEMBER 24) The final wrestling show ever at the Dallas Sportatorium was held on 11/17. It had been widely reported everywhere, including here, that the decision to tear the building down and turn it into a drive-through liquor store had been rescinded. Actually the story was that if the local CWA promotion could get the crowd up to about 2,500 paid, it would show that there was enough interest to save the building. Considering that there were no Freebirds or Von Erichs to be found on 11/17, all the hype and pleading with fans to save the building resulted in 500 fans, by far the largest in the history of the promotion, but still not enough to save the lease. The final match in the building saw Action Jackson & Warrior 2000 beat Al Jackson & King Parsons & Baboose in a handicap match. The CWA will continue to operate, moving their base of operations for weekly Friday night shows to the Longhorn Ballroom, which is a former famous Country-Western spot during the 70s that has housed pro wrestling in the past, and is located only a few blocks from the Sportatorium.

GORILLA MONSOON

(NOVEMBER 10) The condition of long-time WWF icon Bob Marella (Gorilla Monsoon) had improved over the week although as of press time he was still listed in serious condition at Allegheny University Hospital in Philadelphia.

Marella was on a respirator and kidney dialysis much of the past week, and early in the week his condition was listed as grave after a heart attack on 10/26. By the end of the week he was able to be removed from the respirator and doctors were hoping to perform a much needed heart bypass operation when his physical condition improved to where he was considered out of danger.

Doctors had, prior to the heart attack, recommended to Marella that he undergo a heart transplant but he was reluctant. He had more than 90 percent blockage in more than one ventricle.

Marella, a former amateur wrestling star at Ithaca College, made his professional name first as a heel after being given one of the all-time classic ring names, has been part of both the old World Wide Wrestling Federation and current World Wrestling Federation since the mid-60s and a famous title run against then-champion Bruno Sammartino while managed by Wild Red Berry.

He later turned babyface, and was a long-time part-owner of the old Capital Sports (parent company of both the WWWF and early days of the WWF) before selling his stock to Vince McMahon Jr. in 1982. He had remained with the company ever since, both in his visible roles as a television announcer and later figurehead company President, and behind the scenes working the front office and giving the time cues at television tapings.

Phil LaFon

(November 17) Phil LaFon was arrested on 11/5 after a domestic dispute in Calgary. It was a really strange situation as basically someone came to his house looking for a fight over a woman. Both, unknown to the other, were carrying a gun. LaFon pulled his first and had the guy on the ground with the gun in his mouth crying for mercy. At that point the woman, who didn't know what was going on, came over and stabbed the other party. LaFon dropped his gun to stop the woman from slashing the guy's throat and wound up fighting the guy and it was pretty one-sided. In the melee, a gun went off, neighbors called police and they arrived with SWAT helmets and dogs. LaFon was arrested for assault with intent to do bodily harm and the girl was arrested for firing a firearm within city limits. He has a court date on 12/22.

Chapter Forty One

WWF Ins and Outs

Harlem Heat

(January 20) Public Enemy and Harlem Heat are currently working in WCW without contracts. There have been a ton of rumors about Heat going to WWF. Based on what I'm hearing, WWF has so much committed to guys already under long-term contracts with guaranteed money that they're second-guessing a lot of the deals already (does the name Mark Henry come to mind?). Anyway, obviously an exception would be made for really big names, but I'm pretty well sure that medium big names aren't going to get guaranteed $250,000 contracts from WWF right now.

Brakkus

(March 10) Muscle Mag International ran a story on Brakkus (Achim Albrecht) and his switch from pro bodybuilding to pro wrestling. The gist of the story is that he was fed up with bodybuilding. At 34, he was unable to place high enough in contests to justify the huge costs of preparing for shows and talked about being fed up with the drug scene. He said he remarked to Ed Connors, who runs the Gold's Gym chain, that he'd like to do pro wrestling and Connors called Shane McMahon and an interview was arranged and he had the job within a week. He said he signed a paper with Titan saying he wouldn't use any drugs and that he's been surprise tested on three occasions including the night of his pro debut in November.

Jake Roberts

(March 24) Jake Roberts was fired. Two weeks back he took a rental car while on the Texas-Louisiana tour and disappeared for two days including missing a shot. It was just a few weeks back when he was fired, but then re-hired the next day for something similar. I guess his nine lives were up this time. He'd been working in the office helping write television besides working as an occasional in-ring performer when needed.

Big Foot

(March 31) WWF apparently made an offer to the huge bodybuilder (second guy who came out) in the Roddy Piper angle who looked good in 40 seconds. He works indies around Georgia as Big Foot. There was real heat in WCW about WWF making offers to guys who haven't even turned pro from their own Power Plant.

Neville Meyer

(April 21) Neville Meyer, who was the highest ranking person in the history of the Titan Sports company not named McMahon, resigned this past week. Meyer was the co-CEO of the company with Linda McMahon. We really never heard much about him after he was hired. He was supposed to be in charge of taking the business to a new level but nothing changed drastically and his leaving didn't seem to even cause that much of a stir.

Hugo Savinovich

(May 5) Spanish language announcer Hugo Savinovich, 38, was fired after being arrested at his apartment in Stamford, CT on charges of possession of narcotics, child neglect and possession of drug paraphernalia on 4/24. Stamford police arrested Savinovich and two companions when they investigated in his apartment and found malnourished five and six-year-old children and an apartment lined with cockroaches and crack cocaine vials. All three adults were held on $20,000 bond. When the WWF was asked to comment, they said that Savinovich no longer worked for the company.

Mankind

(May 19) In regard to Mankind, while he hasn't signed a new contract, his old one isn't due until the fall but he's begun negotiations for a new one and it is generally believed he is looking to stay since his only real options are ECW and FMW which don't pay nearly as well as he's got a lawsuit out against WCW.

(June 16) Mankind has verbally agreed to but not yet signed a five-year renewal which would put him under contract until November 2002.

Dusty Rhodes

(May 19) For whatever rumors there are about Dusty Rhodes going to WWF, and WWF did design the pieces with the expectations that those rumors would start, Rhodes has one year left on his WCW contract.

PG-13, The Funkettes and Tracy Smothers

(May 26) As far as the status of different wrestlers and rumors, PG-13 is gone after the Road Warriors deal. Apparently the guys think it's that Jerry Lawler had them fired because they're working opposition to Lawler in Tennessee, although that's been denied internally. They were told there is a chance they'll be brought back for the light heavyweight division but that would likely be only for television purposes if it happens at all. J.C. Ice had gotten a lot of heat in his short tenure there. The Funkettes haven't been officially eliminated, but unless things change, don't expect to see them around as a cost-cutting measure. It appears they're trying to get them to drop their per-show price as it's an expensive entourage act, particularly for a wrestler getting no push. Tracy Smothers probably won't be used since he's working ECW and he'd only be used here as a jobber, which would hurt him in ECW.

Michael Cole

(June 23) WWF has hired a new announcer named Michael Cole, who did the Shotgun show over this past weekend with Jim Cornette. Don't know anything about Cole but reports we heard were that it was obvious he didn't know much and Cornette was carrying him.

The Patriot

(July 14) The Patriot, who left AJPW and signed with WWF without apparently informing Giant Baba, was officially fired this past week when word reached Japan about him wrestling Rockabilly on the 6/30 WWF show in Des Moines. Patriot had told the office he needed an operation due to suffering a torn tricep and would be out of action for several months. This was after All Japan created the new threesome called GET of Patriot & Kenta Kobashi & Johnny Ace. Johnny Smith, who is a good worker but on the short side in a promotion usually built around taller guys, and who has a history of being a prelim wrestler here, has joined Kobashi & Ace in the group. In addition, there are rumors in Japan already that Ace will be the next one to join the WWF.

Jim Neidhart

(August 4) Jim Neidhart disappeared as well. The situation with him is that before coming to WWF, he had signed an exclusive contract with Universal Championship Wrestling out of Deer Park, NY and the WWF wasn't aware of that. When the WWF was told by UCW of the existing contract, they wanted Neidhart to legally get out of the deal before they'd put him back in the mix. So the stipulation about Neidhart shaving his beard on Raw on 8/4 was dropped.

Jim Ross

(August 18) Jim Ross has been elevated to Senior Vice President of Titan Sports and is the highest ranking official in the company not named McMahon. He's in charge of things like contract negotiations and talent recruiting along with playing a major role in booking the house shows and PPV shows. The ultimate decisions are, have been and likely always will be in the hands of Vince McMahon.

Jerry Lynn, Jacques Rougeau and The Great Sasuke

(September 8) Jerry Lynn wasn't offered a WWF contract because they have so many people under contract and don't have enough full-time work for those already under contract, but will likely get a lot of TV bookings based on his performance in Chicago. Jacques Rougeau has looked for work and may get some bookings in Canada part-time or be involved in some way in helping promote the Survivor Series in Montreal. There are no plans right now regarding Great Sasuke returning. Sasuke wanted to trade an appearance on a major WWF show in exchange for Undertaker appearing on his 10/10 show but WWF wasn't going for it believing that Undertaker in Japan is worth far more than Sasuke in the U.S. Paul Heyman asked Vince McMahon if he could use Sasuke and his talent on his 11/30 PPV and McMahon gave him the impression they didn't want anything to do with him and to be his guest.

Taka Michinoku

(October 27) A press conference was held on 10/16 in Stamford, CT with Vince McMahon, Jim Ross, Bruce Prichard, Great Sasuke and Victor Quinones to announce the signing of Taka Michinoku. The figures released in Japan, and I'm under the assumption these numbers aren't real although the three-year time frame is, that he signed a three-year-deal at $333,000 per year. They also said that McMahon wrote a check for $250,000 for Great Sasuke and would give it to him if he gave McMahon the old WWF junior heavyweight and light heavyweight belts. That latter deal is a gimmick for sure. As mentioned here before, WWF has wanted New Japan, to stop calling the light heavyweight belt (which is part of the J Crown currently held by Shinjiro Otani) a WWF belt. McMahon claimed that the WWF hasn't recognized either belt since 1984 (actually it would be 1985 when the WWF and New Japan broke off their business relationship). The WWF junior heavyweight title, created in 1978 for Tatsumi Fujinami, was dropped by New Japan in 1985 and replaced in 1986 by the IWGP junior heavyweight title. The WWF will be starting its light heavyweight title tournament on 11/3 in Hershey, PA after numerous delays due to problems working with both Japan and Mexican offices.

Crush

(December 8) Crush was out of action this weekend due to jamming his neck in the angle with Kane on 11/24. In actuality, he's involved in a contract dispute. Don't know the particulars. Either they want to renegotiate his contract for less money, or his contract is coming due and they're offering him less money to stay. Either way, he isn't happy and I'd say it's a solid bet he may be leaving for you know where, not that it's any kind of a major acquisition or anything. They are going to push Chainz now as the leader of the DOA.

STEVIE RICHARDS

(DECEMBER 8) Stevie Richards had a meeting with Titan. Richards was at the ECW show saying that he was offered a spot in DX but turned it down. Those close to the situation confirm he was offered a great spot in the WWF although didn't confirm it was in DX.

Chapter Forty Two

WCW Ins and Outs

Don Frye

(January 27) Don Frye was interviewed recently on a Texas radio station and asked about the rumors of him replacing Steve McMichael in the Four Horseman and he said he's been talking regularly to Ric Flair about it and hopes it happens.

Randy Savage

(February 3) Savage's new contract was for a limited amount of dates and for $1,000,000 per year. Apparently the deal was completed about the time the Savage Slim Jim commercials started appearing once again. WCW is justifying the deal because they were going to lose the Slim Jim sponsorship without Savage, and that brings in about $500,000 per year by itself. We had heard talk that Kevin Nash and Scott Hall were both given raises. Their original deal was $780,000 per year but Nash did a newspaper interview in Detroit and he claimed he was making $900,000.

Mike Tyson

(June 30) WCW is still working on Mike Tyson appearing at the Las Vegas Nitro but with his fight two days earlier, it probably won't be a definite until the last minute.

Jose Lothario

(July 7) WCW attempted to bring in Jose Lothario as a surprise for the show, just to get people talking, but it didn't materialize.

Several Firings

(July 7) WCW has let about a dozen wrestlers go. Don't have all the names but the ones bandied about were Michael Wallstreet, Craig Pittman, Nasty Boys, Jim Duggan, Joe Gomez, Ice Train and Nancy Sullivan. Nancy Sullivan may make a final appearance in Chris Benoit's corner at the PPV show or she may be gone completely already. Supposedly Kevin & Nancy are splitting up in real life, although this has nothing to do with the storyline, although they've been pretending for so long when they weren't that it's like the boy who cried wolf when it comes to them talking about splitting up.

More Firings

(July 14) Add to the list of dearly departed from WCW when their 90 day windows are up to their contracts as Renegade, Lanny Poffo, Col. Rob Parker, Jerry Lynn, David Taylor, Pat Tanaka and the French Canadians. Some of the guys being dumped may get a restructured deal or be taken off guarantee but still used. For example, there is talk that Duggan will be taken off his $250,000 per year deal and work on a per-night deal and mainly be used in a p.r. capacity and not so much if any in the ring. Wallstreet has told friends he's been offered a new deal. Ice Train may be kept around provided he moves to Atlanta, etc. Jim Powers may also be on that list.

Verne Gagne and The Crusher

(August 4) WCW is negotiating to honor both Verne Gagne and The Crusher at upcoming house shows in Minneapolis and Milwaukee respectively. Gagne has so much heat with so many people (I'd guess in the mid-80s that Gagne was, even more than myself or Vince McMahon, the most hated person in the industry) in this industry that it isn't the easiest thing to get people to cooperate about.

Syxx

(August 18) Syxx was fired for a short time. Bischoff was under a lot of heat from the higher-ups for standards violated largely having to do with vulgarity standards. Syxx must have used naughty words and some of his gestures weren't met with the highest of approval either. In the tag match with Flair & Hennig vs. Norton & Bagwell, when Syxx did the run-in, he pulled Flair's tights down and Bischoff claimed it was the straw that broke the camel's back. When he told Hall & Nash what happened, they were ready to walk, and an hour later, everything was fine again.

Rick Martel

(September 1) Rick Martel was in the office for an interview. Martel's original plan was to come in as a tag team with Winnipeg wrestler Don Callis, a Howard Stern lookalike who does really good interviews. WCW told Martel they weren't interested in adding any tag teams. People were saying Martel, 41, was in excellent condition.

Stampede Wrestling

(November 24) Bruce Hart is talking about re-starting Stampede Wrestling in Calgary with an affiliation with WCW as a way for the younger wrestlers to gain experience on the road every night.

Sean Morley

(December 8) Bischoff reportedly told Sean Morley, who has had try-outs with both WWF and WCW in recent weeks, that whatever he's offered by WWF that Bischoff would match or top it.

Jacquelyn

(December 29) Jacquelyn was let go because on the 12/15 show, she was supposed to be attacked and left laying by Elizabeth and she refused to do the angle. She had a lot of heat on the way out for that one, since they put her over Disco Inferno and had her beating up on so many men despite her being so small, and then she refused to sell in an angle where she'd be jumped from behind and it wouldn't be like she'd be beaten up face-to-face by Liz. It's one thing to not do a clean job like Disco got fired for not doing, but another to refuse to do an angle to set up a situation to give her a program that she didn't have.

Ted DiBiase

(December 29) Ted DiBiase is actually thinking seriously of making a comeback. DiBiase, who turns 44 next month, has been out of action a few years since suffering a serious neck injury while wrestling in Japan. He collected on a Lloyd's of London insurance policy signing off that he would never be able to wrestle again.

For him to wrestle, he'd have to pay Lloyd's a figure said to be around $462,000 and he's apparently strongly considering it. During his career, DiBiase was one of the best workers of his era.

Chapter Forty Three

Business Analysis

MAY 5

The first quarter is, at least in the United States, the most important quarter of the year because traditionally that's when all facets of the business are usually at their high point in any given year. What these figures show, which is something that has been obvious all along, and that is that house shows, pay-per-view business and television ratings are three entirely different animals. And the feelings people have close to and inside the industry as to how business is, and how business really is, are often entirely different stories as well.

WWF	**'95**	**'96**	**'97**
Attendance	3,227	5,838	5,718
Gate	$50,447	$84,558	$87,956
Sellout percentage	4.8	18.1	6.6
Cable ratings	2.07	2.00	1.43
PPV buy rate	1.15	1.02	0.67
Avg. PPV revenue	$3.84M	$3.06M	$1.89M

WCW	**'95**	**'96**	**'97**
Attendance	2,020	3,467	4,955
Gate	$21,280	$39,250	$61,027
Sellout percentage	0.0	24.7	38.6
Cable ratings	2.27	2.33	2.20
PPV buy rate	0.96	0.65	0.70
Avg. PPV revenue	$2.63M	$1.96M	$2.06M

AJPW	**'95**	**'96**	**'97**
Attendance	2,290	2,247	2,450
Gate	$98,160	$73,440	$80,752
Sellout percentage	38.2	44.3	37.9
TV ratings	2.13	2.77	3.63

NJPW	'95	'96	'97
Attendance	3,047	3,674	3,280
Gate	$158,410	$169,523	$134,190
Sellout percentage	22.7	71.8	61
TV ratings	2.30	1.93	3.30

Now, let's try to examine what these numbers actually mean, promotion by promotion.

As we all know, the perception seems to be of the World Wrestling Federation as being this company on a major decline, having been passed, even lapped by World Championship Wrestling, and WCW as the most powerful wrestling company on the planet.

In comparing the two promotions, we see that the WWF is still ahead when it comes to house shows, although both major American companies have made tremendous strides in getting people out to the arena since the lull in wrestling's live show popularity from 1992-95. It should be noted that WCW has sold out 38.6 percent of its shows thus far this year while WWF is at 6.6 percent, which means a lot of the difference in average attendance is simply because WCW is playing in smaller-capacity arenas overall, and a lot of the gate differences is because WWF charges higher ticket prices generally to its shows. WCW should close the gap this next quarter with a recent ticket price increase. Over the first three months of the year, the WWF is pretty much when it comes to arena business, at a similar level as last year with no real decline at all, and way ahead of business during the same period in 1995.

However, in comparison to both previous years, the cable television ratings across the board, and not just the Monday night numbers which have actually held up better than the Saturday and Sunday numbers, are in the toilet. As you can see when it comes to WWF, back in 1995 when arena business was 43 percent lower than it is today, television ratings were 45 percent higher. If you ever need anymore facts to show that getting people to watch pro wrestling on television and getting people to attend live shows are two entirely different things, then keep reading because you'll get all the evidence you need.

The alarming numbers from a WWF standpoint are in PPV. Keep in mind that the 1995 figures are a little misleading on the surface in comparison to 1996 and 1997 because 1995 compares two shows, WrestleMania and Royal Rumble, while in both 1996 and 1997 you're throwing in a February In Your House that did decidedly lower numbers. Still, comparing this year with last year, the WWF is down, and this is not in any way a misleading figure, some 34 percent in the PPV division.

The perception is that this is because WCW has taken over, and that really isn't the case either because WCW during the same period has only slightly increased its numbers from last year and is well behind the same period in 1995. That latter pair of facts will probably surprises a lot of people who believe that the buy rates have gone through the roof of late due to the NWO and Nitro, when the buy rates were considerably higher before either was around. And that's throwing in some major hot-shotting this year in the form of an estimated $500,000 to Dennis Rodman and who knows how much to Roddy Piper in addition to Hulk Hogan's huge percentage which has been there for the past three years.

How many of you knew that the TV ratings thus far this year for WCW are down as compared to the same period in both 1995 and 1996? However, since the decline is six percent as compared with the WWF's decline of 29 percent, the perception is that WCW has increased. Of course, WCW has increased tremendously when it comes to house show business, with it hitting yet another level in January. House show business has nearly tripled in the past two years for WCW and is blowing away any kind of figures in the history of the company. This comes at the same time that the company's television ratings and even buy rates have declined compared to the same quarter of the past two years.

Basically what we can gather is that more people are going to wrestling live, and although we don't have figures to back this up here, people are buying a lot more merchandise. However, fewer people are watching on television and ordering PPV shows. Since the PPV revenue per month is far more impressive and important than house show revenue or television advertising revenue (the only real money the companies get from television although in WCW the perception is important because the people who foot the bills live and die by TV ratings), the buy rate numbers when it comes to bottom line dollars are far more important than the house show and television ratings numbers.

For a total gross, as an example, if WWF averages 17 house shows per month at $88,000, that's about $1.5 million coming in, before taking away renting, advertising, transportation and all the other expenses of running an arena schedule. PPV, in a down period for the company, brings in $1.9 million and that's with far less overhead. So as hot as wrestling seems, that, in some ways may also be misleading. From a WCW standpoint, since they run fewer house shows, the PPV revenue is even more important to them than WWF.

From the All Japan standpoint, despite the perception of the company being stale and the lack of heat at the arenas compared to years past, the average attendance is actually slightly up from the past two years and the sellout percentage is roughly the same.

But check out the television ratings. For a stale promotion that based on its traditional nature, lack of angles, lack of new faces on top, lack of heat and an absolutely horrible time slot, it is drawing the best ratings of any major promotion, up 31 percent from the past year and a whopping 70 percent as compared with two years ago, during a period that the perception was that the promotion was hot and the arenas were filled with heat. Heat inside the building for the matches may actually be the single most overrated factor in how hot a promotion is. It's definitely the single most misleading. But that 70 percent increase in ratings really hasn't translated to the company taking in more money at the gate.

New Japan has had a similar marked increase in television ratings, although attendance has slightly declined from last year and it's a little ahead of 1995. If you look at the sellout percentages for New Japan, you see that while arena business has declined from 1996, it's still overall quite a bit stronger than 1995 and television viewership is way up from both the previous years.

In a nutshell, in the United States, television ratings are down, buy rates are down, and at the same time more people are going to live shows now than in years. In Japan, television ratings are through the roof with no logical explanation as to why, since they aren't the priority they are in the United States and the shows have largely been unchanged in format for the past 25 years as compared to the constant tinkering and hot-shotting that has actually resulted in lower ratings in the United States over the past few years. Business live is largely stagnant, although stagnant at a healthy level.

JULY 28

Since we did a business analysis of the first three months of the year in pro wrestling in the 5/5 issue and not all that much has changed in regard to momentum or direction, we are just going to offer these figures comparing the first six months of 1997 with similar periods in 1995 and 1996 for both WWF and WCW.

WWF	**'95**	**'96**	**'97**
Paid attendance	3,275	5,486	5,615
Average gate	$44,658	$80,505	$88,951
Average cable rating	2.13	2.03	1.60
Est. average buy rate	0.95	0.79	0.60
Est. average PPV revenue	$2.66M	$2.19M	$1.60M

WCW			
Paid attendance	2,008	3,502	5,317
Average gate	$20,668	$40,801	$73,484
Average cable rating	2.10	2.17	2.12
Est. average buy rate	0.75	0.56	0.65
Est. average PPV revenue	$2.01M	$1.62M	$1.95M

The major thing to notice in this table when it comes to why budgets are being tightened is that even though WWF's arena attendance average has increased this year, it doesn't make up for the drop of nearly $600,000 per month when it comes to PPV revenue as compared to one year ago. Another note when it comes to average is that this year the WWF has been running 15-18 house shows per month as compared to 22 the previous year so once again while average is up, total revenue would be down even in that category.

WCW, which has been the leader when it comes to television ratings on-and-off for much of the past decade (although it was closer and there were several years like 1995 where the WWF did beat WCW overall when it came to ratings), has almost caught up this year in attendance. The gate differential is largely because it took WCW until well into this year when it raised its ticket prices to basically the same structure, and now in many markets a higher structure, than WWF.

WCW has a substantial lead in ratings, and has taken the lead in PPV although the gap is still relatively small. WCW, on the other hand, had greatly increased its arena revenue to the point of nearly doubling its average income per show. In some instances, due to playing in larger and more costly buildings this year as opposed to last and spending more on advertising, I don't think the actual profit margin would have doubled but it would be a very safe bet to say it's increased dramatically, while at the same time they are up over last year in PPV as well, while TV ratings have only shown a slight decline over the same period last year.

One thing it should be noted when it comes to TV ratings and myth vs. reality, is that the NWO angle is constantly being touted as the reason the ratings are up and that WCW is beating WWF. One has to say the NWO angle is very likely a main cause for the increases at the house shows, certainly in merchandising and buy rates, but the fact of the matter is the ratings over the first six months of 1996—before the NWO came into existence and for the most part only including one month of Scott Hall and maybe a week or two of Kevin Nash, were higher than the first six months of this year. Why do I think I'll be reading next week somewhere how if it wasn't for the NWO that WCW's TV ratings would be in the toilet?

Another interesting note from the WCW comparisons is that even though buy rates are up significantly from last year, if you compare them with the same period in 1995, before Nitro, before WCW became "hot" and without using football and basketball superstars on every PPV, they are actually lower, and PPV is still the leading revenue source for a major league American pro wrestling company nowadays.

SEPTEMBER 29

The question of whether the WWF going live or on tape has anything to do with the ratings has been answered many times over in the past. The answer is it has nothing to do with it because the virtual entirety of the television audience that watches wrestling doesn't follow the product close enough to even know when shows are live or on tape, and those who do follow it that closely are going to watch the taped show anyway.

The unanswered question for this week is whether the venue, in this case a sellout crowd at Madison Square Garden in New York, the most famous arena in the world in the most populous city in the country, makes a difference. Shocking to many, the answer in this case was also a resounding "no."

The WWF Raw show, with all the New York hype over the past month plus about this being an extra special show, and a lot of work in pre-production being done with taped historical features to add to the atmosphere of what was largely a very good television show on 9/22 from MSG drew a 2.33 rating (2.35 first hour; 2.30 second hour) and 3.49 share. That compares with a 2.54 rating on 9/15 with a taped show coming from Muncie, IN with far less hype.

Even more depressing from a WWF standpoint, and astounding, is that when Nitro went off the air at 10:16 p.m. Eastern time, that the Raw audience showed almost no growth, and wound up averaging a 2.33 for the three segments after Nitro was off the air, the same exact average it had for the five head-to-head segments. This meant that of the basically 2.6 million homes watching Nitro, that statistically none (which translated means so few it isn't statistically significant to even mean an 0.1 rating differential) of those homes tuned to USA.

The general feeling when the new season started with the new time slot for Raw was that it would get beaten during the head-to-head segments by Nitro as has been happening the past year plus, but it would pick up greatly in the ratings with the Nitro lead-in once Nitro goes off the air. That has happened in the past, but didn't occur at all this week.

The MSG show drew 14,615 fans, packing the building cut down in seats to the taping television, with 10,672 paying $258,339 and another $97,720 in merchandise. While there have been larger paid attendances for live Raw tapings, with the high New York ticket prices, this was a bigger live gate than at any Raw (or for that matter Nitro) taping in history.

The other pattern becoming prevalent in the new season, is that Nitro now peaks every week from 8:45 to 9 p.m., and does lose a fraction of its audience when Raw and Monday Night Football, and probably more the latter than the former, begin. Although Nitro's ratings remain tremendously impressive against the football competition, there is also a pattern of viewers declining as the show goes on.

The drop at 9 p.m. should be expected and easily explainable, but the huge drop every week before the main events the show is being built around, when in the past the company did phenomenal final quarter numbers, is a telling sign. Perhaps it's been too many weeks without Sting on television doing an end of the show fly-in. Perhaps people have seen the fly-in so much that they don't need to stick around for it anymore, even though it's no longer happening. Probably the wrestlers they've been using to anchor the main events of late, in particular Curt Hennig the past two weeks and Diamond Dallas Page and Lex Luger the weeks before that, are either not over as mainstream TV draws in the case of Hennig or have had their characters flattened out by recent angles in the case of the other two.

Nitro on 9/22 did a 3.69 rating (3.83 first hour; 3.58 second hour) and 5.57 share, which means the head-to-head five segments saw Nitro winning 3.58 to 2.33. Nitro replay did a 1.6 rating and 3.0 share.

Nitro peak was a 4.4 for the segment involving Scott Hall, Syxx, Larry Zbyszko and the quickie match with Hector Garza. The rating stayed strong with the second highest segment a 4.0 for the eight-man Lucha match and the Piper interview, despite the start of Raw (2.1 for MSG nostalgia clips, Ahmed Johnson vs. Rocky Maivia and Austin interview from the stands) and football. From that point Nitro dropped to a 3.6 (Steiners vs. Meng & Barbarian) to Raw's 2.3 (Undertaker and Michaels interview); followed by a Nitro 3.8 (Hogan & Bischoff interview, Savage interview, Savage vs. Richards) to a Raw 2.4 (LOD vs. Faarooq & Kama); a Nitro 3.2 (Raven attacking Richards, Konnan & Norton vs. Booker T) to a Raw 2.6 (Owen vs. Pillman and Austin using the stunner on McMahon) and finally a Nitro 3.3 (Hennig vs. Jarrett and typical NWO finish) to a Raw 2.2 (first half of Cactus Jack vs. Helmsley). The second half of Cactus vs. Helmsley, despite it being an excellent match and Nitro ending, still only drew a 2.2 and the unopposed rating grew only to a 2.3 for the Michaels interview and Undertaker confrontation and 2.5 for Bret vs. Goldust main event.

OCTOBER 27

With the Monday Night ratings war still being the hot topic of discussion and comparisons within the industry, at least in the US, a secondary set of question which hasn't been answered has come up. Who draws what ratings and why?

Wrestlers have tried to talk about who individually draws what to prove who is over, and who isn't, bookers have done the same, and management theoretically pores over the quarter-hours trying to figure out what lesson exactly the viewing patterns of the public is telling them about which individual wrestlers.

Like most of pro wrestling, lots of talk. Lots of figures quoted without understanding. Almost no research.

With the start of the fall season at the beginning of September, we've been compiling all the quarter hours and who was in them in a key position. There are many ways you can do ratings for individuals, but the decision was made that the best is to judge based on how the ratings went up or down as compared with the previous quarter. Obviously if there is a huge audience watching, getting a big rating for a quarter is easier than if you start out. The quarter hour differences, pluses and minuses, tell if more people were tuning on then tuning out when this personality—and this is a personality driven business—was the key part of the show.

With any system, there are flaws. The two key ones right now are the 9 p.m. to 9:15 p.m. quarter hour on Nitro. With the start of the NFL and the start of Raw, you are almost guaranteed to drop at least a few rating points. The other key position is on Raw, during that unpredictable period somewhere between 10 p.m. and 10:30 p.m. when Nitro finally goes off the air. In theory, Raw should pick up viewers during that quarter, although as we've discussed, the reality is that isn't always the case, but in theory that should be a good period for Raw. Aside from that, this system is pretty well fair and fool-proof.

Wrestlers in the first quarter hour, since the show is just starting and there is no plus or minus to figure from, aren't figured into the equation, although the pattern right now for both shows has been to start the show with interviews with the biggest stars.

And before getting into anymore analysis, we'll just present the data as it exists. The only names listed are those who since the start of September, have contributed to at least a .5 plus or minus rating. Wrestlers who aren't listed, and these are the majority, are basically ones that over the course of between 9/1 and 10/13 (the 10/20 shows aren't included in these numbers) have really made no ratings difference.

The Big Winners

+16	Disco Inferno (WCW)
+14	Roddy Piper (WCW)
+12	Chris Jericho (WCW)
+9	Steve Austin (WWF), Alex Wright (WCW)
+8	Syxx (WCW)
+7	Hugh Morrus (WCW), Mortis (WCW)
+6	Ric Flair (WCW), Bill Goldberg (WCW), Brian Pillman (WWF), Vader (WWF)
+5	Rey Misterio Jr. (WCW), Legion of Doom (WWF), Steve Regal (WCW), Max Mini (WWF)

The Big Losers

-25	Scott Hall (WCW)
-18	Head Bangers (WWF)
-12	Jeff Jarrett (WCW), Steiners (WCW), Steve McMichael (WCW)
-9	Curt Hennig (WCW), Konnan (WCW), Ultimo Dragon (WCW)
-8	The Godwinns (WWF)
-7	Hector Garza (WWF)
-6	Lex Luger (WCW), Scott Norton (WCW), Los Boricuas (WWF), Raven (WCW)
-5	Stevie Richards (WCW), Randy Savage (WCW), Bret Hart (WWF), Ahmed Johnson (WWF)

Just looking over the list, the very first impression is that for the most part, it shows that it isn't the personalities that draw the ratings, it's the television show itself, the promotion and the positioning. Keep that in mind not only when it comes to television ratings, but crowd reactions, and really every aspect of this business. How "over" and to what degree is more a matter of positioning than any sort of ability either in the ring or on the mic. If someone is put in the same "group" as the stars and positioned as a star, they become a star, even if they don't draw, flop in their role, or whatever. Once they are positioned to that point, most people to a degree, take it like they are on that level.

This should weaken a lot of leverage of a lot of wrestlers when it comes to contract negotiations because of what they mean to the ratings, when in fact, as individuals, for the most part (the exception being the short-term boost when a guy like a Roddy Piper, or potentially an Ultimate Warrior that were major stars that disappear for a few months and come back) they mean very little. Bret Hart's numbers were negative. Shawn Michaels was only a +2. Hulk Hogan was a +4. Sting was a -1, although based on the last six months since WCW used to do those phenomenal final quarters, I'm sure his numbers would have been as impressive as anyone's up until the last month or two, and that probably does say something about how they've crossed the boundary of going too long with his angle to where it is beginning to erode in interest.

Scott Hall's numbers speak for themselves. Now to a point, based on a different type of positioning (he's done a lot of matches in the 9 p.m. quarter), Hall has simply been the wrong guy at the wrong time. Although the fact is that out of his eight quarters where he has been the focal point, six of them saw the ratings drop from the previous quarter and not all of them can be explained by simply being at the 9 p.m. quarter because some were in more advantageous time slots. And no matter where they've been placed in the show, the ratings have increased significantly ever time Disco Inferno has done a match and every time but once that Roddy Piper has appeared on television on this run.

The single most overlooked aspect of Raw vs. Nitro is if you ask people "on the street" so to speak. Raw seems more popular among the so-called hardcores and Internet types, but those are also largely the teenage and early 20s males that don't make up the bulk of the television audience. Nitro's dominant position has from the start been because of attracting a new audience that hadn't been watching WWF wrestling on Monday nights, largely late 20s and older, which is where the bulk of the population fits. That audience grew up with Hulk Hogan, Roddy Piper, Randy Savage, Ric Flair and the rest, and no doubt that's a big part of it. But I can also say the main response when I've been to places where people ask me about wrestling and bring up the two shows, that 80% of the time people say they watch Nitro ahead of Raw, usually more out of habit than what is on either show, and the first reason they'll bring up is the most simple reason that nobody has been able to grasp but I hear it every time.

The wrestling on Raw is so slow, or its corollary, the wrestlers on Nitro are so much better. For all the desperation tactics Raw throws out, how many times it trots out Steve Austin, how many interviews Shawn Michaels does, it's biggest weakness is the pace of its matches and its excitement level of those matches to the audience in comparison to its competition.

And speaking of ratings, 10/20 was another record setter for both WCW Nitro and pro wrestling in general.

Nitro drew its largest audience ever for an opposed show, doing a 4.54 (4.65 first hour; 4.47 second hour) rating and 6.98 share, breaking the competitive record of a 4.34 set for the 8/4 Nitro from Auburn Hills, MI with the Hulk Hogan vs. Lex Luger main event. On 8/25 and 9/1, with Raw preempted, Nitro both weeks drew a larger audience than this past week at 4.97 and 4.73 respectively (the former with no football competition, the latter against the NFL Monday season opener). Even more impressive is the record was set with competition during the second hour from Monday Night Football, even though the game drew only a 12.0 rating as opposed to the usual 15-16 level, which was probably a contributing factor in the Nitro record rating. In addition, the Nitro replay drew a near record 2.24 rating (the record is 2.31 also set for the 8/4 show) and 4.69 share.

With Raw drawing a healthy 2.96 (2.88 first hour; 3.05 second hour) rating and 4.59 share, it means that the combined ratings for the six head-to-head segments was a 7.39 and a 11.03 share or a total audience watching both shows of 5,398,000 homes. This breaks the record combined audience at 7.11 (which was an 11.86 share since fewer people are watching television as a whole on a Monday night in August as opposed to October) and 5,065,000 homes also set on 8/4.

In a counter-programming move, the USA network and WWF have scheduled a Survivor Series flashback show on 10/28, airing both at 8 p.m. and again at 11 p.m. Eastern time, the same two starting times as the TNT produced "Escape from Devil's Island" premiere movie starring Hulk Hogan and Carl Weathers. The flashback show is being heavily pushed as the night of 100 stars, including Hogan, Savage, Flair, Hennig, Diesel, Razor, and other WCW names featured prominently in the ad, which will be headlined by a match from November 28, 1991 where Undertaker pinned Hogan to win the WWF title.

WWF drew a tremendous 3.8 rating when they did the same type of a special before SummerSlam and should be favored to win a rare wrestling ratings victory against the TNT movie debut. Bischoff in particular showed that the USA network's counter-programming got to him as he made three television references to Vince McMahon being scared of Hogan's movie during the 10/20 Nitro show.

Chapter Forty Four

Supercard Summary

WWF Royal Rumble

After some worries going in, the World Wrestling Federation ended up drawing the second largest paid attendance in the history of pro wrestling in the United States for its Royal Rumble PPV show on 1/19 at the Alamo Dome in San Antonio.

While the show fell short of the 71,000 mark bandied about in all the pre-match publicity, the total in the building was 60,525 fans (it was announced on the PPV show as 60,477 but a later compilation revealed the slightly higher number), with 48,014 paying $480,013, all figures topping even optimistic company expectations a few days before the show. In the final few days they sold 20,000 tickets, mainly at $5 and $7 with discount coupons from Taco Bell that according to locals were being picked up as fast as they were printed.

The only larger paid attendance for a show in the United States was the famous Hulk Hogan vs. Andre the Giant match on March 29, 1987 at the Pontiac Silverdome which drew approximately 78,000 fans legitimately and about 75,800 paid. The WWF has also topped the 48,000 paid mark (actually topped the 64,000 paid mark) on at least three other occasions outside the United States, two events in Canada (Hogan vs. Paul Orndorff and Hogan vs. Ultimate Warrior in Toronto) and one in England (Warrior vs. Randy Savage and Bret Hart vs. Davey Boy Smith double main event at London's Wembley Stadium).

The 1992 WrestleMania at the Hoosier Dome in Indianapolis with a Hulk Hogan vs. Sid and Ric Flair vs. Savage double main event drew 62,167 fans, which was slightly more than the Alamo Dome show, but the paid attendance was less as that show was substantially papered. Tickets were scaled much higher at the Hoosier Dome and the gate was nearly triple the Alamo Dome gate.

The large attendance was fueled by numerous fans getting in as cheap late walk-up buys, which wasn't the case at similar attended shows around the world (bottom price at the New Japan Tokyo Dome shows now is $50 although for years it was $30, while even in 1987 the bottom price at the Silverdome was $9). The actual gate wasn't even in the top echelon even for the United States and actually trailed live gates that several major offices routinely do for major indoor arena shows.

The gate still broke the all-time Texas state record set on May 6, 1984 for the Ric Flair vs. Kerry Von Erich title change at Texas Stadium that drew 32,123 fans (previous state record attendance) and $402,000. Considering how much money was spent in advertising on those two respective shows, this was a long way from being the most profitable house show ever in Texas. By any account, the paid and total crowd were huge successes for the

WWF, which by all accounts did perhaps its best job ever when it comes to local promotion of a show.

The attendance was the story of the show and the saving of the show, which saw Shawn Michaels capture the WWF title from Sid in the main event and Steve Austin win the Royal Rumble in a late swerve. Those at Titan believed too many fans knew the original plan of Bret Hart winning and were concerned, perhaps overly so, that Vic Venum (Vince Russo) had "given it away" (he predicted it ala a Mark Madden gimmick where he knows a planned finish and then predicts it to get himself over) to make himself look smart on their own Live Wire television in the early days of the promotion of this show (Venum later came back the next week after getting heat and said nobody could predict a winner of a bout like a Royal Rumble).

It was the classic case of reactive booking instead of pro-active booking. The problem with reactive booking means those who are supposed to be in control are no longer in control and they are reacting to forces rather than creating and controlling the forces. This is not meant as a knock on it because if the end result is still Shawn Michaels vs. Bret Hart at WrestleMania, the long-term battle plan has changed along the way but has the same ultimate destination.

The change in Rumble plans changed the four corners match on the 2/16 Chattanooga PPV from having the supposed top four in the WWF—Sid, Shawn Michaels, Austin and Bret Hart, to the final four in the Rumble—Bret Hart, Austin, Vader and Undertaker with the title shot at Michaels at WrestleMania being at stake to the winner.

From a match quality standpoint, this wasn't a good show. The Rumble match was a one-man show with nobody else even making a dent. Michaels, bothered by the flu, had his worst PPV match in several years, although in his home town with a crowd that had come largely to see only one match, it came off well as a spectacle and to many hid the workrate. Sid may also have not been at 100% due to having an auto accident nine days earlier—although he had worked three house show dates in the interim—as he did almost nothing.

The crowd shots and generally strong production were the highlights of a show that contained average to fair wrestling. The booking was way below par as only one match, a Mexican trios match that nobody cared about, had a finish that didn't involve either a referee screw-up or outside interference.

I enjoyed the show based on the atmosphere, because the size of the crowd and the heat and emotion in the title match is something that even the best matches on the biggest shows of the year can't duplicate. But if any two other wrestlers in front of that crowd, or those two wrestlers in front of any other crowd, or for that matter any other two wrestlers in front of any other crowd, had move-for-move the same match, it would be a one-star match and people would be vehement about how awful a world title change match it was.

A few other show notes:

- Vince McMahon repeatedly called the crowd "capacity" even after they gave the number during the show at 60,477 and they had been hyping 71,000 for two months.
- After several years, they finally got Jim Ross in the black cowboy hat as a full-time gimmick. Ross was fired a few years back by WWF for among other things, an interview in Pro Wrestling Torch newsletter and because he wouldn't agree to be portrayed as "Good ol' J.R." wearing a black cowboy hat.
- Legendary Montreal wrestler Jacques Rougeau Jr., the father of Raymond, (WWF promoter) Jo Ann and (WCW wrestler) Jacques Jr. did the French language broadcast with his son Ray.
- They had an ad during the show for the Sugar Ray Leonard-Hector Camacho fight which Vince McMahon and Titan Sports are promoting on PPV in March. Expect a lot more hype for that fight as weeks go on.
- The second consecutive last minute "surprise" on a WWF PPV show turned out to be a dud, as the late entrant in the Royal Rumble turned out to be Jerry Lawler, who had been advertised all along in print but never on TV.
- From live reports, the show was generally panned by those there. Reports were that fans leaving the building were happy because the home town wrestler won the title but not happy with the show as a whole.
- Although the crowd in attendance was heavily Mexican and many spoke only Spanish, it appeared almost nobody knew or cared about any of the AAA wrestlers although reports were that the wrestlers in the

two dark matches blew everyone else on the show away when it came to performance.

- This show was heavily promoted in all the Mexican wrestling magazines
- The local San Antonio Express News, which was one of the sponsors of the show, ran several stories leading up to the event and ran the next-day coverage of the event with a large color photo on the front page. As far as I'm concerned, no matter what someone may think of pro wrestling, any time an entertainment event can come to a city the size of San Antonio and draw 60,000 people, it should be front page news.

WCW/NWO Souled Out

You may call it the night that the NWO gimmick was fully exposed. Maybe it'll even go down as a turning point in an ever changing wrestling war at the very worst. At best, it was one real bad night, lucky if only for the fact that one bad show doesn't change the face of wrestling and that the majority of the television viewing wrestling fans don't order PPV and thus didn't see it. Problem is, most of the television viewing wrestling fans who actually spend money on pro wrestling, thus basically keep the wrestling economy going, do order PPV events.

NWO Souled Out—what came off to outsiders as the brainchild of someone intoxicated by his own success to the point of all perspective being lost—was the single worst PPV show in the history of pro wrestling. There have been shows where the quality of the matches were worse, although this would be a bad show by that criterion. There have been shows with less heat and worse atmosphere, although this would be a bad show by those criteria as well. But there has never been a show with such poor announcing and outside wrestling skits, and combined with the bad wrestling, lack of heat and bad atmosphere made it the night the Baltimore Bash and the Philadelphia Halloween Havoc were no longer thought of as the bottom of the PPV barrel.

It was like WCW copied the worst aspects of the first two weeks of Shotgun Saturday Night, and then tried to go even farther to the point it looked like a bar show put on by a person whose brain was so fried by acid that only they knew what world they were in and it had only a semblance of resemblance to the pro wrestling show they were attempting to put together. It was even more amazing coming from a company that was on its biggest roll in its history and is loaded when it comes to talent depth, neither of which were apparent.

The only signs of the success of WCW were the sellout at the Five Seasons Center in Cedar Rapids, IA of 5,120 paying $68,209 who largely felt as ripped off as those at home did that spent $27.95 on this mess. And it will likely turn out to be a fairly significant buy rate for the show since NWO was the in thing in wrestling.

This show, based on crowd reactions, in that an NWO show in a sea of NWO t-shirts saw the NWO wrestlers get booed, or in many cases, ignored in nearly every match sans Scott Hall & Kevin Nash's tag team match. While the name NWO is over, the NWO name can't get anyone over. The NWO's popularity is Hall & Nash. Hogan, trying to play heel and rogue babyface at the same time, is still both a big drawing card based on his past and an obnoxious bore based on his present. The rest of the guys are guys who weren't over, dressed up with the same cool t-shirts as those in the crowd, but still couldn't get over. While Hall & Nash can get away with the teenage lingo or just about anything else in their late 30s because when you're over you can almost do no wrong, both Eric Bischoff and especially Ted DiBiase come off as pitiful trying to act like teenagers in the parking lot during class breaks while in their 40s. Sweet? Not!

The less said about the NWO Beauty Pageant and the members of the washed-up band Jackal the better. If the Oak Ridge Boys, who are a real big name band, in Nashville, their home town, didn't sell one ticket or one PPV buy and ended up as the bathroom break for the live wrestling fans, the idea of trying it again with a worse band just shows that those who don't know anything about the past are doomed to repeat its stupidity.

If that wasn't bad enough, the booking was horrible as well. The Nick Patrick gag went from being a heat seeking missile to a tired worn out screw-job by the climax of one of the worst world title PPV matches in history. A Mexican death match without any Mexicans and without an explanation as to why? A wrestler running another over in a motorcycle and the announcers selling it as a comedy spot rather than a heat spot? And that same wrestler after having been run down, appeared two nights later on a live television show not selling an injury nor did the announcers even acknowledge the incident. A PPV show without even one interview with a wrestler, despite having some of the best interviews in wrestling sitting about four rows deep in the audience?

Suffice to say that if someone wanted to put on the worst show possible on purpose, they could have put on worse matches, but they'd be hard pressed to have a worse show.

UFC 12

There was almost too much news to digest coming out of UFC XII and the circus atmosphere surrounding the political football during the week which made national headlines.

When the week was over, UFC had moved from Niagara Falls, NY to Dothan, AL, had garnered major national media attention; had filed a $32 million lawsuit; had lost a court battle to save the show in New York; had the law they spent $50,000 getting passed to regulate and answer the question of legality in New York state be on the verge of being overturned; had spend an estimated $500,000 (not to mention losing out on as much as $200,000 more by not having the live gate in Niagara Falls) the profit margin and then some, chartering last minute flights and making all the last second changes necessary to save the show; and had introduced a new phenomenon; created a new champion; and unbeknownst to almost anyone created a new martial arts hero in Japan.

The creation of a new monster champion in Mark Coleman, a freestyle wrestler who placed seventh in the 1992 Olympics at 220 pounds, who made Dan Severn submit to a combination headlock and choke in 2:59; and of a new phenom in 19-year-old Vitor Belfort (Vitor Belfort Gracie, the adopted son of Jiu Jitsu legend Carlson Gracie Sr.), who destroyed the competition enroute to winning the heavyweight tournament, paled by comparison with the questions regarding the future of the sport.

If the economics of to maintain a new sport on PPV after the novelty has worn off aren't hard enough, the political problems have made it that much more expensive. Whatever profit margin SEG would have made on the show had to be eaten up by legal fees, refunding the six-figure live gate in Niagara Falls and having to let spectators in free at the new location, the costs of chartering planes, booking last minute hotel rooms, ordering a new production truck, and paying overtime for the basic around-the-clock set-up of getting the Dothan Civic Center and Octagon ready for a PPV show at the last minute.

If anything, it was a miracle the show ran as smoothly from a television standpoint as it did amidst all the commotion.

While the majority of problems were thrust upon SEG, they made things worse by being overconfident about the court case, and then being not totally unprepared, but largely not ready for the last minute move after insisting all week that it was a 100% certainty the events would take place in Niagara Falls despite the court battle being in progress.

This left the entire organization reeling when U.S. Federal Court Judge Miriam Goldman Cederbaum ruled in the early afternoon on 2/6, the day before the show, against SEG's motion to throw out the new rules that were thrown at the group to cripple the show. Cedarbaum ruled that she didn't believe SEG had proven that the imposition of a 114-page rule book governing the event, which totally changed the nature of the event of Ultimate Fighting from the Brazilian sport of Vale Tudo to what would approximate the Japanese sport of shootboxing while wearing amateur boxing headgear (not that any of the particulars involved in writing or ruling on the new laws even knew what either of those sports are), would cause SEG and UFC irreparable damage before the lawsuit itself comes to trial. No final decision has been made by SEG as to whether or not to continue the lawsuit against the state athletic commission, as the company is still hopeful of gaining yet another political reversal in time for a proposed 5/30 show at the Nassau Coliseum and would need the commission on its side at that point in time, although because of the media pressure, it's highly unlikely such a reversal is going to happen.

After the ruling, SEG arranged to move he event to Dothan, originally slated as a back-up site when the new rule book was sent to SEG. SEG officials had made arrangements to possibly hold the event in Dothan on 1/31, however three days later, called the Civic Center and told them they wouldn't be needing the event, after being assured that it was a 100% certainty that they would win the case in court. Panic stricken on Thursday, they called back that afternoon with the building still available and willing to take the booking on short notice.

At that point SEG chartered a jet from Niagara Falls, carrying about 200 fighters, entourages, reporters and fans from around the world on an excursion that none will probably ever forget. With numerous problems, not the least of which was the weight of the octagon which delayed the departure, the plane didn't leave Niagara Falls until midnight. It landed in Montgomery, AL—more than 100 miles away, after 2 a.m., at which point several buses were rented for another two hour plus journey in the middle of the night down Alabama highways to four assorted hotels rented as the last minute, with most not getting into their rooms until 5 a.m. and everyone having to check out by Noon due to a religious convention that had booked all the rooms for Saturday.

After flying and being in a bus all night the night before, it was literally a miracle that someone wasn't hurt more seriously in combat—the very thing the politicians and reporters in New York grandstanding were proclaiming they were attempting to avoid. SEG chartered another plane immediately after the show leaving Dothan and returning to Niagara Falls, where everyone's original flights were booked out of because the idea of flying everyone home from Dothan, which is only served by one airline, would be both a logistical and financial nightmare.

After working around-the-clock, they were still painting the canvas on the octagon at 7 p.m., when the alternate bouts were scheduled to start. As it was, the show started live 15 minutes late, but on time for the PPV. The PPV itself was neither the best nor the worst UFC to date. Most of the matches were short and not really competitive. The only screwed-up aspect of the show was Tank Abbott's performance in doing what was purportedly color commentary on three matches, and that had nothing due to with the change in location.

The debut of the under-200 pound weight class was generally considered a success. Although the announcers never acknowledged and probably didn't understand the importance of it, Pancrase fighter Yoshiki Takahashi became something of a national hero in his home country, at least within the martial arts world, winning his first round match over Wallid Ismael, a Brazilian Vale Tudo fighter of much renown who was brought into UFC with the expectations he'd destroy everyone in the tournament. No Japanese fighter had ever beaten a name Brazilian in a Vale Tudo match, and in this instance, it was a mid-card Pancrase fighter beating someone who many considered as one of the five best BJJ fighter around rather conclusively, and doing so while fighting with what he believed was a broken hand for much of the fight.

In addition, it brought new respect for Pancrase from a martial arts world that somewhat dismissed the entire sport and its performers and their accomplishments within their sport as top level fighters due to it being part of the pro wrestling world (and perhaps for good reason in certain instances because there have been worked matches in Pancrase). Nevertheless, the climax was a letdown as the Pancrase vs. Lions Den grudge match with Takahashi vs. Jerry Bohlander, a grudge the announcers never mentioned (interestingly enough since Ken Shamrock was doing color for those matches), never took place since Takahashi had what was believed at the time to be a broken hand. It was later diagnosed as a severe sprain (ironically with all the talk in the New York media about potential deaths, this was the most serious injury to come out of the matches), which did require minor surgery. The belief is had Takahashi recognized it wasn't a break, he probably could have come out for the championship match.

Even though the natural storyline would demand a match between the two on the 5/30 PPV, that may not be in the cards. The battle plan right now is to have an under-200 tournament on that show, and invite Takahashi back, along with Pancrase's Guy Mezger. Mezger would likely be the favorite in such a tournament, however that would create another problem if things went according to plan, as the two tournament winners are scheduled for a singles match in July to create the first UFC World lightweight champion. However, it has been made clear that Mezger won't fight Bohlander because Lion's Den fighters won't fight each other.

The heavyweight division was all Vitor Belfort, whose boxing prowess proved not to be overrated in the least. With the quickest and most accurate punches of anyone ever in a UFC event, Belfort won his two matches without having to display any real ground fighting technique. The irony of instituting weight classes is that the lightweight champion, Bohlander, likely weighed more than the heavyweight champion, Belfort (Bohlander was announced at 199 but was probably 205, and Belfort, announced at 205, was probably a few pounds lighter than that). Due to Brazilians coming up short in several NHB situations they were expected to win, both in UFC and in EFC, the Carlson Gracie side needed a find like this. The question now regards Belfort's future. His boxing trainer, who also trained Oscar de la Hoya, said Belfort is the second best boxer he's ever trained and could win an Olympic gold medal. There is far more money in being a top flight boxer than in a top flight NHB fighter so there is certainly an economic lure for Belfort to try the more lucrative sport.

Coleman trimmed down from 255 to 240. If anything, he appeared to be more powerful than ever despite coming off a virus contracted in Brazil in November that plagued him for several months. The belief going into the fight is that Coleman's superior strength would give him the early advantage, but if and once the match got past the 5:00 mark, Severn's superior conditioning would turn the tide in his favor. Severn, who told friends that he had trained harder for this match than for anything in his athletic career, came in about ten pounds heavier and stronger than he had in his previous recent UFC appearances. However, it was for naught, as he apparently wrenched his back almost immediately and Coleman, with his incredible grip strength, turned a simple side headlock into a smother choke and Severn had no choice but to tap or pass out, either of which would have meant a loss. Severn, who had talked of retiring from NHB after this match and a possible match with Don Frye had he won, told friends after the matches that he felt he still had a few good matches left in his career.

With no local publicity, the promotion was forced to open the doors for free and packed the 3,100-seat Dothan Civic Center, with the proviso that nobody under 18 would be allowed in the building (although the New York Times reported that teenagers were able to sneak in). The crowd was very enthusiastic and far more knowledgeable about the participants and the game than the promotion feared, so the atmosphere wasn't a letdown. There was basically no acknowledgement by the announcers of the political problems and the last minute move other than a very brief mention in the open about a political storm. However, there were numerous chants by the crowd of "New York sucks," which weren't acknowledged on the air.

Stories regarding the show were the lead story on page one in newspapers in both Dothan, AL and Niagara Falls, and also a first section story for several days in the New York Times, which published an editorial that largely turned the political tide in New York state against the event and ultimately was responsible for the event being moved. The Times event coverage claimed that blood was spilled in seven of the nine matches, although in actuality it in three, none of which were overly bloody by a boxing or pro wrestling standard although the story largely focused on in as bloodsport and used the human cockfight reference. USA Today ran the story on page three on 2/6. Newsday in New York in a column by Ellis Henican blistered promoter Bob Meyrowitz and the UFC, saying that he resembles Satan saying "Since 1994, Meyrowitz has been sending men, two at a time, into violent brawls for public amusement, and he chooses not to protect his fighters with many rules." The column, which ran two days after the PPV show, went on to point out such facts as there are no rounds (true, but that generally makes it more of a cardiovascular sport since it gives conditioning and endurance an advantage over power), no judges (obviously the guy watched the PPV very closely), and no weight classes (he really watched the show closely). He wrote that UFC is a bore and the only thing that saves it is the blood, which he wrote, is what the "low-watt cretins" (the latest euphemism for UFC fans) were shouting for during the Severn-Coleman match. Well, there was no chant for blood during that match, but he did notice the New York sux chants which he attributed to "some of Alabama's lower IQs."

During the week, NHB took several more political lumps. In New York, the state Assembly voted 134-1 to ban NHB events from the state. A similar bill in the state Senate, which wouldn't ban the sport outright but give local politicians the right to ban the events within their jurisdiction, passed by a 33-0 margin. However, on 2/10, State Senate majority leader Joseph Bruno reversed his position and said he would ask the senate to pass the same bill as the assembly totally banning the sport in the state, which Governor George Pataki has already pledged to sign immediately. Bruno said he'd support the outright ban because the rule book implemented by the state athletic commission on the sport had effectively banned it in the state anyway, although Bruno still said that he considered UFC to be less violent than boxing. The Oklahoma legislature overruled the state boxing commission in allowing events with a few rule changes such as were on the most recent Extreme show. The Oklahoma rules that were allowed until the new ruling had banned head-butts and attacking the spine, added five-minute rounds (called phases) and mandated the wearing of gloves.

Not that Meyrowitz and UFC are totally not at fault. There are problems which we speak of regularly. Lack of steroid tests leave an unlevel playing field and change the results and strategies to a great degree. And don't think steroids are some secret that only a chosen few know about or recognize in the fighters. In one match on the show, virtually every insider when it came to predictions was using steroids as their reason for picking one or the other to win, based largely on the effects of steroids during the short and long haul. And they were probably correct since the match went almost exactly according to one of the two expected scenarios.

We still have the unverifiable and obviously phony records, like the alternate named Jackie Lee, who looked like the middle-age cook in the Bruce Lee bio movie, being 98-0. We still have people who have no reasonable chance or ground skills and balance from a competitive wrestling or Jiu Jitsu background, to win, such as Jim Mullen, being put in tournaments, which there is no reason with a four-man field. It's been established what a "real fight," UFC style entails, and Mullen himself, despite whatever the WKA North American championship in kick boxing actually means, admitted in a newspaper interview the week before the fight that he wasn't planning on using his kick boxing skills because he recognized they wouldn't work. Trying to answer ignorant martial artists by putting people from disciplines that have no chance of winning into the event only makes the event look bad to outsiders.

The newspaper advertising and some of the cable advertising that was in the days before the fight listed Ken Shamrock as appearing in the heavyweight tournament. Although there had been talk of this happening at one point, the fact is the two sides had never agreed to terms and it's been known for at least a month that Shamrock wasn't going to be fighting in this show so they were advertising up to the last minute arguably their biggest drawing card for a show he wasn't fighting on.

I'm also confused about having weight divisions but not doing a weigh-in, made only more weird by the idea that the lightweight tournament winner may have weighed more than the heavyweight winner. The idea of putting Tank Abbott, who added nothing, on commentary for three matches backfired even worse than putting him out for one match did a few shows back. One positive is that Bruce Beck did an outstanding job throughout the show, particularly in keeping the commentary going while Abbott was babbling semi-incoherently.

But while far from perfect in many aspects, what the media, the government, the athletic commission and the court system did to SEG was a downright scary commentary on our country. The fact SEG was seemingly oblivious to the end result of this one-sided game and was caught with its pants down at the last minute was no excuse or justification over what was done to them. They had gone through proper procedures to get a bill passed, overwhelmingly as it turned out, signed by the Governor, that clearly legalized their event in New York and stipulated what the rules of such an event were, and then booked a PPV for the state.

The media, ignoring the existing lack of evidence as to serious injuries compared with sports like boxing, football and auto racing, crucified the politicians for passing the bill, citing dangers like a potential for death that the facts didn't support. Politicians reversed their field, but had no legal leg to stand on in getting either the UFC or EFC show stopped in the state until they had time to enact the new law. Instead, they sucker punched SEG by having the commission attempt to sabotage the event with a 114-page rule book completely changing the nature of what the competitors were training for and the sport that was being advertised, despite the existing law having different rules written into it.

Instead of the media calling attention to just what the new rules were about such as the Octagon needing to be 40-feet in diameter (a rule added to force the event out of state because there wasn't time to build a new octagon, not to make it safer), or doing the very small amount of research to realize the brutality of the matches don't live up to the media hype, the imposition of mandatory boxing gloves which are impossible to wrestle in thus nullifying the most physically safe legal maneuvers in the UFC and turning it into a striking battle among some athletes whose specialty isn't striking in many ways, based on how people had trained, actually made the fights more dangerous.

This was a commission that looked the other way the entire decade of the 80s sanctioning pro wrestling events while 90% of those involved were juiced to the gills. And I don't even want to think about the boxing abuses they've looked the other way at. On the very night of the UFC show, Nevada allowed a spaced out fighter with documented recent drug problems into the ring for a world title fight and he basically suffered a nervous breakdown with the nation watching on HBO. But even if the new rules would make the event safer, this is the same thing as one week before that boxing title fight, the commission deemed that any punches to the head would be illegal based on the prospective danger, or, that the two boxers should instead fight under freestyle wrestling rules because the injury rate in freestyle wrestling is less than that of pro boxing.

Or one week before an NFL championship football game, the government ruled that because pro football has such a high injury rate, the two teams instead would be at the last minute forced to square off under baseball or soccer rules instead. That key point was ignored across the board and the commission was praised for making it safe and the promoters, who are hardly without blame, were vilified for moving out of town rather than comply with the new safer rules.

SEG officials have blamed a lot of their problems on Donald Zuckerman, promoter of the rival Extreme Fighting. It was Zuckerman and Extreme's antics in Quebec that got the entire genre basically banned from PPV throughout Canada, a market which was actually more successful on a buy rate basis than the U.S. They blamed Zuckerman for piggy-backing on the expense they put out to get the bill passed, and then blowing it for them by running a show in Manhattan before establishing a safety record in Niagara Falls, which led to the New York Times and New York media flap and for all real purposes ruined both Niagara Falls and their attempt at their biggest show to date at the Nassau Coliseum.

If there was a positive to all the problems, it's that the publicity may have caused an increase in the buy rate, although there is no way whatever buy rate increase would cover the costs incurred by the move. Very preliminary estimates indicated an increase from the 0.5 for Ultimate Ultimate, which would put the group still in the same league as the WWF and WCW shows in January, but with all the added costs destroying the profitability.

With the exception of a Coleman vs. Don Frye championship match which will be the main event, no matches have been finalized for the next PPV show. SEG plans on holding off a potential Coleman vs. Belfort match for quite a while. The question now is until that point, who can they put up against either to give them a competitive match? While Marco Ruas' management has reached an agreement verbally about a potential three show deal culminating with a title match, there is no signed contract in regard to that as reported here last week. With fighters like Ruas, Belfort, Abbott, Ken Shamrock, Dan Severn and Kimo potentially available for singles matches, it's now a matter of matching them up and putting together matches that both sides want. Shamrock wants Abbott, Severn or Belfort, but not Ruas. Abbott wants a Brazilian and claimed Vitor is too small for him and says Kimo will be too easy, but he refuses to fight Shamrock although he knocked him calling him a "sham" on the broadcast.

WWF In Your House 13: Final Four

With the exception of a hot main event that decided its new champion, the WWF's Final Four PPV show on 2/16 in Chattanooga, TN wasn't particularly eventful.

The show was built, more than any WWF PPV show to date, around one match. And that match delivered. Nothing on the undercard was particularly bad, but it was largely routine except for the tag title match that had some good wrestling and creative break-up spots but a totally lame finish. The crowd didn't appear to be into most of the matches except for the main event, nor into the wrestlers as much as would be expected.

The show drew 6,399 fans paying $76,762 or a little shy of being full in the UTC Arena set up for a lesser capacity than usual, curtained off for a 7,500-seat configuration. Very preliminary estimates are that the PPV did not do well. With so much hype on the Thursday special and a lackluster line-up, basically promoted as a one-match show, it figured to do a lower than usual buy rate, but adding the final four match being to determine the new champion figured to at least pick up interest in the show when it came to impulse buys.

Instead of airing a match on the pre-game show, they spent the half-hour hyping the main event. Dok Hendrix announced all four participants' names, and Vader and Steve Austin's names received boos, but only half-hearted, Bret Hart's name received a mixed half-hearted reaction and Undertaker received a substantial, but hardly overwhelming babyface pop. Austin opened doing a long interview. The point where Undertaker came out and Austin's mic didn't work was a planned spot, unlike some other spots both on the Superstars show earlier and later on the PPV where dead mics weren't planned spots. As the pre-game show went on there was a match in the background between the Godwinns and the Head Bangers (won by Godwinns), although the crowd didn't appear to be interested.

Noticeable by their absence from the international broadcast teams were Jacques Rougeau Sr. on the French team and Arturo Rivera on the Spanish team. Even more noticeably absent was Vince McMahon, as Jim Ross and Jerry Lawler handled the announcing. Apparently McMahon wanted to be backstage to make sure all the ego's would be in check in the final four match and everyone understood what was expected of them. Ross did a solid job early, making a series of average to below average matches seem, well, average to below average. He did better than most in the tag match and he and Lawler did a very good job in building excitement into the main event.

WCW SuperBrawl VII

WCW's SuperBrawl '97 from the San Francisco Cow Palace was yet another successful event both from an aesthetic as well as financial standpoint. As is typical of WCW shows, the undercard was largely one good match after another. The main event, while not a disappointment in that who expects a Hulk Hogan match to be any good, was still the worst match on the show. The big shock of this show was the Randy Savage NWO heel turn, helping Hogan beat Roddy Piper in the main event.

Hogan-Piper was another financial windfall for both the two headliners and the company. While buy rates aren't available at press time, it likely did well, but probably not as well as their original meeting at Starrcade. Locally, from my perspective this was the single most anticipated live event in this area in the past 25 years, and that includes the legendary San Francisco Battle Royals of the 70s and the biggest Pat Patterson or Ray Stevens match.

The show sold out nearly two weeks in advance with 13,324 in the building (12,145 paying $192,000). The gate was the third highest in the history of World Championship Wrestling (behind only the Ilio DiPaolo show in Buffalo, NY and the Hogan-Savage match in Las Vegas last Halloween Havoc), although had they booked a larger building, it would have easily broken the company's gate record. It was the largest live gate ever in Northern California. The $93,000 in merchandise sales was the second largest in company history behind only the Nitro in Chicago in January.

The number of signs brought to the show was the most I've ever seen and what was impressive is that it was across the board, not just for the megastars like Hogan, Piper, Hall, Nash, Sting and Flair, but significant for guys like Dean Malenko, Debra McMichael, Konnan, Rey Misterio Jr., Juventud Guerrera, Four Horsemen, etc. They did confiscate ECW signs although a few were visible as the show went on. There were numerous fans with Sting face-paint, more than I've ever seen at a WCW show. The response was such that they've already planned on moving the World War III PPV in late November from the traditional Norfolk to the Oakland Coliseum Arena.

That said, the heat for the show overall was nothing impressive. The only two matches that had real good heat were Kevin Sullivan vs. Chris Benoit and Hogan vs. Piper, although the quality of the wrestling from top-to-bottom on the show was very good. It was an easy thumbs up. Not a card of the year and no matches of the year, but on a 12 match live show, eight of the matches were good and none were all that bad.

WCW Uncensored

Dennis Rodman's first major foray into the world of pro wrestling turned into something of a publicity coup for World Championship Wrestling, probably more important than the otherwise forgettable PPV show that he debuted on.

WCW Uncensored was the typical WCW PPV show of the past year. The lines are familiar. Good undercard.

Terrible main event. Booking with more holes in it than Swiss cheese. Well, in this case, the undercard wasn't as good as most of the shows of the past year. But some of the angles were very good, actually two of them were excellent. The booking holes were large enough to fit The Giant in some of them.

And even if the show blew, and some of it did, in particular the main event, it accomplished something the best of PPV shows don't—it got the company mainstream publicity. Not on the level of the first few WrestleManias. But more than anything WCW has done in its history. Some of it was embarrassing, such at the Atlanta Constitution, which ran a nine-paragraph preview to the PPV show in its Sunday sports section, complete with a Rodman photo, but in every reference, called the promotion he was working for the "WWF," even to the point of saying he would be training at the WWF Power Plant in Atlanta, and that the WWF had a television show called Monday Nitro on TNT that was delivering good ratings. Very little of it was written in a positive manner, but what do you expect when you combine two well respected institutions to the general public like pro wrestling and Rodman?

But it was there, and nobody knew it better than the orchestrator, Hulk Hogan. It was Hogan's influence on Eric Bischoff that got him to match, or exceed the WWF's offer to Rodman for WrestleMania. And WCW scored a major moral victory, being in the Chicago Sun-Times nearly every day promoting its PPV show while WWF had WrestleMania in the same city one week later. ABC radio ran the story on its national news the next morning (well, through the 6 a.m. newscast) reporting it as Rodman wrestling and being in a tag team match with Hogan as his partner in Charleston, SC that they won, and using Tony Schiavone's PPV commentary of his involvement.

However, most major newspapers failed to make mention of Rodman being involved in the wrestling show. Hogan made sure to surgically bind himself to Rodman's side as much as possible at the PPV show, so when the horde of photographers, particularly shooting for every major sports paper in Japan, got their shots of Rodman wearing his NWO t-shirt, guess whose face is side-by-side. Actually the main event seemed more of a backdrop to the real story, the NWO guys posing for photos with Rodman and everyone who has power trying to get themselves hooked up with him for photo ops—which wound up being Hogan, Randy Savage, to a lesser extent Kevin Nash and Scott Hall, and of course, Roddy Piper.

It appears from media reports that Rodman's deal with WCW is that this show was the angle to build for a match on 7/13 in Daytona Beach, FL for the Bash at the Beach PPV. There will only be one match, according to media reports, on the two-show deal, unlike a three-show deal we had speculated on last week. When the Bulls season ends, Rodman will get a few weeks of training in at the Power Plant so they can hopefully choreograph his match well enough to be acceptable, much as they did last summer with the debut match of Kevin Greene and Steve McMichael. The only money figure running around Chicago is that Rodman received $2 million for the deal, but I'd suspect that figure is close to double what the real number is.

The show largely got a mixed response, with many of the thumbs up specifically saying they thought the show was saved by the angle that ended the show, where Sting finally attacked the entire NWO, dropping them all on the back of their heads with Scorpion death drops (a much cooler name for the same move than slop drop), including, just as the show went off the air, Hogan himself. Sting got a thunderous pop, as he should have since they spent six months building up to that moment, and he soaked it in while the credits ran. And true to form of keeping their storylines consistent, the final name in the credits was the WCW Senior Vice President—Eric Bischoff. You mean he really wasn't suspended in real life? Next thing you're gonna tell me is that Kevin Sullivan isn't really doing Jacquelyn.

Uncensored on 3/23 drew 9,295 (7,640 paying $101,184) fans to the North Charleston, SC Coliseum—or 360 shy of a sellout although there were points where the box office was closed and it was sold out for the moment until they opened more seats up. With the exception of future of the Stinger and the Worm, probably the biggest question on the minds of people who viewed the show was—if I was as incompetent at my job as Dusty Rhodes is at his, how long would I last?

Rhodes, whose announcing has gotten progressively worse, if that's even possible, was well past the point of unbearable. He ruins it completely for Tony Schiavone, who really appears to be trying to catch up in a rapidly changing world that Rhodes wants to single-handedly drag back to 1975. The fact that Bobby Heenan has been living off his name and reputation for the past year only makes things worse for Schiavone for having to carry 600 plus pounds of dead weight through all these endless hours of television every month. And people wonder why he has a bad neck.

Not that he was perfect, as he kept speculating about who WCW would get to replace Rick Steiner, and when there was nobody, it only left the audience with an empty feeling as the main event started, thinking WCW was a bunch of wimpy putzes once again. Don't even get me started on Mike Tenay. Or Scott Steiner. Or Rey Misterio Jr.

WWF WrestleMania 13

There may be a PPV show almost every week, but there is still one name that stands above the rest—WrestleMania.

That is largely based on history—it was the first PPV pro wrestling show ever—it was the second show in history to be closed-circuited (a now dead part of wrestling history) on a national basis and it was the show that in many ways saved and paved the ways for what would happen in the pro wrestling industry for the rest of the 1980s. And it is still, and has been, the biggest money pro wrestling show in North America every year it has been in existence.

But the 1980s are long gone. Seven years in pro wrestling, the way it moves and changes with such rapidity, are like dog years, 49 years in some other worlds. And this year's WrestleMania, going in, seemed to have the least interest ever. It was expected to be a one match show. And fortunately for the name WrestleMania, the one match delivered to match of the year caliber.

WrestleMania showed WWF doesn't have the depth of talent as WCW, but we all knew that. And they sunk to WCW levels for a main event by putting Undertaker in with Sid, ending with Undertaker capturing the WWF title for a second time—the fifth WWF title change already in 1997.

But Bret Hart and Steve Austin more than saved the show with a match phenomenal in workrate, intensity, and telling a story, resulting in the expected double turn—Austin to being the loner but top babyface in the promotion; Hart to being the promotion's top heel. With the aid of the blade, tremendous announcing and Hart's performance, Austin's face turn couldn't have been structured any better. Hart's performance in doing three run-ins during the Sid vs. Undertaker title match nearly saved that match as well. And by backing off from Ken Shamrock after the match with Austin, Hart established Shamrock immediately as a force to be reckoned with down the line.

Continuing in the new rougher, more violent and more hardcore image the WWF is attempting to present, the WWF has, in these times of cable censorship, become the World Apology Federation. Faarooq making racial remarks about Ahmed Johnson that would cause him to be practically lynched if it was a white wrestler making the same remarks, is within the bounds as long as we apologize after.

Despite the long-standing policy regarding blood, graphic blood on the second straight PPV, including a close-up shot of the pool of blood in the ring after the match which was a cause of concern the next morning within the cable world, is okay to show in close-ups and as a key part of a storyline because we'll simply apologize. Usage of all the weapons, including the striking with billy clubs—the same things that would get ECW booted from PPV—is okay, we'll just apologize afterwards. We didn't have any swearing, because that was last week's attempted shock and it would be hard to apologize twice for the same thing without the apologies coming off as hollow as they truly seem to be. And how about them putting that black wig on Tony Atlas' head and calling him Chyna? Oh, that wasn't Tony Atlas in a sports bra. Have you ever seen them both at the same time. "Politically Incorrect, and Damn sure going to apologize about it."

This is not meant as a complaint about blood. It was a part of this business since the 40s. When not overdone and turned into an expected cliché, it is often good for business. Certainly in the Hart-Austin match, the blood wasn't used for the sake of providing blood alone, but as part of telling the story of the match and did enhance the drama of the match.

Usage of blood on consecutive PPVs in the wake of last year's letters from Vince McMahon to Ted Turner when WCW used blood does make McMahon come off as a hypocrite of the highest order, but we are talking about wrestling promoters here and situational ethics, let alone any kind of ethics, is about as much as we can hope for. Self mutilation with a razor blade to one's forehead comes off as barbaric to the general public, but the real dangers of it are far less then many practices used regularly within the pro wrestling world.

So, Bret Hart and Steve Austin was awesome. And the Road Warriors Chicago Street fight was a better version of the same match WCW tried the previous week. And the real biggest story of the show? Next year's WrestleMania will be on March 29, 1998 at the Fleet Center in Boston. The same building WCW is about to put tickets on sale (4/10) for a 6/9 Nitro date. Raw is War. Monday night is War. The arena business is War. All is fair in love and a wrestling war. Take no prisoners.

This year's WrestleMania on 3/23 drew a sellout 18,197 fans to the Rosemont Horizon in Chicago (16,467 paying $837,150). It was more than double the largest previous gate for pro wrestling ever in Chicago, and the largest gate for pro wrestling in the United States since the 1993 WrestleMania at Madison Square Garden. The total number of fans and paid attendance was a few hundred more than WCW got for its Nitro at the United Center in January, so WCW's claims of drawing what would be the biggest wrestling crowd of the year in Chicago didn't hold up to the show the knock was specifically designed for.

Best poster award. The guy with the giant scissors with the names Sid and Arn on them. Least creative poster? How about "Austin 3:16?" And what about those R.F. Video plugs and phone number signs? Somebody let me know their publicity agent. Worst crowd shot. During the Hart-Austin match, the shot of Bret's nine-year-old daughter with her hands over her eyes because she was horrified of the violent nature of seeing her dad in such a match. That came off as real exploitation.

WCW Spring Stampede

It was just another Sunday afternoon on 4/6 for WCW's Spring Stampede. It was a show that few were expecting much from, and even fewer were pleasantly surprised when it was over. It didn't have the booking flaws of the Uncensored show three weeks earlier, but the quality of the matches wasn't as consistently good either.

And with WCW being the hot promotion that it is, the show drew a sellout 8,356 fans (7,428 paying $107,115) to the Tupelo, MS Coliseum. The announcing was improved from the depths of Uncensored, largely because Dusty Rhodes was only mildly awful. There were a few funny notes in the announcing. Bobby Heenan, during the confusing Benoit-Malenko finish, in his inimitable way, brought up that they needed to call Banecek (a TV detective series that didn't last very long from a generation ago) to get to the bottom of it, but earlier in the show, when talking about the National Enquirer story this week regarding Rey Misterio Jr. and Jennifer Anniston, only knew of Anniston, one of the country's biggest celebrities, as "one of the women from Friends." Lee Marshall was even funnier, knowing the exact make of Madusa's Harley from the Hog Wild PPV show last August, but not knowing any of the wrestling holds that were used during the Madusa vs. Akira Hokuto match.

Most reprehensible award goes to WCW this year for its handling of the Scott Hall hiatus. Hall has been gone now for a few weeks dealing with personal problems, both marriage and other apparent vices that, as Kevin Nash stated on Nitro six days earlier, are far more important than pro wrestling. However, WCW never addressed to the fans who were buying the PPV the FACT that the company knew weeks in advance that Hall wasn't going to be doing the show. Yet WCW continued to advertise Hall as appearing. Nash did say that he didn't know if Hall was going to be there or not on the previous Monday's Nitro, but it is believed that was his personal doing and not a company directive.

On the weekend television, the subject of Hall was brought up with them hinting that they didn't know if he'd be there or not. But even during the pre-game show, they continued to mention Hall & Nash as defending the tag team titles without even a hint that Hall might not be there. Then, when the show opened, Tony Schiavone announced that Hall wasn't there and that Nash would wrestle in a handicap match, and because doing the handicap match itself (which at one time was being strongly considered) would have been a disaster from a psychological standpoint with Nash as a heel, they created a really contrived angle to get Scott Steiner out of the picture early in the show.

ECW Barely Legal

The debut of Extreme Championship Wrestling on PPV on 4/13 is now history, and perhaps, even historical.

The show was a very slightly toned down version of the product, with a high work rate, a few, well not death defying but certainly injury defying spots, some sloppiness and nervousness, several booking swerves, a few technical problems, some excellent matches and undoubtedly the best pre-game show for a PPV in the history of the business. In the end, the show was stolen by the two oldest performers on the show, the first one of pro wrestling's bonafide legends, and the other one of the most underrated enduring great workers in the history of the industry.

Terry Funk, a few months shy of his 53rd birthday, came out with a stellar dramatic performance in a triangle match, winning over Stevie Richards and Sandman to get a title match that took place immediately thereafter, and then bled heavily and sold big in a short swerve-laden main event which ended with him coming out of the ring as new ECW world heavyweight champion. In the pre-game show, they aired an incredible taped promo of him at his father's grave site talking about winning the title.

Actually the best worker on the show, amazingly enough since he was in a match doing a style that isn't exactly geared for someone who is past 30, let alone 44, was Gran Hamada, the undersized Japanese star who became a lighter weight major star in Mexico in the late 70s. Hamada is one of the few survivors who has remained a top worker from the original class that put junior heavyweight wrestling on the map in Japan in the early 1980s original Tiger Mask era (actually the only other survivor as a top star from that era is Bret Hart).

Hamada has always been something of an unsung star in the business, his prime coming during a period when people of his size weren't given breaks, and a real rarity in that how often does someone make noticeable improvements as a worker updating his style between the ages of 43 and 44? And because he was part of a "cold" match in that it was guys thrown in with no storyline, and since the star of the show and only person who appeared to really be known to the fans was Great Sasuke, he came out of a PPV show where he was the best worker almost totally unsung once again.

He's probably held more major lighter weight world titles than all but a few wrestlers that have ever lived, somewhere in the vicinity of names like Danny Hodge, Rey Mendoza and Perro Aguayo, all bona fide legendary Hall of Fame performers. And Hamada was a far better worker than any of the men mentioned above. But as a Japanese wrestler who was too small for Japan in his youth, and made too many enemies due to some questionable business in his 30s, has now become a small promotion main eventer after basically retiring from his second home in Mexico and is surviving past 40 on more than just reputation, doing the one thing most veteran performers don't do, adapting the 90s style into his repertoire rather than relying on what he did in his youth and mental acuity to get him through.

When it was over, the show had to be considered a major success aesthetically for ECW. It was far from perfect, and the flaws many talked about with the promotion were more than evident, but when it was over, the strong points overwhelmed the weak points.

Very preliminary buy rates estimates at press time with less than 10 percent of the systems reporting were in the 0.2 range, or probably about 26,000 buys and an estimated total company revenue of $210,000 (break even was between $350,000 and $400,000) which, due to the limited number of homes available because so many major systems refused to carry the show, would be a money loser as a show itself. ECW had to guarantee Request a certain number of buys to get them to carry the show.

Paul Heyman was expecting that going in and was majorly downplaying the show's chances of being a money maker and claiming it was more as a way to put on a show with a product content that would get those who didn't carry the first show into changing their position for the future. Some of the losses could be offset in the future by eventual videotape sales and from the live gate.

As a first show, it appeared to do from a buy rate standpoint (which is a fair comparison, total homes wouldn't be) if the early figures are a national indication, well below the debuts of such groups as UWFI, Pancrase and EFC, none of which succeeded on PPV. It would be slightly less than AAA, which also never got a second show but that was more due to disorganization than anything else. However, all the aforementioned groups that are no longer around saw buy rates decline significantly after the first show, which is the general pattern for most events on PPV. UFC, which debuted in 1993 with 80,000 buys, pro boxing and major league pro wrestling are the notable exceptions although all three have suffered consistent gradual declines as a pattern in recent years.

There is a good chance ECW would fall into the category of exceptions, and if the second show on 8/17 were able to clear the vast majority of the cable universe and maintain a 0.2, it would break even or show a small profit to the point it could stay in the game. Meetings with Cablevision and Viewers Choice, both of which didn't carry this show, are expected soon. A decline in buy rate on a second show would make it difficult to continue on PPV. But keep in mind any figures this early are preliminary at best.

There were no major problems or excesses that should prevent this show, if used as a demo tape, to alarm PPV carriers to the point they won't carry the second show. The angles and problems that led to the first show only being available in around half the PPV universe have largely been rectified. A second show was announced for 8/17, which Heyman said will be from a larger building likely in a major market that ECW hasn't run in the past. Heyman is steering clear of running a major show within the New York City limits because of the political climate and because he realizes as a small fish playing with the big fish that he can't afford to make enemies right now.

Joey Styles, doing his first live broadcast, doing the show solo almost completely (Tommy Dreamer and Beulah McGillicutty sat in during the final two matches but Beulah said literally nothing and Dreamer might as well have) was somewhere in the range of very good to great, getting over all the key points, getting enough storyline over for first-timers, and not only calling the key spots but getting the individual Japanese wrestlers over as more than simply nameless faceless clones as several of the major promotion announcers do routinely when foreign talent is imported.

The booking was excellent. The camera work wasn't, particularly early. The guys busted their asses, but there was far more sloppiness than you'd ever see on a major promotion big show. There was heavy juice by Funk, but the juice wasn't used so often on the show that it become a cliché. There were a few swear words—limited to three, all of which were presented in a script beforehand weeks ago to Request. No "f" word and overall the language was kept pretty much inoffensive. The only woman beating was a woman beating a man, Reggie Bennett attempting (and not quite succeeding) a power bomb on Funk. There was some knocking of WWF and WCW, but not a whole lot. Some aspects of the show technically looked second rate, but when the show was over, it was better overall than the vast majority of WWF and WCW shows.

The show drew a sellout of 1,250 to the ECW Arena, which was given a face lift and cleaned up with a new paint job, plus they had a new ring with "ECW Hardcore Wrestling" written on the canvas. The show sold out a few days in advance. The gate had to destroy any previous company records, probably well in excess of $60,000 with 320 tickets at $100 and about 900 others at $40. The show also set a company merchandise record doing just under $20 per head, which is an unheard of figure for almost anything short of a Tokyo Dome show.

Just 24 seconds after the show went off the air, the generator blew and all power for television went off. Had this happened five minutes earlier, it would have destroyed the climax of the show. Heyman along with Funk, Dreamer, Eliminators and a few others got in the ring and thanked the crowd in the ring in a short speech.

AJPW Champion Carnival

Toshiaki Kawada was the winner of All Japan's 1997 Champion Carnival tournament coming out on top in only the second gimmick singles match in the 25-year history of the company.

Kawada came out the winner of a triangle match with Kenta Kobashi and Mitsuharu Misawa on 4/19 at Tokyo's Budokan Hall before an announced sellout of 16,300 fans in what is by tradition the second biggest show of the year (behind only the December tag team tournament finals) for the company. It was the second time that Kawada has captured the Carnival tournament, having won in 1994 in a famous final match beating Steve Williams. Perhaps more significantly, it was the first time Kawada has ever in his career pinned Misawa in a singles match.

With the three wrestlers coming out of the Round Robin tied with 19 points, it was announced that the

Budokan tournament final would consist of each wrestler having a 30-minute singles match against the other two and whomever wound up with the best record out of their two matches would be the champion. If the wrestlers were to all split matches (finish 1-1), the Carnival champion would be determined by who scored the fastest victory.

It started with Misawa and Kobashi going to a 30:00 draw. The storyline of the match was that Misawa was "injured" from a previous match against Jun Akiyama. Kobashi dominated the final 2:30 of the match gaining near falls with at least two brainbusters and a DDT. So Misawa went into the match with Kawada "exhausted" and Kawada destroyed him early until Misawa hit a Frankensteiner. Misawa had a few flurries during the match but Kawada dominated, using his stretch plum submission and a power bomb to gain a pin in 6:09.

This left Kawada vs. Kobashi, and if Kobashi won, he'd win the Carnival, but all Kawada needed was a 30:00 draw to win. As it was, Kawada pinned Kobashi in 21:27 after a series of high kicks. One would expect this sets Kawada up as the next challenger for Misawa's Triple Crown and the match as the more than likely main event for the 6/6 show at Budokan Hall.

The final 15:00 of Misawa-Kobashi and the entire Misawa-Kawada match aired on television on 4/20, and the Kobashi-Kawada match airs on 4/27. Even though the 4/20 show was moved due to other programming to the unlikely time slot of 1:40 a.m. on Sunday, it still drew a 3.7 rating which at that time slot is a 34.2 share.

It was only the second gimmick singles match in the history of the traditional promotion, the other being a Texas death match in 1974 between Giant Baba and Fritz Von Erich.

Misawa made it to the finals with a win over Johnny Ace on 4/17 in Soka, in which they teased the 30:00 draw by going 26:27 before Misawa scored the pin with a Tiger driver. Kawada and Kobashi had already clinched spots in the final after wins on 4/14 and 4/15 respectively. Baba crossed up his patterned booking as many times All Japan will have a situation where a top name needs a win to make the finals on either the final night or the final round-robin night, only to be held to a 30:00 draw that knocks them out of contention.

Final standings were:1. Kawada 10-1-3, 23 points; 2. Kobashi 9-3-2, 20 points and Misawa 9-3-2, 20 points; 4. Akira Taue 9-3, 18 points and Stan Hansen 8-2-2, 18 points and Steve Williams 8-2-2, 18 points; 7. Gary Albright 6-6, 12 points; 8. Johnny Ace 5-7, 10 points; 9. Jun Akiyama 4-7-1, 9 points; 10. Giant Kimala II 3-9, 6 points; 11. Takao Omori 2-10, 4 points and Tamon Honda 2-10, 4 points; 13. Jun Izumida 0-14, injury forfeited most of the tournament.

WWF In Your House 14: Revenge of Taker

Raw certainly overshadowed the final PPV in a six week run with a show every weekend. The 4/20 show from the Rochester War Memorial Auditorium, entitled "Taker's Revenge," was a largely forgettable show with two strong main event matches and a total nothing undercard. The plethora of DQ finishes (three in five PPV matches) run-ins and ref bumps was only made worse by a DQ finish in the Bret Hart vs. Austin main event.

In addition, the mystery surprise protege of Honky Tonk Man turned out to be Billy Gunn, renamed Rockabilly, which caused the crowd to either go into a temporary coma or flock to the bathroom and basically put the final nail in the undercard's coffin. Even with the final two strong matches, the screw-job laden booking and disappointment of a surprise made this a slight thumbs down show. It does continue the competitive situation with WCW in that WCW has the far stronger undercards and WWF has far stronger main event matches on PPV.

The show drew a sellout 6,477 paying $87,414, selling out five days beforehand, again showing just how hot pro wrestling is these days, and drawing the largest gate in the history of pro wrestling in Rochester.

FMW Anniversary Show

Frontier Martial Arts and Wrestling ran its annual Anniversary show, which by tradition is its biggest show of the year, before an announced sellout crowd of 16,000 on 4/29 at the Yokohama Arena.

Although it was probably a trios match with Atsushi Onita and Terry Funk on opposite sides that was the main drawing card, FMW used a women's no rope two sided barbed wire electronic dynamite barricade double hell death match for its two womens championships and the retirement of its long-time poster woman, Megumi Kudo, as the main event.

Perhaps the most noteworthy news from the show was the announcement by Onita that FMW was going to book Kawasaki Baseball Stadium (52,000 capacity), which is currently under renovation, the site of FMW's biggest shows in its history, for a show on 9/28 and he's looking to make it a joint show with the World Wrestling Federation and also looking to include wrestlers from several other Japanese offices. Onita will be meeting with Vince McMahon on 5/1 to discuss a talent cooperation agreement and working together on this show.

Kudo, 27, had what was billed as her final match of a nearly 11-year career that began with the All Japan Women's promotion and saw her involved in the same training camp as such luminaries as Aja Kong and Bison Kimura. Kudo captured both the WWA womens championship and the World Independent womens championships that she had recently lost to Shark Tsuchiya (Eriko Tsuchiya) in 21:46.

Kudo was twice whipped into the explosive barbed wire and blown up with the mini-bombs. She also took a bump onto the explosive barbed wire barricades on the open side of the ring for an even louder explosion. Tsuchiya pulled out a knife and carved up Kudo's face. Kudo made the comeback and Tsuchiya was blown up and finally pinned for the big career finale.

In the other key match, Onita & Masato Tanaka & Wing Kanemura (Yukihiro Kanemura) beat Funk & The Gladiator (Mike Alfonso) & Cactus Jack (which explains the Mankind suspension from Raw because of the booking here at the same time) in a Texas tornado street fight death match in 20:20 when Kanemura pinned Gladiator after coming off the top rope with a chair onto his head.

Funk both threw a fireball at Onita and burned him with a flaming branding iron. Funk, Onita, Tanaka and Kanemura all heavily juiced. Funk and Onita brawled into the crowd with tables and chairs including Onita giving Funk a piledriver on a table. Since Kanemura got the pin, he then challenged Onita to a singles match which may be the big show headliner.

WWF In Your House 15: A Cold Day in Hell

Whether the WWF's Cold Day in Hell PPV was going to be a good or a bad show was far less important than the bigger question the show would begin to answer: Does Ken Shamrock have any potential as an American style pro wrestler by World Wrestling Federation standards?

Based on his first major match, the semi-main event on the 5/11 PPV show from the Richmond, VA Coliseum, the answer seems to be strongly in the affirmative.

After both men worked much of the past week in Calgary under the tutelage of Bret Hart, Shamrock and Vader put together a match reminiscent of Vader's classic Japanese matches with Nobuhiko Takada, but with a little concession to American style thrown in. They did an exceedingly stiff and more of a semi-shoot than most people would realize in what was very close to a UWF-style before fans who didn't quite understand the meaning of a lot of what they were seeing. And because Takada is one of the great workers and pro wrestling athletes of our generation and it is totally unfair to believe Shamrock, with his limited pro wrestling experience, could walk into a new field and already be the level of performer as the elite members of that profession. But it was a good match. Better than anyone had the right to expect. Far better than many people undoubtedly going in would have feared.

In comparison to other celebrity athletes from other sports such as Lawrence Taylor, Reggie White or Steve McMichael, Shamrock had an advantage. He was trained originally to be a pro wrestler by the likes of the late Buzz Sawyer and Nelson Royal. He did work for a few months in late 1989 and early 1990 on a small indie promotion in the Carolinas as Vincent Torelli, the Italian Stallion, even forming an occasional tag team with Ricky Steamboat, in a promotion which included the likes of The Nasty Boys, Robert Fuller and Dean Malenko. He did one tour of All Japan Pro Wrestling under the name Ken Shamrock, where, in his own words, because of lack of experience, he was totally lost.

He wound up hooking up with Malenko and trained in submissions, not by traditional martial arts teachers, but with pro wrestlers like the Malenkos and Karl Gotch. He ended up being booked with the Universal

Wrestling Federation, a worked shoot style group in Japan with the likes of Akira Maeda, Takada, Masakatsu Funaki, Minoru Suzuki, and Yoshiaki Fujiwara, under the name Wayne Shamrock (because Ken Shamrock had done a pro wrestling tour for All Japan and the promotion didn't want him to be confused with another traditional style pro wrestler). That promotion folded just as Shamrock was getting started, and he moved to Pro Wrestling Fujiwara Gumi in 1991.

By 1993, he was a legitimate major wrestling star in Japan, and he, Funaki and Suzuki left PWFG to form Pancrase, taking a major career risk since he had already made a name for himself as a star since Pancrase was designed to largely be a shoot sport, the closest thing to legitimate sport that the pro wrestling world had seen in generations.

Just as Pancrase was getting started, so was Ultimate Fighting in the United States. Shamrock was in the initial UFC PPV show in November of 1993, beating Patrick Smith in the first round, but being choked out by Royce Gracie in the second round. He eventually became the top star in Pancrase and its first world champion winning a tournament in late 1994, giving it up to Minoru Suzuki in 1995 as a business loss, before having a much publicized falling out with the promotion in 1996 over a contract dispute. He became one of the major stars of UFC after going to a 36:00 draw in a rematch with Gracie, and no doubt its highest-paid performer, but fell short of being the dominant superstar that due to his look and charisma, that the company hoped he would turn out to be. When SEG failed to pick up his option on his contract, he looked back at pro wrestling as a new livelihood, but this time pro wrestling of the more traditional sense.

It came down to New Japan and the World Wrestling Federation. What could have beens are just that, but it was the WWF that wanted him more and got him. So they had another highly paid non-pro wrestler on their roster with apparently no idea whatsoever what to do with him. But this is not Chapter Two of the Mark Henry story.

The most obvious, and most lucrative angle, the outsider angle that New Japan would have almost surely done to perfection, was blown in an immediate quest to get him on television for ratings purposes, a mistake in hindsight since there were no ratings to be gotten initially. After a few weeks of being put on television well before he or they were ready with a long-term storyline to build, the buzz was out that this was yet another in the long list of recent WWF booking failures.

But after a few well produced video features and Shamrock himself becoming more comfortable with his position and doing live interviews good enough for pro wrestling while not compromising his character into a cartoon, there was no question the potential was there to be a star—if he could project being a star in the ring.

Vader was both the best and worst opponent for a first encounter. The best, because of his own famous series of matches with Takada and experience at a worked shoot style, to draw from in knowledge of how to not compromise the shooter mystique of his opponent, but at the same time make it entertaining pro wrestling. The worst because it was way too soon for this match to take place. Vader should be the ultimate challenge for Shamrock months after blitzing every prelim wrestler in sight in record time. At that point, his finally being put in a position of jeopardy and his selling much of the match and coming out of the down predicament and coming out with the decisive win would have meant ten times as much. But you can only play the hand that is dealt to you.

When ring announcer Howard Finkel announced that the next match would be the no holds barred match, the response from the nearly full house of 9,381 (7,681 paying $116,547—the largest pro wrestling gate, although far from the largest wrestling crowd, ever in the city along with another $55,000 in merchandise sales) was rather tepid. It was hardly the fever pitch one remembers in years past when a well promoted stipulation would bring a huge crowd buzz just as Finkel said a few words and the crowd registered which match was coming up. But when Shamrock came down the aisle, he got a good response, the best thus far of the show. The crowd didn't take to him as a main event superstar, but they did see him as a star.

The match itself was, as mentioned before, largely based on the three-match Takada-Vader series of 1993-95. But the most important thing wasn't the moves, but how Shamrock came across. His selling was far better than expected. The crowd got with him to actually a surprising degree when he was down. His offense was believable, actually far more believable than all of the far more experienced wrestlers who worked the undercard on the same show. If you consider his experience level, he actually came across in the ring as a Japanese "natural," one of those wrestlers that comes along every few years who in their first few matches you can already see are going to make it to the top. His style is still more suited for Japan, which in a sense is good because it breaks him from the rest of the pack and makes him unique, but bad because it requires a lot more work from the announcers to teach the crowd to register things they've never been taught before such as stiff forearms and muay thai style leg kicks.

But this was also another example of Vader as the single greatest performer of his size in the history of this industry. Exactly how good Shamrock really is at this point and really can be as an American worker may not have been fairly indicated because of who he was in the ring with.

A decade ago, there was a strongman, gymnast, acrobatic, actor, bodybuilder who was trained in Calgary by the name of Tom Magee. He was 6-5, looks of a model, physique of an Ultimate Warrior, one of the strongest men alive, and could do cartwheels and backflips in the ring. In those days where size and physique ruled, here was a guy who was nearly as big as Hulk Hogan and ten times the athlete. He had world champion written all over him. That was, until he was put in the ring.

One night in Rochester, NY at a WWF television taping, he had a dark match with a solid prelim wrestler who was experienced at getting good matches out of total stiffs. Magee was so impressive in that match that it became almost preordained, after the guy's very first WWF match, that he was the next Hulk Hogan, the heir to the throne.

Of course, Tom Magee never made it in pro wrestling. He had no charisma, and he couldn't translate his athletic gifts into making a match. He never had another match one-tenth as good as the match he had in Rochester. About five years later, the wrestling world had changed once again. The guy put on the throne was the solid prelim wrestler. Bret Hart. The moral of the story is you can only take first impressions for what they are. First impressions.

Cold Day in Hell was just another Sunday afternoon PPV show that will largely be forgotten by the end of the week. Shamrock-Vader and the main event, Undertaker vs. Steve Austin, were good matches. The undercard was as lackluster as ever. The show generally lacked heat. The finishes were clean. The outside interference was kept to a minimum so that the one point it was used for storyline (Brian Pillman ringing the bell so Steve Austin couldn't pin Undertaker) added to the show rather than resulted in the feeling of just another screw-job. But it's more and more clear that the WWF is a company that has one tremendous feud on top, and even that one is getting overexposed, and very little depth otherwise. And the undercard performers who should have decent matches on paper somehow seem to get worse by the month.

This hasn't been confirmed, but I believe neither Vince McMahon nor Jim Cornette attended the show due to personal situations. On the broadcast which Jim Ross did with Jerry Lawler, they said that Rose Anderson (a close family friend that McMahon's kids would refer to as "Aunt Rose") had passed away the previous night and Cornette's girlfriend came down with what they at first thought was appendicitis although turned out to be something less serious.

WCW Slamboree

After the longest ring absence of his career, a full eight months after surgery to repair a torn rotator cuff suffered in a Japanese match against Kensuke Sasaki, Ric Flair, the greatest wrestling performer of his and probably anyone else's time returned to the ring at age 48 on his home turf, the Charlotte Independence Arena for Slamboree on 5/18.

The show, almost universally well received, saw Flair and local football hero and last year's NFL sack leader Kevin Greene of the Carolina Panthers and long-time Flair wrestling rival Roddy Piper from the so-called glory days of Mid Atlantic Championship wrestling face Scott Hall & Kevin Nash & Syxx in a match probably more interesting for its behind-the-scenes political ramifications than for anything that took place in the ring.

There had been numerous ideas for the main event, including Flair and Greene, two of the city's biggest sports heroes, on opposites side of the ring due to last year's Steve McMichael-Greene angle figuring McMichael, as a Horseman, should team with Flair and Greene, who was turned on by McMichael and screwed with by Flair in his last appearance, be with a babyface team.

Ideas changed by the moment, and it wound up with Flair & Piper & Greene against the NWO, but when Hulk Hogan decided his movie commitments wouldn't allow him to do the date (or whatever his real reason may have been), Hall & Nash suggested Syxx, an idea Flair and Piper balked at, which led to words being said and some interviews on television on both sides that didn't go anywhere close to how they were scripted. In recent weeks, both sides had gotten on the same page and whatever has been said the past few weeks was all business and not ego, at least as much as that's possible in a business fueled by out of control egos.

Piper, who has creative control of all his angles, attempted to pull out of the match, which led to a booking concession and eventually to Hall, Nash and Syxx agreeing to do a three-way job finish which popped the crowd locally beyond belief. In return, Hall & Nash theoretically get their win back in Moline, IL on 6/15, where Flair and Piper get to do their angle and the two legends of the past generation and long-time friends get to work together and do their thing without worrying much about wrestlers who either have no respect for what they've accomplished in this business, or wrestlers who look at things based on what people can do today as opposed to what they may have done in another place on another day. Of course that latter attitude is forgetting that it is something that can all be thrown out the window when it comes to judging certain individuals.

Flair's return drew a sellout of 9,643 paid and $167,705, the second largest gate in the long and storied history of Charlotte wrestling (a 1985 outdoor stadium match between Flair and Nikita Koloff that drew 27,000 fans remains the all-time record). Merchandise sales topped $100,000, among the largest in company history.

Was it a success? By the standards that made Hulk Hogan the greatest wrestler of all-time, it was. Oh, Hogan isn't the greatest wrestler of all-time? By the standards that made Ric Flair the greatest wrestler of all-time, the reality of being 48 has turned him into a regional version of Hulk Hogan. Hey, there are worst criticisms than being compared with the biggest money maker the sport has. Although none worse to a fan of Flair, comparing him to Flair's fans' symbolic Antichrist.

But standards of people as to what constitutes great change depending on who is their favorite at the moment. To call the reaction to the match great would be fair. To call the match great would be cheapening the standard set by every great match Flair had over the previous 20 years. The match on this day in this building was going to be great to the audience live and on PPV so long as Flair didn't break his leg and won at the end. And so it was, by that standard. If it was any other six guys doing the exact same match, people would recognize that the only real wrestling in the entire match was provided by Syxx.

In some ways this wasn't all that different from all those Hulk Hogan vs. John Studd and King Kong Bundy matches in Hogan's prime, in that the fans live thought they were good matches so long as Hogan didn't break his leg when he fell down from that legdrop and won at the end, not to say this match was THAT bad. When Flair talked about Dick the Bruiser in St. Louis in his mid-50s, he was talking about a fan reality.

In Charlotte, or anywhere in the Carolinas, Flair will still be the biggest draw and most popular star if he chooses to be, in the year 2003, even if he becomes Dick the Bruiser in terms of ring ability. A PPV main event against Hogan for the title, despite the cringes that sound has for many within the company, is still probably the biggest money match the company could put on with the exception of Hogan vs. Sting.

You may say Flair's interviews are out of touch or out of style. But they were still better than Bruiser or Crusher's were when they were drawing big money and a hell of a lot less mobile at an older age. Hey, Sinatra can still draw money today, and in this business, Flair is Sinatra. A bigger star today, as long as he works in small doses, than he was in the day he really was the best.

This show, as with most WCW PPV events, had a strong undercard. Nothing off the charts, but most matches were as good if not better than they figured to be on paper. It also featured easily the worst match of this or many other years, the Steve McMichael-Reggie White fiasco. Terry Taylor, who trained McMichael and Greene for their match with Flair & Arn Anderson last summer, pulled off a miracle. Well, maybe it wasn't a miracle because of the Divine intervention on the other side of the ring. But lightning didn't strike a second time in a different place. White may have put on the single worst performance on a major PPV show since the legends of grown-up Danny Partridge and Peter Brady in a dark match in Chicago. But the match did garner the expected media publicity for WCW, with coverage that night on both CNN and ESPN's sports reports and in the 5/19 USA Today.

WWF King of the Ring

The World Wrestling Federation's fifth annual King of the Ring PPV show had an interesting plot irony.

Hunter Hearst Helmsley was scheduled to win the King of the Ring last year but, largely due to punishment from an incident in Madison Square Garden, wasn't even on the card, having been eliminated in a television preliminary tournament match. Fast forward to this year and Helmsley was eliminated in a television preliminary match, but due to an injury to Vader and several changes in plans, Helmsley was not only put back in the tournament, but given the crown on 6/9 at the Providence Civic Center.

King of the Ring would have to be described as a show that ended up being far better in actuality than it looked on paper. On paper, the tournament didn't look interesting and the only match on the show that appeared to be potentially memorable was Shawn Michaels vs. Steve Austin. Instead it was a solid, although unspectacular show.

Initial plans were for Helmsley to be a first round loser to Ahmed Johnson, as, in fact, he was in their Raw is War match on 5/12 in Newark, DE. After a convoluted explanation necessitated by the injury to Vader making him unable to wrestle Crush on 5/19 in Mobile, Helmsley was put back in the tournament and beat Crush to advance into the tournament. Based on television commercials taped weeks in advance, the final four in the original plans were to be Ahmed Johnson vs. Vader and Goldust vs. Savio Vega, so as it turned out, only Johnson of the originally planned final four were even there.

Helmsley was scheduled to win the tournament last year to start his climb to major stardom, but the plans changed after Helmsley, Shawn Michaels, Diesel (Kevin Nash) and Razor Ramon (Scott Hall) got in the ring for their infamous curtain call in Hall & Nash's final appearance in the WWF before leaving for WCW. Since Hall and Nash were leaving and Michaels was a headliner and top draw that the company seemingly was afraid to discipline, which has led to a year plus worth of future problems by not nipping the original problems in the bud, it was Helmsley whose fate was changed and punished. Not only did he not win at King of the Ring, but he basically spent the entire summer as a jobber before getting a chance to be rebuilt later in the year in the angle where Mr. Perfect was supposed to manage him and he'd get the rub from Perfect's star stature, which also, like most of the WWF's long term plans, didn't materialize in the storyline the way it did when it was first scripted.

The show drew 9,312 fans paying $202,963 in the 16,000-seat arena, although Vince McMahon several times announced it as a capacity crowd on the air while Jim Ross' one crowd reference during the broadcast was a more realistic 10,000 fans. The show also did $74,672 in merchandise business.

WCW The Great American Bash

World Championship Wrestling shattered all attendance and gate records for the Quad Cities with its Great American Bash PPV show on 6/15 from the Mark of the Quad in Moline, IL.

The show drew 9,613 fans (8,538 paying $142,118), which would have broken the area's attendance record set back in the early 60s. The show was about 500 tickets shy of a legitimate sellout and drew an additional $66,000 in merchandise.

It was a rather uneventful show as far as advancing the storyline, and got a mixed response. I thought it was a good show, mixing up good, bad and average matches, most of which came across better than they figured to be on paper, with largely strong booking that had a purpose and storylines within the matches.

Some of the finishes left something to be desired, and it was an overall very good announcing performance by Tony Schiavone as the host, and although The Brain is showing that his brain isn't what it once was, at no point was Dusty Rhodes his stereotypical overbearing personality and Mike Tenay did a great job in the opener. From an organizational standpoint, it's a night-and-day difference with Terry Taylor running things as the

announcers fed the eventual storylines much better than when they appeared to go out and call matches with no clue as to what is going on.

Not to say that even under these circumstances that Bobby Heenan was all there, although he only made one major faux pas, still not understanding the tap submission rule, which was one of the main things this show was designed to get over. In particular, after the replay showed Meng tapping for Chris Benoit's crossface, Heenan was still asking if Meng had submitted or if the referee had stopped the match because Meng had passed out. You'd think after not understanding the tap out on Nitro two weeks back with Barbarian, that he'd have figured it out by now.

With three tap out finishes and only one DQ ending, the booking was often solid in that several undercard matches built up a specific story and paid off on it at the end. However, matches one (Ultimo Dragon vs. Psicosis), four (Glacier vs. Wrath) and seven (Steve McMichael vs. Kevin Greene) had almost the same finish, the old outside interference backfires, which was a little much for one card. Going off the air without an explanation as to what happened to Ric Flair when he simply disappeared defied all credibility. And exactly how many referees were knocked out in the Diamond Dallas Page vs. Randy Savage match? Which was only made worse because as Savage was dropping referees, it was looking way too similar to the Steve Austin vs. Shawn Michaels match that took place seven days earlier.

Tony Schiavone opened the show describing it as the 13th consecutive year that the Great American Bash has been broadcast "to your home." Actually it was the eighth. The first Bash PPV was in 1988, although there were Great American Bash house shows starting with the Charlotte Baseball Stadium show on July 6, 1985 where Ric Flair vs. Nikita Koloff drew 27,000 fans. In both 1986 and 1987 there were Bash summer tours of arenas, and the first Bash PPV was headlined by Ric Flair vs. Lex Luger in 1988. However, there was no Great American Bash, as the name was dropped by WCW, in 1993 or 1994 stemming from debacles of shows under that name in 1991 (among the worst PPV shows ever) and 1992, and the name was brought back in 1995.

WWF In Your House 16: Canadian Stampede

It figured going in that the Canadian Stampede PPV show on 7/6 in Calgary's Saddledome would have a unique bizarro world atmosphere with the heels being cheered. But I'm not sure anyone could have expected what actually took place.

In a show that due to generally weak hype going in, a change in the title match over the last week due to an injury, and coming at the end of a major holiday weekend, figured to be one of the last anticipated PPV shows in WWF history, turned out to be one of its best shows ever. The crowd atmosphere, which put the show over the top even more than the consistently good wrestling, equaled or exceeded nearly any major show in history.

Every match was good, with two of the four matches being excellent. The risk of doing a four-match card, which was not in the original cards but ended up that way after a series of injuries racked a company already plagued with depth problems, paid off at the end with a show the level that even the most optimistic going in couldn't have dreamed would turn out the way it did.

The show drew a paid attendance of 10,974 (12,151 in the building) and gate of $229,598 along with another $65,000 in merchandise, the latter two figures being the largest in each category in the long and illustrious history of pro wrestling in Calgary. It was the third largest crowd ever for wrestling in Calgary trailing a 1991 card (Hulk Hogan vs. Sgt. Slaughter and Ultimate Warrior vs. Undertaker) that drew 11,153 and a 1987 show Hogan vs. King Kong Bundy) which holds the record of 12,034.

The largest crowds for Stampede Wrestling were at the 7,500-seat Calgary Corral since the Saddledome wasn't built in 1984 and Stu Hart only ran one show there. Among the well-known matches that packed the old Corral in the Stampede days were George & Sandy Scott vs. Bill & Dan Miller (1958), Archie "Stomper" Gouldie vs. Dan Kroffat (1973), Al Mills vs. Stu Hart (1958) and Dory Funk Jr. vs. Billy Robinson (1969).

The atmosphere with the Harts being portrayed as the first family of wrestling, in their home towns, working as total babyfaces and being portrayed in the commentary as such which was really weird, ended up with the Hart Family being put over as babyfaces not only by the fans but also by the promotion and the storyline to the degree that almost nobody ever in wrestling PPV history has ever been put over. The only comparison would have been in 1993 when Ric Flair beat Vader in Charlotte for the WCW title, and with all due respect to the magic of that night, this night in a city known for its wrestling crowds being reserved from all the years of seeing guys like Dynamite Kid work matches that were a generation ahead of its time, blew it away.

The amount of media publicity, both with it being the first major match with Bret returning from knee surgery, the first PPV show ever in Calgary and being part of the annual Stampede, was unprecedented in local wrestling annals. Both the Calgary show and the Edmonton show the next night received front page newspaper coverage the next morning. There were stories in the newspaper every day, with features on many of the top wrestlers and numerous autograph sessions including one session for Owen, Bret and Davey Boy which drew an estimated 8,000 people.

For the rest of the world, it was strange at the same time to see Bret Hart, the WWF's lead heel, being presented as a home town legend, getting a Hogan in his prime response, and being shown and portrayed as a role model who had lines a mile long waiting for autographs at public appearances over the weekend and accommodated everyone who asked.

Or how about seeing Owen Hart, the pesky little brother, work a spectacular babyface like performance climaxing with him saving the day and leading the good guys to victory, and then celebrating not only with his entire family in the ring, but hugging his baby.

Or seeing Davey Boy Smith walking his wife down the aisle and kissing her before the match started to a thunderous ovation. Some main event heel.

And what about Brian Pillman, the loose cannon? There he was helping 82-year-old Stu Hart into the ring so the father figure of Calgary wrestling could receive a well-deserved sendoff at the end of the night. Hey, where was the cheap shot clothesline.

In the WWF's quest to overdo things and explain to the rest of the world why the locals were behaving this way and cheering the wrong guys, they probably succeeded in a sense of having an awful lot of fans wondering why they were the ones rooting against the real babyfaces. Those Canadian fans, who in the clips hardly came off as brain surgeons, still seemed in their less than infinite wisdom, to be on the right side. The WWF trying to make sense of the aftermath and move things back to as they were is going to be intriguing. It's almost like you had this dream that you saw one of the best wrestling PPV shows ever, but then you wake up the next morning, and it was almost like it never happened.

WCW Bash at the Beach

So now Dennis Rodman is a bona fide pro wrestler. And the scary part was, he wasn't all that bad.

After doing a couple of angles, Rodman's first appearance as a participant in a pro wrestling match at WCW's Bash at the Beach PPV saw him tear down the house by doing a simple arm drag on Lex Luger. In the tag match at the Ocean Center in Daytona Beach, FL, where Rodman teamed with Hulk Hogan against Luger & The Giant, it wasn't until the 6:30 mark before Rodman tagged in. Rodman, teased his first lock-up seemingly forever (actually it was more than two minutes later), and hit Luger with an arm drag, and then came back and took an arm drag from Luger. The funny part is that Luger probably had to be taught the move this week as well.

After just a few days of practice this past week under the eyes of Terry Taylor and the WCW staff (although from his two minute early stall, it seemed his wrestling hero was more like Larry Zbyszko), Rodman, 36, was not only not an embarrassment in the ring, but actually showed far more aptitude than most trained pro wrestlers with months of training in their first match. His offense, while limited, looked decent. His athletic ability, which is world class, he was able to translate better into wrestling than expected, was naturally his strong point with some high and well timed leap frog spots. His selling was pretty good, certainly for someone in their first match. His ability to work the crowd was very good as he's a natural ham, and he obviously he wasn't about to be intimidated because there was a sellout crowd watching him. And his psychology was there.

Many people joked he was the best of the four participants in the tag match, which wouldn't have been much of an exaggeration, but in reality he was already better in his first match than a main eventer like Sid or Ultimate

Warrior after years in the ring. Guess that's the advantage of having real athletic ability.

To the mainstream, the circus of Rodman's pro wrestling debut was the big story, making CNN, ESPN, television sports show highlight reels, feature stories in several newspapers and some tiny mentions in the sports briefs in others. From a WCW standpoint, it's this type of publicity needed to transfer the years of having the New York advantage that has made the WWF the "name brand" to those who really don't follow pro wrestling. Even though WCW is ahead of WWF when it comes to television viewership and is now in the lead when it comes to PPV revenue, WWF is still the name brand.

Witness the many media stories back in March when Rodman debuted for WCW doing an angle at the Uncensored PPV show on 3/16 that listed Rodman appearing on a WWF show. There probably were sportscasters around the country that mentioned WWF in association with Rodman this time out, but the number dwindled and those mistakes, embarrassing to the WCW empire, certainly weren't in nearly as many high profile positions like their home town Atlanta Journal Constitution as the previous appearance.

The show was actually a bigger deal with the Japanese media. There were likely as many Japanese media present for this show as any U.S. pro wrestling show ever. Part of the lure was Rodman. Part of the lure was Great Muta & Masahiro Chono working as a tag team against the Steiners. And most of it was that hoards of sports media from Japan were already in the U.S. for the debut of Hideki Irabu with the New York Yankees a few days earlier and most of them used Rodman doing pro wrestling as the second stop since they were already in the country.

Virtually all the Japanese sports newspapers had large photos from the match on the front page of the sports section on 7/15, and news of the match was even carried on the nightly NHK (equivalent to PBS) news, a station that virtually never touches pro wrestling (although they did cover Naoya Ogawa's early matches with New Japan). This card was also taped to be the 7/26 "World Pro Wrestling" television show in Japan, focusing on the Rodman and Steiners matches and the entire wrestling television crew from TV-Asahi was there including announcers Tsuji and Masa Saito.

We know Rodman drew the media to the show. We also know, what the media didn't, that Rodman didn't draw the fans to the show although he was a major curiosity point once they got there. What nobody knows yet is Rodman's PPV drawing power. Rodman received a deal that was likely in the $1.5 to $2 million range for reportedly three appearances. The original WCW reports we had received on the Rodman deal were two matches plus the original angle and a Chicago Tribune story on 7/14 reported that Rodman has one more match with WCW on his contract and that the date hasn't been agreed on but indicated it would be before basketball season starts in the fall, although I'm not sure when that would be since the August (Hogan vs. Luger) and October PPV shows are already largely booked without him. September will be War Games, November will be that horrible three-ring Battle Royal gimmick and December will be Hogan vs. Sting.

New Japan is interested in using him for a Dome show but that price tag is still more than they've ever paid anyone (although they offered more to Royce Gracie but that's a totally different situation) and they sellout their Dome shows without him. WCW signed Rodman earlier this year after beating a $1 million offer for two appearances by WWF which wanted to pair Rodman and Goldust as a tag team, shooting the angle at WrestleMania for a match at SummerSlam. To be worth the $750,000 Rodman was paid for this specific appearance, which would rank as among the largest one-day payoffs ever in pro wrestling, WCW needs to draw 83,900 more orders on PPV than it would have without him. Figuring WCW's average PPV shows with Hogan are doing about 200,000 buys, they need to get it up to 284,000 buys or a 1.01 buy rate to make it worth their while. The very preliminary numbers indicate WCW will wind up right about at that figure. Logic would say that for a gimmick like that, a second appearance wouldn't garner anywhere close to that level of curiosity buys.

Of course everything is synergistic and you can argue if they fall short on the buy rate, which would rank with the two Hogan-Flair matches and the first Hogan-Piper as the biggest money matches in company history, they can make it up in ratings. However the Nitro from Chicago with Rodman live saw no ratings bump at all due to Rodman appearing and this week the number was up only one-tenth of a point despite more mainstream pub than ever for WCW from the show the previous night. Mainstream curiosity often translates into more revenue but generally translates better into television ratings for free. If it did, the Bash would have sold out Daytona Beach the first day tickets went on sale.

Usually something like this would be more likely to swell television ratings because it appeals more to the curiosity of the casual person on the street interest that has no interest in spending money on wrestling. The best example of this would be the Lawrence Taylor angle in WWF two years ago, which started a great period of ratings for Monday Night Raw, but drew a hugely disappointing buy rate for WrestleMania—where the money was supposed to have been made on the deal.

As a live show, the Bash drew a sellout of 7,851 fans (6,354 paying $150,870), selling out three days in advance. While media reports will attribute it to Rodman drawing the sellout, the reality isn't nearly as romantic. The fact was this show was, while not a hard sell since it did sellout and the advance was solid, it wasn't selling tickets at the same level of most major WCW events in recent months that get no national publicity despite the Rodman hype locally which started with his angle in March. In fact, the real ticket sales movement didn't come until after the announcement of the Ric Flair vs. Roddy Piper match. The crowd live was said to have been not nearly as hot as most major WCW house shows, but still decent with only the Flair and Hogan matches drawing major crowd heat.

If the Rodman debut was a success, it was tempered a little by a lower profile failure—the debut of Curt Hennig. Hennig, 39, one of the great workers of his era but now out of action for a few years, showed up probably the heaviest he has ever appeared, and looked slow and unimpressive and killed what had been up to this point a hot angle involving Diamond Dallas Page and Randy Savage. Hennig wasn't in the ring much, but his appearance as Page's mystery partner was such a letdown that there was no heat at all for the match.

Part of that was due to a major mistake WCW made before the show went on the air and in television hype weeks ago. Page alluded in his first interview regarding a mystery partner by looking at the sky it would be Sting. Since fans have been waiting for Sting's first match for months, anyone but Sting was going to be a letdown of sorts. It was made worse at the building when before the show, ring announcer Dave Penzer asked the crowd who they thought would be the mystery partner and 90% of the reaction screamed "Sting." In addition, when Hennig did his first interview on the 7/7 Nitro in Memphis, it was a total heel promo. Many people called the turn ahead of time, which only served to make Page look stupid to the fans for trusting a guy who had already done a heel promo as opposed to Page being betrayed.

As is typical with WCW, when it comes to the wrestling, it was the undercard that stole the show, with the two best matches being a cruiserweight title match between Chris Jericho and Ultimo Dragon, and an amazing aerial circus involving Hector Garza & Lizmark Jr. & Juventud Guerrera vs. Psicosis & Villano IV & La Parka.

WWF SummerSlam

There were quite a number of major themes to the WWF's SummerSlam PPV show on 8/3 from the Continental Airlines Arena in East Rutherford, NJ.

There was the main event, where Michaels began the heel turn by "accidentally" hitting Undertaker with a chair as Bret Hart ducked, leading to Hart capturing the WWF title for a record-tying fifth time. Hulk Hogan was the only other wrestler in WWF history with five title reigns. Neither Hogan nor the fifth time tying the record were mentioned in the commentary or storyline leading up to the match or after the match for the obvious political reasons (although Jim Ross did mention at one point during the show that the first WWF show at the Meadowlands was in 1981 headlined by Bruno Sammartino vs. George Steele, which for history buffs, was at the time billed as Sammartino's retirement match).

And there was the crowd, 20,213 strong (17,361 paying $523,154 along with a whopping $202,500 in merchandise sales), selling out about one week in advance. The show broke pro wrestling records in all three categories at the former Meadowlands Arena with the previous records set at the August 28, 1989 SummerSlam event of 17,202 paying $326,658 for a show headlined by Hulk Hogan & Brutus Beefcake vs. Zeus & Randy Savage. The gate will be the second largest of 1997 in North America, trailing only WrestleMania in Chicago.

But overall, despite the WWF riding a major wave of momentum from the U.S. vs. Canada angle storm, the show generally had to be considered a disappointment. The WWF's top talent and the promotion itself, Austin, Hart and Undertaker, showed without question they were over by selling out one week in advance and with the generally strong house show business of late. But the crowd response from the sellout was disappointing, particularly from a live perspective.

Aside from a few carefully choreographed spots during the show and the last few minutes of the Undertaker-Bret title change, there was no real heat in the building, which made the show seem unimpressive to the television viewers who were comparing it with the current industry standards, let alone the spectacular response at the recent Calgary PPV show four weeks earlier and some of the recent Raw tapings. Some there live credited the dead crowd to the idea so many had been at the afternoon tailgate party and boozed it up heavily and by the time the show started, they were all tapped out. There were reports of numerous fans who by midway in the show appeared to be on the verge of falling asleep because of too much partying in the hot sun before the show.

Even discounting the lack of crowd reaction, the match quality wasn't good. There were far too many botched up spots and messed up finishes for a major league show. Owen Hart and Austin were on the way to doing the show-stealer of a match before the injury cut them short and left the match flat, but they were the only ones who were working a great match.

Bret and Undertaker, while not a bad match, was a very long match that was largely identical to all their previous matches until the finish and was certainly nothing out of the ordinary. While the storyline built well, for match quality this would have been a middle-of-the-road quality match at most of the recent PPV shows.

Mankind vs. Hunter Hearst Helmsley had a few spectacular spots, but overall never got serious momentum. The cage prevented the outside the ring spots that are usually the highlight when Mankind has a great match. But the cage didn't prevent the outside interference, which was overdone to the point of silliness when it comes to the whole gimmick of a cage match. Chyna is the only thing in Helmsley's repertoire that the crowd seems to care about so her constant interference is something of an easy out.

None of the other four matches were any good, and about the only moment from any of them the slightest bit memorable would have been Ken Shamrock, bleeding from the mouth, doing his caged lion routine and he "lost it" and took it out on executives and former wrestling stars Pat Patterson and Gerald Brisco and two referees en route to having his name chanted after a match which had to be classified as disappointing.

Except for the main event, most of the finishes came off somewhat botched. Chyna did a run-in one spot early in the cage match, then had to go out of the cage and do the exact same thing for the "real" finish. Goldust and Brian Pillman messed up their finishing sunset flip spot to the point of almost complete embarrassment. Shamrock vs. British Bulldog was technically a DQ finish for Shamrock hitting Bulldog with a dog food can, cheap on its own, but so poorly explained after the fact that virtually everyone at home assumed it was an equally flat double count out finish to end what was only a fair match. The only thing positive to say about the Los Boricuas vs. DOA finish was that at least there was one, and it came about two minutes too late. And Owen Hart and Austin's finish, which was just a matter of one of those nightmarish moments, a momentary panic due to fear of a catastrophic injury with 20,000 peoples eyes glued to them.

While Austin's injury was the major one, a second apparent injury took place involving Ahmed Johnson. Johnson, recovering from recent arthroscopic knee surgery, had just gotten word earlier in the week that his recovery was behind schedule. He had been scheduled to return to the ring this coming weekend but word late in the week was he wouldn't be able to return until early September, and like Marc Mero, would be forced to wear a heavy knee brace. After the spot leading to the finish of the eight-man match, where Johnson was supposed to give Chainz (Brian Lee) a Pearl River plunge on the floor, Johnson seemed to change his mind on the move in mid-air, and it came off more like a power bomb, and apparently re-aggravated the knee.

They did put him in the ring at Raw the next night to do an angle where the NOD turned on him to explain his longer absence and give him an issue to return for, although even before the NOD attack, it was clear in the ring that his knee was gone. With him limited by injury and Chainz limited by lack of ability, it gave the two the additional opportunity to try to set new standards for the category of awful pro wrestling. No word on when he'll return but his first major match had been scheduled against Undertaker on the 9/20 "One Night

Only" England PPV show. Undertaker also screwed up his back taking a superplex off the top rope from Hart, although he wasn't expected to miss any time from it.

NJPW G-1 Climax Tournament

New Japan's answer to March Madness, the seventh annual G-1 Climax tournament every August at Tokyo Sumo Hall, ended with Kensuke Sasaki as the winner, Hiroyoshi Tenzan as the rising star and MVP, and Masahiro Chono in the hospital.

Sasaki, whose first G-1 tournament win and overall biggest career win to this point took place one day before his 31st birthday, had a first round bye, and then became the ultimate NWO-buster by being put over Marcus Bagwell in the second round on 8/2, and both Scott Norton in the semifinals and Tenzan in the finals on 8/3. Tenzan, who along with Satoshi Kojima was also legitimately injured over the three hard-fought days, was put over IWGP heavyweight champion Shinya Hashimoto in the semifinals, where he suffered a knee injury which initial reports are should require arthroscopic surgery. However, due to the storyline, combined with the injury to Chono, Tenzan came out for the finals and won't be missing any action, losing to Sasaki's lariat and Northern lights bomb (his wife's finishing maneuver) in 8:09.

Chono didn't work the third night and reporters at the matches were told that he would be forced to undergo surgery on the ankle after all, which would be taking place this week, and would have to miss the Nagoya Dome show, where he was scheduled against Hashimoto for the IWGP heavyweight title. This may have resulted in New Japan changing the finish of the Hashimoto vs. Tenzan match that night, as it would have been more dramatic for Sasaki to score his biggest career win against Hashimoto than against Tenzan, and from a storyline standpoint it would make sense with Sasaki set to challenge for the IWGP title on 8/31 in Yokohama. However, with New Japan needing a replacement for Chono on 8/10, Tenzan needed the credibility immediately of not only going to the finals, but scoring a clean win over Hashimoto in the G-1.

Tenzan scored the clean win over Hashimoto with a diving head-butt in 14:01 in what was reported as a great match, while Sasaki won his semifinal over Norton in 5:16 with the Northern Lights bomb. The quarterfinals on 8/2 saw Sasaki beat Bagwell in a match of wrestlers with a first round bye in 8:04 with the reverse ipponzei (judo hiptoss); Tenzan pinned Kojima in 11:43 after a moonsault; Norton pinned Great Muta in a battle of NWO members in 6:31 with a powerslam and Hashimoto beat Chono in 5:45. The Muta-Norton match saw the two shake hands at the beginning but Muta blew the mist in Norton's face. Muta then was beating on Norton outside the ring using objects until Bagwell washed the green out of Norton's eyes to start the comeback. Bagwell wound up fighting outside the ring against fellow NWO members Tenzan and Hiro Saito. Finish saw Muta go for a Frankensteiner off the top but Norton held on, and powerslammed him for the win.

Reports are that the first night was just shy of a sellout with 10,500 fans, and that the second and third shows were complete sellouts of 11,000. The third show, a Sunday afternoon card, had been sold out for weeks in advance, with the gate the second and third night around an estimated $600,000.

Chono, who had suffered a badly injured ankle delivering an atomic drop to Dusty Wolfe at WCW's World Wide tapings in Orlando, FL two weeks earlier, announced he was going to work the tournament and his scheduled title match on 8/10. This also may have been initially scheduled as a title change, and he would also work the main event on New Japan 8/31 show at Yokohama Arena since it was the Riki Choshu Memorial Night.

The actual injuries suffered in Florida were a dislocated right ankle, torn ligaments in the ankle and a broken heel bone. An operation was recommended by both the doctors in Florida and by the New Japan doctors when he returned, which would have put Chono out of action until November. Chono decided not only against the operation because of the important matches on the immediate schedule, but to also work the big shows rather than take time off. Chono worked his first round match on 8/1, getting his expected win over Michiyoshi Ohara in 18:39 of what was said to have been a very dramatic match due to Ohara's working on Chono's left ankle. However, apparently it was during this match that the injury was re-aggravated.

In the second round, he faced Hashimoto. On the house mic, Chono challenged Hashimoto not to attack his bad leg so as to not make it a handicap match. Chono opened by kicking the hell out of Hashimoto using a special shoe to protect the injury. Hashimoto sold it like he was knocked out in the ring. In apparent desperation, Hashimoto went after the bad leg. This saw the rest of the NWO, Tenzan, Norton, Bagwell and Hiro Saito hit the ring and several New Japan wrestlers hit the ring for a brawl. This allowed Chono to attack Hashimoto and use his favorite STF, but Hashimoto made the ropes. Hashimoto made the big comeback, using a standing ankle lock before the referee stopped the match in just 5:45.

New Japan held a press conference on 8/4 to officially announce Tenzan as Hashimoto's opponent for the Nagoya Dome, since New Japan couldn't get any major last minute help from WCW to fill the slot (not that there's anyone in WCW who would mean a lot except possibly Norton since he has two pins earlier this year against Hashimoto challenging for the IWGP title) because the Road Wild PPV makes it impossible for anyone on that show to work Nagoya. They didn't make an announcement regarding the main event on 8/31 in Yokohama which was initially scheduled as Chono & Great Muta & Tenzan vs. Choshu & Tatsumi Fujinami & Genichiro Tenryu.

Kojima apparently suffered a concussion in his match on 8/2 where he lost to Tenzan in the tournament and attempted to wrestle in a six-man tag the next night. He collapsed in the ring during the match and was pinned by Akira Nogami, and he was taken out by a stretcher to the hospital.

Even though on paper the G-1 shows didn't look anywhere close to the level of last year, reports we had were that all three shows were great with most of the matches being good and that Tenzan and Tadao Yasuda put on career performances.

One of the surprises was the major league pro wrestling debut of Don Frye (who about nine years ago did work a half-dozen or so indie dates in Arizona), facing Kazuyuki Fujita on 8/2. This was reported as having the most heat of any match on that show. Fujita, a New Japan rookie whose credentials include being a Japanese national champion in amateur wrestling, got a tremendous crowd reaction for hanging in with Frye, particularly getting him in a submission where Frye needed a rope break. Frye made the comeback doing punches from the mount before using what I believe was a crooked head scissors for the victory at 6:40. However, Frye, who was managed by former pro wrestler Brad Rheingans, "turned heel" by refusing to break the hold until Naoya Ogawa hit the ring and started throwing kicks. The place went wild as Frye and Ogawa squared off until New Japan wrestlers pulled them both apart, but not before Antonio Inoki was in the ring as well. Frye faces former UFC fighter Cal Worsham at the Nagoya Dome, building toward a match with Ogawa that is scheduled to take place on 1/4 at the Tokyo Dome.

There was also a three-day long storyline involving injured Shiro Koshinaka trying to get Tatsumi Fujinami & Kengo Kimura to join the depleted ranks to Heisei Ishingun. This led to Kimura teaming with Nogami & Akitoshi Saito on 8/2 and a match on 8/3 where Fujinami & Kimura & Nogami beat Kojima & Manabu Nakanishi & Junji Hirata. Also on 8/3 in the undercard, Tatsuhito Takaiwa got the biggest win of his career in a non-title match beating J Crown champion El Samurai in 16:42 to set himself up for a future title match.

The G-1 first round matches on 8/1 saw Kojima pin Steve Regal in 9:45 with a diamond cutter; Tenzan pinned Yasuda in 10:39 with a moonsault; Norton pinned Hirata with a powerslam in 6:31; Chono beat Ohara with a chicken wing and cross face submission in 18;39; Muta pinned Manabu Nakanishi in 10:25 after a Frankensteiner off the top rope and Hashimoto beat Kazuo Yamazaki in 11:25 with the armbreaker. Yamazaki didn't tap out, but ref Masao Hattori stopped the match.

WCW ROAD WILD

With PPV shows coming with such frequency, there are going to be good ones and bad ones. The industry is moving at such a ridiculously frantic pace that there is no time to savor the good ones or dwell on the bad ones, because for the most part by the end of next night, they are already old news.

WCW's Road Wild was one of the bad ones. That in itself isn't a big story because WWF and WCW have their bad ones. But the reasons why are a huge story.

There have been inner demons festering within WCW during this period of outward success. We know about the good and often great ratings, the best house show business in company history and a talent pool with depth when it comes to both marketable names and those who work at a world class level that would be the envy of virtually any wrestling promotion in the history of the industry. We also know about the egos involved, and the problems that entails.

The failure of Road Wild as a show points more to the problems with egos and decision making than to the poor show as a measuring stick of where the promotion is today.

To start with, there's the very concept. The Sturgis rally is a big deal to biker enthusiasts around the country. It doesn't mean crap to anyone else. The idea of doing a show on location outdoors near the mountains in front of the bikers was a novel concept last year, much like the beach show in Los Angeles in 1995. As a concept, it failed, like the beach show, but every time you take a new chance in this business you take the risk of it failing. But since it gave those in charge of the company and some of the top wrestlers a chance to ride their Harleys from Detroit (or Minneapolis) to Sturgis for a week, which apparently is more akin to their leisure time than riding waves, it was done again.

WCW is in a lot different situation than it was in 1995. Today in any major market, a WCW PPV event will, between ticket sales and merchandise, gross from a low of $150,000 to a high of around $300,000. So doing a free show is basically giving away the opportunity for a tremendous amount of revenue. One can argue that Eric Bischoff turned the profitability of the company around far more than that, and doing shows that are fun for the boss and a few of the boys that like to ride and hang out in that atmosphere is just a perk of the company's success.

But the show suffered for it. The whole situation, with the ring on a platform, limited greatly the out of the ring antics and flying moves because the ring itself was elevated so much higher than the ground and made the risk factor such that a lot of out of the ring antics weren't even attempted. This hurt the excitement of the matches last year, and this year did so even more because most of the high fliers were kept off the card since their talents couldn't be used properly. And that handicap was already going to take the workrate down a couple of notches.

Luckily for WCW, the live crowd, something of a problem last year, wasn't much of one this year. Well, at least until the end of the show, but that has been consistent with a lot of crowds with a lot of promotions ever since television not so subtly encourages them the end of a show signifies the time they have free license to throw objects to their hearts content at the performers. Hulk Hogan got a rock thrown upside his head, and had to call an in-ring audible, and shielded his head with the title belt as he and his cohorts changed the title change celebration to an indoor event backstage while the befuddled announcers were left sitting there trying to kill time at the end of a show that was about ten minutes short.

But that was the least of the problems. Fact is, the crowd was totally different than expected. It was more wrestling fans than bikers with nothing to do. Harlem Heat, the biggest heels on the show last year because of their skin color, got no racist heat at all. Hulk Hogan, the big babyface last year because virtually nobody in the audience even knew about his turn, was a total heel this year. The crowd knew the storylines and reacted, most notably when it comes to the Jeff Jarrett/Steve McMichael stealing the wife storyline.

Road Wild was ruined before it ever started. The setting was strike one. The backstage maneuvering was strike two. And the results of that maneuvering, the lame hastily-put together finishes up and down the show, were strike three. Booker Terry Taylor had put together a show and subsequent bookings for the next couple of months built around three title changes on this show—Chris Jericho to regain the cruiserweight title from Alex Wright, The Steiners to finally win the tag team titles from Kevin Nash & Scott Hall, and Hulk Hogan to regain the WCW heavyweight title from Lex Luger. The fact that some fans knew this ahead of time, which has caused WCW and other promotions in the past to change long-term plans, had absolutely nothing to do with the fact two of the three never took place. And the result is there are cards booked with matches that make no sense and will likely have to be re-done.

What exactly happened wasn't clear. The belief is that Hall & Nash went to Bischoff and told him that they thought there had been too many title changes of late and it was ruining the credibility of the titles. At least that's where everyone was placing the blame. On the surface, they have a valid point. Bischoff agreed. Which may have been the correct thing to do. The problem was, if that was the case, it needed to have been done before all the plans were made. And the fact that it was Hall & Nash who came to that conclusion at the same time they were going to drop the titles does give that viewpoint something of a conflict of interest. The whole idea beforehand for Hall & Nash to lose the titles was to then put them into singles programs, with the Nash-Giant program thought to be a potential big moneymaker.

So just before the beginning of the show, the three title changes had been switched to zero. This threw the 8/21 Clash of the Champions, the company's next major show (not to mention all the upcoming house shows) for a loop since it was supposed to be built around three title matches, all of which became almost obsolete. The Steiners were to defend the tag titles against Dean Malenko & Chris Benoit. Well, the Steiners don't have the belts. Chris Jericho's cruiserweight title defense against Eddie Guerrero is out, since Jericho didn't win the title back as planned. And Ultimo Dragon's TV title defense against Alex Wright, which was booked that way because Wright was going to lose the cruiser belt and then be elevated to TV champ, also looks to be in jeopardy because he didn't lose the cruiser belt, and one would think if Bischoff believes Hall & Nash to have a valid point, that point would be undermined by having Wright beat Dragon.

Oh yeah, you're asking. What about Hogan beating Luger? Wasn't the one good thing done on Monday the post-match celebration really getting the emphasis back on the world title belt as the focal point of the promotion? If that's the case, why kill it all by changing the title back five nights later with such a ridiculous cliché of a finish? Yet another NWO star dresses up as Sting and causes Lex Luger to lose. The announcers again destroy whatever credibility they have left by all acting as if it was the real Sting doing it despite it being the same angle they've done a million times over the past year. What gives? Well, there is one ultimate authority in WCW, and when he showed up, zero title changes moved back to one although at this point with the show about to start, nobody had figured out a finish to accomplish this.

All the changes meant all new finishes, most of which were really bad, particularly in the Steiners vs. Hall & Nash. The fact the work rate wasn't too hot, largely because of the setting the matches taking place meant the fliers were mostly kept off the show, didn't help matters. The one title change that probably made the least sense to take place on that night of the three (although Hogan did have to regain the belt shortly because the big money match they've been building for more than one year is Hogan vs. Sting and Hogan needs to be champion for that match to reach its money potential) was the one that did because it specifically involved Hogan, Hogan's creative control of his programs, and Hogan not winning back the belt.

If you're keeping score, Hall & Nash won their power struggle with Taylor, who has now become this month's version of Kevin Sullivan, a booker who does all the work, takes all the heat, and then gets overruled almost all the time. But Hogan beat Hall & Nash again, because even though they were able to maintain their tag belts they were supposed to lose, they weren't able to keep Luger with the belt he was supposed to lose.

And everyone else in WCW were the big losers. Several of the wrestlers who were told what they'd be doing on the show and after the show ended up feeling lied to. Those involved with promotion were advertising matches that make no sense now and will probably have to be changed. And the booking team has to change its basic game plan, to a game plan that once implemented, may be changed again to render it useless once again, if any part of the plan gives any of the stars a bug up their ass.

So much for As the World Turns. But As the World Turns was far more entertaining than the mess on the dirt. Road Wild on 8/10 in Sturgis, SD drew a crowd estimated by various sources live as between 6,000 and 10,000. Judging from the overhead shots it looked in the 6,000 to 7,000 range—larger than last year but obviously smaller than the 9,500 at the beach in 1995. Tony Schiavone was in the Pinocchio role, having to say over and over again that the crowd was 20,000. Can you believe one week earlier in Auburn Hills at the Palace when they really had nearly 18,000 in the building, not one announcer mentioned a crowd figure? This time, when they half less than half of that, they give the ridiculous lie that was apparent to everyone viewing.

Pinocchio statement No. 2, repeated often on Nitro the next night was that the Hogan-Luger match was the most watched title match in pro wrestling history. Whoa! Pro wrestling history takes in a lot and while the audience was the largest ever for a competitive situation on cable since the Monday night wars began in late 1995 which doesn't exactly constitute the beginning of time, that statement isn't even close to true. There have been title matches with ten times the television audience of Hogan-Luger. The very preliminary buy rate estimate coming from Request is 0.77 (the very preliminary numbers are always higher than they turn out because the people who report back the quickest are the ones who are the happiest), which has to be considered good. This would be roughly the same as the preliminary figures for SummerSlam at an 0.79 buy rate.

ECW Hardcore Heaven

One would have thought the inauguration of Shane Douglas as the theoretical long-term standard bearer as ECW champion would have been the most memorable part of the company's second PPV show on 8/16 from the Fort Lauderdale War Memorial Auditorium. But instead, despite Douglas winning the title in what was generally conceded to have been the best match on the show, the lasting thought was what ECW feared most. The show looked minor league.

The wrestling was for the most part okay, although nobody except Sabu came out of the show as breaking out of the pack. But the production, lighting, look and sound came off more like a Herb Abrams PPV than the alternative to WWF and WCW that ECW attempts to present itself as. The overall reaction to the show was mixed, and really it would be almost impossible not to get some positive reaction to the show considering ECW does have its fan base which is as fanatical to its product as any fan base for a wrestling promotion in the world. There were many who loved the show. But those who didn't like the show, and that appeared to have been the majority, reacted nearly as vociferously with numerous callers saying it was the best PPV show of the year and almost as many others saying it was the worst.

The show seemed thrown together in spots, unlike the first ECW PPV show in April which was planned out far in advance and was one of the best shows of the year. Reports were that Request TV didn't get a script until literally the last minute. ECW officials were frantically trying to find "surprises" during the last week, to the point they were even looking for Jim Duggan's phone number. As it was, they got Jake Roberts and Dory Funk, who were both good for nice pops, but played no part into any real storyline development.

Paul Heyman described the card as a good live house show but a terrible PPV television show. Reports from those who attended the show live would concur as among those there it got almost all thumbs ups. The show suffered with an attempt to get creative that fell totally flat in the show-long Sandman ambulance ride. Heyman said that the next PPV show, which will be 11/30 from Monaca, PA (suburban Pittsburgh) would be more like an ECW Arena or television shoot with two or three cameras, with more concentration on planning ahead of time and of the show quality itself and less on making sure not to offend people.

Heyman felt he had to be careful when it came to what aired on television since they were under the gun with many cable systems to back up their claim that they were no different then the other wrestling groups on PPV, thus pulling back the camera shots from the blood ala WCW, cutting back on the swearing so as not to give whomever his enemies are ammunition to hurt future events and to get over the hump with Viewers Choice and some of the other companies that to this point are refusing to carry the show. The only swearing came in the first few minutes when Rick Rude said "F*** you (Tod) Gordon." They even toned down not using phrases like this being the "most extreme" wrestling in the world and toned down referring to Dreamer as "the innovator of violence."

Once again several, perhaps many, ECW fans who are supposedly such loyal pro-company advocates don't have any clue of the big picture. With the company trying to tone down slightly in order to be on the right side of some cable company executive's "offensive" compass (which is also not selling out, but simply trying to conduct business in today's real world climate rather than some mixed up fantasy about what hardcore is supposed to mean) many fans were out there doing crude chants trying to get themselves over and not having one clue about how their actions could potentially effect the PPV future of the company they profess to care so much about, particularly because there is a possibility, although unlikely at present but there had been negotiations up until about a month or two ago, for Viewers Choice to take over Request and VC has yet to approve of running ECW PPV events.

If everything in regards to that scenario would go wrong for ECW, and the odds are strongly against it, they could lose PPV exposure. The objections there are to the show, whether valid or not and since it's PPV where you have to make a conscious choice to order the show so really like with UFC, these decisions not to carry the events are really unsettling and kind of scary, have to do with violence and obscenities. But if the people who profess to love the product so much can't figure out the score, they can potentially be the cause of it taking a giant step backwards as well.

Very early estimates indicate the show did between an 0.20 and 0.23 buy rate, or about 35,000 buys, which would be an estimated 13 to 20 percent drop from the first show but would also make a profit crudely estimated by those who really don't know the costs of around $90,000. For a second show, it held up far better than Pancrase, EFC or UWFI but didn't show the growth momentum of UFC at the same stage (UFC went from about 80,000 buys to 100,000 buys in a significantly larger universe from show one to show two).

On Monday, Michael Klein at Viewers Choice said that they hadn't made a decision about carrying the next show but that they have discussions with ECW scheduled for the future. Others in Viewers Choice did confirm that they've agreed to carry the 10/17 UFC show, which saves that product from the almost sure extinction that a decision by VC not to carry it would have resulted in. There were rumors that VC would put ECW on, but on its Hot Choice Channel which is a secondary channel that would be in just over half the PPV homes that the major VC channels are. While it wouldn't clear ECW universally besides the systems such as Time Warner and Cablevision that have decided system-wide not to carry the event, it would at least up the exposure by several million homes from what it was for this show.

In response to all the protests to Cablevision from ECW fans including Joey Styles, who resides in Stamford, CT, the company issued a release defending its position. It claimed that by reviewing videotapes of the television show that the level of violence is incompatible with its own standards on violence on television. The strange double-standard of that reasoning is those same television shows air on Cablevision on broadcast and cable channels that anyone has access to with no steps taken to avoid them airing, yet PPV, where one has to go through specific steps to pay and see it, is being kept off the airwaves. It defended its broadcasting adult entertainment channels on PPV because it has a standard of violence that those also have to adhere to.

The angle where Sandman showed up and took Sabu out of the three-way title match appears to build up a singles match between the two at the next PPV, which will likely be a ladder match. The usage of Sunny just before the finish in the Jerry Lawler vs. Tommy Dreamer match may result in a Chris Candido & Sunny vs. Dreamer & Beulah match either on that show or an arena show later this year to be marketed for videotape. Because of Sunny's name in the WWF, the novelty of her doing a wrestling match on PPV would be a coup as far as getting some mainstream fans who don't know much about ECW curious about getting the show.

Roberts may or may not return to ECW, but Heyman said that he wouldn't be putting Roberts in the ring as a wrestler and would likely never advertise him as appearing on a show ahead of time due to his track record, but may use him once every few months as a surprise in an angle since he'll get a big pop and he recognizes his major star power in small doses. Apparently Heyman was frantically calling WWF at the last minute trying to get the okay to use Sunny because his original plan was for Roberts to be the ultimate surprise, but then Roberts arrived so late that they were afraid he wasn't going to get there and they changed the plans and then he arrived. There was apparently some thought of using Roberts to go into Roberts vs. Dreamer, but that appears to be totally out the window.

Although the crowd, which packed the 1,800-seat auditorium, came off as dead, except for a few big pops for carefully choreographed spots, the crowd at the end of the show did seem to be enjoying it at the end when the wrestlers were in the crowd as the show went off the air and the fans chanted "ECW." A little less than half the crowd chanted for the encore curtain call, similar to what happened at the ECW Arena for the first PPV. It's not known exactly what was paid and papered in the crowd. ECW offered free tickets to anyone who flew down from Philadelphia as part of a travel package, which drew 101 people and there were also 40 people who flew in from Tokyo, although they paid for their ringside tickets. The actual advance one week out was 800 tickets (we had reported 1,000 last week) and we were told the market was going to be heavily papered in the final days to fill the building.

Before the show went on the air, they shot an angle in the building where two members of the rap band "Insane Clown Posse" were in the ring putting over their favorite wrestler, Rob Van Dam. Van Dam then turned on them, giving one a spin kick and another a Tiger driver and put him in a camel clutch. Sabu came out in a suit, trying to look like The Sheik (and he is looking more and more like him by the day) and joined in until Sandman made the save. That didn't last long as Sabu threw a chair at Sandman and Van Dam kicked a chair into Sandman's head. Sabu came off the top rope with a chair and then put the chair on Sandman while he and Van Dam both came off the top rope at the same time onto him. Sandman did a stretcher job and was taken out in an ambulance.

As the show went on, they did a storyline where they had a helicopter which they called the "Extreme Chopper" follow the ambulance, which supposedly Sandman had commandeered and was driving (and he actually was driving it). The story was that since Sandman didn't know Florida, he was totally lost trying to find the building and supposedly we were told how he was stopping for directions at convenience stores to get directions, beer and cigarettes. Supposedly he mistakenly went to the Knight Center (another building wrestling used to be held at in nearby Miami before the Arena was built) before, just as the main event started, he showed back up at the right building. At this point he started caning supposed police officers.

The lack of believability of these segments that played throughout the show made it again seem like an Abrams show in that they were copying bad ideas that WWF and WCW had done in the past and doing low rent (not that renting the chopper for the show was all that cheap) versions of them. To make matters worse, Lance Wright, who was doing the remote from the helicopter, froze, and never got across the points he was supposed to get across.

There was the strong insinuation that Sandman was drinking while driving and even though this is all fantasy (although Sandman really was driving), it rubs me the wrong way really badly to glorify drinking while driving even if the gimmick of the performer is to be a drunk and the nature of the audience they play to.

There was a lot of talk before hand about doing that segment totally as a pre-tape (which is how WWF or WCW would have done it) in case of screw-ups, but it was done live. No doubt the Posse angle was pre-taped in case using non wrestlers in an angle looked bad.

There were complaints from the fans live about the audience as a whole, in that they were said to have been really rude to the Japanese fan contingent with chants of "USA" at them and "We Want a War." Much of live the crowd also knew Jake Roberts was there because of the nature of how the wrestlers had to enter the arena.

WWF In Your House 17: Ground Zero

About the only thing to say about the WWF Ground Zero PPV show on 9/7 from Louisville, KY, is that it was the first three-hour In Your House show presented at a $29.95 price tag. How that increase in price on a monthly basis affects the buy rates and overall PPV revenue, which should increase significantly, is a lot more of a story than what turned out to be a wilder product and maybe an overall slightly-above average show.

The event sold out weeks in advance in the 6,000-seat Louisville Gardens, with 4,963 paying $82,228 and another $44,184 in merchandise. Probably the most memorable thing on the show was the angle where Steve Austin gave Jim Ross a stone cold stunner. The first ever match of Undertaker vs. Shawn Michaels was notable for yet another world-class performance by Michaels. The fact Bret Hart beat Patriot in the WWF title match should have surprised nobody, but the near burial of Patriot, just a few weeks after arriving in the WWF, was. The Head Bangers winning the WWF tag team title in the Fatal Four way, which given the workrate was an appropriate name for the match, was a surprise, although the finish, where Austin giving Owen Hart a stone cold stunner causing his duo with Davey Boy Smith to lose, shouldn't have been.

The next attempt to push the minis from Mexico highlighted their ability to do spots, but the attempt to turn them into 1960s "mighty midgets" doing the Sky Low Low and Fuzzy Cupid spots were woefully outdated. The triangle match was a strong worst match of the year candidate. There really isn't much to say about Brian

Christopher vs. Scott Putski since due to Putski's injury early on, the match was stopped well before it had gotten going. Brian Pillman vs. Goldust was the beginning of what appears to be a very long soap operaish angle, and to their credit, their match was a lot better than their first meeting at SummerSlam.

50 Years of Funk

The other legendary Texas wrestling family, the Funks, had a celebration and an ending of an era as well on 9/11 in Amarillo at the Fairgrounds Coliseum.

It was billed as 50 years of Funk—as Dory Funk Sr. came from Indiana to Texas in 1947 and eventually became the biggest wrestling star and owner of the territory based in Amarillo until his death in 1973. It was also billed as the final match for Terry Funk in his home town where he started wrestling in 1965. Terry and Vicki Funk promoted the show, combining talent from the WWF, ECW, FMW and JD for a card that will air on Japanese cable television. The main event, Terry Funk against Bret Hart, was also taped for a movie, tentatively titled "Beyond the Mat," a documentary to be produced by Barry ("Nutty Professor") Blaustein in conjunction with Ron Howard and with two of the ECW matches scheduled to air on the television show this week.

The show drew nearly a full house of 3,800. The highlight, even more than the live crowd that responded well to nearly every match, no matter how good or bad the quality was, was a ceremony before the Funk-Hart match. After Hiromichi Fuyuki, who Funk will wrestle for the old NWA Texas heavyweight title on 9/28 at Kawasaki Baseball Stadium, came out to issue a challenge, all the ECW wrestlers on the show along with Paul Heyman, Dory Funk, and Terry's wife and family got in the ring. Heyman gave Funk much deserved credit for helping take ECW to the level it has reached and presented him with a replica ECW world heavyweight title belt which he said was for being the lifetime ECW champion. Hart, who was accompanied to the ring by father Stu and brothers Ross and Bruce, then said that he believed Terry Funk was the single greatest wrestler in the history of the business and mentioned that as a kid he spent a lot of time living with both Dory and Terry and he thought that Amarillo wrestling was the greatest wrestling that there ever was.

Among the people backstage who weren't part of the live show included Taka Michinoku, Sam Houston and Grizzly Smith. The show was promoted locally off six weeks of ECW television, that aired past midnight on the NBC affiliate. The crowd there recognized and reacted to the ECW wrestlers, although only Sandman got a great pop coming out. It appears that Heyman and Funk will try to promote another show in Amarillo in early 1998 which would be a total ECW card.

WCW Fall Brawl

WCW's PPV show of the week, Fall Brawl on 9/14 from the Lawrence Joel Coliseum in Winston-Salem, NC, was the typical WCW offering. A strong undercard with the match quality in the so-so range after the mid-point. The general reports were favorable, but not enthusiastically so. In this case, the main event that the show was built around, War Games, was among the worst War Games ever as a match, but the ending and post-match were among the most dramatic.

The show drew a sellout 11,939 (11,024 paid) with a $213,330 gate, slightly more than last year's War Games in the same building but a much higher gross with the increase in ticket prices. In all the WCW print advertising in the market, they listed Hulk Hogan as appearing on the show which is blatant false advertising because it was known months in advance that he was skipping this show. The general belief as to why the teams in War Games weren't announced until the day before the show is only partly the typical lack of organization, but also because the way the Nitro hype was going, to make people think that perhaps Hogan and Sting would be on opposite sides until the announcement of the complete line-up of Team WCW six days before the show.

Because of an angle during the show that involved Larry Zbyszko, he was brought in to do color instead of Dusty Rhodes, which turned out to be a major plus. The booking was top-notch in that the matches that needed controversial finishes for storyline reasons had them, and the waters weren't muddied underneath to where it seemed like screw-job city because everything underneath was a clean finish.

WWF One Night Only

The World Wrestling Federation ran its first ever PPV show primarily for the British market on 9/20 before a sellout crowd of 11,000 fans at the NEC Arena in Birmingham, England. The show aired live in the United Kingdom, on tape delay on PPV in Canada, and has been released for the U.S. market on home video.

Our reports indicated it was a very good show, with the final three matches being the highlight of the show, headlined by Shawn Michaels winning the European title from Davey Boy Smith in a match that Smith dedicated to his sister, Traci, who came out to the ring with him and is suffering from bone cancer. The basic idea for this title change, making Michaels the first ever "Grand Slam" champion (WWF, IC, WWF tag team and European) in company history, appears to build up a second PPV for the United Kingdom, likely coming from Smith's home town of Manchester, England, sometime in the spring of 1998.

It was the same promotional gimmick used by the WWF last year to build up the Royal Rumble PPV where Shawn Michaels regained the WWF title in his home town of San Antonio. The fact Michaels was given the title in the wake of the incident in Muncie, IN where he was swearing (nicely edited off television), calling out Undertaker who wasn't there, and running around in biker shorts and "stuffing" his crotch makes one wonder just how much Vince McMahon really didn't know about the incident before hand.

Throwing all that out, from a pure business perspective, this is a viable tried-and-true wrestling angle, with a heartbreaking loss by the top babyface (in that market) to set up a return. If the Michaels deal wasn't an angle, which is something I'd be skeptical of at this point, than the WWF is stupid to put a belt on Michaels in the state he's in, not to mention his track record of how many times coming up with excuses and reasons to never drop back belts he's given.

For WWF in England, the first PPV show was expected to do well based on the novelty of it being the first non-boxing event ever on PPV in that country, but it becomes less and less of a novelty with each successive show. Rather than "waste" having your largest expected audience with a blow-off, you use the largest audience to do a major angle to try and keep it for the next show. But it doesn't appear that this title change was planned more than a week in advance unless the communication within the company has broken down, because on Raw two days after the switch, there were localized promos all over the country running for matches in October talking about Bulldog's matches as being European title matches.

WWF In Your House 18: Badd Blood

Under the cloud of the death of Pillman, WWF ran its Badd Blood PPV show on 10/5 in St. Louis at the Kiel Center. The show drew a legitimate sellout of 21,151 fans (17,404 paying $212,550; $101,155 in merchandise). It would have been the second largest crowd in the long and storied history of St. Louis wrestling, trailing the famous Strangler Lewis vs. Jim Londos stadium match in 1934 that drew 35,000.

I really can't give a fair assessment of the show. It appeared that none of the matches were any good except the main event, which was a strong candidate for match of the year. I'd give the show a thumbs in the middle, but it's hard to really give you any feelings on the show.

WCW Halloween Havoc

In an era where fan behavior at wrestling has led to problems often more than weekly at wrestling matches, WCW decided to encourage the problem with a lame fan out of the audience angle as the closing scene in its Halloween Havoc PPV show.

Havoc on 10/26 from the MGM Grand Garden Arena in Las Vegas, which will hold a short-lived title as the largest grossing wrestling event in WCW history, was the typical WCW PPV fare. Good undercard matches and a weak finish. In this case, more exaggerated than usual.

The Rey Misterio Jr. vs. Eddie Guerrero mask vs. cruiserweight title, won by Misterio Jr., in a finish apparently not finalized until just minutes before the show started, was arguably the single best match on a WCW PPV show dating back more than six years to the prime of Ric Flair and the February 24, 1991 War Games match from Phoenix. Because of sentimental and memorable reasons, some may compare it with the Jushin Liger vs.

Brian Pillman match in 1992, but this match was clearly due to the sport advancing over five years, of a higher quality if both were judged by the same standards. Ultimo Dragon vs. Yuji Nagata opened with an excellent match as well.

But the show had its disasters, including but not limited to Hulk Hogan vs. Roddy Piper, Steve McMichael vs. Alex Wright and Disco Inferno vs. Jacquelyn, which had better work than the aforementioned two but from a logic standpoint came off as a vindictive company trying to punish a wrestler for reasons having nothing to do with putting on a good show. Even with the bad being exceedingly bad, no show with a match the caliber of the Misterio Jr. match and backed up with three other good matches on the card could get a thumbs down from me.

The show drew a legitimate sellout of 12,457 fans, with 10,138 paying $297,508 and another $102,340 in merchandise sales. The live gate was the all-time record for WCW, breaking the Boston Nitro record set earlier in the year, but its a record that has already been topped by the advance for the 11/23 World War III PPV in Auburn Hills, MI.

There really wasn't much to say about the show other then the new cage used for the first time in the Hulk Hogan vs. Roddy Piper match looked to legitimately be about 20 feet high, which would make it as high a cage as wrestling has ever seen. The typical pro wrestling "15 foot cage" is eight feet high, and the monstrous cage used by AAA in Los Angeles noted for the spectacular dive by Mascarita Sagrada onto Jake Roberts, was probably no more than 12 feet.

As awesome as the height of the cage was, it was incredible that Randy Savage, just weeks before his 45th birthday and coming off a serious ankle injury just a few months ago, did a leap off the top of the cage to set up the finish of the Hogan-Piper match. The fact that he actually missed Hogan, who he was supposed to hit to set up Piper's sleeper hold finish, can be forgiven for the combination of guts and insanity it took to even consider doing such a move.

It was largely like watching two PPVs in some way. The first three matches, largely with wrestlers who learned their trade in other countries and announced by Mike Tenay, were the beginnings of an excellent show. Starting with match four, it was among the worst PPV shows in years with only the Savage vs. Diamond Dallas Page match as a saving grace.

After the match was over and the NWO group of Hogan, Savage and Eric Bischoff had Piper handcuffed to the cage as if they were going to crucify him, a plant fan with Sting make-up hopped the advance in an incredibly lame attempt at a shoot angle. The fan got away from one of the fake Stings (who appeared to be Bobby Walker) and ended up being attacked by Savage and Hogan, with Hogan throwing his lame work punches that weren't even hitting the guy as the cameras focused on that, and security stood there and did nothing and as the fan was pulled from the cage as the show went off the air.

Last year, when fans began throwing garbage at the NWO during PPV shows, it created a ripple effect to where fans thought buying a ticket to live shows gave them the license to hurl garbage at the wrestlers when the show was over. While no wrestlers have been seriously injured by this trend, fans at arenas have been hit and cut with bottles. One of the draws of Nitro itself, along with the PPV shows, Raw and ECW tapings, is for fans themselves to get on television with their antics and signs and get their five seconds of fame. There is nothing wrong with this trend so long as nobody gets hurt and perhaps, so long as fan behavior doesn't reach the stage of being lewd. But when it is glorified that a fan hits the ring to attack the heels, in the atmosphere we're in now, you can guarantee it'll happen again.

It's already happened a few times on Nitro. It's just been lucky so far that the fans have been people who small referees are able to snatch. Some day a guy the size of Roadblock (who actually got into the pro wrestling business based on an incident where he took down and was beating up One Man Gang—he was actually trying to get at Hogan but Gang was a closer target) will be the one wanting to impress his friends, or a drunk college football lineman on a dare from his teammates, and on live television, the situation could be dangerous, not only with the guy ruining a match or perhaps popping a wrestler, but a wrestler perhaps having to protect himself and breaking his hand in the process, and if nobody who runs wrestling today has figured it out yet, the injury rate in this business is alarming enough to begin with.

Very preliminary buy rate estimates are almost through the roof with very serious belief that this show could be the best buy rate of the year, which is saying something because it went in with nowhere near the media publicity of the Rodman show and didn't involve any non-wrestling talent, which again shows that to the general public, putting Hogan and Piper in a cage because of their name value, despite them both being washed up in the ring, still means more than anything else, just as putting Hogan and Flair together again in a program will still mean big business.

There were a lot of fans who left the matches before the Hogan-Piper match started, and fans were leaving in droves during the post-match angle while Piper was still getting annihilated. Another bad sign is that one of the reasons Hogan-Piper has such little heat was because fans were waiting for Sting to do a run-in at the end since they used his name and teased it in the interviews earlier in the show and were looking around for it, and left even more disappointed when the real Sting never showed up.

WWF Survivor Series

In the wake of all that insanity came the show itself, on 11/9 at the Molson Center in Montreal. Survivor Series live drew a sellout crowd of 20,593 (18,101 paying an all-time province record $447,284).

The show, when it was over, was overshadowed by the finish of the main event and the aftermath. Before the show had even started, it was guaranteed the show would be upstaged by the main event, both the quality of which and the backstage maneuvering, negotiating, professionalism and ultimately threat of double-crossing rather than anything that took place underneath.

As it was, it was the same broken record. The lack of talent depth in the WWF was made even more glaring in a show format that requires so many wrestlers to work the show. Even more glaring was that the problem seems to be in the picking of talent. Historically, the WWF has always been known as a "big-man" territory. In the 80s that served them in good stead because they were controlling the fan base into the idea that the steroid look was superior, and then continued to parade out an assembly line of guys who weren't generally very good workers, but provided the fans with what they wanted.

In the 90s, for numerous reasons, mainly media and government pressure, things had to change, which is where Bret Hart and Shawn Michaels, talented mid-card performers that were generally considered in the 80s as not to have any main event potential due to their size, got their shot at superstardom. But even in those days, WWF still marketed successfully some marginally talented and even untalented big men to the top of its cards.

If you look at the undercards of WWF vs. WCW, in WCW you are filled with small men who wow the crowds with matches that get over. WWF has the same big men doing an outdated style of plodding brawling that gets no heat on the big shows, and generally Michaels and/or Steve Austin or Hart are there at the end to save the show. WCW still has the terrible main event matches, but it can't be argued with the results of the buy rates and that is those terrible over-40 wrestlers that work on top draw the casual fans through their name recognition.

But for every Kane, which is a gimmick that seems to be hitting it big, you have far too many Crushes, Interrogators, Brian Lees, Justin Hawk Bradshaws and Kama Mustafas who are all huge men with no fan appeal, or men like Faarooq and Ahmed Johnson with little ability in the ring and some, but not overwhelming, fan appeal. The wrestlers in first two matches on this show were a lot worse than I see locally with independent wrestlers with little experience. And the wrestlers they are scouting on the independent scene are close to Brian Lees than to Shawn Michaels', both in terms of size and talent, if you get my drift.

It's hard for me to understand, because the concept of when everyone in the ring is 6'5", that there are no big men in the ring who can get away with slow moving and a lack of action, but when everyone in the ring is 5'9", than a 6'3" wrestler can get away with doing big-man spots and still have a good match because size in the ring is all illusion based on who one is in the ring with.

Yet we saw two horrible matches with a bunch of 6'5" guys, and no smaller, faster guys because with the exception of Taka Michinoku, the promotion has lagged to the point they are way behind the eight-ball so to speak. The political situation isn't entirely the company's fault based on who they have to deal with and WCW trying to corner the market, in making deals to shore up their depth by adding the new dimension, but the weaknesses have never been more glaring than the first few matches on this show.

WCW WORLD WAR 3

For a company with more talent depth than perhaps any wrestling company in history, there is really no excuse to present a line-up that appeared going in to be so weak on paper as WCW did for World War III on 11/23.

And the line-up was every bit the precursor for the show. Sure, the show did great business—a near sellout crowd of 17,128, with 15,735 paying $407,831 plus another $139,191 in merchandise, at the Palace in Auburn Hills, MI. The gate figure destroyed the record set just a few weeks earlier at Halloween Havoc in Las Vegas of $297,508. It fell just shy of the company's all-time attendance records set on 6/9 in Boston of 18,003 fans and 16,025 paid. But most of the tickets were purchased before the matches were announced, largely coming off a successful 8/4 Nitro appearance in the same building which actually drew more people into the building because it was somewhat papered.

With the three-ring 60 man Battle Royal gimmick, which has never worked in the past from a television standpoint on top and too many of the heavy hitters off the undercard, it was a poor show from a company with far too much talent to have an excuse for such a card. It wasn't as if it was big names getting a lot of heat while shortcutting their way through bad matches, but it was a lot of people who aren't over being put in a position above their league but from a working and perception standpoint, and the crowd responding in kind.

The Battle Royal itself was shot better than the distracting three-ring 20:00 long test patterns with multiple announcing teams from the previous two years, but the match itself may have been the worst of the three. Certainly it was the most uneventful, with only one slim fabric of a storyline presented, the constant near eliminations of Rey Misterio Jr., and the ball was even dropped on that one as he went out before the finals and the cameras didn't catch nor did the announcers notice when he was eliminated after all the teases. The entire NWO being together at the finish was the same as last year, but last year at least had a more exciting finish.

Misterio Jr. and Eddie Guerrero stole the show, but in the words of Jim Cornette, it was petty theft. They had what would have been an incredible match had any two other wrestlers in this world done it with inventing new moves and some incredible spots, but due to a little sloppiness and hesitation after missed spots by Misterio Jr., it fell well short of the match of the year standard they had set last month and that people were going in with the inflated expectations of.

The other good match on paper from last month, Ultimo Dragon vs. Yuji Nagata was good, but again, not nearly on the level as their previous match, perhaps due to Dragon not being 100% after elbow surgery, and lacked heat. Ric Flair vs. Curt Hennig had the expected good psychology, and the selling of the legs was as good as anything you would see in pro wrestling (partially because some of the pain appeared to be real), but Hennig these days is inconsistent at best, and Flair has his good days and his bad days, and this was one of those days where he made the effort to have a good day but somehow didn't.

ECW NOVEMBER TO REMEMBER

Extreme Championship Wrestling's third PPV show seemed to finalize a lot of answers to lingering questions.

Can the company over the long haul make a go of it? At its level, yes. Can the company remain a PPV entity? Again, at its level, yes, although there are potential monkey wrenches in the road they'll have to dodge, but if left to a free economy, probably yes but at a certain level. Is the company a legitimate threat to WWF or WCW as far as being a major mainstream entity? Absolutely not.

The November to Remember PPV, billed ahead of time as ECW's showcase event of the year, fell far short of the mark in that regard. As a promotion, it was the most successful by far in company history. For a group that has only drawn 2,000 fans on two occasions in its nearly five year history, it destroyed all existing company records with a sellout crowd of 4,634 (4,218 paying about $103,900, plus another $43,930 in merchandise which are phenomenal figures for a company of that size) at the Golden Dome in Monaca, PA on 11/30.

Of the three ECW PPV's to date, this would have to rank in the middle as far as a show. It was nowhere near the quality of the "Barely Legal" show in April. It was superior to the "Hardcore Heaven" in August, although that is more due to production improvements than a major improvement in the quality of the show itself. Based on the response here, the general feeling is that to its audience, ECW can do no wrong even when nearly everything goes wrong, as in August. To people who are fans of WWF or WCW and try to judge it by those standards, it naturally doesn't come close when it comes to production, but also the difference in wrestling quality for the most part is noticeable, even with a generally much higher level of effort and considering the somewhat inconsistent product of late by the WWF and WCW. But those people aren't for the most part interested in buying the show to begin with. It's a niche group buying, and a successful one, every bit like FMW in Japan, and in its own way like shoot groups in Japan as well although as diametrically opposite from that as possible, although with not quite the same level of popularity.

ECW throws in enough swerves and turns into every match for those into constant gratification to have something to hold onto, and has enough consistent "hot" spots during the match (although not done in a manner building a match) to satisfy people who buy the show for "highlight reel" spots or attend to chant "ECW." The crowd reactions couldn't touch most WCW and WWF Monday night shows, but is still better than most of what qualifies as pro wrestling, and they did react to spots designed to get the big reactions, the suicidal spots, the low blows and the run-ins. Reports from those live said the crowd heat was never all that good throughout the show except for the Dreamer finish, but that the show was killed live by the Sabu-Sandman match and dead for the last two matches.

But that is missing the point as well. The human toll makes the injury rate in WWF or WCW, or for that matter in a Demolition Derby, seem tame. Some people would argue that what they do isn't even pro wrestling, because things like making it look somewhat plausible (not that any pro wrestling except shoot style looks the slightest bit plausible to begin with) and working without holes big enough to shoot Dusty Rhodes through doesn't exist here.

But that would also be missing the entire point and looking at this business with blinders on. Pro wrestling is whatever enough people are willing to buy. What works economically is what pro wrestling is. Pro wrestling is not limited to what the WWF, WCW or even New Japan and All Japan are doing. ECW, or FMW, or IWA, are all pro wrestling as long as they can survive economically. They cease to be pro wrestling when they can't survive, not when they stop working under standards set and associated with pro wrestling in times past or even times present elsewhere. On that account, ECW is a big success coming from nowhere and being a genuine player, albeit a secondary player, in the PPV industry. No, they aren't New Japan, or even WWF. Nor are they RINGS or Kingdom or for that matter Lucha Libre, nor are RINGS and Kingdom anything like WCW. But they are all pro wrestling, just as Country, Top 40, Rap and Classical music are all under the umbrella as music.

At the same time, missed and blown spots are missed and blown spots and just because they're done by wrestlers who are over with the crowd and forgiven in an ECW ring as opposed to by wrestlers who are over with the mainstream in WCW and the fans don't groan because they are superstars doesn't make them any less blown in either setting.

The injury toll for the show was huge, and probably contributed to a great deal of the show being an overall disappointment. Tommy Rogers injured his neck early in his match with Chris Candido. He's scheduled to undergo a myelogram (shooting a large needle in his spine) this coming week.

Tommy Dreamer injured his good ankle because he's spent so long favoring the bad one, early in his match with Rob Van Dam, and was practically immobile the entire match, although that didn't stop him from working a long match. He was hospitalized after the match, but was mobile by the next day and will still be working this weekend.

Sandman injured his shoulder, then his arm, and banged up his ribs in acting like the sloppiest most inebriated kamikaze pilot in a match with Sabu that was either a demolition derby classic or the single worst match of 1997, depending upon how you view pro wrestling. His injury list included both wrists being swollen, sore ribs and a badly bruised up side and at press time it was recommended that he not wrestle this coming weekend although his condition for the weekend was listed as iffy at press time.

Shane Douglas, who was going to need elbow surgery to clear up bone chips to begin with before the match took place, in taking so many big bumps, made the injury even worse. He'll be undergoing an elbow operation this week, although that was actually planned before the match and the spots in the match where Bigelow destroyed his arm were to be used as the storyline reason for the elbow injury.

To the surprise of nobody, Douglas regained the ECW title from Bam Bam Bigelow in the main event of a match that went far too long, largely due to them giving Sabu vs. Sandman the hook after "only" 21 minutes. What was a surprise was the lack of crowd reaction for most of the match, particularly with Douglas challenging for the title in his hometown. The attempt to work a match similar to Ric Flair vs. Vader from Starrcade '93, the hometown babyface against the monster, largely failed even though it was the most professional looking match of the show as Bigelow's offense and demeanor and ability to get over as a monster was not at the Vader level of '93, and Douglas simply isn't over in his home city anywhere close to Flair in his.

The surprises turned out to be the return of Stevie Richards, which was, despite attempts to hide it, figured to be an inevitability at some point although maybe not this week; and appearances by WWF performers Brakkus, Al Snow, Doug Furnas and Phil LaFon, all in cameo roles. There were hints of a WWF vs. ECW feud, although it's not been made clear if that'll be the focus of the promotion. As it turned out, neither porn star Jenna Jameson or the Insane Clown Posse rap group appeared on the show as advertised.

During the final week before the show, there were talks with WCW regarding Chris Benoit and also talks with Dan Severn. Depending on who you wish to believe, the Benoit situation went something like this. Either a) As a settlement offering in a proposed lawsuit by ECW against WCW that still has yet to be filed, WCW and ECW made an agreement that Benoit would work this PPV. This fell through by the end of the week when Paul Heyman never called Eric Bischoff back to confirm details; or b) There had been negotiations on WCW providing talent to ECW in exchange for ECW dropping the proposed legal action, and that dates on both Benoit and Eddie Guerrero had been talked about, but that no settlement terms have been reached and that ECW was interested in Benoit and Guerrero for big market house shows but not looking at using Benoit on this PPV show.

In regards to Severn, Candido called Severn two nights before the show and offered an angle which would result in a confrontation with Taz. Severn turned down the offer because it came as such a last minute thing but left the lines of communication open and ECW is still considering using Severn against Taz, although Paul Heyman recognizes how carefully everything would have to be put together in such an angle so as not to expose everything Taz has been built up as and at the same time get Severn, who has yet to do a job in a pro wrestling scenario since he first made his name in UFC, to agree to the scenario. Brakkus, who was trained by Candido, was a last minute decision to fill that hole.

An appearance by Benoit would have been interesting politically since Furnas, LaFon, Snow and Brakkus from WWF were on the show. There was a similar situation in Puerto Rico on Thanksgiving night where there was actually a singles match between a WCW wrestler (La Parka, although he was booked through Promo Azteca, which sent a crew of wrestlers to Puerto Rico for the weekend, and not WCW) against a WWF wrestler (Jesus "Huracan" Castillo), although there is a very good chance that neither the WWF nor WCW were aware of this taking place before the fact since it was in Puerto Rico and both got their bookings independently of their U.S. offices.

There was some concern expressed by WWF regarding the relationship between the groups, something to the effect that WWF gave ECW free television commercials for the PPV that aired on its weekend USA Network show and sends them talent free of charge. There is no problem when it comes to the storyline knocks at WWF and Vince McMahon on television or riling the ECW fans against WWF fans for a storyline inter-promotional feud. Where the potential problems exist is the idea that inside the ECW dressing room, some of the wrestlers seem to be under the impression the worked feud is a shoot and that some of the wrestlers in ECW see and talk about the WWF as an enemy promotion when the WWF sees it as them doing many favors for ECW.

From a political standpoint, there was a lot of blood on the show, most of it blading and some of it appeared to be hardway (Van Dam in particular). There were no camera close-ups of the blood, which caused some complaints from people who bought the show figuring it was guaranteed blood, but that caution needs to be there at this point in time due to the realities of maintaining a PPV presence. If you don't get that by now, get your hand out of the sand and into reality. The spot where Sabu came off the top rope on Beulah could be a problem if it gets a bug under the wrong person's butt. The one surprise was Sabu pulling out a fork and hitting Sandman with it, since after the Erich Kulas incident, it was believed that one of the few stipulations Request made was no stabbing like motions with blunt instruments to the head.

WWF In Your House 19: D-Generation X

The WWF D-Generation X concept as the top heel contingent is of course almost a total knockoff on the WCW concept of the NWO.

The trendy misspellings, the gestures designed to get heels over as cult babyfaces, the personalities (ironically key members of both groups, Kevin Nash, Scott Hall and Syxx in WCW and Shawn Michaels and Hunter Hearst Helmsley in WWF, were all members of the so-called Kliq that was riding high in WWF during Nash's reign as WWF champion) are all basically the same. In fact, there would be no D-Generation X heel group in WWF as the company never would have gone in such a direction had WCW not been so successful taking the same direction, and now WWF is trying to take that direction one step farther.

And so it was fitting that the WWF's PPV named after its top heel contingent was about the same as WCW's in January, the infamous NWO Souled Out show. Really, the only difference between the shows is that the Souled Out show had better wrestling in the undercard, and the WWF show had a stronger main event in the ring, which sounds like a broken record since it's the same comparison every month between the PPV shows of the two groups—and the WWF show did have better announcing, but that is hardly huge praise when one considers what it is being compared with.

DX had a good, but not great opener, a good main event with a weak finish, a "surprise" appearance by Owen Hart which was only a matter of time before it happened, and one of the worst mid-cards in the history of PPV, a collection of matches that each in their own way proved to be more unsatisfying than the one before it.

The show on 12/7 at the Springfield, MA Civic Center drew a sellout 6,358 fans paying $112,864 with another $44,000 in merchandise. There was nothing on the show that came off as all that heated with the exception of Steve Austin's match with Rocky Maivia. And when the show was over, with the exception of the return of Hart, who will wind up doing an angle based on the double-cross of his brother and feud with DX, and perhaps the strangest sight was of Jim Cornette doing the Mean Gene, Todd Pettengill, Dok role as the pre-show pitchmaster to hype last minute buys. With Sunny on the shelf due to a broken foot (as has been reported she was stepped on by her horse), it was The Jackal who was with Kevin Kelly in the 900 line room.

Not that WWF is alone in this or that WCW hasn't had more of a problem with it in recent years, but there were more physiques than at anytime in the past three or four years with the telltale side effects (swollen nipples, crater like acne of the back) and more muscular physiques associated with steroid use. And it's not just limited to the women. And the guy who wrecked his rental car wasn't even on the show.

WCW Starrcade

For nearly 16 months, Sting, one of the most popular wrestlers in the country over the past decade, was kept on the shelf with a new stoic brooding character taken from "The Crow" movie as an attempt for him to reach the "franchise" level of drawing card that had been long predicted for him and that he had never reached despite being thrust into that position numerous times.

With carefully orchestrated theatrics and regular run-ins as time was running out on Monday nights, some segments of which were actually totally botched up, Sting had become the No. 2 merchandise seller in the business behind Steve Austin. All this while never wrestling a match. At first, Sting was to make his triumphant return to the ring in February 1997 at the Cow Palace for SuperBrawl, but the gimmick was working so well they decided to hold him out for almost all of 1997—climaxing with his winning the WCW title from Hulk Hogan at Starrcade.

It was obvious the gimmick was paying off big. Anticipation for the match reached a level unseen in pro wrestling in this country in many years. The signing of the contract during a break-in on a Hogan movie on TNT drew one of the largest made-for-cable movie ratings in history. Nitro's numbers grew throughout the year, peaking to an unheard of 4.1 average during the final quarter of 1997 despite head-up competition from Monday Night Football (whose ratings declined 10 percent over the previous year this season). When tickets for the first pro wrestling show ever scheduled for 12/28 at the MCI Arena in Washington, DC were put on sale two months earlier, WCW had already broken its all-time gate record. And the buy rate record was almost sure to follow.

It would turn a great phrase to say that 16 months of work was exposed about halfway through Sting's walk down the aisle and before he ever got in the ring. The mythical super hero turned human right before the fans' very eyes. It wasn't as if it was a bad wrestling match that did it, although the match itself was bad. But you could see the big initial pop after all the hype and special effects didn't even last until Sting made it to the ring. The match itself was a struggle. The finish was totally botched up. Sting did leave as champion. But after WCW's most successful quarter in history, the record-breaking show raised more questions about the future than answers the record revenue will provide.

And that was hardly the only question. Probably the most important question of all regarded Kevin Nash, scheduled to wrestle The Giant for the second straight PPV show. The day before the show, WCW received word that Nash had suffered a mild heart attack at his home in Phoenix. Nash, who is 39, has a family history of heart problems including his father dying of a heart attack before the age of 40.

Nobody was exactly clear as to the actual story, as there were also reports it was thought to be a heart attack but actually a bad case of indigestion (which medically that mistake is not unusual to be made) causing massive chest pains, or massive chest pains from an anxiety attack suffered due to stress because his father-in-law has a serious health problem, which coincidentally enough is the exact same problem Undertaker had a few weeks ago which caused his blood pressure and heartbeat to go through the roof and caused him to miss a house show, and the health problem is said to be the same life-threatening health problem that Undertaker's father is undergoing. The only thing anyone seemed to know for sure is that Nash was undergoing tests to see what kind of a problem it actually was.

A man who legitimately has a bad heart is one hell of a risk, even with the style he works, in the ring, yet there didn't seem to be nearly the concern one would expect from a lot of parties close to the situation if a superstar in the business was suffering a serious health problem that could keep him out of action for a long time. The reports were that Nash's father-in-law was in bad health with a life threatening bowel problem, the same condition as Undertaker's father. Others were openly questioning it believing that Nash had somehow found out the finish (and he was supposed to do the job) and everything else was a cover reason. Others speculated that even though there was probably some truth to some of the stories it was a combination of both the former and the latter.

It's really become a screwed up business when someone may have suffered a legitimate major health scare and his friend at the same time may have suffered a legitimate dislocated knee (Hunter Hearst Helmsley), but since they were friends and their group is building up a tremendous track record of excuses to avoid doing jobs (Helmsley was scheduled to drop the European title to Owen Hart at the Nassau Coliseum on 12/29 but showed up injured from the show the previous day in Hamilton, ONT; although at the same time Scott Hall has actually done a lot more jobs than he's given credit for) so many within the industry don't believe a thing anymore.

It's a problem that ultimately was industry created. When promoters create an environment where the wrestlers themselves feel they are being manipulated and worked and doing angles specifically to fool the boys breeds that problem even worse, it is only natural for the wrestlers themselves once they get in a position of power to try and play the game back. In an industry that needs some level of trust for a cohesive product, but never really has true trust because the business is built on a house of lies, even though the health of the industry is near peak levels, the foundation of the industry has never been so completely screwed up.

Nash had managed to postpone his first PPV match with The Giant, originally scheduled for World War III, claiming his knee hadn't recovered from arthroscopic surgery a few months back and his entire ring time over the past several months consisted of the cameo at the end of the Battle Royal. He got out of numerous other booked house show matches with Giant (he did a few just before his injury) due to the knee surgery. But he had also told people that he wasn't going to work a program with The Giant and in recent weeks before any of these problems surfaced had told people he wasn't doing the match at Starrcade for a variety of reasons, among them because he didn't think it had been promoted correctly and because he didn't want to do the program to begin with.

And Nash wasn't the only problem on the show. Konnan called and said that his girlfriend had given birth to a premature stillborn child and that he couldn't leave Mexico. This left a hole in the six-man tag match. The company wanted Randy Savage to fill the spot, and in negotiations to get him to fill the spot literally a few hours before the show was going on the air, had to agree to change the originally planned finish of The Steiners & Ray Traylor going over. To get Savage to agree, the finish was changed to where Savage got to score the pin using the elbow off the top on Scott Steiner. This left Scott Steiner visibly livid to the point he had major words with booker Terry Taylor and they tried to alleviate him by letting him do so many big moves at the end for saves before doing the job, although he still wasn't happy at all.

Dean Malenko was originally mad because he had asked for Starrcade off because his wife was due at about that time. He was told if his wife was in labor or had given birth, that he didn't have to do the show and that Rey Misterio Jr. would sub for him in the match against Eddie Guerrero. Apparently he was also unhappy about Guerrero vs. Malenko being advertised on the television the previous weekend when he believed the company had a good idea that he wasn't going to be there. Malenko's wife Julie gave birth to a girl on 12/25, and the plan was to put Misterio Jr. against Guerrero in the match.

However, with Konnan and Nash both no-showing at basically the 11th hour and the company knowing basically all along that the advertised Raven vs. Chris Benoit match also wasn't going to take place due to Raven not being fully recovered from his inflamed pancreas, at that point they felt it important not to have another no-show and actually chartered a jet on the last day for Malenko to come in for the show.

It is too early to get any kind of a realistic estimate on the buy rate. WCW sources were predicting ahead of time 500,000 buys, which would be about a 1.7 which would be the most buys for any PPV show in this industry dating back to the heyday of the WWF on PPV around seven years ago. WCW's all-time record was probably around 310,000 buys for the Hogan-Piper Halloween Havoc cage match. Due to the holidays, even preliminary estimates are sketchy at best but the early numbers are looking to be in the 1.55 range which would be around 435,000 buys.

The show destroyed WCW's all-time gate record doing an even $543,000 (as it turns out, the old record set for World War III on 11/23 in Auburn Hills was actually $395,831 and not the $407,831 which was originally listed here) and also setting the company all-time one-night merchandise record at $161,961. The paid attendance for the sold out show was a company record of 16,052, breaking the old mark of 16,025 set for the Nitro on 6/9 in Boston. The total in the building was in the 17,500 range, falling slightly short of the company record of 18,003 set for the Nitro in Boston. On the broadcast, Tony Schiavone, using his best Monsoonian figures, numerous times gave the attendance at 24,000. Even though it was the biggest WCW paid attendance in history, it was not even the biggest of the weekend in North American pro wrestling as the WWF drew a sellout of 18,304 (16,620 paid) for its 12/26 house show at the Rosemont Horizon in suburban Chicago headlined by Undertaker vs. Shawn Michaels, and they even had the match.

The show was bad. Despite it being a full house, the crowd heat wasn't there. It appeared the people came only to see the main event, and they recognized quickly it wasn't what they had bargained for. Nearly every match on the show was worse than one would think it would be (Bischoff-Zbyszko was the only one that would have been better, and that's only because how high could expectations have been going in), and only one or two of the matches looked good on paper to begin with. The main events were fiascos, particularly after all the hype. Of course the title change itself got a big pop, but when does a world title change not get a big pop? And to

WCW's credit, the one thing that did come off well was the post-match celebration with the ring filling up with WCW wrestlers to celebrate Sting's win.

The other big story was the finish. The story was scheduled to be that since Hogan was doing the job, he'd dominate on offense. Since Nick Patrick was going to turn heel as a ref (in a role that was originally designed for Earl Hebner however WCW either never made a strong enough effort to contact Dave and Earl Hebner or they turned down the offer, but it's obvious that was what the original role in this match was booked for), he had to play it straight the entire match.

After a lackluster match, which even saw "boring" chants two minutes in, Hogan delivered his foot to the face and leg drop finish. At this point the plan was for Patrick to deliver a fast count and have Sting still kick out before three, but Patrick would rule it as a pin, leading to Bret Hart's avenging the wrong done to him at Survivor Series and getting the match restarted and taking over as ref leading to Sting winning with the scorpion submission in the middle.

A funny thing happened. Patrick didn't count fast. Why is a bigger mystery than the weird gravitational pull from the alignment of the stars that resulted in Kevin Nash, Royce Gracie and Hunter Hearst Helmsley all coming up injured within days of each other just prior to all having to suffer either symbolic worked or realistic beatings. You can mistime a ref bump. You can blow a move. But how do you blow a fast count? The only reasonable answer to this is Hogan changed the spot in the ring and Patrick didn't want to cross Hogan because of all the power he wields even though the plan was different.

Coming off the Hart-Michaels deal which has been the catalyst for everything in the business since, is Bischoff, Hogan and nobody else, perhaps Sting, decided to do a non fast count when there was supposed to be a fast count an angle (is your head spinning yet), but that doesn't make sense either because why did they have the announcers sell it as a fast count the next day so hard when it wasn't and if that was the case the guy who got screwed and made a fool of would have been Hart, who if anything, this company wasn't trying to portray in that matter after the last company did? Sting did try to kick out but Hogan didn't sell it by flying off, giving the first assumption some more validity.

I'd say coming in the wake of the Hart-Michaels deal that the most likely scenario is that Hogan, who no doubt was negotiating for all he was worth as far as getting whatever he could out of doing the job, apparently was able to manipulate the finish into appearing that he actually won the match cleanly and he was screwed by Hart, which wasn't the idea the fans were supposed to have. On TV the next night, they didn't even acknowledge the original story wasn't executed in the original manner, trying to sell the entire show that Patrick gave a fast count and Hart wouldn't stand for it.

By all appearances, Hogan pinned Sting pretty much clean (he did hold the tights but that's a normal heel finish). Hart then came out and prevented the ref from ringing the bell, punched out Patrick, who told Hart he had counted three trying to say he'd never let a ref screw a wrestler like that, playing off the Survivor Series finish (amazing how one finish can be the backbone of the top angles in two promotions at the same time), and got in the ring to take over as referee. As both Marcus Bagwell and Scott Norton failed in run-ins, teased by having a similar run-in finish cost Lex Luger his match with Bagwell, Sting clamped on the scorpion after signaling that the hold was almost a tribute to Hart by the eye contact made, and Hart ruled it was a submission and called for the bell.

With the finish from the previous night messed up and thus really unable to ever be shown on television (basically it's okay to have the fans spend $28 to buy the replay to see a fast count that isn't but never to see it for free), it was decided after the dust settled to change directions once again. A match was held on Nitro the next night in Baltimore, with the gimmick being that the finish wouldn't be shown on television and likely used as a tease for the debut of the Thursday show and they'd basically do the same finish with a few minor ramifications. So on Nitro the next night, they hyped a Sting-Hogan title rematch for the main event. About six minutes into the match, at about 10:04 p.m., just as ref Randy Anderson was bumped after being in the wrong place when Sting did the Stinger splash, the show abruptly went off the air.

Naturally there were more complaints about this the next day at Turner Broadcasting than anything WCW has ever pulled in its history, although that reaction was by design and not unexpected. Nitro had set a precedent for the last 18 months at least of staying with the main event until the finish (broken once before as a way to garner ratings for the debut of the Robin Hood series by pretending Hogan and The Giant were doing a 40 minute match and showing taped clips purported as being live as the show was on the air). This actually would have been the earliest the show had gone off the air in recent memory despite having nothing but the Nitro replay to follow on TNT and it being billed as the biggest match in Nitro history.

After the show went off the air, with Anderson down, Nick Patrick did a run-in as referee. Hogan again hit the legdrop and this time Patrick did the planned fast count (the clip that will be used forever more) and just as he was hitting three for the super fast count this time, Sting kicked out although it was basically a dead heat as to which happened first. Sting got up and clotheslined Patrick. The match continued with Sting getting Hogan in the scorpion and Anderson reviving and calling for the bell. It should be noted that both nights when Hogan "submitted" to the scorpion, in neither instance did he tap out.

J.J. Dillon grabbed the belt and went to give it to Sting, but at this point Bischoff and Dillon ended up in a tug-of-war over the belt, ending when Bischoff KO'd Dillon with a kick. Sting then dropped Bischoff using the reverse DDT to the biggest pop of the night. As the NWO guys came for the run-in on Sting, they were cut off by the WCW guys, with the biggest reaction coming again to Hart fighting with Hall, but also out there were Lex Luger, Diamond Dallas Page, Ray Traylor, The Giant, The Steiners, Jim Duggan (?) and others.

What I expect to happen from this is that they'll talk about the controversial ending on the weekend television and also on Nitro and tease that the clip will air on the first Thursday show on 1/8. At that point they'll announce the title is held up and set up a rematch either for the Souled Out PPV on 1/24 or SuperBrawl at the Cow Palace on 2/22, with it more likely being at the latter, and whatever finish likely setting up a Hogan-Bret Hart match. At this point the only matches official for Souled Out are Luger vs. Savage and Zbyszko vs. Hall and I'd guess Ultimo Dragon defending the cruiserweight title against Eddie Guerrero.

In the much-hyped match for Nitro, WCW President Bischoff had his first pro wrestling match at the age of 41. Going into the match with what was said to have been a serious knee injury, perhaps a broken kneecap suffered in training for the match that may require surgery (although he was not limping on television the next night), Bischoff did reasonably well for his first match. However, it was nothing close to reasonably well for the semi-main event on the biggest show in company history. Even with 44-year-old announcer Larry Zbyszko somewhat smaller than in his active days (and maybe in a little better shape), he was so much larger than Bischoff that his attempts to sell Bischoff's weak-appearing offense turned the match from a heat seeking missile into an almost ridiculous farce within two minutes.

To make things worse, on a night where so much went wrong, in the finish, where Bischoff was supposed to kick Zbyszko in the head in a loaded kick pad with Scott Hall putting an object in the pad, the object went flying out of Bischoff's kick pad into the air just before the kick made contact with Zbyszko's head. Zbyszko had to sell that blow as a knockoff, and Hart, who had teased a heel turn as ref throughout the match, suddenly "shocked" everyone by punching out Bischoff, as he did McMahon, when Bischoff offered him the huge money, thus, I guess, showing publicly that he wasn't a sellout (the announcers never explain what the storylines are since everything is dual storyline nowadays so who knows what the real idea behind that was).

Hall did a run-in but was quickly put in the scorpion by Hart, which actually got the biggest pop of the show up to that point. Zbyszko then choked Bischoff with his black belt, and Hart got off a laid out Hall, and raised Zbyszko's hand signifying that WCW retained Nitro. As for the big question about Thursday, well, if you've got any good ideas for a Thursday night show, email them to Eric quickly because they're starting on 1/8. And if you've heard any rumors of the concept, they're only rumors because everything right now is up in the air.

Chapter Forty Five

The Big Shows Directory: Domestic PPV Events

The most interesting thing to note when it comes to big shows from 1997 is that when it comes to traditional pro wrestling, out of 27 PPV shows from WWF, WCW and ECW, only nine of them were any good and none since September. During a period when competition should elevate the product, it has when it comes to less wrestling and more angles on television, but when it comes to the PPV and house shows, that hasn't been the case.

Now more than at any time in the past, house shows are something that the stars try and get out of doing and all but the youngest, hungriest or a few dedicated types use them to largely go through the motions knowing there is no emphasis from the company and having good or bad matches doesn't affect your stock because the fans don't remember because cities are run so infrequently, and the promoters don't care at all.

Both WWF and WCW only had four good shows out of 12 PPV shows based on readers' reaction, and if you look back at these shows, it isn't a case of so much product making standards too high for reader satisfaction. If anything, based on the shows and poll results and comparisons to prior years, standards in some ways are easier than ever.

Before 1997 started, we figured that competition would result in better shows and better matches, and really, the opposite was the case even though 1997 from a newsworthy standard of strange out of the ring occurrences, was the most interesting year probably in the history of the business. In 1996, WWF put on nine good PPV shows out of 12 while WCW put on four out of ten based on reader responses (and for whatever reason, my opinion is that as a general rule of thumb people judge WWF on easier standards because equally bad WWF and WCW shows will often get thumbs in the middles on WWF and thumbs downs on WCW). ECW, which is often judged by the easiest standard of all because it caters more to hardcore fans, still only managed to put on one good PPV show out of three.

From a business standpoint, WCW's business across the boards showed huge increases. We'll deal with attendance (a gigantic increase) and television ratings in future issues (actually television ratings did not improve much if at all, as for every new viewer on Monday, with Nitro averaging a 3.2 in 1996 and a 3.7 in 1997, there was an equal and possibly greater corresponding loss of viewers over the weekend for the product as the weekend ratings on TBS have never been lower), but the company showed a huge increase in both buys and revenue.

WWF, on the other hand, while having a strong year at the gate, did improve its television ratings but that was on the strength of increasing the weekend numbers (Raw averaged a 2.7 in 1996 and a 2.7 in 1997), decreased over the course of the year when it came to PPV buys, but due to increasing the price of the "B" shows from $19.95 to $29.95, it showed a sizable revenue increase overall which was probably the key factor in putting the company on its most solid financial footing in several years.

Any predictions for 1998 are foolish. All we can say for sure is that it will be another year of change. The key issues at the beginning of the year are WCW's Thursday television show, WWF's usage of Mike Tyson and the ensuing media publicity both good and bad that will result from it, how far the companies can push the envelope without even more serious fan problems resulting, a lack of discipline that has resulted in an environment where titles will less and less be won and lost in the ring and clean victories in main events will be something reserved for Japan and Mexico.

WWF ROYAL RUMBLE
(January 19, San Antonio, TX)
Attendance: 60,525 (48,014 paid)
Live gate: $480,013
Est. buy rate/revenue:
0.7/$2.18 million
Thumbs up/down/middle:
100 (42.4%), 92 (39.0%), 44 (18.6%)
Best match: 70 - Royal Rumble, 45 - Shawn Michaels vs. Sid
Worst match: 66 - Canek & Hector Garza & Perro Aguayo vs. Heavy Metal & Jerry Estrada & Fuerza Guerrera, 29 - Undertaker vs. Vader
Highlights: Shawn Michaels regained the WWF title for a second time pinning Sycho Sid in 13:49 in his home town (**). Steve Austin, who had actually been eliminated behind both refs back, got back in the ring and threw out Bret Hart in 50:29 to win the annual Royal Rumble (***). An attempt to forge an alliance with AAA in Mexico, which wound up being short-lived, saw a six-man match with Hector Garza & Perro Aguayo & Canek beating Jerry Estrada & Heavy Metal & Fuerza Guerrera in a match that didn't get over live (*). Vader pinned Undertaker in 13:19 due to outside help from Paul Bearer (*1/4). Hunter Hearst Helmsley retained the IC title pinning Goldust in 16:50 (**).

WCW/NWO SOULED OUT
(January 25, Cesar Rapids, IA)
Attendance: 5,120 sellout
Live gate: $68,209
Est. buy rate/revenue:
0.47/$1.37 million
Thumbs up/down/middle:
4 (1.4%), 276 (97.2%), 4 (1.4%)
Best match: 157 - Syxx vs. Eddie Guerrero, 21 - Chris Jericho vs. Masahiro Chono
Worst match: 141- Hulk Hogan vs. The Giant, 8 - Big Bubba vs. Hugh Morrus
Highlights: Generally considered as among the worst PPV events of all-time. Main event saw WCW champion Hulk Hogan and The Giant go to a non decision in 11:00. When this match took place, it was considered almost a given to win worst match of the year, but the year had some incredibly bad major matches (-*1/2). Eddie Guerrero retained the U.S. title beating Syxx in 13:48 (****). Steiners supposedly won the WCW tag titles from Scott Hall & Kevin Nash in 14:43 when ref Randy Anderson came out of the stands to count the fall after Nick Patrick was bumped. The decision was reversed on television the next day (**1/4). Between the beauty contest and the announcing, it more than made up in infamy for the fact that a lot of shows, including this year, have actually presented worse wrestling.

UFC 12: JUDGEMENT DAY
(February 7, Dothan, AL)
Attendance: 3,100 sellout
Live gate: $0
Est. buy rate/revenue:
0.55/$896,000
Thumbs up/down/middle:
132 (88.0%), 8 (5.3%), 10 (6.7%)
Best match: 101 - Yoshiki Takahashi vs. Wallid Ismail, 7 - Mark Coleman vs. Dan Severn
Worst match: 72 - Jerry Bohlander vs. Nick Sanzo, 8 - Mark Coleman vs. Dan Severn
Highlights: After a move literally the day before after losing a court fight when the New York State Athletic Commission, spurred on by a series of negative articles in the New York Times, decided to re-write the rule book as a legal technicality to force UFC out of the state when a law passed specifically legalizing the event, the event moved to Dothan, AL where all the tickets were given away because of such a last minute deal. The show was headlined by Mark Coleman capturing the UFC heavyweight title from Dan Severn with a headlock choke in 2:59 and the UFC debut of 19-year-old Brazilian Vitor Belfort, who captured the heavyweight tournament. Jerry Bohlander won the UFC's first-ever under-200 pounds tournament.

WWF FINAL FOUR
(February 16, Chattanooga, TN)
Attendance: 6,399
Live gate: $76,762
Est. buy rate/revenue:
0.5/$1.04 million
Thumbs up/down/middle:
123 (70.7%), 11 (6.3%), 40 (23.0%)
Best match: 132 - Final Four
Worst match: 83 - Faarooq & Crush & Savio Vega vs. Flash Funk & Goldust & Bart Gunn, 17 - Rocky Maivia vs. Hunter Hearst Helmsley
Highlights: Bret Hart captured the WWF title for the fourth time winning a final-four match for the title vacated three days earlier by Shawn Michaels in 24:05 over Steve Austin, Vader and Undertaker when Undertaker was distracted by the eliminated Austin, allowing Hart to cradle him from behind in an excellent headliner (****1/4). Owen Hart & Davey Boy Smith retained the WWF tag titles losing via DQ against Phil LaFon & Doug Furnas in 10:30 (***1/4). Rocky Maivia retained the IC title pinning Hunter Hearst Helmsley in 12:39 (*3/4)

WCW SUPERBRAWL VII
(February 23, San Francisco, CA)
Attendance: 13,324 sellout (12,145 paid)
Live gate: $192,000

Est. buy rate/revenue:
0.75/$2.20 million
Thumbs up/down/middle:
151 (84.8%), 10 (5.6%), 17 (9.6%)
Best match: 61 - Konnan & La Parka & Villano IV vs. Juventud Guerrera & Ciclope & Super Calo, 35 - Dean Malenko vs. Syxx
Worst match: 87 - Hulk Hogan vs. Roddy Piper, 34 - Harlem Heat vs. Faces of Fear vs. Public Enemy
Highlights: Hulk Hogan retained the WCW title beating Roddy Piper in 10:52 due to outside interference from Randy Savage (*1/4). The Giant & Lex Luger beat Scott Hall & Kevin Nash in another apparent tag team title change that was overruled the next day in 8:53. Luger was injured as an angle, and although advertised, was not allowed to participate so Giant went at it alone. Luger then showed up, tagged in, and racked Nash for the win but it was overruled since Luger wasn't medically allowed to be there (***1/2). Eddie Guerrero retained the U.S. title beating Chris Jericho (***1/4). Prince Iaukea retained the WCW TV title pinning Rey Misterio Jr. (***1/4). Syxx won the WCW cruiserweight title from Dean Malenko in 11:57 due to distraction in the finish from Guerrero (***1/4)

WCW UNCENSORED

(March 16, North Charleston, SC)
Attendance: 9,295 (7,640 paid)
Live gate: $101,184
Est. buy rate/revenue:
0.89/$2.61 million
Thumbs up/down/middle:
87 (39.7%), 95 (43.4%), 37 (16.9%)
Best match: 114 - Dean Malenko vs. Eddie Guerrero, 32 - Harlem Heat vs. Public Enemy
Worst match: 97 - Three team elimination match, 38 - Glacier vs. Mortis
Highlights: A triangle match, which appeared to be booked on acid, saw Team NWO of Kevin Nash, Scott Hall, Randy Savage & Hulk Hogan beat Team Piper (Chris Benoit & Piper & Jeff Jarrett & Steve McMichael) and Team WCW (The Giant & Lex Luger & Scott Steiner as they took Rick Steiner out of the picture with an angle earlier in the show) in 19:22 when it came down to Hogan and Luger, but Savage interfered causing Luger to get pinned. After the match, Dennis Rodman, who was actually the focal point of the match to the point Hogan was surgically attached to his hip for photo ops from all the media, ended up spray painting NWO on Luger's back (*). As became the WCW pattern throughout the year, the poor main event was backed by a strong undercard as Dean Malenko won the U.S. title from Eddie Guerrero in 19:14 (***3/4), Ultimo Dragon pinned Psicosis in 13:17 (***1/2), Harlem Heat beat Public Enemy in a tornado match (**1/2) and a disappointing match where Prince Iaukea retained the TV title beating Rey Misterio Jr. in 13:41 (*1/2).

WWF WRESTLEMANIA 13

(March 23, Rosemont, IL)
Attendance: 18,197 sellout (16,467 paid)
Live gate: $837,150
Est. buy rate/revenue:
0.77/$2.46 million
Thumbs up/down/middle:
206 (78.9%), 38 (14.6%), 14 (6.5%)
Best match: 253 - Bret Hart vs. Steve Austin
Worst match: 84 - Four corners tag match, 63 - Rocky Maivia vs. Sultan
Highlights: One of probably the two or three greatest matches in the history of WrestleMania was the Bret Hart win over Steve Austin in an I Quit match with Ken Shamrock as ref in 22:05. The win also featured a double turn—Hart into a heel and Austin into a babyface, the latter becoming arguably the hottest star in the business for the remainder of the year and inarguably the biggest merchandise seller. Hart won, but Austin never submitted (*****). Hart-Austin shared double co-billing with the WWF title match where Undertaker won the title from Sycho Sid in 21:19 (*1/4). In a street fight, Legion of Doom & Ahmed Johnson beat Faarooq & Crush & Savio Vega in 10:45 (***1/2), Owen Hart & Davey Boy Smith retained the WWF tag titles going to a double count out with Vader & Mankind in 16:08 (**1/2) and Rocky Maivia pinned Sultan in 9:45 to retain the IC title (*1/4)

EFC IV

(March 28, Des Moines, IA)
Attendance: 750
Est. buy rate/revenue:
0.12/$172,000
Thumbs up/down/middle:
101 (98.1%), 2 (1.9%), 0 (0.0%)
Best match: 39 - Kevin Jackson vs. John Lober, 32 - Kenny Monday vs. John Lewis
Worst match: 68 - Gary Myers vs. Tom Glanville
Highlights: Arguably the single best NHB show to date, but for financial reasons the end of the EFC promotion which folded a few weeks later. The highlights were the NHB debuts of two gold medal winning Olympic wrestlers, Kevin Jackson (1992 gold at 181 pounds) and Kenny Monday (1988 gold at 163). Jackson beat John Lober in 1:12 of the second round via submission, while Monday knocked out John Lewis at 4:09. In the main event, Maurice Smith retained his EFC title beating Murakami Kazunari in 4:20 with the single most devastating knockout punch in American NHB history.

WCW SPRING STAMPEDE
(*April 6, Tupelo, MS*)
Attendance: 8,356 sellout (7,428 paid)
Live gate: $107,115
Est. buy rate/revenue:
0.58/$1.75 million
Thumbs up/down/middle:
10 (6.5%), 89 (57.8%), 55 (35.7%)
Best match: 93 - Ultimo Dragon vs. Rey Misterio Jr., 31 - Diamond Dallas Page vs. Randy Savage
Worst match: 57 - Public Enemy vs. Jarrett & McMichael, 30 - Four Corners match
Highlights: Another poor WCW PPV, this time without the booking problems of the past, but also sans the good undercard wrestling for the most part. The pre-show hype built the card around a four-corners match with Lex Luger, The Giant and Harlem Heat where Giant basically gave Luger the win to earn a future WCW title shot in 18:18 (*), although the final position was given to Diamond Dallas Page's lift into superstardom when Randy Savage put him over in 15:38 of a no DQ match (***1/4). Dean Malenko retained the U.S. title going to a no contest with Chris Benoit in a match plagued with far too many run-ins (***1/4), Prince Iaukea retained the TV title beating Steven Regal in 10:01 (*1/2) and one excellent opening match with Rey Misterio Jr. beating Ultimo Dragon in 14:55 (****1/4)

ECW BARELY LEGAL
(*April 13, Philadelphia, PA*)
Attendance: 1,170 sellout
Live gate: $66,000
Est. buy rate/revenue:
0.26/$400,000
Thumbs up/down/middle:
283 (82.5%), 29 (8.5%), 31 (9.0%)
Best match: 208 - Great Sasuke & Gran Hamada & Masato Yakushiji vs. Mens Teioh & Dick Togo & Taka Michinoku, 51 - Terry Funk vs. Stevie Richards vs. Sandman
Worst match: 195 - Shane Douglas vs. Pit Bull #2, 21 - Eliminators vs. Dudleys
Highlights: The long-awaited debut of ECW on PPV was built around the first singles match between Sabu and Taz, and Terry Funk's quest to win the ECW title just before his 53rd birthday. Funk won a triangle match over Sandman and Stevie Richards (****) to earn his title shot where he beat Raven due to Tommy Dreamer's interference in 7:20 (***1/4). Taz beat Sabu in their first meeting doing the same double-turn as in the Bret Hart-Steve Austin match in 17:49 (***1/4), Shane Douglas retained the TV title beating Pit Bull #2 in 20:43 (3/4*), Eliminators regained the tag titles beating The Dudleys in 6:11 (**3/4) and in one of the best U.S. matches of the year, Great Sasuke (who had just worked the previous night against Jushin Liger at the Tokyo Dome) & Gran Hamada & Masato Yakushiji beat Dick Togo & Mens Teioh & Taka Michinoku in 16:55 (****1/2).

WWF REVENGE OF TAKER
(*April 20, Rochester, NY*)
Attendance: 6,477 sellout
Live gate: $87,414
Est. buy rate/revenue:
0.5/$1.08 million
Thumbs up/down/middle:
61 (36.5%), 81 (48.5%), 25 (15.0%)
Best match: 75 - Bret Hart vs. Steve Austin, 56 - Undertaker vs. Mankind
Worst match: 94 - Jesse Jammes vs. Rockabilly, 14 - Owen Hart & Davey Boy Smith vs. Legion of Doom
Highlights: Largely a forgettable show with two good main events, a nothing undercard, and three DQ finishes in five matches. Steve Austin beat Bret Hart via DQ in 21:09 (***3/4) in the main event, while Undertaker pinned Mankind in 17:26 to retain the WWF title (***3/4). Savio Vega beat Rocky Maivia via count out so Maivia kept the IC title in 8:33 (3/4*) and Legion of Doom beat tag champs Owen Hart & Davey Boy Smith via DQ in 10:11 (3/4*)

WWF A COLD DAY IN HELL
(*May 11, Richmond, VA*)
Attendance: 9,381 sellout (7,681 paid)
Live gate: $116,547
Est. buy rate/revenue:
0.57/$1.27 million
Thumbs up/down/middle:
33 (23.4%), 70 (49.6%), 38 (27.0%)
Best match: 81 - Ken Shamrock vs. Vader, 46 - Undertaker vs. Steve Austin
Worst match: 34 - Ahmed Johnson vs. NOD, 27 - Jesse Jammes vs. Rockabilly
Highlights: Described as just another Sunday afternoon PPV show that would be forgotten in a week, Undertaker pinned Steve Austin in 20:06 to retain the WWF title using the tombstone after some distraction from Brian Pillman (***). Even more noteworthy on the show was the WWF in-ring debut of Ken Shamrock, who beat Vader with an ankle lock in 13:21 (***1/4).

WCW SLAMBOREE
(*May 18, Charlotte, NC*)
Attendance: 9,643 sellout
Live gate: $167,705
Est. buy rate/revenue:
0.60/$1.88 million
Thumbs up/down/middle:
112 (77.8%), 12 (8.3%), 20 (13.9%)

Best match: 66 - Steve Regal vs. Ultimo Dragon, 50 - Roddy Piper & Ric Flair & Kevin Greene vs. Scott Hall & Kevin Nash & Syxx
Worst match: 78 - Steve McMichael vs. Reggie White, 26 - Glacier vs. Mortis
Highlights: The return of Ric Flair to the ring after being out of action for eight months after rotator cuff surgery ended up with him teaming with Roddy Piper and local football hero Kevin Greene to beat Scott Hall & Kevin Nash & Syxx in a match that had more controversy before it took place because of Hulk Hogan's not doing the match and Syxx being in the main event. Officially Hall did the job via pin to Flair's figure four while Piper had Nash in the sleeper and Greene had powerslammed Syxx to give the fans a happy ending in a match that had great heat and emotion overwhelming so-so wrestling (**1/2). Future NFL Hall of Famer Reggie White made his pro wrestling debut, and unlike people like Greene and Lawrence Taylor, White was a total embarrassment being in one of the worst matches of the year, losing to Steve McMichael in 15:17 (-**). In title matches, Steve Regal regained the WCW TV title from Ultimo Dragon in 16:04 (***3/4) and Dean Malenko retained the U.S. title beating Jeff Jarrett due to outside interference from McMichael in 15:03 (***).

UFC 13: ULTIMATE FORCE

(May 30, Augusta, GA)
Attendance: 5,100 (4,100 paid)
Live gate:
Est. buy rate/revenue:
0.50/$897,000
Thumbs up/down/middle:
124 (96.1%), 4 (3.1%), 1 (0.8%)
Best match: 48 - Tank Abbott vs. Vitor Belfort, 38 - Enson Inoue vs. Royce Alger
Worst match: 14 - Tito Ortiz vs. Wesley Albritton, 13 - Tony Halme vs. Randy Couture
Highlights: The myth of Tank Abbott fell to the reality of Vitor Belfort in just 53 seconds of the main event. U.S. national Greco-roman champion Randy Couture debuted in NHB beating pro wrestler Tony Halme and Steven Graham to capture the heavyweight tournament, while Pancrase's Guy Mezger won the under-200 division beating Cal State-Bakersfield wrestler Tito Ortiz.

WWF KING OF THE RING

(June 8, Providence, RI)
Attendance: 9,312
Live gate: $202,963
Est. buy rate/revenue:
0.50/$1.59 million
Thumbs up/down/middle:
100 (66.7%), 29 (19.3%), 21 (14.0%)
Best match: 118 - Shawn Michaels vs. Steve Austin, 35 - Mankind vs. Hunter Hearst Helmsley
Worst match: 42 - Goldust vs. Crush, 20 - Legion of Doom & Sycho Sid vs. Owen Hart & Davey Boy Smith & Jim Neidhart
Highlights: Undertaker pinned Faarooq in 13:43 to retain the WWF title in a match better than it seemed on paper when distraction in the NOD caused Undertaker to use a tombstone to get the title (**1/4). Shawn Michaels actually got louder cheers than Steve Austin in their double disqualification match at 22:29 (****) while Hunter Hearst Helmsley captured the King of the Ring tournament that had been promised him one year earlier beating Mankind in 19:26 of the finals (***1/2).

WCW GREAT AMERICAN BASH

(June 15, Moline, IL)
Attendance: 9,613 (8,538 paid)
Live gate: $142,118
Est. buy rate/revenue:
0.60/$1.88 million
Thumbs up/down/middle:
41 (30.8%), 52 (39.1%), 40 (30.1%)
Best match: 55 - Ultimo Dragon vs. Psicosis, 35- Diamond Dallas Page vs. Randy Savage
Worst match: 44 - Konnan vs. Hugh Morrus, 17 - Steve McMichael vs. Kevin Greene
Highlights: Randy Savage pinned Diamond Dallas Page due to outside help from Scott Hall in a wild falls count anywhere lights out match main event in 16:56 (***3/4). Kevin Nash & Scott Hall retained the WCW tag titles beating Ric Flair & Roddy Piper when Flair was fighting with Syxx backstage leaving Piper by himself in 10:02 (**1/4). In yet another battle of football players, Kevin Greene pinned Steve McMichael in 9:21 (**). Greene showed incredible potential as a wrestler being able to work a match that good with McMichael, which most seasoned top stars were unable to do. In a womens title vs. retirement match, Akira Hokuto beat Madusa in 11:41 (***) and Madusa never has resurfaced in WCW despite still being under contract.

WWF CANADIAN STAMPEDE

(July 6, Calgary, Canada)
Attendance: 12,151 (10,974 paid)
Live gate: $229,598 (Canadian)
Est. buy rate/revenue:
0.59/$1.32 million
Thumbs up/down/middle:
256 (99.6%), 1 (0.4%), 0 (0.0%)
Best match: 169 - Bret & Owen Hart & Jim Neidhart & Brian Pillman & Davey Boy Smith vs. Goldust & Legion of Doom & Steve Austin & Ken Shamrock, 42 - Great Sasuke vs. Taka Michinoku

Worst match: 74 - Godwinns vs. Blackjacks (pre-game show), 45 - Undertaker vs. Vader
Highlights: For a show that had little interest coming in and only four matches, it was arguably not only the best PPV show of the year but the best in the history of the WWF. All four matches were good to excellent, with The Hart Foundation (Bret & Owen Hart & Davey Boy Smith & Brian Pillman & Jim Neidhart) as unbelievable babyfaces in Calgary despite being portrayed as heels on television beating Steve Austin & Legion of Doom & Ken Shamrock & Goldust when Owen pinned Austin in 24:31 (****1/4). Undertaker retained the WWF title pinning Vader in 12:39 (***1/4). In a match designed to set up Great Sasuke as the star of the WWF's light heavyweight division, it was Taka Michinoku, in doing the job, who got over and by the end of the year was the WWF's champion (****) and Mankind went to a double count out with HHH (***).

WCW BASH AT THE BEACH
(July 13, Daytona Beach, FL)
Attendance: 7,851 sellout (6,354 paid)
Live gate: $150,870
Est. buy rate/revenue:
0.89/$2.79 million
Thumbs up/down/middle:
149 (71.6%), 29 (13.9%), 30 (14.4%)
Best match: 86 - Hector Garza & Juventud Guerrera & Lizmark Jr. vs. La Parka & Psicosis & Villano IV, 71 - Ultimo Dragon vs. Chris Jericho
Worst match: 57 - Jeff Jarrett vs. Steve McMichael, 36 - Hulk Hogan & Dennis Rodman vs. Lex Luger & The Giant
Highlights: Lex Luger & The Giant beat Hulk Hogan & Dennis Rodman in 22:30 when Luger beat Hogan with the torture rack submission to set up their singles feud later in the year. After the match Luger racked Rodman and also Randy Savage. While not a good wrestling match per se, it was far better than anyone had the right to expect considering the participants and had super heat (*1/2). In other top matches, Roddy Piper beat Ric Flair (***1/4) in a surprisingly good match, Scott Hall & Randy Savage beat Diamond Dallas Page & debuting Curt Hennig in 9:35 (1/2*), Jeff Jarrett kept the U.S. title beating Steve McMichael in 6:56 (DUD), Chris Benoit beat Kevin Sullivan in a loser must retire match in 13:10 (***1/2), Rick & Scott Steiner earned a tag title shot beating Great Muta & Masahiro Chono in 11:37 (***1/4), Chris Jericho retained the WCW cruiserweight title pinning Ultimo Dragon in 12:55 (****1/4) and a tremendous six-man saw Juventud Guerrera & Hector Garza & Lizmark Jr. beat La Parka & Psicosis & Villano IV in 10:08 (****1/4).

UFC 14: SHOWDOWN
(July 27, Birmingham, AL)
Attendance:
Live gate:
Est. buy rate/revenue:
0.53/$850,000
Thumbs up/down/middle:
110 (90.9%), 5 (4.1%), 6 (5.0%)
Best match: 113 - Mark Coleman vs. Maurice Smith
Worst match: 49 - Joe Moreiera vs. Yuri Vaulin
Highlights: In UFC's most memorable match of the year, Maurice Smith captured the heavyweight title beating Mark Coleman in what was something of a title unification match with Smith holding the strap of th defunct EFC. Up to that point it had been a night for the wrestlers with Kevin Jackson winning the under-200 pound tournament with ease, and Mark Kerr capturing the heavyweight tournament with little competition.

WWF SUMMERSLAM
(August 3, East Rutherford, NJ)
Attendance: 20,213 sellout (17,361 paid)
Live gate: $523,514
Est. buy rate/revenue:
0.8/$2.76 million
Thumbs up/down/middle:
111 (45.3%), 107 (43.7%), 27 (11.0%)
Best match: 99 - Bret Hart vs. Undertaker, 57 - Steve Austin vs. Owen Hart
Worst match: 97 - Los Boricuas vs. DOA, 37 - Legion of Doom vs. Godwinns
Highlights: The injury to Steve Austin several minutes before the scheduled conclusion of an IC title match against Owen Hart, which Austin won at 16:16, took the luster away from one of the big shows of the year (**3/4). In the main event, Bret Hart regained the WWF title from Undertaker when special ref Shawn Michaels hit Undertaker with a chair, thus turning heel, when Hart ducked in 28:09 (***). In other key matches, Mankind beat Hunter Hearst Helmsley in a cage match in 16:25 (**1/2) and Davey Boy Smith retained the European title beating Ken Shamrock via DQ in 7:29 (*3/4).

WCW ROAD WILD
(August 9, Sturgis, SD)
Attendance: 6,500
Live gate: $0
Est. buy rate/revenue:
0.65/$2.09 million
Thumbs up/down/middle:
8 (6.0%), 119 (88.8%), 7 (5.2%)
Best match: 35 - Alex Wright vs. Chris Jericho, 10 - Steiners vs. Scott Hall & Kevin Nash
Worst match: 27 - Hulk Hogan vs. Lex Luger, 13 - Diamond Dallas Page vs. Curt Hennig

Highlights: Hulk Hogan, who had lost the WCW title to Lex Luger six days earlier, regained it due to Scott Hall, as an impostor Sting, hitting Luger with a baseball bat. Marcus Bagwell, Syxx, Vincent and Kevin Nash all interfered as well in 16:15 (1/2*). In a match that was originally to be a tag title change but the finish was changed at the 11th hour, Steiners beat Kevin Nash & Scott Hall via DQ in 15:29 (*3/4), while Giant pinned Randy Savage in 6:05 (*), Curt Hennig beat Diamond Dallas Page in 9:41 (3/4*), Ric Flair pinned Syxx in 11:06 (*1/4) and Alex Wright pinned Chris Jericho to keep the cruiserweight title in 13:03 (***).

ECW HARDCORE HEAVEN

(August 17, Fort Lauderdale, FL)
Attendance: 1,950 (1,650 paid)
Live gate: $60,000
Est. buy rate/revenue:
0.21/$325,000
Thumbs up/down/middle:
104 (42.3%), 137 (55.7%), 5 (2.0%)
Best match: 97 - Shane Douglas vs. Terry Funk vs. Sabu, 37 - Al Snow vs. Rob Van Dam
Worst match: 53 - Bam Bam Bigelow vs. Spike Dudley, 34 - Tommy Dreamer vs. Jerry Lawler
Highlights: In a night that for the most part didn't work including one of the worst skits in recorded history where Sandman was drinking and driving an ambulance looking for the arena, Shane Douglas won a three-way dance over ECW champion Sabu and Terry Funk by pinning Funk in 26:37 (***1/2). In an inter-promotional match, Tommy Dreamer pinned Jerry Lawler in 18:57 with outside interference from Jake Roberts and Sunny among others (1/2*) and The Dudleys retained the ECW tag titles beating PG-13 in 10:58 (**).

WWF GROUND ZERO

(September 7, Louisville, KY)
Attendance: 4,963 sellout
Live gate: $82,228
Est. buy rate/revenue:
0.45/$1.58 million
Thumbs up/down/middle:
62 (42.2%), 39 (26.5%), 46 (31.3%)
Best match: 73 - Shawn Michaels vs. Undertaker, 32 - Bret Hart vs. Patriot
Worst match: 84 - Faarooq vs. Crush vs. Savio Vega, 29 - Four-corners tag match
Highlights: Undertaker and Shawn Michaels battled to a no contest in 16:03 (although with the pre-match brawl it went closer to 23:00) in the main event (***3/4) of a fairly forgettable show. Bret Hart retained the WWF title via submission over The Patriot with the sharpshooter in 19:20 (***1/4) and Head Bangers won the WWF tag titles in a four-corners match over Owen Hart & Davey Boy Smith, Godwinns and Legion of Doom in an awful match (DUD).

WCW FALL BRAWL

(September 14, Winston-Salem, NC)
Attendance: 11,939 sellout (11,024 paid)
Live gate: $213,330
Est. buy rate/revenue:
0.53/$1.74 million
Thumbs up/down/middle:
68 (68.0%), 20 (20.0%), 12 (12.0%)
Best match: 41 - Eddie Guerrero vs. Chris Jericho, 23 - Alex Wright vs. Ultimo Dragon
Worst match: 30 - Giant vs. Scott Norton, 22 - War Games
Highlights: Team NWO of Marcus Bagwell & Kevin Nash & Syxx & Konnan beat Team Horseman of Ric Flair & Chris Benoit & Steve McMichael who were to team with Curt Hennig, who did basically the same injury angle he did one year earlier in WWF with Hunter Hearst Helmsley to screw Marc Mero, and ended up turning on Flair and the Horseman causing them to lose the War Games in 19:37 (**1/2). The second half of the show was so-so, but the first half was tremendous. Lex Luger & Diamond Dallas Page beat Scott Hall & Randy Savage when Larry Zbyszko counted as Luger pinned Hall in 10:19 (**), Giant pinned Scott Norton with a choke slam in 5:27 (*), Alex Wright kept the TV title pinning Ultimo Dragon in 18:43 (***1/2) and Eddie Guerrero kept the cruiserweight title beating Chris Jericho in 17:19 (***3/4).

WWF BADD BLOOD

(October 5, St. Louis, MO)
Attendance: 21,151 sellout (17,404 paid)
Live gate: $212,550
Est. buy rate/revenue:
0.6/$2.11 million
Thumbs up/down/middle:
72 (49.7%), 34 (23.4%), 39 (26.9%)
Best match: 119 - Shawn Michaels vs. Undertaker
Worst match: 39 - Los Boricuas vs. DOA, 31 - Head Bangers vs. Godwinns
Highlights: Under the cloud of Brian Pillman's death a few hours earlier, WWF went on with the show with few highlights aside from arguably the greatest cage match in history where Shawn Michaels beat Undertaker in 29:59 due to interference from Kane to earn the next WWF title shot (*****) and a ceremony honoring former NWA champions like The Funks, Harley Race, Jack Brisco, Gene Kiniski and Lou Thesz along with long-time St. Louis promoter Sam Muchnick. Bret Hart & Davey Boy Smith beat what was advertised as a flag match but the rules changed at the last minute to be a regular match over Vader & Patriot in 23:13,

Owen Hart won the vacant IC title in the tourney finals from Faarooq in 7:12 and Godwinns won the tag titles from Head Bangers in 12:17, all of which were subdued at best performances.

IWF THE CONTENDERS
(*October 11, Sioux City, IA*)
Attendance: 250
Live gate:
Est. buy rate/revenue:
0.03/$72,000
Thumbs up/down/middle:
11 (14.1%), 56 (71.8%), 11 (14.1%)
Best match: 37 - Frank Shamrock vs. Dan Henderson, 13 - Tom Erikson vs. Tsuyoshi Kikuchi
Worst match: 17 - Townsend Saunders vs. Andre Pedernarias, 9 - Dennis Hall vs. Joao Roque
Highlights: In a show which featured a tremendous caliber of athletes but a poor concept, John Perretti attempted to get stars of NHB through the PPV censors that were destroying NHB by doing a submissions only show between wrestlers and submission experts. The scoring rules were never explained. The matches, featuring no strikes and lots of defensive moves were generally boring. Most of the wrestlers had trouble with the submission fights' guards. The wrestling contingent was furious because the wrestlers, without the ability to strike and head-butt from the top, couldn't do much due to lack of submission skill. The Jiu Jitsu contingent was furious because they thought the rules favored the wrestlers when it came to point systems. Nobody bought the show. And a few days later, this group was defunct. The star of the show was Frank Shamrock, who made two-time Olympic wrestler Dan Henderson submit in just 56 seconds to an ankle lock. Kenny Monday, one of the great wrestlers of his era, lost to an ankle lock in just 45 seconds against Matt Hume. Tom Erikson, America's best freestyle heavyweight, won via decision against RINGS' Tsuyoshi Kikuchi.

UFC 15: COLLISION COURSE
(*October 17, Bay St. Louis, MS*)
Attendance: 1,500 sellout
Live gate:
Est. buy rate/revenue:
0.5/$708,000
Thumbs up/down/middle:
139 (96.5%), 2 (1.4%), 3 (2.1%)
Best match: 64 - Vitor Belfort vs. Randy Couture, 50 - Carlao Baretto vs. Dave Beneteau
Worst match: 24 - Mark Kerr vs. Gregory Stott, 23 - Mark Kerr vs. Dwane Cason
Highlights: Randy Couture derailed Vitor Belfort in an upset in 8:17 as the biggest story of one of the best UFC shows in history. In the main event, Maurice Smith made late out-of-shape replacement Tank Abbott quit due to leg kicks in 8:11 while Mark Kerr went to 7-0 in easily winning his second straight heavyweight tournament. UFC would end up losing Kerr due to legal problems after this show. The show also featured one of the closest and best UFC matches in history with David Beneteau upsetting Carlao Barreto via decision after 15:00.

WCW HALLOWEEN HAVOC
(*October 16, Paradise, NV*)
Attendance: 12,457 sellout (10,138 paid)
Live gate: $297,508
Est. buy rate/revenue:
1.1/$3.62 million
Thumbs up/down/middle:
90 (43.5%), 82 (39.6%), 35 (16.9%)
Best match: 183 - Rey Misterio Jr. vs. Eddie Guerrero, 7 - Randy Savage vs. Diamond Dallas Page
Worst match: 83 - Hulk Hogan vs. Roddy Piper, 37 - Alex Wright vs. Steve McMichael
Highlights: This show will best be remembered for the third match on the show, where Rey Misterio Jr. won the cruiserweight title from Eddie Guerrero in a match where he was originally scheduled to lose his mask in 13:51 (****3/4). Otherwise it was a lackluster show headed up by a main event that'll forever be known as the "Age in the Cage" match where Roddy Piper won a poor non-title match over Hulk Hogan in 13:37 (DUD). Randy Savage beat Diamond Dallas Page when Hogan, dressed as Sting, interfered in 18:07 (***1/4), Lex Luger beat Scott Hall in 13:02 with Larry Zbyszko as ref (3/4*), Curt Hennig beat Ric Flair via DQ in 13:57 (*3/4).

WWF SURVIVOR SERIES
(*November 9, Montreal, Canada*)
Attendance: 20,593 sellout (18,101 paid)
Live gate: $447,284 Canadian
Est. buy rate/revenue:
0.89/$3.14 million
Thumbs up/down/middle:
81 (35.8%), 87 (38.5%), 58 (25.7%)
Best match: 147 - Bret Hart vs. Shawn Michaels, 23 - Kane vs. Mankind
Worst match: 77 - Truth Commission vs. DOA, 55 - Jesse Jammes & Billy Gunn & Godwinns vs. Head Bangers & Blackjacks
Highlights: Shawn Michaels defeated Bret Hart to win the WWF title in 12:11 of the famous double-cross finish in the historical climax of the show when Vince McMahon ordered ref Earl Hebner, a long-time close friend of Hart's, to call for the bell and rule it a submission without Hart's knowledge some five minutes before the match was scheduled to end.

With Hart actually reversing the hold as the bell was called, a large percentage of fans watching realized it was all screwed up (***3/4). That finish took all the attention away from the show, which included Steve Austin regaining the IC title from Owen Hart in 4:04 in a match well below par because both men were wrestling injured (*) topping off a series of elimination tag team matches.

WCW WORLD WAR 3

(November 23, Auburn Hills, MI)
Attendance: 17,128 (15,735 paid)
Live gate: $395,831
Est. buy rate/revenue:
0.56/$1.84 million
Thumbs up/down/middle:
27 (21.1%), 87 (68.0%), 14 (10.9%)
Best match: 77 - Eddie Guerrero vs. Rey Misterio Jr., 13 - Ric Flair vs. Curt Hennig
Worst match: 40 - Battle Royal, 38 - Alex Wright vs. Steve McMichael
Highlights: Another poor show headlined by the annual three-ring 60 man Battle Royal won by Scott Hall in 29:48. It was noteworthy as Battle Royal rules were changed from over-the-top eliminations to simply rolling someone under the ropes would be an elimination (1/2*), and for Hulk Hogan (who arrived unadvertised) and Kevin Nash (dressed as Sting), the highest paid performers on the show both coming out only for the finish. Curt Hennig retained the U.S. title pinning Ric Flair in 17:57 (**1/2). Eddie Guerrero retained the cruiserweight title pinning Rey Misterio Jr. in 12:42 (****). Steiners retained the WCW tag titles beating Steven Regal & David Taylor in 9:45 when Rick pinned Regal after a sky high bulldog (**) and Perry Saturn pinned Disco Inferno to retain the TV title in 8:19 (1/4*).

ECW NOVEMBER TO REMEMBER

(November 30, Monaca, PA)
Attendance: 4,634 sellout (4,218 paid)
Live gate: $103,900
Est. buy rate/revenue:
0.20/$400,000
Thumbs up/down/middle:
71 (36.2%), 102 (52.0%), 23 (11.7%)
Best match: 36 - Chris Candido & Lance Storm vs. Jerry Lynn & Tommy Rogers, 32 - Sabu vs. Sandman
Worst match: 88 - Sabu vs. Sandman, 32 - Taz vs. Pit Bull #2
Highlights: While ECW couldn't live up to its expectations and hype from previous years when it came to putting on better shows than its much larger opposition, this show clearly established them as a PPV promotion for the long haul as they maintained their buy rate after a disastrous second show. Shane Douglas, in his home town, regained the ECW title from Bam Bam Bigelow in 25:02 of a so-so match (*3/4). Sabu pinned Sandman in 20:55 of a tables and ladders legal match that was among the worst matches of the decade (-***1/2). Tommy Dreamer went to a non-decision against Rob Van Dam in 16:02 (**3/4). Tracy Smothers & Little Guido retained the ECW tag titles in a four-corners match beating the Dudleys, Axl Rotten & Balls Mahoney and the Gangstanators (*1/2) while Taz beat Pit Bull #2 in 1:29 to retain the TV title (1/2*).

WWF D-GENERATION X

(December 7, Springfield, MA)
Attendance: 6,358 sellout
Live gate: $112,864
Est. buy rate/revenue:
0.40/$1.51 million
Thumbs up/down/middle:
22 (17.2%), 96 (75.0%), 10 (7.8%)
Best match: 83 - Taka Michinoku vs. Brian Christopher, 26 - Shawn Michaels vs. Ken Shamrock
Worst match: 60 - Sgt. Slaughter vs. Hunter Hearst Helmsley, 44 - Marc Mero vs. Butterbean
Highlights: D-Generation X, in the spirit of the NWO which the concept was a knockoff of, delivered its own poor show loaded with run-in DQ finishes and poor matches. In the main event, Shawn Michaels retained the WWF title losing via run-in DQ to Ken Shamrock in 18:29 (***). In a match he was asked and refused to drop the title in, Steve Austin retained the IC title, which he voluntarily vacated the next night, by pinning Rocky Maivia in 5:12 (**1/4). In another of the series of worst matches of the year, Hunter Hearst Helmsley beat Sgt. Slaughter in a Boot Camp match in 17:39 (-**), while Billy Gunn & Jesse Jammes retained the WWF tag titles beating Legion of Doom via DQ in 10:33 (DUD), in a worked Tough Man match, Butterbean beat Marc Mero via DQ at :10 or found four (DUD) and Taka Michinoku became the first WWF light heavyweight champion actually recognized in the United States (another version of the title had bounced around Japan and Mexico for 16 years) by pinning Brian Christopher in 12:02 (***).

WCW STARRCADE

(December 29, Washington, D.C.)
Attendance: 17,500 sellout (16,052 paid)
Live gate: $543,000
Est. buy rate/revenue:
1.6/$5.58 million
Thumbs up/down/middle:
26 (9.4%), 216 (78.0%), 35 (12.6%)
Best match: 138 - Eddie Guerrero vs. Dean Malenko, 19 - Chris Benoit vs. Perry Saturn
Worst match: 69 - Bill Goldberg vs. Steve McMichael, 67 - Hulk Hogan vs. Sting

Highlights: The biggest money PPV show in more than five years ended with Sting, having been held out of the ring for 16 months, returning to beat Hulk Hogan for the WCW title in 12:54 when Bret Hart, playing off the famous Survivor Series finish, punched ref Nick Patrick who was supposed to have screwed Sting on the finish, and ruled Hogan submitted to a scorpion deathlock. Patrick was supposed to fast count as Hogan pinned Sting, however it was a normal count, making the Hart attack of Patrick and taking over make little sense (1/4*). It was the climax of the biggest year in WCW history, but it was yet another poor show even without much of an undercard. In a match billed where Nitro was at stake, 44-year-old announcer Larry Zbyszko beat 41-year old WCW President Eric Bischoff via DQ in 11:12 with Hart also as referee (1/4*). Diamond Dallas Page pinned Curt Hennig with the diamond cutter to win the U.S. title in 10:52 (**). Eddie Guerrero retained the cruiserweight title pinning Dean Malenko after a frog splash in 14:57 (**3/4).

1997 YEAR END TABULATIONS

WWF

Total shows:	12
Thumbs up shows:	4
Thumbs down shows:	1
In the middle shows:	7
Average buy rate:	0.61 (-9.0%)
Average revenue:	$1.84m (+10.8%)

WCW

Total shows:	12
Thumbs up shows:	4
Thumbs down shows:	5
In the middle shows:	3
Average buy rate:	0.77 (+20.3%)
Average revenue:	$2.45m (+36.1%)

UFC

Total shows:	5
Thumbs up shows:	4
Thumbs down shows:	1
In the middle shows:	0
Average buy rate:	0.52 (-1.9%)
Average revenue:	$838,000 (-21.7%)

ECW

Total shows:	3
Thumbs up shows:	1
Thumbs down shows:	2
In the middle shows:	0
Average buy rate:	0.22
Average revenue:	$375,000

Chapter Forty Six

The Big Shows Directory: Major International Events

NJPW WRESTLING WORLD IN TOKYO DOME
(January 4, Tokyo, Japan)
Attendance: 62,500 sellout
Television rating: 11.3
Highlights: In a show where the primary draw was the tradition of the 1/4 big show, Shinya Hashimoto retained the IWGP heavyweight title pinning Riki Choshu in 18:04 with a brainbuster DDT (****). The other two major titles changed hands, as Tatsumi Fujinami & Kengo Kimura, the first-ever IWGP tag team champions (having won the belts in 1985) regained them for the fourth time beating Masahiro Chono & Hiroyoshi Tenzan in 16:10 when Fujinami made Chono submit to the dragon sleeper. Jushin Liger won the J Crown from WCW cruiserweight champion (the WCW title wasn't at stake in this match) Ultimo Dragon in 18:21 (***3/4). Power Warrior (Kensuke Sasaki) pinned Great Muta in 16:09 (***1/4). 53-year-old Antonio Inoki beat 48-year-old former karate star Willie Williams in a horrible match in 4:13 in the first meeting between the two since a legendary match in 1980 (-*). The undercard was mainly Big Japan vs. New Japan matches, which New Japan winning all but one. A trivial note underneath is that Super Liger (Chris Jericho) debuted pinning Koji Kanemoto. This was supposed to set up Liger's main feud for 1997, however management decreed this idea didn't work, the match never even aired on television and Super Liger was never heard from again.

RINGS BATTLE DIMENSION
(January 4, Tokyo, Japan)
Attendance: 11,800
Highlights: Volk Han captured the tournament for the second time (previous win in 1994) beating Kiyoshi Tamura in 12:36 with an achilles tendon submission and in a surprise, Bitzsade Tariel captured third place beating Yoshihisa Yamamoto in 6:19. In what would prove to be an interest result with the year over, Akira Maeda in a worked match defeated EFC (and eventual UFC) champion Maurice Smith in 5:35.

NJPW SUMO HALL
(February 16, Tokyo, Japan)
Attendance: 11,000 sellout
Highlights: Shinya Hashimoto retained the IWGP heavyweight title beating Kazuo Yamazaki with a brainbuster in 18:55 (***). Tatsumi Fujinami & Kengo

Kimura retained the IWGP tag team titles beating Satoshi Kojima & Manabu Nakanishi in 14:41 (**1/4). Great Muta pinned Shiro Koshinaka in 12:43 with a moonsault (**1/2). Jushin Liger retained the J Crown pinning Koji Kanemoto in 19:26 (****3/4).

AJPW BUDOKAN HALL
(*March 1, Tokyo, Japan*)
Attendance: 16,300 sellout
Highlights: Mitsuharu Misawa retained the Triple Crown pinning Steve Williams in 27:52 (***1/4) and Akira Taue & Toshiaki Kawada retained the Double tag team titles beating Gary Albright and future Kingdom wrestler Yoshihiro Takayama in 14:12 when Kawada made Takayama submit to the stretch plum (*3/4). The Misawa-Williams match was also a high-water mark for the company doing a 5.0 rating in the post-midnight Sunday time slot.

AJW WRESTLING QUEENDOM
(*March 23, Yokohama, Japan*)
Attendance: 5,000
Highlights: A disappointing crowd turned out to see Kyoko Inoue retain her own newly-created Triple Crown of the WWWA world title, the All-Pacific title and the IWA world title pinning Aja Kong in 29:29 (***1/2). Tomoko Watanabe & Kumiko Maekawa retained the WWWA tag titles beating Takako Inoue & Mariko Yoshida in 28:00 (***3/4), and Kaoru Ito pinned Manami Toyota in 29:29 to earn a future Triple Crown title shot.

RINGS NK HALL
(*March 28, Tokyo, Japan*)
Attendance: 6,872 sellout
Highlights: In the first meeting between the biggest name of the past in the promotion (Akira Maeda) and his apparent successor by year's end in the main event slot (Kiyoshi Tamura), Maeda won with a choke sleeper in 7:54. The two actually had wrestled many years earlier in Tamura's first pro match where Maeda had scored a win in the old UWF promotion.

NJPW TOKYO DOME
(*April 12, Tokyo, Japan*)
Attendance: 50,000 (heavily papered)
Television rating: 10.3
Highlights: Of a show that was added to the schedule when New Japan thought it had a deal for a Shinya Hashimoto vs. Ken Shamrock match which would have been an easy sellout, when Shamrock pulled out to join the WWF, New Japan moved Naoya Ogawa, a three-time former world heavyweight champion in judo who was to debut on the card, into the main event against Hashimoto, and to create him as a superstar, put him over in a non-title match in 9:25 (**1/4). Riki Choshu & Kensuke Sasaki won the IWGP tag team titles from Tatsumi Fujinami & Kengo Kimura in 15:39 (**1/4), Great Muta pinned Masahiro Chono in 14:09, but after the match the two shook hands, continuing a long storyline that resulted in Muta joining the NWO (*1/2). Antonio Inoki beat Tiger King (Satoru Sayama) in 6:46 with a cobra twist submission (*). Jushin Liger retained the J Crown beating Great Sasuke in 20:08 (***3/4).

AJPW CHAMPION CARNIVAL FINALS
(*April 19, Tokyo, Japan*)
Attendance: 16,300 sellout
Highlights: Toshiaki Kawada won the Champion Carnival in only the second gimmick match in the history of the All Japan promotion (the other being a Giant Baba vs. Fritz Von Erich death match in 1975). Mitsuharu Misawa, Kawada and Kenta Kobashi all finished the round-robin with 19 points, with Kawada going 8-1-3, Kobashi going 9-2-1 and Misawa going 9-2-1. First, Misawa and Kobashi went to a 30:00 draw in a classic match (****1/2), followed by Kawada scoring his first pinfall victory of his career in a singles match against the tired Misawa in 6:09 (***3/4). Kobashi vs. Kawada followed, with Kawada winning that match as well in 21:27 of a match below par for the two (***3/4).

PANCRASE NK HALL
(*April 27, Tokyo, Japan*)
Attendance: 7,000 sellout
Highlights: Yuki Kondo, 21, after just 15 months as a pro wrestler, became the youngest ever King of Pancrase beating Masakatsu Funaki in 15:12. Paul Varelans of same UFC infamy made his only Pancrase show of the year losing 4-1 to Ryushi Yanagisawa after they went 15:00. Noted traditional style pro wrestler Taka Michinoku made his first and only shoot match losing to Keiichiro Yamamiya in 7:36 to an armlock. Bas Rutten beat Kiuma Kunioku by a 1-0 score after the two went the time limit.

FMW ANNIVERSARY SHOW
(*April 29, Yokohama, Japan*)
Attendance: 16,000 sellout
Highlights: Megumi Kudo, 27, in her final match of her career captured both the WWA world championship and Independent womens championship beating Shark Tsuchiya in 21:46 in an explosive barbed wire match. In the other key match on the show, Atsushi Onita & Masato Tanaka & Wing Kanemura beat Terry Funk & The Gladiator & Cactus Jack in 20:20 when Kanemura pinned Gladiator.

NJPW STRONG STYLE EVOLUTION
(*May 3, Osaka, Japan*)

Attendance: 53,000 sellout

Highlights: The first pro wrestling show at the Osaka Dome was a show more notable for the crowd and having top WCW than for anything in the ring. Main event saw Shinya Hashimoto avenge his defeat from a few weeks earlier and beat Naoya Ogawa in 10:20 to retain the IWGP heavyweight title after a series of savage kicks when Tiger King threw in the towel (***1/4). Satoshi Kojima & Manabu Nakanishi surprisingly captured the IWGP tag team from Riki Choshu & Kensuke Sasaki in 11:34 when Kojima used a dragon sleeper on Choshu (***1/4). Antonio Inoki & Tiger King beat Jushin Liger & Yoshiaki Fujiwara in 10:42 with Inoki beating Fujiwara with a choke sleeper (**1/2). In matches involving WCW talent, Kevin Nash & Scott Hall & Masahiro Chono beat Steiners & Keiji Muto (**), Marcus Bagwell & Scott Norton upset Lex Luger & The Giant due to outside help from Hiroyoshi Tenzan (1/2*), and NWO Sting & Syxx beat Tadao Yasuda & Takashi Iizuka (*1/2). The best match on the show was a best-of-three fall opener in which Koji Kanemoto & Shinjiro Otani & Dick Togo & Mens Teioh & Hanzo Nakajima won two straight falls from Super Delfin & Gran Hamada & Great Sasuke & Norio Honaga & El Samurai in 21:11 (****), however that combination New Japan vets & Michinoku faces vs. New Japan young juniors & Michinoku heels never got off the ground as political problems from WCW stemming from Great Sasuke and Taka Michinoku working for WWF later in the year ended the New Japan/Michinoku business relationship. A shockingly good match saw Shiro Koshinaka beat former tag partner Kengo Kimura in 13:34 (***3/4)

NJPW BUDOKAN HALL

(June 5, Tokyo, Japan)

Attendance: 14,000

Highlights: In a head-to-head battle between All Japan and New Japan in All Japan's traditional big show arena, New Japan came up just short of a sellout for a match where Shinya Hashimoto retained the IWGP heavyweight title beating Keiji Muto on 26:01 after two DDT's (***1/2). In a match of the year candidate and the match in which Koji Kanemoto opened up everyone's eyes as to his standing as one of the best all-around workers in the business, the finals of the Top of the Super Junior tournament saw El Samurai pin Kanemoto in 23:51 (*****). Satoshi Kojima & Manabu Nakanishi retained the IWGP tag team titles beating NWO Sting & Masahiro Chono in 14:15 (**3/4). In other top bouts, in a rematch of a famous feud from 14 years earlier, Tiger King (Satoru Sayama) beat Kuniaki Kobayashi (1/2*) and an eight-man tag saw Gran Naniwa & Dr. Wagner Jr. & Chris Jericho & Jushin Liger beat Shinjiro Otani & Hanzo Nakajima & Yoshihiro Tajiri & Tatsuhito Takaiwa (****).

AJPW BUDOKAN HALL

(June 6, Tokyo, Japan)

Attendance: 16,300 sellout

Highlights: Coming off his win in the Champion Carnival, Toshiaki Kawada challenged Mitsuharu Misawa for the Triple Crown with Misawa winning in 31:22 in another strong match of the year candidate (*****). The semifinal saw Kenta Kobashi & Johnny Ace & The Patriot debut as the GET trio beating Steve Williams & Gary Albright & The Lacrosse in 22:00 (**1/4). However, Patriot then quit the promotion to join WWF and the trio ended just after the big push began.

NJPW MAKOMANAI ICE ARENA

(July 6, Sapporo, Japan)

Attendance: 10,000 sellout

Highlights: New Japan's first show at the new building in Sapporo was a big success with Riki Choshu & Shinya Hashimoto beating Keiji Muto & Masahiro Chono in 12:39 when Choshu pinned Chono (***1/4). El Samurai captured the J Crown pinning Jushin Liger in 19:40 (***3/4) while Naoya Ogawa beat Kazuo Yamazaki in 8:30 (**1/2) and Antonio Inoki & Tiger King beat Kazuyuki Fujita & Kensuke Sasaki in 9:34 (**1/4).

AJPW BUDOKAN HALL

(July 25, Tokyo, Japan)

Attendance: 16,300 sellout

Highlights: Mitsuharu Misawa retained the Triple Crown pinning Akira Taue in 20:25 in a great match (****1/4), and in the promotion's worst major match of not only the year but the entire decade , Steve Williams & Gary Albright captured the double tag team titles beating Kenta Kobashi & Johnny Ace in 29:36 when Williams pinned Kobashi (DUD).

NJPW G-1 CLIMAX TOURNAMENT

(August 1-3, Tokyo, Japan)

Attendance:

10,500/11,000 sellout/11,000 sellout

Highlights: Kensuke Sasaki began his unbelievable August push winning the G-1 Climax tournament one day before his 31st birthday pinning Hiroyoshi Tenzan, who turned in a career performance despite suffering a severe knee injury before the finals in 8:09 (***3/4). Masahiro Chono was also injured in the tournament, forcing him to cancel his main event one week later against Shinya Hashimoto for the IWGP title at the first Nagoya Dome show. On 8/2, Don Frye, a UFC superstar and 1996 Ultimate Ultimate champion, made his major league pro wrestling debut beating Kazuyuki Fujita in a surprisingly good match (**1/2).

NJPW FOUR HEAVEN IN NAGOYA DOME

(August 10, Nagoya, Japan)

Attendance: 43,500 sellout

Highlights: Shinya Hashimoto retained the IWGP heavyweight title pinning Hiroyoshi Tenzan in 17:09 with a DDT in a brutal main event on the first pro wrestling event ever at the new Nagoya Dome (***1/2). Great Muta used the green mist to beat Naoya Ogawa in 6:39 (1/2*), Kazuo Yamazaki & Kensuke Sasaki captured the IWGP tag team titles from Satoshi Kojima & Manabu Nakanishi in 12:31 when Sasaki pinned Nakanishi with his Northern Lights bomb (***), Tatsumi Fujinami pinned Riki Choshu in 6:48 in what was billed as their final singles match ever (*1/2), Don Frye beat Cal Worsham in a worked UFC style match (1/2*), Shinjiro Otani won the J Crown pinning El Samurai in 18:05 (****) and Koji Kanemoto pinned Jushin Liger in 21:51.

NJPW FINAL POWER HALL

(August 31, Yokohama, Japan)

Attendance: 18,000 sellout

Highlights: New Japan ended arguably the biggest month in history for any promotion, following a sold out Nagoya Dome and successful G-1 with a nearly $2 million house celebrating the impending retirement of Riki Choshu. Choshu's protege, Kensuke Sasaki, completed his own Triple Crown during the month beating Shinya Hashimoto to win the IWGP heavyweight title with a Northern Lights bomb in 16:54 of a disappointing main event (**1/4). In the other top match, Choshu & Genichiro Tenryu & Tatsumi Fujinami beat Great Muta & Hiroyoshi Tenzan & Hiro Saito in 8:56 when Choshu pinned Saito with a lariat (*). Among those honoring Choshu after the show were Tenryu, Fujinami, Akira Maeda (making his first appearance at a New Japan show in ten years), long-time tag team partner Animal Hamaguchi, his daughter world freestyle champion Kyoko Hamaguchi and of course, Antonio Inoki. In other top matches, Naoya Ogawa beat Scott Norton in 6:25 (DUD), Shinjiro Otani retained the J Crown beating Koji Kanemoto via submission with the dragon sleeper in 20:20 (***3/4) and Jushin Liger pinned Tatsuhito Takaiwa in 17:00.

AJPW BUDOKAN HALL

(September 6, Tokyo, Japan)

Attendance: 16,300 sellout

Highlights: In an excellently worked match but somewhat taken down by the lack of heat, Mitsuharu Misawa retained the Triple Crown pinning Jun Akiyama in 24:57 using a Tiger driver (****). In the other top matches, Steve Williams & Gary Albright & Yoshihiro Takayama beat Tamon Honda & Toshiaki Kawada & Akira Taue in 17:30 (**), and Hayabusa & Jinsei Shinzaki of FMW beat Kenta Kobashi & Kentaro Shiga in 20:32 (***1/2).

WWF ONE NIGHT ONLY

(September 20, Birmingham, England)

Attendance: 11,000 sellout

Highlights: Shawn Michaels captured the European title from Davey Boy Smith in 24:00 with outside interference from Rick Rude, Chyna and Hunter Hearst Helmsley on the first WWF PPV show in England (all North American-based WWF PPV shows air in England on free television). Bulldog was originally scheduled to win the belt via pinfall, but when Michaels refused to put Bulldog over, the finish was changed to build for a future rematch where Michaels would lose, that of course never was going to take place. In a match where the crowd reaction was split, more in favor of Undertaker, Bret Hart retained the title winning via DQ when Undertaker refused to stop choking and punching Hart on the ropes in 28:00. Head Bangers retained the WWF tag titles beating Savio Vega & Miguel Perez in 14:00. Due to disputes in negotiations with the leading cable companies, the show wasn't cleared in much of England, and overall reports are that in the places it was cleared its buy rate was disappointing, well below the level of major boxing events.

NJPW BUDOKAN HALL

(September 23, Tokyo, Japan)

Attendance: 12,800

Highlights: It was a show based around wrestlers against UFC fighters as New Japan's Shinya Hashimoto beat Zane Frazier, a Vale Tudo veteran of matches in the U.S., Brazil and Japan including a KO win within seconds in a shoot match against Kendo Nagasaki at 1:05 of the third round(1/4*); Naoya Ogawa beat Brian Johnston in 11:14 (1/4*) in the latters' pro wrestling debut, and Don Frye won his rematch against former national freestyle champion and New Japan rookie star Kazuyuki Fujita in 6:02 (**1/4). In the pro wrestling matches on the show, Great Muta & Masahiro Chono defeated IWGP tag team champions Kensuke Sasaki & Kazuo Yamazaki in a non-title match when Muta walked out and Keiji Muto returned, but then joined the NWO and pinned Sasaki after a moonsault in 17:30 (*1/2) and Shinjiro Otani retained the J Crown pinning Tatsuhito Takaiwa.

FMW KAWASAKI BASEBALL STADIUM

(September 28, Kawasaki, Japan)

Attendance: 40,000

Highlights: Atsushi Onita pinned Wing Kanemura in 17:41 of a disappointing no rope barbed wire electrified dynamite land mines time bomb death match. In apparently one of the great tag matches of all-time, Kenta Kobashi & Maunukea Mossman of All Japan beat Jinsei Shinzaki & Hayabusa from FMW in 21:30. Masato Tanaka won both the Independent and Brass Knux titles from The Gladiator in another great match. Vader beat Ken Shamrock in a UFC rules cage match in a match Shamrock was scheduled to lose, however the finish came early at 7:17 because Shamrock began coughing up blood from a previous injury. In other key matches, Terry Funk retained the so-called NWA Texas heavyweight title pinning Hiromichi Fuyuki in 12:23, Shark Tsuchiya won the vacant WWA and Independent womens titles pinning Aja Kong in 18:25 and Mr. Gannosuke & Hisakatsu Oya retained the FMW World Brass Knux tag titles beating Gedo & Jado in 15:02.

MPW ANNIVERSARY SHOW

(October 10, Tokyo, Japan)

Attendance: 6,000

Highlights: A solid very good show climaxed with Great Sasuke pinning Taka Michinoku in 28:12 with a german suplex (***3/4). The basic Michinoku style six-man tag saw Super Delfin & Naohiro Hoshikawa & Masato Yakushiji beat Dick Togo & Mens Teioh & Shoichi Funaki in 18:44 (****1/4) while Undertaker was brought in for a match with Jinsei Shinzaki with Undertaker going over in 12:08 (*) and the original Tiger Mask, without the hood wrestling as Satoru Sayama, beat 1979-80 Mexican rival El Satanico in 6:38 with an armbreaker (*1/2).

KPW PRIDE ONE

(October 11, Tokyo, Japan)

Attendance: 37,000 (30,000 paid)

Buy rate: 8.0

Highlights: A poor show ending with the "funeral" of mythical shooting legend Nobuhiko Takada as he was easily handled by Rickson Gracie losing to an armbar in just 4:47. Dan Severn and Kimo went to a boring 30:00 draw in which Severn would have won the match on points but both men's reputations as shooters in Japan was damaged in the process while unheralded Akira Shoji held Renzo Gracie to a 30:00 draw in a match that Shoji probably would have garnered had their been judges although it was a close match and the best match on the show, which included at least a few worked matches.

AJPW 25TH ANNIVERSARY SHOW

(October 21, Tokyo, Japan)

Attendance: 16,300 sellout

Highlights: Mitsuharu Misawa retained his Triple Crown beating Kenta Kobashi in 32:55 of another Match of the year type performance (****1/2). In perhaps his worst major singles match of his career, Toshiaki Kawada pinned Yoshihiro Takayama in 18:22 (DUD) while Akira Taue pinned Johnny Ace in 16:54 (***3/4).

NJPW FINAL POWER HALL IN FUKUOKA

(November 2, Fukuoka, Japan)

Attendance: 40,000

Highlights: A largely disappointing show with the exception of some of the junior heavyweight matches. The main event was anti-climactic with IWGP tag team champions Keiji Muto & Masahiro Chono beating Tatsumi Fujinami & Genichiro Tenryu in 21:33 when Chono made Fujinami submit to the STF (*3/4). Shinya Hashimoto beat former K-1 and Vale Tudo competitor Hubert Numrich of Germany with a facelock in 1:04 of the second round (*). In the actual top drawing match on the show, IWGP heavyweight champion Kensuke Sasaki scored his first singles victory of his career against mentor Riki Choshu in 11:34 using Choshu's lariat as the finisher (**1/4). In other mixed matches, Naoya Ogawa beat Holland kickboxer Erwin Vreeker in 3:19 of a terrible match (-*1/2) and Don Frye beat Kazuo Yamazaki in 12:21 (**1/2). Shinjiro Otani retained the J Crown pinning Wild Pegasus (Chris Benoit) in 19:28 in easily the best match on the show (****1/4). The other strong juniors match saw the first ever teaming of the two biggest junior heavyweight stars of the modern era, Tiger King & Jushin Liger as they beat Koji Kanemoto & Tatsuhito Takaiwa in 14:18 when Liger pinned Takaiwa after a super fisherman buster (***3/4).

AJPW REAL WORLD TAG LEAGUE FINAL

(December 5, Tokyo, Japan)

Attendance: 15,500

Highlights: Toshiaki Kawada & Akira Taue won the tournament for the second consecutive year, once again beating Mitsuharu Misawa & Jun Akiyama in the finals at 30:52 when Taue pinned Akiyama after a high kick in an early candidate for next year's match of the year (*****). To create a rematch of the 1996 final match, also a match of the year calibre event, both teams were 7-1-1 in the round-robin, finishing ahead of Gary Albright & Steve Williams and Kenta Kobashi & Johnny Ace, who tied for third with 6-1-2 records.

NJPW SUPER GRADE TAG TOURNAMENT

(December 8, Osaka, Japan)

Attendance: 6,500 sellout

Highlights: IWGP tag team champions Keiji Muto & Masahiro Chono captured the tournament beating Shinya Hashimoto & Manabu Nakanishi in 23:33 when Muto made Hashimoto submit to the figure four leg lock (****). Hashimoto & Nakanishi made it to the finals beating Kazuo Yamazaki & Kensuke Sasaki in 15:24 when Hashimoto made Yamazaki submit to a Fujiwara armbar as both teams tied for second place at 5-2 records during the round-robin (***3/4). Shinjiro Otani retained the J Crown pinning Kendo Ka Shin after a dragon suplex in 14:16 (****).

PANCRASE YOKOHAMA BUNKA GYM

(December 20, Yokohama, Japan)
Attendance: 5,500 sellout
Highlights: Masakatsu Funaki won the King of Pancrase title for a second time beating protege Yuki Kondo with an armbar in 2:20. NHB star Igor Zinoviev made his Pancrase debut going to a 13:00 draw with Osami Shibuya, but suffering a cracked right wrist in the process.

UFC ULTIMATE JAPAN

(December 21, Yokohama, Japan)
Attendance: 5,000 (heavily papered)
Est. buy rate:
Thumbs up/down/middle:
31 (28.2%), 56 (50.9%), 23 (20.9%)
Best match: 29 - Conan Silviera vs. Kazushi Sakuraba, 14 - Frank Shamrock vs. Kevin Jackson 14
Worst match: 32 - Vitor Belfort vs. Joe Charles, 9 - Maurice Smith vs. Randy Couture
Highlights: Arguably UFC's weakest show to date viewed by its largest audience with network television coverage in Japan but overall a live promotional flop with heavy papering. Randy Couture captured the UFC heavyweight title beating Maurice Smith via decision after the 21:00 time limit expired with neither man seriously damaging the other but Couture having more control and more aggressiveness. Frank Shamrock became the UFC's first under-200 champion beating Kevin Jackson in just :14 with an armbar. Kazushi Sakuraba, a pro wrestler from the Kingdom promotion won the UFC's weirdest tournament to date beating Conan Silviera in 3:45 after the two had a match earlier in the show that Silviera initially won via ref stop but it was then overruled. In one of the most controversial fights in UFC history, boxer Vitor Belfort didn't throw a punch the entire fight in beating hand-picked opponent Joe Charles in 4:04 with an armbar.

Chapter Forty Seven

1997 PPV Drawing Cards

Based on buy rate points in total for the year having appeared in PPV main events. The number in parenthesis is the age of the wrestler as of 1/1/98.

	Wrestler	Pts	Shows	Avg
1.	Hulk Hogan (44)	6.65	7	.95
2.	Undertaker (32)	4.24	7	.61
3.	Bret Hart (40)	4.05	6	.68
4.	Steve Austin (33)	3.43	6	.57
5.	Roddy Piper (46)	3.34	4	.84
6.	Shawn Michaels (32)	3.09	5	.62
7.	Lex Luger (39)	3.01	4	.75
8.	The Giant (26)	2.83	4	.71
9.	Kevin Nash (39)	2.02	3	.67
10.	Sting (38)	1.90	1	1.90
11.	Ric Flair (48)	1.73	3	.58
12.	Maurice Smith (36)	1.67	4	.42
13.	Ken Shamrock (33)	1.52	3	.51
14.	Scott Hall (38)	1.49	2	.75
14.	Randy Savage (45)	1.49	2	.75

In approximate total revenue generated, Hogan's 6.65 total points works out to about 1,862,000 total PPV buys or about $52,042,900 in total generated revenue or about $21,858,000 for WCW; $4,163,000 for the middle-men (Viewers Choice and Request TV) and $26,021,450 for the cable television companies (TCI, Time Warner, Cablevision, et al). If you want to figure his actual worth to WCW as a PPV box office attraction, take the WCW non-Hogan PPV revenue average and multiply it by 12 (the number of PPV shows WCW produced). Then figure the difference between the revenue they actually generated and the revenue they would have generated without him by multiplying the non-Hogan PPV revenue number over 12 shows, divided by two because he had opponents who deserve credit for the increase over the average as well.

The 1997 value of Hulk Hogan on PPV to WCW was approximately $5,617,000. In other words, if Hogan's deal still is 25% of the company gross on all PPV shows he appears, that is almost a perfect formula this year when figuring out what his name meant as a draw, as the actual perfect figure would be he increased revenue 25.6% per show which actually means if Hogan's figure still is 25%, the company is actually not making any extra profit by having Hogan work the shows over the course of the year either as whatever extra he's drawing he would be getting himself and also there is little doubt they spend more money in advertising on the PPV shows he appears on so that cuts down the profit margin.

But taking everything into consideration, if Hogan earned $5 million last year in WCW it was money well spent. If he earned $6 million, it probably still was money well spent, although any more than that wouldn't be.

Taking the same formula into account, Undertaker's value to the WWF on PPV would be negligible as the shows he headlined drew no better than the shows he didn't, which would apply for Austin and everyone else on the list except for Hart, Piper, Michaels and Sting. Those were the only five wrestlers who could make any claim to have actually drawn added money on their own on PPV in 1997, and in the case of Michaels, the figure is almost negligible as well.

By the same formula, Hart's value to WWF for the year on PPV alone based on his raising the buy rates on the shows he appeared would be $1,422,500, thus when all the arguments are said and done on that subject he was not overpaid last year even in comparison to the salary structure of the other headliners in the company as his PPV revenue increase over the average paid for almost his entire salary, and that doesn't include his value when it came to house show attendance, television ratings or any sale of his merchandise since his contract was such that he actually didn't receive any cut of his merchandise or get any kind of bonus for appearing, let alone main eventing on PPV, even if the PPV show did well.

Piper's value would be $408,500; Michaels' value would be $123,300 and Sting's would be $2,059,600 even though he only worked one match all year. Based on the respective earnings of the five names (Hogan, Hart, Piper, Michaels and Sting) who made any difference in the company average buy rate and considering what each earned during the year, the most underpaid of the five, despite the fact he probably earned about $1 million and only wrestled one PPV match all year, would be Sting.

Chapter Forty Eight

1997 Final Match Quality Ratings

Based on major show matches covered in the Observer during 1997, based on having three or more singles or tag team matches on major shows this year. Ranking for respective years in parenthesis.

Singles	1997	1996	+-
Steve Austin	3.04 (20)	2.63	0.41
Marcus Bagwell	1.81	----	----
Chris Benoit	3.00	3.79 (10)	-0.79
Masahiro Chono	2.30	2.93	-0.63
Riki Choshu	2.58	2.70	-0.12
Crush	0.33	----	----
Shane Douglas	1.67	----	----
Ultimo Dragon	3.80 (10)	4.13 (5)	-0.33
Tommy Dreamer	1.92	----	----
Faarooq	1.05	----	----
Ric Flair	2.19	2.75	-0.56
Don Frye	1.94	----	----
The Giant	0.75	1.33	-0.58
Glacier	0.67	----	----
Goldust	1.45	1.86	-0.41
Eddie Guerrero	3.75 (12)	3.39 (15)	0.36
Billy Gunn	0.42	----	----
Bret Hart	3.79 (11)	3.20 (19)	0.59
Owen Hart	2.31	----	----
Hunter Hearst Helmsley	2.00	1.92	0.08
Shinya Hashimoto	2.73	2.94	-0.21
Curt Hennig	1.75	----	----
Hulk Hogan	0.40	0.70	-0.30
Prince Iaukea	2.08	----	----

Singles	1997	1996	+-
Jeff Jarrett	1.33	2.00	-0.67
Chris Jericho	3.21 (19)	2.94	0.27
Ahmed Johnson	0.88	1.88	-1.00
Koji Kanemoto	4.38 (1)	----	----
Toshiaki Kawada	3.45 (15)	3.50 (13)	-0.05
Kenta Kobashi	4.38 (1)	4.31 (1)	0.07
Shiro Koshinaka	2.67	3.39 (15)	-0.72
Jushin Liger	3.96 (6)	3.88 (9)	0.08
Lex Luger	0.75	----	----
Rocky Maivia	1.45	----	----
Dean Malenko	3.39 (17)	3.44 (14)	-0.05
Mankind	2.53	3.05 (20)	-0.52
Steve McMichael	0.54	----	----
Shawn Michaels	3.58 (14)	4.00 (7)	-0.42
Taka Michinoku	3.69 (13)	----	----
Mitsuharu Misawa	4.23 (3)	4.17 (3)	0.06
Rey Misterio Jr.	3.43 (16)	4.14 (4)	-0.71
Keiji Muto	2.04	3.54 (12)	-1.50
Scott Norton	1.13	----	----
Naoya Ogawa	1.46	----	----
Shinjiro Otani	3.97 (5)	4.25 (2)	-0.28
Diamond Dallas Page	2.32	2.36	-0.04
Roddy Piper	1.50	----	----
Psicosis	3.83 (7)	----	----
Steven Regal	2.08	----	----
Sabu	1.58	----	----
El Samurai	4.04 (4)	3.30 (17)	0.74
Kensuke Sasaki	3.00	2.54	0.46
Great Sasuke	3.83 (7)	3.96 (8)	-0.13
Randy Savage	2.67	2.00	0.67
Ken Shamrock	2.81	----	----
Syxx	2.83	2.67	0.16
Tatsuhito Takaiwa	3.83 (7)	----	----
Akira Taue	2.92	4.05 (6)	-1.13
Taz	2.06	----	----
Hiroyoshi Tenzan	3.29 (18)	2.46	0.83
Tiger King	1.08	----	----
Undertaker	2.59	2.55	0.04
Vader	2.75	2.50	0.25
Rob Van Dam	2.75	----	----
Savio Vega	0.25	1.83	-1.58
Alex Wright	1.63	----	----
Kazuo Yamazaki	2.69	2.11	0.58

Tag Teams	1997	1996	+-
Fujinami & Kimura	2.57 (8)	----	----
Hall & Nash	2.44 (10)	1.85	0.59
Godwinns	0.25	0.85	-0.60
Owen Hart & Bulldog	2.17	2.67 (10)	-0.50
Harlem Heat	2.25	2.08	0.17
Hashimoto & Nakanishi	3.06 (5)	----	----
Kawada & Taue	3.57 (2)	4.38 (2)	-0.81

Kobashi & Ace	3.38 (3)	----	----
Legion of Doom	0.38	2.06	-1.68
Luger & Giant	1.83	----	----
Kojima & Nakanishi	3.00 (6)	----	----
Misawa & Akiyama	4.35 (1)	4.56 (1)	-0.21
Muto & Chono	2.48 (9)	----	----
Sasaki & Yamazaki	2.96 (7)	----	----
Steiners	2.11	3.08 (6)	-0.97
Tenzan & NWO Sting	0.58	----	----
Williams & Albright	3.17 (4)	----	----

While recognizing the limitations of a system where wrestlers (and teams) are ranked based on the average rating of their major show matches during the previous year (ie. quality of opponents isn't taken into consideration; restraints based on promotional decision of time allotment and limitations and changes thrown in at the last minute; and the subjectivity of rating matches to begin with), there is a lot that can be learned from these numbers.

These numbers are a better indication of consistency throughout the year then memories of only the best or worst that survive the year. They also tell stories of whose work truly improved and dropped off as opposed to people swayed by illusory improvement of someone getting a bigger push or more television time. And they do tell just how pathetic 1997 was when it came to tag team wrestling in the United States, although I'm sure most realize you didn't need to see numbers to figure that out.

In running down notes on the various people, here are more items to be considered:

Steve Austin was actually at a 3.94 clip before suffering the neck injury in the SummerSlam match with Owen Hart. Had he not suffered the injury, he'd have been in contention and possibly even been the most consistently productive performing wrestler in the United States for the year.

Although Marcus Bagwell received tons of support and will finish strongly in the Most Improved Wrestler category, that is more due to his heel role garnering him more of a television push and an improvement in persona based on being given a chance. It has nothing to do with actually having better matches.

Chris Benoit may very well be the single best junior heavyweight worker in the business and best overall worker in the United States, but he was buried with weak opponents and feuds all year long. While a drop of .79 in most cases would be a significant decline, upon closer look at his opponents, this is one case where the numbers have to be disregarded.

On the other hand, the decline in the work of Masahiro Chono is significant for a wrestler that is arguably the most important wrestler in arguably the most successful company in the world. Chono is another whose reputation as a worker exceeds his actual work and where these numbers actually do tell a story.

As they do for the actual level of worker Ric Flair was in 1997.

Although we haven't heard it much over the past year, Dustin Runnels (Goldust) always had a reputation for being a good, although not great worker. It was a rep garnered many years ago in WCW, but he's only shown limited spurts of that rep since joining the WWF. For two years now he's actually been a below average worker in the ring.

Eddie Guerrero going into Starrcade was actually the top rated North American worker for 1997, but the subpar (by his standards, not for others) match on that card nudged him into fourth place behind Psicosis, Ultimo Dragon and Bret Hart.

For all the talk of Hart slipping, he actually had better big show matches in 1997 than he did in 1996. Quite frankly, more likely than not, had the Michaels match went to its fruition with the added four more minutes of near falls, it almost surely would have been better than a **** match and Hart would have been the top rated North American wrestler of the year. This isn't to make any statements about his drawing power or whether he was worth what his contract says or if he's a better choice to be on top than Shawn Michaels, only that when it came to the big shows, in the ring, Hart is still at the top of not only his game but of *the* game.

Despite having one of the best heads of hair in the business, when it comes to production in the ring, Hunter Hearst Helmsley was overall an average wrestler in 1996 and an average wrestler in 1997. He had an improved push during the year and was positioned as a superstar, but overall his work nor his ability to get over gave no backing to the new push. He's doing well in his new role, but getting that role had more to do with he was one of Shawn Michaels' few friends in the company and his look (and throughout the years there are numerous people in the business who have made tons of money based on their look with no ability in the ring).

The fact that Shinya Hashimoto's decline was fairly small over the last year is actually amazing. There is not one major star in the business, not Benoit, not anyone, who was put in the ring in major singles matches with such a poor quality of opponents and to pull some actual good matches out of the likes of Naoya Ogawa (twice, and nobody else has come close to have matches with Ogawa at that level), and even bad matches out of Zane Frazier and Hubert Numrich and still keep a 2.73 average for the year shows Hashimoto to really be one of the best in the business.

If anyone was still judging Curt Hennig as a wrestler based on the fact he was top-five in the world in his prime, check out the numbers and if you figure in that his bouts have been against Page and Flair, both of whom even at this stage can't be considered below average on their own, you'll see his actual nickname at this stage of the game is either Mr. Slightly Below Average or the $750,000 lemon.

Jeff Jarrett declined, but there isn't a guy who wouldn't having to work a program with Steve McMichael.

Chris Jericho must be one of the most underrated workers in the business.

I'm amazed Ahmed Johnson has fared as well as he has the past two years.

It takes a long time to accept people at the level they are. I've noticed in awards when it comes to bests and worsts and improvement that often there is what I'd call a one year latency period, in that people don't notice improvements and declines in talent until sometimes a year after it takes place. Case in point—Koji Kanemoto. Based on the full year, there was not a better worker in the business. But since Kanemoto was always considered a top-20 level guy, most would tab his improvement this year to maybe cracking the top ten when he not only cracked the top ten, but plowed through it.

On the other hand we have Toshiaki Kawada. There are a lot of people, myself included, who immediately would rank Mitsuharu Misawa, Kenta Kobashi and Kawada as the three best heavyweight wrestlers in the world. As you can see, both Misawa and Kobashi unquestionably deserve that reputation. Kawada, for two years running, has finished No. 13 and No. 15, despite having numerous Match of the Year type efforts. Fact is, Kawada, unlike Misawa and Kobashi, sometimes has real bad nights on real big shows. No doubt when Kawada turns it on, he's equal to anyone in this business, but what these numbers show is that both of the last two years his consistency hasn't been enough to crack the top ten even if his best matches are.

I guess whatever rep Kenta Kobashi has garnered is deserved. Finishing No. 1 two straight years says a lot. Sure, it helps when you get three major singles matches with Misawa so he's been positioned where he should do well, but positioning alone isn't going to make someone No. 1 two straight (and if we'd done these numbers before I'd guess Kobashi would be at or near the top for many years before that).

For Jushin Liger to have a year like he did coming back from a brain tumor which at first thought could be a career-ender, is probably the single most under-publicized story of 1997. Liger has been so good for so long that his work is taken for granted. In the ring, he is for consistency the greatest junior heavyweight of all-time. There are others, like Benoit, who are in his class, but on a nightly basis going back for the last nine years, he may be the best worker in the business.

Dean Malenko is consistently very good. What a revelation.

Shawn Michaels is, well, you can see the numbers. You can argue Shawn vs. Bret till the cows come home and it really doesn't matter. Shawn didn't get a good match out of Sid despite being in his home city before 60,000 fans. But Bret probably couldn't either. Bret got a better match out of Del Wilkes than Shawn did out of Ken Shamrock (from most accounts, Bret's house show matches with Shamrock were better than Shawn's television and PPV matches with Shamrock although Shamrock should be a better opponent for Bret since Bret had a hand in training him). Bret's England PPV match with Undertaker and Shawn's first PPV match with Undertaker were of similar quality, although Michaels' cage match with Undertaker was one of the best performances by anyone all year. Michaels is a great worker, but on a consistent basis he's also not the best in the business.

Misawa's numbers aren't a surprise. Actually, if you throw in tag team matches, he was better than Kobashi or Kanemoto. Kobashi did have one horrendous match on a big show (a tag match with he and Johnny Ace vs. Steve Williams & Gary Albright) this year while Misawa's worst matches were still ***1/4 stars and that's with 15 major show singles and tag matches and not all against Kobashi and Kawada—more than any wrestler in the business during the year, 11 of which were **** or better.

Misterio Jr's decline can be summed up in two words—Prince Iaukea (whose illusory better than average rating can be summed up by Rey Misterio Jr.). Take the Prince matches out and you've got a 3.85 rating which again would be the top in North America for the year. In 1996, Misterio Jr. had the most consistent great matches in North America because he was largely booked against his best possible opponents on big shows, Ultimo Dragon, Juventud Guerrera, Psicosis, Dean Malenko and Jushin Liger among others. This year he had Iaukea and Konnan.

The numbers tell the story about Keiji Muto in 1997. He's gone from being one of the best workers in the business to probably the most inconsistent (although even in the past he was inconsistent). He can still be a great worker when he's got the working shoes on. But he laced those boots up a whole lot less this year than last year. He's probably the equivalent in Japan to Randy Savage in his prime where he is a great worker, but he often sucks. Savage's work plunged for years to where everyone wrote him off as being washed up. But as this year shows, he still has a lot left in him. Muto shows enough flashes to see he's got a lot of great matches left in him, but he was sure inconsistent this year. And when he doesn't have his lucky boots on, his matches smell like week-old fish.

Shinjiro Otani is one of the best. What a shock, huh?

Diamond Dallas Page is the Most Improved Wrestler in the business? Talk about the illusion based on positioning. In 1996, he had to work with guys like Booty Man so he deserved some slack. This year his big matches were against the likes of a revitalized Randy Savage, a good friend in Marcus Bagwell, and a guy with a great rep (although living off it) in Curt Hennig and he did no better. Page has a lot of charisma. His timing of when to do moves can be great and he did an incredible job of getting his finisher over. His interviews can be great. His major stardom in this business is because Hall & Nash sold for him and Sting and just about nobody else, because he was given ample TV and because positioning is almost everything. But is he one of the best workers in the business? His talk and push are so good that a lot of people believe it, and hey, that's what this business is all about. Except he's not.

Amazing that there wasn't a North American worker in the business that was more consistent in big show matches than a WCW TV jobber (Psicosis)? Are he and El Samurai the single most underrated workers in the business today?

Savage's numbers seem to be an accurate indication that for whatever reason he's probably wrestling the best he has in many years.

Tatsuhito Takaiwa is the Most Improved Wrestler in the business? Going from an opening match wrestler with potential to No. 7 as a worker over a one year period is sort of unheard of.

Akira Taue's 1996 was a lucky number based on so many singles matches with great opponents. His 1997 number isn't so much an indication of a big decline as much as a reality check.

Hiroyoshi Tenzan has been the most improved wrestler of the year when it comes to an unheralded improvement. If you don't believe it, check out of a tape of the Yasuda match. But his tag team work doesn't hold up to his singles.

The only real comments in regard to tag teams is just how pathetic the list is overall, and how the Steiners and LOD are living off their reputations, the latter more than the former.

Chapter Forty Nine

Wrestling Observer Newsletter Awards

CATEGORY A AWARDS

Winners determined by points voted on a 5-3-2 basis. First place votes in parenthesis.

WRESTLER OF THE YEAR

1.	Mitsuharu Misawa (338)	2,288
2.	Bret Hart (72)	758
3.	Kenta Kobashi (79)	722
4.	Steve Austin (79)	705
5.	Shawn Michaels (51)	510
6.	Shinya Hashimoto (10)	345
7.	Shinjiro Otani (19)	208
8.	Koji Kanemoto (18)	197
9.	Toshiaki Kawada (3)	194
10.	Rey Misterio Jr. (12)	191

Honorable Mention

Jushin Liger 154, Eddie Guerrero 87, Dean Malenko 74, Maurice Smith 74

Previous Winners

1980 - Harley Race, 1981 - Ric Flair, 1982 - Ric Flair, 1983 - Ric Flair, 1984 - Ric Flair, 1985 - Ric Flair, 1986 - Ric Flair, 1987 - Riki Choshu, 1988 - Akira Maeda, 1989 - Ric Flair, 1990 - Ric Flair, 1991 - Jumbo Tsuruta, 1992 - Ric Flair, 1993 - Vader, 1994 - Toshiaki Kawada, 1995 - Mitsuharu Misawa, 1996 - Kenta Kobashi

MOST OUTSTANDING WRESTLER

1.	Mitsuharu Misawa (143)	1,002
2.	Rey Misterio Jr. (114)	894
3.	Shinjiro Otani (82)	713
4.	Kenta Kobashi (59)	680

5.	Koji Kanemoto (47)	544
6.	Eddie Guerrero (48)	538
7.	Shawn Michaels (65)	484
8.	Chris Benoit (43)	467
9.	Ultimo Dragon (23)	275
10.	Dean Malenko (20)	215

Honorable Mention

Toshiaki Kawada 185, Manami Toyota 119, Jushin Liger 110, Taka Michinoku 91, Bret Hart 78, Jun Akiyama 72

Previous Winners

1986 - Ric Flair, 1987 - Ric Flair, 1988 - Tatsumi Fujinami, 1989 - Ric Flair, 1990 - Jushin Liger, 1991 - Jushin Liger, 1992 - Jushin Liger, 1993 - Kenta Kobashi, 1994 - Kenta Kobashi, 1995 - Manami Toyota, 1996 - Rey Misterio Jr.

BEST BOX OFFICE DRAW

1.	Hulk Hogan (235)	1,576
2.	Shinya Hashimoto (137)	1,176
3.	Steve Austin (76)	746
4.	Riki Choshu (58)	537
5.	Bret Hart (33)	466
6.	Roddy Piper (9)	329
7.	Shawn Michaels (17)	323
8.	Ric Flair (8)	182
9.	Mitsuharu Misawa (2)	131
10.	Undertaker (5)	111

Honorable Mention

Nobuhiko Takada 90, Atsushi Onita 78

Best Babyface Previous Winners

1980 - Dusty Rhodes, 1981 - Tommy Rich, 1982 - Hulk Hogan, 1983 - Hulk Hogan, 1984 - Hulk Hogan, 1985 - Hulk Hogan, 1986 - Hulk Hogan, 1987 - Hulk Hogan, 1988 - Hulk Hogan, 1989 - Hulk Hogan, 1990 - Hulk Hogan, 1991 - Hulk Hogan, 1992 - Sting, 1993 - Atsushi Onita, 1994 - Atsushi Onita, 1995 - Perro Aguayo, 1996 - Shawn Michaels

Best Heel Previous Winners

1980 - Larry Zbyszko, 1981 - Don Muraco, 1982 - Buzz Sawyer, 1983 - Michael Hayes, 1984 - Roddy Piper, 1985 - Roddy Piper, 1986 - Michael Hayes, 1987 - Ted DiBiase, 1988 - Ted DiBiase, 1989 - Terry Funk, 1990 - Ric Flair, 1991 - The Undertaker, 1992 - Rick Rude, 1993 - Vader, 1994 - Love Machine, 1995 - Masahiro Chono, 1996 - Steve Austin

FEUD OF THE YEAR

1.	Steve Austin vs. The Hart Foundation (157)	1,212
2.	WCW vs. NWO (116)	891
3.	Bret Hart vs. Shawn Michaels (93)	715
4.	Otani & Kanemoto vs. Liger & Samurai (47)	362
5.	New Japan vs. NWO (38)	353
6.	Michinoku Seikigun vs. Kaientai DX (11)	287
7.	Diamond Dallas Page vs. Randy Savage (18)	259
8.	Eddie Guerrero vs. Rey Misterio Jr. (12)	244
9.	El Hijo del Santo vs. Negro Casas (23)	155
10.	Jerry Lawler vs. ECW (17)	148

Honorable Mention

Sabu vs. Taz 130, Dean Malenko vs. Eddie Guerrero 122, Shawn Michaels vs. Undertaker 119, Mitsuharu Misawa vs. Toshiaki Kawada 91

Previous Winners

1980 - Bruno Sammartino vs. Larry Zbyszko, 1981 - Andre the Giant vs. Killer Khan, 1982 - Ted DiBiase vs. Junkyard Dog, 1983 - Freebirds vs. Von Erichs, 1984 - Freebirds vs. Von Erichs, 1985 - Ted DiBiase vs. Jim Duggan, 1986 - Hulk Hogan vs. Paul Orndorff, 1987 - Jerry Lawler vs. Austin Idol & Tommy Rich, 1988 - Midnight Express vs. Fantastics, 1989 - Ric Flair vs. Terry Funk, 1990 - Jumbo Tsuruta vs. Mitsuharu Misawa, 1991 - Tsuruta & company vs. Misawa & company, 1992 - Moondogs vs. Jerry Lawler & Jeff Jarrett, 1993 - Bret Hart vs. Jerry Lawler, 1994 - Gringo Locos vs. Mexican AAA, 1995 - Dean Malenko vs. Eddie Guerrero, 1996 - WCW vs. NWO

TAG TEAM OF THE YEAR

1.	Mitsuharu Misawa & Jun Akiyama (222)	1,448
2.	Toshiaki Kawada & Akira Taue (146)	1,375
3.	Kenta Kobashi & Johnny Ace (25)	521
4.	Etsuko Mita & Mima Shimoda (44)	392
5.	Shinjiro Otani & Koji Kanemoto (34)	367
6.	Owen Hart & Davey Boy Smith (42)	342
7.	Perry Saturn & John Kronus (41)	335
8.	Rick & Scott Steiner (24)	319
9.	Keiji Muto & Masahiro Chono (28)	244
10.	Dick Togo & Mens Teioh (22)	215

Honorable Mention

Sabu & Rob Van Dam 183, Scott Hall & Kevin Nash 159, Harlem Heat 134, Manabu Nakanishi & Satoshi Kojima 92, Legion of Doom 71

Previous Winners

1980 - Terry Gordy & Buddy Roberts, 1981 - Terry Gordy & Jimmy Snuka, 1982 - Stan Hansen & Ole Anderson, 1983 - Ricky Steamboat & Jay Youngblood, 1984 - Road Warriors, 1985 - Dynamite Kid & Davey Boy Smith, 1986 - Bobby Eaton & Dennis Condrey, 1987 - Bobby Eaton & Stan Lane, 1988 - Bobby Eaton & Stan Lane, 1989 - Shawn Michaels & Marty Jannetty, 1990 - Rick & Scott Steiner, 1991 - Mitsuharu Misawa & Toshiaki Kawada, 1992 - Terry Gordy & Steve Williams, 1993 - Brian Pillman & Steve Austin, 1994 - Love Machine & Eddie Guerrero, 1995 - Mitsuharu Misawa & Kenta Kobashi, 1996 - Mitsuharu Misawa & Jun Akiyama

MOST IMPROVED

1.	Tatsuhito Takaiwa (138)	923
2.	Rocky Maivia (45)	488
3.	Marcus Bagwell (45)	391
4.	Maunukea Mossman (39)	340
5.	Ken Shamrock (47)	304
6.	Koji Kanemoto (28)	255
7.	Alex Wright (15)	155
8.	Yoshihiro Tajiri (19)	154
9.	Disco Inferno (17)	154
10.	NWO Sting (19)	138

Honorable Mention

Johnny Smith 137, Mortis 132, Kendo Ka Shin 92, Manabu Nakanishi 82, Yuji Nagata 79, Hayabusa 75, Tomoko Kuzumi 73

Previous Winners

1980 - Larry Zbyszko, 1981 - Adrian Adonis, 1982 - Jim Duggan, 1983 - Curt Hennig, 1984 - The Cobra (George Takano), 1985 - Steve Williams, 1986 - Rick Steiner, 1987 - Big Bubba Rogers, 1988 - Sting, 1989 - Lex Luger, 1990 - Kenta Kobashi, 1991 - Dustin Rhodes, 1992 - El Samurai, 1993 - Tracy Smothers, 1994 - Diesel (Kevin Nash), 1995 - Johnny B. Badd, 1996 - Diamond Dallas Page

BEST ON INTERVIEWS

1.	Steve Austin (252)	1,643
2.	Ric Flair (53)	695

3.	Shane Douglas (39)	520
4.	Bret Hart (40)	505
5.	Arn Anderson (62)	370
6.	Shawn Michaels (29)	354
7.	Mankind (31)	347
8.	Kevin Nash (30)	316
9.	Hulk Hogan (3)	78
10.	Brian Pillman	63

Previous Winners

1981 - Lou Albano and Roddy Piper (tied), 1982 - Roddy Piper, 1983 - Roddy Piper, 1984 - Jimmy Hart, 1985 - Jim Cornette, 1986 - Jim Cornette, 1987 - Jim Cornette, 1988 - Jim Cornette, 1989 - Terry Funk, 1990 - Arn Anderson, 1991 - Ric Flair, 1992 - Ric Flair, 1993 - Jim Cornette, 1994 - Ric Flair, 1995 - Cactus Jack, 1996 - Steve Austin

MOST CHARISMATIC

1.	Steve Austin (178)	1,267
2.	Ric Flair (102)	998
3.	Shawn Michaels (114)	956
4.	Sting (56)	383
5.	Hulk Hogan (23)	283
6.	Diamond Dallas Page (4)	205
7.	Riki Choshu (29)	199
8.	Roddy Piper (8)	146
9.	Bret Hart (7)	129
10.	Undertaker (3)	95

Honorable Mention

La Parka 85

Previous Winners

1980 - Ric Flair, 1981 - Michael Hayes, 1982 - Dusty Rhodes and Ric Flair (tied), 1983 - Ric Flair, 1984 - Ric Flair, 1985 - Hulk Hogan, 1986 - Hulk Hogan, 1987 - Hulk Hogan, 1988 - Sting, 1989 - Hulk Hogan, 1990 - Hulk Hogan, 1991 - Hulk Hogan, 1992 - Sting, 1993 - Ric Flair, 1994 - Atsushi Onita, 1995 - Shawn Michaels, 1996 - Shawn Michaels

BEST TECHNICAL WRESTLER

1.	Dean Malenko (214)	1,519
2.	Chris Benoit (82)	939
3.	Shinjiro Otani (63)	785
4.	Ultimo Dragon (50)	485
5.	Mitsuharu Misawa (56)	420
6.	Volk Han (38)	345
7.	Kiyoshi Tamura (54)	308
8.	Eddie Guerrero (24)	291
9.	Koji Kanemoto (18)	272
10.	Bret Hart (14)	143

Honorable Mention

Kenta Kobashi 140, Daisuke Ikeda 97, Rey Misterio Jr. 94, Steve Regal 79, Ken Shamrock 73

Previous Winners

1980 - Bob Backlund, 1981 - Ted DiBiase, 1982 - Tiger Mask (Satoru Sayama), 1983 - Tiger Mask (Satoru Sayama), 1984 - Dynamite Kid and Masa Saito (tied), 1985 - Tatsumi Fujinami, 1986 - Tatsumi Fujinami, 1987 - Nobuhiko Takada, 1988 - Tatsumi Fujinami, 1989 - Jushin Liger, 1990 - Jushin Liger, 1991 - Jushin Liger, 1992 - Jushin Liger, 1993 - Hiroshi Hase, 1994 - Chris Benoit, 1995 - Chris Benoit, 1996 - Dean Malenko

BRUISER BRODY MEMORIAL AWARD (BEST BRAWLER)

1.	Mankind (266)	1,654
2.	Chris Benoit (121)	841
3.	Tommy Dreamer (87)	752
4.	Sandman (17)	363
5.	Terry Funk (25)	317
6.	New Jack (21)	292
7.	Sabu (16)	228
8.	David Finlay (6)	221
9.	Wing Kanemura (12)	191
10.	Mayumi Ozaki (19)	155

HONORABLE MENTION

Steve Austin 120, Masato Tanaka 110, Aja Kong 85

PREVIOUS WINNERS

1980 - Bruiser Brody, 1981 - Bruiser Brody, 1982 - Bruiser Brody, 1983 - Bruiser Brody, 1984 - Bruiser Brody, 1985 - Stan Hansen, 1986 - Terry Gordy, 1987 - Bruiser Brody, 1988 - Bruiser Brody, 1989 - Terry Funk, 1990 - Stan Hansen, 1991 - Cactus Jack, 1992 - Cactus Jack, 1993 - Cactus Jack, 1994 - Cactus Jack, 1995 - Cactus Jack, 1996 - Mankind

BEST FLYING WRESTLER

1.	Rey Mysterio Jr. (412)	2,502
2.	Taka Michinoku (45)	811
3.	Great Sasuke (22)	692
4.	Juventud Guerrera (9)	408
5.	Sabu (16)	328
6.	Hayabusa (19)	243
7.	Ultimo Dragon	220
8.	Shinjiro Otani (10)	219
9.	Psicosis (20)	175
10.	Mr. Aguila (4)	167

HONORABLE MENTION

Hector Garza 99, Koji Kanemoto 90

PREVIOUS WINNERS

1981 - Jimmy Snuka, 1982 - Tiger Mask (Satoru Sayama), 1983 - Tiger Mask (Satoru Sayama), 1984 - Dynamite Kid, 1985 - Tiger Mask (Mitsuharu Misawa), 1986 - Tiger Mask (Mitsuharu Misawa), 1987 - Owen Hart, 1988 - Owen Hart, 1989 - Jushin Liger, 1990 - Jushin Liger, 1991 - Jushin Liger, 1992 - Jushin Liger, 1993 - Jushin Liger, 1994 - Great Sasuke, 1995 - Rey Misterio Jr., 1996 - Rey Misterio Jr.

MOST OVERRATED

1.	Hulk Hogan (224)	1,451
2.	Lex Luger (87)	1,018
3.	Kevin Nash (35)	417
4.	Roddy Piper (19)	299
5.	Sycho Sid (23)	277
6.	Kensuke Sasaki (28)	252
7.	Triple H (15)	166
8.	Steve McMichael (15)	158
9.	Shane Douglas (13)	138
10.	Scott Hall (13)	117

Honorable Mention
The Giant 101, Taz 86, Sandman 79

Previous Winners
1980 - Mr. Wrestling II, 1981 - Pedro Morales, 1982 - Pedro Morales, 1983 - Bob Backlund, 1984 - John Studd, 1985 - Hulk Hogan, 1986 - Hulk Hogan, 1987 - Dusty Rhodes, 1988 - Dusty Rhodes, 1989 - Ultimate Warrior, 1990 - Ultimate Warrior, 1991 - Ultimate Warrior, 1992 - Erik Watts, 1993 - Sid Vicious, 1994 - Hulk Hogan, 1995 - Hulk Hogan, 1996 - Hulk Hogan

MOST UNDERRATED

1.	Flash Funk (92)	666
2.	Chris Benoit (100)	662
3.	Psicosis (52)	649
4.	Juventud Guerrera (47)	570
5.	Al Snow (54)	440
6.	La Parka (15)	209
7.	Chris Jericho (17)	189
8.	Chris Candido (22)	165
9.	Johnny Smith (19)	119
10.	Marcus Bagwell (12)	118

Honorable Mention
Ultimo Dragon 112, Silver King 99, Billy Kidman 78

Previous Winners
1980 - Iron Sheik, 1981 - Buzz Sawyer, 1982 - Adrian Adonis, 1983 - Dynamite Kid, 1984 - Brian Blair, 1985 - Bobby Eaton, 1986 - Bobby Eaton, 1987 - Brad Armstrong, 1988 - Tiger Mask (Mitsuharu Misawa), 1989 - Dan Kroffat, 1990 - Bobby Eaton, 1991 - Terry Taylor, 1992 - Terry Taylor, 1993 - Bobby Eaton, 1994 - Brian Pillman, 1995 - Skip (Chris Candido), 1996 - Leif Cassidy

BEST PROMOTION

1.	New Japan Pro Wrestling (311)	2,270
2.	All Japan Pro Wrestling (115)	1,529
3.	World Championship Wrestling (131)	1,337
4.	Extreme Championship Wrestling (39)	677
5.	World Wrestling Federation (77)	646
6.	RINGS	97
7.	EMLL	84
8.	Michinoku Pro	72
9.	Pancrase	70
10.	Frontier Martial Arts Wrestling	64

Previous Winners
1983 - Jim Crockett Promotions, 1984 - New Japan Pro Wrestling, 1985 - All Japan Pro Wrestling, 1986 - Mid South Sports, 1987 - New Japan Pro Wrestling, 1988 - New Japan Pro Wrestling, 1989 - Universal Wrestling Federation Japan, 1990 - All Japan Pro Wrestling, 1991 - All Japan Pro Wrestling, 1992 - New Japan Pro Wrestling, 1993 - All Japan Pro Wrestling, 1994 - AAA, 1995 - New Japan Pro Wrestling, 1996 - New Japan Pro Wrestling

BEST WEEKLY TELEVISION SHOW

1.	New Japan World Pro Wrestling (141)	1,558
2.	All Japan Pro Wrestling 30 (142)	1,292
3.	WCW Monday Nitro (144)	1,225
4.	Extreme Championship Wrestling (119)	1,118
5.	WWF Raw is War (76)	802
6.	EMLL (12)	155

7.	WCW Saturday Night (7)	96
8.	Promo Azteca	49
9.	WWF Shotgun Saturday Night	34
10.	WWF Superstars	33

Previous Winners

1983 - New Japan World Pro Wrestling, 1984 - New Japan World Pro Wrestling, 1985 - Mid South Wrestling, 1986 - Universal Wrestling Federation (Mid South), 1987 - CWA 90 Minute Memphis Wrestling, 1988 - New Japan World Pro Wrestling, 1989 - All Japan Pro Wrestling, 1990 - All Japan Pro Wrestling, 1991 - All Japan Pro Wrestling, 1992 - All Japan Pro Wrestling, 1993 - All Japan Pro Wrestling, 1994 - Extreme Championship Wrestling, 1995 - Extreme Championship Wrestling, 1996 - Extreme Championship Wrestling

MATCH OF THE YEAR

1.	Bret Hart vs. Steve Austin (3/23) (125)	1,070
2.	Mitsuharu Misawa vs. Kenta Kobashi (1/20) (133)	1,013
3.	Undertaker vs. Shawn Michaels (10/5) (99)	899
4.	Eddie Guerrero vs. Rey Misterio Jr. (10/26) (57)	643
5.	Mitsuharu Misawa vs. Toshiaki Kawada (6/6) (64)	560
6.	El Samurai vs. Koji Kanemoto (6/5) (43)	446
7.	Misawa/Akiyama vs. Kawada/Taue (12/6) (37)	317
8.	Michinoku Pro Six Man (4/13) (5)	138
9.	Mitsuharu Misawa vs. Kenta Kobashi (10/21) (20)	119
10.	Jushin Liger vs. Shinjiro Otani (2/9) (10)	83

Honorable Mention

Bret Hart vs. Shawn Michaels (11/9) 82, The Hart Foundation vs. Steve Austin & Ken Shamrock & Goldust & Legion of Doom (7/6) 70, Ultimo Dragon vs. Dean Malenko (12/29) 66, Hector Garza & Juventud Guerrera & Lizmark Jr. vs. La Parka & Psicosis & Villano IV (7/13) 62

Previous Winners

1980 - Bob Backlund vs. Ken Patera, 1981 - Pat Patterson vs. Sgt. Slaughter (4/21), 1982 - Tiger Mask (Satoru Sayama) vs. Dynamite Kid (8/5), 1983 - Ric Flair vs. Harley Race (11/24), 1984 - Freebirds vs. Von Erichs (7/4), 1985 - Tiger Mask (Mitsuharu Misawa) vs. Kuniaki Kobayashi (6/12), 1986 - Ric Flair vs. Barry Windham (2/14), 1987 - Ricky Steamboat vs. Randy Savage (3/29), 1988 - Ric Flair vs. Sting (3/27), 1989 - Ric Flair vs. Ricky Steamboat (4/2), 1990 - Jushin Liger vs. Naoki Sano (1/31), 1991 - Rick & Scott Steiner vs. Hiroshi Hase & Kensuke Sasaki (3/21), 1992 - Dan Kroffat & Doug Furnas vs. Kenta Kobashi & Tsuyoshi Kikuchi (5/25), 1993 - Manami Toyota & Toshiyo Yamada vs. Dynamite Kansai & Mayumi Ozaki (4/11), 1994 - Razor Ramon vs. Shawn Michaels (3/20), 1995 - Manami Toyota vs. Kyoko Inoue (5/7), 1996 - Mitsuharu Misawa & Jun Akiyama vs. Steve Williams & Johnny Ace (6/7)

ROOKIE OF THE YEAR

1.	Mr. Aguila (202)	1,356
2.	Chris Chetti (73)	1,053
3.	Don Frye (79)	876
4.	Kazuyuki Fujita (64)	542
5.	Naoya Ogawa (46)	530
6.	Yoshinobu Kanemaru (29)	448
7.	Jason Godsey (20)	120
8.	Brackus (4)	70
9.	Ernest Miller	60
10.	Bulldog Raines (1)	37

Previous Winners

1980 - Barry Windham, 1981 - Brad Armstrong and Brad Rheingans (tied), 1982 - Steve Williams, 1983 - Road Warriors, 1984 - Tom Zenk and Keiichi Yamada (tied), 1985 - Jack Victory, 1986 - Bam Bam Bigelow, 1987 - Brian Pillman, 1988 - Gary Albright, 1989 - Dustin Rhodes, 1990 - Steve Austin, 1991 - Johnny B. Badd, 1992 - Rey Misterio Jr., 1993 - Jun Akiyama, 1994 - Mikey Whipwreck, 1995 - Perro Aguayo Jr., 1996 - The Giant

BEST TELEVISION ANNOUNCER

1.	Mike Tenay (222)	1,738
2.	Joey Styles (173)	1,350
3.	Jim Ross (95)	1,115
4.	Jim Cornette (15)	324
5.	Tsuji (36)	254
6.	Tony Schiavone (6)	200
7.	Jerry Lawler (11)	197
8.	Larry Zbyszko (3)	122
9.	Bruce Beck (1)	122
10.	Bobby Heenan	56

Previous Winners

1981 - Gordon Solie, 1982 - Gordon Solie, 1983 - Gordon Solie, 1984 - Lance Russell, 1985 - Lance Russell, 1986 - Lance Russell, 1987 - Lance Russell, 1988 - Jim Ross, 1989 - Jim Ross, 1990 - Jim Ross, 1991 - Jim Ross, 1992 - Jim Ross, 1993 - Jim Ross, 1994 - Joey Styles, 1995 - Joey Styles, 1996 - Joey Styles

WORST TELEVISION ANNOUNCER

1.	Dusty Rhodes (292)	1,812
2.	Rick Rude (18)	531
3.	Eric Bischoff (27)	441
4.	Lee Marshall (47)	433
5.	Larry Zbyszko (32)	395
6.	Vince McMahon (29)	358
7.	Bobby Heenan (14)	344
8.	Tony Schiavone (25)	227
9.	Jerry Lawler (12)	134
10.	Michael St. John (9)	127

Honorable Mention:

Joey Styles 86

Previous Winners

1984 - Angelo Mosca, 1985 - Gorilla Monsoon, 1986 - David Crockett, 1987 - David Crockett, 1988 - David Crockett, 1989 - Ed Whalen, 1990 - Herb Abrams, 1991 - Gorilla Monsoon, 1992 - Gorilla Monsoon, 1993 - Gorilla Monsoon, 1994 - Gorilla Monsoon, 1995 - Gorilla Monsoon, 1996 - Steve McMichael

BEST MAJOR WRESTLING CARD

1.	WWF Canadian Stampede (7/6) (182)	1,133
2.	ECW Barely Legal (4/13) (139)	1,083
3.	WWF WrestleMania (3/23) (35)	288
4.	WCW Starrcade '96 (12/29) (22)	257
5.	EFC IV (3/28) (4)	226
6.	WCW SuperBrawl (2/23) (14)	184
7.	WCW Bash at the Beach (7/13) (16)	178
8.	New Japan Tokyo (6/5) (22)	171
9.	UFC Ultimate Ultimate '96 (12/7) (3)	145
10.	All Japan Women (8/20) (12)	119

Honorable Mention:

WCW Slamboree (5/18) 100, New Japan Wrestling World in Tokyo Dome (1/4 96), WCW Halloween Havoc (10/26) 87, WWF Royal Rumble (1/19), WWF SummerSlam (8/3) 77, WWF One Night Only (9/20) 72

Previous Winners

1989 - WCW Baltimore Great American Bash (7/23), 1990 - WWF/New Japan/All Japan U.S. and Japan Wrestling Summit (4/13), 1991 - WCW Wrestle War (2/24), 1992 - All Japan Women Wrestlemarinpiad (4/25), 1993 - All Japan Women Dream Slam I (4/2), 1994 - New Japan Super J Cup (4/16), 1995 - Weekly Pro Wrestling Multi-promotion show (4/2), 1996 - WAR Super J Cup Second Stage (12/13/95)

CATEGORY B AWARDS

Winners determined by first placed votes.

WORST MAJOR WRESTLING CARD

1.	WCW Souled Out (1/25)	341
2.	WCW World War III (11/23)	41
3.	ECW Hardcore Heaven (8/16)	32
4.	WCW Road Wild (8/9)	30
5.	WCW Uncensored (3/16)	22
6.	WCW Halloween Havoc (10/26)	17
7.	WWF Survivor Series (11/9)	13
8.	ECW November to Remember (11/30)	13
9.	KRS Pride One (10/11)	12
10.	WWF Royal Rumble (1/19)	7

Previous Winners

1989 - WWF WrestleMania (4/2), 1990 - WCW Clash XIII (11/20), 1991 - WCW Great American Bash (7/14), 1992 - WCW Halloween Havoc (10/25), 1993 - WCW Fall Brawl (9/19), 1994 - UWF Blackjack Brawl (9/25), 1995 - WCW Uncensored (3/29), 1996 - WCW Uncensored (3/24)

BEST WRESTLING MANEUVER

1.	Diamond Dallas Page - Diamond Cutter	66
2.	Koji Kanemoto - Reverse Frankentoyota	60
3.	Rey Misterio Jr. - Springboard Huracanrana	57
4.	Hector Garza - Corkscrew Plancha	49
5.	Taka Michinoku - Springboard Plancha	40
6.	Steve Austin - Stone Cold Stunner	40
7.	Taka Michinoku - Michinoku Driver II	29
8.	El Samurai - Top Rope Reverse DDT	25
9.	Tatsuhito Takaiwa - Triple Power Bomb	24
10.	Tommy Rogers - Tomokaze	17
=10.	Chris Jericho - Spike Super Frankensteiner	17

Honorable Mention

Marcus Bagwell - Buff Blockbuster 16, Great Sasuke - Sasuke Special 16, Juventud Guerrera - Air Juvi 13, Ultimo Dragon - Running Liger Bomb 12, Bret Hart - Figure Four around post 11, Chaparita Asari - Sky Twister Press 11, Rey Misterio Jr. - Springboard Plancha into Huracanrana on Floor 9, Shinjiro Otani - Springboard DDT 8, Ultimo Dragon - Asai Moonsault 6

Previous Winners

1981 - Jimmy Snuka - Superfly Splash, 1982 - Super Destroyer (Scott Irwin) - Superplex, 1983 - Jimmy Snuka - Superfly Splash, 1984 - Davey Boy Smith - Power Clean in combination with Dynamite Kid Dropkick off the top rope, 1985 - Tiger Mask (Mitsuharu Misawa) - Tope with mid-air flip, 1986 - Chavo Guerrero - Moonsault Bodyblock, 1987 - Keiichi Yamada (Jushin Liger) - Shooting Star Press, 1988 - Keiichi Yamada (Jushin Liger) - Shooting Star Press, 1989 - Scott Steiner - Frankensteiner, 1990 - Scott Steiner - Frankensteiner, 1991 - Masao Orihara - Moonsault off top rope to floor, 1992 - Too Cold Scorpio - Scorpio Splash, 1993 - Vader - Moonsault, 1994 - Great Sasuke - Sasuke Special, 1995 - Rey Misterio Jr. - Flip Dive into Frankensteiner on floor, 1996 - Ultimo Dragon - Running Liger Bomb

MOST DISGUSTING PROMOTIONAL TACTIC

1.	WWF - Melanie Pillman interview on Raw the day after Brian's death	183

2.	WWF - Double-cross of Bret Hart at Survivor Series	166
3.	WWF - Promising Bret Hart and delivering a midget	29
4.	WWF - Racial angles	27
5.	WWF - Brian Pillman/Marlena angle	21
6.	NWO - Spoof of Arn Anderson's retirement	18
7.	WWF/WCW - Encouraging fans to throw things/hit the ring	12
8.	ECW - Not firing New Jack	7
9.	WWF - Goldust/Marlena break-up angle	6
10.	WCW - Advertising Hall on PPV when knew he wouldn't be there	5

Previous Winners

1981 - LeBelle Promotions usage of The Monster saying he was built in a laboratory, 1982 - Bob Backlund as WWF champion, 1983 - WWF pretending Eddie Gilbert had re-broken his neck after original neck injury in a car accident, 1984 - Blackjack Mulligan faking heart attack by Championship Wrestling from Florida, 1985 - Usage of Mike Von Erich's near fatal illness to sell Cotton Bowl tickets, 1986 - Equating an angle of Chris Adams' blindness with the death of Gino Hernandez by World Class, 1987 - World Class' handling of Mike Von Erich's death, 1988 - Fritz Von Erich fake brush with death by World Class, 1989 - Jose Gonzalez babyface push by WWC, 1990 - Atsushi Onita stabbing angle with Jose Gonzalez, 1991 - WWF exploiting Persian Gulf War for WrestleMania angle, 1992 - Erik Watts push, 1993 - Cactus Jack amnesia angle, 1994 - WCW retiring Ric Flair, 1995 - WCW Gene Okerlund 900 line come-ons and lies, 1996 - WWF tease and usage of New Razor and Diesel

READERS PERSONAL FAVORITE WRESTLER

1.	Chris Benoit	80
2.	Ric Flair	67
3.	Steve Austin	60
4.	Shawn Michaels	39
5.	Manami Toyota	36
6.	Shinjiro Otani	31
7.	Jushin Liger	26
8.	Super Delfin	25
9.	Rey Misterio Jr.	25
10.	Bret Hart	20

Honorable Mention

Eddie Guerrero 13, Mankind 13, Kenta Kobashi 13, Undertaker 12, Takako Inoue 12, Mitsuharu Misawa 11, Koji Kanemoto 11, Toshiaki Kawada 10, Brian Pillman 10, Volk Han 10

Previous Winners

1984 - Ric Flair, 1985 - Ric Flair, 1986 - Ric Flair, 1987 - Ric Flair, 1988 - Ric Flair, 1989 - Ric Flair, 1990 - Ric Flair, 1991 - Ric Flair, 1992 - Ric Flair, 1993 - Ric Flair, 1994 - Sabu, 1995 - Manami Toyota, 1996 - Ric Flair

READERS LEAST FAVORITE WRESTLER

1.	Hulk Hogan	148
2.	Shawn Michaels	66
3.	Kevin Nash	46
4.	Lex Luger	40
5.	Hunter Hearst Helmsley	27
6.	Taz	24
7.	Goldust	18
8.	Shane Douglas	14
9.	Glacier	9
10.	Bret Hart	9

Honorable Mention

Steve McMichael 8, Sycho Sid 8

Previous Winners

1984 - Ivan Putski, 1985 - Hulk Hogan, 1986 - Hulk Hogan, 1987 - Dusty Rhodes, 1988 - Dusty Rhodes, 1989 - Ultimate Warrior, 1990 - Ultimate Warrior, 1991 - Hulk Hogan, 1992 - Erik Watts, 1993 - Sid Vicious, 1994 - Hulk Hogan, 1995 - Hulk Hogan, 1996 - Hulk Hogan

WORST WRESTLER

1.	Hulk Hogan	93
2.	Steve McMichael	61
3.	Lex Luger	55
4.	Interrogator	52
5.	Ahmed Johnson	36
6.	Roddy Piper	33
7.	Sandman	32
8.	Jim Duggan	17
9.	Sycho Sid	16
10.	Jimmy Valiant	14

Honorable Mention

Rusher Kimura 13, Giant Baba 12, Brian Lee 11, Vincent 9

Previous Winners

1984 - Ivan Putski, 1985 - Uncle Elmer (Stan Frazier), 1986 - Mike Von Erich, 1987 - Junkyard Dog, 1988 - Ultimate Warrior, 1989 - Andre the Giant, 1990 - Junkyard Dog, 1991 - Andre the Giant, 1992 - Andre the Giant, 1993 - The Equalizer (Dave Sullivan), 1994 - Dave Sullivan, 1995 - Renegade, 1996 - Loch Ness

WORST TAG TEAM

1.	Godwinns	198
2.	Legion of Doom	36
3.	Meng & Barbarian	35
4.	Recon & Sniper	26
5.	Kevin Nash & Scott Hall	25
6.	Billy Gunn & Jesse Jammes	23
7.	Blackjacks	23
8.	Public Enemy	21
9.	High Voltage	17
10.	Buh Buh Ray & D-Von Dudley	15

Honorable Mention

Glacier & Ernest Miller 12, Head Bangers 10

Previous Winners

1984 - The Crusher & Baron Von Raschke, 1985 - Uncle Elmer (Stan Frazier) & Cousin Junior (Lanny Kean), 1986 - Junkyard Dog & George Steele, 1987 - Jimmy Valiant & Bugsy McGraw, 1988 - Nikolai Volkoff & Boris Zhukov, 1989 - Warlord & Barbarian, 1990 - Giant Baba & Andre the Giant, 1991 - Giant Baba & Andre the Giant, 1992 - Bushwhackers, 1993 - Colossal Kongs, 1994 - Bushwhackers, 1995 - Dick Slater & Bunkhouse Buck, 1996 - Godwinns

WORST TELEVISION SHOW

1.	USWA	124
2.	WCW Pro	78
3.	WWF Live Wire	67
4.	WCW Monday Nitro	55
5.	WWF Shotgun Saturday Night	44
6.	WWF Raw is War	39
7.	WWF Superstars	32

8.	WCW Saturday Night	31
9.	WCW Main Event	18
10.	WCW World Wide	13
=10.	AAA	13

Previous Winners

1984 - WWF All-Star Wrestling, 1985 - Championship Wrestling from Florida, 1986 - California Championship Wrestling, 1987 - World Class Championship Wrestling, 1988 - AWA on ESPN, 1989 - ICW Wrestling, 1990 - AWA on ESPN, 1991 - Herb Abrams UWF, 1992 - GWF on ESPN, 1993 - GWF on ESPN, 1994 - WCW Saturday Night, 1995 - WCW Saturday Night, 1996 - AWF Warriors of Wrestling

WORST MANAGER

1.	Sonny Onoo	175
2.	Debra McMichael	43
3.	Sable	42
4.	James Vandenburg	39
5.	Jackyl	38
6.	Teddy Long	30
7.	Uncle Cletus	24
8.	Iron Sheik	17
9.	Jacquelyn	16
10.	Jimmy Hart	10

Honorable Mention

Ted DiBiase 9, Hillbilly Jim 8

Previous Winners

1984 - Mr. Fuji, 1985 - Mr. Fuji, 1986 - Paul Jones, 1987 - Mr. Fuji, 1988 - Mr. Fuji, 1989 - Mr. Fuji, 1990 - Mr. Fuji, 1991 - Mr. Fuji,1992 - Mr. Fuji, 1993 - Mr. Fuji, 1994 - Mr. Fuji, 1995 - Mr. Fuji, 1996 - Sonny Onoo

WORST MATCH OF THE YEAR

1.	Hulk Hogan vs. Roddy Piper (10/26)	182
2.	Sabu vs. Sandman (11/30)	158
3.	Reggie White vs. Steve McMichael (5/18)	71
4.	Shane Douglas vs. Pit Bull #2 (4/13)	28
5.	Hulk Hogan vs. The Giant (1/25)	22
6.	World War III Battle Royal (11/23)	22
7.	DOA vs. Truth Commission (11/9)	20
8.	Faarooq vs. Crush vs. Savio Vega (9/7)	15
9.	Bret Hart vs. Shawn Michaels (11/9)	13
10.	Steve McMichael vs. Alex Wright (10/26)	8

Honorable Mention

Hulk Hogan vs. Lex Luger (8/9) 7, Disco Inferno vs. Jacquelyn (10/26) 7

Previous Winners

1984 - Fabulous Moolah vs. Wendi Richter (7/23), 1985 - Fred Blassie vs. Lou Albano, 1986 - Roddy Piper vs. Mr. T (4/2), 1987 - Hulk Hogan vs. Andre the Giant (3/29), 1988 - Hiroshi Wajima vs. Tom Magee (4/21), 1989 - Andre the Giant vs. Ultimate Warrior (10/31), 1990 - Sid Vicious vs. Night Stalker (11/20), 1991 - P.N. News & Bobby Eaton vs. Terry Taylor & Steve Austin (7/14), 1992 - Rick Rude vs. Masahiro Chono (10/25), 1993 - Four Doinks (Bushwhackers & Men on a Mission) vs. Bam Ban Bigelow & Head Shrinkers & Bastion Booger (11/24), 1994 - Jerry Lawler & Queasy & Cheesy & Sleazy vs. Doink the Clown & Dink & Wink & Pink (11/23), 1995 - Sting vs. Tony Palmore (1/4), 1996 - Hulk Hogan & Randy Savage vs. Ric Flair & Arn Anderson & Meng & Barbarian & Kevin Sullivan & Ze Gangsta & Ultimate Solution & Lex Luger (3/24)

WORST FEUD OF THE YEAR

1.	DOA vs. Boricuas vs. NOD	99
2.	Legion of Doom vs. Godwinns	63
3.	Hulk Hogan vs. Roddy Piper	62
4.	WCW vs. NWO	43
5.	Glacier & Miller vs. Wrath & Mortis	27
6.	Ahmed Johnson vs. Nation of Domination	22
7.	Disco Inferno vs. Jacquelyn	22
8.	Jeff Jarrett vs. Steve McMichael	21
9.	Shawn Michaels vs. Bret Hart	12
10.	NWO vs. Ray Traylor	11

Previous Winners

1984 - Andre the Giant vs. John Studd, 1985 - Sgt. Slaughter vs. Boris Zhukov, 1986 - Machines (Andre the Giant & Bill Eadie) vs. King Kong Bundy & John Studd, 1987 - George Steele vs. Danny Davis, 1988 - Midnight Rider (Dusty Rhodes) vs. Tully Blanchard, 1989 - Andre the Giant vs. Ultimate Warrior, 1990 - Ric Flair vs. Junkyard Dog, 1991 - Hulk Hogan vs. Sgt. Slaughter, 1992 - Ultimate Warrior vs. Papa Shango, 1993 - Undertaker vs. Giant Gonzalez, 1994 - Jerry Lawler vs. Doink the Clown, 1995 - Hulk Hogan vs. Dungeon of Doom, 1996 - Big Bubba vs. John Tenta

WORST ON INTERVIEWS

1.	Ahmed Johnson	211
2.	Alex Wright	39
3.	Lex Luger	38
4.	Roddy Piper	28
5.	Hunter Hearst Helmsley	26
6.	Road Warriors	21
7.	Shawn Michaels	18
8.	Ken Shamrock	14
9.	Jacquelyn	13
10.	Scott Steiner	11
=10.	Raven	11

Honorable Mention

Marc Mero 9, The Giant 8, Steve McMichael 8

Previous Winners

1984 - Jimmy Snuka, 1985 - Thunderbolt Patterson, 1986 - Mike Von Erich, 1987 - Bugsy McGraw, 1988 - Steve Williams, 1989 - Ultimate Warrior, 1990 - Ultimate Warrior, 1991 - Ultimate Warrior, 1992 - Ultimate Warrior, 1993 - Mr. Fuji, 1994 - Dave Sullivan, 1995 - Hulk Hogan, 1996 - Ahmed Johnson

WORST PROMOTION

1.	United States Wrestling Association	251
2.	World Wrestling Federation	89
3.	AAA	68
4.	World Championship Wrestling	52
5.	Big Japan Pro Wrestling	52
6.	Extreme Championship Wrestling	31
7.	Music City Wrestling	30
8.	World Wrestling Council	24
9.	Frontier Martial Arts Wrestling	12
10.	Catch Wrestling Association	11

Honorable Mention

National Wrestling Alliance 9, Louisville IWA 9

Previous Winners

1986 - AWA, 1987 - World Class, 1988 - AWA, 1989 - AWA, 1990 - AWA, 1991 - Herb Abrams UWF, 1992 - GWF, 1993 - WCW, 1994 - WCW, 1995 - WCW, 1996 - AWF

BEST BOOKER

1.	Paul Heyman	252
2.	Riki Choshu	88
3.	Terry Taylor	77
4.	Shohei Baba	59
5.	Jushin Liger	58
6.	Vince McMahon	39
7.	Great Sasuke	26
8.	Eric Bischoff	22
9.	Kevin Sullivan	18
10.	Konnan	9

Previous Winners

1986 - Dusty Rhodes, 1987 - Vince McMahon, 1988 - Eddie Gilbert, 1989 - Shohei Baba, 1990 - Shohei Baba, 1991 - Shohei Baba, 1992 - Riki Choshu, 1993 - Jim Cornette, 1994 - Paul Heyman, 1995 - Paul Heyman, 1996 - Paul Heyman

PROMOTER OF THE YEAR

1.	Riki Choshu	311
2.	Eric Bischoff	132
3.	Vince McMahon	61
4.	Paul Heyman	57
5.	Shohei Baba	51
6.	Steve Nelson	9
7.	Konnan	7
8.	Masami Ozaki	7
9.	Atsushi Onita	6
10.	Antonio Pena	4

Previous Winners

1988 - Vince McMahon, 1989 - Akira Maeda, 1990 - Shohei Baba, 1991 - Shohei Baba, 1992 - Shohei Baba, 1993 - Shohei Baba, 1994 - Shohei Baba, 1995 - Riki Choshu, 1996 - Riki Choshu

SHOOTER OF THE YEAR

1.	Maurice Smith	346
2.	Vitor Belfort	48
3.	Dan Severn	47
4.	Mark Kerr	41
5.	Don Frye	33
6.	Yuki Kondo	32
7.	Mark Coleman	19
8.	Randy Couture	17
9.	Frank Shamrock	15
10.	Tom Erikson	12

Honorable Mention

Masakatsu Funaki 11, Bas Rutten 11, Kevin Jackson 9

SHOOT MATCH OF THE YEAR

1.	Maurice Smith vs. Mark Coleman (7/27)	357

2.	Vitor Belfort vs. Randy Couture (10/17)	43
3.	Lisa Hunt vs. Donna Cauthen (4/12)	35
4.	Carlos Baretto vs. David Beneteau (10/17)	26
5.	Wallid Ismail vs. Yoshiki Takahashi (2/7)	13
6.	Rickson Gracie vs. Nobuhiko Takada (10/11)	12
7.	Kimo vs. Paul Varelans (12/7/96)	11
8.	Frank Shamrock vs. Tsuyoshi Kousaka (9/26)	9
9.	Don Frye vs. Tank Abbott (12/7/96)	7
10.	Frank Shamrock vs. John Lober (1/20)	7

BEST GIMMICK

1.	Stone Cold Steve Austin	93
2.	NWO	69
3.	Kane	68
4.	Dude Love	35
5.	Degeneration X	32
6.	Oz Academy	31
7.	Sting	29
8.	Raven's Nest	17
9.	Al Snow's Head	13
10.	Full Blooded Italians	10

HONORABLE MENTION:

Chyna 7

PREVIOUS WINNERS

1986 - Adrian Street, 1987 - Ted DiBiase Million Dollar Man, 1988 - Rick Steiner Varsity Club, 1989 - Jushin Liger, 1990 - Undertaker, 1991 - Undertaker, 1992 - Undertaker, 1993 - Undertaker, 1994 - Undertaker, 1995 - Disco Inferno, 1996 - NWO

WORST GIMMICK

1.	New Goldust	68
2.	Truth Commission	58
3.	Glacier	57
4.	Degeneration X	30
5.	Rockabilly	28
6.	Dude Love	25
7.	NWO	17
8.	Sting	12
9.	Kane	9
10.	Flash Funk	9

PREVIOUS WINNERS

1986 - Adorable Adrian Adonis, 1987 - Adorable Adrian Adonis, 1988 - Midnight Rider (Dusty Rhodes), 1989 - Ding Dongs, 1990 - Gobbledy Gooker, 1991 - Oz, 1992 - Papa Shango, 1993 - Shock Master, 1994 - Dave Sullivan, 1995 - Goldust, 1996 - New Razor, Diesel and Double J

MOST EMBARRASSING WRESTLER

1.	New Goldust	176
2.	Hulk Hogan	105
3.	Shawn Michaels	49
4.	Glacier	26
5.	Godwinns	21
6.	Roddy Piper	19

7.	Sandman	16
8.	Jim Duggan	15
9.	New Jack	15
10.	Interrogator	9

Previous Winners

1986 - Adrian Adonis, 1987 - George Steele, 1988 - George Steele, 1989 - Andre the Giant, 1990 - Dusty Rhodes, 1991 - Van Hammer, 1992 - Papa Shango, 1993 - Bastion Booger, 1994 - Doink the Clown, 1995 - Hulk Hogan, 1996 - Hulk Hogan